U0856384

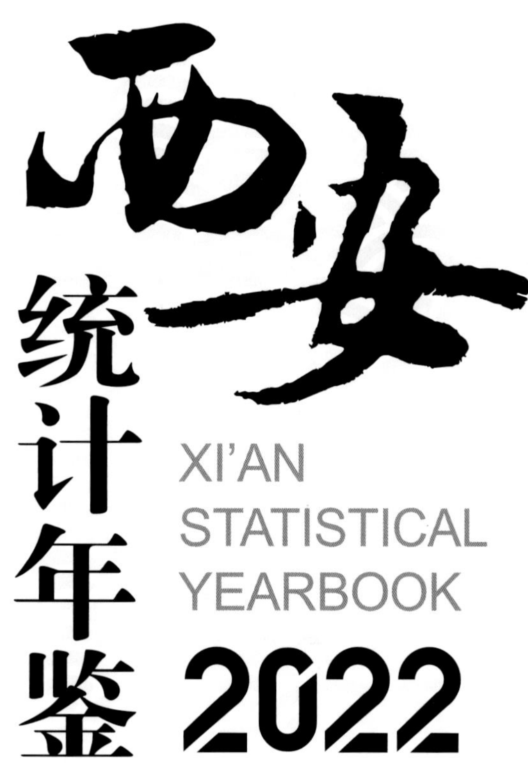

中英文对照 Chinese/English

中国统计出版社
China Statistics Press

西安市统计局
XI'AN MUNICIPAL BUREAU OF STATISTICS
国家统计局西安调查队
NBS SURVEY OFFICE IN XI'AN

图书在版编目（CIP）数据

西安统计年鉴. 2022 = Xi'an Statistical Yearbook 2022 : 汉英对照 / 西安市统计局, 国家统计局西安调查队编. -- 北京 : 中国统计出版社, 2022.9
ISBN 978-7-5037-9905-1

Ⅰ. ①西… Ⅱ. ①西… ②国… Ⅲ. ①统计资料－西安－2022－年鉴－汉、英 Ⅳ. ①C832.411-54

中国版本图书馆CIP数据核字(2022)第148267号

西安统计年鉴2022

作　　者 / 西安市统计局　国家统计局西安调查队
责任编辑 / 钟　钰
装帧设计 / 西安乐成品牌策划设计有限公司
出版发行 / 中国统计出版社有限公司
地　　址 / 北京市丰台区西三环南路甲6号
邮政编码 / 100073
电　　话 / 邮购（010）63376909　书店（010）68783171
网　　址 / http://www.zgtjcbs.com
印　　刷 / 西安第一印刷厂
经　　销 / 新华书店
开　　本 / 890mm × 1240mm 1/16
字　　数 / 1098千字
印　　张 / 44　彩页1.25
版　　别 / 2022年9月第1版
版　　次 / 2022年9月第1次印刷
定　　价 / 260.00元　Price:260.00yuan(RMB)

本书附同版本CD-ROM一张，光盘内容以书面文字为准。
如有印装差错，由本社发行部调换。

《西安统计年鉴2022》编辑部

总编辑：张民伟　韩国军

副总编辑：秦来生　赵群洁　陈瑾瑜　李　红　连　鹏　陈　英　边可为　朱　强　焦卫冬　董　军　李云耀

编辑部主任：连　鹏

编辑部副主任：罗延庆　李　芬　杨　骏

编辑人员：（以姓氏笔画为序）

马　琰　马建华　王　贞　王　峰　王义龙　白　敏　冯　乐　冯军魁　刘　婷　刘栋婷　刘晓敏　安海军　孙国伟　李　玫　李　娜　张　珂　张　静　张　磊　陈小兵　罗朝晖　赵　晖　贾海宇　贾薪蓉　栾立森　高小琴　席锋旭　黄雪冰　康　敏　景春玲　曾文元　薛　丰

执行编辑：赵　博　罗　茜　孟　刚　张　熠　王　慧

英文翻译：史　可　刘　航　闫小溪　李宇徽　李怡馨　赵婧媛　董　骋

XI'AN STATISTICAL YEARBOOK 2022

EDITORLAL STAFF

Editors-in-chief: Zhang Minwei　Han Guojun

Associate Editors-in-chief: Qin Laisheng　Zhao Qunjie　Chen Jinyu　Li Hong　Lian Peng　Chen Ying　Bian Kewei　Zhu Qiang　Jiao Weidong　Dong Jun　Li Yunyao

Director of Editorial Department: Lian Peng

Deputy Directors of Editorial Department: Luo Yanqing　Li Fen　Yang Jun

Editorial Staff: (in order of number of strokes of the Chinese character of the surname)

Ma Yan　Ma Jianhua　Wang Zhen　Wang Feng　Wang Yilong　Bai Min　Feng Le　Feng Junkui　Liu Ting　Liu Dongting　Liu Xiaomin　An Haijun　Sun Guowei　Li Mei　Li Na　Zhang Ke　Zhang Jing　Zhang Lei　Chen Xiaobin　Luo Zhaohui　Zhao Hui　Jia Haiyu　Jia Xinrong　Luan Lisen　Gao Xiaoqin　Xi Fengxu　Huang Xuebing　Kang Min　Jing Chunling　Zeng Wenyuan　Xue Feng

Executive Editors: Zhao Bo　Luo Qian　Meng Gang　Zhang Yi　Wang Hui

English Translators: Shi Ke　Liu Hang　Yan Xiaoxi　Li Yuhui　Li Yixin　Zhao Jingyuan　Dong Cheng

编者说明

一、《西安统计年鉴2022》系统收录了全市、区县及开发区2021年经济、社会各方面统计数据，以及重要历史年份主要统计数据，是一部全面记载西安市国民经济和社会发展情况的大型连续性统计文献资料和重要工具书。

二、本年鉴正文内容分为二十二个篇章：（一）综合；（二）基本单位；（三）国民经济核算；（四）人口、从业人员与职工工资；（五）固定资产投资；（六）财政；（七）物价指数；（八）人民生活；（九）城市公用事业；（十）环境保护；（十一）农业；（十二）工业；（十三）能源；（十四）建筑业；（十五）运输、邮电和信息化；（十六）国内贸易；（十七）对外经济贸易和旅游；（十八）规模以上服务业；（十九）金融业；（二十）教育和科技；（二十一）文化、体育、卫生、社会福利和其他；（二十二）企业调查。同时，为方便读者使用，各篇章前设有简要说明和主要统计指标，对本篇章的主要内容、资料来源以及历史变动情况予以简要概述，篇末附有《主要统计指标解释》。

三、本年鉴统计资料的统计标准，按当时国家统计制度执行，有关指标的涵义、口径、范围、计算方法等，在不同时期可能有所不同，使用时请注意。如国民经济行业分类按GB/T4754—2017标准执行。

四、为便于国内外读者查阅，本年鉴全部内容均采用中英文对照编辑。

五、本年鉴中，国民经济核算部分的2018年数据为全国第四次经济普查数据，2003-2017年数据为第四次经济普查修订数据；工业部分的2018年数据为第四次经济普查数据；国内贸易部分的1993-2017年为第四次经济普查修订数据；农业部分的2007-2017年农林牧渔业总产值、产量等和2013-2017年畜产品等为依据第三次农业普查调整后数据；2011-2019年常住人口及相关指标数据为依据第七次全国人口普查修订数据；固定资产投资数据主要为增长速度等相对指标数据；科技数据（除部门数据）、创新活动为2020年数据。

六、数据口径：本年鉴2021年数据，基本单位、国民经济核算、农业、工业、建筑业、国内贸易、服务业、能源（部分）、固定资产投资、常住人口、从业人员和职工工资、信息化、企业调查、水资源等指标数据不含西安（西咸新区）—咸阳共管区。户籍人口、土地面积等指标数据为西安原口径。其他指标数据口径详见各部分说明或各表下具体注释。

七、本年鉴中的部分指标合计数或相对数由于单位取舍不同产生的计算误差均未作机械调整。

八、本年鉴所使用的计量单位均依据2021年相关统计报表制度。

九、本年鉴使用的符号说明："..."表示数据不足本表最小单位；"空白"表示该项统计指标无数据或数据不详；"#"表示其中项；"*"表示另有注解。

感谢社会各界长期以来对《西安统计年鉴》的广泛关注和大力支持。为进一步做好工作，更好地为广大读者服务，希望社会各界提出宝贵意见。

PREFACE

I. *Xi'an Statistical Yearbook 2022* is a periodical statistic yearbook that records the economic and social development of Xi'an all-around in 2021 and some selected data series in important historical years. With its features of comprehensive and intensive information, this book provides data covering the situation of social and economic developments in Xi'an.

II. The book contains twenty-two parts, 1.General Survey; 2.Basic Unit; 3.National Economic Account; 4.Population、Employment and Wages; 5.Investment in Fixed Assets; 6.Government Finance; 7.Price Indices; 8.People's Livelihood; 9.Urban Public Utilities; 10.Environmental Protection; 11.Agriculture; 12.Industry; 13.Energy; 14.Construction; 15.Transportation、Post and Informatization; 16.Domestic Trade; 17.Foreign Trade; 18. Service Industry; 19.Financial Intermediation; 20.Education、Science and Technology; 21.Culture、Sports、Public Health、Social Welfare and Other Social Activities; 22.Enterprises Investigation. Meanwhile, for the reader's convenience, a brief explanation and major statistical indicators are provided before each chapter, and the main contents、sources and historical changes of this chapter are briely summarized. The end of part is accompanied by the interpretation of major statistical indicators.

III. The data of various years in conformity with to the statistical standards prescribed by the national statistical system of the time. The meaning、scope and calculating method of indicators may have some differences in different periods, which readers must pay attention. For example, national industries classification is carried out according to standard GB/T4754 -2017.

IV. For the convenience of being consulted by foreigners, the book is a Chinese-English bilingual edition.

V. In this yearbook, the data on national economy accounting in 2018 is the Fourth National Economic Census data, and the data from 2003 to 2017 are the revised data of the Fourth Economic Census. The 2018 data of the industrial part is the Fourth Economic Census data. The domestic trade data from 1993 to 2017 is revised from the Fourth Economic Census.The total output value and output of agriculture、forestry、animal husbandry and fishery from 2007 to 2017 and the livestock products from 2013 to 2017 are adjusted data of the Third Agricultural General Census. The data on permanent population and related indicators from 2011 to 2019 is revised from the Seventh National Population Census; The data on fixed asset investment are mainly relative indicators such as growth rate. Science and technology data (except department data) and innovation activities were data in 2020.

VI. Statistical scope: Data of 2021 in this yearbook, the basic unit、national economic accounting、agriculture、industry、construction industry、domestic trade、services、energy、investment in fixed assets、permanent resident population、labor and wages、informatization、enterprise survey、water resources does not include Xixian New District. Household registered population、land area are Xi'an original caliber data. The scope of other data is the description of each part or notes under the table.

VII. Statistical discrepancies due to rounding are not adjusted automatically in this yearbook.

VIII. Unit of measurement is used in this yearbook according to the 2021 statistics system.

Ⅸ. Explanations of symbols used in this yearbook:

"..." indicates the data is less than the minimum unit in this table;

(Blank) shows the data is not available;

\# shows the one of items;

* indicates some other explanatory note.

Here we would like to express our sincere thanks to the people for their concern and support of the Xi'an statistical yearbook. To do better and provide better service to readers, we hope that the whole of society fields can propose constructive advice.

地区生产总值（亿元）

Gross Domestic Product (100 million yuan)

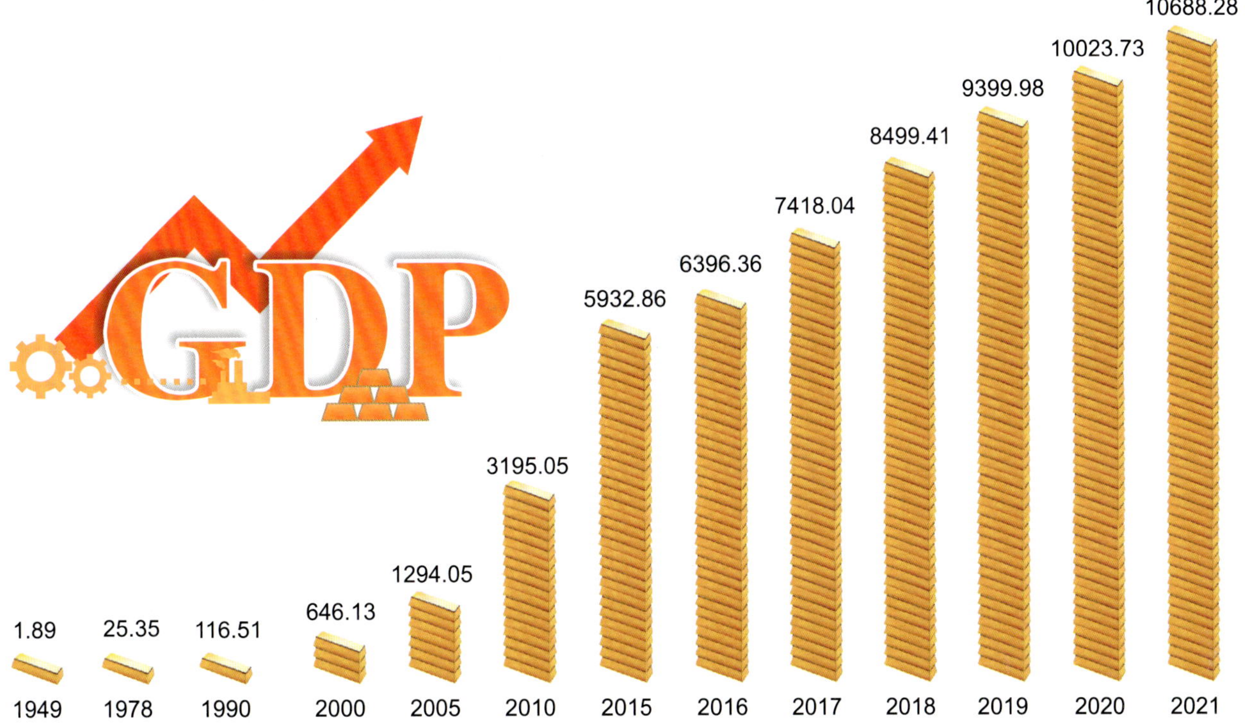

地区生产总值指数（以上年为100）

Indices of Gross Domestic Product (preceding year=100)

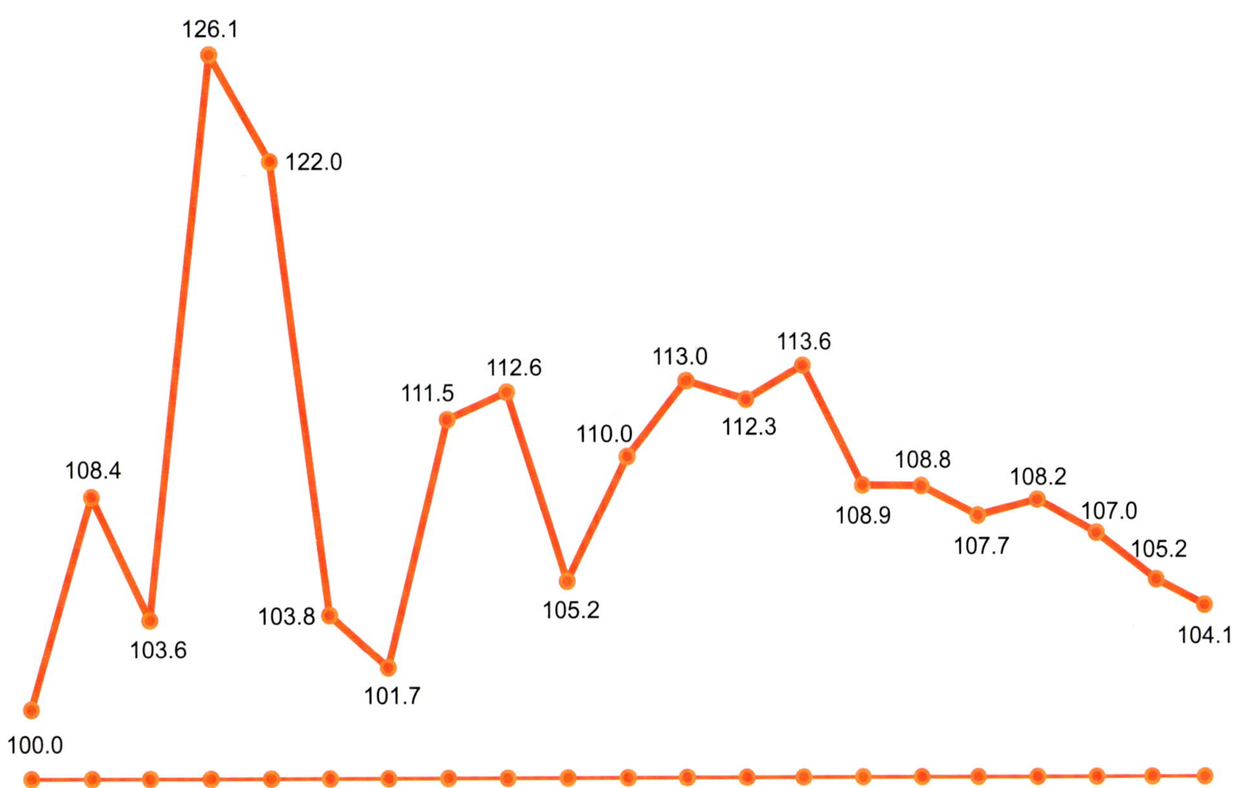

地区生产总值构成（%）

Composition of Gross Domestic Product (%)

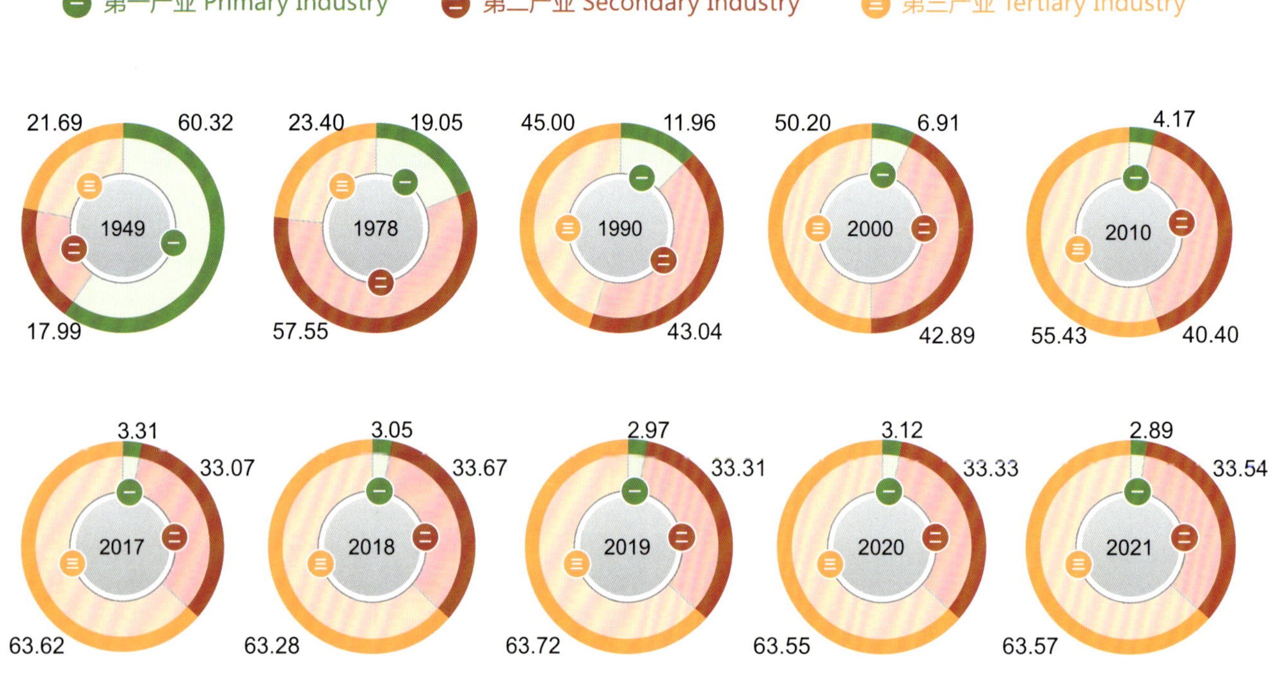

人均GDP（元/人）

Per Capita GDP (yuan/person)

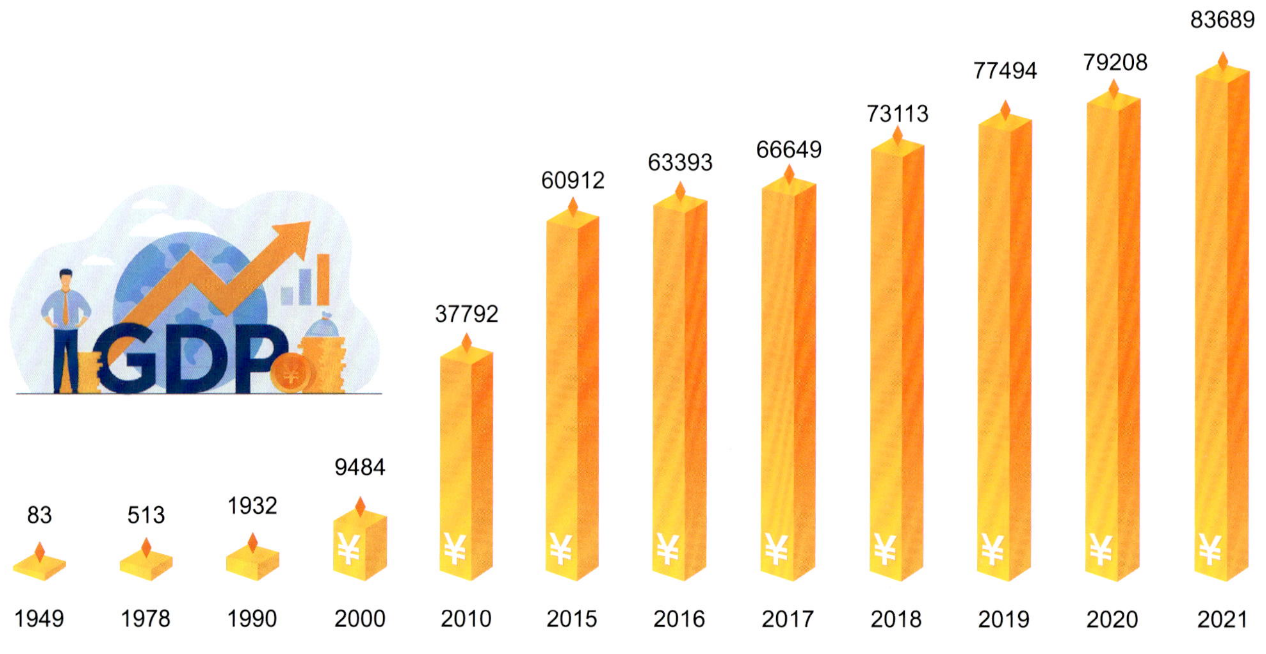

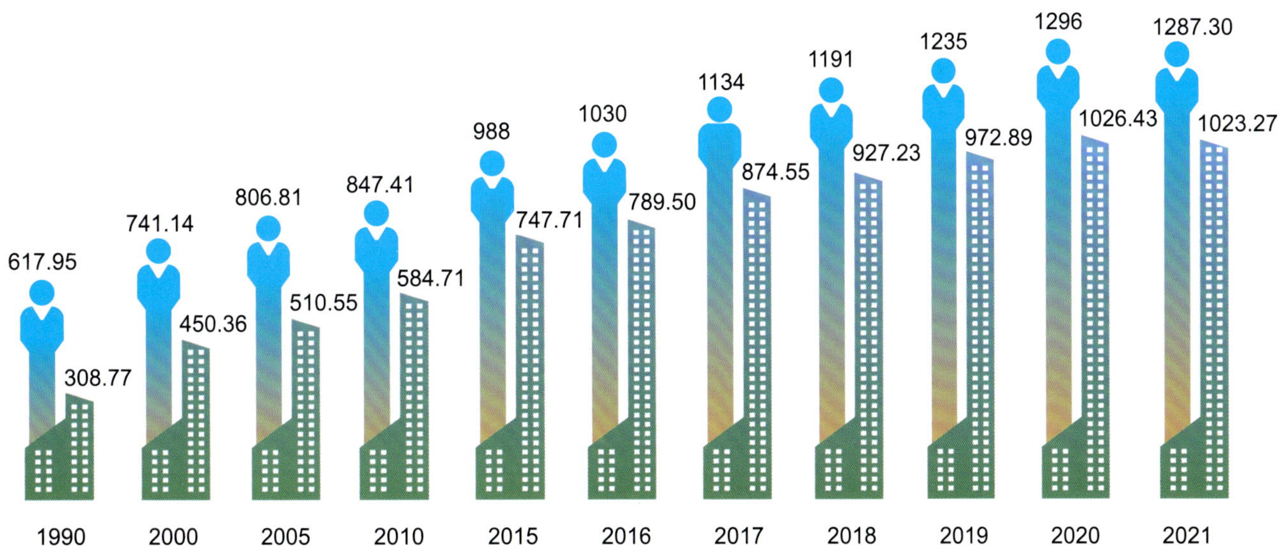

全社会从业人数（万人）

Social Workers (10 000 persons)

固定资产投资比上年增长速度（%）

Growth Rate of Investment in Fixed Assets (%)

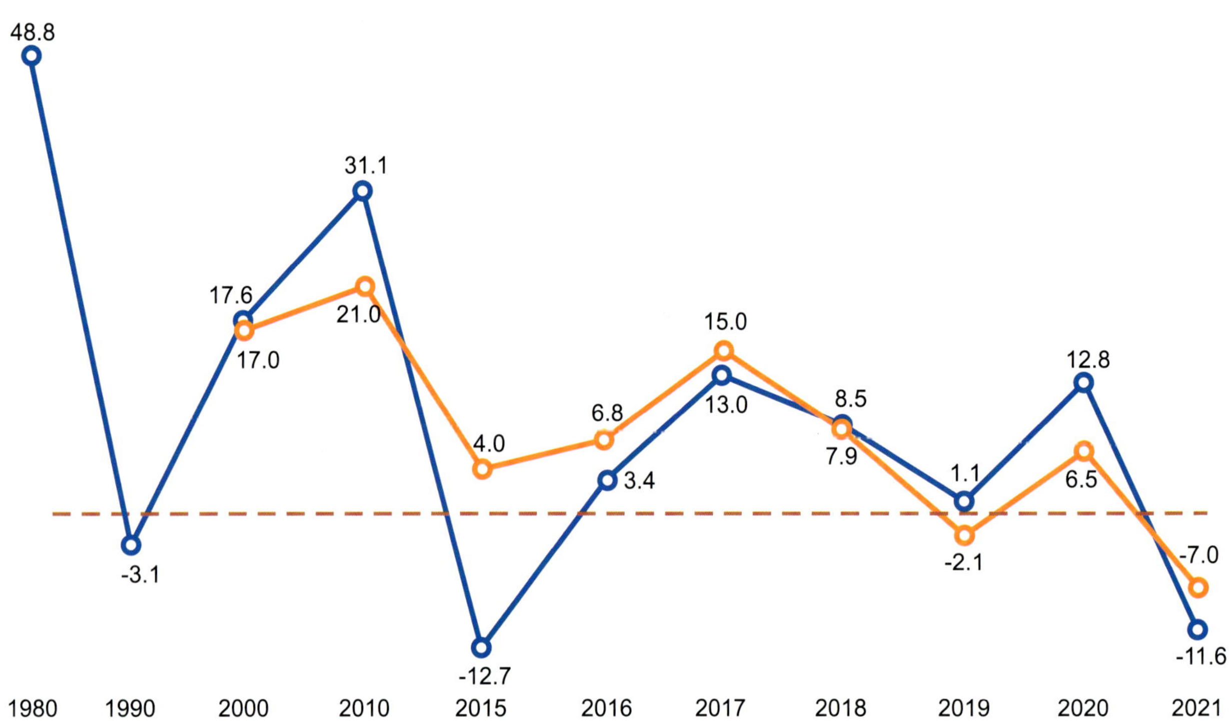

商品房销售面积（万平方米）

Floor Space of Commercialized Buildings Sold (10 000 sq.m)

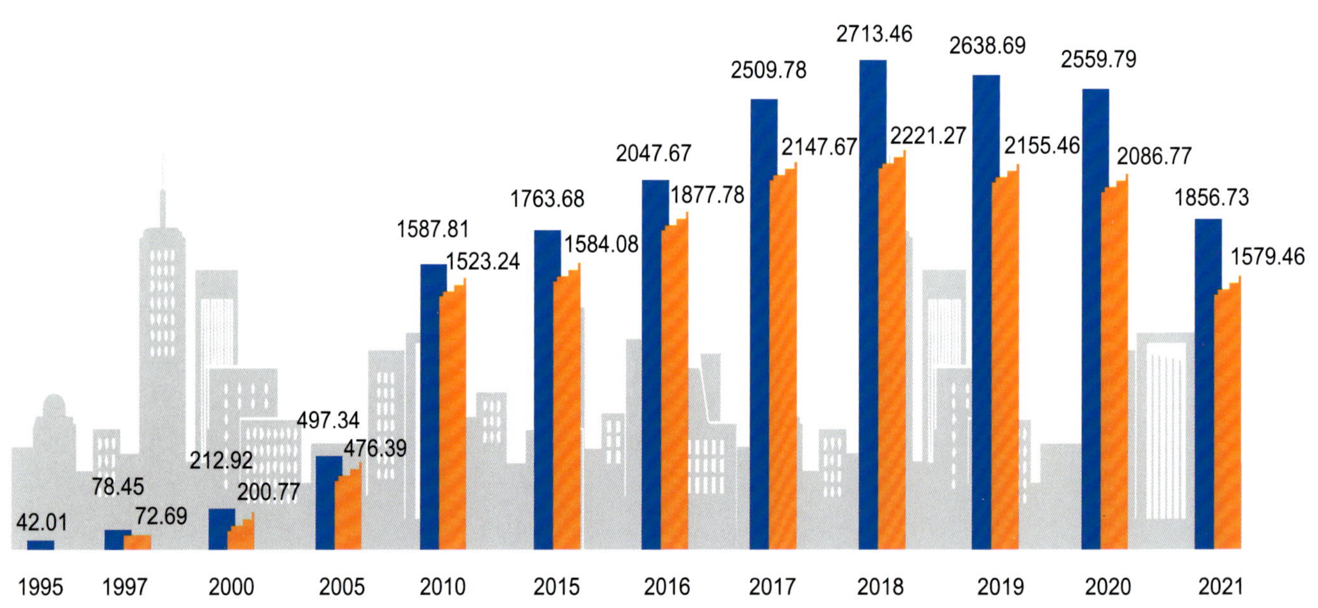

农林牧渔业总产值（亿元）

Gross Output Value of Farming,Forestry,
Animal Husbandry and Fishery (100 million yuan)

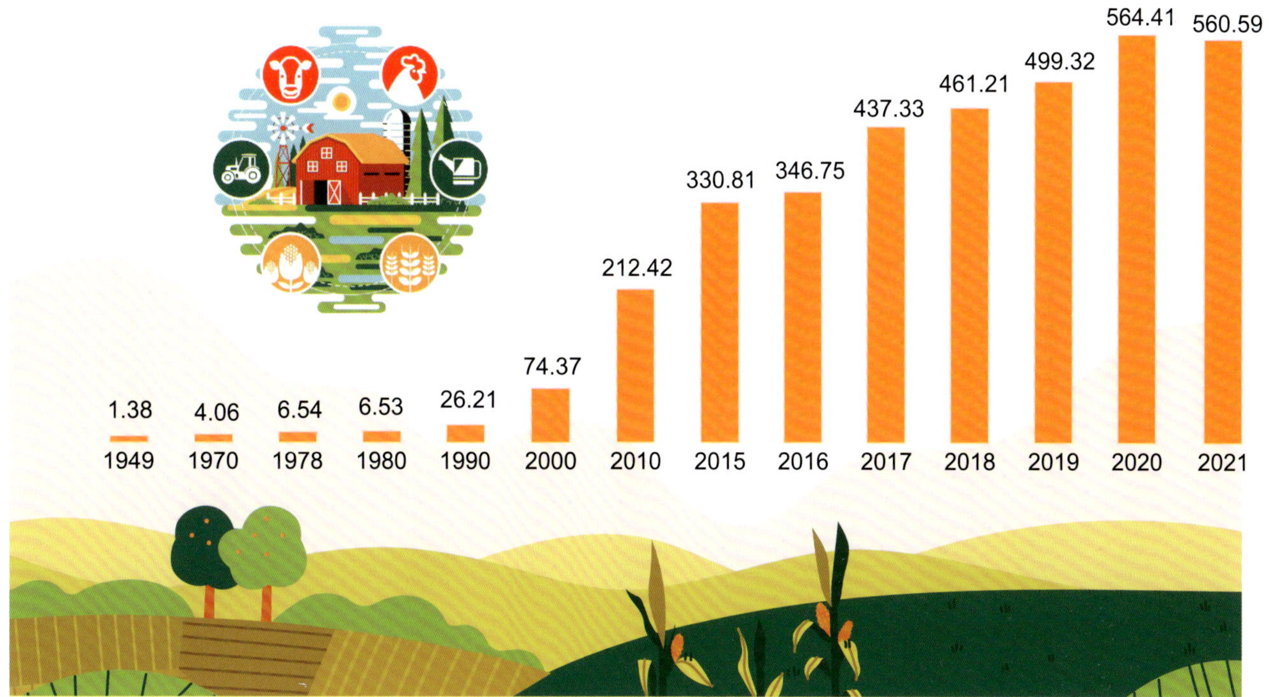

粮食产量（万吨）

Grain Product (10 000 tons)

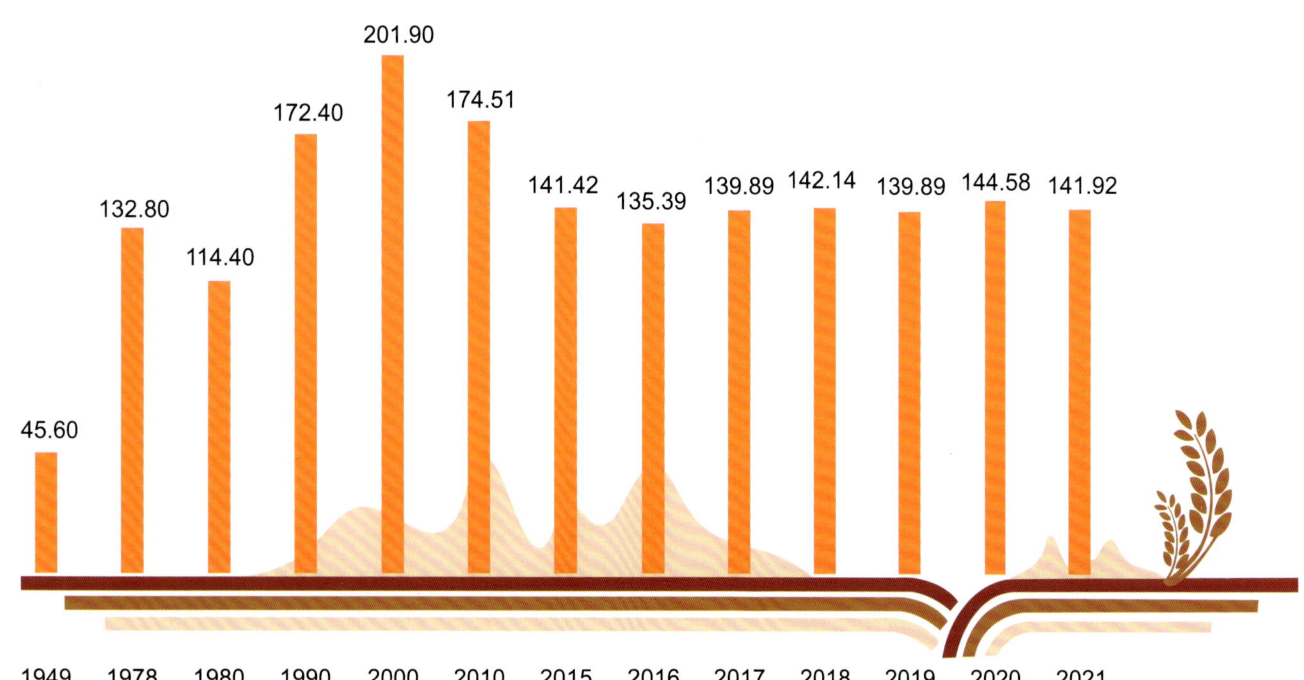

蔬菜产量（万吨）
Vegetables Product (10 000 tons)

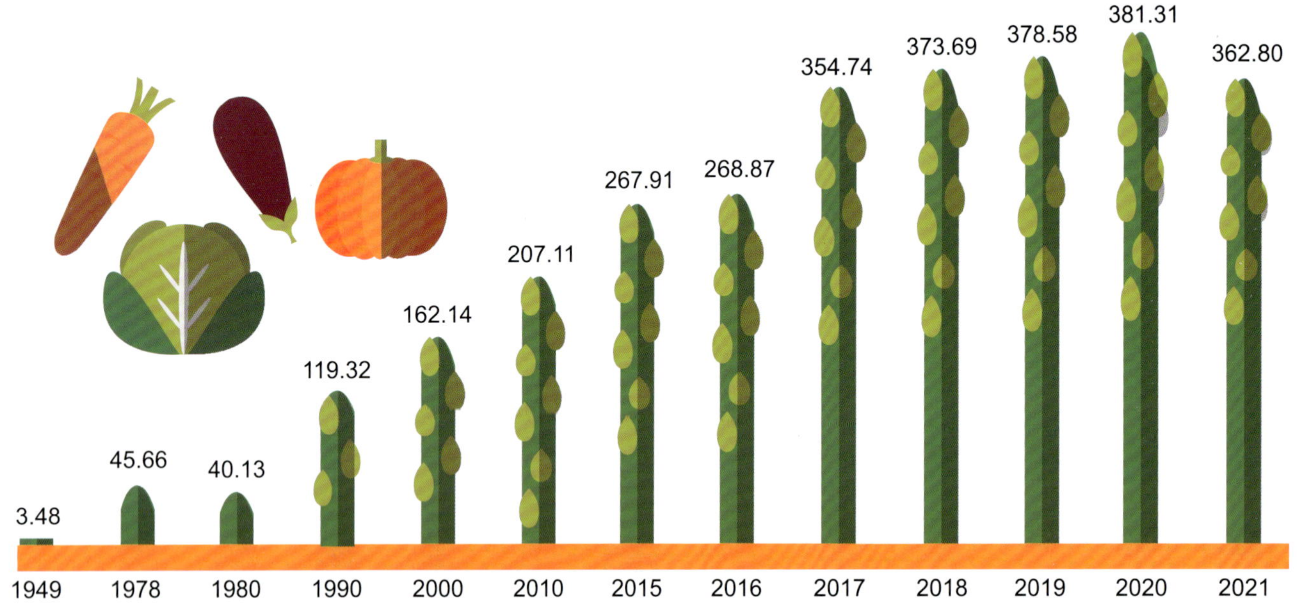

规模以上工业企业主要产品产量
Major Output of Industrial Products Enterprises Above Designated Size

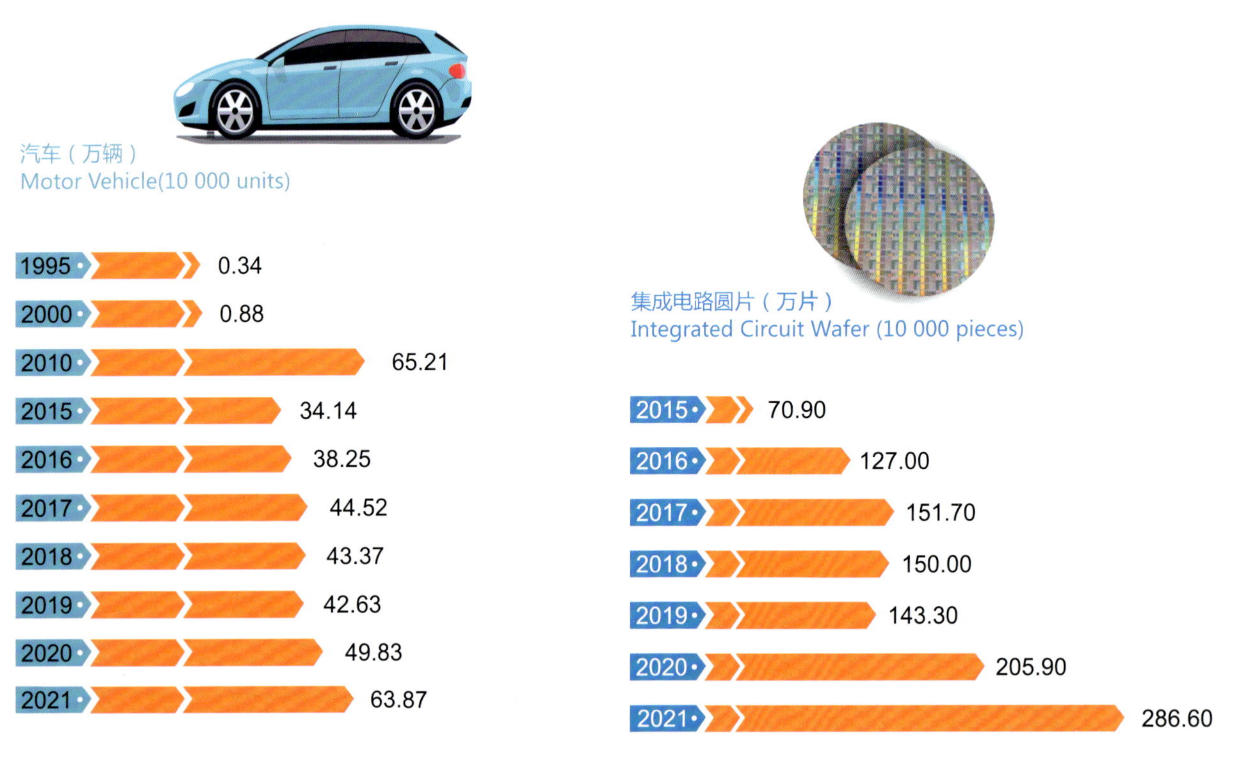

交通
Traffic

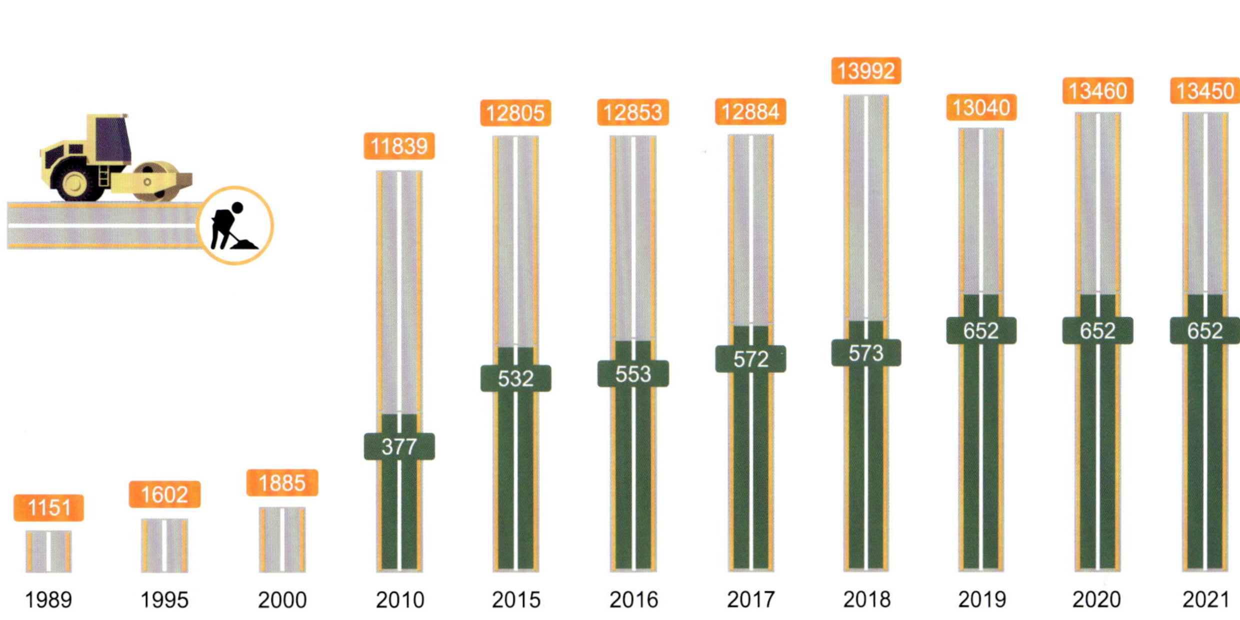

全社会车辆数（万辆）
Possession of Civil Vehicles (10 000 units)

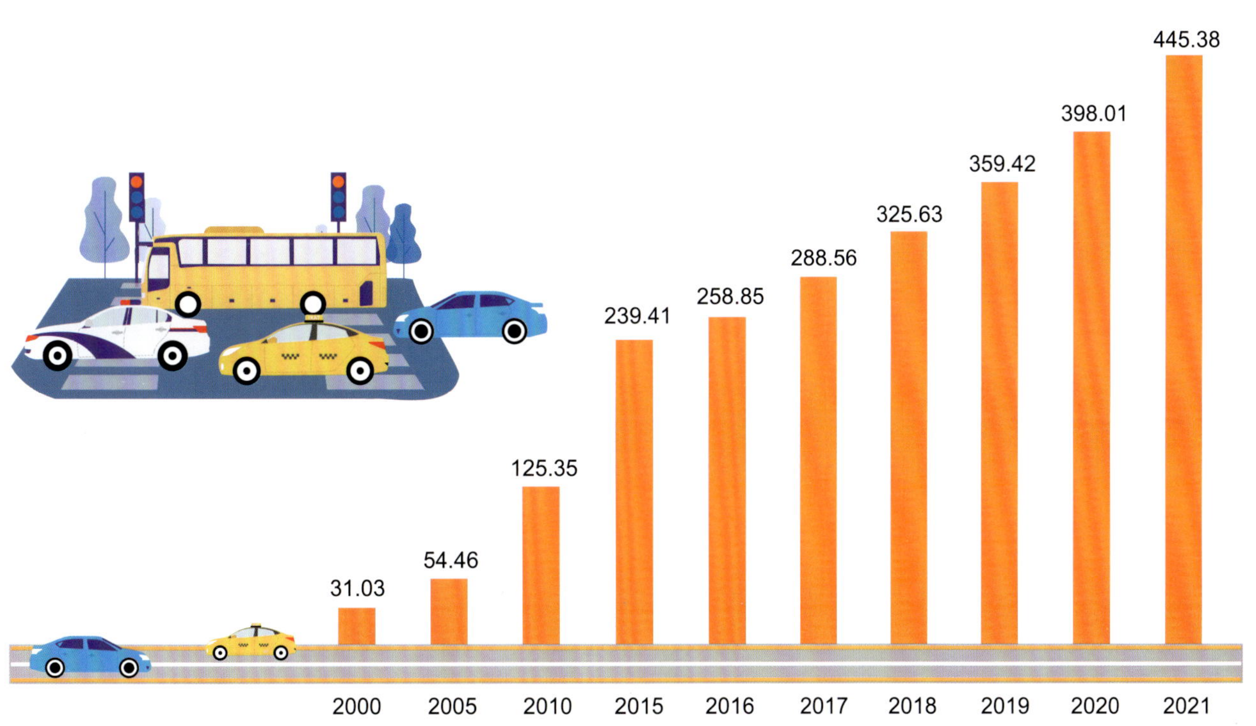

社会消费品零售总额（亿元）
Total Retail Sales of Consumer Goods (100 million yuan)

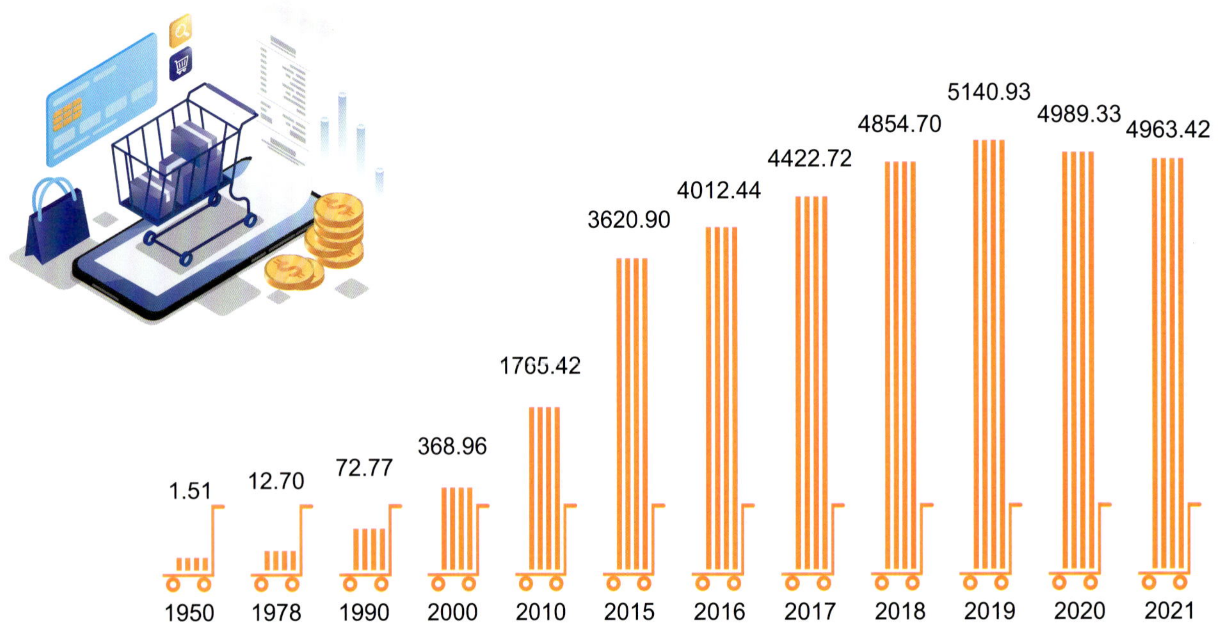

实际利用外资（亿美元）
Actual Utilized Foreign Investment (USD 100 million)

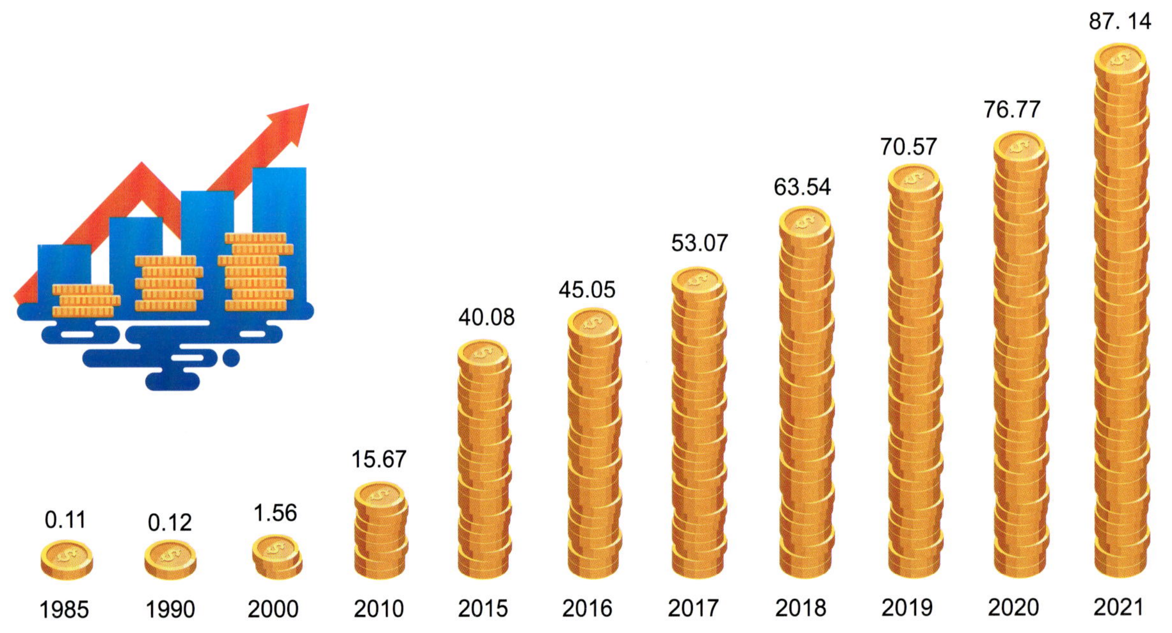

进出口总值

Total Value of Imports and Exports

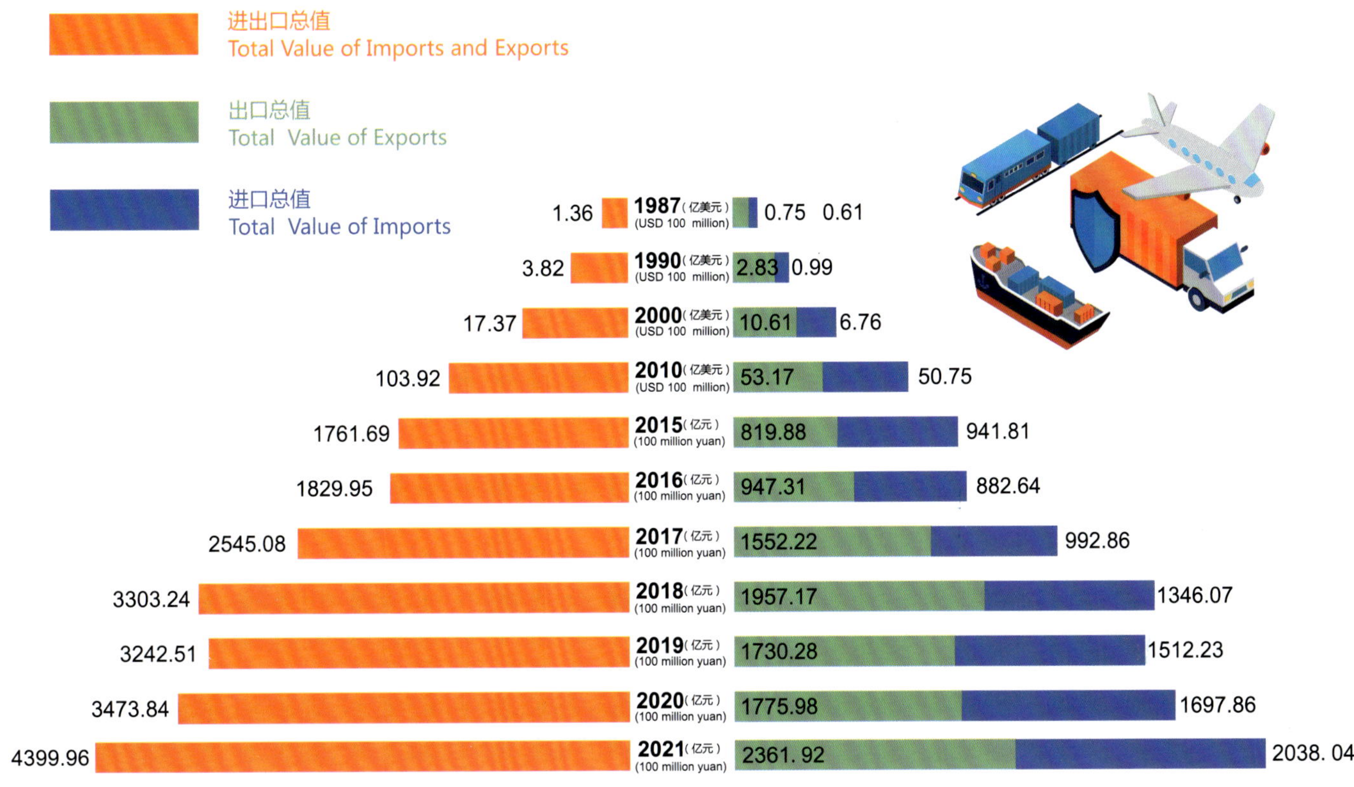

旅游人数及收入

Number of Tourists and Tourism Earnings

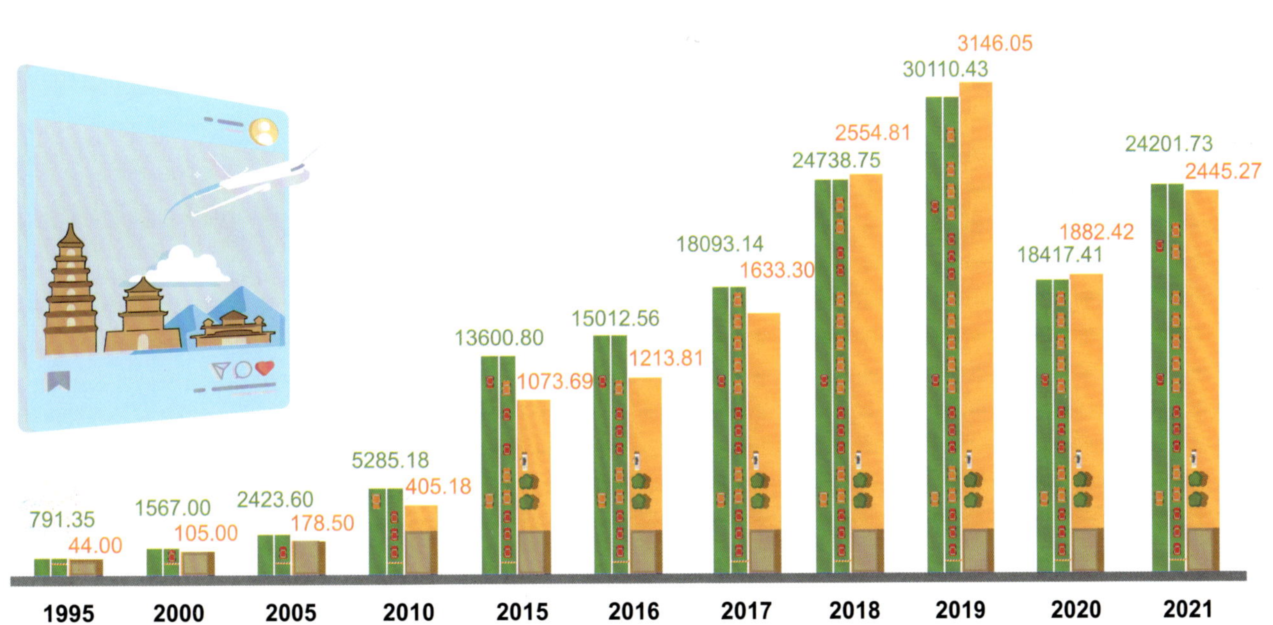

财政收支（亿元）

Government Revenue and Expenditure (100 million yuan)

地方财政一般公共预算收入
General Public Budgetary
Revenue of Local Government
地方财政一般公共预算支出
General Public Budgetary
Expenditure of Local Government
41.39
46.50
73.05
97.82
241.86
371.62
650.99
917.24
641.07
942.52
654.50
1045.09
684.70
1151.87
702.56
1247.02
724.14
1347.58
856.00
1474.62
2000
2005
2010
2015
2016
2017
2018
2019
2020
2021

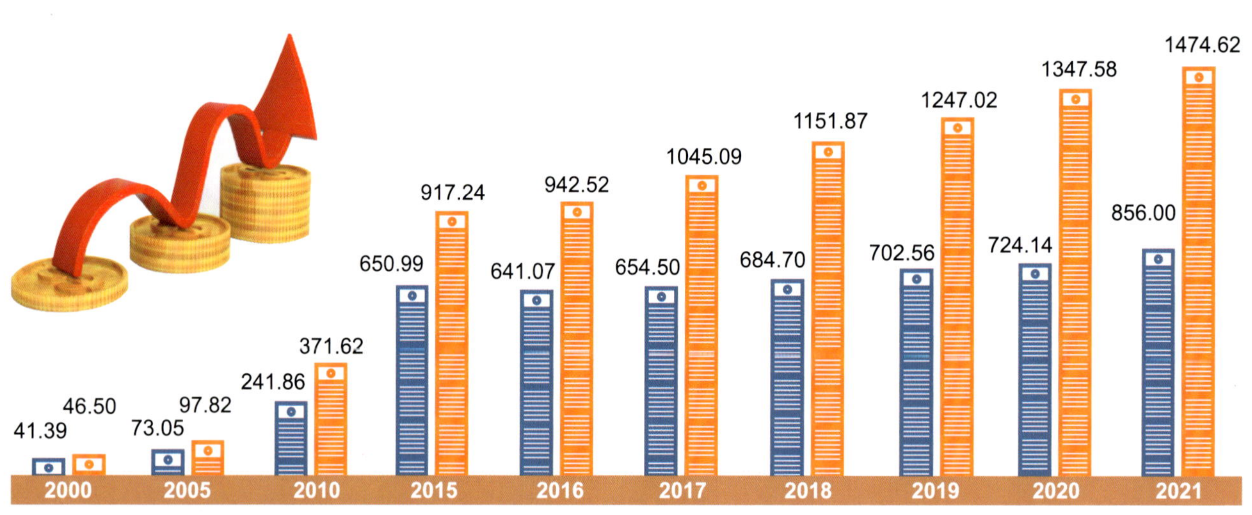

金融机构人民币存贷款年末余额（亿元）

Year-end Deposit and Loans in Financial Institutions (100 million yuan)

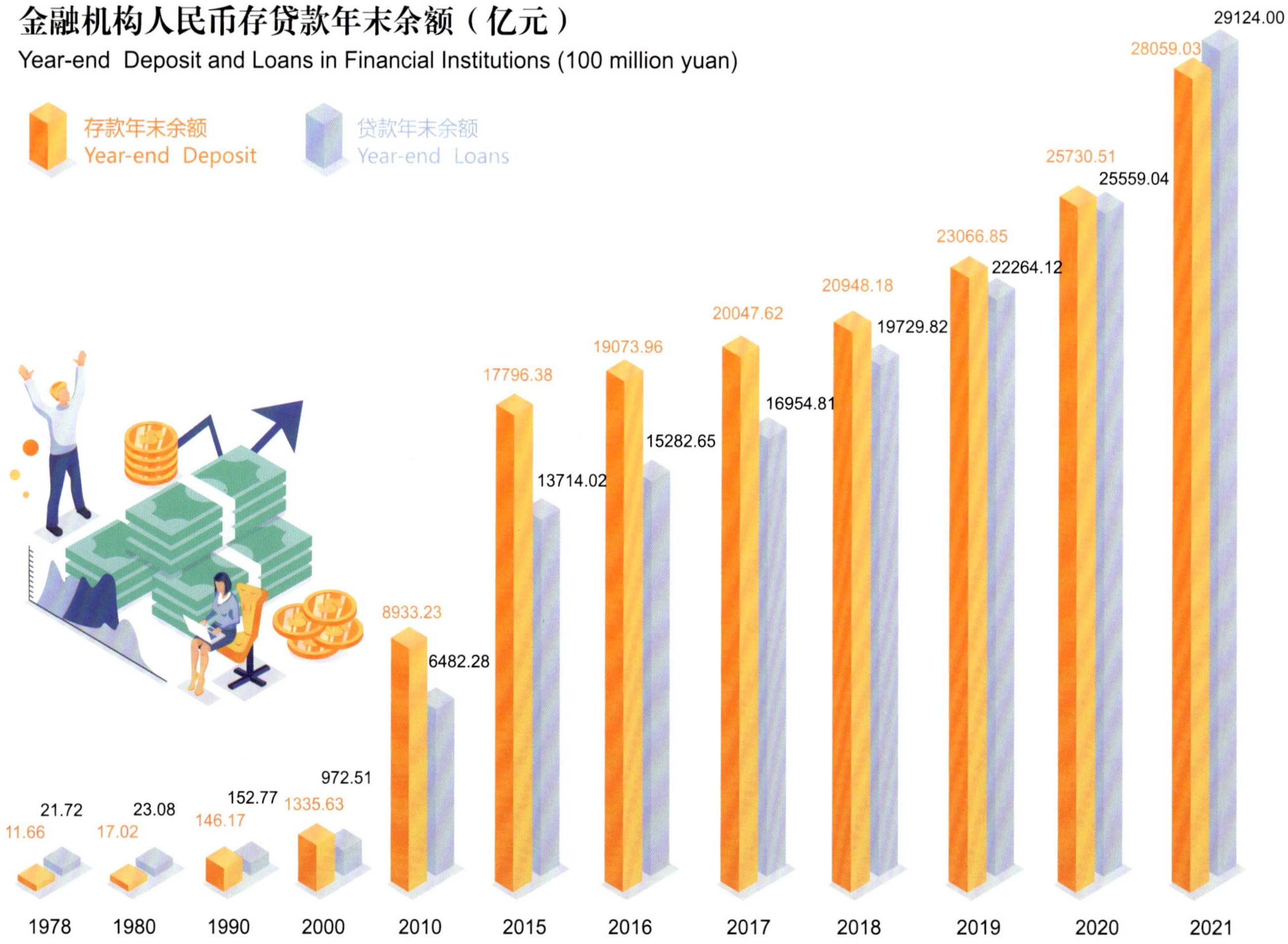

存款年末余额
Year-end Deposit
贷款年末余额
Year-end Loans
11.66
21.72
17.02
23.08
146.17
152.77
1335.63
972.51
8933.23
6482.28
17796.38
13714.02
19073.96
15282.65
20047.62
16954.81
20948.18
19729.82
23066.85
22264.12
25730.51
25559.04
28059.03
29124.00
1978
1980
1990
2000
2010
2015
2016
2017
2018
2019
2020
2021

城市公共运营车辆（辆）

City Operating Vehicles (unit)

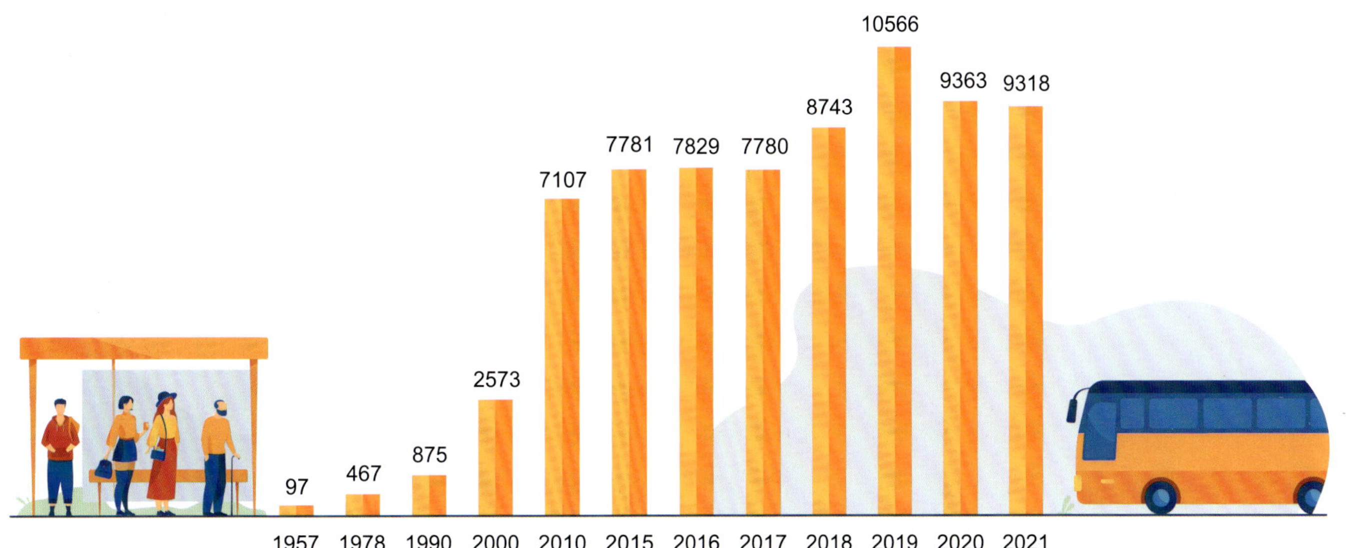

地铁运营线路长度（公里）

Length of Subway Lines in Operation (km)

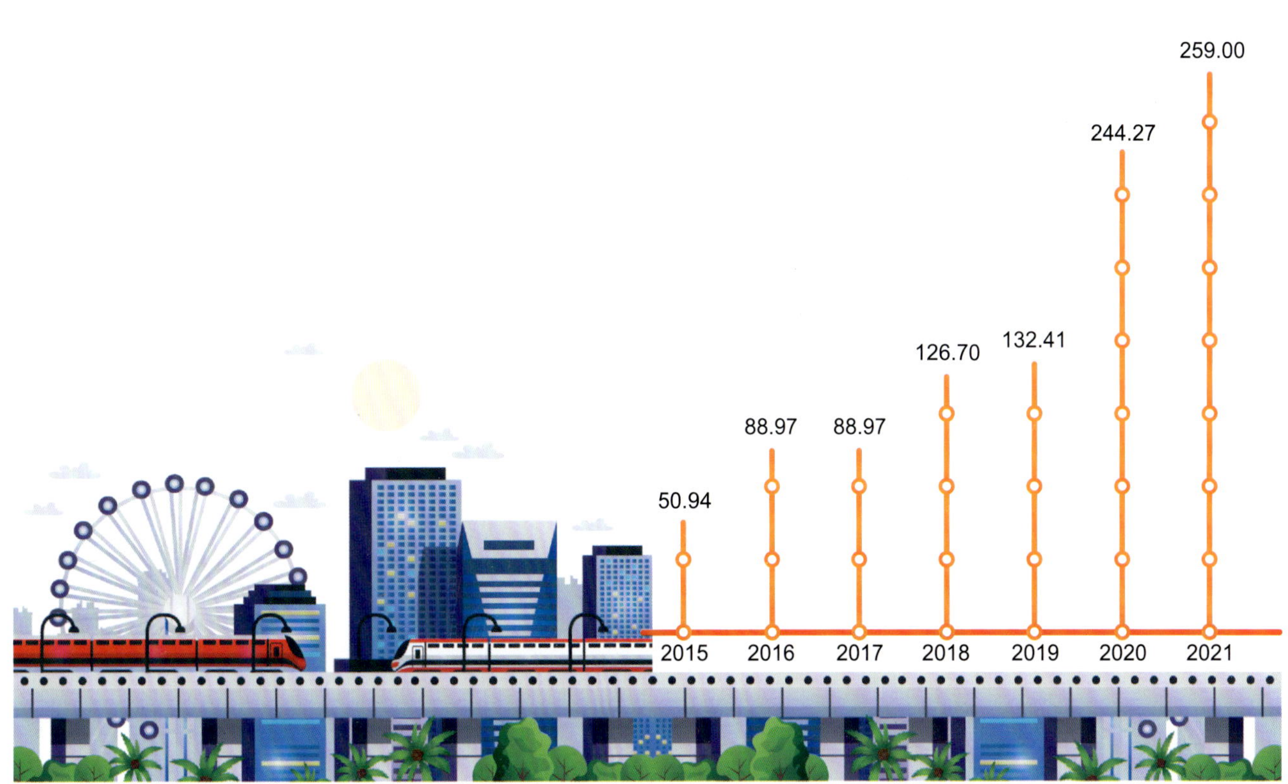

绿地面积（公顷）
Green Area (hectare)

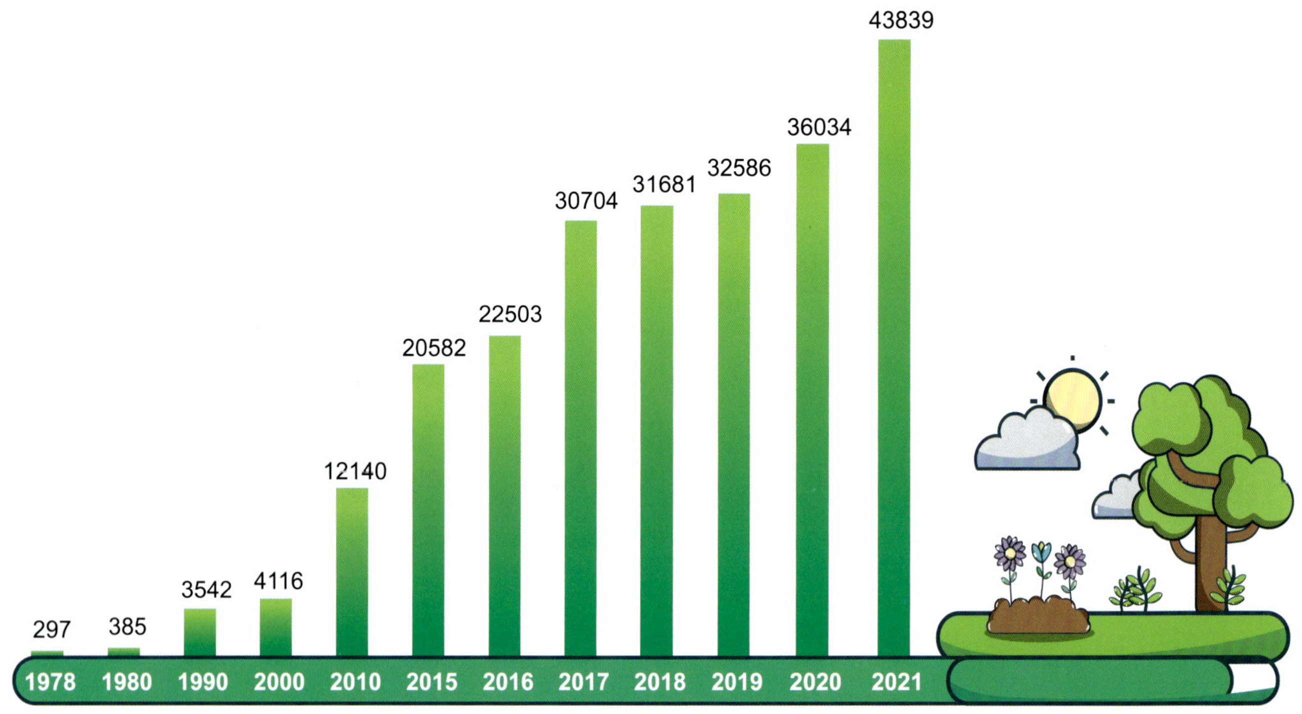

天然气供气总量（万立方米）
Total Natural Gas Supply (10 000 cu.m)

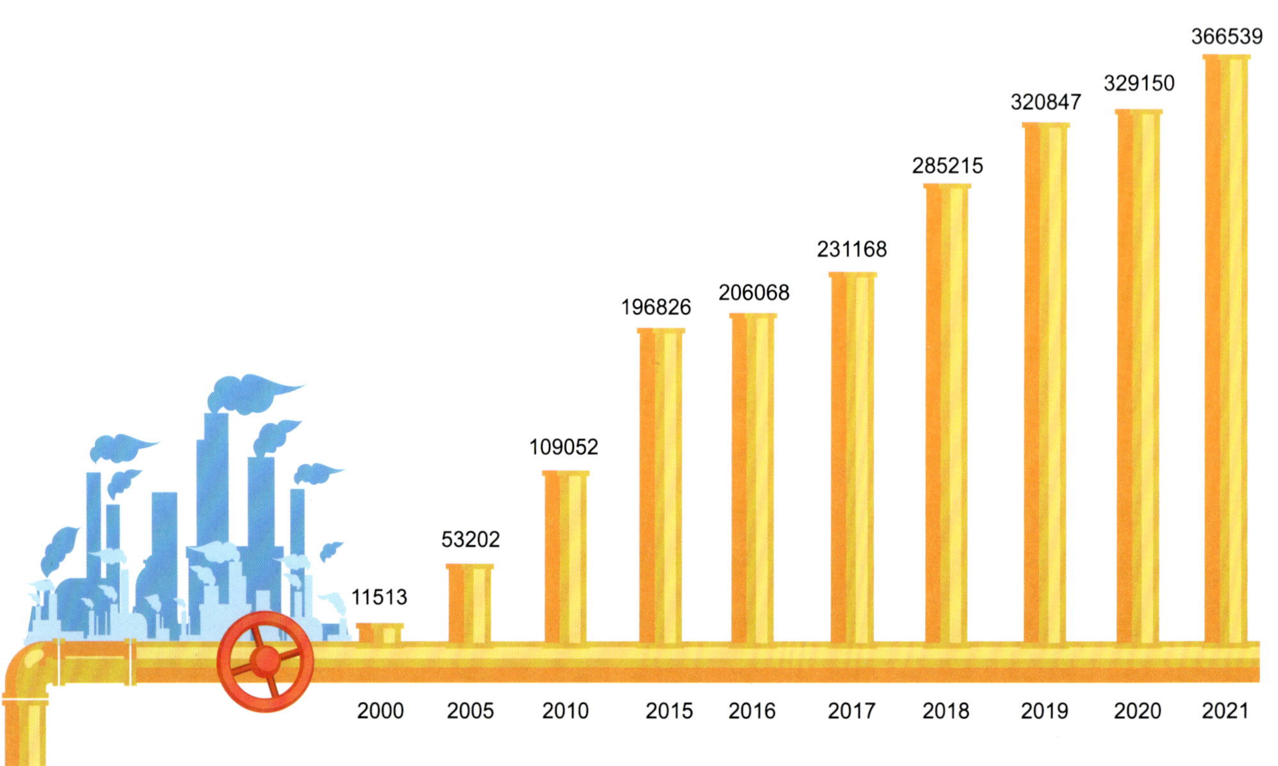

普通教育在校学生（万人）
Total Enrollment of Regular Education (10 000 persons)

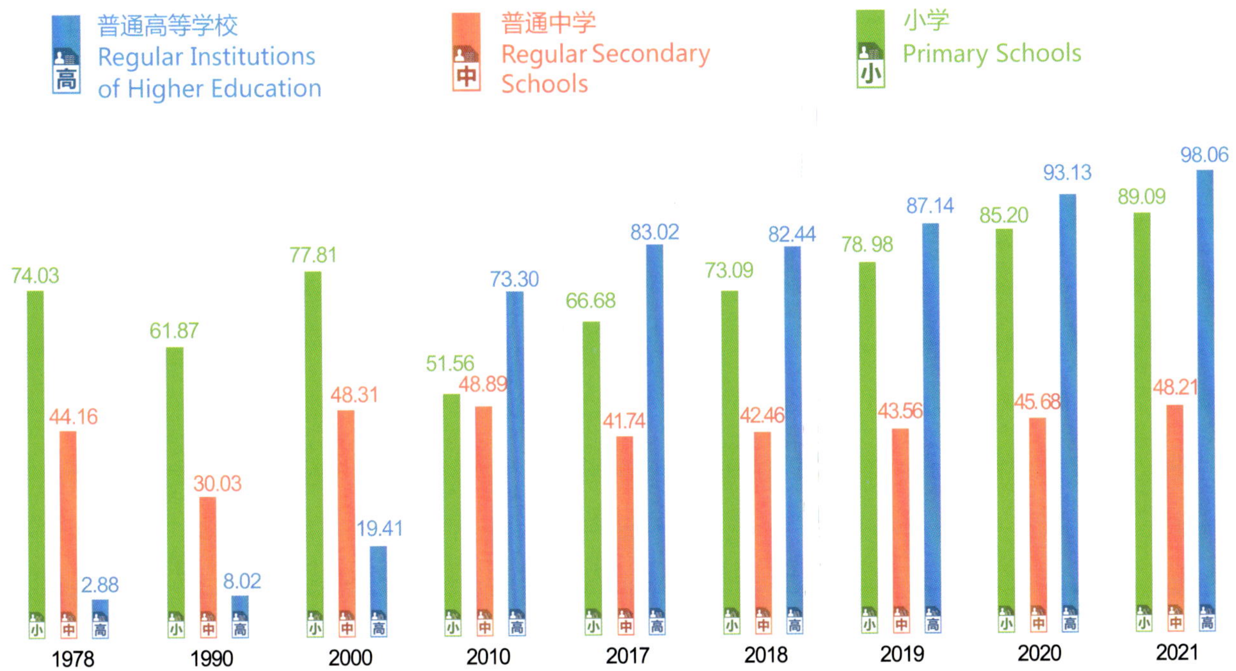

专任教师（万人）
Full-time Teachers (10 000 persons)

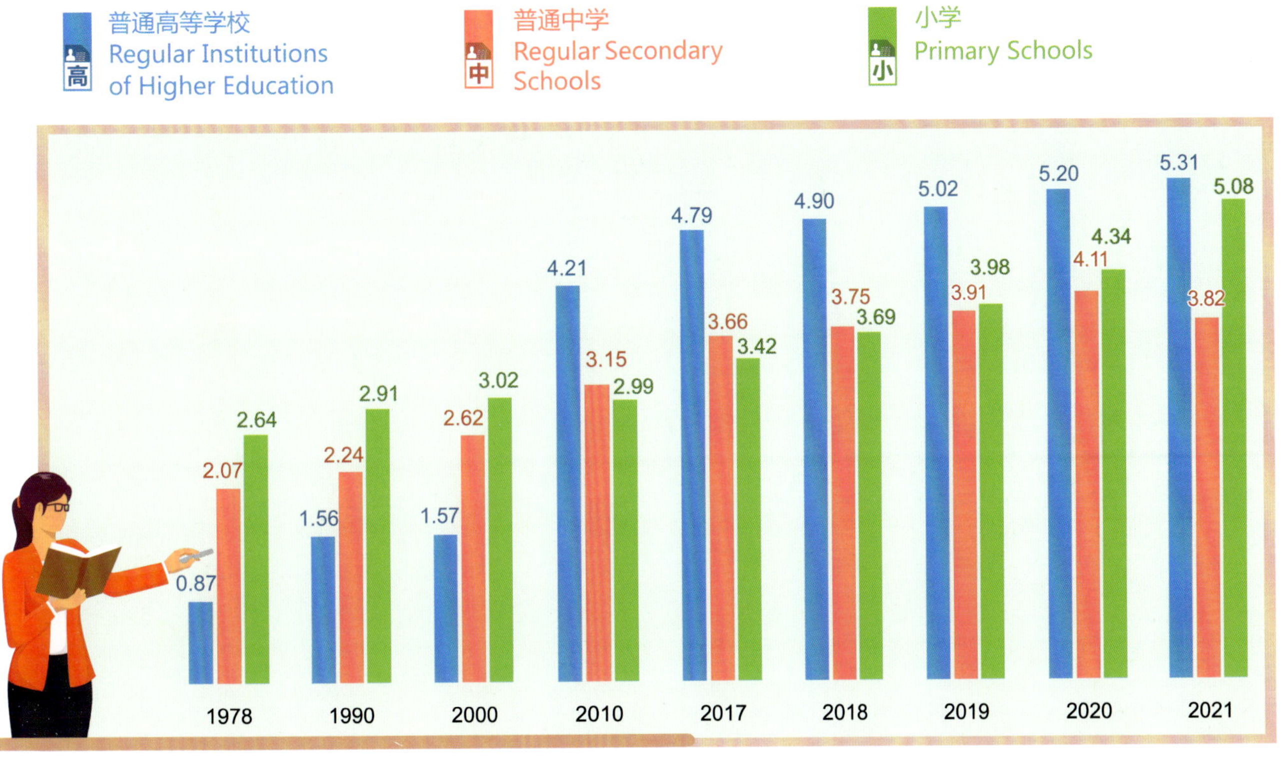

城乡居民收入比（以农村居民人均可支配收入为 1）

The Residents Income Ratio Between Urban and Rural (rural per capita disposable income=1)

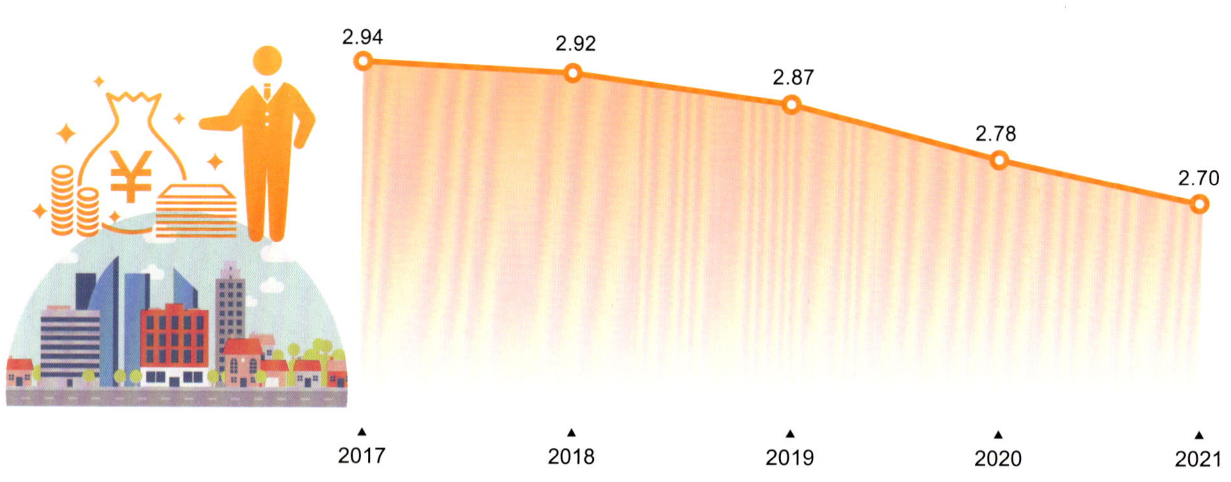

价格指数（以上年价格为100）

Price Index (the price of preceding year=100)

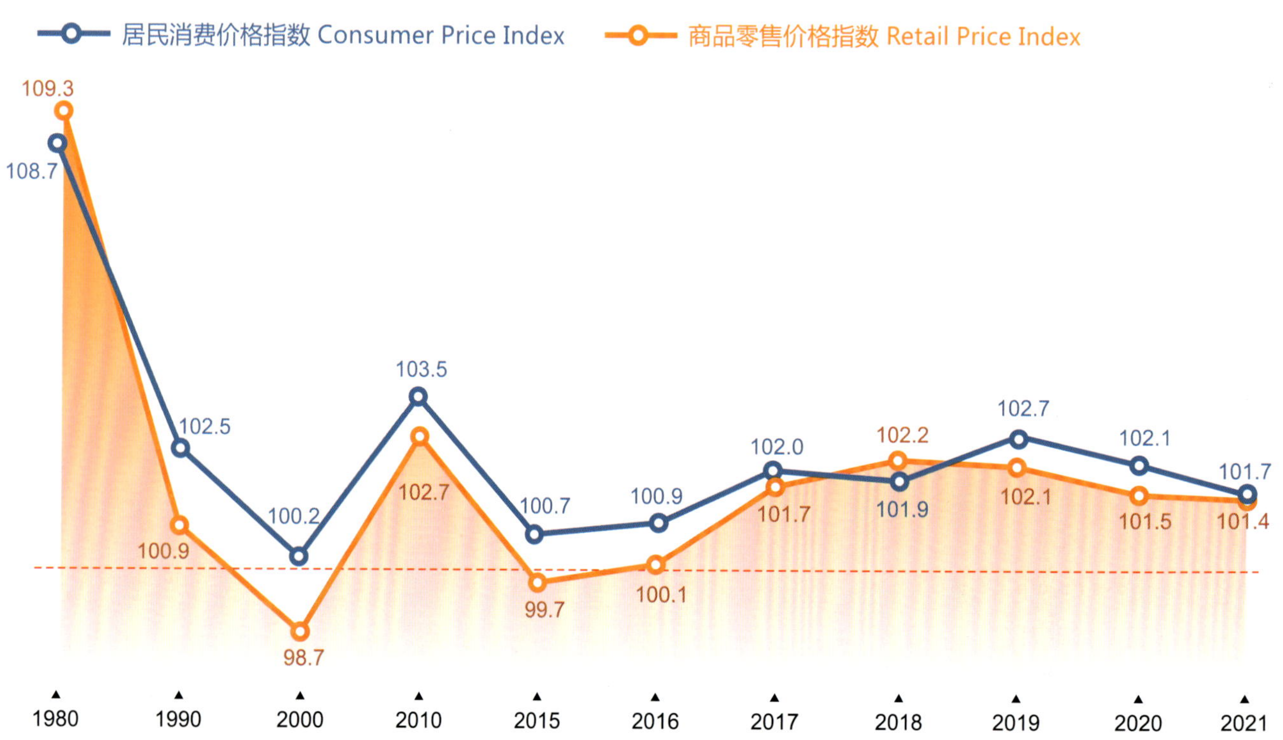

目　　录

CONTENTS

一、综　　合

GENERAL SURVEY

二、基本单位

BASIC UNIT

三、国民经济核算

NATIONAL ECONOMIC ACCOUNTS

四、人口、从业人员与职工工资

POPULATION，EMPLOYEES AND WAGES

五、固定资产投资

INVESTMENT IN FIXED ASSETS

六、财　　政

GOVERNMENT FINANCE

七、物价指数

PRICE INDICES

八、人民生活

PEOPLE'S LIVELIHOOD

九、城市公用事业

URBAN PUBLIC UTILITIES

十、环境保护

ENVIRONMENT PROTECTION

十一、农　业

AGRICULTURE

十二、工　业

INDUSTRY

十三、能　源
ENERGY

十四、建筑业
CONSTRUCTION

十五、运输邮电和信息化
TRANSPORT，POSTAL TELECOMMUNICATION SERVICE AND INFORMATIZATION

十六、国内贸易

DOMESTIC TRADE

十七、对外经济贸易和旅游

FOREIGN TRADE AND ECONOMIC COOPERATION TOURISM

十八、规模以上服务业

SERVICE INDUSTRY OBOVE DESIGNATED SIZE

十九、金融业

FINANCIAL INDUSTRY

二十、教育和科技

EDUCATION, SCIENCE AND TECHNOLOGY

二十一、文化、体育、卫生、社会福利和其他

CULTURE, SPORTS, PUBLIC HEALTH, SOCIAL WELFARE INSTITUTIONS AND OTHER SOCIAL ACTIVITIES

二十二、企业调查

ENTERPRISES INVESTIGATION

西安市2021年国民经济和社会发展统计公报[1]

西安市统计局　国家统计局西安调查队

2022年4月6日

2021年，是党和国家历史上具有里程碑意义的一年，也是西安发展进程中极不平凡的一年。在以习近平同志为核心的党中央坚强领导下，全市上下坚持以习近平新时代中国特色社会主义思想为指导，全面贯彻党的十九大和十九届历次全会精神，深入贯彻习近平总书记来陕考察重要讲话重要指示精神，贯通落实“五项要求”“五个扎实”，统筹疫情防控和经济社会发展，坚持稳中求进工作总基调，主动服务和融入新发展格局，经济社会发展大局稳定，创新活力加速释放，民生保障有力有效，高质量发展持续推进。

一、综合[2]

根据市（区）生产总值统一核算结果，全年地区生产总值[3]（初步核算）10688.28亿元，按可比价格计算，比上年增长4.1%，两年平均增长[4]4.6%。其中，第一产业增加值308.82亿元，增长6.1%；第二产业增加值3585.20亿元，增长0.9%；第三产业增加值6794.26亿元，增长5.7%。三次产业构成为2.89∶33.54∶63.57。全年人均地区生产总值83689元。非公有制经济增加值占地区生产总值比重53.5%。

图1：2017-2021年地区生产总值（亿元）

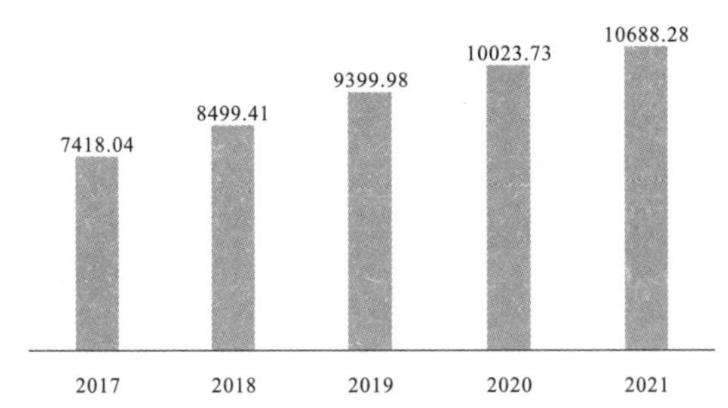

图2：2021年三次产业增加值占地区生产总值比重（%）

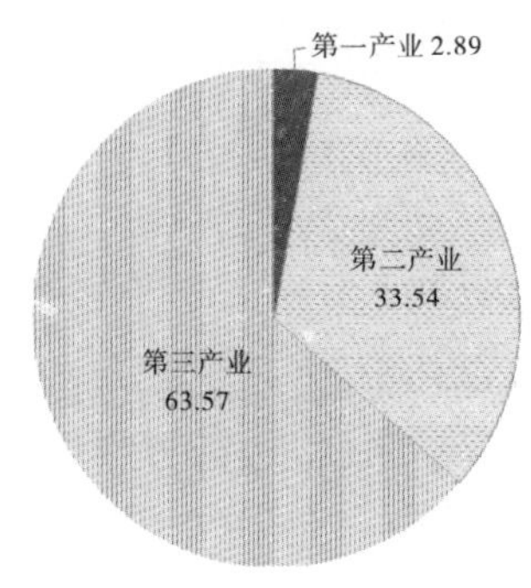

全年居民消费价格比上年上涨1.7%，其中，食品烟酒价格上涨1.9%。商品零售价格上涨1.4%。新建商品住宅销售价格上涨7.5%，二手住宅销售价格上涨6.3%。

图3：2021年居民消费价格月度涨跌幅度（%）

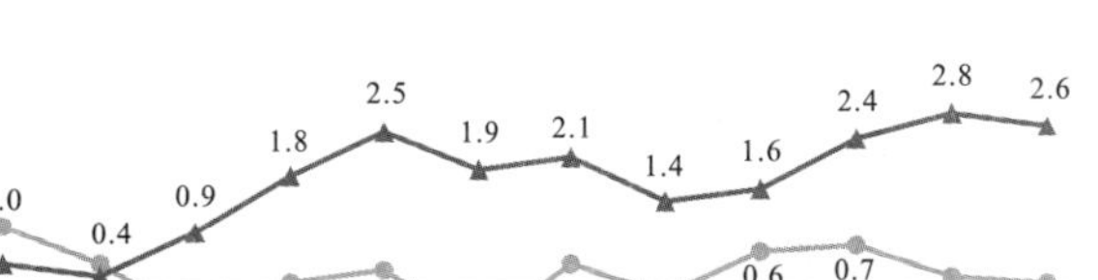

表1：2021年居民消费价格涨跌幅度

指标	涨跌幅度（%）
居民消费价格	1.7
其中：食品烟酒	1.9
衣着	1.1
居住	2.0
生活用品及服务	0.3
交通和通信	2.8
教育文化和娱乐	3.7
医疗保健	−1.7
其他用品和服务	1.5

年末全市常住人口（含西咸共管区）[5]1316.30万人。其中，男性人口672.13万人，占51.06%；女性人口644.17万人，占48.94%。性别比为104.34（以女性为100，男性对女性的比例）。人口城镇化率79.49%。人口出生率8.44‰，死亡率7.51‰，自然增长率0.93‰。

全年新增城镇就业15.98万人，城镇失业人员再就业4.07万人。年末城镇登记失业率为3.6%。

全年新登记市场主体50.09万户，比上年增长11.5%。年末累计在册各类市场主体269.02万户，增长10.7%。

二、农业

全年粮食种植面积386.44万亩，比上年下降2.0%；蔬菜种植面积106.60万亩，增长1.9%；瓜果种植面积14.47万亩，增长1.4%；油料种植面积5.47万亩，增长7.5%；棉花种植面积0.07万亩，下降11.2%。

全年粮食产量141.92万吨，比上年增长1.3%，其中，夏粮产量72.34万吨，增长2.5%；秋粮产量69.58万吨，增长0.1%。肉类产量4.93万吨，增长11.0%；奶类产量13.86万吨，增长0.1%；禽蛋产量4.77万吨，下降7.7%；蔬菜产量362.80万吨，下降0.2%；园林水果产量101.01万吨，增长4.3%。

表2：2021年主要农产品产量及其增长速度

产品名称	单位	产量	比上年增长（%）
粮食	万吨	141.92	1.3
蔬菜	万吨	362.80	-0.2
园林水果	万吨	101.01	4.3
肉类	万吨	4.93	11.0
其中：猪肉	万吨	3.40	23.5
奶类	万吨	13.86	0.1
禽蛋	万吨	4.77	-7.7
猪年末存栏数	万头	32.00	9.8
牛年末存栏数	万头	5.26	1.4
羊年末存栏数	万只	7.48	3.9
家禽年末存栏数	万只	572.22	-8.9

三、工业和建筑业

全年规模以上工业[6]增加值比上年增长5.7%。

全年规模以上工业中，战略性新兴产业[7]总产值比上年增长27.6%，占规模以上工业总产值的比重为49.9%；高技术制造业[8]总产值增长26.6%，占规模以上工业总产值的比重为35.5%。

全年规模以上工业中，装备制造业[9]总产值增长23.4%，占规模以上工业总产值的比重为74.0%。其中，计算机、通信和其他电子设备制造业增长33.8%，电气机械和器材制造业增长38.2%，汽车制造业增长12.1%，金属制品业下降4.4%，铁路、船舶、航空航天和其他运输设备制造业增长10.1%，仪器仪表制造业下降6.3%，通用设备制造业增长10.7%，专用设备制造业增长9.0%。

表3：2021年规模以上工业主要行业产值增长速度

行业	比上年增长（%）
汽车制造业	12.1
铁路、船舶、航空航天和其他运输设备制造业	10.1
电气机械和器材制造业	38.2
医药制造业	-21.6
通用设备制造业	10.7
专用设备制造业	9.0
计算机、通信和其他电子设备制造业	33.8
仪器仪表制造业	-6.3
金属制品业	-4.4
电力、热力生产和供应业	9.7

表4：2021年规模以上工业主要产品产量及其增长速度

产品名称	单位	产量	比上年增长（%）
小麦粉	万吨	23.8	-63.1
饮料	万吨	201.9	24.3
乳制品	万吨	54.5	-6.5
汽车	万辆	63.9	28.3
其中：新能源汽车	万辆	26.9	348.3
智能手机	万台	4917.2	37.6
3D打印设备	台	218	44.4
交流电动机	万千瓦	277.2	14.9
充电桩	个	32000	33.3
单晶硅	万千克	165.1	0.7
多晶硅	万千克	272.0	83.7
电力电缆	万千米	23.3	22.0
光缆	万芯千米	986.7	8.1
光纤	万千米	809.4	10.6
电子元件	亿只	442.0	877.9
集成电路	亿块	59.5	6.1
集成电路圆片	万片	286.6	39.2
锂离子电池	万只	2179.6	5.2
汽车用发动机	万千瓦	804.1	35.1
气体压缩机	万台	98.4	18.1
太阳能电池	万千瓦	1542.5	306.1

全年全社会建筑业增加值1552.18亿元，占地区生产总值比重为14.5%。全市具有资质等级的总承包和专业承包建筑业企业完成建筑业总产值5404.47亿元，比上年增长5.6%，其中，国有及国有控股企业总产值4266.66亿元，增长6.6%。所有资质等级企业签订合同额15151.18亿元，增长7.5%。

四、服务业

全年批发和零售业增加值837.62亿元，比上年下降1.4%；交通运输、仓储和邮政业增加值382.92亿元，增长6.7%；住宿和餐饮业增加值153.50亿元，增长4.8%；金融业增加值1174.47亿元，增长6.0%；房地产业增加值849.55亿元，下降1.0%；其他服务业增加值3294.69亿元，增长9.3%。全年规模以上服务业[10]企业营业收入3075.96亿元，比上年增长10.1%。其中，信息传输、软件和信息技术服务业营业收入增长14.7%。

全年货物运输总量27047.65万吨，比上年增长5.2%；货物运输周转量505.48亿吨公里，增长0.6%。旅客运输总量10632.47万人次，下降25.8%；旅客运输周转量220.44亿人公里，下降4.8%。国际（地区）航线97条，比上年增加5条，境外航班通航3810架次。年末全市机动车保有量445.38万辆，比上年末增加47.37万辆。其中，私人汽车保有量369.06万辆，增加32.25万辆。

表5：2021年客货运输量及其增长速度

指标	单位	绝对数	比上年增长（%）
货物运输总量	万吨	27047.65	5.2
公路	万吨	26526.76	5.2
铁路	万吨	481.34	2.2
民航	万吨	39.56	5.1
旅客运输总量	万人次	10632.47	–25.8
公路	万人次	3332.21	–55.5
铁路	万人次	4282.93	14.4
民航	万人次	3017.33	–2.9

全年邮政行业业务收入（不包括邮政储蓄银行直接营业收入）101.51亿元，比上年增长11.2%。快递服务企业业务量7.87亿件，增长17.2%；业务收入84.18亿元，增长11.2%。全年电信业务总收入168.19亿元，比上年增长8.7%。年末移动电话用户1759.00万户，固定互联网宽带接入用户[11]615.87万户。

五、国内贸易

全年社会消费品零售总额4963.42亿元，比上年增长0.8%。其中，限额以上企业（单位）消费品零售额[12]2419.82亿元，下降3.8%。在限额以上企业（单位）中，按经营地统计，城镇消费品零售额2413.30亿元，下降3.8%；乡村消费品零售额6.52亿元，下降16.4%。按消费类型统计，商品零售2307.11亿元，下降4.6%；餐饮收入112.71亿元，增长17.2%。

在限额以上企业（单位）商品零售额中，粮油、食品类零售额比上年下降6.4%，服装、鞋帽、针纺织品类下降6.9%，化妆品类下降8.1%，金银珠宝类增长31.2%，日用品类增长14.2%，体育、娱乐用品类增长24.7%，书报杂志类增长5.1%，家用电器和音像器材类下降4.0%，文化办公用品类增长4.1%，石油及制品类下降8.4%，汽车类下降2.8%。

全年限额以上企业（单位）中，网上商品零售额[13]652.91亿元，占限额以上消费品零售额的27.0%，比上年提高3.4个百分点。

六、固定资产投资

全年固定资产投资（不含农户）比上年下降11.6%。

按产业分，第一产业投资比上年下降55.2%；第二产业投资下降16.0%，其中，工业投资下降15.8%；第三产业投资下降10.6%。民间投资[14]下降4.7%，基础设施投资[15]下降18.1%，文化产业投资增长26.3%。

表6：2021年主要行业固定资产投资（不含农户）增长速度

行业	比上年增长（%）
固定资产投资（不含农户）	–11.6
制造业	–12.7
其中：农副食品加工业	–19.1
通用设备制造业	4.1
电气机械及器材制造业	6.1
计算机、通信和其他电子设备制造业	11.7
建筑业	15.0
交通运输、仓储和邮政业	–7.4
其中：铁路运输业	229.3
道路运输业	–10.2
水利、环境和公共设施管理业	–20.3
卫生和社会工作	39.6
文化、体育和娱乐业	–5.8
公共管理和社会组织	35.1

全年房地产开发投资比上年下降7.0%。其中，住宅投资下降1.6%，办公楼投资下降25.9%，商业营业用房投资下降13.8%。商品房销售面积1856.73万平方米，下降27.0%。年末商品房待售面积[16]144.50万平方米，比上年末下降3.4%。

七、对外经济

全年进出口总值4399.96亿元，比上年增长26.5%。其中，出口总值2361.92亿元，增长33.0%；进口总值2038.04亿元，增长19.8%。对"一带一路"沿线国家进出口总值704.76亿元，增长29.0%。

在进出口总值中，加工贸易进出口2522.08亿元，增长20.4%，占进出口总值的57.3%；一般贸易进出口

1055.32亿元，增长41.0%，占进出口总值的24.0%。

主要进口商品中，机电产品进口1510.31亿元，增长13.8%。主要出口商品中，机电产品出口2319.36亿元，增长32.6%；农产品出口21.15亿元，下降2.7%；基本有机化学品出口15.65亿元，增长12.3%。

全年实际使用外资87.14亿美元，比上年增长13.5%。

八、财政金融

全年一般公共预算收入855.96亿元，比上年增长18.2%，其中，税收收入682.44亿元，增长19.4%。一般公共预算支出1474.94亿元，比上年增长9.5%。

年末金融机构本外币存款余额28510.03亿元，比上年末增长9.5%；人民币存款余额28059.03亿元，增长9.0%，其中，住户存款余额11996.54亿元，增长9.9%。金融机构本外币贷款余额29411.25亿元，增长14.0%；人民币贷款余额29124.00亿元，增长13.9%。

全年证券市场各类证券交易总额72489.51亿元，比上年增长23.9%。年末全市拥有境内上市公司48家，比上年末增加6家。总股本856.84亿股，总市值13697.47亿元。

年末全市共有保险机构70家，比上年末增加3家。全年保费收入583.27亿元，比上年增长5.9%。全年赔款给付支出176.54亿元，增长11.2%。

九、人民生活和社会保障

根据城乡一体化住户调查，全年全体居民人均可支配收入38701元，比上年增长8.2%。其中，城镇居民人均可支配收入46931元，增长7.4%；农村居民人均可支配收入17389元，增长10.4%。城乡居民收入比为2.70，比上年缩小0.08。

城镇居民人均可支配收入中，工资性收入27872元，比上年增长6.6%；经营净收入2790元，增长2.0%；财产净收入5344元，增长15.3%；转移净收入10925元，增长7.1%。

农村居民人均可支配收入中，工资性收入10632元，比上年增长15.2%；经营净收入2702元，增长1.9%；财产净收入384元，增长1.4%；转移净收入3671元，增长5.1%。

图4：2021年城镇居民人均可支配收入构成（%）

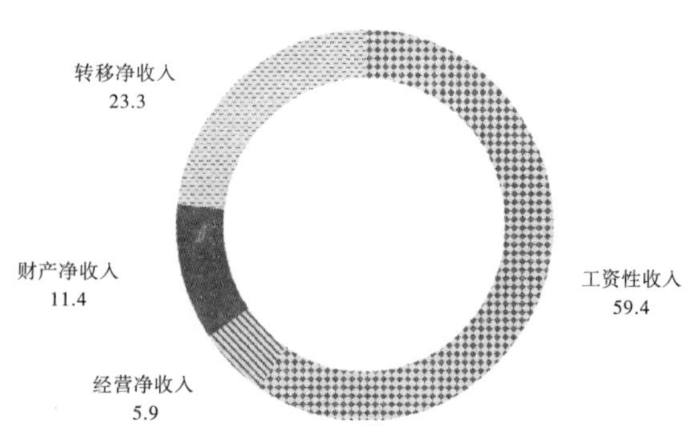

图5：2021年农村居民人均可支配收入构成（%）

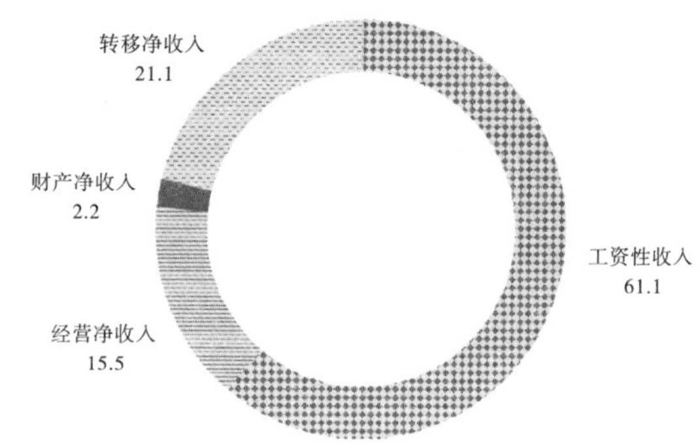

全年全体居民人均消费支出24829元，比上年增长12.0%。其中，城镇居民人均消费支出28810元，增长11.6%；农村居民人均消费支出14521元，增长12.1%。

年末全市参加医疗保险人数1094.10万人，其中，城乡居民医疗保险参保人数684.04万人，城镇职工基本医疗保险（含生育保险）参保人数410.06万人。基本养老保险参保人数814.12万人，其中，城镇企业职工养老保险参保人数528.42万人。失业保险参保人数259.76万人，工伤保险参保人数299.27万人。

年末全市共有提供住宿的养老机构[17]143个，床位2.86万张，收养人数1.15万人。年末城市低保对象1.39万户、1.98万人，发放低保金1.77亿元；农村低保对象2.98万户、7.84万人，发放低保金5.38亿元。7975人享受农村特困人员救助供养，发放供养金1.51亿元。

十、科技、教育、文化、卫生健康和体育

年末全市国家级高新技术企业7140家，比上年末增加1906家。专利授权量64131件，比上年增长41.2%。其中，发明专利授权量14055件。全年技术市场合同交易额2209.49亿元，增长34.0%。

全市普通高等学校（本专科）63所，在校学生81.44万人，毕业生18.89万人。研究生培养单位43所，在校学生16.44万人，毕业生3.61万人。普通中学501所，在校学生48.21万人，毕业生14.00万人。小学1170所，在校学生89.09万人，毕业生10.96万人。

年末全市共有博物馆（不含私营）136座，各级别文物保护单位428处。公共图书馆14个，总流通217.54万人次；市级群众艺术馆1个，文化馆14个，艺术表演团体16个。全年举办各类会展活动307场，其中，举办国际性会展活动10场，全国性会展活动52场；参展参会148万人次。

年末全市共有各类卫生机构7123个，其中，医院375个，社区卫生服务中心（站）264个，卫生院113个。各类卫生技术人员12.33万人，其中，执业（助理）医师4.33万人，注册护士5.70万人。各类卫生机构床位7.95万张，其中，医院床位7.39万张。

全年举办各类群众体育展示表演和竞赛活动共计600项次，我市培养输送运动员参加国际、国内各项比赛获得金牌22枚、银牌25枚、铜牌50枚。

十一、资源、环境和应急管理

全年各类建设用地供应量7.99万亩，其中，供应工业用地1.14万亩。公共供水综合生产能力290万立方米/日。

全年规模以上工业综合能源消费量584.77万吨标准煤，比上年下降2.3%。全社会用电量489.37亿千瓦时，增长17.9%。其中，工业用电量153.75亿千瓦时，增长12.9%。

全年空气质量优良天数265天，比上年增加15天。颗粒物（PM_{10}）年平均浓度为82微克/标立方米，下降5.7%；颗粒物（$PM_{2.5}$）年平均浓度为41微克/标立方米，下降19.6%。城市主要饮用水源水质达标率为100%。区域环境噪声等效声级均值为56.2分贝，道路交通噪声等效声级均值为68.7分贝。

全年发生各类生产安全事故195起、死亡174人，分别比上年下降14.1%和1.7%。其中，道路运输事故[18] 128起、死亡106人；工矿商贸事故66起、死亡67人。

注释：

[1]本公报中2021年数据均为初步统计数。部分数据因四舍五入的原因，存在分项与合计不等的情况。

[2]由于西咸新区数据口径变更为西咸新区直管区，地区生产总值、农业、工业、建筑业、国内贸易、投资等指标增速按可比口径计算。

[3]生产总值、三次产业及相关行业增加值绝对数按现价计算，增长速度按不变价格计算。2017-2020年数据为最终核实数。

[4]两年平均增速是指以2019年同期数为基数，采用几何平均的方法计算的增速。

[5]常住人口包含西安（西咸新区）—咸阳共管区为1316.30万人，不含西安（西咸新区）—咸阳共管区为1287.30万人。

[6]规模以上工业统计标准为年主营业务收入2000万元及以上的工业法人单位。

[7]工业战略性新兴产业包括新一代信息技术产业，高端装备制造产业，新材料产业，生物产业，新能源汽车产业，新能源产业，节能环保产业七大产业中的工业相关行业。

[8]高技术制造业包括医药制造业，航空、航天器及设备制造业，电子及通信设备制造业，计算机及办公设备制造业，医疗仪器设备及仪器仪表制造业，信息化学品制造业。

[9]装备制造业包括金属制品业，通用设备制造业，专用设备制造业，汽车制造业，铁路、船舶、航空航天和其他运输设备制造业，电气机械和器材制造业，计算机、通信和其他电子设备制造业，仪器仪表制造业。

[10]规模以上服务业统计范围包括:年营业收入2000万元及以上的交通运输、仓储和邮政业，信息传输、软件和信息技术服务业，水利、环境和公共设施管理业，卫生行业法人单位；年营业收入1000万元及以上的房地产业（不含房地产开发经营），租赁和商务服务业，科学研究和技术服务业，教育行业法人单位；年营业收入500万元及以上的居民服务、修理和其他服务业，文化、体育和娱乐业，社会工作行业法人单位。

[11]固定互联网宽带接入用户是指报告期末在电信企业登记注册，通过xDSL、FTTx+LAN、FTTH/0以及其他宽带接入方式和普通专线接入公众互联网的用户。

[12]限额以上企业（单位）消费品零售额的统计标准为年主营业务收入2000万元及以上的批发业企业（单位）、500万元及以上的零售业企业（单位）、200万元及以上的住宿和餐饮业企业（单位）。

[13]网上商品零售额是指企业（单位）通过公共网络交易平台（包括自建网站和第三方平台）取得订单，售给个人、社会集团非生产、非经营用的实物商品金额（含增值税），付款可以在网上进行，也可以在网下进行。公共网络包括计算机互联网、移动互联网等。

[14]民间固定资产投资是指具有集体、私营、个人性质的内资企事业单位以及由其控股（包括绝对控股和相对控股）的调查单位建造或购置固定资产的投资。

[15]基础设施投资包括电力、热力、燃气及水的生产和供应业，交通运输、邮政业，电信、广播电视和卫星传输服务业，互联网和相关服务业，水利、环境和公共设施管理业投资。

[16]商品房待售面积是指报告期末已竣工的可供销售或出租的商品房建筑面积中，尚未销售或出租的商品房屋建筑面积，包括以前年度竣工和本期竣工的房屋面积，但不包括报告期已竣工的拆迁还建、统建代建、公共配套建筑、房地产公司自用及周转房等不可销售或出租的房屋面积。

[17]提供住宿的养老机构为正常运营机构数。

[18]道路运输事故为公路客运、公交客运、出租客运、网络约车、旅游客运、租赁、教练、货运、危化品运输、工程救险、校车，包括企业通勤车在内的其他营运性车辆或其他生产经营性车辆等十二类道路运输车辆在从事相应运输活动中发生人员伤亡的事故。

数据口径：

2021年7月，西安市全面代管西咸新区，指标数据逐步调整为仅包含西咸新区直管区口径，不再包含西安（西咸新区）—咸阳共管区。国内贸易、教育、卫生等部分指标由于此变化数据小于去年。进出口、客货运、存贷款、专利等指标数据为西安行政区划口径。

资料来源：

本公报中粮食产量、畜禽产量、物价、居民收入及消费支出数据来自国家统计局西安调查队；城镇新增就业、登记失业率、社会保障数据来自市人力资源和社会保障局；市场主体、专利数据来自市市场监督管理局；财政数据来自市财政局；进出口数据来自西安海关；实际使用外资数据来自市投资合作局；公共图书馆、群众艺术馆、文化馆数据来自市文化和旅游局；博物馆数据来自市文物局；客货运量数据来自市交通运输局；机动车数据来自市公安局；邮政业务数据来自市邮政管理局；电信业务数据来自中国移动西安分公司、中国电信西安分公司、中国联通西安分公司；金融数据来自中国人民银行西安分行营业管理部；证券、保险、期货数据来自市金融工作局；教育数据来自市教育局；科技数据来自市科学技术局；会展数据来自市商务局；体育数据来自市体育局；医疗保险数据来自市医疗保障局；卫生数据来自市卫生健康委员会；社会服务、低保、农村特困人员救助供养数据来自市民政局；建设用地数据来自市自然资源和规划局；供水数据来自市水务局；用电数据来自国网陕西省电力公司西安供电公司；环境监测数据来自市生态环境局；安全生产数据来自市应急管理局；其他数据均来自市统计局。

Statistical Communique of Xi'an City On 2021 National Economic and Social Development[1]

Xi'an Municipal Bureau of Statistics and NBS Survey Office in Xi'an

April 6, 2022

The year 2021 was a year of milestone significance in the history of the Communist Party of China and the People's Republic of China, as well as an extraordinary year in the development of Xi'an. Under the strong leadership of the Central Committee of the Communist Party of China (CPC) with Comrade Xi Jinping as the core, the whole city took Xi Jinping Thought on Socialism with Chinese Characteristics for a New Era as the guideline, fully implemented the spirits of the 19th CPC National Congress and the Plenary Sessions of the 19th Central Committee of the CPC, earnestly implemented the guiding principles of Xi's speeches made during his visit in Shaanxi, thoroughly implemented the "Five Requirements" for promoting sustained and sound economic growth, advancing agricultural modernization, strengthening cultural advancements, ensuring and improving people's wellbeing, and exercising strict governance over the Party, coordinated pandemic prevention and control and economic and social development, upheld the underlying principle of pursuing progress while ensuring stability, and took an initiative in serving and getting integrated into the new developmental paradigm. The overall economic and social development was stable; innovation and vitality were unleashed in an accelerated manner; people's livelihood was strongly and effectively safeguarded; high-quality development was continuously promoted.

I. General Outlook[2]

According to the unified accounting results of the city (district), the gross domestic product (GDP) [3] was 1068.828 billion yuan based on preliminary estimation in 2021, up 4.1% over the previous year with the average two-year growth [4] of 4.6%. Of this, the added value of the primary industry reached 30.882 billion yuan, up 6.1%. The added value of the secondary industry was 358.52 billion yuan, up 0.9%. The added value of the tertiary industry reached 679.426 billion yuan, up 5.7%. The three industries constitute 2.89 : 33.54 : 63.57. The annual GDP per capita of the city was 83689 yuan. The added value of the non-public sector accounted for 53.5% of GDP.

Table 1 District GDP from 2017 to 2021 (100 million yuan)

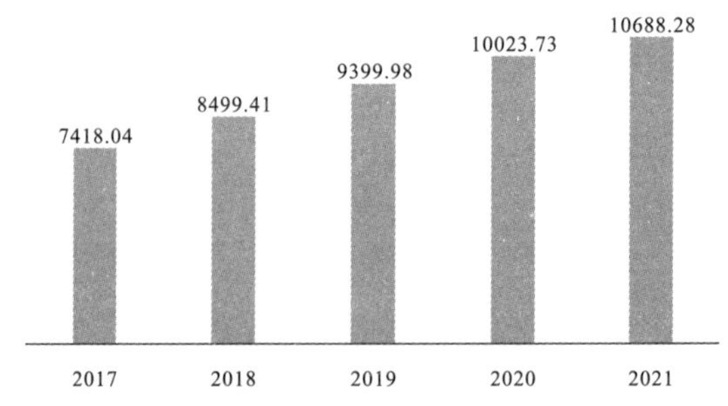

Table 2 Proportion of added value of three industries to GDP in 2021 (%)

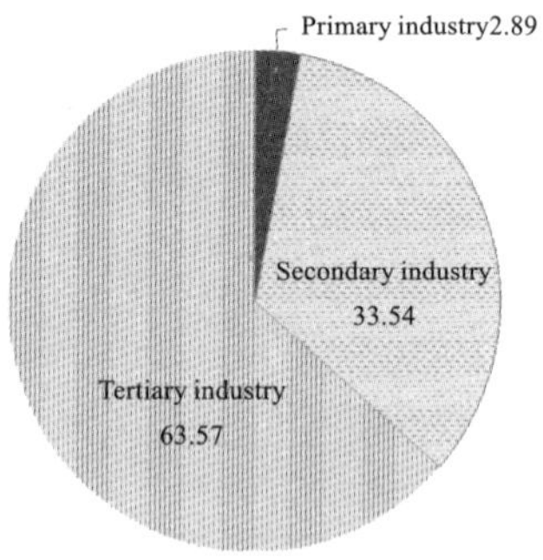

The consumer price index rose by 1.7%, of which the prices of food, tobacco and alcohol rose by 1.9%. Retail prices rose 1.4%. Sales prices of new commercial residential buildings rose by 7.5% and sales prices of second-hand housing rose by 6.3%.

Table 3 Monthly changes of consumer prices in 2021(%)

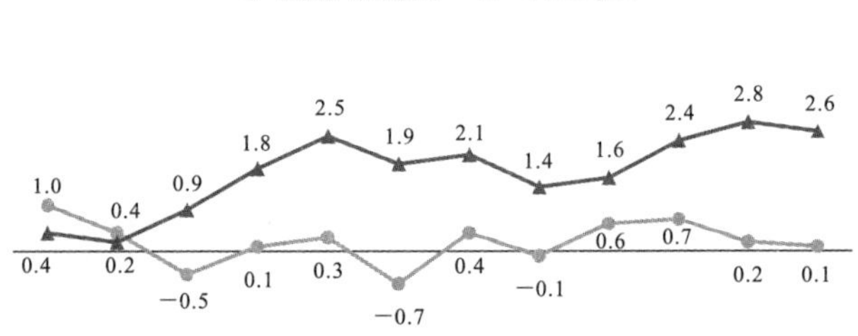

Sheet 1 Increase and decrease rate of consumer prices in 2021(%)

Item	Rise or fall (%)
Consumer price	1.7
Food, alcohol and tobacco	1.9
Dress	1.1
Housing	2.0
Articles and services for daily use	0.3
Transportation and Communications	2.8
Education, culture and entertainment	3.7
Health care	-1.7
Other supplies and services	1.5

By the end of the year, the city's permanent resident population (including mutually controlled Xixian New Area)[5] reached 13163000. Of the total, the male population was 6721300, accounting for 51.06%; the female population was 6441700, accounting for 48.94%. The sex ratio was 104.34 (104.34 males per 100 females). The urbanization rate was 79.49%. The birth rate was 8.44‰, the death rate was 7.51‰, and the natural growth rate was 0.93‰.

A total of 159800 urban jobs were created in the year, and 40700 unemployed urban workers were re-employed. The registered urban unemployment rate was 3.6% at the end of the year.

The number of newly registered market entities was 500900 in the year, an increase of 11.5% over the previous year. By the end of the year, a total of 2690200 market entities of all kinds were registered, an increase of 10.7%.

II. Agriculture

The total sown area of grain was 3.8644 million mu, down 2.0% from the previous year. The sown area of vegetables was 1.066 million mu, up 1.9%; the sown area of melon and fruit was 144700 mu, up 1.4 %; the sown area of oil-bearing crops was 54700 mu, up 7.5%; the sown area of cotton was 700 mu, down 11.2 %.

The total output of grain of the year was 1.4192 million tons, up 1.3% from the previous year. Of the total, the output of summer grain was 723400 tons, up 2.5%; the output of autumn grain was 695800 tons, up 0.1%.The output of meat was 49300 tons, up 11.0%; the output of milk was 138600 tons, up 0.1%; the output of eggs was 47700 tons, down 7.7%; the output of vegetables was 3.628 million tons, down 0.2%; the output of garden fruits was 1.0101 million tons, up 4.3%.

Sheet 2 The main Product of Agriculture Production in 2021

Name of Product	Units	Output	Growth over the last year (%)
Grain	10,000 tons	141.92	1.3
Vegetable	10,000 tons	362.80	-0.2
Garden fruit	10,000 tons	101.01	4.3
Meat	10,000 tons	4.93	11.0
#Pork	10,000 tons	3.40	23.5
Milk	10,000 tons	13.86	0.1
Poultry egg	10,000 tons	4.77	-7.7
Year-end Pig on hand	10,000 head	32.00	9.8
Year-end Ox on hand	10,000 head	5.26	1.4
Year-end Sheep on hand	10,000 head	7.48	3.9
Year-end Fowl on hand	10,000 head	572.22	-8.9

III. Industry and Construction

The total value added of industrial enterprises above the designated size[6] increased by 5.7% over the previous year.

In 2021, of the industrial enterprises above the designated size, the value added of strategic emerging industries [7] increased by 27.6% from the previous year, accounting for 49.9% of the total value of the industrial enterprises above the designated size; the value added of high-tech manufacturing industry [8] increased by 26.6% from the previous year, accounting for 35.5% of the total value of the industrial enterprises above the designated size.

In 2021, of the industrial enterprises above the designated size, the value of the equipment manufacturing industry [9] increased by 23.4%, accounting for 74.0% of the total value of the industrial enterprises above the designated size. Among them, computers, communications and other electronic equipment manufacturing rose 33.8%, electrical machinery and equipment manufacturing industry rose38.2%, automobile manufacturing industry rose12.1%, metal products industry declined 4.4%, railway, shipbuilding, aerospace and other transportation equipment manufacturing industry increases 10.1%, the instrumentation manufacturing industry fell 6.3%, general equipment manufacturing rose 10.7%, and special equipment manufacturing rose 9.0%.

Sheet 3 Growth rate of out value of major industrial industries above the designated size in 2021 (%)

Industry	Growth over the last year (%)
Automobile manufacturing industry	12.1
Railway ship, aerospace and other transportation	10.1
Electrical machinery and equipment manufacturing	38.2
Pharmaceutical manufacturing industry	-21.6
General equipment manufacturing	10.7
Special equipment manufacturing	9.0
Computers, communications and other electronic equipment manufacturing	33.8
Instrumentation manufacturing industry	-6.3
Metal products industry	-4.4
Electricity and heat production and supply industry	9.7

Sheet 4 Output and growth rate of major products of industrial enterprises above the designated size in 2021

Product	Unit	Output	Growth over the last year (%)
Wheat meal	10,000 tons	23.8	-63.1
Drink	10,000 tons	201.9	24.3
Dairy	10,000 tons	54.5	-6.5
Automobile	10,000 units	63.9	28.3
#new energy vehicle	10,000 units	26.9	348.3
Smartphones	10,000 units	4917.2	37.6
3D printing equipment	unit	218	44.4
AC motors	10,000 kilowatts	277.2	14.9
Charging station	unit	32000	33.3
Monocrystalline silicon	10,000 kg	165.1	0.7
Polycrystalline silicon	10,000 kg	272.0	83.7
Electric cable	10,000 km	23.3	22.0
Optical cable	10,000 core kilometers	986.7	8.1
Optical fiber	10,000 km	809.4	10.6
Electronic component	100 million units	442.0	877.9
Integrated circuit	100 million units	59.5	6.1
Integrated circuit chip	10,000 units	286.6	39.2
Lithium-ion battery	10,000 units	2179.6	5.2
Automobile engine	10,000 kilowatts	804.1	35.1
Gas compressor	10,000 units	98.4	18.1
Solar cell	10,000 kilowatts	1542.5	306.1

The added value of the construction industry reached 155.218 billion yuan, accounting for 14.5% of the district GDP. The total value of general contracting and specialized contracting construction enterprises with qualification grades reached 540.447 billion yuan, up 5.6%, among which the output value of state-owned and state holding enterprises was 426.666 billion yuan, up 6.6%. The value of contracts signed by enterprises of all levels of qualification reached 1515.118 billion yuan, up 7.5%.

IV. Service Sector

The added value of wholesale and retail businesses amounted to 83.762 billion yuan, down 1.4% over the previous year; transportation, warehousing and postal services added 38.292 billion yuan, up 6.7%;the added value of the accommodation and catering industry reached 15.35 billion yuan, up 4.8%; the added value of the financial sector reached 117.447 billion yuan, up 6.0%;the added value of the real estate industry reached 84.955 billion yuan, down 1.0%; the added value of other services is 329.469 billion yuan, up 9.3%.The annual operating revenue of service enterprises above the designated size [10] was 307.596 billion yuan, an increase of 10.1% over the previous year, with the operating revenue of information transmission, software and information technology services increasing by 14.7%. Cargo transport totaled 270.4765 million tons, an increase of 5.2% over the previous year. Cargo transport turnover reached 50.548 billion ton-km, up 0.6%. The total number of passenger trips reached 106.3247 million, down 25.8%; passenger traffic amounted to 22.044 billion passenger-km, down 4.8%. There were 97 international (district) routes, up five from a year ago, and 3810 overseas flights. At the end of the year, the number of motor vehicles in the city was 4453800, an increase of 473700 over the previous year. Among them, the number of private car PARC reached 3690600, up 322500.

Sheet 5 Passenger and freight transportation volume and growth in 2021

Indicator	Unit	Absolute number	Growth over the last year (%)
Total cargo transportation	10,000 tons	27047.65	5.2
Highway	10,000 tons	26526.76	5.2
Railway	10,000 tons	481.34	2.2
Civil aviation	10,000 tons	39.56	5.1
Total passenger transportation	10,000 person-times	10632.47	-25.8
Highway	10,000 person-times	3332.21	-55.5
Railway	10,000 person-times	4282.93	14.4
Civil aviation	10,000 person-times	3017.33	-2.9

The total revenue (excluding the direct operating revenue of postal savings banks) of postal services reached 10.151 billion yuan, up 11.2% over the previous year. The express delivery business volume was 787 million pieces, an increase of 17.2% over the previous year, with revenue increasing 11.2% to 8.418 billion yuan. The total revenue of telecom business reached 16.819 billion yuan, up 8.7%. By the end of the year, there were 17.59 million mobile phone users, as well as fixed Internet broadband access users[11] 6.1587 million households.

V. Domestic Trade

Total retail sales of consumer goods of the year were 496.342 billion yuan, an increase of 0.8% over the previous year, with the retail sales of consumer goods by enterprises (units) above the designated size [12] falling 3.8% to 241.982 billion yuan. Among enterprises (units) above the designated size, according to local statistics, the retail sales of consumer goods in urban areas reached 241.33 billion yuan, down 3.8%. Rural retail sales of consumer goods were 652 million yuan, down 16.4%. According to consumption patterns, retail sales of goods were 230.711 billion yuan, down 4.6%; food and beverage revenue was 11.271 billion yuan, up 17.2%.

For the retail sales of goods among enterprises (units) above the designated size, the retail sales were down 6.4% in grain, oil, and food from a year earlier, down 6.9% in clothing, shoes, hats, needles andtextiles, down 8.1% in cosmetics, up 31.2% in gold and silver jewelry, up 14.2% in daily necessities, up 24.7% in sports and entertainment products, up 5.1% in books, newspapers and magazines, down 4.0% in household appliances and audio-visual equipment, up 4.1% in cultural office supplies, down 8.4% in oil and products, and down 2.8% in motor vehicles.

Among enterprises (units) above the designated size, the online retail sales of goods [13] were 65.291 billion yuan, accounting for 27.0% of the total retail sales of enterprises (units) above the designated size, up 3.4 percentage points over the previous year.

VI. Investment in Fixed Assets

In 2021, investment in fixed assets (excluding rural households) fell by 11.6% over the previous year.

In terms of industries, investment in the primary industry decreased by 55.2% compared with the previous year. Investment in the secondary industry increased by 16.0%, of which industrial investment decreased by 15.8%. Investment in the tertiary industry decreased by 10.6%. Private investment in fixed assets [14] decreased by 4.7% over the previous year; infrastructureinvestment[15] decreased by 18.1%,and cultural industryinvestment increased by 26.3%.

Sheet 6 Growth rate of fixed assets investment by industry (excluding farmers) in 2021

Industry	Growth rate(%)
Investment fixed assets (excluding farmers)	-11.6
Manufacturing	-12.7
#Agriculture, forestry animal husbandry and fishery	-19.1
General equipment manufacturing	4.1
Electrical machinery and equipment manufacturing	6.1
Computers, communications and other electronic equipment manufacturing	11.7
Construction	15.0
Transportation, warehousing and postal services	-7.4
#Transportation by railway	229.3
Transportation by highway	-10.2
Water, environmental and public utility management	-20.3
Health and social work	39.6
Culture, sports and entertainment	-5.8
Public administration and social organization	35.1

The investment in real estate development decreased by 7.0% over the previous year. Among them,residential investment fell by 1.6%,investment in office buildings fell by 25.9%, and investment in commercial premises fell by 13.8%. The sales area of commercial housing was 18.5673 million square meters, down 27.0%. At the end of the year, the area of commercial housing for sale[16] was 1.445 million square meters, down 3.4% from the previous year.

VII. Foreign Economic Relations

Imports and exports totaled 439.996 billion yuan in the year, up 26.5% from the previous year. Among them, exports reached 236.192 billion yuan, up 33.0%; imports reached 203.804 billion yuan, up 19.8%. Import and export to countries along the "the belt and road initiative" countries reached 70.476 billion yuan, an increase of 29.0%.

Of the total value of imports and exports, processing trade totaled 252.208 billion yuan, up 20.4% and accounting for 57.3% of the total value. Imports and exports in general trade totaled 105.532 billion yuan, up 41.0% and accounting for 24.0% of the total value of imports and exports.

The main imports included mechanical and electrical products, which reached 151.031 billion yuan, up 13.8%. The main exports were mechanical and electrical products, which totaled 231.936 billion yuan, up 32.6%; the export of agricultural products reached 2.115 billion yuan, down 2.7%; the export of organic chemicals came to 1.565 billion yuan, up 12.3%.

The actual use of foreign capital reached 8.714 billion US dollars, an increase of 13.5% over the previous year.

VIII. Finance and Financial Intermediation

In 2021, general public budget revenue was 85.596 billion yuan, an increase of 18.2% over the previous year, of which the tax revenue was 68.244 billion yuan, a decrease of 19.4%. The general public budget expenditure was 147.494 billion yuan, an increase of 9.5% over the previous year.

At the end of the year, the balance of local and foreign currency deposits of financial institutions was 2851.003 billion yuan, an increase of 9.5% over that at the end of the previous year. The deposit balance of RMB was 2805.903 billion yuan, up 9.0%, among which, the household deposit balance was 1199.654 billion yuan, up 9.9%, The balance of domestic and foreign currency loans of financial institutions was 2941.125 billion yuan, up 14.0%. The balance of RMB loans was 2912.4 billion yuan, up 13.9%.

All kinds of securities traded on the stock market totaled 7248.951 billion yuan last year, an increase of 23.9% over the previous year. At the end of the year, the city had 48 domestic listed companies, six more than the previous year, The total listed capital was 85.684 billion shares and the total market value was 1369.747 billion yuan.

At the end of the year, there were 70 insurance institutions in the city, up three from a year ago. The annual premium income was 58.327 billion yuan, an increase of 5.9% over the previous year. The government paid 17.654 billion yuan in damages, an increase of 11.2% over the previous year.

IX. People' s Livelihoodand Social Security

According to the household survey of urban-rural integration, the per capita disposable income of residents in the whole city was 38701 yuan, an increase of 8.2% over the previous year. Among them, the per capita disposable income of urban residents was 46931 yuan, an increase of 7.4%; the per capita disposable income of rural residents was 17389 yuan, an increase of 10.4%. The income ratio of urban and rural residents was 2.70, which was 0.08 smaller than that of the previous year.

Among the per capita disposable income of urban residents, the wage income was 27872 yuan, an increase of 6.6% over the previous year; the net operating income was 2790 yuan, an increase of 2.0%; the net property income was 5344 yuan, an increase of 15.3%; the net transfer income was 10925 yuan, an increase of 7.1%.

Among the per capita disposable income of rural residents, the wage income was 10632 yuan, an increase of 15.2% over the previous year; the net operating income was 2702 yuan, an increase of 1.9%; the net property income was 384 yuan, an increase of 1.4%; the net transfer income was 3671 yuan, an increase of 5.1%.

Table 4 Composition of per capita disposable income of urban residents in 2021 (%)

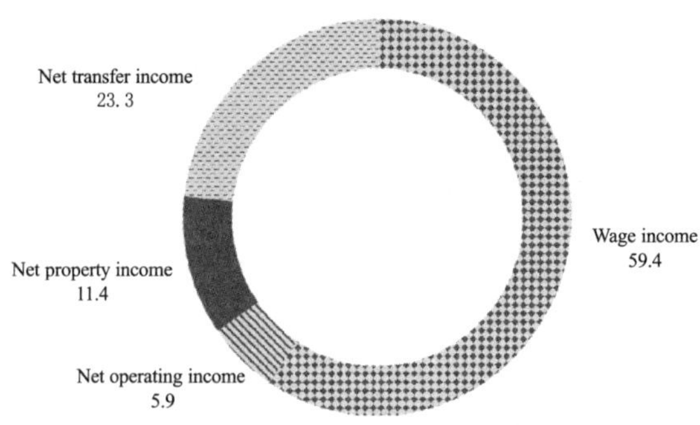

Table 5 Composition of per capita disposable income of rural residents in 2021 (%)

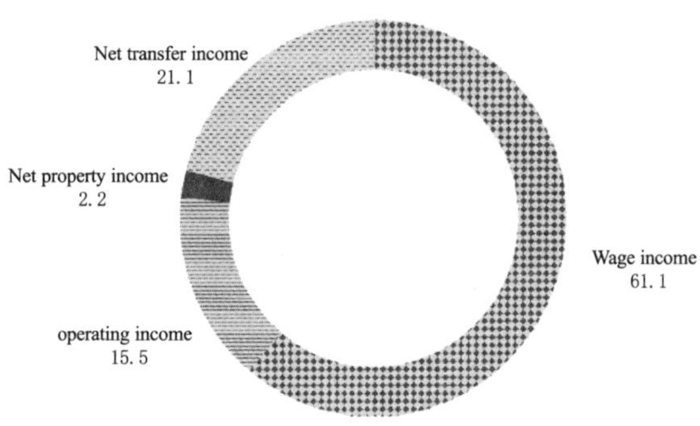

In 2021, the per capita consumption expenditure of residents in the whole city was 24829 yuan, up 12.0% from the previous year. Among them, the per capita consumption expenditure of urban residents was 28810 yuan, up 11.6%; the per capita consumption expenditure of rural residents was 14521 yuan, an increase of 12.1%.

At the end of the year, a total of 10941000 people participated in medical insurance in the city, of which the number of urban and rural residents participating in medical insurance was 6840400, and the number of urban workers participating in basic medical insurance (including maternity insurance) was 4100600. There were 8141200 people participating in basic old-age insurance, of which 5284200 were participating in old-age insurance for urban enterprise employees. There were 2597600 people participating in unemployment insurance and 2992700 people participating in industrial injury insurance.

There were 143 old-age care institutions [17] providing accommodation in the city, with 28600 beds and 11500 adoptions at the end of the year. At the end of the year, there were 13900 households, or 19800 people, receiving urban subsistence allowances, and 177 million yuan of subsistence allowances were paid; there were 29800 households, or 78400 people, receiving rural minimum living allowances, and 538 million yuan of minimum living allowances were paid. A total of 7975 people enjoyed assistance and support for poor people in rural areas, and paid 151 million yuan of support funds.

X. Science and technology, education, culture, health and sports

At the end of the year, there were 7140 state-level high-tech enterprises, an increase of 1906 over the previous year. There were 64131 patents granted, up 41.2% over the previous year, with 14055 invention patents granted. The technology market contract transactions amounted to 220.949 billion yuan, an increase of 34.0%.

There were 63 colleges and universities in Xi' an, with814400 students and 188900 graduates. There were 43 postgraduate training institutions with 164400 students and 36100 graduates. There were 501 ordinary middle schools with 482100 students and 140000 graduates. There were 1170 primary schools with 890900 students and 109600 graduates.

The city had 136 museums (excluding private ones) and 428 cultural relic protection units at all levels at the end of the year. There were 14 public libraries, with a total circulation of 2175400 people; there were one municipal mass art gallery, 14 cultural centers and 16 art performance groups. Totally 307 exhibition events were held throughout the year, ten of which were international events and 52 national exhibition activities. The annual number of participants reached 1.48 million.

By the end of the year, there were 7123 health institutions of all kinds in the city, among which 375 were hospitals, 264 were community health service centers (stations) and 113 were health centers. There were 123300 health technicians of all kinds, including 43300 practicing doctors (including assistant doctors) and 57000 registered nurses. There were 79500 beds in various health institutions, of which 73900 were in hospitals.

A total of 600 mass sports exhibitions and competitions were held throughout the year.

The city trained athletes to participate in international and domestic competitions and won 22 gold medals, 25 silver medals and 50 bronze medals.

XI.Resources, Environment and Emergency Management

The supply of various types of construction land was 79900 mu in 2021, of which, the supply of industrial land was 11400 mu. The comprehensive production capacity of the public water supply reached 2.9 million cubic meters per day,

The comprehensive energy consumption of industrial enterprises above the designated size was 5847700 tons of standard coal in the year, down 2.3% over the previous year. The electricity consumption in the city totaled 48937 billion kilowatt hours, an increase of 17.9%. Among them, industrial electricity consumption amounted to 15.375 billion kilowatt hours, an increase of 12.9%.

There are 265 days with good air quality throughout the year, an increase of 15 days over the previous year. The average annual concentration of particulate matter (PM_{10}) was 82 $\mu g/m^3$, down 5.7% and that of particulate matter ($PM_{2.5}$)was 41 $\mu g/m^3$, down 19.6%. The water quality of centralized drinking water source in the whole city reaches the standard rate of 100%.The average equivalent sound level of regional environmental noise was 56.2 dB, and the average equivalent sound level of road traffic noise was 68.7 dB.

There were 195 production safety accidents and 174 deaths, down 14.1% and 1.7% over the previous year, respectively. Among them, there were 128 traffic and transportation accidents [18], with 106 deaths; 66 industrial, mining and trade accidents, with 67 deaths.

Notes:

[1] The 2021 data in this communique are preliminary statistics. Some of the data is rounded, there is a breakdown and total unequal.

[2]As the data of Xixian New Area has been adjusted to be subject to the area directly controlled by Xixian New Area, the growth of GDP, agriculture, industry, construction, domestic trade, investment and other indicators should be calculated on a comparable basis.

[3] The absolute value-added value of GDP, tertiary industries and related industries is calculated at current prices, and the growth rate is calculated at constant prices. The data from 2017 to 2020 are the final verified data.

[4] The average two-year growth is the geometric mean of the growth with the data of the same period in 2019 as the base.

[5]The permanent resident population includes 13.163 million people mutually managed by Xi' an (Xixian New Area) and Xianyang, but excludes 12.873 million people mutually managed by Xi' an (Xixian New Area) and Xianyang.

[6] The statistical standards for industries above the scale are industrial legal entities with annual main business income of 20 million yuan or more.

[7] Industrial strategic emerging industries include new generation information technology industry, high-end equipment manufacturing industry, new materials industry, biological industry, new energy automobile industry, new energy industry, energy conservation and environmental protection industry.

[8] High-tech manufacturing includes pharmaceutical manufacturing, aviation, spacecraft and equipment manufacturing, electronic and communication equipment manufacturing, computer and office equipment

manufacturing, medical instrument equipment and instrumentation manufacturing, and information chemicals manufacturing.

[9] Equipment manufacturing industry includes metal products industry, general equipment manufacturing industry, special equipment manufacturing industry, automobile manufacturing industry, railway, ship, aerospace and other transportation equipment manufacturing industry, electrical machinery and equipment manufacturing industry, computer, communication and other electronic equipment manufacturing industry, and instrumentation manufacturing industry.

[10] The statistical scope of service industries above designated size includes: transportation, warehousing and postal services, information transmission, software and information technology services, water conservancy, environment and public facilities management, and health industry legal entities with annual operating income of 20 million yuan or more; Real estate industry (excluding real estate development and operation), leasing and business services, scientific research and technical services, and education industry legal entities with annual operating income of 10 million yuan or more; Legal entities in residential service, repair and other service industries, culture, sports and entertainment industries, and social work industries with annual operating income of 5 million yuan or more.

[11] Fixed Internet broadband access users refer to those who are registered with telecommunications enterprises at the end of the reporting period and access the public Internet through xDSL, FTTx+LAN, FTTH/O and other broadband access methods and ordinary dedicated lines.

[12]The statistical standards of retail sales of consumer goods for enterprises above designated size are wholesale enterprises (units) with annual main business income of 20 million yuan or above, retail sales enterprises (units) with annual retail sales of 5 million yuan or above, and accommodation and catering enterprises (units) with annual sales of 2 million yuan or above.

[13] Retail sales of online goods refer to the amount of physical goods (including value-added tax) sold to individuals and social groups for non-production and non-business use through public online trading platforms (including self-built websites and third-party platforms) that enterprises (units) obtain orders from. Payment can be made online or offline. Public network includes computer Internet, mobile Internet and so on.

[14]Private fixed assets investment refers to the investment in the construction or purchase of fixed assets by domestic funded enterprises and institutions with the nature of collective, private and individual, and the survey units that are controlled by them (including absolute holding and relative holding).

[15] Infrastructure investment includes the production and supply of electricity, heat, gas and water, transportation, postal services, telecommunications, radio and television and satellite transmission services, Internet and related services, water conservancy, environment and public facilities management.

[16] For commercial buildings that have been completed by the end of the reporting period and that are available for sale or rent, the floor space thereof for sale refers to the floor space that has not been sold or rented out, including floor space completed within and before this reporting period, but excluding floor space of government-built buildings or demolition and relocation projects, government-entrusted buildings, public buildings, or real estate companies' own buildings and swing space that cannot be sold or rented out.

[17] The number of old-age care institutions in operation refers to those providing accommodation.

[18] Traffic and transportation accidents refer to deaths or injuries of people engaged in transportation via twelve types of road transport vehicles, including passenger transport on highway, by bus, taxi, ride-hailing, passenger travel, as well as leasing, coaching, freight, transportation of dangerous chemicals, engineering rescue, school bus, corporate commuter vehicles and other production and operation vehicles.

Data Caliber:

As the city of Xi'an took full custody of Xixian New area in July 2021, data of indicators has been gradually adjusted to only cover areas directly controlled by Xixian New area, and exclude areas mutually controlled by Xi'an (Xixian New area) and Xianyang. Therefore, the data of some indicators such as domestic trade, education and health are smaller than last year. The data of imports and exports, passenger transport and freight, deposits and loans, patent and so on are subject to Xi'an.

Data sources: Grain output, livestock and poultry output, price and per capita disposable income data in this communique are from the Xi'an Survey Team of the National Bureau of Statistics. New urban employment, registered unemployment rate and social security data are from Xi'an Human Resources and Social Security Bureau. Market entities and patent data are from Xi'an Administration for Market Regulation. The financial data are from the municipal Finance Bureau. Import and export data from Xi'an Customs. Data on utilization of foreign capital came from municipal Investment Cooperation Bureau. Data of public libraries, public art museums and cultural centers are obtained from the Municipal Administration of Culture and Tourism. Museum data comes from the Municipal Cultural Relics Bureau. Passenger and freight transportation data comes from the Municipal Transportation Bureau. Motor vehicle data comes from the Municipal Public Security Bureau. The postal service data are from the municipal Postal administration. The telecom business data came from Xi'an Branch of China Mobile, Xi'an Branch of China Telecom and Xi'an Branch of China Unicorn. The monetary and financial data are from the Operation Management Department of Xi'an Branch of the People's Bank of China. The data of securities and insurance are from the Municipal Finance Work Bureau. The education data came from the municipal Education Bureau. The science and technology data are from the municipal Science and Technology Bureau. Exhibition data from municipal Bureau of Commerce. The sports data are from the municipal Sports Bureau. Health data from the municipal Health and Health Commission. Data on social services, subsistence allowances and assistance and support for people in extreme poverty in rural areas are from the Civil Affairs Bureau. The construction land data comes from the Municipal Natural Resources and Planning Bureau. Water supply data come from Municipal Water Bureau. Electricity consumption data are from Xi' an Power Company of State Grid Shaanxi Electric Power Company. Environmental monitoring data from municipal Bureau of Ecology and Environment. The safety production data come from the municipal Emergency management Bureau. Other data are from the municipal Bureau of Statistics.

1 综　合

GENERAL SURVEY

资料整理：杨　骏　王　慧

Data management：Yang Jun　Wang Hui

数据审核：罗延庆

Data audit：Luo Yanqing

第一部分　综合

一、简要说明

本章资料主要包括西安市行政区划、自然地理、自然资源、气象、国民经济和社会发展等综合资料，由西安市统计局综合处根据局内各专业处及有关部门统计资料进行整理和编辑。

二、主要指标

地区生产总值（亿元）	10688.28	比上年增长	4.1%
农林牧渔业总产值（亿元）	560.59	比上年增长	6.6%
固定资产投资额（亿元）	–	比上年下降	11.6%
社会消费品零售总额（亿元）	4963.42	比上年增长	0.8%
财政一般公共预算收入（亿元）	856.00	比上年增长	18.2%
财政一般公共预算支出（亿元）	1474.62	比上年增长	9.4%
进出口总值（亿元）	4399.96	比上年增长	26.5%
城镇常住居民人均可支配收入（元）	46931	比上年增长	7.4%
农村常住居民人均可支配收入（元）	17389	比上年增长	10.4%

1　GENERAL SURVEY

Ⅰ.Brief Introduction

This chapter consists of mainly unified data of administrative divisions, natural geography, natural resources, meteorology, national economy and social development of Xi'an city. It is compiled by Integration Division according to the reported data from other divisions of the Xi'an Bureau of Statistics and other departments of the municipal government.

Ⅱ. Major Indicators

Indicator	Value	Increase over Preceding Year
Gross Domestic Product (100 mil. Yuan)	10688.28	4.1%
Gross Output Value of Farming, Forestry, Animal, Husbandry and Fishery (100 mil. Yuan)	560.59	6.6%
Investment In Fixed Assets (100 mil. Yuan)	–	–11.6%
Total Retail Sales of Consumer Goods (100 mil. Yuan)	4963.42	0.8%
Government General Public Budgetary Revenue (100 mil. Yuan)	856.00	18.2%
Government General Public Budgetary Expenditures (100 mil. Yuan)	1474.62	9.4%
Total Value of Imports and Exports (100 mil.Yuan)	4399.96	26.5%
Per Capita Disposable Income of Urban Households (Yuan)	46931	7.4%
Per Capita Disposable Income of Rural Households (Yuan)	17389	10.4%

1-1 行政区划（2021年）

Administrative Divisions(2021)

单位：个 (unit)

地 区	Region	乡镇及街道办 Township and Urban Subdistrict Office	镇数 Township	街道办事处 Urban Subdistrict Office	村民委员会 village committees	社区居委会 Neighbourhood committees
西安市	**Xi'an**	**191**	**41**	**150**	**1927**	**1323**
新城区	Xincheng	9		9		108
碑林区	Beilin	8		8		98
莲湖区	Lianhu	9		9		131
灞桥区	Baqiao	9		9	76	75
未央区	Weiyang	12		12	50	201
雁塔区	Yanta	10		10	41	164
阎良区	Yanliang	7		7	73	32
临潼区	Lintong	23		23	226	45
长安区	Chang'an	25		25	232	88
高陵区	Gaoling	7		7	86	29
鄠邑区	Huyi	14		14	193	18
蓝田县	Lantian	19	18	1	337	14
周至县	Zhouzhi	20	19	1	237	16
西咸新区	Xixian New Area	19	4	15	192	142

注：本表数据来源市民政局。2021年基层社会组织数量（村民委员会、社区居委会）统计口径包含6个开发区：高新区村委会156个、居委会70个；港务区村委会28个、居委会14个；经开区居委会17个；浐灞生态区居委会28个；航天基地居委会9个；曲江新区居委会24个。

1-2 土地面积和常住人口密度(2021年)

Statistics on Land Area and Density of Permanent Population (2021)

地 区	Region	土地面积 Area 绝对数(平方公里) Absolute Value (sq.km)	比重(%) Proportion (%)	常住人口(万人) Total of Permanent Population (10 000 persons)	常住人口密度(人/平方公里) Density of Permanent Population (person/sq.km)
西安市	**Xi 'an**	**10096.89**	**100.0**	**1287.30**	
市区	**Urban districts**	**5145.70**	**51.0**	**1078.13**	
新城区	Xincheng	30.13	0.3	62.25	20660
碑林区	Beilin	23.37	0.2	76.96	32931
莲湖区	Lianhu	38.32	0.4	102.93	26861
灞桥区	Baqiao	324.50	3.2	102.96	3173
未央区	Weiyang	264.41	2.6	158.83	
雁塔区	Yanta	151.44	1.5	208.66	13778
阎良区	Yanliang	244.55	2.4	30.73	1257
临潼区	Lintong	915.98	9.1	68.13	744
长安区	Chang'an	1588.54	15.7	162.24	
高陵区	Gaoling	285.03	2.8	45.75	1605
鄠邑区	Huyi	1279.43	12.7	58.69	
二县	**Two Counties**	**4951.19**	**49.0**	**105.53**	**213**
蓝田县	Lantian	2005.96	19.8	49.54	247
周至县	Zhouzhi	2945.23	29.2	55.99	190
西咸新区	**Xixian New Area**			**103.64**	

注：1.本表土地面积数据来源于市自然资源和规划局，为西安原口径数据。表中土地面积数据为2020年数据。
2.因土地面积数据为原口径数据，暂不计算全市、市区及相关区人口密度。

1–3 自然状况和资源（2021年）

Natural Conditions and Resources(2021)

指　标	Item	2021
一、自然状况	**Natural Conditions**	
土地总面积（平方公里）	Total Land Area (sq.km)	10096.89
#市区面积	Urban Area	5145.70
气候（市区）	Climate (Urban)	
年平均气温（℃）	Annual Average Temperature (℃)	15.5
年降水量（毫米）	Total Annual Precipitation(mm)	1005.8
日照总时数（小时）	Total Sunshine Time (hour)	1910.6
平均风速（米/秒）	Average Wind-speed (m/sec.)	2.2
二、自然资源	**Natural Resources**	
林业用地面积（千公顷）	Area of Forestland(1 000 hectare)	593.43
水资源总量（亿立方米）	Total Water Resources(100 million cu.m)	60.90
#天然地表水资源总量	Total Savageness Surface Water Resource	54.16
地下水资源总量（亿立方米）	Total Underground Water Resource(100 million cu.m)	17.70

注：1.本表数据来源于市气象局、市自然资源和规划局、市水务局等。
2.本表水资源总量等市水务局相关指标数据含西咸新区直管区，其他指标数据为西安原口径数据。
3.本表林业用地面积数据为2020年调整数据。土地面积为2020年数据。

1-4 气象情况（2021年）

Climate Condition(2021)

地 区	Region	平均气温（℃）Average Temperature（℃）	日照时数（小时）Sunshine Time (hour)	降水天数（天）Raining days (day)	年降水量（毫米）Total Annual Precipitation (mm)	平均风速（米/秒）Average Wind-speed (m/second)
市 区	Urban	15.5	1910.6	130	1005.8	2.2
灞桥区	Baqiao	13.7		115	1287.3	1.5
阎良区	Yanliang	14.4		82	952.6	2.1
临潼区	Lintong	15.2	1928.7	96	1108.7	1.8
长安区	Chang'an	14.0	1760.7	113	1160.6	1.3
高陵区	Gaoling	14.7	1910.2	123	875.3	2.0
鄠邑区	Huyi	14.6	1720.9	142	982.4	1.6
蓝田县	Lantian	13.4	2936.5	118	1320.5	1.5
周至县	Zhouzhi	14.3	1826.6	144	1022.0	1.6
西咸新区	Xixian New Area	14.4	1743.2	92	933.6	1.9

注：本表数据来源于市气象局。灞桥区、阎良区为区域气象站，无日照监测资料。下同。

1-5 市区及远郊区县各月平均气温（2021年）

Average Temperature of Xi'an and the Districts and Outer Suburban of Each Month (2021)

单位：℃ (℃)

月 份	Month	市区 Urban	灞桥区 Baqiao	阎良区 Yanliang	临潼区 Lintong	长安区 Chang'an	高陵区 Gaoling	鄠邑区 Huyi	蓝田县 Lantian	周至县 Zhouzhi	西咸新区 Xixian New Area
一月	January	2.7	1.7	0.8	2.6	0.5	1.1	1.5	-0.8	1.5	1.1
二月	February	7.8	6.3	5.5	7.6	5.1	6.0	6.4	4.5	6.5	5.7
三月	March	11.7	10.5	10.6	11.3	10.6	10.9	10.9	10.3	10.8	10.8
四月	April	15.0	12.8	14.2	14.8	13.7	14.5	14.3	13.4	14.0	14.2
五月	May	21.7	19.8	20.8	21.5	20.4	20.9	21.1	19.7	20.6	20.8
六月	June	26.8	24.0	26.6	26.7	25.0	26.9	25.8	24.8	25.1	25.9
七月	July	27.3	25.0	27.0	26.7	26.5	27.1	27.0	25.7	26.5	27.0
八月	August	25.7	23.2	26.8	25.2	24.4	25.5	24.9	24.0	24.5	25.3
九月	September	21.5	20.0	21.0	21.3	20.9	21.2	21.2	20.5	20.9	21.3
十月	October	13.6	11.7	13.0	13.6	12.7	13.4	13.0	12.6	12.6	12.9
十一月	November	8.1	7.0	6.1	8.2	6.0	6.7	7.0	5.0	6.6	6.3
十二月	December	3.6	2.6	0.9	3.2	1.6	1.9	2.6	0.7	2.3	1.9

注：本表数据来源于市气象局。

1-6 市区及远郊区县各月日照时数（2021年）

Sunshine Duration of Xi'an and the Districts and Outer Suburban of Each Month (2021)

单位：小时 (hour)

月 份	Month	市区 Urban	临潼区 Lintong	长安区 Chang'an	高陵区 Gaoling	鄠邑区 Huyi	蓝田县 Lantian	周至县 Zhouzhi
一月	January	161.8	162.3	145.3	158.1	145.7	204.7	154.9
二月	February	160.4	159.3	159.9	158.0	148.5	199.8	167.6
三月	March	145.9	152.9	131.3	147.7	111.9	232.9	126.1
四月	April	112.5	99.9	103.9	111.1	92.8	236.6	102.5
五月	May	228.2	229.8	200.1	232.2	212.1	339.3	227.5
六月	June	183.1	187.9	163.6	178.5	155.0	309.3	160.6
七月	July	190.8	196.1	175.9	190.8	175.6	328.1	181.4
八月	August	174.7	177.1	156.6	174.2	154.1	292.4	144.0
九月	September	139.5	140.5	136.0	140.3	145.2	218.9	153.1
十月	October	73.4	77.5	68.2	75.1	62.5	175.7	64.3
十一月	November	183.1	183.8	170.4	183.2	155.0	210.0	181.9
十二月	December	157.2	161.6	149.5	161.0	150.7	188.8	162.7

注：本表数据来源于市气象局。

1-7 市区及远郊区县各月降水天数（2021年）

Precipitation Days of Xi'an and the Districts and Outer Suburban of Each Month (2021)

单位：天 (day)

月 份	Month	市区 Urban	灞桥区 Baqiao	阎良区 Yanliang	临潼区 Lintong	长安区 Chang'an	高陵区 Gaoling	鄠邑区 Huyi	蓝田县 Lantian	周至县 Zhouzhi	西咸新区 Xixian New Area
一月	January	1	2		2	2	2	2	2	2	2
二月	February	5	7	5	5	5	5	8	5	8	5
三月	March	6	6	2	6	8	12	8	6	11	5
四月	April	12	12	9	11	15	14	18	16	20	8
五月	May	7	7	8	7	8	6	10	8	11	8
六月	June	7	10	9	7	10	14	13	12	13	8
七月	July	8	10	9	10	11	10	14	11	15	10
八月	August	8	14	8	9	11	13	14	14	15	8
九月	September	15	17	18	15	18	16	17	16	18	16
十月	October	12	16	12	14	16	18	20	17	20	13
十一月	November	5	7	2	5	4	8	10	4	7	5
十二月	December	4	7	0	5	5	5	8	7	5	4

注：本表数据来源于市气象局。

1-8 市区及远郊区县各月降水量（2021年）

Amount of Precipitation of Xi'an and the Districts and Outer Suburban of Each Month (2021)

单位：毫米 (mm)

月份	Month	市区 Urban	灞桥区 Baqiao	阎良区 Yanliang	临潼区 Lintong	长安区 Chang'an	高陵区 Gaoling	鄠邑区 Huyi	蓝田县 Lantian	周至县 Zhouzhi	西咸新区 Xixian New Area
一月	January	1.2	2.6	0.0	1.8	1.6	1.5	1.5	2.7	1.1	1.6
二月	February	29.3	38.9	32.7	35.2	36.9	29.9	26.9	35.9	17.6	26.0
三月	March	14.3	21.8	11.3	14.7	17.4	14.4	16.9	23.2	15.7	14.4
四月	April	81.6	117.7	72.6	113.1	87.4	78.6	60.6	96.7	81.6	68.2
五月	May	59.9	80.1	33.6	52.9	71.1	36.3	73.5	60.1	81.8	68.4
六月	June	72.7	87.2	60.8	66.5	81.3	60.2	79.7	78.4	82.8	82.2
七月	July	159.4	128.9	200.9	201.3	131.1	95.9	73.9	216.5	58.2	89.9
八月	August	188.0	263.0	114.3	173.1	190.4	154.0	178.1	262.7	200.6	185.5
九月	September	288.9	377.4	325.5	335.7	398.2	300.7	354.8	404.2	347.5	289.3
十月	October	96.5	119.2	90.9	87.2	112.8	90.3	93.0	105.8	119.6	91.9
十一月	November	9.0	33.5	10.0	19.3	18.0	10.6	13.1	18.5	6.1	9.0
十二月	December	5.0	17.0	0.0	7.9	14.4	2.9	10.4	15.8	9.4	7.2

注：本表数据来源于市气象局。

1-9 市区及远郊区县各月平均风速（2021年）

Average Wind Speed of Xi'an and the Districts and Outer Suburban Districts(2021)

单位：米/秒 (m/s)

月份	Month	市区 Urban	灞桥区 Baqiao	阎良区 Yanliang	临潼区 Lintong	长安区 Chang'an	高陵区 Gaoling	鄠邑区 Huyi	蓝田县 Lantian	周至县 Zhouzhi	西咸新区 Xixian New Area
一月	January	1.9	1.7	2.5	1.9	1.5	1.7	1.6	1.4	1.5	1.8
二月	February	2.2	1.7	2.6	2.0	1.4	2.0	1.7	1.6	1.6	1.9
三月	March	2.4	1.7	2.5	1.9	1.4	2.2	1.5	1.7	1.6	2.3
四月	April	2.6	1.5	2.3	1.9	1.2	2.3	1.6	1.6	1.6	2.2
五月	May	2.3	1.6	2.4	2.0	1.5	2.2	1.9	1.7	2.0	2.3
六月	June	2.0	1.5	1.9	2.0	1.2	2.1	1.6	1.5	1.9	1.9
七月	July	2.3	0.9	1.2	1.8	1.2	2.1	1.5	1.4	1.6	2.0
八月	August	2.2	1.0	2.0	1.7	1.0	2.0	1.4	1.4	1.5	2.0
九月	September	2.1	1.4	1.8	1.7	1.1	1.8	1.4	1.4	1.4	1.8
十月	October	2.1	1.5	1.8	1.8	1.1	1.9	1.5	1.3	1.5	1.9
十一月	November	1.9	2.2	2.1	1.7	1.4	1.8	1.6	1.5	1.7	1.7
十二月	December	1.8	1.2	2.0	1.4	1.1	1.5	1.3	1.3	1.5	1.5

注：本表数据来源于市气象局。

1-10 主要年份国有土地使用权出让、划拨情况

The Transfer and Allocation of State-Owned Land Use Right in Representative Years

项 目	Item	2010	2014	2015	2016	2017	2018	2019	2020	2021
国有土地使用权出让	**Lease of the Use Right of State-owned Land**									
出让地块(宗)	Land leased (item)	386	506	416	457	397	387	540	619	443
协议	Agreement	173	109	72	82	69	79	116	117	62
招标	Invitation for Bid	3								
拍卖	Auction	11				25	203	171	89	45
挂牌交易	Listed Transaction	199	397	344	375	303	105	253	413	336
出让面积（公顷）	Area of Totally Leased Land (hectare)	1364	1789	1294	1599	1736	1623	2157	2812	2036
土地使用权出让总收入（万元）	**Total Revenue from Leasing of the Use Right(10 000 yuan)**	**358098**	**183901**	**109116**	**2832632**	**3988818**	**5738433**	**8221571**	**12462600**	**12427737**
国有土地使用权划拨	**Administrative Allocation of the Use Right of State-owned Land**									
划拨地块（宗）	Land Allocated (item)	108	152	141	132	130	116	205	167	211
划拨面积（公顷）	Area of Land Allocated(hectare)	1027	1739	1209	1135	1411	3099	4605	2312	3288

注：1.本表数据来源于市自然资源和规划局。
2.2016年起土地使用权出让总收入包括协议出让和招拍挂出让收入。
3.2019年起包含西咸新区。

1-11 主要年份国民经济和社会发展总量与速度指标

指　标	Item	总量指标 Total quantity index 1995	2000	2005	2010
人口与就业	Population and Employment				
人口	Population				
年底户籍总人口（万人）	Population at the Year-end(10 000 persons)	648.21	688.01	741.73	782.73
城镇人口	Urban Population	255.71	285.79	333.14	374.64
乡村人口	Rural Population	392.50	402.20	408.60	408.10
男性人口	Male Population	334.75	355.18	382.02	398.80
女性人口	Female Population	313.46	332.83	359.71	383.93
就业	Employment				
全社会从业人员数（万人）	Employment(10 000 persons)	372.60	389.10	415.83	477.58
#非私营单位在岗职工人数	Number of Employees of non-private units	141.17	109.62	119.73	130.70
城镇登记失业人数（万人）	Registered Unemployed in Urban Areas(10 000 persons)	5.92	3.85	8.45	10.46
宏观经济	Macroeconomic Indicator				
国民经济核算	National Accounts				
地区生产总值（亿元）	Gross Domestic Product(100 mil. yuan)	330.35	646.13	1294.05	3195.05
第一产业	Primary Industry	41.40	44.65	66.01	133.22
第二产业	Secondary Industry	135.33	277.13	511.19	1290.93
第三产业	Tertiary Industry	153.62	324.35	716.86	1770.89
#工业	Industry	112.50	218.44	393.51	875.97
建筑业	Construction	22.83	58.69	117.68	414.96
固定资产投资	Investment in Fixed Assets				
固定资产投资（不含农户）	Investment in Fixed Assets(excluding farmers)	88.50	203.01	776.33	3104.92
#房地产开发投资	Real Estate Investment	21.65	51.85	225.23	842.34
按经济成分划分:	By Economic Component				
国有单位	State-owned	69.08	159.60	373.70	1348.76
集体单位	Collective-Owned	9.78	14.65	59.23	326.44
个体经济	Self-employed Individual	11.13	24.40	79.04	54.73
其他经济	Other	13.43	33.72	323.13	1520.63
财政	Public Finance				
地方财政一般公共预算收入（亿元）	General Public Budgetary Revenue of Local Government (100 mil. yuan)	18.21	41.39	73.05	241.86
地方财政一般公共预算支出（亿元）	General Public Budgetary Expenditure of Local Government (100 mil. yuan)	18.42	46.50	97.82	371.62
物价指数（上年=100）	Price Indices（preceding year=100）				
商品零售价格指数	Retail Price Index	114.6	98.7	99.7	102.7
居民消费价格指数	Consumer Price Index	117.0	100.2	100.3	103.5
工业生产者出厂价格指数	Producer Price Indices (PPI) for Manufactured Goods	110.8	99.4	103.9	102.3
利用外资	Utilization of Foreign Capital				
利用外资签定协议额（万美元）	Amount of Foreign Capital for Utilization Through Signed Contracts or Agreements(USD 10 000)	28956	54123	121499	119689
外商实际直接投资额（万美元）	Amount of Foreign Capital Actually Utilized (USD 10 000)	18653	15633	57113	156653

注：1.国民经济核算2003—2017年为第四次全国经济普查修订数据。2018年为第四次全国经济普查数据。2019-2020年为最终核算数。2021年为初步核算数。
2.2009年及以前年份财政收支为一般预算收支与基金预算收支之和。部分历史年份数据有所修订。
3.由于2010年固定资产投资起报点的变化，指数和平均增长速度为可比口径。
4.2015年，市公安局提供户籍人口分类为“城镇人口”和“乡村人口”，2015年之前，分类为“非农业人口”和“农业人口”。自2020年开始，无户籍“城镇人口”和“乡村人口”指标数据。

Total and Speed Index of National Economy and Social Development in Representative Years

					速度指标（%）				Indices and Growth Rates (%)		
					指数（2021年比以下各年）(2021 as percentage of the following years)				平均增长速度 Average Annual Growth Rate		
2015	2018	2019	2020	2021	2005	2010	2015	2020	2006-2010	2011-2015	2016-2020
815.66	922.82	956.74	977.97	999.45	134.7	127.5	122.4	102.2	1.1	0.8	3.7
545.95	639.62	668.57							2.4	7.8	
269.70	283.20	288.20							…	-7.9	
412.23	461.51	477.13	486.50	496.21	129.9	124.4	120.4	102.0	0.9	0.7	3.4
403.43	461.31	479.61	491.47	503.24	139.9	131.2	124.8	102.4	1.3	1.0	4.0
528.06	621.22	645.86	664.45	686.53	153.0	133.2	120.6	103.3	2.8	2.0	3.1
181.86	181.76	192.14	197.11	191.34	157.6	144.4	103.7	97.1	1.8	6.8	1.3
10.74	12.48	12.52	13.76	15.77	183.9	148.8	144.7	114.6	4.4	0.5	4.8
5932.86	8499.41	9399.98	10023.73	10688.28	476.2	248.7	148.7	104.1	13.9	10.9	7.4
191.91	258.98	279.13	312.75	308.82	217.5	163.3	127.7	106.1	5.9	5.0	3.8
2070.47	2861.86	3130.80	3340.97	3585.20	397.0	220.7	138.8	100.9	12.5	9.7	6.6
3670.48	5378.56	5990.06	6370.01	6794.26	563.7	274.8	155.6	105.7	15.5	12.1	8.0
1242.18	1707.90	1816.23	1854.35	2099.65	371.2	225.2	143.9	106.4	10.5	9.4	6.2
857.40	1210.79	1370.63	1535.76	1552.18	519.5	224.9	134.7	94.6	18.2	10.8	7.3
5086.93					1071.0	267.8	127.7	88.4	31.9	15.9	7.6
1831.67					1045.1	279.4	128.4	93.0	30.2	16.8	6.7
1826.62					818.2	226.7	132.7	82.0	29.3	11.3	10.1
158.14					70.4	12.8	20.8	87.5	40.7	-9.4	-25.0
80.47									-7.1	13.2	
3100.75					1343.1	285.4	111.2	95.5	36.6	20.7	3.1
650.99	684.70	702.56	724.14	856.00	1584.2	474.6	169.0	118.2	27.3	22.9	7.4
917.24	1151.87	1247.02	1347.58	1474.62	1470.6	386.7	155.3	109.4	30.6	20.0	7.3
99.7	102.2	102.1	101.5	101.4					2.5	1.7	1.5
100.7	101.9	102.7	102.1	101.7					3.1	2.6	1.9
98.5	101.1	101.6	100.2						2.2	0.1	0.2
193684	475508	196410	735596	84579	34.7	35.2	21.8	11.5	-0.3	10.1	13.6
400833	635370	705738	767702	871421	1464.8	534.1	208.7	113.5	22.4	20.7	13.0

5.由于2017年部分指标包含有西咸新区数据，速度指标为同口径计算数据。
6.本表数据2021年数据口径情况详见总说明和相关章节表下注释。
7.农业部分数据依据三农普数据对2007-2017年进行了修订。畜牧业数据2013-2017年为三农普修订数据。下同。
8.投资有关数据2018年起为相对数据，与投资总量相关的指标，暂不计算。下同。
9.2020年之前城镇非私营单位在岗职工人数为全部单位在岗职工人数。
10.2021年起，因调查方案变动，西安不出工业生产者出厂价格指数数据。

1-11 续表1

指 标	Item	总量指标 Total quantity index			
		1995	2000	2005	2010
产 业	**Industry**				
农业	**Agriculture**				
农林牧渔业总产值（亿元）	Gross Output Value of Farming，Forestry, Animal Husbandry and Fishery(100 mil yuan)	75.46	74.37	106.54	212.42
主要农产品产量（万吨）	Output of Major Farm Products(10 000 tons)				
粮 食	Grain	175.30	201.90	205.50	174.51
奶 类	Milk				
蔬 菜	Vegetables	133.60	162.14	195.70	207.11
水 果	Fruits	24.10	34.36	51.29	66.11
肉 类	Meat				
水产品	Aquatic Products	0.85	1.14	0.94	1.19
工业	**Industry**				
规模以上工业企业主要经济指标（亿元）	Main Economic Indicators of Industrial Enterprises above Designated Size(100 mil yuan)				
资产总计	Total Assets		958.05	1503.85	3592.13
主营业务收入	Revenue from Principal Business		420.42	980.97	3011.19
利润总额	Profits		16.11	28.72	245.37
从业人员年平均人数（万人）	Annual Average Employees(10 000 persons)		43.25	37.92	47.11
主要工业产品产量	Output of Major Industrial Products				
布（亿米）	Cloth(100 mil.m)	3.03	2.48	2.70	2.38
机制纸及纸板（万吨）	Machine-Made Paper(10 000ton)	36.44	5.47	22.19	49.60
发电量（亿千瓦小时）	Electricity(100 million kWh)	22.00	19.00	48.00	96.94
钢材（万吨）	Steel Products(10 000ton)	31.44	10.00	24.02	110.77
汽车（万辆）	Motor Vehicles(10 000 units)	0.30	0.90	4.10	65.21
建筑业	**Construction**				
建筑业企业年末从业人数（人）	Number of Employees in Construction Enterprises at the end of year(person)		136718	158311	539000
建筑业总产值（亿元）	Gross Output Value(100 mil. yuan)	42.55	105.93	326.65	1334.00
房屋建筑施工面积（万平方米）	Floor Space of Buildings under Construction (10 000 sq.m)	601.70	793.30	1801.20	4592.57
房屋建筑竣工面积（万平方米）	Floor Space of Buildings Completed (10 000 sq.m)	177.15	336.80	569.01	1391.91

注：1.规模以上工业2018年为第四次全国经济普查数据。
2.由于2010年规模以上工业起报点的变化，指数和平均增长速度为可比口径计算。

continued 1

					速度指标（%） Indices and Growth Rates(%)							
2015	2018	2019	2020	2021	指数（2021年比以下各年） (2021 as percentage of the following years)				平均增长速度 Average Annual Growth Rate		
					2005	2010	2015	2020	2006-2010	2011-2015	2016-2020
330.81	461.21	499.32	564.41	560.59	237.1	169.7	129.7	106.6	6.8	5.5	4.0
141.42	142.14	139.89	144.58	141.92	85.5	79.3	97.1	101.3	1.5	-4.0	-0.8
7.68	11.52	12.37	14.03	13.86	142.3	94.9	94.2	100.1	8.5	0.1	-1.2
267.91	373.69	378.58	381.31	362.80	193.7	149.8	114.0	99.8	5.3	5.6	2.7
73.33	89.15	97.18	100.93	101.01	256.0	155.0	124.8	104.3	10.6	4.4	3.7
7.21	5.45	5.14	4.56	4.93	76.8	102.3	86.7	111.0	-5.6	3.4	-4.8
1.42	1.35	1.36	1.13	1.32	140.4	110.8	93.0	116.8	5.7	3.6	-4.5
6740.26	8409.16	9449.95	10638.17	11999.61	814.1	340.7	181.5	112.8	19.0	13.4	10.0
4374.11	6055.58	6483.80	6650.76	7895.23	760.6	248.0	170.6	118.7	25.1	7.8	7.5
206.88	399.52	325.60	466.63	444.48	1335.4	156.4	185.5	95.3	53.6	-3.4	14.2
50.59	51.87	49.75	50.16	53.70	130.1	104.7	97.6	107.1	4.4	1.4	-1.8
1.04	1.28	1.21	0.99	1.13	38.3	43.6	99.6	104.2	-2.5	-15.3	-0.9
12.22	15.39	11.38	4.22	3.52	11.3	5.1	20.5	87.7	17.5	-24.4	-25.2
158.68	172.76	155.00	154.27	167.67	304.3	150.7	92.0	106.1	15.1	10.4	-2.8
37.03	33.40	31.47	39.99	37.88	267.0	58.0	173.3	95.0	35.8	-19.7	12.8
34.14	43.37	42.63	49.83	63.87	1557.5	98.1	187.0	128.2	73.9	-12.1	7.8
596245	740351	835995	867328	751733	469.9	138.1	124.8	86.9	27.8	2.0	7.5
2650.41	3925.72	4514.38	5124.37	5404.47	1651.3	404.3	203.6	105.6	41.0	14.7	14.0
11979.16	15855.39	17174.05	20218.75	22452.11	1224.8	480.2	184.2	111.1	20.6	21.1	10.6
2712.01	2755.17	2726.28	3486.09	3319.74	549.0	224.4	115.2	95.5	19.6	14.3	3.8

1-11 续表2

指 标	Item	总量指标 Total quantity index			
		1995	2000	2005	2010
交通运输	**Transportation**				
货运量（万吨）	Freight Traffic(10 000 tons)	9590	6999	12051	34323
铁 路	Railways	3317	3101	540	706
公 路	Highways	6268	3890	11505	33610
民用航空	Civil Aviation	5	8	6	7
客运量（万人次）	Passenger Traffic(10 000 persons-times)	9069	8068	10479	30294
铁 路	Railways	2678	2130	1796	2781
公 路	Highways	6128	5578	8294	26536
民用航空	Civil Aviation	263	360	389	977
邮电通信业	**Post and Telecommunication Services**				
邮电业务总量（亿元）	Total Business Revenue(100 mil. yuan)	7.65	46.16	132.04	323.11
函 件（万件）	Number of Letters Delivered(10 000 pieces)	14647	8230	9526	8176
固定电话年末用户数（万户）	Local fixed telephone end users(10 000 subscribers)	29.95	124.26	321.48	261.77
城市电话用户	Urban Telephone Subscribers	29.11	107.24	271.40	228.27
乡村电话用户	Rural Telephone Subscribers	0.84	17.02	50.08	33.50
移动电话用户（万户）	Number of Mobile Telephone Subscribers (10 000 subscribers)		73.10	419.96	1423.08
互联网年末宽带用户（万户）	Number of Subscribers of Intemet Services (10 000 subscribers)			33.93	146.18
国内贸易	**Domestic Trade**				
社会消费品零售总额（亿元）	Total Retail Sales of Consumer Goods (100 mil. yuan)	188.35	368.96	698.37	1765.42
对外经济贸易	**Foreign Trade**				
进出口总值（万美元）	Total Value of Exports and Imports(USD 10 000)	137510	173696	390146	1039273
出口总值	Exports	110163	106062	263441	531729
进口总值	Imports	27347	67634	126705	507544
旅游	**Tourism**				
旅游者人数（万人次）	Number of Tourists(10 000 persons)	791.35	1567.00	2423.60	5285.18
旅游总收入（亿元）	Earnings from Tourism (10 000yuan)	44.00	105.00	178.50	405.18
金融业	**Financial Intermediation**				
金融机构（不含外资）人民币存款余额（亿元）	Balance of Deposits in Domestic Funded Financial Institutions (100 mil. yuan)	359.51	1335.63	3599.70	8863.36
金融机构（不含外资）人民币贷款余额（亿元）	Balance of Loans in Domestic Funded Financial Institutions (100 mil. Yuan)	334.50	972.52	2158.10	6420.72
保险公司保费收入（亿元）	Insurance premium income (100 million Yuan)	4.70	13.58	44.94	129.38
保险公司赔款及付给金额（亿元）	Indemnity Insurance and Amount Paid (100 million yuan)	1.70	1.39	9.50	26.39

注：1.2006年铁路数据按新口径统计；2018年起铁路数据为西铁局西安口径数据。
2.2006年国际互联网络用户改为互联网宽带用户。
3.1993—2017年社会消费品零售总额为第四次全国经济普查修订数据。2018年为第四次全国经济普查数据。
4.2014年起，海关不发布进出口美元口径数据，为了数据可持续性，使用年均汇率折算为美元口径。

continued 2

					速度指标（%） Indices and Growth Rates (%)						
2015	2018	2019	2020	2021	指数（2021年比以下各年） (2021 as percentage of the following years)				平均增长速度 Average Annual Growth Rate		
					2005	2010	2015	2020	2006-2010	2011-2015	2016-2020
46270	26219	27426	25713	27048				105.2	23.3		
848	497	487	471	481				102.2	5.5		
45401	25691	26901	25204	26527				105.2	23.9		
21	31	38	38	40				105.1	3.1		
26904	26057	26315	14338	10632				74.2	23.7		
3982	6037	6332	3745	4283				114.4	9.1		
19625	15555	15261	7486	3332				44.5	26.2		
3297	4465	4722	3107	3017				97.1	20.2		
331.53	739.53	1421.70	1721.55	2039.02	1544.1	631.1	614.9	118.4	19.6	0.5	39.0
1707	1081	1028	902	810	8.4	10.0	47.5	89.8	-3.0	-26.9	-12.0
292.08	262.28	250.08	238.95	240.32	74.7	91.7	82.2	100.6	-4.0	2.2	-4.0
261.45	237.78	229.46	219.78	218.92	80.6	95.8	83.7	99.6	-3.4	2.8	-3.4
30.63	24.50	20.62	19.17	21.40	42.9	63.9	70.0	111.6	-7.7	-1.8	-8.9
1767.00	1858.09	1711.36	1704.47	1759.00	418.8	123.6	99.5	103.2	27.6	4.4	-0.7
289.97	392.48	438.65	479.24	615.87	1817.0	421.7	212.7	128.5	33.9	14.7	10.6
3620.90	4854.70	5140.93	4989.33	4963.42	751.1	300.2	147.9	100.8	20.4	15.4	8.0
2828479	4991748	4700323	5036454	6820057	1749.0	656.6	241.3	135.4	21.6	39.6	12.2
1316350	2957605	2508203	2574853	3661042	1389.4	688.4	278.0	142.2	15.1	35.3	14.3
1512129	2034142	2192120	2461601	3159015	2494.3	622.8	209.0	128.3	32.0	43.9	10.3
13600.80	24738.75	30110.43	18417.41	24201.73	998.9	457.9	177.9	131.4	21.6	37.0	6.2
1073.69	2554.81	3146.05	1882.42	2445.27	1369.5	603.3	227.6	129.9	15.1	38.4	11.9
17682.94	20811.95	22891.88	25600.53	27967.15	776.7	315.5	158.2	109.2	19.7	14.8	7.7
13604.89	19610.88	22135.23	25456.70	29044.20	1345.5	452.3	213.5	114.1	24.4	16.2	13.3
263.02	478.56	522.85	550.43	583.24	1299.2	451.2	222.0	106.0	23.6	15.2	15.9
87.62	130.82	141.42	157.75	176.54	1857.1	668.4	201.4	111.9	24.8	27.1	12.5

1-11 续表3

指　标	Item	总量指标 Total quantity index			
		1995	2000	2005	2010
教育、科技、文化	**Education, Science and Technology and Culture**				
教育	**Education**				
专任教师数（人）	Full-time Teachers(person)				
#普通高等学校	Institutions of Higher Education	15914	15679	29498	42098
普通中等专业学校	Regular Specialized Secondary Schools	2533	3172	2130	1845
普通中学	Regular Middle Schools	21984	26230	31094	31506
小 学	Primary Schools	30270	30215	29647	29944
在校学生数（万人）	Students Enrollment(10 000 person)				
#普通高等学校	Institutions of Higher Education	11.67	19.41	53.06	73.30
普通中等专业学校	Regular Specialized Secondary Schools	3.74	6.02	6.16	6.80
普通中学	Regular Schools	32.32	48.31	55.74	48.90
小 学	Primary Schools	79.36	77.81	60.47	51.60
科技	**Science and Technology**				
国家级高新技术企业数（个）	Hi-tech Enterprises (unit)				827
企事业单位累计授权专利数（件）	Accumulated patents awarded(unit)	3164	6139	11670	31999
文化	**Culture**				
图书馆总藏量（千册件）	Total Collections in Library (1000 Volume-time)	2830	3214	3671	4465
文化馆、站（个）	Cultural Centers or Stations (unit)	201	251	192	197
电视节目制作时间（时）	Time for TV Programs Production(hour)	5738	11871	27377	29626
家庭、生活、环境	**Family, People's Livelihood and Environment**				
家庭	**Family**				
家庭总户数（户籍人口）（万户）	Total Number of Households(10 000 household)	171.25	187.08	203.04	226.71
城镇常住居民平均每户家庭人口（人）	Average Household Size in Urban Areas(person)	3.88	2.99	2.93	2.81
农村常住居民平均每户家庭人口（人）	Average Household Size in Rural Areas(person)	4.60	4.30	4.22	3.94
婚姻	**Marriages and Divorces**				
结婚（对）	Number of Marriages(couple)	47236	46415	49962	83645
离婚（对）	Number of Divorces(couple)	4296	5161	12747	19060
居住	**Housing**				
城镇居民人均现住房建筑面积（平方米）	Per Capita Building Area of Urban Residents (sq.m)	13.05	14.82	16.38	28.70
农村居民人均现住房建筑面积（平方米）	Per Capita Building Area of Rural Residents(sq.m)	21.77	28.31	36.73	66.73

注：1.2008年及以前图书馆总藏量为图书馆藏书量。
2.2005年以前城镇居民人均现住房总建筑面积为城镇人均住房使用面积。
3.2014年城乡居民人均住房面积为城乡住户调查一体化改革后新口径数据，与往年不可比。
4.结婚和离婚对数2018年数据含西咸新区与往年不可比，增速暂不计算。

continued 3

					速度指标（%）				Indices and Growth Rates(%)		
2015	2018	2019	2020	2021	指数（2021年比以下各年）(2021 as percentage of the following years)				平均增长速度 Average Annual Growth Rate		
					2005	2010	2015	2020	2006-2010	2011-2015	2016-2020
47768	49018	50236	51996	53139	180.2	126.2	111.3	102.2	7.4	2.6	1.7
1228	958	918	970	974	45.8	52.7	79.3	100.4	-2.8	-7.8	-4.6
33014	37539	39143	41133	38196	115.7	114.1	108.9	92.9	0.3	0.9	3.2
28748	36878	39836	43423	50767	157.9	156.2	164.7	116.9	0.2	-1.1	7.1
84.83	82.44	87.14	93.13	98.06	184.9	133.8	115.6	105.3	6.7	3.0	1.9
3.47	2.48	2.79	3.02	2.03	32.9	30.0	58.4	67.2	1.9	-12.5	-2.8
41.37	42.46	43.56	45.68	48.21	83.2	95.0	112.4	105.5	-2.6	-3.3	1.3
56.62	73.09	78.98	85.20	89.09	139.5	163.8	149.1	104.6	-3.1	1.9	7.3
1316	2620	3673	5234	7140		862.9	542.5	136.4		9.7	31.7
103910	206703	240826	286233	350364	3004.4	1095.6	337.3	122.4	22.4	26.6	22.5
6522	7711	8012	7977	8628	235.3	193.6	132.4	108.2	4.0	7.9	4.1
199	202	202	204	204	95.6	93.3	92.4	100.0	0.6	0.2	-1.6
43563	45731	58427	30016	41152	150.3	138.9	94.6	137.1	1.6	8.0	-7.2
253.13	290.41	300.95	310.59	321.21	158.0	141.7	126.9	103.4	2.2	2.2	4.2
2.8	2.8	2.8	2.8	2.9	99.0	103.2	103.6	103.6	-0.8	-0.1	
3.6	3.7	3.7	3.5	3.4	80.6	86.3	94.4	97.1	-1.6	-1.8	-0.6
80790	93007	87315	75887	76004				100.2	10.9	-0.7	
22748	42034	45329	41785	30108				72.1	8.4	3.6	
32.1	34.4	34.8	34.9	35.2			109.8	100.9	11.9		1.7
50.7	51.4	49.1	50.2	46.8			92.2	93.2	12.7		-0.2

1-11 续表4

指 标	Item	总量指标 Total quantity index			
		1995	2000	2005	2010
生活	**People's Livelihood**				
城镇居民人均可支配收入（元）	Per Capita Annual Disposable Income of Urban Households (yuan)	4153	6364	9628	22244
农村居民人均可支配收入（元）	Per Capita Annual Disposable Income of Rural Residents(yuan)	1353	2344	3460	7750
住户存款（亿元）	Household deposits(100 mil. Yuan)	291.46	675.83	1716.76	3641.09
工资	**Wages**				
在岗职工工资总额（亿元）	The Gross Salary of Workers(100 mil. yuan)	67.23	101.68	211.14	501.76
城镇非私营单位从业人员年平均工资（元）	Aunual Average Wage of Stuff and Workers in Urban Non-privite Enterprises(yuan)	4763	9179	17728	37870
卫生	**Health Care**				
医院、卫生院（个）	Number of Hospitals(unit)	368	426	479	412
执业（助理）医师（人）	Licensed (Assistant) Doctors (person)	18846	18750	17730	18763
医院、卫生院床位数（张）	Number of Hospital Beds(unit)	28265	28697	30087	36796
市政建设	**City Construction**				
自来水供应量（万立方米）	Volume of Tap Water Supply(10 000 cu.m)	35885	30273	35776	41089
自来水供水管道长度（公里）	Length of Water Supply Pipelines(km)	1066	2237	2315	2416
城市天然气供气总量 （万立方米）	Volume of Natural Gas Supply in Urban Areas (10 000 cu.m)	8419	11513	53202	109052
城市公共运营车辆（辆）	Total Number of Public Buses and Trolley Buses(unit)	977	2573	4762	7107
道路长度（公里）	Length of Paved Roads(km)	835	975	1382	2662
绿地面积（公顷）	Areas of Green Land(hectare)	5603	4116	4867	12140
环境、灾害	**Environment and Disaster**				
工业废水排放量（万吨）	Volume of Waste Water up to the Standard for Discharge(10 000 tons)	12479	9145	16969	13840
火灾发生数（起）	Number of Fire Disasters(case)	426	1040	2664	1825
火灾事故损失额（万元）	Fire Loss(10 000 yuan)	742	472	1566	2224
交通事故发生数（起）	Number of Traffic Accidents(case)	3065	4099	4903	2323
交通事故损失额（万元）	Loss of Traffic Accidents(10 000 yuan)	1103	1116	2024	737

注：1.城镇非私营单位从业人员年平均工资2012年前为城镇非私营单位在岗职工年平均工资。
2.2014年及以后城乡居民人均收入为新口径数据。2013年及以前“农村居民人均可支配收入”为“农村居民人均纯收入”。依据2018年新口径对2017年城乡居民收入进行了衔接，其他年份不可比。
3.人民银行西安分行对住户存款部分历史年份数据进行了修订。2015年之前住户存款为储蓄存款。
4.市政建设大部分指标2017年起包含西咸新区，与以前年份不可比，故不计算相关增速指标。

continued 4

					速度指标（%） Indices and Growth Rates (%)						
2015	2018	2019	2020	2021	指数（2021年比以下各年） (2021 as percentage of the following years)				平均增长速度 Average Annual Growth Rate		
					2005	2010	2015	2020	2006-2010	2011-2015	2016-2020
33188	38729	41850	43713	46931	617.4	267.2	152.4	107.4	18.2	15.1	7.2
14072	13286	14588	15749	17389	764.5	341.5	167.8	110.4	17.5	15.3	8.7
6571.18	8360.33	9553.29	10913.05	11996.54	699.2	329.7	182.7	109.9	13.3	12.5	10.7
1202.01	1622.72	1903.84	2081.05	2223.66	1017.8	428.5	178.8	106.9	18.9	19.1	10.8
60557	83821	92359	99315	111078	629.4	294.7	184.2	111.8	16.4	9.8	10.5
395	462	477	476	488	91.3	106.2	110.9	102.5	-3.0	-0.8	1.6
26626	33776	38469	40714	43289	235.7	222.5	156.8	106.3	1.1	7.3	8.1
51345	65552	69107	68426	75684	240.2	196.3	140.7	110.6	4.1	6.9	4.9
56055	90394	75392	76944	82379				107.1	2.8	6.4	
4371	4960	4977	5991	6364				106.2	0.9	12.6	
196826	285215	320847	329150	366539				111.4	15.4	12.5	
7781	8743	10566	9363	9318	195.8	131.1	119.8	99.5	8.3	1.8	3.8
3571	4712	5142	5284	5877				111.2	14.0	6.1	
20582	31681	32586	36034	43839				121.7	20.1	11.1	
5204	4163	3914	2998	3813	23.7	28.9	76.7	127.2	-4.0	-17.8	-9.6
2590	2066	1871	3034	5348	200.8	293.4	206.4	176.3	-7.3	7.3	3.2
2402	1783	1887	2387	4462	285.4	200.7	185.8	186.9	7.3	1.5	-0.1
2392	3153	2973	2835	2776	56.6	119.5	116.0	97.9	-13.9	0.6	3.5
1470	2191	1809	1738	1548	76.4	210.2	105.3	89.1	-18.3	14.8	3.4

1-12 主要年份国民经济和社会发展结构指标

单位：%

指　标	Item	1995	2000	2005
人口与就业	**Population and Employment**			
人　口	**Population**			
城乡结构	Structure			
城镇人口	Urban Population	39.45	41.54	44.91
乡村人口	Rural Population	60.55	58.46	55.09
性别结构	Sexual Structure			
男	Male	51.64	51.62	51.50
女	Female	48.36	48.38	48.50
就　业	**Employment**			
全社会从业人员产业结构	Industrial Structure of the Whole Society			
第一产业	Primary Industry	41.17	37.78	32.78
第二产业	Secondary Industry	29.43	27.57	27.46
第三产业	Tertiary Industry	29.40	34.65	39.76
宏观经济	**Macro Economy**			
国民经济核算	**National Accounting**			
地区生产总值产业结构	Industrial Structure of GDP			
第一产业	Primary Industry	12.53	6.91	5.10
第二产业	Secondary Industry	40.97	42.89	39.50
第三产业	Tertiary Industry	46.50	50.20	55.40
投　资	**Investment**			
报表种类结构	By classification			
固定资产投资（不含农户）	Investment in Fixed Assets (excluding farmers)	85.57	87.36	92.96
#房地产开发投资	Real Estate Investment	20.93	22.31	27.00
经济成分结构	Registion Status Composition			
国有经济	State-owned Enterprises Investment	66.79	68.68	44.75
集体经济	Collective-owned Enterprises Investment	9.46	6.30	7.09
个体经济	Self-employed Individual	10.76	10.50	9.46
其他经济	Other	12.99	14.51	38.69
财　政	**Government Finance**			
财政收入结构	Structure of Government Revenue			
中　央	Central Government		31.94	58.30
地　方	Local Governments		68.06	41.70

注：1.2015年，市公安局提供户籍人口分类为"城镇人口"和"乡村人口"，2015年之前，分类为"非农业人口"和"农业人口"。
2.本表2008年以后财政收入结构中地方指地方财政一般公共预算收入。

Structural Indicators of National Economic and Social Development in Representative Years

(%)

2010	2014	2015	2016	2017	2018	2019	2020	2021
47.86	51.29	66.93	66.94	67.12	69.31	69.88		
52.14	48.71	33.07	33.06	32.88	30.69	30.12		
50.95	50.59	50.54	50.49	50.29	50.01	49.87	49.75	49.65
49.05	49.41	49.46	49.51	49.71	49.99	50.13	50.25	50.35
25.65	19.71	20.39	19.50	18.98	16.30	15.70	15.05	14.52
29.65	28.49	24.53	23.72	22.73	24.79	25.48	23.45	22.21
44.70	51.80	55.08	56.78	58.29	58.91	58.83	61.50	63.27
4.17	3.44	3.23	3.07	3.31	3.05	2.97	3.12	2.89
40.40	38.59	34.90	33.45	33.07	33.67	33.31	33.33	33.54
55.43	57.97	61.87	63.48	63.62	63.28	63.72	63.55	63.57
95.52	96.25	98.47	98.18	98.77				
25.91	29.84	35.46	37.67	30.88				
41.49	32.46	35.36	44.92	54.62				
10.04	3.44	3.06	2.93	2.03				
1.68	1.41	1.56	1.57	1.24				
46.78	62.69	60.02	50.58	42.10				
37.28	29.61	28.94	31.68	35.63	39.86	40.83	39.89	40.48
47.36	57.25	58.39	56.45	47.96	46.88	45.80	46.98	46.23

1-12 续表1

单位：%

指　标	Item	1995	2000	2005
产　业	**Industry**			
农　业	**Agriculture**			
农林牧渔业总产值结构	Structure of Gross Output Value of Farming, Forestry,Animal Husbandry and Fishery			
农　业	Farming	68.03	69.23	61.69
林　业	Forestry	0.96	1.14	1.23
牧　业	Animal Husbandry	30.29	28.58	30.96
渔　业	Fishery	0.72	1.05	0.69
农林牧渔专业及辅助性活动	Services in Support of Farming,Forestry,Animal Husbandry and Fishery			5.43
建筑业	**Construction**			
建筑业总产值结构	Structure of Gross Output Value of Construction Industry			
房屋建筑业	Building Construction	12.84	9.28	34.05
土木工程建筑业	Civil Engineering Construction	86.27	88.50	56.59
建筑安装业	Installation of Construction			
建筑装饰和其他建筑业	Decoration and others	0.89	2.22	9.36
交通运输业	**Transportation**			
客运量结构	Structure of Passenger Traffic			
铁　路	Railways	29.53	26.40	17.14
公　路	Highways	67.57	69.14	79.15
民　航	Civil Aviation	2.90	4.46	3.71
货运量结构	Structure of Freight Traffic			
铁　路	Railways	34.59	44.30	26.92
公　路	Highways	65.36	55.58	73.04
民　航	Civil Aviation	0.05	0.12	0.04
国内贸易	**Domestic Trade**			
社会消费品零售总额结构	Composition of Retail Sales of Consumer Goods			
城　镇	Urban Area	88.95	87.99	90.17
农　村	Rural Area	11.05	12.01	9.83
教育文化、卫生、人民生活	**Education and Culture，Health Care，People's Livelihood**			
教　育	**Education**			
在校学生结构	Structure of Student Enrollment			
#普通高等学校	Institutions of Higher Education	8.81	12.44	28.48
普通中等专业学校	Regular Specialized Secondary Schools	2.84	3.84	3.33
普通中学	Regular Schools	24.55	30.93	29.89
小 学	Primary Schools	59.91	49.89	32.45

continued 1

(%)

2010	2014	2015	2016	2017	2018	2019	2020	2021
65.40	67.95	68.06	68.00	68.81	70.04	69.97	69.53	69.65
1.26	2.69	2.96	2.95	3.10	3.67	3.70	4.18	3.46
25.35	19.60	18.54	17.93	16.67	14.74	14.56	15.06	14.94
0.60	0.74	0.59	0.57	0.52	0.57	0.44	0.33	0.46
7.39	9.02	9.85	10.56	10.90	10.98	11.33	10.90	11.49
24.63	41.58	38.41	36.69	36.64	37.73	39.84	39.49	37.19
68.61	49.43	51.84	53.63	54.13	54.84	52.80	53.49	55.19
4.39	5.32	5.91	6.61	6.30	4.88	4.79	4.42	4.86
2.37	3.67	3.84	3.07	2.93	2.55	2.56	2.60	2.76
9.18	13.65	14.80	17.74	18.53	23.17	24.06	26.12	40.28
87.59	74.97	72.95	66.63	64.24	59.70	57.99	52.21	31.34
3.23	11.38	12.25	15.63	17.24	17.14	17.94	21.67	28.38
2.06	2.14	1.83	3.58	3.90	1.90	1.78	1.83	1.78
97.92	97.81	98.12	96.32	96.00	97.99	98.09	98.02	98.07
0.02	0.05	0.05	0.10	0.10	0.12	0.14	0.15	0.15
96.00	96.85	96.70	96.61	96.43	98.05	98.02	97.84	96.83
4.00	3.15	3.30	3.39	3.57	1.95	1.98	2.16	3.17
32.60	33.16	32.78	31.38	29.13	27.52	27.44	27.80	28.40
3.02	1.58	1.34	1.17	0.96	0.83	0.88	0.90	0.59
21.74	16.53	16.00	15.37	14.65	14.18	13.72	13.64	13.96
22.95	20.88	21.88	22.58	23.40	24.40	24.87	25.44	25.80

1-12 续表2

单位：%

指 标	Item	1995	2000	2005
专任教师结构	Structure of Full-time Teachers			
#普通高等学校	Institutions of Higher Education	21.25	19.89	29.93
普通中等专业学校	Regular Specialized Secondary Schools	3.38	4.02	2.16
普通中学	Regular Middle Schools	29.37	33.21	31.55
小 学	Primary Schools	40.41	38.34	30.08
人民生活	**People's Livelihood**			
城镇居民消费结构	Consumption Structure of Urban Residents			
食品烟酒	Food,Tobacco and Alcohol	44.68	36.46	37.04
衣 着	Clothing	12.67	8.13	9.03
居 住	Residence	6.49	11.23	9.10
生活用品及服务	Living Articles and Services	13.75	11.33	4.73
交通和通信	Transport and Communication Services	5.58	6.93	9.67
教育文化娱乐	Recreation, Education and Culture Services	9.05	13.74	17.18
医疗保健	Medical and Health Care Services	3.27	7.23	9.45
其他用品和服务	Other Commodities and Services	4.51	4.95	3.80
农村居民消费结构	Consumption Structure of Rural Residents			
食品烟酒	Food,Tobacco and Alcohol	50.31	36.63	36.34
衣 着	Clothing	8.39	6.65	6.11
居 住	Residence	5.92	21.41	17.76
生活用品及服务	Living Articles and Services	5.17	5.47	5.11
交通和通信	Transport and Communication Services	8.09	4.21	8.19
教育文化娱乐	Recreation, Education and Culture Services	18.53	14.49	16.15
医疗保健	Medical and Health Care Services	1.78	6.93	8.19
其他用品和服务	Other Commodities and Services	1.81	4.21	2.15
卫 生	**Health Care**			
卫生技术人员结构	Medical Technical Personnel by Types			
执业（助理）医师	Licensed（Assistant） Doctors	45.42	44.82	41.96
注册护士	Registered Nurses	32.68	34.29	33.14
药 师	Junior Paramedics	8.78	8.31	7.30
技 师	Technicians	5.21	5.21	5.33
卫生监督员	Health Supervisors			
其 他	Others	7.91	7.37	12.27

注：2014年及以后为城乡住户调查一体化改革后数据，居民消费结构与2014年之前不可比。

continued 2

(%)

2010	2014	2015	2016	2017	2018	2019	2020	2021
32.47	33.87	34.52	32.63	30.90	30.74	29.97	29.13	28.85
1.42	0.97	0.89	0.84	0.64	0.60	0.55	0.54	0.53
24.30	23.62	23.86	23.50	23.58	23.54	23.35	23.04	20.74
23.10	20.57	20.52	21.41	22.03	23.13	23.76	24.33	27.56
31.29	29.21	29.59	29.26	29.44	27.08	26.80	28.08	26.98
11.11	9.09	8.78	8.22	8.12	7.91	7.65	6.65	5.99
9.33	17.89	17.78	17.87	17.84	20.01	21.00	24.21	25.69
7.56	7.21	7.42	7.59	7.57	7.86	7.26	7.16	6.47
12.06	14.16	13.31	13.67	13.00	11.74	11.85	11.21	10.32
14.66	12.60	12.48	12.29	12.61	13.93	13.69	10.60	11.45
9.50	7.32	7.92	8.14	8.28	8.97	8.95	9.80	10.60
4.49	2.53	2.72	2.96	3.15	2.50	2.79	2.30	2.50
32.54	29.93	28.18	26.86	27.27	24.43	25.45	27.98	28.94
6.55	7.44	7.12	6.65	6.50	5.94	6.25	6.09	5.68
24.41	21.99	23.28	23.38	23.54	23.60	23.10	24.25	23.67
6.53	6.97	6.60	7.59	7.85	7.67	7.22	5.81	5.69
8.45	10.66	10.70	10.76	10.69	11.71	11.85	12.59	12.58
11.20	10.26	11.68	11.86	11.90	13.26	13.15	11.41	11.91
8.54	11.07	10.68	11.17	10.47	12.05	11.46	10.37	9.82
1.78	1.68	1.76	1.73	1.79	1.34	1.51	1.51	1.71
33.16	32.66	32.69	32.30	32.71	33.28	34.27	34.60	35.11
40.01	42.28	42.74	43.50	44.15	45.77	46.22	46.18	46.24
5.36	4.88	4.86	4.72	4.54	4.36	4.20	4.09	3.92
8.11	5.63	5.76	5.86	5.94	5.95	5.91	5.94	6.82
								0.35
13.36	14.56	13.97	13.62	12.66	10.64	9.40	9.19	**7.56**

1-13 主要年份国民经济和社会发展比例和效益指标

指　标	Item	1995
人口与就业	**Population and Employment**	
人口	**Population**	
出生率（‰）	Birth Rate(‰)	11.95
死亡率（‰）	Death Rate(‰)	4.98
自然增长率（‰）	Natural Growth Rate(‰)	6.79
就业	**Employment**	
就业者负担人口	Dependency Ratio	1.7
三次产业就业者比例	Employment Ratio by Type of Industry	
（以第一产业为100）	(Employment in primary industry=100)	
第一产业	Primary Industry	100
第二产业	Secondary Industry	71.5
第三产业	Tertiary Industry	71.4
城镇登记失业率（%）	Unemployment Rate in Urban Areas(%)	3.1
宏观经济	**Macro Economy**	
国民经济核算	**National Accounting**	
三次产业增加值比例	Ratio of Value-added by Type of Industry	
（以第一产业为100）	(Employment in primary industry=100)	
第一产业	Primary Industry	100
第二产业	Secondary Industry	326.9
第三产业	Tertiary Industry	371.1
全社会劳动生产率（元／人）	Overall Labor Productivity(yuan/person)	8963
第一产业	Primary Industry	2698
第二产业	Secondary Industry	12404
第三产业	Tertiary Industry	14488
人均地区生产总值（元）	Per Capita GDP(yuan)	5131
固定资产投资	**Investment in Fixed Assets**	
全社会固定资产投资相当于地区生产总值比例（%）	Proportion of Investment in fixed Assets to GDP(%)	31.3
房屋建筑面积竣工率（%）	Rate of Floor Space of Buildings Completed in Construction(%)	33.4
固定资产交付使用率（%）	Rate of Fixed Assets Completed in Capital Construction and Put into Use(%)	70.7
建设项目建成投产率（%）	Rate of Projects Completed in Capital Construction and Put into Use(%)	43.7
财政	**Finance**	
财政总收入相当于地区生产总值比例（%）	Proportion of Government Revenue to GDP(%)	5.5
一般公共预算支出相当于地区生产总值比例(%)	Proportion of Government General Public Budgeary Expenditures to GDP(%)	5.6
利用外资	**Utilization of Foreign Capital**	
外商实际直接投资额相当于利用外资协议金额比例（%）	Proportion of Foreign Capital Actually Used to Total Amount of Foreign Capital for Utilization by Signed Contracts or Agreements (%)	64.4

注：本表财政收入数据2009年及以前为一般预算财政收入和基金收入之和。依据部门历史年份修订结果对财政相关数据进行了重新计算。本表涉及常住人口计算的指标数据依据第七次全国人口普查数据进行了修订。

Proportions of National Economic and Social Development and Benefit Index in Representative Years

2000	2005	2010	2011	2012	2013	2014	2015	2016	2017	2018	2019	2020	2021
13.07	9.58	9.73	9.71	10.13	9.57	10.11	10.15	11.54	12.62	12.47	12.32	9.14	8.44
5.96	5.16	5.34	5.38	5.57	5.37	5.47	5.51	5.40	5.42	5.48	5.53	7.48	7.51
7.11	4.42	4.39	4.33	4.56	4.20	4.64	4.64	6.14	7.20	6.99	6.79	1.66	0.93
1.8	1.8	1.8	1.8	1.8	1.8	1.8	1.8	1.9	1.9	1.9	1.9	1.9	1.9
100	100	100	100	100	100	100	100	100	100	100	100	100	100
73.0	83.8	124.0	125.0	141.3	137.2	144.6	120.3	121.7	119.7	152.1	162.3	155.9	153.0
91.7	121.3	183.3	184.7	206.5	243.3	262.9	270.1	291.3	307.1	361.4	374.8	408.8	435.7
3.4	4.3	4.2	3.9	3.5	3.4	3.4	3.4	3.3	3.3	3.3	3.3	3.6	3.6
100	100	100	100	100	100	100	100	100	100	100	100	100	100
620.7	774.4	969.0	916.6	953.3	1066.0	1123.5	1078.9	1087.9	1000.1	1105.1	1121.6	1068.3	1160.9
726.4	1086.0	1329.3	1275.5	1359.5	1550.4	1687.5	1912.6	2064.6	1924.4	2076.8	2146.0	2036.8	2200.1
16367	31356	67973	77893	86490	94907	104867	111837	119867	130668	139628	148372	152998	158230
2960	4747	11129	13883	15351	16204	17783	18045	18483	22470	24156	27552	31067	30935
25443	45258	93218	102201	110093	124045	141911	147176	166245	186251	197683	196560	208563	232548
24024	44611	83586	96232	106847	111886	118682	129488	136009	144404	150770	160613	161554	161196
9484	16158	37792	43723	48530	53624	58829	60912	63393	66649	73113	77494	79208	83689
36.0	64.5	101.7	88.3	97.1	103.5	105.9	87.1	81.2	101.9				
42.0	28.1	6.9	10.0	8.7	13.2	11.4	6.8	9.9	11.2	6.4	6.3	4.9	2.6
74.0	52.8	38.4	40.4	42.4	37.1	42.5	40.3	38.3	43.4	26.9	33.6	37.2	20.9
44.2	54.2	53.9	54.9	56.1	56.1	62.5	61.0	64.6	62.4	36.3	55.3	42.0	31.9
9.5	12.7	16.0	17.1	17.2	18.2	18.3	18.8	17.8	18.4	17.2	16.3	15.4	17.3
7.2	7.6	11.6	13.0	13.7	14.7	14.7	15.5	14.7	14.1	13.6	13.3	13.4	13.8
28.9	47.0	130.9	167.0	68.8	124.3	145.0	207.0	441.2	114.1	133.6	359.3	104.4	1030.3

1-13 续表1

指 标	Item	1995
能　源	**Energy**	
单位生产总值能耗降低率（%）	Decreasing Rate of Energy Consumption per Unit GDP(%)	
产　业	**Industries**	
农业	**Agriculture**	
每个农林牧渔业劳动力农产品	Output of Farm Products per Farming,Forestry,Animal	
生产量（公斤）	Husbandry and Fishery Husbandry and Fishery Laborer (kg)	
粮食	Grain	1150
蔬菜	Vegetables	877
禽蛋	Poultry Eggs	
肉类	Meat	
水产品	Aquatic Products	6
每公顷播种面积农产品产量（公斤）	Output of Farm Crops per Hectare of Sown Area(kg)	
粮食	Grain	3806
油料	Oil-bearing Crops	1753
蔬菜	Vegetables	34800
工业	**Industry**	
规模以上工业企业经济效益	Economic Benefit of Industrial Enterprises above Designated Size	
总资产贡献率（%）	Ratio of Total Assets to Industrial Output Value (%)	
资产负债率（%）	Assets-Liability Ratio (%)	
流动资产周转次数（次／年）	Rate of Annual Turnover Working Capitals(times/year)	
成本费用利润率（%）	Ratio of Profits to Cost (%)	
产品销售率（%）	Proportion of Industrial Products Sold(%)	
全员劳动生产率（元／人）	Overall Labor Productivity (yuan/person)	
建筑业	**Construction**	
技术装备率(元／人)	Value of Machinery per Laborer(yuan/person)	5990
产值利润率（%）	Ratio of Per-tax Profits to Gross Output Value(%)	3.5
全员劳动生产率（元／人）	Overall Labor Productivity(yuan/person)	37689
（按总产值计算）	(in terms of gross output value per employee)	
邮电通信业	**Postal and Telecommunication Services**	
电话普及率（含移动电话）（部/百人）	Access to Telephones, National(include mobilphone) (set/100 persons)	7.9
移动电话普及率（部/百人）	Access to Mobile Telephones(set/100 persons)	0.5

continued 1

2000	2005	2010	2011	2012	2013	2014	2015	2016	2017	2018	2019	2020	2021
		2.06	3.56	3.51	3.57	5.89	3.20	3.83	4.61	5.99	4.78	7.52	-0.94
1382	1493	1497	1438	1480	1398	1276	1346	1323	1267	1456	1430	1469	1462
1110	1421	1777	1844	2012	2249	2338	2549	2628	3214	3827	3870	3874	3737
					45	43	49	61	48	54	55	53	49
					61	64	69	67	53	56	53	46	51
8	7	10	10	12	13	13	14	13	13	14	14	11	14
4342	4796	4682	4772	4949	4886	4831	5132	5052	4947	5082	5122	5313	5509
1526	1821	1950	2027	1992	1948	1519	2099	1408	2173	2180	2157	2135	2166
37797	35231	39798	40668	42990	45271	38085	48711	39152	50851	52027	52717	52258	51051
	8.4	12.2	8.6	7.7	8.5	7.4	5.7	6.4	7.2	7.3	5.4	6.1	5.4
65.0	65.0	57.6	57.7	59.4	59.5	59.7	57.3	55.7	53.0	54.8	53.9	55.2	57.4
1.0	1.3	1.7	1.5	1.5	1.5	1.4	1.3	1.3	1.4	1.3	1.2	1.1	1.1
4.2	3.1	8.8	5.2	4.5	5.2	5.2	4.8	6.0	6.6	6.7	5.1	7.1	5.7
97.1	97.5	97.1	97.4	96.7	95.7	94.9	94.5	96.0	97.3	96.2	94.0	93.0	92.4
29496	82815	188483	194105	230032	264324	275288	268182	277240	294393				
6805	13332	9461	28669	12216	10339		12712	14193	10051	10005	7964	7562	7118
3.4	4.8	4.4	4.4	2.8	2.6	2.3	2.3	3.1	2.8	3.0	2.5	3.0	3.4
74347	206337	321340	334172	479232	354419	347000	406962	422421	411690	457729	449583	497584	540075
31.2	100.0	199.0	212.5	231.4	264.9	242.9	208.4	196.5	187.6	178.0	158.8	150.0	155.3
10.6	56.6	168.0	182.0	197.3	230.8	211.0	178.8	168.9	163.5	156.0	138.6	131.5	136.6

1-13 续表2

指 标	Item	1995
国内贸易	**Domestic Trade**	
人均批发零售和住宿餐饮业消费品零售额（元）	Per Capita Retail Sales of Wholesale,Retail Trade and Accommodation Catering Trade (yuan)	1997
对外经济贸易	**Foreign Trade**	
进出口总额相当于地区生产总值比例（%）	Proportion of Total Imports & Exports to GDP(%)	34.76
旅游	**Tourism**	
每一游客花费（元）	Expenditure per International Tourist(yuan)	556
金融业	**Finance and Insurance**	
金融机构存款相当于地区生产总值比例（%）	Bank Deposits as Percentage of GDP(%)	108.83
金融机构贷款相当于地区生产总值比例（%）	Bank Loans as Percentage of GDP(%)	101.26
教育、科技、文化	**Education, Science and Technology and Culture**	
教育	**Education**	
毕业率（%）	Graduation Rate(%)	
小学	Primary Schools	
初中	Junior Schools	
学校教师负担系数	Student-teacher Ratio	
高等学校	Colleges and Universities	6.83
中等学校	Secondary Schools	14.42
小学	Primary Schools	26.22
文化	**Culture**	
每百万人有艺术表演团体（个）	Number of Troupes per Million Persons(unit)	3.39
每百万人有公共图书馆（个）	Number of Public Libraries per Million Persons(unit)	2.31
家庭、生活、环境	**Family, People's Livelihood and Environment**	
家庭	**Family**	
城市居民家庭	Urban Households	
平均每一劳动力负担人口（人）	Persons supported by Each Laborer (person)	1.8
农村居民家庭	Rural Households	
平均每一劳动力负担人口（人）	Persons supported by Each Laborer (person)	1.6
卫生	**Health Care**	
每万人医院数（个）	Number of Hospitals per 10 000 Persons(unit)	0.60
每万人医生数（人）	Number of Doctors per 10 000 Persons(person)	29.10
每万人医院床位数（张）	Number of Hospital Beds per 10 000 Persons(unit)	43.60
市政建设	**City Construction**	
城市自来水普及率（%）	Percentage of Households with Access to Tap Water(%)	
城市用气普及率（%）	Percentage of Households with Access to Tap Gas (%)	
人均公园绿地面积（平方米）	Per Capita Public Green Areas (sq.m)	3.80

continued 2

2000	2005	2010	2011	2012	2013	2014	2015	2016	2017	2018	2019	2020	2021
4122	9160	20882	24751	28106	31336	34571	37176	39767	40875	41761	42382	39426	38427
22.25	24.79	21.54	20.94	18.72	22.11	27.47	29.69	28.61	34.31	38.86	34.49	34.67	41.17
645	737	767	797	820	801	792	789	809	903	1033	1045	1022	1010
206.71	278.17	277.41	272.99	275.61	275.51	270.11	298.05	296.38	268.85	244.86	243.53	255.40	261.66
150.51	166.77	200.96	197.70	195.86	200.19	207.57	229.31	237.00	226.90	230.73	235.48	254.00	271.73
		100.4	100.2	100.17	99.82	99.69	99.64	99.78	99.76	99.99	99.83	99.69	98.34
		99.7	100.6	98.74	99.27	99.93	98.31	98.67	99.28	99.24	99.02	99.13	97.85
12.38	17.99	17.41	17.92	18.15	18.05	18.27	17.76	17.62	17.33	16.82	17.35	17.91	18.45
17.84	18.47	17.78	16.91	16.43	15.07	14.01	13.88	13.05	12.78	13.10	13.06	12.89	14.38
25.75	20.38	17.22	18.06	17.15	17.66	18.94	19.70	19.32	19.52	19.82	19.83	19.62	17.55
3.20	2.56	1.53	3.38	2.08	1.92	1.88	1.82	1.75	1.59	1.51	1.46	1.39	1.40
2.18	2.02	1.77	1.69	1.64	1.60	1.56	1.32	1.26	1.15	1.09	1.05	1.16	1.16
2.2	2.1	1.9	1.8	1.9	1.8	1.3	1.3	1.3	1.3	1.3	1.3	1.3	1.3
1.6	1.6	1.5	1.5	1.5	1.5	1.4	1.4	1.4	1.4	1.5	1.6	1.5	1.4
0.57	0.59	0.49	0.41	0.41	0.41	0.40	0.40	0.38	0.40	0.39	0.39	0.37	0.38
25.30	21.98	22.14	24.30	25.22	25.52	25.85	26.95	27.05	27.18	28.36	31.15	31.42	33.63
38.72	37.29	43.42	42.01	44.40	47.21	49.04	51.97	51.46	53.36	55.04	55.96	52.80	58.79
98.95	99.00	98.77	99.95	100	100	100	100	100	99.25	97.85	98.27	98.67	99.40
81.51	91.30	97.02	97.46	98.19	98.68	98.71	98.79	98.89	96.07	99.90	99.96	99.87	99.95
5.12	5.63	9.11	9.89	10.22	10.70	11.22	11.47	11.61	12.04	9.97	9.97	11.79	11.80

1-14 主要年份平均每天主要社会经济活动

指　标	Item	1995	2000
一、每天创造的财富	**Daily Production**		
地区生产总值（万元）	Gross Domestic Product(10 000 yuan)	9050.7	17702.2
第一产业	Primary Industry	1134.3	1223.3
第二产业	Secondary Industry	3707.7	7592.6
第三产业	Tertiary Industry	4208.8	8886.3
工业	Industry	3082.2	5984.7
建筑业	Construction	625.5	1608.0
批发和零售业	Wholesale and Retail Trade	909.6	1804.7
交通运输、仓储和邮政业	Transport, Storage, Post & Telecommunication Services	674.0	1178.4
住宿和餐饮业	Hotels and Catering Services		505.8
财政总收入（万元）	Total Government Revenue(10 000 yuan)	498.8	1686.8
财政一般公共预算支出（万元）	Government General Public Budgetary Expenditures(10 000 yuan)	504.7	1274.0
粮食（吨）	Grain(ton)	4801	5532
奶类（吨）	Milk(ton)		
蔬菜（吨）	Vegetables(ton)	3660	4442
肉类（吨）	Meat(ton)		
水产品（吨）	Aquatic Products(ton)	23	31
布（万米）	Cloth(10 000 m)	83	77
发电量（万千瓦小时）	Electricity(10 000 kWh)	610	534
钢材（吨）	Steel(ton)	861	274
汽车（辆）	Motor Vehicle(unit)	8	25
二、每天消费量	**Daily National Consumption**		
社会消费品零售总额（万元）	Total Retail Sales of Consumer Goods (10 000 yuan)	5160	10108
三、每天其他经济活动	**Other Daily Economic Activities**		
竣工住宅面积（平方米）	Floor Space of Buildings Completed (sq.m)	6927	14930
货运量（万吨）	Freight Traffic(10 000 tons)	26.3	19.2
客运量（万人次）	Passenger Traffic(10 000 person-times)	24.8	22.1
邮电业务总量（万元）	Business Volume of Postal and Telecommunication Services(10 000 yuan)	209.6	1264.7
进出口总值（万美元）	Total Value of Imports and Exports (USD 10 000)	110.2	475.9
出口值	Exports	82.5	290.6
进口值	Imports	27.7	185.3
外商实际直接投资额（万美元）	Foreign Capital Actually Used(USD 10 000)	51.1	42.8
旅游者人数（人次）	Number of Tourists (person-time)	21681	42932
四、每天人口变动和婚姻	**Daily Population Changes and Marriages**		
出　生（人）	Births(person)	211	247
死　亡（人）	Deaths(person)	88	113
结　婚（对）	Marriages(couple)	129	129
离　婚（对）	Divorces(couple)	12	14

注：本表财政收入数据2009年及以前为一般预算财政收入和基金收入之和。依据部门历史年份修订结果对财政相关数据进行了重新计算。

Major Social and Economic Activities Per Day in Representative Years

2005	2010	2014	2015	2016	2017	2018	2019	2020	2021
35453.4	87535.6	152794.0	162544.1	175242.7	203234.0	232860.5	257533.7	274622.7	292829.6
1808.5	3649.9	5248.8	5257.8	5387.9	6719.5	7095.3	7647.4	8568.5	8460.8
14005.2	35367.9	58970.7	56725.2	58616.2	67203.3	78407.1	85775.3	91533.4	98224.7
19640.0	48517.5	88574.5	100561.1	111238.6	129311.2	147357.8	164111.2	174520.8	186144.1
10781.1	23999.2	38000.8	34032.3	34326.3	39362.2	46791.8	49759.7	50804.1	57524.7
3224.1	11368.8	21688.8	23490.4	25206.8	28694.2	33172.3	37551.5	42075.6	42525.5
3823.8	9026.8	15131.8	16146.0	16413.2	17903.8	19429.0	21594.2	21785.5	22948.5
1619.7	3679.2	5803.6	6565.2	7366.8	8151.8	8674.8	9535.1	9600.3	10491.0
1303.8	2628.2	3448.2	3887.1	3927.1	4204.1	4498.4	5142.2	3888.5	4205.5
4489.6	13991.5	27936.7	30547.4	31114.5	37389.3	40010.7	42024.4	42232.9	50728.1
2680.0	10181.4	22453.2	25129.9	25822.5	28632.6	31558.1	34164.9	36920.0	40400.6
5631	4781	3857	3875	3709	3833	3894	3833	3961	3888
		222	210	217	319	316	339	384	380
5362	5674	7065	7340	7366	9719	10238	10372	10447	9940
		194	198	188	161	149	141	125	135
26	33	39	39	37	38	37	37	31	36
74	65	33	29	33	35	35	33	27	31
1316	2656	4920	4347	4411	4842	4733	4247	4227	4594
658	3035	1175	1015	1203	1504	915	862	1096	1038
112	1787	1027	935	1048	1220	1188	1168	1365	1750
19133	48368	89790	99203	109930	121170	133005	140847	136694	135984
16400	12287	40078	22632	36472	36683				
33.0	94.0	115.2	126.8	65.4	69.9	71.8	75.1	70.4	74.1
28.7	83.0	70.5	73.7	64.9	66.5	71.4	72.1	39.3	29.1
3617.7	8852.3	8016.4	9083.1	10496.2	12050.7	20261.1	38950.7	47165.8	55864.0
1068.9	2847.3	6833.5	7749.3	7547.9	10327.4	13676.0	12877.6	13798.5	18685.1
721.8	1456.8	3276.7	3606.4	3907.3	6298.6	8103.0	6871.8	7054.4	10030.3
347.1	1390.5	3556.8	4142.8	3640.6	4028.8	5573.0	6005.8	6744.1	8654.8
156.5	429.2	1014.5	1098.2	1234.2	1453.9	1740.7	1933.5	2103.3	2387.5
66400	144799	328767	372625	411303	495702	677774	824943	504587	663061
210	225	238	241	277	330	335	341	325	298
63	124	129	131	130	142	147	153	265	265
137	229	250	221	212	194	255	239	208	208
35	52	60	62	70	79	115	124	114	82

1-15 各区县国民经济和社会发展主要指标（2021年）

指 标	Item	新城区 Xincheng	碑林区 Beilin	莲湖区 Lianhu
一、年底总人口（常住人口）（万人）	**Population at the Year-end Permanent population(10 000 persons)**	**62.25**	**76.96**	**102.93**
二、地区生产总值（亿元）	**Gross Domestic Product(100 mil. yuan)**	**639.96**	**1098.86**	**831.08**
第一产业	Primary Industry			
第二产业	Secondary Industry	182.29	232.76	257.88
第三产业	Tertiary Industry	457.67	866.10	573.20
三、固定资产投资（不含农户）增长速度	**The growth rate of Investment in Fixed Assets (excluding farmers)**	**20.8**	**-19.1**	**-23.2**
#房地产开发投资增长速度	The growth rate of Real Estate	44.1	57.9	-2.2
四、财政一般公共预算收入（万元）	**General Public Budgetary Revenue(10 000 yuan)**	**226272**	**410933**	**400385**
财政一般公共预算支出（万元）	General Public Budgetary Expenditure(10 000 yuan)	342964	310000	394009
五、农林牧渔业总产值（万元）	**Gross Output Value of Farming,Forestry Animal Husbandry and Fishery(10 000 yuan)**			
主要农产品产量(万吨)	Output of Major Farm Products(10 000 tons)			
粮食	Grain			
蔬菜	Vegetables			
瓜果	Melon and Fruit			
肉类(吨)	Meat (Ton)			
奶类(吨)	Milk (Ton)			
六、规模以上工业企业营业收入（亿元）	**Business Revenue of Industrial Enterprises above Designated Size(100 mil. yuan)**	**334.43**	**15.55**	**340.22**
七、建筑业	**Construction**			
房屋建筑施工面积（万平方米）	Floor Space of Buildings under Construction (10 000 sq.m)	777.41	6628.91	3310.31
房屋建筑竣工面积（万平方米）	Floor Space of Buildings Completed(100 mil. yuan)	46.43	1072.81	466.11
八、社会消费品零售总额（亿元）	**Total Retail Sales of Consumer Goods (100 mil. yuan)**	**253.36**	**592.05**	**518.55**
九、城镇居民人均可支配收入（元）	**Per Capita Annual Disposable Income of Urban Households (yuan)**	**54302**	**53643**	**53816**
农村居民人均可支配收入（元）	Per Capita Disposable Income of Rural Households (yuan)			
十、医疗机构数（个）	**Number of Health Care Institutions(unit)**	**292**	**472**	**453**
卫生技术人员（人）	Number of Medical Technical Personnel (person)	14582	15714	14044
床位数（张）	Number of Beds(unit)	9497	9504	9560

Major Indicators of National Economy and Social Development by Region (2021)

灞桥区 Baqiao	未央区 Weiyang	雁塔区 Yanta	阎良区 Yanliang	临潼区 Lintong	长安区 Chang'an	高陵区 Gaoling	鄠邑区 Huyi	蓝田县 Lantian	周至县 Zhouzhi	西咸新区 Xixian New Area
102.96	**158.83**	**208.66**	**30.73**	**68.13**	**162.24**	**45.75**	**58.69**	**49.54**	**55.99**	**103.64**
606.85	**1437.23**	**2725.20**	**264.84**	**260.11**	**1269.45**	**384.72**	**266.05**	**151.70**	**146.39**	**590.13**
18.02	1.29		33.08	42.89	34.22	31.80	31.98	33.09	42.24	40.22
184.64	624.26	630.14	95.40	67.76	706.31	202.15	125.62	25.07	14.23	221.24
404.19	811.68	2095.06	136.36	149.46	528.92	150.77	108.45	93.54	89.92	328.67
0.3	**-12.5**	**-7.0**	**-34.5**	**-23.1**	**0.9**	**-58.9**	**9.1**	**9.3**	**-8.8**	**-19.1**
37.1	-25.3	-9.4	-21.0	-29.3	2.1	-51.7	49.3	323.6	11.1	-17.0
201166	**341533**	**492942**	**88991**	**140817**	**239588**	**141552**	**88595**	**45132**	**26449**	**1064896**
296719	390285	375501	237076	475822	518904	345484	374032	537650	435722	1506859
333120	**22050**		**566427**	**804561**	**590455**	**627125**	**564710**	**608535**	**753511**	**735412**
2.07			11.98	36.60	17.87	12.41	20.17	18.12	10.78	11.92
7.15	0.91		74.83	55.07	20.24	63.09	30.50	12.94	22.80	75.26
0.17	0.04		22.76	5.41	3.28	1.04	4.63	2.91	0.08	3.68
843	2.00		2756	12893	4066	4303	6931	7373	8447	1642
3551	237.00		21307	63717	7316	9044	7412	18661	5269	2123
192.73	**1257.67**	**726.58**	**359.29**	**288.54**	**2365.18**	**1137.89**	**606.11**	**64.41**	**25.24**	**443.62**
526.90	5918.46	3077.44	65.75	61.68	645.08	57.23	84.17	18.03	4.15	1276.58
4.31	805.07	652.68	43.25	11.52	42.00	29.21	22.01	9.79	1.46	113.10
530.32	**827.04**	**1139.20**	**31.59**	**63.09**	**229.38**	**180.68**	**46.11**	**41.82**	**38.03**	**472.21**
45389	**50655**	**55109**	**45863**	**34744**	**47197**	**43704**	**27922**	**26739**	**25266**	**28358**
21385			18746	17588	18956	19448	16372	17309	15691	16725
455	**533**	**713**	**187**	**530**	**627**	**230**	**430**	**570**	**502**	**590**
5367	12976	19073	2791	4066	9181	3447	4598	2618	3311	3603
3249	6971	9312	2136	3669	7116	2994	3205	2171	2628	2378

主 要 统 计 指 标 解 释

行政区划 指国家对行政区域的划分。根据有关法规规定，我国的行政区域划分如下：（1）全国分为省、自治区、直辖市；（2）省、自治区分为自治州、县、自治县、市；（3）自治州分为县、自治县、市；（4）县、自治县分为乡、民族乡、镇；（5）直辖市和较大的市分为区、县；（6）国家在必要时设立的特别行政区。

气候 指地球与大气之间长期能量交换与质量交换所形成的一种自然环境状态，它是多种因素综合作用的结果。气候既是人类生活和生产的环境要素之一，又是供给人类生活和生产的重要资源。气温、降水、湿度等气象要素的多年平均值是用来描述一个地区气候状况的主要参数，而各种气象要素某年、某月的平均值（或总量）则可以反映出该时期天气气候状况的重要特征。

自然资源 指人类可以直接从自然界获得，并用于生产和生活的物质资源。自然资源一般可以分成可再生资源和非再生资源两大类。可再生资源指在较短时间内可以再生、可以循环利用的资源，包括土地资源、水资源、气候资源、生物资源和海洋资源等。非再生资源指在使用后不能再生的资源，包括矿产资源和地热能源。

土地资源 土地指陆地的表层部分，它主要由岩石、岩石的风化物和土壤构成。土地资源按利用类型可以分为农用地、建筑用地和未利用地。农用地包括耕地、园地、林地、牧草地和水面。建筑用地包括居民点及工矿用地、交通用地和水利设施用地。未利用地指农用地和建筑用地以外的土地，包括滩涂、荒漠、戈壁、冰川和石山等。

耕地面积 指经过开垦用以种植农作物并经常进行耕耘的土地面积。包括种有作物的土地面积、休闲地、新开荒地和抛荒未满三年的土地面积。

森林面积 指由乔木树种构成，郁闭度0.2以上（含0.2）的林地或冠幅宽度10米以上的林带的面积，即有林地面积。森林面积包括天然起源和人工起源的针叶林面积、阔叶林面积、针阔混交林面积和竹林面积，不包括灌木林地面积和疏林地面积。

林业用地面积 指生长乔木、竹类、灌木、沿海红树林等林木的土地面积，包括有林地、灌木林、疏林地、未成林造林地、迹地、苗圃等。

水资源总量 指评价区内降水形成的地表和地下产水总量，即地表产流量与降水入渗补给地下水量之和，不包括过境水量。

地表水资源量 指评价区内河流、湖泊、冰川等地表水体中可以逐年更新的动态水量，即当地天然河川径流量。

地下水资源量 指评价区内降水和地表水对饱水岩土层的补给量，包括降水入渗补给量和河道、湖库、渠系、渠灌田间等地表水体的入渗补给量。

气温 指空气的温度，我国一般以摄氏度（℃）为单位表示。气象观测的温度表是放在离地面约1.5米处通风良好的百叶箱里测量的，因此，通常说的气温指的是离地面1.5米处百叶箱中的温度。其统计计算方法为：

月平均气温是将全月各日的平均气温相加，除以该月的天数而得。

年平均气温是将12个月的月平均气温累加后除以12而得。

降水量 指从天空降落到地面的液态或固态（经融化后）水，未经蒸发、渗透、流失而在地面上积聚的深度。其统计计算方法为：

月降水量是将全月各日的降水量累加而得。

年降水量是将12个月的月降水量累加而得。

日照时数 指太阳实际照射地面的时间。其统计方法与降水量相同。

平均增长速度 平均增长速度表明社会经济现象在一个较长的时期内逐期平均增长变化的程度，它不能根据各个环比增长速度直接求得，但与平均发展速度之间存在着一定的数量关系：平均增长速度 = 平均发展速度 – 1。

平均发展速度 是一种根据环比发展速度计算的序时平均数，由于各时期对比的基础不同，所以计算平均发展速度不能采用一般的序时平均数的计算方法，计算方法分为水平法和累计法。水平法，又称几何平均法，即将环比发展速度按连乘法用几何平均数公式计算。累计法，也称方程法，根据一段时期内各年发展水平总和与基期水平的关系，列出方程式计算平均发展速度。水平法着重考虑最后一年所达到的发展水平；累计法着重考虑整个时期累计发展水平的总量。

本年鉴内所列的平均增长速度，均用“水平法”计算。从某年到某年平均增长速度的年份，均不包括基期年在内。

Explanatory Notes on Main Statistical Indicators

Divisions of Administrative Areas refers to the division of administrative areas by the State. The relative laws stipulate that (1)the whole country is divided into provinces, autonomous regions and municipalities directly under the Central Government;(2)provinces and autonomous regions are further divided into autonomous prefectures, counties, autonomous counties and cities; (3)autonomous prefectures are further divided into counties, autonomous counties and cities; (4)counties and autonomous counties are further divided into townships, ethnic townships and towns; (5)municipalities directly under the Central Government and large cities are divided into districts and counties, (6)the State shall, when necessary, establish special administrative regions.

Climate refers to the natural environmental status formed by the long-term exchange of energy and mass between the earth and the atmosphere, and is the result of interaction of many factors. Climate is both one of the environment factors and also the important resources for living and production activities of the human being. The average values across several years of meteorological factors such as temperature, rainfall and humidity are used as important parameters to describe the climate of a region, while the average values (or total values)of a given year or month of meteorological factors reflect the key characteristics of climate for that period of time.

Natural Resources refer to material resources that could be obtained from the nature by human being and used for production and living. Natural resources in general can be classified as renewable resources and non-renewable resources. Renewable resources refer to resources that could be renewed and recycled during a relatively short period of time, including land resource, water resource, climate resource, biology resource and marine resource. Non-renewable resources include resources that could not be renewed, such as minerals and geothermal resource.

Land Resource Land refers to the surface of the earth, consisting of mainly rocks and its whethering and earth. Land resource can be classified, by its utilization, as land for agriculture, land for construction and unused land. Land for agriculture includes cultivated land, plantation land, forestland, grassland and waters. Land for construction includes land for residential purpose, for manufacturing and mining, for transportation and for water-conservancy projects. Unused land refers to land other than land for agriculture and construction, including beaches, deserts, Gobi, glaciers and rock mountains.

Area of Cultivated Land refers to area of land reclaimed for the regular cultivation of various farm crops, including crop-cover land, fallow, newly reclaimed land and land laid idle for less than 3 years.

Forest Area refers to the area of trees and bamboo grow with canopy density above 0.2, the area of shrubby tree according to regulations of the government, the area of forest land inside farm land and the area of trees planted by the side of villages, farm houses and along roads and rivers.

Area of Afforested Land refers to area for land for trees bamboo, bushes and mangrove, including forest-covered land, bush-covered land, sparse forest land, land planned for afforestation and nurseries of young trees.

Total Water Resources refers to total volume of water resources measured as run-off for surface water from rainfall and recharge for groundwater in a given area, excluding transit water.

Surface Water Resources refers to total renewable resources which exist in rivers, lakes, glaciers and other collectors from rainfall and are measured as run-off of rivers.

Groundwater Resources refers to replenishment of aquifers with rainfall and surface water.

Temperature refers to the air temperature. China uses centigrade as the unit. The thermometry used for weather observation is put in a breezy shutter, which is 1.5 meters high from the ground. Therefore, the commonly used temperature refers to the temperature in the breezy shutter 1.5 meters away from the ground. The calculation method is as follows:

Monthly average temperature is the summation of average daily temperature of one month divided by the actual days of that particular month.

Annual average temperature is the summation of monthly average of a year divided by 12 months.

Volume of Precipitation refers to the deepness of liquid state or solid state (thawed)water falling from the sky to the ground that has not been evaporated, infiltrated or run off. The calculation method is as follows:

Monthly precipitation is the summation of daily precipitation of a month.

Annual precipitation is the summation of 12 months precipitation of a year.

Sunshine Hours refer to the actual hours of sun irradiating the earth. The calculation method is the same as that of the precipitation.

Average Annual Growth Rate shows the average growth rate of social and economic development during a longer period. It can not be directly calculated by chain based growth rate. The relation is:

Average Annual Growth Rate=Average Speed of Development - 1

Average speed of development is the time series average of speed which calculated by chain based.Because the reference bases during the different periods are not same, average speed of development can not be calculated by the general method. Level approach and accumulative approach for calculating average speed of development rate are applied. The "level approach" , or the method of calculating the geometric average, is derived by the formula of geometric average of the chain-based speeds of development, or comparing the level of the last year of the interval with that of the beginning year; the other is called the "accumulative approach" or the "algebraic average" , "equation" method, which is derived by the summation of the actual figure of each year in the interval divided by the figure in the base year. The level approach focuses on the level of the last year, while the accumulative approach emphasizes the aggregate development in the duration.

The average annual growth rates listed in the Yearbook are calculated by the level approach except for the growth rate of investment in fixed assets. The base year is not listed in the duration for which average annual growth rates are computed.

2 基本单位

BASIC UNIT

资料整理：张 奇 张 斌
Data management：Zhang Qi Zhang Bin
数据审核：曾文元
Data audit：Zeng Wenyuan

第二部分　基本单位

一、简要说明

本章资料主要包括法人单位、产业活动单位和企业一套表调查单位数等资料，由西安市统计局普查中心提供，数据不包含西安（西咸新区）—咸阳共管区，本年统计年鉴一套表调查单位数为年报数，使用时请注意。

二、主要指标

法人单位数（个）	312523	比上年增长	7.6%
产业活动单位数（个）	333627	比上年增长	6.9%
规模以上工业企业数（个）	1699	比上年增长	4.0%
限额以上批发零售住宿餐饮业企业数（个）	3175	比上年增长	8.9%
资质内建筑业企业数（个）	1402	比上年增长	3.0%
房地产开发经营企业数（个）	1092	比上年下降	9.6%
规模以上服务业企业数（个）	2367	比上年增长	0.5%

2　BASIC UNIT

Ⅰ.Brief Introduction

This chapter consists of unified data of enterprises and industrial active unites and investigation unit in "Enterprises Data in One sheet", provided by census center of Xi'an Municipal Bureau of statistics. The data does not include Xixian New District. Data of " Enterprises Data in One Sheet" in this Yearbook Reserch from the number of annual reports, please note that when used.

Ⅱ.Major Indicators

		Increase over Preceding Year
Number of Enterprises (unit)	312523	7.6%
Number of Industrial Active Units (unit)	333627	6.9%
Number of Industrial Enterprises above Designed Size (unit)	1699	4.0%
Number of Enterprises about Wholesale、Retail、Accommodation and Catering above Designed Size (unit)	3175	8.9%
Number of Qualified Construction Enterprises (unit)	1402	3.0%
Number of Real Estate Development Enterprises (unit)	1092	–9.6%
Number of service Enterprises above Designed Size (unit)	2367	0.5%

2-1 按登记注册类型分法人单位数（2021年）

Number of Impersonal Entities by Status of Registration(2021)

单位：个 (unit)

分 组	Classify	法人单位数 Number of Enterprises	企业 Enterprises
总 计	**Total**	**312523**	**292749**
#非公有制企业法人	Non-public corporate	287824	287824
按登记注册类型分	**Grouped by Status of Registration**		
（一）内资	Domestic Funded Enterprises	311214	291440
国有	State-owned Enterprises	5917	890
集体	Collective-owned Enterprises	1567	981
股份合作	Cooperative Enterprises	181	158
联营	Joint Ownership Enterprises	64	33
国有联营	State Joint Ownership Enterprises	8	5
集体联营	Collective Joint Ownership Enterprises	23	15
国有与集体联营	Joint State-collective Ownership Enterprises	6	5
其他联营	Other Joint Ownership Enterprises	27	8
有限责任公司	Limited Liability Corporations	14432	14330
国有独资公司	State Sole Funded Corporations	674	674
其他有限责任公司	Other Limited Liability Corporations	13758	13656
股份有限公司	Share-holding Corporations Limited	635	632
私营	Private Enterprises	275226	273854
私营独资	Private-funded Enterprises	5267	4579
私营合伙	Private Partnership Enterprises	1583	1334
私营有限责任公司	Private Limited Liability Corporations	267019	266596
私营股份有限公司	Private Share-holding Corporations Ltd.	1357	1345
其他	Other Domestic Funded Enterprises	13192	562
（二）港澳台商投资	Enterprises with Funds from Hong Kong, Macao and Taiwan	474	474
与港澳台商合资经营	Joint-venture with Funds from Hong Kong,Macao and Taiwan	119	119
与港澳台商合作经营	Cooperative Enterprises with Funds from Hong Kong Macao and Taiwan	9	9
港澳台商独资	Enterprises with Sole Investment from Hong Kong Macao and Taiwan	238	238
港澳台商投资股份有限公司	Share-holding Corporations Ltd. with funds from Hong Kong, Macao & Taiwan	11	11
其他港澳台商投资	Other Enterprises with Funds from Hong Kong, Macao and Taiwan	97	97
（三）外商投资	Foreign Funded Enterprises	835	835
中外合资经营	Sino-foreign Joint Ventures	265	265
中外合作经营	Sino-Foreign Cooperation Enterprises	5	5
外资企业	Foreign Owned Enterprises	505	505
外商投资股份有限公司	Limited Company Funded by Foreign Investment	28	28
其他外商投资	Other Foreign Funded Enterprises	32	32

2-2 按国民经济行业分法人单位数（2021年）

Number of Impersonal Entities by Industry of the National Economy(2021)

单位：个 (unit)

分　组	Classify	法人单位数 Number of Enterprises	企业 Enterprises
总　计	**Total**	**312523**	**292749**
（一）农、林、牧、渔业	Agriculture,Forestry,Animal Husbandry and Fishery	6102	2238
农业	Farming	2708	914
林业	Forestry	990	296
畜牧业	Animal Husbandry	1205	492
渔业	Fishery	40	20
农、林、牧、渔专业及辅助性活动	Agriculture, Forestry, Animal husbandry, Fishery and Auxiliary Activities	1159	516
（二）采矿业	Mining	220	220
煤炭开采和洗选业	Mining and Washing of Coal	6	6
石油和天然气开采业	Extraction of Petroleum and Natural Gas	11	11
黑色金属矿采选业	Mining of Ferrous Metal Ores	6	6
有色金属矿采选业	Mining of Non-ferrous Metal Ores	11	11
非金属矿采选业	Mining and Processing of Nonmetal Ores	82	82
开采专业及辅助性活动	Mining Professional and Auxiliary Activities	92	92
其他采矿业	Mining of Other Ores	12	12
（三）制造业	Manufacturing	19802	19764
农副食品加工业	Processing of Food from Agricultural Products	540	520
食品制造业	Manufacture of Foods	567	565
酒、饮料和精制茶制造业	Manufacture of Beverages	211	211
烟草制品业	Manufacture of Tobacco	6	6
纺织业	Manufacture of Textile	139	138
纺织服装、服饰业	Manufacture of Textile Wearing Apparel	206	203
皮革、毛皮、羽毛及其制品和制鞋业	Manufacture of Leather, Fur,Feather and Related Products and Footware	20	19
木材加工和木、竹、藤、棕、草制品业	Timber Processing,Bamboo,Cane,Palm Fiber and Straw Products	670	665
家具制造业	Manufacture of Furniture	616	616
造纸及纸制品业	Manufacture of Paper and Paper Products	408	408
印刷和记录媒介复制业	Printing,Reproduction of Recording Media	658	658
文教、工美、体育和娱乐用品制造业	Manufacture of Articles For Culture,Education and Sport Activities	340	338

2-2 续表1 continued 1

单位：个 (unit)

分 组	Classify	法人单位数 Number of Enterprises	企业 Enterprises
石油、煤炭及其他燃料加工业	Processing of Petroleum, Coal and Other Fuel	61	61
化学原料和化学制品制造业	Manufacture of Raw Chemical Materials and Chemical Products	839	839
医药制造业	Manufacture of Medicines	328	328
化学纤维制造业	Manufacture of Chemical Fibers	17	17
橡胶和塑料制品业	Manufacture of Rubber and Manufacture of Plastics	551	551
非金属矿物制品业	Manufacture of Non-metallic Mineral Products	1615	1615
黑色金属冶炼和压延加工业	Smelting and Pressing of Ferrous Metals	159	159
有色金属冶炼和压延加工业	Smelting and Pressing of Non-ferrous Metals	197	197
金属制品业	Manufacture of Metal Products	1629	1629
通用设备制造业	Manufacture of General Purpose Machinery	2784	2784
专用设备制造业	Manufacture of Special Equipment	2065	2064
汽车制造业	Manufacture of Motor Vehicle	331	331
铁路、船舶、航空航天和其他运输设备制造业	Railways,Shipbuilding,Aerospace and Other Transportation Equipment Manufacturing Industry	426	426
电气机械和器材制造业	Manufacture of Electric Equipment and Machinery	1449	1449
计算机、通信和其他电子设备制造业	Manufacture of Communication Equipment,Computers and other Electronic Equipment	1216	1215
仪器仪表制造业	Manufacture of Measuring Instruments and Machinery	794	794
其他制造业	Other Manufacturing	137	137
废弃资源综合利用	Recycling and Disposal of Waste	106	106
金属制品、机械和设备修理业	Metal Products,Machinery and Equipment Repair Industry	717	715
（四）电力、热力、燃气及水生产和供应业	Production and Distribution of Electricity,Heat ,Gas and Water	632	627
电力、热力生产和供应业	Production and Supply of Electric Power and Heat Power	383	381
燃气生产和供应业	Gas mining and supplying industry	76	75
水的生产和供应业	Production and Supply of Water	173	171
（五）建筑业	Construction Industry	48463	48463
房屋建筑业	Construction of Building	11155	11155
土木工程建筑业	Civil Engineering	13808	13808
建筑安装业	Architectural Installation	5959	5959
建筑装饰、装修和其他建筑业	Architectural Decoration and Other Construction	17541	17541
（六）批发和零售业	Wholesale and Retail Trades	92054	89415
批发业	Wholesale Trade	48173	45934

2-2 续表2 continued 2

单位：个 (unit)

分 组	Classify	法人单位数 Number of Enterprises	企业 Enterprises
零售业	Retail Trade	43881	43481
（七）交通运输、仓储和邮政业	Traffic, Transport, Storage and Post	5776	5485
铁路运输业	Transport Via Railway	19	19
道路运输业	Transport Via Road	3749	3725
水上运输业	Water Transport	151	151
航空运输业	Air Transport	85	84
管道运输业	Transport Via Pipeline	4	4
多式联运和运输代理业	Multimodal Transport and Transportation Agency	681	681
装卸搬运和仓储业	Loading,Unloading,portage,storge and management of Land industry	923	658
邮政业	Post	164	163
（八）住宿和餐饮业	Hotels and Catering Services	6316	6315
住宿业	Hotels	2205	2204
餐饮业	Catering Services	4111	4111
（九）信息传输、软件和信息技术服务业	Information Transmission, Software and Information Technology	21889	21855
电信、广播电视和卫星传输服务	Telecom & Other Information Transmission Services	742	742
互联网和相关服务	Internet and Relevant Services	3366	3357
软件和信息技术服务	Software Industry	17781	17756
（十）金融业	Financial Intermediation	1468	1462
货币金融服务	Monetary and Financial Services	527	523
资本市场服务	Capital Market Services	440	439
保险业	Insurance	196	196
其他金融业	Other Financial Intermediation	305	304
（十一）房地产业	Real Estate	13954	13943
房地产业	Real Estate	13954	13943
（十二） 租赁和商务服务业	Leasing and Business Services	42165	41436
租赁业	Leasing	4218	4213
商务服务业	Business Services	37947	37223
（十三）科学研究和技术服务业	Scientific Research, Technical Sevice	21028	20420
研究与试验发展	Research and Experimental Development	2509	2428
专业技术服务业	Professional Technical Services	12557	12337
科技推广和应用服务业	Services of Science and Technology Exchanges and Promotion	5962	5655

2-2 续表3 continued 3

单位：个 (unit)

分 组	Classify	法人单位数 Number of Enterprises	企业 Enterprises
（十四）水利、环境和公共设施管理业	Management of Water Conservancy, Environment and Public Facilities	2792	2618
水利管理业	Management of Water Conservancy	147	80
生态保护和环境治理业	Environmental Management	372	348
公共设施管理业	Management of Public Facilities	1741	1669
土地管理业	Lang management	532	521
（十五）居民服务、修理和其他服务业	Services to Households and Other Services	7226	7161
居民服务业	Services to Households	2902	2851
机动车、电子产品和日用产品修理业	The Repair Service Industry for Motor Vehicle、Electronic	3131	3129
其他服务业	Other Services	1193	1181
（十六）教育	Education	6136	2536
教育	Education	6136	2536
（十七）卫生和社会工作	Health, Social Security	2218	1291
卫生	Health	1755	1172
社会工作	Social Work	463	119
（十八）文化、体育和娱乐业	Culture, Sports and Entertainment	7870	7500
新闻和出版业	Journalism and Publishing Activities	199	177
广播、电视、电影和录音制作业	Broadcasting,Movies,Television and Audiovisual Activities	1681	1667
文化艺术业	Cultural and Art Activities	2007	1752
体育	Sports Activities	865	820
娱乐业	Entertainment	3118	3084
（十九）公共管理、社会保障和社会组织	Public Management and Social Organizaion	6412	
中国共产党机关	Organs of Communist Party of China	152	
国家机构	Government Agencies	1675	
人民政协、民主党派	People's Political Consultative Conference and Democratic Parties	19	
社会保障	Social Security	53	
群众团体、社会团体和其他成员组织	Mass organizations、Social Groups and other members of the organization	1670	
基层群众自治组织及其他组织	Autonomous Organizations at the Grassroots Level and other Organizations	2843	
（二十）国际组织	International Organizations		
国际组织	International Organizations		

2-3 各区县法人单位数（2021年）

Number of Impersonal Entities by Region and Development Zone(2021)

单位：个 (unit)

区 县	Region	法人单位数 Number of Enterprises	企业 Enterprises
总 计	**Total**	**312523**	**292749**
新城区	Xincheng	12381	11674
碑林区	Beilin	24841	23889
莲湖区	Lianhu	31072	30114
灞桥区	Baqiao	19542	18668
未央区	Weiyang	59069	58070
雁塔区	Yanta	92335	90948
阎良区	Yanliang	5152	4511
临潼区	Lintong	6209	4658
长安区	Chang'an	16489	14733
高陵区	Gaoling	5697	4735
鄠邑区	Huyi	8428	6285
蓝田县	Lantian	4974	3393
周至县	Zhouzhi	8869	4658
西咸新区	Xixian New Area	17465	16413

2-4 按登记注册类型分产业活动单位数（2021年）

Number of Industrial Active Units by Status of Registion (2021)

单位：个　　　　(unit)

分 组	Classify	产业活动单位数 Number of Industrial Active Units	企业 Enterprises
总计	**Total**	**333627**	**312233**
按登记注册类型分	Grouped by Status of Registion		
（一）内资	Domestic Funded Enterprises	330461	309067
国有	State-owned Enterprises	8035	1560
集体	Collective-owned Enterprises	1849	1157
股份合作	Cooperative Enterprises	249	226
联营	Joint Ownership Enterprises	75	42
国有联营	State Joint Ownership Enterprises	11	8
集体联营	Collective Joint Ownership Enterprises	25	17
国有与集体联营	Joint State-collective Ownership Enterprises	7	6
其他联营	Other Joint Ownership Enterprises	32	11
有限责任公司	Limited Liability Corporations	17469	17367
国有独资公司	State Sole Funded Corporations	813	813
其他有限责任公司	Other Limited Liability Corporations	16656	16554
股份有限公司	Share-holding Corporations Limited	2632	2629
私营	Private Enterprises	286875	285500
私营独资	Private-funded Enterprises	5386	4696
私营合伙	Private Partnership Enterprises	1626	1376
私营有限责任公司	Private Limited Liability Corporations	278225	277802
私营股份有限公司	Private Share-holding Corporations Ltd.	1638	1626
其他	Other Enterprises	13277	586

2-4 续表 continued

单位：个 (unit)

分 组	Classify	产业活动单位数 Number of Industrial Active Units	企业 Enterprises
（二）港澳台商投资	Enterprises with Funds from Hong Kong,Macao and Taiwan	839	839
与港澳台商合资经营	Joint-venture with Funds from Hong Kong,Macao and Taiwan	152	152
与港澳台商合作经营	Cooperative Enterprises with Funds from Hong Kong Macao and Taiwan	13	13
港澳台商独资	Enterprises with Sole Investment from Hong Kong Macao and Taiwan	470	470
港澳台商投资股份有限公司	Share-holding Corporations Ltd. with funds from Hong Kong, Macao & Taiwan	53	53
其他港澳台商投资	Other Enterprises with Funds from Hong Kong,Macao and Taiwan	151	151
（三）外商投资	Foreign Funded Enterprises	2327	2327
中外合资经营	Sino-foreign Joint Ventures	363	363
中外合作经营	Sino-Foreign Cooperation Enterprises	8	8
外资企业	Foreign Owned Enterprises	1661	1661
外商投资股份有限公司	Limited Company Funded by Foreign Investment	171	171
其他外商投资	Other Foreign Funded Enterprises	124	124

2-5 按国民经济行业分产业活动单位数（2021年）

Number of Industrial Active Units by Industry of the National Economy (2021)

单位：个 (unit)

分 组	Classify	产业活动单位数 Number of Industrial Active Units	企业 Enterprises
总 计	**Total**	**333627**	**312233**
（一）农、林、牧、渔业	Agriculture,Forestry,Animal Husbandry and Fishery	6154	2252
农业	Farming	2713	919
林业	Forestry	992	296
畜牧业	Animal Husbandry	1208	494
渔业	Fishery	41	21
农、林、牧、渔专业及辅助性活动	Agriculture, Forestry, Animal husbandry, Fishery and Auxiliary Activities	1200	522
（二）采矿业	Mining	233	233
煤炭开采和洗选业	Mining and Washing of Coal	7	7
石油和天然气开采业	Extraction of Petroleum and Natural Gas	13	13
黑色金属矿采选业	Mining of Ferrous Metal Ores	6	6
有色金属矿采选业	Mining of Non-ferrous Metal Ores	12	12
非金属矿采选业	Mining and Processing of Nonmetal Ores	82	82
开采专业及辅助性活动	Mining Professional and Auxiliary Activities	101	101
其他采矿业	Mining of Other Ores	12	12
（三）制造业	Manufacturing	20381	20342
农副食品加工业	Processing of Food from Agricultural Products	559	538
食品制造业	Manufacture of Foods	600	598
酒、饮料和精制茶制造业	Manufacture of Beverages	220	220
烟草制品业	Manufacture of Tobacco	6	6
纺织业	Manufacture of Textile	143	142
纺织服装、服饰业	Manufacture of Textile Wearing Apparel	213	210
皮革、毛皮、羽毛及其制品和制鞋业	Manufacture of Leather, Fur,Feather and Related Products and Footware	22	21
木材加工和木、竹、藤、棕、草制品业	Timber Processing,Bamboo,Cane,Palm Fiber and Straw Products	681	676
家具制造业	Manufacture of Furniture	627	627
造纸及纸制品业	Manufacture of Paper and Paper Products	417	417
印刷和记录媒介复制业	Printing,Reproduction of Recording Media	676	676
文教、工美、体育和娱乐用品制造业	Manufacture of Articles For Culture,Education and Sport Activities	346	344

2-5 续表1 continued 1

单位：个 (unit)

分组	Classify	产业活动单位数 Number of Industrial Active Units	企业 Enterprises
石油、煤炭及其他燃料加工业	Processing of Petroleum, Coal and Other Fuel	63	63
化学原料和化学制品制造业	Manufacture of Raw Chemical Materials and Chemical Products	867	867
医药制造业	Manufacture of Medicines	348	348
化学纤维制造业	Manufacture of Chemical Fibers	17	17
橡胶和塑料制品业	Manufacture of Rubber and Manufacture of Plastics	569	569
非金属矿物制品业	Manufacture of Non-metallic Mineral Products	1686	1686
黑色金属冶炼和压延加工业	Smelting and Pressing of Ferrous Metals	161	161
有色金属冶炼和压延加工业	Smelting and Pressing of Non-ferrous Metals	198	198
金属制品业	Manufacture of Metal Products	1668	1668
通用设备制造业	Manufacture of General Purpose Machinery	2837	2837
专用设备制造业	Manufacture of Special Equipment	2130	2129
汽车制造业	Manufacture of Motor Vehicle	344	344
铁路、船舶、航空航天和其他运输设备制造业	Railways,Shipbuilding,Aerospace and Other Transportation Equipment Manufacturing Industry	434	434
电气机械和器材制造业	Manufacture of Electric Equipment and Machinery	1499	1499
计算机、通信和其他电子设备制造业	Manufacture of Communication Equipment,Computers and other Electronic Equipment	1243	1242
仪器仪表制造业	Manufacture of Measuring Instruments and Machinery	813	813
其他制造业	Other Manufacturing	143	143
废弃资源综合利用	Recycling and Disposal of Waste	106	106
金属制品、机械和设备修理业	Metal Products,Machinery and Equipment Repair Industry	745	743
（四）电力、热力、燃气及水生产和供应业	Production and Distribution of Electricity,Heat ,Gas and Water	720	714
电力、热力生产和供应业	Production and Supply of Electric Power and Heat Power	434	431
燃气生产和供应业	Gas mining and supplying industry	101	100
水的生产和供应业	Production and Supply of Water	185	183
（五）建筑业	Construction	49504	49504
房屋建筑业	Construction of Building	11478	11478
土木工程建筑业	Civil Engineering	14066	14066
建筑安装业	Architectural Installation	6143	6143
建筑装饰、装修和其他建筑业	Architectural Decoration and Other Construction	17817	17817
（六）批发和零售业	Wholesale and Retail Trades	99249	96605
批发业	Wholesale Trade	49209	46967

2-5 续表2 continued 2

单位：个 (unit)

分 组	Classify	产业活动单位数 Number of Industrial Active Units	企业 Enterprises
零售业	Retail Trade	50040	49638
（七）交通运输、仓储和邮政业	Traffic, Transport, Storage and Post	6549	6250
铁路运输业	Transport Via Railway	39	39
道路运输业	Transport Via Road	4086	4054
水上运输业	Water Transport	158	158
航空运输业	Air Transport	101	100
管道运输业	Transport Via Pipeline	7	7
多式联运和运输代理业	Multimodal Transport and Transportation Agency	820	820
装卸搬运和仓储业	Loading,Unloading,portage,storge and management of Land industry	963	698
邮政业	Post	375	374
（八）住宿和餐饮业	Hotels and Catering Services	7446	7445
住宿业	Hotels	2421	2420
餐饮业	Catering Services	5025	5025
（九）信息传输、软件和信息技术服务业	Information Transmission, Software and Information Technology	22745	22709
电信、广播电视和卫星传输服务	Telecom & Other Information Transmission Services	988	987
互联网和相关服务	Internet and Relevant Services	3459	3449
软件和信息技术服务	Software Industry	18298	18273
（十）金融业	Financial Intermediation	3947	3935
货币金融服务	Monetary and Financial Services	2075	2065
资本市场服务	Capital Market Services	655	654
保险业	Insurance	860	860
其他金融业	Other Financial Intermediation	357	356
（十一）房地产业	Real Estate	15147	15136
房地产业	Real Estate	15147	15136
（十二） 租赁和商务服务业	Leasing and Business Services	44308	43540
租赁业	Leasing	4387	4382
商务服务业	Business Services	39921	39158
（十三）科学研究和技术服务业	Scientific Research, Technical Sevice	21980	21327
研究与试验发展	Research and Experimental Development	2572	2490
专业技术服务业	Professional Technical Services	13250	12998
科技推广和应用服务业	Services of Science and Technology Exchanges and Promotion	6158	5839

2-5 续表3 continued 3

单位：个 (unit)

分　组	Classify	产业活动单位数 Number of Industrial Active Units	企业 Enterprises
（十四）水利、环境和公共设施管理业	Management of Water Conservancy, Environment and Public Facilities	2908	2704
水利管理业	Management of Water Conservancy	164	86
生态保护和环境治理业	Environmental Management	383	353
公共设施管理业	Management of Public Facilities	1804	1722
土地管理业	Lang management	557	543
（十五）居民服务、修理和其他服务业	Services to Households and Other Services	7606	7536
居民服务业	Services to Households	3072	3019
机动车、电子产品和日用产品修理业	The Repair Service Industry for Motor Vehicle、Electronic	3300	3298
其他服务业	Other Services	1234	1219
（十六）教育	Education	6806	2764
教育	Education	6806	2764
（十七）卫生和社会工作	Health, Social Security	2442	1471
卫生	Health	1968	1346
社会工作	Social	474	125
（十八）文化、体育和娱乐业	Culture, Sports and Entertainment	8166	7766
新闻和出版业	Journalism and Publishing Activities	207	183
广播、电视、电影和录音制作业	Broadcasting,Movies,Television and Audiovisual Activities	1741	1726
文化艺术业	Cultural and Art Activities	2068	1788
体育	Sports Activities	943	898
娱乐业	Entertainment	3207	3171
（十九）公共管理、社会保障和社会组织	Public Management and Social Organizaion	7336	
中国共产党机关	Organs of Communist Party of China	156	
国家机构	Government Agencies	2542	
人民政协、民主党派	People's Political Consultative Conference and Democratic Parties	19	
社会保障	Social Security	62	
群众团体、社会团体和其他成员组织	Mass organizations、Social Groups and other members of the organization	1701	
基层群众自治组织及其他组织	Autonomous Organizations at the Grassroots Level and other Organizations	2856	
（二十）国际组织	International Organizations		
国际组织	International Organizations		

2-6 各区县产业活动单位数（2021年）

Number of Industrial Active Units by Region and Development Zone (2021)

单位：个 (unit)

区 县	Region	产业活动单位数 Number of Industrial Active Units	企业 Enterprises
总 计	**Total**	**333627**	**312233**
新城区	Xincheng	13528	12819
碑林区	Beilin	26921	25965
莲湖区	Lianhu	32990	32019
灞桥区	Baqiao	20693	19723
未央区	Weiyang	62076	61021
雁塔区	Yanta	97876	96460
阎良区	Yanliang	5771	4982
临潼区	Lintong	7173	5296
长安区	Chang'an	17596	15783
高陵区	Gaoling	6413	5283
鄠邑区	Huyi	9095	6794
蓝田县	Lantian	5672	3721
周至县	Zhouzhi	9480	5103
西咸新区	Xixian New Area	18343	17264

2-7 按统计机构分企业一套表调查单位数（2021年）

Number of Survey Units by Statistical Agencies of "One Sheet" (2021)

单位：个 (unit)

区县、开发区	Region	合计 Total	规模以上工业 Industrial Enterprises above Designed Size	限额以上批发零售住宿餐饮业 Above wholesale and Retail Accommodation and Catering Industry	资质内建筑业 Qualified Construction Enterprises	房地产开发经营企业 Real Estate Development Enterprises	规模以上服务业 Service Enterprises above Designed Size
全　市	**Total**	**9735**	**1699**	**3175**	**1402**	**1092**	**2367**
新城区	Xincheng	452	5	244	69	20	114
碑林区	Beilin	675	7	322	154	15	177
莲湖区	Lianhu	502	30	200	88	40	144
灞桥区	Baqiao	192	52	40	35	32	33
未央区	Weiyang	389	16	159	77	58	79
雁塔区	Yanta	622	40	209	153	62	158
阎良区	Yanliang	150	58	30	26	22	14
临潼区	Lintong	226	95	55	37	12	27
长安区	Chang'an	206	33	54	31	48	40
高陵区	Gaoling	259	120	56	20	33	30
鄠邑区	Huyi	208	99	53	16	29	11
蓝田县	Lantian	132	56	30	16	14	16
周至县	Zhouzhi	100	19	40	16	17	8
西咸新区	Xixian New Area	1065	246	313	100	204	202
高新区	Hi-Tech Industries Development Zone	1630	417	382	242	129	460
经开区	Economic Development Zone	1294	247	465	184	71	327
曲江新区	Qujiang New District	545		128	60	83	274
航空基地	National Aviation Hi-tech Industrial Base	114	57	16	10	16	15
航天基地	National Civil Aerospace Industrial Base	333	74	96	33	60	70
浐灞生态区	Chan-ba Ecological District	303	5	118	26	85	69
国际港务区	International Trade & Logistics Park	338	23	165	9	42	99

注：由于统计口径不同，一套表调查单位数与各专业有差异。

2-8 各区县企业一套表调查单位数（2021年）

Number of Survey Units of "One Sheet" by Region and Development Zone (2021)

单位：个 (unit)

区 县 Region		合计 Total	规模以上工业 Industrial Enterprises above Designed Size	限额以上批发零售住宿餐饮业 Above wholesale and Retail Accommodation and Catering Industry	资质内建筑业 Qualified Construction Enterprises	房地产开发经营企业 Real Estate Development Enterprises	规模以上服务业 Service Enterprises above Designed Size
全　市	**Total**	**9735**	**1699**	**3175**	**1402**	**1092**	**2367**
新城区	Xincheng	453	5	243	69	22	114
碑林区	Beilin	672	8	323	157	15	169
莲湖区	Lianhu	506	30	200	88	40	148
灞桥区	Baqiao	697	79	275	57	114	172
未央区	Weiyang	1683	170	646	270	173	424
雁塔区	Yanta	2492	265	691	428	251	857
阎良区	Yanliang	263	115	46	35	38	29
临潼区	Lintong	238	95	56	37	19	31
长安区	Chang'an	769	242	182	87	117	141
高陵区	Gaoling	386	213	71	21	38	43
鄠邑区	Huyi	262	143	57	19	31	12
蓝田县	Lantian	131	56	30	16	13	16
周至县	Zhouzhi	118	32	42	18	17	9
西咸新区	Xixian New Area	1065	246	313	100	204	202

2-9 按区县和国民经济行业分法人单位数（2021年）

单位：个

区 县	Region	合计 Total	农、林、牧、渔业 Agriculture Forestry Animal Husbandry and Fishery	采矿业 Mining	制造业 Manufacturing	电力、热力、燃气及水生产和供应业 Production and Distribution of Electricity,Heat, Gas and Water
全 市	**Total**	**312523**	**6102**	**220**	**19802**	**632**
新城区	Xincheng	12381	4	3	296	6
碑林区	Beilin	24841	2	7	215	13
莲湖区	Lianhu	31072	14	4	453	21
灞桥区	Baqiao	19542	327	5	1523	41
未央区	Weiyang	59069	100	104	2969	100
雁塔区	Yanta	92335	205	40	4154	130
阎良区	Yanliang	5152	197	1	904	28
临潼区	Lintong	6209	739	1	829	22
长安区	Chang'an	16489	597	9	1690	46
高陵区	Gaoling	5697	566	12	977	23
鄠邑区	Huyi	8428	1029	10	1731	37
蓝田县	Lantian	4974	575	3	570	73
周至县	Zhouzhi	8869	1450	9	418	27
西咸新区	Xixian New Area	17465	297	12	3073	65

Number of Impersonal Entities by Region and Development Zone and Industry of the National Economy (2021)

(unit)

建筑业 Construction	批发和零售业 Wholesale and Retail Trades	交通运输、仓储和邮政业 Traffic Transport Storage and Post	住宿和餐饮业 Hotels and Catering Services	信息传输、软件和信息技术服务业 Information Transmission, Software and Information Technology	金融业 Financial Intermediation
48463	**92054**	**5776**	**6316**	**21889**	**1468**
1300	5128	240	446	514	62
3252	8847	190	738	1575	100
4346	11321	621	893	1998	76
3184	6453	686	304	766	186
10191	23575	1218	854	2618	230
15134	20544	706	1853	11800	615
930	977	209	86	197	18
1003	1091	142	114	147	13
3140	2936	260	404	1009	72
749	1219	209	94	139	6
1053	1414	143	107	183	38
637	1305	70	96	70	5
1033	3041	387	91	100	12
2511	4203	695	236	773	35

2-9 续表

单位：个

区 县	Region	房地产业 Real Estate	租赁和商务服务业 Leasing and Business Services	科学研究和技术服务业 Scientific Research Technical Services	水利、环境和公共设施管理业 Management of Water Conservancy, Environment and Public Facilities
全 市	**Total**	**13954**	**42165**	**21028**	**2792**
新城区	Xincheng	614	1632	590	69
碑林区	Beilin	1344	4256	1620	91
莲湖区	Lianhu	1386	4757	2249	253
灞桥区	Baqiao	743	2418	936	232
未央区	Weiyang	2780	7031	3378	347
雁塔区	Yanta	4402	15528	8935	864
阎良区	Yanliang	238	474	191	58
临潼区	Lintong	172	537	212	68
长安区	Chang'an	695	1998	1073	172
高陵区	Gaoling	315	429	187	53
鄠邑区	Huyi	272	599	443	120
蓝田县	Lantian	109	235	111	94
周至县	Zhouzhi	134	386	137	228
西咸新区	Xixian New Area	750	1885	966	143

continued

(unit)

居民服务、修理和其他服务业 Services to Households Repairs and Other Services	教育 Education	卫生和社会工作 Health and Social Work	文化、体育和娱乐业 Culture Sports and Entertainment	公共管理、社会保障和社会组织 Public Administration Social Security and Social Organizations	国际组织 International Orgnizations
7226	**6136**	**2218**	**7870**	**6412**	
365	321	152	281	358	
699	514	222	745	411	
727	569	275	701	408	
512	336	129	438	323	
1256	588	248	939	543	
1983	1263	435	3225	519	
109	144	46	78	267	
142	291	70	149	467	
437	581	193	507	670	
156	166	43	103	251	
102	338	115	135	559	
62	246	63	87	563	
82	409	118	137	670	
594	370	109	345	403	

2-10 按区县和机构类型分法人单位数（2021年）

Number of Impersonal Entities by Agencies Types of Legal Entities Corporate Units and Region and Development Zone(2021)

单位：个 (unit)

区 县	Region	法人单位数 Number of Enterprises	企业法人 Business Entity	事业法人 Institution Entity	机关法人 Government Entity	社会团体 Social Organization	其他 Other
全 市	**Total**	**312523**	**292749**	**3826**	**1003**	**1366**	**13579**
新城区	Xincheng	12381	11674	224	89	110	284
碑林区	Beilin	24841	23889	287	71	172	422
莲湖区	Lianhu	31072	30114	279	74	126	479
灞桥区	Baqiao	19542	18668	168	63	32	611
未央区	Weiyang	59069	58070	337	123	92	447
雁塔区	Yanta	92335	90948	332	92	176	787
阎良区	Yanliang	5152	4511	128	50	65	398
临潼区	Lintong	6209	4658	260	69	46	1176
长安区	Chang'an	16489	14733	500	90	51	1115
高陵区	Gaoling	5697	4735	138	50	35	739
鄠邑区	Huyi	8428	6285	336	65	103	1639
蓝田县	Lantian	4974	3393	214	69	87	1211
周至县	Zhouzhi	8869	4658	379	65	214	3553
西咸新区	Xixian New Area	17465	16413	244	33	57	718

2-11 按区县和登记注册类型分企业法人单位数（2021年）

Number of the Corporate Units by Types of Corporate Registration and Region and Development Zone (2021)

单位：个 (unit)

区 县	Region	企业单位数 Number of Enterprises	内资企业 Domestic Investment Enterprises	国有企业 State-owned Enterprises	集体企业 Collective-owned Enterprises	股份合作企业 Share-holding Corporative Enterprises	联营企业 Joint Ownership Enterprises
全 市	**Total**	**292749**	**291440**	**890**	**981**	**158**	**33**
新城区	Xincheng	11674	11655	97	132	6	6
碑林区	Beilin	23889	23788	132	124	27	1
莲湖区	Lianhu	30114	30046	144	145	16	4
灞桥区	Baqiao	18668	18573	46	61	12	1
未央区	Weiyang	58070	57895	56	57	11	1
雁塔区	Yanta	90948	90415	152	81	37	3
阎良区	Yanliang	4511	4486	24	32	7	
临潼区	Lintong	4658	4645	41	64	4	3
长安区	Chang'an	14733	14614	56	73	16	4
高陵区	Gaoling	4735	4711	25	19	2	3
鄠邑区	Huyi	6285	6252	27	65	9	
蓝田县	Lantian	3393	3386	23	38	2	2
周至县	Zhouzhi	4658	4657	34	37	2	1
西咸新区	Xixian New Area	16413	16317	33	53	7	4

2-11 续表 continued

单位：个 (unit)

区 县	Region	有限责任公司 Limited Liability Corporations	股份有限公司 Share-holding Corporative Ltd.	私营企业 Private Enterprises	其他企业 Other Enterprises	港、澳、台商投资企业 Enterprises with Funds from Hong Kong, Macao and Taiwan	外商投资企业 Enterprises with Foreign Investment
全 市	**Total**	**14330**	**632**	**273854**	**562**	**474**	**835**
新城区	Xincheng	865	43	10491	15	10	9
碑林区	Beilin	907	32	22556	9	45	56
莲湖区	Lianhu	881	37	28810	9	26	42
灞桥区	Baqiao	1476	38	16938	1	51	44
未央区	Weiyang	1909	75	55779	7	70	105
雁塔区	Yanta	4560	224	84971	387	162	371
阎良区	Yanliang	207	12	4201	3	10	15
临潼区	Lintong	154	4	4366	9	7	6
长安区	Chang'an	1352	86	12974	53	30	89
高陵区	Gaoling	268	21	4372	1	7	17
鄠邑区	Huyi	290	7	5853	1	15	18
蓝田县	Lantian	147	12	3155	7	3	4
周至县	Zhouzhi	114	8	4405	56		1
西咸新区	Xixian New Area	1200	33	14983	4	38	58

主要统计指标解释

企业（单位）登记注册类型 企业或企业产业活动单位的登记注册类型，依据在市场监管部门登记注册的类型划分。机关、事业单位和社会团体及其他组织的登记注册类型，依据主要经费来源和管理方式，根据实际情况进行划分。

国有企业 指企业全部资产归国家所有，并按《中华人民共和国企业法人登记管理条例》规定登记注册的非公司制的经济组织。不包括有限责任公司中的国有独资公司。

集体企业 指企业资产归集体所有，并按《中华人民共和国企业法人登记管理条例》规定登记注册的经济组织。

股份合作企业 指以合作制为基础，由企业职工共同出资入股，吸收一定比例的社会资产投资组建，实行自主经营，自负盈亏，共同劳动，民主管理，按劳分配与按股分红相结合的一种集体经济组织。

联营企业 指两个及两个以上相同或不同所有制性质的企业法人或事业单位法人，按自愿、平等、互利的原则，共同投资组成的经济组织。联营企业包括国有联营企业、集体联营企业、国有与集体联营企业和其他联营企业。

有限责任公司 指根据《中华人民共和国公司登记管理条例》规定登记注册，由两个以上，五十个以下的股东共同出资，每个股东以其所认缴的出资额对公司承担有限责任，公司以其全部资产对其债务承担责任的经济组织。有限责任公司包括国有独资公司以及其他有限责任公司。

股份有限公司 指根据《中华人民共和国公司登记管理条例》规定登记注册，其全部注册资本由等额股份构成并通过发行股票筹集资本，股东以其认购的股份对公司承担有限责任，公司以其全部资产对其债务承担责任的经济组织。

私营企业 指由自然人投资设立或由自然人控股，以雇佣劳动为基础的营利性经济组织。包括按照《公司法》《合伙企业法》以及《个人独资企业法》规定登记注册的私营独资企业、私营合作企业、私营有限责任公司、私营股份有限公司和个人独资企业。

与港澳台商合资经营企业 指港澳台地区投资者与内地企业依照《中华人民共和国中外合资经营企业法》及有关法律的规定，按合同规定的比例投资设立，分享利润和分担风险的企业。

与港澳台商合作经营企业 指港澳台地区投资者与内地企业依照《中华人民共和国中外合作经营企业法》及有关法律的规定，依照合作合同的约定进行投资或提供条件设立，分配利润、分担风险和亏损的企业。

港澳台商独资经营企业 指依照《中华人民共和国外资企业法》及有关法律的规定，在内地由港澳台地区投资者全额投资设立的企业。

港澳台商投资股份有限公司 指根据国家有关规定，经商务部（原外经贸部）批准设立，其中港、澳、台商的股本占公司注册资本的比例达25%以上的股份有限公司。凡其中港、澳、台商的股本占公司注册资本的比例小于25%的，属于内资企业中的股份有限公司。

中外合资经营企业 指外国企业或外国人与中国内地企业依照《中华人民共和国中外合资经营企业法》及有关法律的规定，按合同规定的比例投资设立，分享利润和分担风险的企业。

中外合作经营企业 指外国企业或外国人与中国内地企业依照《中华人民共和国中外合作经营企业法》及有关法律的规定，依照合作合同的约定进行投资或提供条件设立，分配利润、分担风险和亏损的企业。

外资企业 指依照《中华人民共和国外资企业法》及有关法律的规定，在中国内地由外国投资者全额投资设立的企业。

外商投资股份有限公司 指根据国家有关规定，经商务部（原外经贸部）批准设立，其中外资的股本占公司注册资本的比例达25%以上的股份有限公司。凡其中外资股本占公司注册资本的比例小于25%的，属于内资企业中的股份有限公司。

机关、事业单位和社会团体

机关：包括国家权力机关、国家行政机关、国家监察机关、司法机关、政党机关、政协组织和其他机关法人；机关法人单位的本部，以及国家权力机关分支机构、国家行政机关分支或派出机构、监察机关分支机构、人民法院分支机构、人民检察院分支机构等。

①国家权力机关：指全国人民代表大会及其常务委员会、地方各级人民代表大会及其常务委员会和办事机构。

②国家行政机关：指国务院和地方各级人民政府及其工作部门，以及地区行政行署。

③国家监察机关：指行使监察职能的机关。

④国家司法机关：指国家审判机关和检察机关。

⑤政党机关：指中国共产党各级机关和所属办事机构、各民主党派各级机关和办事机构。

⑥政协组织：指中国人民政治协商会议全国委员会和地方各级委员会及其办事机构。

事业单位 包括①经机构编制部门批准成立和登记或备案，领取《事业单位法人证书》，取得法人资格的单位；②事业法人单位的本部及分支机构或派出机构。

社会团体 指中国公民自愿组成，为实现会员共同意愿，按照其章程开展活动的非营利性社会组织。包括①经各级民政部门核准登记，领取《社会团体法人登记证书》的各类社会团体；②由各级机构编制管理部门直接管理其机构编制的群众团体；③经国务院批准可以免于登记的社会团体。

Explanatory Notes on Main Statistical Indicators

The types of registration of enterprises (units) The types of registration of enterprises or industrial activity units of enterprises shall be divided into the types of registration of government organs, public institutions, social organizations and other organizations according to the types of registration registered in the market supervision departments, and shall be divided according to the main sources of funds and ways of management according to the actual situation.

State–owned Enterprises refer to non-corporation economic units where the entire assets are owned by the State and which have been registered in accordance with the Regulation of the People's Republic of China on the Management of Registration of Corporate Enterprises. Not included from this category are solely State-funded corporations in the limited liability corporations.

Collective–owned Enterprises refer to economic units where the assets are owned collectively and which have been registered in accordance with the Regulation of the People's Republic of China on the Management of Registration of Corporate Enterprises.

Cooperative Enterprises refer to a form of collective economic units (enterprises)where capitals come mainly from employees as their shares, with certain proportion of capital from the outside, where production is organized on the basis of independent operation, independent accounting for profits and losses, joint work, democratic management, and a distribution system that integrates remuneration according to work with dividend according to capital share.

Joint Ownership Enterprises refer to economic units established by two or more corporate enterprises or corporate institutions of the same or different ownership, through joint investment on the basis of voluntary participation, equality, and mutual benefits. They include State joint ownership enterprises; collective joint ownership enterprises; joint State-collective enterprises; and other joint ownership enterprises.

Limited Liability Corporations refer to economic units established with investment from 2 to 50 investors and registered in accordance with the Regulation of the People's Republic of China on the Management of Registration of Corporations, each investor bearing limited liability to the corporation depending on its share of investment, and the corporation bearing liability to its debt to the maximum of its total assets. Limited liability corporations include solely State-funded limited liability corporations and other limited liability corporations.

Share–holding Corporations Ltd. refer to economic units registered in accordance with the Regulation of the People's Republic of China on the Management of Registration of Corporations, with total registered capital divided into equal shares and raised through issuing stocks. Each investor bears limited liability to the corporation depending on the holding of shares, and the corporation bears liability to its debt to the maximum of its total assets.

Private Enterprises refer to profit-making economic units invested and established by natural persons, or controlled by natural persons using employed labour-it includes in this category are private limited liability corporations, private share-holding corporations Ltd., private partnership enterprises and Law on Individual Proprietorship provision for the registration of prirate propretorship enterprises, private partnerships, private limited liability companies and individual proprietorship enterprises.

Other Domestic–funded Enterprises refer to domestic-funded economic units other than those mentioned above.

Joint Venture Enterprises with Funds from Hong Kong, Macau and Taiwan are enterprises established by investors from Hong Kong, Macau and Taiwan with enterprises in the mainland of China in accordance with the Law of the People's Republic of China on Sino-foreign Equity Joint Ventures and other relevant laws, where the establishment of the investment and the sharing of profits and risks are stipulated under joint venture contracts.

Cooperative Enterprises with Funds from Hong Kong, Macau and Taiwan established by investors from Hong Kong, Macau and Taiwan with enterprises in the mainland of China in accordance with the Law of the People's Republic of China on Sino-foreign Contractual Joint Venture and other relevant laws, where the investment or provision of facilities and the sharing of profits and risks and are stipulated under cooperative contracts.

Enterprises with Sole (exclusive)Investment from Hong Kong, Macau and Taiwan refer to enterprises established in the mainland of China with exclusive investment from investors from Hong Kong, Macau and Taiwan in accordance with the Law of the People's Republic of China on Wholly Foreign-owned Enterprises and other relevant laws.

Share–holding Corporations Ltd. with Investment from Hong Kong, Macau and Taiwan refer to share- holding corporations Ltd. established with the approval from the former Ministry of Foreign Trade and Economic Relations in line with relevant State regulations, where the share of investment from Hong Kong, Macau or Taiwan businessmen exceeds 25% of the total registered capital of the corporation. In case the share of investment from Hong Kong, Macau or Taiwan is less than 25% of thetotal registered capital, the enterprise is to be classified as domestic-funded share-holding corporation Ltd.

Joint Venture Enterprises with Foreign Investment refer to enterprises jointly established by foreign enterprises or foreigners with enterprises in themainland of China in accordance with the Law of thePeople's Republic of China on Sino-foreign Equity Joint Ventures and other relevant laws, where the sharing of investment, profits and risks is stipulated under contract.

Cooperative Enterprises with Foreign Investment refer to enterprises jointly established by foreign enterprises or foreigners with enterprises in the mainland of China in accordance with the Law of the People's Republic of China on Sino-foreign Contractual Joint Venture and other relevant laws, According to the enterprise that invests or provides conditions for establishment in accordance with the terms of the cooperation contract, distributes profits and shares risks and losses.

Enterprises with Sole (exclusive)Foreign Investment refer to enterprises established in the mainland of China with exclusive investment from foreign investors in accordance with the Law of the People's Republic of China on Wholly Foreign-owned Enterprises and other relevant laws.

Share–holding Corporations Ltd. with Foreign Investment refer to share-holding corporations Ltd. established with the approval from the former Ministry of Foreign Trade and Economic Relations in line with relevant State regulations, where the share of investment from foreign investors exceeds 25% of the total registered capital of the corporation. In case the share of foreign investment is less than 25% ofthe total registered capital, the enterprise is to be classified as domestic-funded share-holding corporation Ltd.

Administrative Organization, Institutions and Social organizations

Administrative organization including organs of state power, organs of state administration, organs of state supervision, judicial organs, organs of political parties, organizations of the CPPCC and other organs as legal persons; The headquarters of a legal entity of a state organ, a branch of a state organ of power, a branch of a state administrative organ or its dispatched organ, a branch of a supervisory organ, a branch of a people's court, a branch of a people's procuratorate, etc.

(1)The organs of state power: The National People's Congress and its Standing Committee, the local people's congresses at various levels and their standing committees and administrative bodies.

(2)State administrative organs: refer to the State Council and local people's governments at various levels and their working departments, as well as regional administrative agencies.

(3)State supervisory organs refer to organs that exercise supervisory functions.

(4) National judicial organs: refers to the national judicial organs and procurator organs.

Political party organs: refer to the organs and subordinate offices of the Communist Party of China at all levels, and the organs and offices of the democratic parties at all levels.

The CPPCC refers to the National Committee of the Chinese People's Political Consultative Conference (CPPCC) and local committees at all levels and their administrative bodies.

Public institutions include (1) approved by the establishment of institutions and registration or record, get the "institution legal person certificate", obtain the legal person status of the unit; (2) The headquarters and branches or dispatched offices of the institution as legal person.

Social organizations refer to non–profit social organizations formed by Chinese citizens voluntarily to carry out activities in accordance with their articles of association in order to realize the common wishes of members. Including (1) approved by the civil affairs departments at all levels to register, get the "social organization legal person registration certificate" of all kinds of social organizations; (2) The establishment management departments at all levels shall directly manage the mass organizations with their establishment; (3) Social organizations which may be exempted from registration with the approval of the State Council.

3 国民经济核算

NATIONAL ECONOMIC ACCOUNTS

资料整理：张　冲　张　洁　段　斐　刘晓敏　刘　航
Data management：Zhang Chong Zhang Jie Duan Fei Liu Xiaomin Liu Hang
数据审核：张　静
Data audit：Zhang Jing

第三部分　国民经济核算

一、简要说明

1.本章资料反映西安市国民经济核算情况。

2.本章资料包括西安市生产总值、构成和指数，非公有制经济增加值及占比等。地区生产总值是根据不同产业部门、不同行业的特点和资料来源情况而采用不同方法计算的。非公有制经济增加值测算执行的是《陕西省统计局关于非公有制经济增加值测算的暂行办法（修订版）》。

3.本年鉴公布的地区生产总值以及有关的指标数据，如果遇到普查或者重大核算方法改革，在能够获得更详细的基础资料的情况下，地区生产总值的历史数据还会发生变动。

2016年，国家改革研发支出的核算方法，将能够为所有者带来经济利益的研发支出不再作为中间消耗，而是作为固定资本形成处理。根据新的核算方法，在四经普修订时对以前年份进行了调整性修订。

2003–2017年数据为第四次经济普查修订结果，2018年数据为第四次经济普查数据，2019–2020年数据为最终核算数，2021年数据为初步核算数，2011–2019年人均GDP数据依据第七次全国人口普查修订的常住人口数据进行了修订。

4.2012年，根据国家质检总局和国家标准委颁布的《国民经济行业分类》（GB/T 4754–2011），国家统计局对《三次产业划分规定》进行了修订，将“农、林、牧、渔业”中的“农、林、牧、渔服务业”，“采矿业”中的“开采辅助活动”，“制造业”中的“金属制品、机械和设备修理业”等三个大类一并调入第三产业。2013年（含）之后三次产业分类执行国家统计局2012年制定的新《三次产业划分规定》。

5.2004年（含）之前人均GDP按户籍人口计算，2005年（含）之后按常住人口计算。

6.国民经济核算数据绝对数按当年价格计算，指数按可比价格计算。

二、主要指标

地区生产总值（亿元）	10688.28	比上年增长	4.1%
第一产业	308.82	比上年增长	6.1%
第二产业	3585.20	比上年增长	0.9%
第三产业	6794.26	比上年增长	5.7%
人均地区生产总值（元／人）	83689	比上年增长	0.9%

3 NATIONAL ECONOMIC ACCOUNTS

I.Brief introduction

1.Data in this chapter reflects the National Economic accounting situation of Xi'an.

2.Data in this chapter includes Xi'an GDP, composition, index, the added value and the proportion of the non-public sectors of the economy, etc.Data of GDP are based on different approaches in accordance with different features of various sectors, industry and data sources. The estimation of the non-public sectors of the economy is based on Interim Measures of Shaanxi Provincial Bureau on the Estimation of Value Added of the Non-Public Sectors of the Economy (Revised Edition).

3.For data of GDP and related indicators published in the Yearbook, if there are census or reformation of significant accounting method, historical data of GDP may also undergo change under the circumstance that more specific data can be obtained.

In 2016, National Bureau of Statistics reforms the Methodology of Research and Development Expenditure. It regulates that R&D expenditure which will bring economic benefit for the owners should be treated as Fixed Assets instead of Intermediate Consumption. According to new accounting method,the previous years were revised in the fourth national economic census.

The data from 2003 to 2017 were revised according to the fourth Economic Census,the data of 2018 is the results of The Fourth Economic Census,data from 2019 to 2020 were final accounting data, and data of 2021 is preliminary accounting data,the per capita GDP data from 2011 to 2019 was revised according to the resident population data revised by the Seventh National Census.

4.Classification Rules of Three Strata of Industry was adjusted by National Bureau of Statistics of China in accordance with Industrial Classification for National Economic Activities (GB/T 4754-2011) in 2012, which was promulgated by AQSIQ and SAC. Services in support of agriculture, forestry, animal husbandry and fishery, support activities for mining, repair service of metal products, machinery and equipment are categorized into the Tertiary Industry. Industrial classification is based on adjusted Classification Rules of Three Strata of Industry (2012) since 2013.

5.Per capita GDP was calculated by register population before 2005, but since 2005 it is based on permanent resident population.

6.Data on national accounts are calculated at current prices, and the indices are calculated at constant prices.

Ⅱ.Major Indicators

		Increase over Preceding Year
Gross Domestic Production (100 million yuan)	10688.28	4.1%
Primary Industry	308.82	6.1%
Secondary Industry	3585.20	0.9%
Tertiary Industry	6794.26	5.7%
Per Capita Gross Domestic Product (yuan/person)	83689	0.9%

3-1 主要年份地区生产总值

Gross Domestic Product in Representative Years

(本表按当年价格计算) (Data in the table are calculated at current prices)
单位：亿元 (100 million yuan)

年 份 Year	地区生产总值 Gross Domestic Product	第一产业 Primary Industry	第二产业 Secondary Industry	第三产业 Tertiary Industry	人均地区生产总值（元/人） Per Capita GDP (yuan/person)
1952	3.37	1.59	0.88	0.90	135
1965	12.76	2.62	7.22	2.92	323
1970	17.76	3.13	10.96	3.67	412
1975	21.33	4.14	12.63	4.56	448
1978	25.35	4.83	14.59	5.93	513
1980	31.66	4.73	18.69	8.24	623
1983	35.89	5.22	20.14	10.53	674
1984	44.14	7.45	24.17	12.52	817
1985	57.58	8.76	30.83	17.99	1049
1986	65.78	9.59	33.86	22.33	1178
1987	80.16	10.73	37.69	31.74	1409
1988	99.22	11.47	46.58	41.17	1711
1989	109.38	12.78	48.91	47.69	1861
1990	116.51	13.94	50.15	52.42	1932
1991	136.14	17.17	57.06	61.91	2224
1992	164.85	18.78	69.22	76.85	2662
1993	229.56	22.58	110.88	96.10	3661
1994	289.82	31.68	128.27	129.87	4563
1995	330.35	41.40	135.33	153.62	5131
1996	406.95	46.94	161.63	198.38	6246
1997	488.82	51.33	197.97	239.52	7424
1998	525.85	51.91	216.32	257.62	7906
1999	577.29	45.53	243.35	288.41	8599
2000	646.13	44.65	277.13	324.35	9484
2001	734.86	45.87	312.90	376.09	10628
2002	826.68	47.77	353.58	425.33	11831
2003	926.12	50.72	402.22	473.18	13052
2004	1092.35	60.21	464.95	567.19	15155
2005	1294.05	66.01	511.19	716.86	16158
2006	1512.56	70.44	612.69	829.42	18567
2007	1857.75	82.42	763.07	1012.26	22476
2008	2313.26	102.46	940.42	1270.38	27736
2009	2689.06	106.09	1105.01	1477.96	31994
2010	3195.05	133.22	1290.93	1770.89	37792
2011	3791.71	165.43	1516.30	2109.98	43723
2012	4370.16	181.12	1726.70	2462.35	48530
2013	4960.23	182.60	1946.58	2831.05	53624
2014	5576.98	191.58	2152.43	3232.97	58829
2015	5932.86	191.91	2070.47	3670.48	60912
2016	6396.36	196.66	2139.49	4060.21	63393
2017	7418.04	245.26	2452.92	4719.86	66649
2018	8499.41	258.98	2861.86	5378.56	73113
2019	9399.98	279.13	3130.80	5990.06	77494
2020	10023.73	312.75	3340.97	6370.01	79208
2021	10688.28	308.82	3585.20	6794.26	83689

注：1.2004年（含）之前人均GDP按户籍人口计算，2005年（含）之后按常住人口计算。
2.2013年（含）之后三次产业分类依据国家统计局2012年制定的新《三次产业划分规定》。
3.2017年开始西咸新区由西安代管，统计范围发生变化，之前年份则不含西咸新区咸阳部分数据（下同）。2021年数据不包含西安（西咸新区）—咸阳共管区。
4.2003-2017年数据为第四次经济普查修订结果（下同）。2018年数据为第四次经济普查数据。2019-2020年数据为最终核算数（下同）。
5.2021年数据为初步核算数（下同）。
6.2011-2019年人均GDP数据依据第七次全国人口普查修订的常住人口数据进行了修订。

3-2 主要年份地区生产总值指数（上年=100）

Indices of Gross Domestic Product in Representative Years (preceding year = 100)

(本表按可比价格计算) (Data in the table are calculated at constant prices)

年份	Year	地区生产总值 Gross Domestic Product	第一产业 Primary Industry	第二产业 Secondary Industry	第三产业 Tertiary Industry	人均地区生产总值 Per Capita GDP
1952		103.6	92.2	137.5	123.7	
1965		126.1	134.1	133.0	106.7	
1970		122.0	109.4	140.0	100.1	
1975		103.8	92.6	107.1	107.5	
1978		101.7	101.6	99.4	108.2	
1980		111.5	83.3	119.7	116.5	
1985		112.6	107.5	111.8	116.9	
1986		111.4	107.7	108.4	118.8	
1987		113.6	100.8	109.1	126.6	
1988		111.4	81.2	115.5	114.7	
1989		106.7	103.0	104.5	110.8	
1990		105.2	103.0	102.5	109.6	
1991		109.8	118.6	108.6	108.6	108.2
1992		115.6	109.4	118.1	115.0	114.3
1993		123.9	112.5	142.7	108.4	122.3
1994		110.3	98.4	110.6	113.2	108.8
1995		110.0	104.5	112.1	108.6	108.5
1996		114.9	106.8	118.8	111.7	113.5
1997		114.4	109.1	116.7	112.4	113.2
1998		113.3	106.5	117.5	108.8	112.1
1999		112.2	97.4	115.7	110.1	111.2
2000		113.0	103.5	115.1	111.5	111.4
2001		113.1	102.5	115.3	112.6	111.4
2002		113.3	103.1	115.0	113.0	112.1
2003		113.1	101.8	117.5	110.5	111.4
2004		113.1	106.2	115.5	111.7	111.4
2005		112.3	107.5	109.8	115.1	110.5
2006		112.9	106.8	110.5	115.2	111.0
2007		115.1	104.5	113.0	117.4	113.4
2008		114.8	107.6	113.2	116.4	113.8
2009		113.0	104.9	110.7	115.1	112.2
2010		113.6	105.7	115.0	113.2	112.9
2011		112.6	105.4	111.7	113.9	109.8
2012		111.9	106.0	110.4	113.4	107.7
2013		111.2	104.4	112.6	110.7	108.3
2014		109.7	105.0	109.4	110.2	107.0
2015		108.9	104.4	104.6	112.1	106.0
2016		108.8	103.3	107.2	110.0	105.1
2017		107.7	105.0	105.1	109.4	103.6
2018		108.2	103.3	107.1	109.1	103.6
2019		107.0	104.3	106.2	107.6	102.5
2020		105.2	103.0	107.4	104.1	100.8
2021		104.1	106.1	100.9	105.7	100.9
平均每年增长	**Yearly Average Growth Rates**					
“一五”时期	**The First Five-Year Plan Period**	**15.8**	**5.9**	**37.7**	**16.9**	
“二五”时期	**The Second Five-Year Plan Period**	**2.0**	**-3.7**	**2.5**	**8.4**	
1963-1965年	**Readjust Period**	**14.2**	**16.1**	**23.4**	**0.3**	
“三五”时期	**The Third Five-Year Plan Period**	**7.1**	**0.1**	**11.7**	**5.4**	
“四五”时期	**The Fourth Five-Year Plan Period**	**5.0**	**4.0**	**5.3**	**5.0**	
“五五”时期	**The Fifth Five-Year Plan Period**	**6.0**	**-0.7**	**6.5**	**10.1**	
“六五”时期	**The Sixth Five-Year Plan Period**	**10.7**	**7.9**	**10.4**	**12.9**	
“七五”时期	**The Seventh Five-Year Plan Period**	**9.6**	**-1.3**	**7.9**	**15.9**	
“八五”时期	**The Eighth Five-Year Plan Period**	**13.8**	**8.5**	**17.8**	**10.7**	**12.3**
“九五”时期	**The Ninth Five-Year Plan Period**	**13.6**	**4.6**	**16.8**	**10.9**	**12.3**
“十五”时期	**The Tenth Five-Year Plan Period**	**13.0**	**4.2**	**14.6**	**12.6**	**11.4**
“十一五”时期	**The Eleventh Five-Year Plan Period**	**13.9**	**5.9**	**12.5**	**15.5**	**12.7**
“十二五”时期	**The Twelfth Five-Year Plan Period**	**10.9**	**5.0**	**9.7**	**12.1**	**7.8**
“十三五”时期	**The Thirteenth Five-Year Plan Period**	**7.4**	**3.8**	**6.6**	**8.0**	**3.1**
“十四五”时期	**The Fourteenth Five-Year Plan Period**	**4.1**	**6.1**	**0.9**	**5.7**	**0.9**

注：2011-2019年、“十二五”“十三五”时期人均GDP指数依据第七次全国人口普查修订的常住人口数据进行了修订。

3-3 主要年份地区生产总值指数（1952年＝100）

Indices of Gross Domestic Product in Representative Years (1952=100)

（本表按可比价格计算） (Data in the table are calculated at constant prices)

年 份 Year	地区生产总值 Gross Domestic Product	第一产业 Primary Industry	第二产业 Secondary Industry	第三产业 Tertiary Industry
1952	100.0	100.0	100.0	100.0
1965	341.6	173.3	1048.3	329.2
1970	481.6	174.3	1821.0	428.6
1975	614.2	211.9	2362.5	547.9
1978	678.7	231.3	2560.8	643.8
1980	821.4	204.2	3237.2	885.2
1983	988.4	222.5	3846.2	1154.4
1984	1213.6	278.2	4748.8	1388.7
1985	1366.8	299.1	5310.6	1632.4
1986	1523.1	322.3	5756.7	1928.9
1987	1730.0	324.9	6280.6	2441.6
1988	1926.3	263.7	7256.6	2801.2
1989	2054.8	271.6	7583.1	3104.6
1990	2162.5	279.7	7772.7	3403.6
1991	2374.4	331.7	8441.2	3696.3
1992	2744.8	362.9	9969.1	4250.7
1993	3400.8	408.2	14225.9	4607.8
1994	3751.1	401.8	15733.8	5216.0
1995	4126.2	419.9	17637.6	5664.6
1996	4741.0	448.5	20953.5	6327.4
1997	5423.7	489.3	24452.7	7112.0
1998	6145.1	521.1	28731.9	7737.9
1999	6894.8	507.6	33242.8	8519.4
2000	7791.1	525.4	38262.5	9499.1
2001	8811.7	538.5	44116.7	10696.0
2002	9983.7	555.2	50734.2	12086.5
2003	11294.6	565.2	59612.7	13355.6
2004	12778.7	600.2	68852.7	14918.2
2005	14345.3	645.3	75600.2	17170.8
2006	16198.7	689.1	83538.2	19780.8
2007	18644.8	720.1	94398.2	23222.7
2008	21407.9	774.9	106858.8	27031.2
2009	24195.2	812.8	118292.7	31112.9
2010	27478.5	859.2	136036.6	35219.8
2011	30951.8	905.6	151952.8	40115.3
2012	34625.8	959.9	167755.9	45490.8
2013	38514.2	1002.1	188893.2	50358.3
2014	42250.1	1052.2	206649.1	55494.8
2015	46001.9	1098.5	216155.0	62209.7
2016	50063.9	1134.8	231718.1	68430.7
2017	53913.8	1191.8	243508.6	74863.2
2018	58318.6	1231.1	260797.7	81675.8
2019	62400.9	1284.0	276967.2	87883.2
2020	65645.7	1322.5	297462.8	91486.4
2021	68337.2	1403.2	300140.0	96701.1

3-4 主要年份地区生产总值构成

Composition of Gross Domestic Product in Representative Years

(本表按当年价格计算) (Data in the table are calculated at current prices)

单位：% (%)

年 份	Year	地区生产总值 Gross Domestic Product	第一产业 Primary Industry	第二产业 Secondary Industry	第三产业 Tertiary Industry
1952		100	47.18	26.11	26.71
1965		100	20.53	56.58	22.89
1970		100	17.62	61.71	20.67
1975		100	19.41	59.21	21.38
1978		100	19.05	57.55	23.40
1980		100	14.94	59.03	26.03
1985		100	15.21	53.54	31.25
1986		100	14.58	51.47	33.95
1987		100	13.39	47.02	39.59
1988		100	11.56	46.95	41.49
1989		100	11.68	44.72	43.60
1990		100	11.96	43.04	45.00
1991		100	12.61	41.91	45.48
1992		100	11.39	41.99	46.62
1993		100	9.84	48.30	41.86
1994		100	10.93	44.26	44.81
1995		100	12.53	40.97	46.50
1996		100	11.53	39.72	48.75
1997		100	10.50	40.50	49.00
1998		100	9.87	41.14	48.99
1999		100	7.89	42.15	49.96
2000		100	6.91	42.89	50.20
2001		100	6.24	42.58	51.18
2002		100	5.78	42.77	51.45
2003		100	5.48	43.43	51.09
2004		100	5.51	42.56	51.93
2005		100	5.10	39.50	55.40
2006		100	4.66	40.51	54.83
2007		100	4.44	41.07	54.49
2008		100	4.43	40.65	54.92
2009		100	3.95	41.09	54.96
2010		100	4.17	40.40	55.43
2011		100	4.36	39.99	55.65
2012		100	4.14	39.51	56.35
2013		100	3.68	39.24	57.08
2014		100	3.44	38.59	57.97
2015		100	3.23	34.90	61.87
2016		100	3.07	33.45	63.48
2017		100	3.31	33.07	63.62
2018		100	3.05	33.67	63.28
2019		100	2.97	33.31	63.72
2020		100	3.12	33.33	63.55
2021		100	2.89	33.54	63.57
“一五”时期	**The First Five-Year Plan Period**	**100**	**32.88**	**43.92**	**23.20**
“二五”时期	**The Second Five-Year Plan Period**	**100**	**18.08**	**58.63**	**23.29**
1963-1965年	**Readjust Period**	**100**	**19.36**	**55.38**	**25.26**
“三五”时期	**The Third Five-Year Plan Period**	**100**	**18.60**	**57.33**	**24.07**
“四五”时期	**The Fourth Five-Year Plan Period**	**100**	**20.46**	**59.59**	**19.95**
“五五”时期	**The Fifth Five-Year Plan Period**	**100**	**18.41**	**57.69**	**23.90**
“六五”时期	**The Sixth Five-Year Plan Period**	**100**	**16.03**	**55.01**	**28.96**
“七五”时期	**The Seventh Five-Year Plan Period**	**100**	**12.42**	**46.11**	**41.47**
“八五”时期	**The Eighth Five-Year Plan Period**	**100**	**11.44**	**43.52**	**45.04**
“九五”时期	**The Ninth Five-Year Plan Period**	**100**	**9.09**	**41.45**	**49.46**
“十五”时期	**The Tenth Five-Year Plan Period**	**100**	**5.55**	**41.95**	**52.50**
“十一五”时期	**The Eleventh Five-Year Plan Period**	**100**	**4.28**	**40.74**	**54.98**
“十二五”时期	**The Twelfth Five-Year Plan Period**	**100**	**3.71**	**38.21**	**58.08**
“十三五”时期	**The Thirteenth Five-Year Plan Period**	**100**	**3.10**	**33.37**	**63.53**
“十四五”时期	**The Fourteenth Five-Year Plan Period**	**100**	**2.89**	**33.54**	**63.57**

3-5 主要年份分行业增加值

The Value added by Industry in Representative Years

(本表按当年价格计算)　　(Data in the table are calculated at current prices)
单位：亿元　　(100 million yuan)

年 份 Year	地区生产总值 Gross Domestic Product	农、林、牧、渔业 Farming Forestry Animal Husbandry Fishery	工业 Industry	建筑业 Construction	批发和零售业 Wholesale and Retail Trades
1992	164.85	18.78	61.33	7.89	18.16
1993	229.56	22.58	98.88	12.00	22.63
1994	289.82	31.68	110.52	17.75	27.83
1995	330.35	41.40	112.50	22.83	33.20
1996	406.95	46.94	132.52	29.11	44.51
1997	488.82	51.33	161.97	36.00	59.31
1998	525.85	51.91	175.00	41.32	64.93
1999	577.29	45.53	194.00	49.35	70.27
2000	646.13	44.65	218.44	58.69	65.87
2001	734.86	45.87	246.90	66.00	78.38
2002	826.68	47.77	280.20	73.38	91.57
2003	926.12	50.72	319.26	82.96	94.95
2004	1092.35	60.21	372.18	92.77	123.27
2005	1294.05	66.01	393.51	117.68	139.57
2006	1512.56	70.44	465.70	146.99	164.33
2007	1857.75	82.42	569.08	193.99	184.91
2008	2313.26	102.46	672.60	267.82	225.20
2009	2689.06	106.09	763.81	341.20	278.87
2010	3195.05	133.22	875.97	414.96	329.48
2011	3791.71	165.43	1009.29	507.01	406.26
2012	4370.16	181.12	1140.83	585.87	460.05
2013	4960.23	197.76	1268.22	698.54	512.26
2014	5576.98	207.89	1387.03	791.64	552.31
2015	5932.86	209.58	1242.18	857.40	589.33
2016	6396.36	216.34	1252.91	920.05	599.08
2017	7418.04	270.83	1436.72	1047.34	653.49
2018	8499.41	286.33	1707.90	1210.79	709.16
2019	9399.98	309.68	1816.23	1370.63	788.19
2020	10023.73	346.17	1854.35	1535.76	795.17
2021	10688.28	343.70	2099.65	1552.18	837.62

注：1999年（含）之前，批发和零售业与住宿和餐饮业无法分类，故1999年（含）之前批发和零售业数据包含批发和零售业、住宿和餐饮业数据。

3-5 续表 continued

(本表按当年价格计算)
单位：亿元

(Data in the table are calculated at current prices)
(100 million yuan)

年份 Year	交通运输、仓储和邮政业 Transport，Storage and Post	住宿和餐饮业 Accommodation and Catering Trade	金融业 Financial Intermediation	房地产业 Real Estate	其他服务业 Others Services
1992	15.21		16.28	1.58	25.62
1993	18.01		20.59	1.97	32.90
1994	22.02		31.19	3.76	45.07
1995	24.60		35.20	4.90	55.72
1996	32.73		40.15	7.42	73.57
1997	43.02		37.50	8.74	90.95
1998	48.64		32.95	11.95	99.15
1999	55.35		30.37	14.42	118.00
2000	43.01	18.46	33.00	16.96	147.05
2001	45.50	21.97	36.21	21.38	172.65
2002	48.25	25.27	43.48	26.90	189.86
2003	46.99	25.34	47.96	32.39	225.55
2004	49.06	35.03	58.05	37.68	264.11
2005	59.12	47.59	79.33	45.90	345.36
2006	69.07	53.60	95.95	55.31	391.17
2007	78.02	67.89	141.69	70.93	468.83
2008	98.93	81.61	170.78	92.18	601.69
2009	110.55	79.27	198.58	124.92	685.79
2010	134.29	95.93	237.40	188.10	785.70
2011	160.29	114.66	278.09	245.14	905.54
2012	184.19	124.39	350.92	280.17	1062.63
2013	194.73	121.00	446.54	303.30	1217.89
2014	211.83	125.86	597.14	343.69	1359.59
2015	239.63	141.88	683.26	427.42	1542.19
2016	268.89	143.34	743.09	474.39	1778.27
2017	297.54	153.45	834.19	562.78	2161.71
2018	316.63	164.19	916.94	658.64	2528.84
2019	348.03	187.69	976.23	797.58	2805.73
2020	350.41	141.93	1064.25	855.93	3079.76
2021	382.92	153.50	1174.47	849.55	3294.69

3-6 主要年份分行业增加值指数（上年=100）

Indices of the Value added by Industry in Representative Years(preceding year = 100)

（本表按可比价格计算） (Data in the table are calculated at constant prices)

年 份 Year	地区生产总值 Gross Domestic Product	农、林、牧、渔业 Farming Forestry Animal Husbandry Fishery	工业 Industry	建筑业 Construction	批发和零售业 Wholesale and Retail Trades
1992	115.6	109.4	118.1	118.2	130.7
1993	123.9	112.5	143.7	135.6	108.0
1994	110.3	98.4	106.8	141.3	103.1
1995	110.0	104.5	108.1	136.6	109.6
1996	114.9	106.8	117.1	126.8	116.0
1997	114.4	109.1	116.4	117.8	124.0
1998	113.3	106.5	116.1	123.4	110.7
1999	112.2	97.4	114.0	122.8	106.4
2000	113.0	103.5	113.8	120.1	111.4
2001	113.1	102.5	116.3	111.8	110.5
2002	113.3	103.1	116.4	109.3	115.3
2003	113.1	101.8	115.7	124.9	112.0
2004	113.1	106.2	114.5	119.3	109.0
2005	112.3	107.5	106.7	121.1	110.5
2006	112.9	106.8	108.5	117.2	112.9
2007	115.1	104.5	111.7	117.3	113.3
2008	114.8	107.6	111.8	117.5	114.0
2009	113.0	104.9	106.7	121.9	121.7
2010	113.6	105.7	114.0	117.3	110.9
2011	112.6	105.4	111.9	111.2	117.7
2012	111.9	106.0	110.8	109.4	111.2
2013	111.2	104.8	112.4	113.9	108.4
2014	109.7	105.2	108.3	112.3	107.6
2015	108.9	105.1	103.7	107.3	105.0
2016	108.8	104.1	108.2	106.3	103.9
2017	107.7	104.8	105.0	104.8	104.6
2018	108.2	103.5	108.3	107.1	106.1
2019	107.0	104.4	103.9	109.2	108.8
2020	105.2	103.1	105.9	109.1	101.8
2021	104.1	106.0	106.4	94.6	98.6

注：1999年（含）之前，批发和零售业与住宿和餐饮业无法分类，故1999年（含）之前批发和零售业数据包含批发和零售业、住宿和餐饮业数据。

3-6 续表 continued

（本表按可比价格计算） (Data in the table are calculated at constant prices)

年 份 Year	交通运输、仓储和邮政业 Transport，Storage and Post	住宿和餐饮业 Accommodation and Catering Trade	金融业 Financial Intermediation	房地产业 Real Estate	其他服务业 Others Services
1992	111.3		107.6	119.5	112.2
1993	102.7		109.7	107.4	111.4
1994	102.5		126.9	160.7	114.8
1995	102.6		103.7	119.7	113.6
1996	115.1		98.7	130.8	114.2
1997	122.4		87.0	109.6	115.1
1998	114.4		88.8	138.3	110.3
1999	111.9		90.6	118.6	117.0
2000	111.7	111.7	107.7	116.6	111.7
2001	111.6	114.2	103.6	123.5	114.2
2002	106.1	116.5	104.6	106.0	116.5
2003	110.5	112.3	111.1	105.7	110.2
2004	112.3	116.9	108.4	107.7	112.5
2005	112.4	123.4	110.7	108.8	117.8
2006	112.6	116.5	109.5	118.7	117.3
2007	110.9	116.1	123.2	123.1	118.3
2008	109.2	107.5	112.3	108.7	121.6
2009	110.6	103.2	121.2	130.8	111.5
2010	116.3	112.0	114.3	133.4	110.6
2011	112.7	109.4	114.7	117.9	111.8
2012	110.4	105.4	125.4	110.8	112.7
2013	104.6	100.3	124.0	113.2	108.2
2014	105.8	100.2	120.4	107.0	109.5
2015	109.3	110.5	116.4	113.5	113.1
2016	109.0	101.2	111.9	110.9	111.9
2017	106.8	103.9	106.5	109.1	113.6
2018	106.1	104.7	105.3	105.8	112.3
2019	107.5	105.2	106.9	108.2	107.9
2020	101.1	81.3	106.7	100.5	106.9
2021	106.7	104.8	106.0	99.0	109.3

3-7 主要年份三次产业贡献率

Three Industries Contribution Rate in Representative Years

（本表按可比价格计算） (Data in the table are calculated at constant prices)

单位：% (%)

年 份 Year	地区生产总值 Gross Domestic Product	第一产业 Primary Industry	第二产业 Secondary Industry	第三产业 Tertiary Industry
2000	100	1.8	66.9	31.3
2001	100	1.3	50.4	48.3
2002	100	1.5	49.4	49.1
2003	100	0.8	59.2	40.0
2004	100	2.4	54.3	43.3
2005	100	2.9	37.6	59.5
2006	100	2.7	32.2	65.1
2007	100	1.4	33.3	65.3
2008	100	2.2	33.9	63.9
2009	100	1.6	30.8	67.6
2010	100	1.6	40.4	58.0
2011	100	1.8	37.4	60.8
2012	100	2.0	35.0	63.0
2013	100	1.3	43.9	54.8
2014	100	1.7	38.4	59.9
2015	100	1.5	20.6	77.9
2016	100	1.2	28.6	70.2
2017	100	2.2	23.4	74.4
2018	100	1.4	29.8	68.8
2019	100	2.0	29.9	68.1
2020	100	1.8	48.2	50.0
2021	100	4.4	7.6	88.0

3-8 主要年份三次产业对地区生产总值增长的拉动

Contribution of the Three Strata of Industry to GDP Growth in Representative Years

（本表按可比价格计算） (Data in the table are calculated at constant prices)
单位：% (%)

年份 Year	地区生产总值 Gross Domestic Product	第一产业 Primary Industry	第二产业 Secondary Industry	第三产业 Tertiary Industry
2000	13.0	0.2	8.7	4.1
2001	13.1	0.2	6.6	6.3
2002	13.3	0.2	6.6	6.5
2003	13.1	0.1	7.8	5.2
2004	13.1	0.3	7.1	5.7
2005	12.3	0.4	4.6	7.3
2006	12.9	0.3	4.2	8.4
2007	15.1	0.2	5.0	9.9
2008	14.8	0.3	5.0	9.5
2009	13.0	0.2	4.0	8.8
2010	13.6	0.2	5.5	7.9
2011	12.6	0.2	4.7	7.7
2012	11.9	0.2	4.2	7.5
2013	11.2	0.1	4.9	6.2
2014	9.7	0.2	3.7	5.8
2015	8.9	0.1	1.8	7.0
2016	8.8	0.1	2.5	6.2
2017	7.7	0.2	1.8	5.7
2018	8.2	0.1	2.4	5.7
2019	7.0	0.1	2.1	4.8
2020	5.2	0.1	2.5	2.6
2021	4.1	0.2	0.3	3.6

3-9 分行业增加值（2020-2021年）

Value added by Industry(2020-2021)

（本表增加值按当年价格计算，指数按不变价计算） (The data of value added are calculated at current prices,the indices are calculated at constant prices)

单位：亿元 (100 million yuan)

指 标	Item	增加值 Value Added		指数（上年=100） Index(preceding year=100)	
		2020	2021	2020	2021
地区生产总值	**Gross Domestic Product**	**10023.73**	**10688.28**	**105.2**	**104.1**
农、林、牧、渔业	Farming Forestry Animal Husbandry Fishery	346.17	343.70	103.1	106.0
工业	Industry	1854.35	2099.65	105.9	106.4
建筑业	Construction	1535.76	1552.18	109.1	94.6
批发和零售业	Wholesale and Retail Trades	795.17	837.62	101.8	98.6
交通运输、仓储及邮政业	Transport,Storage and Post	350.41	382.92	101.1	106.7
住宿和餐饮业	Accommodation and Catering Trade	141.93	153.50	81.3	104.8
金融业	Financial Intermediation	1064.25	1174.47	106.7	106.0
房地产业	Real Estate	855.93	849.55	100.5	99.0
其他服务业	Others Services	3079.76	3294.69	106.9	109.3
第一产业	Primary Industry	312.75	308.82	103.0	106.1
第二产业	Secondary Industry	3340.97	3585.20	107.4	100.9
第三产业	Tertiary Industry	6370.01	6794.26	104.1	105.7

3-10 各区县生产总值（2021年）

Gross Domestic Product by Region (2021)

（本表按当年价格计算）　　(Data in the table are calculated at current prices)
单位：亿元　　(100 million yuan)

区 县	Region	地区生产总值 Gross Domestic Product	第一产业 Primary Industry	第二产业 Secondary Industry	第三产业 Tertiary Industry	人均地区生产总值（元） Per Capita GDP (yuan)
全 市	**Total**	**10688.28**	**308.82**	**3585.20**	**6794.26**	**83689**
新城区	Xincheng	639.96		182.29	457.67	103178
碑林区	Beilin	1098.86		232.76	866.10	143868
莲湖区	Lianhu	831.08		257.88	573.20	81148
灞桥区	Baqiao	606.85	18.02	184.64	404.19	59188
未央区	Weiyang	1437.23	1.29	624.26	811.68	91418
雁塔区	Yanta	2725.20		630.14	2095.06	131792
阎良区	Yanliang	264.84	33.08	95.40	136.36	86790
临潼区	Lintong	260.11	42.89	67.76	149.46	38328
长安区	Chang'an	1269.45	34.22	706.31	528.92	79133
高陵区	Gaoling	384.72	31.80	202.15	150.77	85541
鄠邑区	Huyi	266.05	31.98	125.62	108.45	45717
蓝田县	Lantian	151.70	33.09	25.07	93.54	30727
周至县	Zhouzhi	146.39	42.24	14.23	89.92	26214
西咸新区（直管区）	Xixian New Area	590.13	40.22	221.24	328.67	57545

注：本表数据为初步核算数。

3-11 各区县生产总值指数（上年＝100）（2021年）

Indices of Gross Domestic Product by Region(preceding year = 100) (2021)

（本表按可比价格计算） (Data in the table are calculated at constant prices)

区 县	Region	地区生产总值 Gross Domestic Product	第一产业 Primary Industry	第二产业 Secondary Industry	第三产业 Tertiary Industry	人均地区生产总值 Per Capita GDP
全 市	**Total**	**104.1**	**106.1**	**100.9**	**105.7**	**100.9**
新城区	Xincheng	106.6		106.5	106.6	106.0
碑林区	Beilin	101.1		85.9	105.9	98.4
莲湖区	Lianhu	100.3		89.6	105.7	97.1
灞桥区	Baqiao	107.7	96.3	106.7	108.7	103.2
未央区	Weiyang	103.7	81.8	101.0	105.8	99.0
雁塔区	Yanta	104.1		101.1	105.0	99.7
阎良区	Yanliang	104.1	103.0	100.1	107.1	102.7
临潼区	Lintong	103.6	107.6	98.9	104.6	103.0
长安区	Chang'an	107.8	106.5	109.7	105.6	103.4
高陵区	Gaoling	100.1	106.3	95.1	106.0	96.5
鄠邑区	Huyi	108.1	107.7	110.8	105.3	106.4
蓝田县	Lantian	106.2	108.4	102.4	106.4	106.2
周至县	Zhouzhi	105.4	108.7	97.1	105.2	105.1
西咸新区（直管区）	Xixian New Area	103.7	106.5	102.0	104.5	100.1

注：本表数据为初步核算数。

3-12 主要年份非公有制经济增加值

The Added Value of Non-public-owned Economic in Representative Years

（本表按当年价格计算） (Data in the table are calculated at current prices)

年 份 Year	非公有制经济增加值 （亿元） the Added Value of Non-public-owned Economic (100 million yuan)	非公有制经济增加值 占GDP比重（%） the Added Value of Non-public-owned Economic Percentage to GDP（%）
2005	560.32	43.3
2006	673.09	44.5
2007	854.57	46.0
2008	1101.11	47.6
2009	1309.57	48.7
2010	1587.94	49.7
2011	1916.95	50.6
2012	2246.26	51.4
2013	2589.24	52.2
2014	2939.07	52.7
2015	3132.55	52.8
2016	3377.28	52.8
2017	3931.72	53.0
2018	4539.52	53.4
2019	5109.00	54.4
2020	5322.60	53.1
2021	5721.03	53.5

注：1.2005-2018年数据根据第四次经济普查GDP修订结果相应进行了调整。2019-2020年数据为最终核实数。
2.2021年数据为初步核算数。

主 要 统 计 指 标 解 释

生产总值（GDP） 是按市场价格计算的一个地区（或国家）所有常住单位在一定时期内生产活动的最终成果。生产总值有三种表现形态，即价值形态、收入形态和产品形态。从价值形态看，它是所有常住单位在一定时期内生产的全部货物和服务价值超过同期中间投入的全部非固定资产货物和服务价值的差额，即所有常住单位的增加值之和；从收入形态看，它是所有常住单位在一定时期内创造并分配给常住单位和非常住单位的初次收入分配之和；从产品形态看，它是所有常住单位在一定时期内最终使用的货物和服务价值与货物和服务净出口价值之和。在实际核算中，生产总值有三种计算方法，即生产法、收入法和支出法。三种方法分别从不同的方面反映生产总值及其构成。

人均生产总值 即"人均GDP"，常作为发展经济学中衡量经济发展状况的指标，是最重要的宏观经济指标之一，它是人们了解和把握一个国家或地区的宏观经济运行状况的有效工具。将一个国家核算期内（通常是一年）实现的国内生产总值与这个国家的常住人口（或户籍人口）相比进行计算，得到人均生产总值。

三次产业 指根据社会生产活动历史发展的顺序对产业结构的划分。目前我国的三次产业划分是：

第一产业是指农、林、牧、渔业（不含农、林、牧、渔服务业）。

第二产业是指采矿业（不含开采辅助活动），制造业（不含金属制品、机械和设备修理业），电力、热力、燃气及水生产和供应业，建筑业。

第三产业即服务业，是指除第一产业、第二产业以外的其他行业。

劳动者报酬 指劳动者因从事生产活动所获得的全部报酬。包括劳动者获得的各种形式的工资、奖金和津贴，既包括货币形式的，也包括实物形式的，还包括劳动者所享受的公费医疗和医药卫生费、上下班交通补贴、单位支付的社会保险费、住房公积金等。

生产税净额 指生产税减生产补贴后的余额。生产税指政府对生产单位从事生产、销售和经营活动以及因从事生产活动使用某些生产要素（如固定资产、土地、劳动力）所征收的各种税、附加费和规费。生产补贴与生产税相反，指政府对生产单位的单方面转移支出，因此视为负生产税，包括政策亏损补贴、价格补贴等。

固定资产折旧 指一定时期内为弥补固定资产损耗按照规定的固定资产折旧率提取的固定资产折旧，或按国民经济核算统一规定的折旧率虚拟计算的固定资产折旧。它反映了固定资产年当期生产中的转移价值。各类企业和企业化管理的事业单位的固定资产折旧是指实际计提的折旧费；不计提折旧的政府机关、非企业化管理的事业单位和居民住房的固定资产折旧是按照统一规定的折旧率和固定资产原值计算的虚拟折旧。原则上，固定资产折旧应按固定资产当期的重置价值计算，但是目前我国尚不具备对全社会固定资产进行重估价的基础，所以暂时只能采用上述办法。

营业盈余 指常住单位创造的增加值扣除劳动者报酬、生产税净额和固定资产折旧后的余额。它相当于企业的营业利润加上生产补贴，但要扣除从利润中开支的工资和福利等。

三次产业贡献率 各产业不变价增加值增量与不变价GDP增量之比。

三次产业拉动率 GDP增长速度与各产业贡献率之乘积。

非公有制经济 非公有制经济是指国民经济中除国有经济和集体经济以外的部分，对其中的混合制经济要依据实收资本之间的比例，按经济成分对各主要经济总量进行划分。

Explanatory Notes on Main Statistical Indicators

Gross Domestic Product (GDP) refers to the final products at market prices produced by all resident units in a country (or a region) during a certain period of time. Gross domestic product is expressed in three different perspectives,namely value,income,and products respectively. GDP in its value perspective refers to the total value of all goods and services produced by all resident units during a certain period of time, minus the total value of input of goods and services of the nature of non-fixed assets; in other words, it is the sum of the value-added of all resident units. GDP from the perspective of income includes the primary income created by all resident units and distributed to resident and non-resident units. GDP from the perspective of products refers to the value of all goods and services for final demand by all resident units plus the net exports of goods and services during a given period of time. In the practice of national accounting,gross domestic product is calculated from three approaches,namely production approach,income approach and expenditure approach, which reflect gross domestic product and its composition from different angles.

Per capita gross domestic product: "per capita GDP", often used as a measure of economic development in development economics, it is one of the most important macroeconomic indicators, and people's understanding and grasp of a country or a region effective tool of macroeconomic performance. The gross domestic product (GDP) of a country's accounting period (usually one year) is divided by the country's resident population (or household population), resulting in per capita GDP.

Three Strata of Industry refer to the division of industrial structure according to the historical clevelopment order of social production activities. In China economic activities are categorized into the following three strata of industry:

Primary industry refers to agriculture, forestry, animal husbandry and fishery excluding agriculture,forestry,animal husbardry and fishery services.

Secondary industry refers to mining and quarrying, manufacturing, production and supply of electricity, water and gas, and construction.

Tertiary industry refers to all other economic activities not included in the primary or secondary industries.

Compensation of Employees refers to the total payment of various forms to employees for the productive activities they are engaged in. It includes wages, bonuses and allowances, which the employees earn in cash or in kind. It also includes the free medical services provided to the employees and the medicine expenses, transport subsidies and social insurance, and housing fund paid by the employers.

Net Taxes on Production refers to taxes on production less subsidies on production. The taxes on production refers to the various taxes, extra charges and fees levied on the production units on their production, sale and business activities as well as on the use of some factors of production, such as fixed assets, land and labour in the production activities they are engaged in. In contrast to taxes on production, subsidies on production refer to the unilateral government transfer to the production units and are therefore regarded as negative taxes on production. They include subsidies on the loss due to implementation of government policies, price subsidies, etc.

Depreciation of Fixed Assets refers to the depreciation of fixed assets in a given period, drawn in accordance with the stipulated depreciation rate for the purpose of compensating the wear-and-tear loss of the fixed assets or the depreciation of fixed assets imputed in accordance with the stipulated unified depreciation rate in the national economic accounting system. It reflects the value of transfer of the fixed assets in the production of the current period. The depreciation of fixed assets in various enterprises and institutions managed as enterprises refers to the depreciation expenses actually drawn. In government agencies and institutions not managed as enterprises which do not draw the depreciation expenses, as well as for the houses of residents, the depreciation of fixed assets is the imputed depreciation, which is calculated in accordance with the stipulated unified depreciation rate. In principle,the depreciation of fixed assets should be calculated on the basis of the re-purchased value of the fixed assets. However, currently the conditions in China do not facilitate the revaluation of all the fixed assets. Therefore, only the above-mentioned methods can be adopted at present.

Operating Surplus refers to the balance of the value added created by the resident units after deducting the labourers remuneration, net taxes on production and the depreciation of fixed assets. It is equivalent to the business profit of the enterprises plus subsidies to production, but the wages and welfare expenses paid from the profits should be deducted.

Three Industry Contribution Rate The ratio of all industries incremental value added to GDP increment at constant prices.

Three Industries Pulling Rate The product of GDP growth rate and the contribution rate of each industry.

Non-public Economy It refers to the part of in addition to state-owned economy and collective economy in the national economy, On which the mixed-economy should be divided according to the major economic components of total economic output based on the proportion in paid-in capital.

4 人口、从业人员与职工工资

POPULATION,EMPLOYEES AND WAGES

资料整理：杨晓柳　张　磊
Data management：Yang Xiaoliu Zhang Lei
数据审核：李　娜
Data audit：Li Na

第四部分　人口、从业人员与职工工资

一、简要说明

（一）人口部分反映西安市人口发展变化基本情况。

1.年末常住人口、性别比例、年龄比例、城镇人口比例以及人口出生率、人口死亡率和人口自然增长率等数据，根据人口普查、1%人口抽样调查或年度人口变动情况抽样调查推算所得，2006–2009年年末常住人口根据2010年第六次全国人口普查数据进行了调整。2011–2019年年末常住人口根据2020年第七次全国人口普查数据进行了修订。2021年年末常住人口不含西安（西咸新区）—咸阳共管区。

2.户籍人口资料数据来源于西安市公安局人口统计年报，为西安原口径数据。

3.人口统计调查方法。目前人口统计调查有：在逢“0”的年份进行全国人口普查；在逢“5”的年份进行全国1%人口抽样调查；其余年份进行人口变动情况抽样调查。

（二）就业部分反映西安市劳动就业与工资的基本情况。

1.主要内容包括全社会从业人员数、城镇非私营单位从业人员数、城镇非私营单位从业人员工资、城镇登记失业率等。（城镇登记失业人数及失业率数据由市人力资源与社会保障局提供并整理）

2.统计范围和调查方法

城镇非私营单位是指城镇地区全部非私营法人单位，具体包括国有单位、集体单位、联营经济、股份制经济、外商投资经济、港澳台投资经济等单位。工资统计是统计单位的从业人员，而个体从业人员、自由职业者等非单位从业人员不在工资统计范围内。

城镇私营单位主要是指在内资法人单位中由自然人投资设立或由自然人控股，以雇佣劳动为基础的营利性经济组织，包括按照《公司法》《合伙企业法》《私营企业暂行条例》规定登记注册的私营有限责任公司、私营股份有限公司、私营合伙企业和私营独资企业。

根据统计调查制度，对一套表法人单位采用全面调查的方法，对非一套表法人单位采用抽样调查的方法。

3.数据发布

由于劳动工资统计调查方法改变，从业人员与职工工资部分自2020年起取消按登记注册类型及机构类型分组数据。

二、主要指标

年末户籍人口（万人）	999.45	比上年增长	2.2%
人口自然增长率（‰）	0.93	比上年下降	0.73个千分点
常住人口（万人）	1287.30	比上年增长（同口径）	1.6%
男女性别比（以女性为100）	104.34	比上年减少	0.05个百分点
户籍人口密度（人／平方公里）	990	比上年增加	21人/平方公里
城镇非私营单位在岗职工年平均工资（元）	115574	比上年增长	10.7%

4 POPULATION,EMPLOYEES AND WAGES

Ⅰ.Brief Introduction

(Ⅰ) Population part reflects the basic conditions of development and changes of population in Xi'an.

1. Permanent population at the year-end, proportion of population by sex, proportion of population by age, proportion of urban population, birth rate, death rate and natural growth rate of population. The data are estimated by Xi'an Bureau of Statistics on the basis of population censuses, the one percent sample survey on population, or annual sample surveys on population changes. Permanent Population at the Year-end from 2006 to 2009 have been adjusted in accordance with the flash sums of the 6th National Population Census in 2010. The resident population and from 2011 to 2019 were revised according to the data of the seventh national census in 2020. Permanent population at the end of 2021 excludes area mutually controlled by Xi'an (Xixian New Area) -Xianyang.

2. The total population with residence registration are obtained from the annual reports of population of Xi'an Public Security Bureau. It is the original caliber data of Xi'an.

3. Investigation methods. The statistical surveys on population are as follows:

The national populationcensus is conducted in the year ending with 0; the national 1 percent population sample survey is conducted in the year ending with 5; sample survey on population changes are conducted in the rest of the years.

(Ⅱ) The employment chapter reflects the basics of employment and wages in Xi'an.

1. It mainly includes the number of all employed persons, the number of employed persons and their wages in urban non-private units, and the registered urban unemployment rate. (The data on the number of registered urban unemployed persons and the registered unemployment rate is provided and processed by the Xi'an Human Resources and Social Security Bureau.)

2. Statistical Coverage and Survey Methods

Urban non-private units refer to all non-private legal units in urban areas, including state-owned units, collective units, joint ownership units, foreign-funded units and units with funds from Hong Kong, Macao & Taiwan. Wages of employed persons in urban non-private units are the persons employed in those units, except the self-employed and freelancers.

Urban private units refer to wage labor-based for-profit units invested and established or controlled by natural persons in domestic legal units, including private limited liability corporations, private shareholding corporations limited, partnership corporations and private sole proprietorship corporations registered in accordance with Company law, Partnership Enterprise Law and Provisional Regulations on Private Enterprises.

According to the statistical survey system, a comprehensive survey method is adopted for a set of legal entities, and a sample survey method is adopted for a non-set of legal entities.

3. Data Release

Due to the change in labor and wage statistics and survey methods, grouping data on the wages of employed persons and workers based on registration type and organization type has been abolished since 2020.

Ⅱ.Major Indicators

		Increase over Preceding Year
Total registered Population of Year-end(10 000 persons)	999.45	2.2%
Natural Growth Rate(‰)	0.93	-0.73per thousand
Permanent Population(10 000 persons)	1287.30	1.6%(Same caliber)
Sex Ratio (Female=100)	104.34	-0.05percentage points
Density of Population (person/sq.km)	990	21person/sq.km
Annual Average Wage of Staff and Workers in Urban Non-privite Enterprises(yuan)	115574	10.7%

4-1 主要年份人口数、人口密度和人口发展情况

Population, Population Density and Population Development in Representative Years

单位：万人 (10 000 persons)

年 份 Year	总人口 Total Population	市区 Urban Area	女性人口 Number of Female	城填人口 Urban Population	人口密度（人/平方公里）Density of Population (person/sq.km)	总人口指数（上年为100）Total Population Index (100 for preceding year) 全市 Whole City	市区 Urban Area
1952	252.92	92.42	118.81	57.61	254	102.6	103.1
1965	400.05	179.88	190.72	136.39	401	102.5	103.4
1970	435.12	188.12	210.47	139.12	436	101.9	101.4
1978	498.10	210.15	241.82	159.98	499	101.7	102.7
1980	511.91	221.19	249.26	172.85	513	101.4	102.6
1985	553.11	245.76	268.40	201.90	554	101.6	102.2
1986	563.97	251.80	273.30	205.92	565	102.0	102.5
1987	574.46	257.69	278.12	210.25	575	101.9	102.3
1988	585.85	264.94	283.68	216.99	587	102.0	102.8
1989	597.36	270.80	289.44	222.54	598	102.0	102.2
1990	608.89	275.69	295.29	226.98	610	101.9	101.8
1991	615.48	419.29	298.13	230.85	617	101.1	152.1
1992	623.20	429.54	301.92	236.45	624	101.3	102.4
1993	630.91	435.41	305.30	240.85	632	101.2	101.4
1994	639.45	442.30	309.17	248.35	641	101.4	101.6
1995	648.21	448.65	313.46	255.71	645	101.4	101.4
1996	654.87	454.68	316.60	261.28	653	101.0	101.3
1997	662.06	461.17	320.18	267.52	663	101.1	101.4
1998	668.22	466.31	323.20	271.75	669	100.9	101.1
1999	674.50	463.56	326.12	276.14	676	100.9	99.4
2000	688.01	483.10	332.83	285.79	689	102.0	104.2
2001	694.84	489.88	336.04	292.62	696	101.0	101.4
2002	702.59	497.38	339.51	300.05	704	101.1	101.5
2003	716.58	510.26	346.26	312.88	718	102.0	102.6
2004	725.01	516.30	350.85	318.50	717	101.2	101.2
2005	741.73	533.21	359.71	333.14	734	102.3	103.3
2006	753.11	540.97	365.74	343.78	745	101.5	101.5
2007	764.25	549.19	371.84	353.85	756	101.5	101.5
2008	772.30	554.73	376.76	363.87	764	101.1	101.0
2009	781.67	561.58	382.39	370.66	773	101.2	101.2
2010	782.73	562.65	383.93	374.64	774	100.1	100.2
2011	791.83	568.77	389.31	391.31	783	101.2	101.1
2012	795.98	572.76	392.04	398.40	788	100.5	100.7
2013	806.93	580.60	398.15	409.82	799	101.4	101.4
2014	815.29	587.16	402.83	418.16	807	101.0	101.1
2015	815.66	588.43	403.43	545.95	808	100.0	100.2
2016	824.93	629.24	408.39	552.21	817	101.1	106.9
2017	845.09	649.08	420.11	567.26	837	102.4	103.2
2018	922.82	725.58	461.31	639.62	914	109.2	111.8
2019	956.74	821.31	479.61	668.57	948	103.7	113.2
2020	977.97	842.39	491.47		969	102.2	102.6
2021	999.45	863.76	503.24		990	102.2	102.5

注：本表为公安年报数据，系户籍人口。2016年起公安年报调整至11月30日，市区数1991年增加临潼、长安，2016年增加高陵，行政区划面积自2012年发生变更，调整了2012年和2013年户籍人口密度。2015年公安局户籍改革，按统计上城乡划分标准统计城镇与乡村人口。户籍人口为西安原口径数据。2019-2020年计算的人口密度所使用的土地面积为2018年数据。由于部门制度变化，自2020年开始，城镇人口数据暂不提供。

4-2 主要年份人口自然变动情况

Natural Population Movements in Representative Years

单位：万人 (10 000 persons)

年 份	出生 Birth		死亡 Death		自然增长率（‰）	迁入人口	迁出人口
	人数	出生率（‰） Birth Rate	人数	死亡率（‰） Death Rate	Natural Growth Rate	Immigrant	Emigrant
Year	Population	（‰）	Population	（‰）	（‰）	Population	Population
1985	8.95	16.30	3.01	5.48	10.82	11.60	8.74
1986	10.14	18.15	2.78	4.97	13.18	11.79	8.39
1987	9.76	17.14	2.83	4.97	12.17	12.58	9.26
1988	9.42	16.24	2.89	4.98	11.26	13.54	8.97
1989	11.78	19.92	3.04	5.13	14.79	12.73	10.15
1990	12.40	20.55	3.45	5.72	14.83	11.82	9.86
1991	8.73	14.25	3.26	5.33	8.92	8.98	6.09
1992	8.98	14.49	3.39	5.48	9.01	13.94	9.54
1993	9.25	14.75	3.37	5.38	9.37	11.50	8.33
1994	8.08	12.71	3.16	4.97	7.74	13.40	8.59
1995	7.69	11.95	3.21	4.98	6.97	14.41	8.85
1996	7.26	11.15	3.41	5.24	5.91	11.94	8.88
1997	6.84	10.38	3.12	4.75	5.63	12.58	8.62
1998	6.40	9.62	3.10	4.66	4.96	10.89	8.36
1999	6.19	9.22	3.88	5.78	3.44	12.58	9.23
2000	8.90	13.07	4.06	5.96	7.11	17.12	9.23
2001	5.11	7.39	2.89	4.19	3.20	15.16	10.83
2002	5.34	7.64	3.08	4.41	3.23	13.90	9.41
2003	6.02	8.48	3.32	4.68	3.80	20.60	9.15
2004	6.63	9.19	4.23	5.87	3.32	15.56	10.19
2005	7.67	9.58	4.13	5.16	4.42	22.61	9.46
2006	8.13	9.98	4.45	5.46	4.52	17.23	11.75
2007	8.27	10.00	4.53	5.48	4.52	19.90	14.01
2008	8.47	10.15	4.65	5.57	4.58	18.49	15.04
2009	8.47	10.08	4.73	5.63	4.45	16.84	13.14
2010	8.23	9.73	4.51	5.34	4.39	14.09	13.50
2011	8.25	9.71	4.57	5.38	4.33	14.21	11.74
2012	8.64	10.13	4.75	5.57	4.56	12.55	13.10
2013	8.20	9.57	4.60	5.37	4.20	10.83	8.60
2014	8.70	10.11	4.71	5.47	4.64	9.10	7.61
2015	8.80	10.15	4.78	5.51	4.64	8.08	11.61
2016	10.12	11.54	4.74	5.40	6.14	6.21	4.68
2017	12.03	12.62	5.17	5.42	7.20	25.22	4.94
2018	12.23	12.47	5.38	5.48	6.99	76.53	8.02
2019	12.45	12.32	5.59	5.53	6.79	30.81	6.21
2020	11.85	9.14	9.69	7.48	1.66	22.45	7.28
2021	10.86	8.44	9.67	7.51	0.93	22.65	7.46

注：2004年以前为公安年报数据。迁入人口和迁出人口为公安年报数据。公安数据为西安原口径数据。2010年、2020年出生、死亡、自然增长率根据人口普查数据推算得出。2005-2009年、2011-2019年及2021年出生、死亡、自然增长率为人口变动抽样调查推算数据。

4-3 主要年份人口年龄构成和抚养比

Population Age Composition and Dependency Ratio in Representative Years

单位：% (%)

年份 Year	各年龄段人口比重 Proportion of Population of All Ages 0-14岁 0-14 years old	15-64岁 15-64 years old	65岁及以上 65 year old and above	总抚养比 Total Dependency Ratio	少年儿童 Children	老年人口 Elderly Population
1990	25.71	69.08	5.21	44.76	37.21	7.55
2000	22.27	71.26	6.47	40.33	31.25	9.08
2010	12.89	78.65	8.46	27.15	16.39	10.76
2011	12.57	78.33	9.10	27.66	16.04	11.62
2012	12.54	78.02	9.44	28.17	16.07	12.10
2013	12.46	77.88	9.66	28.40	16.00	12.40
2014	12.52	77.46	10.02	29.10	16.16	12.94
2015	12.56	76.94	10.50	29.98	16.33	13.65
2016	12.76	76.35	10.89	30.97	16.71	14.26
2017	13.63	75.20	11.17	32.97	18.12	14.85
2018	13.75	74.96	11.29	33.40	18.34	15.06
2019	13.90	74.41	11.69	34.39	18.68	15.71
2020	15.65	73.45	10.90	36.14	21.30	14.84
2021	15.59	72.37	12.04	38.18	21.54	16.64

注：1990年、2000年、2010年、2020年数据根据人口普查数据加工整理，2011-2019年、2021年数据根据人口变动抽样调查数据推算，自2017年起数据包含西咸新区，2021年数据不含西安（西咸新区）—咸阳共管区。抚养比指0-14岁、65岁及以上人口与15-64岁人口的之比。

4-4 全市及各区县人口数和户数（2021年）

Population and Households by Region (2021)

单位：万人 (10 000 persons)

区县	Region	总户数（万户） Number of Households (10 000 households)	总人口 Total Population	按性别划分 Grouped by Sex 男 Male	女 Female	迁入人口（人） Immigrant Population (person)	迁出人口（人） Emigrant Population (person)
全市	**Total**	**321.21**	**999.45**	**496.21**	**503.24**	**226507**	**74552**
新城区	Xincheng	18.60	53.44	26.29	27.15	9716	4089
碑林区	Beilin	23.48	73.35	36.12	37.23	19761	9351
莲湖区	Lianhu	28.14	78.10	38.04	40.06	20602	6610
灞桥区	Baqiao	23.40	70.04	33.98	36.06	16121	3727
未央区	Weiyang	36.20	109.79	52.91	56.89	49491	12280
雁塔区	Yanta	45.51	143.15	69.67	73.48	64177	17225
阎良区	Yanliang	9.04	27.65	13.84	13.81	1881	1258
临潼区	Lintong	24.08	73.21	37.03	36.18	3836	1985
长安区	Chang'an	42.02	132.71	65.77	66.94	24812	6733
高陵区	Gaoling	11.84	37.84	18.63	19.21	4864	1313
鄠邑区	Huyi	19.29	64.48	32.92	31.56	3992	2292
蓝田县	Lantian	20.22	65.76	34.17	31.59	4081	3755
周至县	Zhouzhi	19.40	69.93	36.86	33.07	3173	3934

注：本表均为公安年报数据，为西安原口径数据。表中数据未机械配平。

4-5 全市及各区县常住人口数和人口变动情况（2021年）

Permanent Population and Population Changes by Region (2021)

区 县	Region	常住人口（万人） Permanent Population (10 000 persons)	城镇 Urban	出生率（‰） Birth Rate (‰)	死亡率（‰） Death Rate (‰)	自然增长率（‰） Natural Growth Rate (‰)
全 市	**Total**	**1287.30**	**1023.27**	**8.44**	**7.51**	**0.93**
新城区	Xincheng	62.25	62.25	6.74	6.72	0.02
碑林区	Beilin	76.96	76.96	6.14	6.06	0.08
莲湖区	Lianhu	102.93	102.93	6.93	6.31	0.62
灞桥区	Baqiao	102.96	100.99	8.45	7.55	0.90
未央区	Weiyang	158.83	158.83	8.57	7.28	1.29
雁塔区	Yanta	208.66	208.66	8.83	6.61	2.22
阎良区	Yanliang	30.73	17.95	7.80	7.41	0.39
临潼区	Lintong	68.13	24.92	7.65	7.64	0.01
长安区	Chang'an	162.24	103.33	8.94	8.46	0.48
高陵区	Gaoling	45.75	30.04	9.94	8.52	1.42
鄠邑区	Huyi	58.69	26.18	9.15	8.67	0.48
蓝田县	Lantian	49.54	17.43	9.05	9.66	-0.61
周至县	Zhouzhi	55.99	16.93	10.12	9.99	0.13
西咸新区	Xixian New Area	103.64	75.87	9.35	7.36	1.99

注：本表数据均为人口变动抽样调查推算数据。2021年西咸新区数据不含西安（西咸新区）—咸阳共管区。

4-6 全市及各区县常住人口数和人口变动情况（2020年）

Permanent Population and Population Changes by Region (2020)

区 县	Region	常住人口（万人） Permanent Population (10 000 persons)	城镇 Urban	出生率（‰） Birth Rate (‰)	死亡率（‰） Death Rate (‰)	自然增长率（‰） Natural Growth Rate (‰)
全 市	**Total**	**1296.00**	**1026.43**	**9.14**	**7.48**	**1.66**
新城区	Xincheng	61.80	61.80	6.87	6.71	0.16
碑林区	Beilin	75.80	75.80	6.19	6.03	0.16
莲湖区	Lianhu	101.90	101.90	8.28	6.27	2.01
灞桥区	Baqiao	102.10	100.13	9.51	7.52	1.99
未央区	Weiyang	155.60	155.60	9.64	7.26	2.38
雁塔区	Yanta	204.90	204.90	9.42	6.59	2.83
阎良区	Yanliang	30.30	17.67	8.81	7.39	1.42
临潼区	Lintong	67.60	24.68	8.25	7.62	0.63
长安区	Chang'an	158.70	100.98	9.35	8.44	0.91
高陵区	Gaoling	44.20	29.00	10.85	8.49	2.36
鄠邑区	Huyi	57.70	25.71	9.14	8.62	0.52
蓝田县	Lantian	49.20	16.80	9.22	9.63	-0.41
周至县	Zhouzhi	55.70	16.22	10.80	9.94	0.86
西咸新区	Xixian New Area	130.50	95.36	10.24	7.33	2.91

注：本表数据根据人口普查数据推算得出。城镇人口数未机械配平。

4-7 主要年份常住人口数

Permanent Population in Representative Years

单位：万人 (10 000 persons)

年 份 year	年末常住人口 Permanent Population (year-end)	城镇 Urban	乡村 Rural
2000	741.14	450.36	290.78
2005	806.81	510.55	296.26
2006	822.52	530.94	291.58
2007	830.54	548.99	281.55
2008	837.52	565.16	272.36
2009	843.46	581.40	262.06
2010	847.41	584.71	262.70
2011	887	620.00	267.00
2012	914	659.26	254.74
2013	936	689.01	246.99
2014	960	714.94	245.06
2015	988	747.71	240.29
2016	1030	789.50	240.50
2017	1134	874.55	259.45
2018	1191	927.23	263.77
2019	1235	972.89	262.11
2020	1296	1026.43	269.57
2021	1287.30	1023.27	264.03

注：2000年常住人口为普查数据。2005-2009年、2021年常住人口为人口变动抽样调查推算数据。2010年、2020年常住人口为年末常住人口数，根据人口普查数据推算得出。2011-2019年常住人口依据第七次人口普查数据进行修订。2017-2020年常住口径数据为大西安范围，含西咸新区。2021年数据不含西安（西咸新区）—咸阳共管区。

4-8 主要年份社会从业人数

单位：万人

年 份 Year	合计 Total	一、按城乡分 Grouped by Urban Area and Rural Area				
		1.城镇 Urban	国有经济 State-owned Enterprises	集体经济 Collective Enterprises	其他经济 Others	2.乡村 Village
1985	**296.80**	129.07	96.80	29.07	3.20	167.73
1986	**299.45**	132.82	101.28	28.43	3.11	166.63
1987	**312.16**	138.56	104.58	30.72	3.26	173.60
1988	**327.76**	142.24	106.46	30.73	5.05	185.52
1989	**332.65**	145.65	108.80	30.44	6.41	187.00
1990	**343.06**	147.93	110.95	29.78	7.20	195.13
1991	**347.65**	149.48	111.87	29.80	7.81	198.17
1992	**357.51**	151.67	113.19	29.97	8.51	205.84
1993	**363.70**	155.72	112.98	29.77	12.97	207.98
1994	**364.56**	154.88	113.39	27.97	13.52	209.68
1995	**372.60**	158.80	113.79	25.58	19.43	213.80
1996	**379.29**	164.54	113.29	24.82	26.43	214.75
1997	**385.14**	169.52	112.44	23.52	33.56	215.62
1998	**393.95**	177.20	106.06	21.50	49.64	216.75
1999	**400.43**	180.27	105.08	20.50	54.69	220.16
2000	**389.10**	176.45	103.46	18.40	54.59	212.65
2001	**389.30**	177.94	100.47	17.10	60.37	211.36
2002	**397.16**	181.85	100.54	16.90	64.41	215.31
2003	**404.92**	183.23	94.51	16.78	71.94	221.69
2004	**409.57**	187.53	93.43	15.41	78.69	222.04
2005	**415.83**	192.53	93.27	14.47	84.79	223.30
2006	**422.15**	196.16	84.46	14.41	97.29	225.99
2007	**436.36**	214.27	90.58	11.88	111.81	222.09
2008	**448.05**	224.20	90.17	10.60	123.43	223.85
2009	**462.52**	239.39	90.83	7.63	140.93	223.13
2010	**477.58**	252.54	94.01	5.48	153.05	225.04
2011	**495.99**	265.43	91.62	5.33	168.48	230.56
2012	**514.57**	287.65	95.33	5.10	187.22	226.92
2013	**530.71**	308.04	86.06	7.29	214.69	222.67
2014	**532.92**	316.59	84.83	6.67	225.09	216.33
2015	**528.06**	327.68	84.52	5.29	237.87	200.38
2016	**539.18**	335.07	87.15	4.85	243.07	204.11
2017	**596.21**	370.33	86.06	4.46	279.81	225.88
2018	**621.22**	398.23	80.83	3.53	313.87	222.99
2019	**645.86**	421.75	75.84	3.28	342.63	224.11
2020	**664.45**	443.29				221.16
2021	**686.53**	473.06				213.47

注：1.第一产业从业人员中包括城镇农林牧渔及服务业企业人员。
2.因劳动工资统计调查制度改变，自2020年起，取消分登记注册类型、机构类型分组数据，下同。

Number of Social Laborers in Representative Years

(10 000 persons)

二、按三次产业分 Grouped by Industry		
第一产业 Primary Industry	第二产业 Secondary Industry	第三产业 Tertiary Industry
135.89	98.61	62.30
127.46	100.61	71.38
130.36	107.75	74.05
138.87	108.12	80.77
142.21	106.40	84.04
149.64	106.74	86.68
152.24	108.19	87.22
154.75	110.22	92.54
154.02	114.02	95.66
153.51	108.53	102.52
153.39	109.67	109.54
153.43	109.17	116.69
153.23	109.46	122.45
153.00	110.45	130.50
154.64	110.58	135.21
147.03	107.26	134.81
145.09	108.96	135.25
143.04	111.62	142.50
146.67	109.09	149.16
141.81	111.70	156.06
136.31	114.20	165.32
135.10	116.09	170.96
133.33	125.06	177.97
127.87	130.23	189.95
122.13	131.57	208.82
117.27	145.40	214.91
121.05	151.33	223.61
114.92	162.35	237.30
110.45	151.50	268.76
105.02	151.85	276.05
107.68	129.51	290.87
105.12	127.88	306.18
113.17	135.52	347.52
101.25	154.02	365.95
101.37	164.54	379.95
99.97	155.84	408.64
99.69	152.50	434.34

4-9　按国民经济行业分从业人数（2021年）

单位：万人

行　业	Sector	合计 Total
总计	**Total**	**686.53**
（一）农、林、牧、渔业	Agriculture,Forestry,Animal Husbandry and Fishery	99.69
（二）采矿业	Mining	4.86
（三）制造业	Manufacturing	79.39
（四）电力、热力、燃气及水生产和供应业	Production and Supply of Electricity,Gas,Heat and Water	7.18
（五）建筑业	Construction	61.07
（六）批发和零售业	Wholesale and Retail Trades	114.65
（七）交通运输、仓储和邮政业	Traffic,Transport,Storage and Post	42.30
（八）住宿和餐饮业	Hotels and Catering Services	64.17
（九）信息传输、软件和信息技术服务业	Information Transmission,Software and Information Technology Services	18.50
（十）金融业	Financial Intermediation	13.15
（十一）房地产业	Real Estate	19.68
（十二）租赁和商务服务业	Leasing and Business Services	31.02
（十三）科学研究和技术服务业	Scientific Research and Technical Services	21.07
（十四）水利、环境和公共设施管理业	Management of Water Conservancy,Environment and Public Facilities	3.64
（十五）居民服务、修理和其他服务业	Services to Households,Repairs and Other Services	31.06
（十六）教育	Education	33.67
（十七）卫生和社会工作	Health and Social Work	23.37
（十八）文化、体育和娱乐业	Culture,Sports and Entertainment	4.94
（十九）公共管理、社会保障和社会组织	Public Administration,Social Security and Social Organizations	13.12
（二十）国际组织	International Organizations	

Number of Employed Persons Grouped by Industry of the National Economy (2021)

(10 000 persons)

城镇非私营 Urban Non-Private Units	城镇私营及个体劳动者 Urban Private Enterprises and Individual Labors	乡村从业人员 Rural Employed Persons
202.90	**270.16**	**213.47**
0.22	2.40	97.07
4.71	0.15	
39.50	24.90	14.99
6.37	0.81	
19.48	24.92	16.67
10.50	83.86	20.29
18.40	12.77	11.13
5.03	47.30	11.84
10.36	7.23	0.91
11.06	1.33	0.76
8.53	11.15	
6.18	15.85	8.99
13.94	6.41	0.72
2.63	1.01	
0.48	17.95	12.63
20.90	5.64	7.13
10.79	3.59	8.99
2.21	2.73	
11.61	0.16	1.35

4-10 城镇非私营单位从业人员情况（2021年）

单位：人

分组	Classify	单位从业人员 Employed Persons	女性 Female
总计	**Total**	**2029002**	**801903**
（一）农、林、牧、渔业	Agriculture,Forestry,Animal Husbandry and Fishery	2178	630
（二）采矿业	Mining	47091	14966
（三）制造业	Manufacturing	394967	121639
（四）电力、热力、燃气及水生产和供应业	Production and Supply of Electricity,Gas,Heat and Water	63710	19156
（五）建筑业	Construction	194816	35233
（六）批发和零售业	Wholesale and Retail Trades	105043	56886
（七）交通运输、仓储和邮政业	Traffic,Transport,Storage and Post	184048	44550
（八）住宿和餐饮业	Hotels and Catering Services	50262	29243
（九）信息传输、软件和信息技术服务业	Information Transmission,Software and Information Technology Services	103563	35992
（十）金融业	Financial Intermediation	110564	66370
（十一）房地产业	Real Estate	85250	38104
（十二）租赁和商务服务业	Leasing and Business Services	61768	20315
（十三）科学研究和技术服务业	Scientific Research and Technical Services	139445	43109
（十四）水利、环境和公共设施管理业	Management of Water Conservancy,Environment and Public Facilities	26339	9755
（十五）居民服务、修理和其他服务业	Services to Households,Repairs and Other Services	4817	2466
（十六）教育	Education	209039	131158
（十七）卫生和社会工作	Health and Social Work	107868	79656
（十八）文化、体育和娱乐业	Culture,Sports and Entertainment	22139	11070
（十九）公共管理、社会保障和社会组织	Public Administration,Social Security and Social Organizations	116096	41605
（二十）国际组织	International Organizations		

注：自2018年开始，表名中“全部单位”改为“城镇非私营单位”。下同。

Basic Facts on Employees in Urban Non-Private Units (2021)

(person)

在岗职工合计 Total Fully Employed Staff and Workers	其他从业人员 Other Employed Persons	单位从业人员 平均人数 Average Employment	在岗职工合计 Staff and Workers	其他从业人员 Other Employed Persons
1913381	**115621**	**2067547**	**1924011**	**143536**
2097	81	2153	2076	77
46971	120	46842	46238	604
389591	5376	397382	392430	4952
63370	340	78147	77022	1125
180007	14809	187593	174066	13527
101661	3382	105633	101746	3887
182166	1882	223168	218893	4275
45004	5258	50555	45103	5452
102562	1001	99361	98244	1117
66639	43925	116316	65906	50410
83522	1728	85323	83609	1714
51169	10599	61360	51721	9639
135527	3918	132192	127814	4378
25348	991	26798	25352	1446
4660	157	5014	4874	140
196675	12364	210121	197215	12906
104762	3106	105493	102360	3133
21138	1001	22581	21453	1128
110511	5585	115445	109916	5529

4-11 主要年份城镇非私营单位分行业从业人员年平均工资

单位：元

分 组	Classify	2010	2011
总计	**Total**	**37870**	**41679**
（一）农、林、牧、渔业	Agriculture,Forestry,Animal Husbandry and Fishery	21436	23567
（二）采矿业	Mining	32154	38551
（三）制造业	Manufacturing	26663	34698
（四）电力、热力、燃气及水生产和供应业	Production and Distribution of Electricity,Gas and Water	39508	47705
（五）建筑业	Construction	26875	29773
（六）批发和零售业	Wholesale and Retail Trades	25103	27996
（七）交通运输、仓储和邮政业	Traffic,Transport,Storage and Post	41737	48231
（八）住宿和餐饮业	Hotels and Catering Services	19647	22925
（九）信息传输、软件和信息技术服务业	Information Transmission,Software and Information Technology Services	45904	51135
（十）金融业	Financial Intermediation	63952	72195
（十一）房地产业	Real Estate	45273	34626
（十二）租赁和商务服务业	Leasing and Business Services	30267	31549
（十三）科学研究和技术服务业	Scientific Research and Technical Services	55456	64448
（十四）水利、环境和公共设施管理业	Management of Water Conservancy,Environment and Public Facilities	25322	26009
（十五）居民服务、修理和其他服务业	Services to Households,Repairs and Other Services	26443	23993
（十六）教育	Education	53084	54442
（十七）卫生和社会工作	Health and Social Work	44035	48836
（十八）文化、体育和娱乐业	Culture,Sports and Entertainment	31925	34717
（十九）公共管理、社会保障和社会组织	Public Administration,Social Security and Social Organizations	39964	42163
（二十）国际组织	International Organizations		

Average Wages of Urban Non-private Employees by Industry in Representative Years

(yuan)

2012	2013	2014	2015	2016	2017	2018	2019	2020	2021
44533	**49350**	**54573**	**60557**	**67205**	**75262**	**83821**	**92359**	**99315**	**111078**
31846	36658	42881	43426	48626	52020	72890	81373	90218	90398
33489	40605	42116	46645	108827	118026	99400	106393	143464	148993
38957	44321	49482	56686	61434	66067	73733	80703	90921	100250
55409	59955	61252	65887	69092	77674	70021	75545	103286	113155
35828	39507	48275	52783	60475	68025	73963	81621	93794	104178
34382	37362	40915	46203	48210	55793	62362	68787	71766	81090
48760	54147	59189	62816	63583	69469	88547	97746	86829	92594
26637	29497	30914	33746	37507	41147	42970	46523	44332	49963
63328	67495	100550	109448	137210	142407	150081	167240	174214	215565
75652	97140	104433	106807	108569	114884	108643	114753	108142	148346
37567	44832	48120	52423	56979	57970	65726	72780	79854	83972
34291	42109	46828	52637	54395	53474	54940	62628	65332	75315
68274	69951	69958	72731	79539	86199	103604	118277	129654	143774
29938	38429	43033	45356	44062	48277	54127	59967	67155	67194
25103	32066	32478	37019	35721	35979	56707	62097	52864	57174
54581	59143	58451	63761	71635	86672	98158	103991	112030	117034
56764	61602	59892	61623	74797	86521	99523	108493	114177	120894
40833	50201	57239	61561	65974	70202	74588	81117	84900	92669
47691	49893	47000	51681	59437	77660	84567	90877	97134	99757

4-12 主要年份城镇非私营单位从业人数及工资总额

年 份 year	单位从业人员 （万人） Number of Employed Persons (10 000 persons)	从业人员工资总额 （亿元） Remuneration of Employed Persons (100mil. Yuan)	城镇非私营单位从业人员年平均工资 （元） Annual Average Wage of Employees in Urban Non-private Units(yuan)
1978	93.56	6.28	688
1980	103.09	8.17	818
1985	127.04	14.17	1148
1986	132.78	16.87	1311
1987	135.48	19.13	1446
1988	137.56	22.81	1702
1989	139.86	25.64	1873
1990	141.55	29.48	2133
1991	142.86	26.88	2276
1992	144.51	30.80	2545
1993	146.03	43.25	2999
1994	142.37	58.87	4172
1995	141.17	67.23	4763
1996	140.60	75.64	5407
1997	138.89	80.83	5785
1998	138.78	82.85	6900
1999	115.88	90.13	7764
2000	112.45	103.80	9179
2001	113.93	123.12	10786
2002	115.77	138.88	12138
2003	116.68	155.95	13504
2004	118.15	184.63	15473
2005	123.66	215.67	17728
2006	125.10	250.87	20475
2007	129.40	319.23	25012
2008	130.85	379.29	29749
2009	135.64	450.48	34032
2010	140.38	520.88	37870
2011	154.33	658.73	41679
2012	165.59	770.86	44533
2013	198.42	1031.46	49350
2014	199.41	1151.53	54573
2015	198.46	1255.75	60557
2016	199.19	1358.95	67205
2017	202.29	1542.35	75262
2018	196.23	1677.57	83821
2019	211.31	1992.54	92359
2020	213.57	2175.60	99315
2021	202.90	2296.59	111078

注：因1989年以前，西安市行政区划有几次调整，本表按1989年西安行政区划对1989年前的历史数据进行了修订。

Number of Urban Non-Private Employees and Remuneration in Representative Years

城镇国有单位 从业人员年平均工资 （元） Annual Average Wage of Employees in State-owned Units(yuan)	城镇集体单位 从业人员年平均工资 （元） Annual Average Wage of Employees in Urban Collective Units(yuan)	城镇非私营其他经济 类型单位从业人员年平均工资 （元） Average Wages of Urban Non-private Basic Facts on Employees in other Units(yuan)
705	609	
849	699	
1215	923	1409
1388	1048	1659
1544	1107	1583
1842	1216	2065
2010	1385	2188
2290	1545	2044
2435	1657	2966
2758	1709	3504
3274	1910	3551
4588	2337	5243
5168	2837	5863
5858	3216	6225
6204	3437	7487
7445	3964	6942
8238	4374	8217
9742	5178	9451
11570	5431	10781
12877	6230	12543
14217	6892	14215
15994	7428	17030
18420	7612	19066
21392	8494	21859
25696	9768	27400
30246	10834	33344
34611	11940	37307
38122	12505	40721
45217	23241	37643
47493	29988	41218
52782	34591	47462
54138	41006	55766
60301	43291	61590
66295	48098	68847
76682	54755	74999
87096	53048	82239
101187	49998	88142

4-13 城镇非私营单位从业人员工资总额（2021年）

单位：万元

分 组	Classify	单位从业人员工资总额 Total Wages of Employment
总计	**Total**	**22965940**
（一）农、林、牧、渔业	Agriculture,Forestry,Animal Husbandry and Fishery	19460
（二）采矿业	Mining	697911
（三）制造业	Manufacturing	3983757
（四）电力、热力、燃气及水生产和供应业	Production and Supply of Electricity, Gas,Heat and Water	884278
（五）建筑业	Construction	1954296
（六）批发和零售业	Wholesale and Retail Trades	856585
（七）交通运输、仓储和邮政业	Traffic,Transport,Storage and Post	2066399
（八）住宿和餐饮业	Hotels and Catering Services	252584
（九）信息传输、软件和信息技术服务业	Information Transmission,Software and Information Technology Services	2141867
（十）金融业	Financial Intermediation	1725506
（十一）房地产业	Real Estate	716475
（十二）租赁和商务服务业	Leasing and Business Services	462136
（十三）科学研究和技术服务业	Scientific Research and Technical Services	1900578
（十四）水利、环境和公共设施管理业	Management of Water Conservancy,Environment and Public Facilities	180068
（十五）居民服务、修理和其他服务业	Services to Households,Repairs and Other Services	28667
（十六）教育	Education	2459125
（十七）卫生和社会工作	Health and Social Work	1275348
（十八）文化、体育和娱乐业	Culture,Sports and Entertainment	209258
（十九）公共管理、社会保障和社会组织	Public Administration,Social Security and Social Organizations	1151642
（二十）国际组织	International Organizations	

Total Wages of Urban Non-Private Units Employees (2021)

(10 000 yuan)

在岗职工 工资总额 Total Wages of Employed Staff and Workers	其他从业人员 工资总额 Remuneration of Other Employed Persons	从业人员年 平均工资 （元） Average Wages of Employees (yuan)
22236570	**729370**	**111078**
19232	228	90398
696952	959	148993
3952166	31591	100250
879183	5095	113155
1832888	121408	104178
836083	20502	81090
2046104	20295	92594
243739	8845	49963
2127254	14613	215565
1514701	210805	148346
710361	6114	83972
413224	48912	75315
1868396	32182	143774
175340	4728	67194
28061	606	57174
2394213	64912	117034
1252101	23247	120894
203527	5731	92669
1132904	18738	99757

4-14 主要年份城镇登记失业人数及失业率

Registered Unemployed Persons and Unemployment Rate in Urban Area in Representative Years

年 份 year	城镇登记失业人员数（万人） Real Number of Registered Unemployed Persons(10 000 persons)	城镇登记失业率（%） Registered Unemployment in Urban Area(%)
2002		3.7
2003		4.5
2004	8.29	4.3
2005	8.45	4.3
2006	8.74	4.3
2007	8.77	4.3
2008	9.40	4.2
2009	10.02	4.3
2010	10.46	4.2
2011	10.37	3.9
2012	9.60	3.5
2013	10.13	3.4
2014	10.84	3.4
2015	10.74	3.4
2016	11.29	3.3
2017	11.51	3.3
2018	12.48	3.3
2019	12.52	3.3
2020	13.76	3.6
2021	15.77	3.6

注：本表数据由西安市人力资源和社会保障局提供。

主要统计指标解释

人口数 指一定时点、一定地区范围内的有生命的个人的总和。年度统计的年末人口数，指每年12月31日24时的人口数。

常住人口 指实际经常居住在某地区一定时间（半年以上，含半年）的人口。常住人口包括户口在本辖区人也在本辖区居住的人，户口在本辖区之外但在户口登记地半年以上的人，户口待定（无户口和口袋户口）的人，户口在本辖区但离开本辖区半年以下的人。

城镇人口和乡村人口 城镇人口是指居住在城镇范围内的全部常住人口；乡村人口是除上述人口以外的全部人口。

出生率（又称粗出生率） 指在一定时期内（通常为一年）平均每千人所出生的人数的比率，一般用千分率表示。其计算公式为：

出生率＝年出生人数／年平均人数×1000‰

式中：出生人数指活产婴儿，即胎儿脱离母体时（不管怀孕月数），有过呼吸或其他生命现象。年平均人数指年初、年底人口数的平均数，也可用年中人口数代替。

死亡率（又称粗死亡率） 指在一定时期内（通常为一年）一定地区的死亡人数与同期内平均人数（或期中人数）之比，一般用千分率表示。本资料中的死亡率指年死亡率，其计算公式为：

死亡率＝年死亡人数／年平均人数×1000‰

人口自然增长率 指在一定时期内（通常为一年）人口自然增加数（出生人数减死亡人数）与该时期内平均人数（或期中人数）之比，一般用千分率表示。计算公式为：

人口自然增长率＝（本年出生人数—本年死亡人数）／年平均人数×1000‰。

从业人员 指在16周岁及以上，从事一定社会劳动并取得劳动报酬或经营收入的人员。这一指标反映了一定时期内全部劳动力资源的实际利用情况，是研究我国基本国情国力的重要指标。

单位从业人员 指在各级国家机关、政党机关、社会团体及企业、事业单位中工作，取得工资或其他形式的劳动报酬的全部人员。包括在岗职工、再就业的离退休人员、民办教师以及在各单位中工作的外方人员和港澳台方人员、兼职人员、借用的外单位人员和第二职业者。不包括离开本单位仍保留劳动关系的职工。各单位的就业人员反映了各单位实际参加生产或工作的全部劳动力。

城镇私营和个体就业人员 城镇私营就业人员指在工商管理部门注册登记，其经营地址设在县城关镇（含城关镇）以上的私营企业就业人员；包括私营企业投资者和雇工。城镇个体就业人员指在工商管理部门注册登记，并持有城镇户口或在城镇长期居住，经批准从事个体工商经营的就业人员；包括个体经营者和在个体工商户劳动的家庭帮工和雇工。

国有单位 指资产归国家所有的经济组织。包括按《中华人民共和国企业法人登记管理条例》规定登记注册的非公司制的经济组织，以及中央、地方各级国家机关、事业单位和社会团体。

集体单位 指生产资料归集体所有，并按《中华人民共和国企业法人登记管理条例》规定登记注册的经济组织。

其他单位 包括股份合作单位、联营单位、有限责任公司、股份有限公司、港澳台商投资单位以及外商投资单位等其他登记注册类型单位。

在岗职工 指在本单位工作并由单位支付工资的人员，以及有工作岗位，但由于学习、病伤产假等原因暂未工作，仍由单位支付工资的人员。

职工工资总额 指各单位在一定时期内直接支付给本单位全部职工的劳动报酬总额。工资总额的计算原则应以直接支付给职工的全部劳动报酬为根据。各单位支付给职工的劳动报酬以及其他根据有关规定支付的工资，不论是计入成本的还是不计入成本的，不论是按国家规定列入计征奖金税项目的，还是未列入计征奖金税项目的，不论是以货币形式支付的还是以实物形式支付的，均包括在工资总额内。

职工平均工资 指企业、事业、机关单位的职工在一定时期内平均每人所得的货币工资额。它表明一定时期职工工资收入的高低程度，是反映职工工资水平的主要指标。计算公式为：

职工平均工资＝报告期实际支付的全部职工工资总额/报告期全部职工平均人数

城镇登记失业人员 指有非农业户口，在一定的劳动年龄内，有劳动能力，无业而要求就业，并在当地就业服务机构进行求职登记的人员。

城镇登记失业率 指城镇登记失业人数同城镇从业人数与城镇从业人数与城镇登记失业人数之和的比。计算公式为：

$$\text{城镇登记失业率}=\frac{\text{城镇登记失业人数}}{\text{（城镇单位就业人员–使用的农村劳动力–聘用的离退休人员–聘用的港澳台及外方人员）+不在岗职工+城镇私营业主+城镇个体户主+城镇私营企业及个体就业人员+城镇登记失业人数}}\times 100\%$$

Explanatory Notes on Main Statistical Indicators

The annual statistics on total population is taken at midnight, the 31st of December, not including residents in Taiwan province, Hong Kong SAR and Macao SAR and Chinese national residing abroad.

Permanent population refers to the population of actual habitual residence in a certain area six months or over six months. Permanent popul ation include the accounts in this area which are also living in this area, accounts outside this area but with more than half a year of household registration, accounts to be determined including people without accounts or pockets of accounts, and accounts in the area but leaving this area less than six months.

Urban Population and Rural Population Urban population refers to all people residing in cities and towns, while rural population refers to population other than urban population.

Birth Rate (or Crude Birth Rate) refers to the ratio of the number of births to the average population (or mid-period population) during a certain period of time (usually one year), expressed in ‰. Birth rate in the chapter refers to annual birth rate. The following formula is used:

$$\text{Birth Rate}=\frac{\text{Number of Births}}{\text{Annual Average Population}}\times 1000‰$$

Number of births in the formula refers to live births, i.e. when a baby has breathed or showed any vital phenomena regardless of the length of pregnancy.

Annual average population is the average of the number of population at the beginning of the year and that at the end of the year. Sometimes it is substituted by the mid-year population.

Death Rate (or Crude Death Rate) refers to the ratio of the number of deaths to the average population (or mid-period population) during a certain period of time (usually one year), expressed in ‰. Death rate in the chapter refers to annual death rate. The following formula is used:

$$\text{DeathRate}=\frac{\text{Number of Deaths}}{\text{Annual Average Population}}\times 1000‰$$

Natural Growth Rate of Population refers to the ratio of natural increase in population (number of births minus number of deaths) in a certain period of time (usually one year) to the average population (or mid-period population) of the same period, expressed in ‰. The following formula is applied:

Natural Growth Rate of Population =(Number of Births-Number of Deaths)/Annual Average Population× 1000‰

Employed Persons refer to the ones aged 16 and over who are engaged in gainful employment and thus receive remuneration payment or earn business income. This indicator reflects the actual utilization of total labour force during a certain period of time and is often used for the research on China's economic situation and national power.

Persons Employed in Various Units refer to all the persons working in government agencies of various levels, political and party organizations, social organizations, enterprises and institutions, and receiving wages or other forms of payment. They include fully-employed staff and workers, re-employed retirees, teachers in the schools run by the local people, foreigners and Chinese compatriots from Hong Kong, Macao, and Taiwan working in various units, part-time employees, employees of other units working temporarily at current posts, and employees holding the second job, but do not include persons who have left their working units while keeping their labour contract (employment relation) unchanged. This indicator reflects the total number of laborers actually engaged in production or other operations in various units.

Persons Employed in Private Enterprises and Self- Employed Individuals in Urban Areas Persons employed in private enterprises refer to the persons employed in the private enterprises which have been registered at the departments of industrial and commercial administration for which the business operation are situated at a county town (i.e. a town where the county government is located), or at urban areas with administrative hierarchy higher than a county town. The self-employed individuals in urban areas refer to persons who hold the certificates of residence in urban areas or have resided in the urban areas for a long time and have been registered at the departments of industrial and commercial administration and approved to be engaged in individual industrial or commercial business, including self-employed persons as well as helpers and hired labourers who work in individual households.

State-owned Units refer to economic units whose assets are owned by the state, including non-corporation units registered according to Regulation of the People's Republic of China on the Registration of Enterprises and

Corporations, state organs, institutions and social organizations at the central-level and local levels.

Collective-owned Units refer to economic units registered according to Regulation of the People's Republic of China on the Registration of Enterprises and Corporations where the means of production are collectively owned.

Units of Other Types of Ownership refer to units registered with other types of ownership, including cooperative units, joint ownership units, limited liability corporations, share holding corporations, units funded by entrepreneurs from Hong Kong, Macao, and Taiwan, and foreign- funded units.

Employed Staff and Workers refer to persons who work in, and receive wages from their working units, including persons who have their work posts but are temporarily absent from work for reasons of study or on sick, injury or maternal leave and still receive wages from their working units.

Total Wage Bill refers to the total remuneration payment to employed persons in various units during a certain period of time. The calculation of total wage bill is based on the total remuneration payment to employed persons . Therefore, all the wages and salaries and other payments to employed persons are included in the total wage bill regardless of sources, reckoning the cost of production or not, category, listing as items of premium taxation or not, and forms, paying in cash or in kind.

Average Wage refers to the average wage in money terms per person during a certain period of time for employed persons in enterprises, institutions, and government agencies, which reflects the general level of wage income during a certain period of time and is calculated as follows:

$$\text{AverageWage} = \frac{\text{TotalWage Billof Employed Personsat Reference Time}}{\text{Average Number of Persons Employedat Reference Time}}$$

Registered Unemployed Persons in Urban Areas refer to the persons with non-agricultural household registration at certain working ages (16 years old to retirement age), who are capable of working, unemployed and willing to work, and have been registered at the local employment service agencies to apply for a job.

Registered Unemployment Rate in Urban Areas refers to the ratio of the number of urban registered unemployed to the number of urban employed and the sum of the number of urban employed and the number of urban registered unemployed. The formula is as follows:

$$\text{Registered Unemployment rate in urban areas} = \frac{\text{numberof registered urban unemployed persons}}{\begin{array}{c}\text{number of persons employed in}\\ \text{urbanunits-employed rurallabour force}\\ \text{re-employed retirees - HongKong,}\\ \text{Macao,Taiwan or foreign employees}\\ \text{+ laid-off staff and workers+owners of}\\ \text{urban private Enterprises+ owners of}\\ \text{urbanself-employed Individuals + employees}\\ \text{ofurbanprivate Enterprises+employees of}\\ \text{urbanself- employed Individuals+ registered}\\ \text{unemployed persons in urbanareas}\end{array}} \times 100\%$$

5 固定资产投资

INVESTMENT IN FIXED ASSETS

资料整理：席锋旭　张　驰
Data management：Xi Fengxu Zhang Chi
数据审核：席锋旭
Data audit：Xi Fengxu

第五部分　固定资产投资

一、简要说明

1.本章资料反映西安固定资产投资的基本情况、固定资产投资的结构和比例关系、固定资产投资的资金来源及固定资产投资的效果等。主要包括项目投资、房地产开发投资和分区县、开发区投资情况等。

2.固定资产投资统计的资料来源主要为国家统计局的全面统计报表。

3.统计口径的变化。

自1997年起，除房地产开发投资、非农户投资、农户投资及城镇和工矿区私人建房投资外，固定资产投资的统计起点由5万元提高到50万元。

自2006年起，非农户固定资产投资统计改为按项目统计，调查方法由抽样调查改为全面统计报表，起点提高到50万元。城镇和工矿区私人建房投资改为按项目统计，起点为50万元。

自2011年起，除房地产开发投资、农户投资外，固定资产投资项目统计起点，由计划总投资50万元提高到500万元；统计范围从城镇扩大到农村企事业组织，并将这一统计范围定义为“固定资产投资（不含农户）”。

4.由于国家统计局对《固定资产投资统计报表制度》进行了修订，取消了“房屋施工面积”“房屋竣工面积”“房屋竣工价值”等相关指标，本年鉴所公布的2021年度“房屋施工面积”“房屋竣工面积”“房屋竣工价值”等相关指标数据，均为房地产开发口径。

5.2021年数据不含西安（西咸新区）—咸阳共管区。

二、主要指标

固定资产投资（不含农户）	比上年下降	11.6%
#国有经济单位	比上年下降	18.0%
集体经济单位	比上年下降	12.5%
#房地产开发投资	比上年下降	7.0%
商品房销售面积	比上年下降	27.0%
全市新增固定资产	比上年下降	49.6%
全市竣工住宅面积	比上年下降	41.9%

5 INVESTMENT IN FIXED ASSETS

I. Brief Introduction

1. This chapter reflects the scale and speed of investment in fixed assets in Xi'an, the structure and proportional relationship of investment in fixed assets, the source of funds for investment in fixed assets and the effects of them during a certain period of time, mainly including project investment, real estate development, farmer investment by Region and Development Zone.

2. The data sources for the statistics of investment in fixed assets mainly come from complete statistical report forms.

3. Changes in Statistical Scope

Since 1997, the cut-off point of projects covered by statistics of investment in fixed assets are raised from an investment of 50,000 yuan to 500,000 yuan, except investment in real estate development, non-farm household investment, farm household investment and private investment in housing construction in urban areas and industrial and mining areas.

Since 2006, statistics on investments in fixed assets of rural non-farm households are changed to project-based. Survey method is changed from sample survey to the system of reporting forms with complete enumeration. The cut-off point has been raised to 500,00 yuan.Statistics on private investment in housing construction in urban areas and industrial and mining areas have become project-based. The cut-off point has been raised to 500,000 yuan.

Since 2011, except investment in real estate development and rural household investment, the cut-off point of statistics on investments in fixed assets are raised, amount of intended investment are raised from 500,000 yuan to 5000,000. The scope of investment statistics expends from urban to rural enterprises, and this scope of statistics is defined "investments in fixed assets(non-farm)" .

4. As the National Bureau of Statistics revised the Statistical Report System of Fixed Assets Investment and canceled the relevant indicators such as housing construction area housing completion area and "housing completion value", the relevant indicators such as"housing construction area", "housing completion area" and "housing completion value" published in this yearbook in 2021 are all real estate development standards.

5. The data in 2021 excludes areas mutually controlled by Xi'an(Xixian New Area)-Xian yang.

II. Major Indicators

	Increase over Preceding Year
Investment In Fixed Assets (Non-Farm)	-11.6%
State-owned Enterprises	-18.0%
Collective-owned Enterprises	-12.5%
Real Estate Development	-7.0%
Floor Space of Commercialized Buildings Sold	-27.0%
Investment Newly Increased Fixed Assets	-49.6%
Total Floor Space of Building Completed	-41.9%

5-1　主要年份按类别分固定资产投资增长速度

The Growth Rate of Total Investment in Fixed Assets by Classifications in Representative Years

单位：%　　(%)

年　份 Year	固定资产投资 Investment in Fixed Assets	房地产开发投资 Real Estate Investment
1980	48.8	
1985	35.1	
1986	28.4	
1987	24.9	
1988	5.5	
1989	-2.4	
1990	-3.1	
1991	10.6	120.9
1992	28.6	65.2
1993	102.9	122.6
1994	10.2	62.7
1995	20.5	80.1
1996	9.6	13.9
1997	-1.9	0.1
1998	45.7	54.8
1999	24.5	15.9
2000	17.6	17.0
2001	26.6	30.0
2002	19.6	17.7
2003	45.1	57.3
2004	37.3	35.9
2005	26.8	32.7
2006	25.2	26.9
2007	37.9	35.5
2008	33.3	39.5
2009	32.5	28.9
2010	31.1	21.0
2011	30.0	18.3
2012	29.9	28.6
2013	21.3	24.5
2014	15.2	10.4
2015	-12.7	4.0
2016	3.4	6.8
2017	13.0	15.0
2018	8.5	7.9
2019	1.1	-2.1
2020	12.8	6.5
2021	-11.6	-7.0

注：2017年后数据为含西咸数据。
2021年省统计局给各市区已不反馈全社会固定资产投资数据，为做到数据统一，本表只反映固定资产投资情况。

5-2 主要年份按经济类型分固定资产投资增长速度

The Growth Rate of Investment in Fixed Assets by Economic Type in Representative Years

单位：% (%)

年 份 Year	合计 Total	国有经济 State-owned	集体经济 Collective-owned	个体经济 Self-employed Individual	其他经济 Others
1985	35.1	34.8	72.0	79.0	
1986	28.4	29.3	-28.7	0.3	
1987	24.9	22.9	54.6	7.7	
1988	5.5	6.9	24.0	5.6	
1989	-2.4	-2.1	-21.5	1.7	
1990	-3.1	-4.3	-1.4	-24.3	
1991	10.6	10.0	56.9	48.9	
1992	28.6	31.2	-35.8	22.3	
1993	102.9	86.2	109.0	31.3	
1994	10.2	8.5	36.6	54.0	13.9
1995	20.5	6.8	136.2	10.3	102.6
1996	9.6	16.8	-10.7	12.3	-7.0
1997	-1.9	-4.0	17.0	20.9	13.1
1998	45.7	46.0	-22.7	-29.9	64.7
1999	24.5	20.7	72.6	53.2	33.2
2000	17.6	16.9	7.6	50.4	8.9
2001	26.6	10.0	0.1	58.1	74.7
2002	19.6	13.9	-6.6	15.8	35.3
2003	45.1	32.4	63.0	64.3	47.4
2004	37.3	24.3	79.4	-33.3	94.5
2005	26.8	13.5	47.9	61.5	41.4
2006	25.2	7.3	86.9	35.8	38.5
2007	37.9	18.9	87.1	70.6	27.0
2008	33.3	45.7	19.2	-72.5	60.8
2009	32.5	34.3	17.4	94.1	29.0
2010	31.1	44.6	12.6	-44.1	28.9
2011	30.0	24.8	10.4	36.4	18.9
2012	29.9	37.9	-24.6	10.8	27.4
2013	21.3	6.6	12.9	2.1	32.7
2014	15.2	8.2	-7.5	-1.4	21.0
2015	-12.7	-4.7	-22.2	-3.4	-16.2
2016	3.4	15.9	-17.5	1.5	-15.3
2017	13.0	19.4	-9.9	15.0	21.2
2018	8.5	-2.9	-54.5		8.6
2019	1.1	5.1	44.2		-3.3
2020	12.8	14.5	-51.1		11.1
2021	-11.6	-18.0	-12.5		-4.5

注：集体经济：包括城镇集体和农村集体。
个体经济：私营个体投资。
2017年后数据为含西咸数据。

5-3 主要年份按产业分全市固定资产投资增长速度

The Growth Rate of Total Investment in Fixed Assets in the Whole City by Three Strata of Industry in Representative Years

单位：%　　　　　　　　　　　　　　　　　　　　　　　　　　　　　　　　　　　　　　　(%)

年份 Year	全市固定资产投资 Total Investment in Fixed Assets in The Whole City	第一产业 Primary Industry	第二产业 Secondary Industry	工业 Industry	第三产业 Tertiary Industry
1980	48.8	3.2	68.5	65.0	36.1
1985	35.1	-5.3	58.3	61.7	18.5
1986	28.4	-11.1	24.4	29.8	33.5
1987	24.9	18.8	31.5	34.5	18.6
1988	5.5	-21.1	1.2	-0.5	10.6
1989	-2.4	-13.3	-0.1	2.7	-4.5
1990	-3.1	92.3	-7.6	-7.9	0.3
1991	10.6	8.0	13.1	12.8	8.3
1992	28.6	-63.0	25.0	23.3	34.0
1993	102.9	-30.0	57.1	52.3	145.4
1994	10.2	-57.1	10.4	15.2	10.3
1995	20.5	366.7	6.5	7.2	28.4
1996	9.6	-7.1	-9.9	-12.5	19.0
1997	-1.9	84.6	-8.9	-10.6	0.6
1998	45.7	100.0	49.4	37.9	44.3
1999	24.5	95.8	12.9	21.9	28.1
2000	17.6	-19.1	43.5	49.4	10.0
2001	26.6	13.2	10.7	12.7	32.9
2002	19.6	398.8	17.4	11.7	18.6
2003	45.1	-22.1	12.0	14.6	57.1
2004	37.3	1.2	17.3	22.0	42.3
2005	26.8	55.6	47.7	46.8	22.7
2006	25.2	90.9	48.0	47.0	19.4
2007	37.9	1.6	39.4	38.8	38.0
2008	33.3	132.8	24.3	24.3	34.9
2009	32.5	3.0	24.0	24.3	35.3
2010	31.1	62.8	21.3	12.6	33.1
2011	30.0	22.2	21.3	18.5	31.8
2012	29.9	130.5	41.5	48.1	26.2
2013	21.3	-26.4	46.3	50.2	17.8
2014	15.2	2.7	28.3	38.8	12.2
2015	-12.7	32.8	-8.2	-5.8	-14.7
2016	3.4	-10.1	-12.3	-12.0	8.3
2017	13.0	2.3	-10.2	-10.6	18.6
2018	8.5	20.8	28.6	28.7	5.4
2019	1.1	-21.0	1.5	2.0	1.3
2020	12.8	-43.6	15.5	15.2	12.8
2021	-11.6	-55.2	-16.0	-15.8	-10.6

5-4 全市按资金来源及建设性质分全市固定资产投资增长速度（2021年）

The Growth Rate of Total Investment in Fixed Assets in the Whole City by Sources of Funds and Type of Construction (2021)

单位：% (%)

指　标	Item	增长速度 Growth
一、投资总额	**Total Investment**	**-11.6**
（一）按资金来源分	Grouped by Funds Source	
1. 国家预算内投资	State Budgetary Funds	-28.3
2. 国内贷款	Domestic Loans	-11.5
3. 债券	Bonds	222.2
4. 利用外资	Utilization of Foreign Funds	-2.9
5. 自筹资金	Self-raising Funds	-12.4
6. 其他资金	Others	-10.2
（二）按构成分	Grouped by Composition of Funds	
1. 建筑安装工程	Construction and Installation Projects	-14.9
2. 设备、工器具购置	Purchasing of Equipment and Instruments	-13.2
3. 其他费用	Others	0.6
（三）按建设性质分	Grouped by Type of Construction	
#新建	New Construction	-19.7
扩建	Expansion	76.5
改建和技术改造	Reconstruction and Technical Transformation	-15.8
二、房屋施工面积	**Floor Space Under Construction**	**2.2**

5-5 主要年份全市新增固定资产投资及房屋竣工面积增长速度

The Growth Rate of Newly Added Fixed Assets and Floor Spaces Completed of Municipal Units in Representative Years

单位：% (%)

年 份 Year	新增固定资产 Newly Increased Fixed Assets	房屋竣工面积 Floor Space of Buildings Completed	住宅 Residential Buildings
1980	44.2	38.3	41.7
1985	1.1	-4.6	-5.9
1986	55.5	22.7	20.8
1987	24.8	-11.5	-23.5
1988	0.6	-12.3	-14.1
1989	-1.4	-15.8	-14.3
1990	22.4	18.7	26.5
1991	-12.0	-12.5	-13.7
1992	25.0	10.5	17.6
1993	86.7	26.0	28.6
1994	32.8	9.7	27.3
1995	13.0	26.4	37.0
1996	-4.1	-7.1	-1.3
1997	4.7	12.7	14.8
1998	27.6	2.2	-3.8
1999	48.2	77.9	99.8
2000	26.3	5.0	-1.1
2001	11.7	-3.1	-7.8
2002	18.6	11.7	-3.2
2003	40.4	18.7	18.9
2004	-6.3	-15.4	-13.8
2005	56.4	45.7	20.1
2006	10.6	6.0	-2.6
2007	47.5	39.4	59.4
2008	8.6	-33.4	-25.4
2009	39.8	37.3	18.6
2010	17.7	-49.3	-36.7
2011	86.7	58.9	65.3
2012	36.1	32.0	38.0
2013	6.2	-31.2	-29.4
2014	32.1	66.0	74.1
2015	-17.2	-40.3	-43.5
2016	-4.7	69.9	61.2
2017	24.6	5.5	0.6
2018	-12.2	-44.5	-53.0
2019	26.2	5.6	22.4
2020	25.0	-28.4	-19.0
2021	-49.6	-46.6	-41.9

5-6 全市固定资产投资增长速度（2021年）

The Growth Rate of Total Investment in Fixed Assets in the Whole City (2021)

单位：% (%)

指 标	Item	固定资产投资 Investment in Fixed Assets	房地产开发投资 Real Estate Investment
一、本年完成投资	**Investment Completed This Year**	**-11.6**	**-7.0**
#住宅	Residential Buildings	-2.6	-1.6
（一）按登记注册类型分	**Grouped by Registraion Status**		
内资	Domestic Funded Enterprises	-12.1	-7.2
国有	State-owned Enterprises	-10.4	322.4
集体	Collective-owned Enterprises	-84.6	
股份合作	Cooperative Enterprises	-45.5	
联营	Joint Ownership Enterprises		
国有联营	State Joint Ownership Enterprises		
集体联营	Collective Joint Ownership Enterprises		
国有与集体联营	Joint State-collective Ownership Enterprises		
其他联营	Other Joint Ownership Enterprises		
有限责任公司	Limited Liability Corporations	-18.6	-10.4
国有独资公司	State-funded Corporations	-26.7	-9.1
其他有限责任公司	Other Limited Liability Corporations	-15.4	-10.6
股份有限公司	Stock Limited Corporation	-49.4	-98.8
私营	Private Enterprises	9.3	-7.6
私营独资	Private -funded Enterprises	-65.4	-48.8
私营合伙	Private Limited Liability Corporations	-77.3	
私营有限责任公司	Private Limited Liability Corporations	11.0	-6.4
私营股份有限公司	Private Share Holding Corporations	-38.3	-100.0
其他	Others	-56.3	
港澳台商投资	Enterprises Funded by Hong Kong, Macao and Taiwan	-20.8	34.0
与港澳台合资经营	Joint-venture Enterprises	-72.5	-41.7
与港澳台合作经营	Cooperative Enterprises		
港澳台独资	Wholly Funded from Hong Kong,Macao and Taiwan	15.9	99.3

5-6 续表 continued

单位：% (%)

指 标	Item	固定资产投资 Investment in Fixed Assets	房地产开发投资 Real Estate Investment
港澳台投资股份有限公司	Share-holding Corporations Ltd.	181.2	181.2
其他港澳台投资	Investment From HongKong,Macao,Taiwan		
外商投资	Foreign Owned Enterprises	-1.4	-13.0
中外合资经营	Joint-venture Enterprises	37.7	-42.0
中外合作经营	Cooperation Enterprises		
外资企业	Foreign Funded Enterprises	-3.8	-6.1
外商投资股份有限公司	Share-holding Corporations Ltd. With Foreign Funds		
其他外商投资	Foreign Investment	-37.9	
（二）按建设性质分	**Grouped by Type of Construction**		
#新建	New Construction	-19.7	
扩建	Expansion	76.5	
改建和技术改造	Reconstruction	-15.8	
（三）按构成分	**Grouped by Composition**		
1. 建筑安装工程	Construction and Installation Projects	-14.9	-15.3
2. 设备、工器具购置	Purchasing of Equipment and Instruments	-13.2	-14.1
3. 其他费用	Others	0.6	10.7
二、本年新增固定资产	**Newly Increase in Fixed Assets This Year**	**-49.6**	**-52.1**
三、房屋面积	**Floor Space**		
房屋施工面积	Floor Space of Buildings Under Construction	2.2	2.2
#住宅	Residential Buildings	1.4	1.4
房屋竣工面积	Floor Space of Buildings Completed	-46.6	-46.6
#住宅	Residential Buildings	-41.9	-41.9
四、本年房屋竣工价值	**Value of the Building Completed This Year**	**-50.3**	**-50.3**
#住宅	Residential Buildings	-48.2	-48.2

5-7 按国民经济行业分全市固定资产投资增长速度（2021年）

The Growth Rate of Investment in Fixed Assets in the Whole Country by Industry (2021)

单位：%　　　　(%)

行　业	Sector	固定资产投资 Investment in Fixed Assets	工业企业技术改造 Technological Transformation of Industrial Enterprises
本年完成固定资产投资	**Grouped by Sector**	**-11.6**	**40.6**
（一）农、林、牧、渔业	Agriculture,Forestry,Animal Husbandry and Fishery	-55.8	
（二）采矿业	Mining	-30.0	-13.5
（三）制造业	Manufacturing	-12.7	52.2
农副食品加工业	Processing of Food from Agricultural Products	-19.1	-43.6
食品制造业	Manufacture of Foods	-22.1	25.9
酒、饮料和精制茶制造业	Wine,Soft Drinks and Refined Tea Industry	105.9	-13.0
烟草制品业	Tobacco Processing	-86.6	
纺织业	Textile Industry	-54.5	-100.0
纺织服装、服饰业	Textile,Apparel Industry		
皮革、毛皮、羽毛及其制品和制鞋业	Leather,Fur,Feather(eiderdown) and Their Products Industry	-42.8	-100.0
木材加工和木、竹、藤、棕、草制品业	Timber Processing,Bamboo,Cane, Palm Fiber and Straw Products	160.0	
家具制造业	Furniture Manufacturing	-77.3	
造纸及纸制品业	Papermaking and Paper products	-89.8	-96.6
印刷和记录媒介复制业	Printing,Record Medium Reproduction	-74.1	-5.2
文教、工美、体育和娱乐用品制造业	Culture,Education,Craft Art,Sports and Entertainment Goods Manufacturing Industry	804.0	
石油、煤炭及其他燃料加工业	Oil,Coal and Other Fuel Processing Industries	18.9	35.0
化学原料和化学制品制造业	Raw Chemical Materials and Chemical Products	9.9	-1.4
医药制造业	Medical and Pharmaceutical Products	-30.8	-62.1
化学纤维制造业	Chemical Fiber	-100.0	-100.0
橡胶和塑料制品业	Rubber and Plastic Products Industry	-78.7	-31.8
非金属矿物制品业	Nonmetal Mineral Products	-44.1	-26.6
黑色金属冶炼和压延加工业	Smelting and Pressing of Ferrous Metals	-57.1	-81.5
有色金属冶炼和压延加工业	Smelting and Pressing of Nonferrous Metals	-55.9	-48.0
金属制品业	Metal Products	-45.9	-59.1

5-7 续表 continued

单位：% (%)

行 业	Sector	固定资产投资 Investment in Fixed Assets	工业企业技术改造 Technological Transformation of Industrial Enterprises
通用设备制造业	General Equipment Manufacturing Industry	4.1	-65.7
专用设备制造业	Special Purpose Equipment	-30.0	-21.2
汽车制造业	Automotive Manufacturing	-36.8	176.6
铁路、船舶、航空航天和其他运输设备制造业	Railroad,Marine,Aerospace and other Transportation Equipment Manufacturing	-36.2	-54.7
电气机械和器材制造业	Electric Equipment and Machinery	6.1	170.1
计算机、通信和其他电子设备制造业	Communication Equipment,Computer and Other Electronic Equipment Manufacturing Industry	11.7	102.7
仪器仪表制造业	Instrument Manufacturing Industry	-52.9	-30.6
其他制造业	Other Manufacturing	-46.8	-6.7
废弃资源综合利用业	Comprehensive Utilization of waste Resources	-54.1	262.7
金属制品、机械和设备修理业	Metal Products,Machinery and Equipment Repair Industry	186.8	-55.4
（四）电力、热力、燃气及水生产和供应业	Production & Supply of Electricity,Heat,Gas & Water	-30.1	-57.2
（五）建筑业	Construction	15.0	
（六）批发和零售业	Wholesale and Retail Trades	-49.3	
（七）交通运输、仓储和邮政业	Transport,Storage and Post	-7.4	
（八）住宿和餐饮业	Hotels and Catering Services	-50.9	
（九）信息传输、软件和信息技术服务业	Information Transmission,Computer Service and Software	4.6	
（十）金融业	Financial Intermediation	-82.7	
（十一）房地产业	Real Estate	485.8	
（十二）租赁和商务服务业	Leasing and Business Services	19.8	
（十三）科学研究和技术服务业	Scientific Research,Technical Service and Geologic Prospecting	16.6	
（十四）水利、环境和公共设施管理业	Management of Water Conservancy,Environment and Public Facilities	-20.3	
（十五）居民服务、修理和其他服务业	Services to Households,Repairs and Other Services	-38.6	
（十六）教育	Education	-46.5	
（十七）卫生和社会工作	Health and Social Work	39.6	
（十八）文化、体育和娱乐业	Culture,Sports and Entertainment	-5.8	
（十九）公共管理、社会保障和社会组织	Public Administration,Social Security and Social Organizations	35.1	
（二十）国际组织	International Organizations		

5-8 按国民经济行业分民间投资增长速度（2021年）

The Growth Rate of Private Investment of Municipal Units by Industry (2021)

单位：%　(%)

行　业	Sector	民间投资 Private Investment	占民间投资比重 Rate
民间投资总计	**Total**	**-4.7**	**100.0**
（一）农、林、牧、渔业	Agriculture,Forestry,Animal Husbandry and Fishery	-70.5	0.2
（二）采矿业	Mining	-39.9	
（三）制造业	Manufacturing	-11.8	10.8
（四）电力、热力、燃气及水生产和供应业	Production & Supply of Electricity,Heat, Gas & Water	-2.5	1.4
（五）建筑业	Construction		
（六）批发和零售业	Wholesale and Retail Trades	-54.2	0.2
（七）交通运输、仓储和邮政业	Transportation,Storage and Post	183.3	2.5
（八）住宿和餐饮业	Hotels and Catering Services	-54.0	0.5
（九）信息传输、软件和信息技术服务业	Information Transmission,Computer Service and Software	-66.5	0.2
（十）金融业	Financial Intermediation		
（十一）房地产业	Real Estate	-12.6	62.8
（十二）租赁和商务服务业	Leasing and Business Services	-11.4	2.3
（十三）科学研究和技术服务业	Scientific Research and Technical Service	-57.6	0.3
（十四）水利、环境和公共设施管理业	Management of Water Conservancy,Environment and Public Facilities	89.0	14.6
（十五）居民服务、修理和其他服务业	Services to Households,Repairs and Other Services	311.5	
（十六）教育	Education	3.3	1.5
（十七）卫生和社会工作	Health and Social Work	-30.5	1.3
（十八）文化、体育和娱乐业	Culture,Sports and Entertainment	-1.3	1.3
（十九）公共管理、社会保障和社会组织	Public Administration,Social Security and Social Organizations	450.2	0.1
（二十）国际组织	International Organizations		

5-9 按国民经济行业分基础设施投资增长速度（2021年）

The Growth Rate of Investment for Basic Infrastructure of Municipal Units by Industry (2021)

单位：% (%)

指 标	Item	比去年同期增长± Increase Over the Same Period Last Year	比重 Rate
基础设施投资总计	**Total Investment of Infrastructure**	**-18.1**	**100.0**
一、电力、热力、燃气及水生产和供应业	**Production and Supply of Electricity,Heat,Gas and Water**	**-30.1**	**7.3**
电力、热力的生产和供应业	The Production and Supply of Electricity and Heat	-41.4	3.7
燃气的生产和供应业	The Production and Supply of Gas	21.3	0.4
水的生产和供应业	The Production and Supply of Water	-15.4	3.1
二、交通运输和邮政业	**Traffic,Transport and Post**	**-3.4**	**21.7**
铁路运输业	Railway Transport Industry	229.3	1.5
道路运输业	The Road Transport Industry	-10.2	16.3
水上运输业	Water Transportation		
航空运输业	The Air Transport Industry	9.4	3.7
管道运输业	Pipeline Transportation	-100.0	
多式联运和运输代理服务业	Multimodal Transport and Transport Agency Services	-58.8	0.1
装卸搬运	Handling Service	-59.2	
邮政业	The Postal Service	-61.4	0.1
三、信息传输业	**Information Transmission**	**-21.2**	**3.2**
电信、广播电视和卫星传输服务	Telecommunications,Radio and Television and Satellite Transmission Services	-15.8	3.0
互联网和相关服务	Internet and Related Services	-58.0	0.2
四、水利、环境和公共设施管理业	**Management of Water Conservancy,Environment and Public Facilities**	**-20.3**	**67.8**
水利管理业	Water Resources Management Industry	-18.8	2.9
生态保护和环境治理业	Ecological Protection and Environmental Control Industries	-19.9	2.1
公共设施管理业	Public Facilities Management Industry	-20.4	62.8

5-10 全市固定资产投资资金来源增长速度（2021年）

The Growth Rate of Source of Funds for Total Fixed Assets Investment of Whole City (2021)

单位：% (%)

指 标	Item	固定资产投资 Investment in Fixed Assets	房地产开发 Real Estate
一、本年资金来源合计	**Total of Sources of Funds This Year**	**-5.5**	**2.3**
1. 上年末结余资金	Balance of Last Year	11.3	11.1
2. 本年实际到位资金	Fully Funded Capital this Year	-8.2	-0.4
（1）国家预算资金	State Budgetary Funds	-25.6	
（2）国内贷款	Domestic Loans	-8.2	6.1
（3）债券	Bonds	234.3	
（4）利用外资	Utilization of Foreign Funds	0.7	
（5）自筹资金	Self-raising Funds	-9.1	2.0
（6）其他资金来源	Others	-6.9	-3.7
二、各项应付款合计	**Total Sums of Money to be Paid This Year**	**-8.1**	**-4.9**

5-11 按国民经济行业分施工项目（2021年）

Construction Project Grouped by Industry in the Whole City (2021)

行 业	Sector	本年新增固定资产增长速度（%）The Growth Rate of Newly Increased Fixed Assets This Year(%)
总计	**Total**	**-49.6**
（一）农、林、牧、渔业	Agriculture,Forestry,Animal Husbandry and Fishery	-31.6
（二）采矿业	Mining	84.9
（三）制造业	Manufacturing	-74.6
（四）电力、热力、燃气及水生产和供应业	Production & Supply of Electricity,Heat, Gas & Water	-68.6
（五）建筑业	Construction	
（六）批发和零售业	Wholesale and Retail Trades	-95.9
（七）交通运输、仓储和邮政业	Transportation,Storage and Post	-55.3
（八）住宿和餐饮业	Hotels and Catering Services	-58.6
（九）信息传输、软件和信息技术服务业	Information Transmission,Computer Service and Software	2.1
（十）金融业	Financial Intermediation	-90.1
（十一）房地产业	Real Estate	-48.0
（十二）租赁和商务服务业	Leasing and Business Services	-28.0
（十三）科学研究和技术服务业	Scientific Research and Technical Service	-59.3
（十四）水利、环境和公共设施管理业	Management of Water Conservancy,Environment and Public Facilities	-22.5
（十五）居民服务、修理和其他服务业	Services to Households,Repairs and Other Services	-16.3
（十六）教育	Education	-58.1
（十七）卫生和社会工作	Health and Social Work	22.7
（十八）文化、体育和娱乐业	Culture,Sports and Entertainment	-60.4
（十九）公共管理、社会保障和社会组织	Public Administration,Social Security and Social Organizations	-93.2
（二十）国际组织	International Organizations	

5-11 续表 continued

行 业	Sector	施工项目个数（个）Number of Constructing Projects(unit)	本年新开工 Newly Started This Year	本年投产项目个数（个）Projects put into Use (unit)
总计	**Total**	**3011**	**1122**	**960**
（一）农、林、牧、渔业	Agriculture,Forestry,Animal Husbandry and Fishery	73	36	51
（二）采矿业	Mining	1		1
（三）制造业	Manufacturing	735	244	215
（四）电力、热力、燃气及水生产和供应业	Production & Supply of Electricity,Heat, Gas & Water	170	63	50
（五）建筑业	Construction	1		
（六）批发和零售业	Wholesale and Retail Trades	27	8	7
（七）交通运输、仓储和邮政业	Transportation,Storage and Post	131	38	53
（八）住宿和餐饮业	Hotels and Catering Services	49	19	11
（九）信息传输、软件和信息技术服务业	Information Transmission,Computer Service and Software	103	50	30
（十）金融业	Financial Intermediation	2		
（十一）房地产业	Real Estate	158	61	35
（十二）租赁和商务服务业	Leasing and Business Services	89	31	19
（十三）科学研究和技术服务业	Scientific Research and Technical Service	78	25	21
（十四）水利、环境和公共设施管理业	Management of Water Conservancy,Environment and Public Facilities	1011	422	374
（十五）居民服务、修理和其他服务业	Services to Households,Repairs and Other Services	5	1	2
（十六）教育	Education	222	63	60
（十七）卫生和社会工作	Health and Social Work	85	40	19
（十八）文化、体育和娱乐业	Culture,Sports and Entertainment	48	14	8
（十九）公共管理、社会保障和社会组织	Public Administration,Social Security and Social Organizations	23	7	4
（二十）国际组织	International Organizations			

5-12 全市固定资产投资效果（2021年）

Achievements of Total Assets Investment of Whole City (2021)

指　标	Item	固定资产投资 Investment in Fixed Assets	房地产开发投资 Real Estate Investment
一、建设项目投产率（%）	**Rate of Projects Put Into Use(%)**	**31.9**	
施工项目个数（个）	Number of Constructing Projects(unit)	3011	
本年投产项目个数（个）	Number of Projects Put into Use(unit)	960	
二、固定资产交付使用率（%）	**Rate of Fixed Assets Put into Use(%)**	**20.9**	**7.7**
本年新增固定资产增长速度（%）	The Growth Rate of Newly Increased Fixed Assets This Year(%)	-49.6	-52.1
本年完成投资增长速度（%）	The Growth Rate of Investment Completed This Year(%)	-11.6	-7.0
三、建设周期（年）	**Construction Period(year)**	**5.9**	**8.5**
计划总投资增长速度（%）	The Growth Rate of Total Planned Investment(%)	0.3	8.5
本年完成投资额增长速度（%）	The Growth Rate of Investment Completed This Year(%)	-11.6	-7.0
四、房屋建筑面积竣工率（%）	**Completion Rate of Buildings(%)**	**2.6**	**2.6**
本年房屋施工面积增长速度（%）	The Growth Rate of Floor Space of the Constructing Buildings This Year(%)	2.2	2.2
本年房屋竣工面积增长速度（%）	The Growth Rate of Floor Space of the Buildings Completed This Year(%)	-46.6	-46.6

注：本表从2020年度起，“房屋建筑面积竣工率”及分项指标口径为房地产开发统计口径。

5-13 固定资产投资新增生产能力或效益（2021年）

Newly Increased Production Capacity or Project Efficiency through Investment (2021)

能源名称	Name	累计新增生产能力或效益 Cumulative Newly Increased Production Capacity or Project Efficiency
石油加工：蒸馏设备能力（处理万吨/年）	Oil Processing:Distillation Equipment Capacity (10 000 tons/year)	
石油加工：裂变设备能力（处理万吨/年）	Oil Processing:Fission Equipment Capacity (10 000 tons/year)	
太阳能发电（万千瓦）	Solar Energy(10 000 kW)	
其他发电（万千瓦）	Others(10 000 kW)	
输电线路长度（11万伏及以上）（公里）	Length of Transmission Lines(above 110 000 VA)(km)	
载货汽车制造（辆/年）	Truck Manufacturing(car/year)	508
客车制造（辆/年）	Bus Manufacturing(car/year)	
轿车制造（辆/年）	Car Manufacturing(car/year)	
其他汽车制造（辆/年）	Other cars Manufacturing(car/year)	4500
啤酒（万吨/年）	Beer(10 000 tons/year)	
白酒（万吨/年）	White Spirit(10 000 tons/year)	
其他酒（万吨/年）	Other Alcohols(10 000 tons/year)	
新建公路（公里）	Newly Highways(km)	
#高速公路（公里）	Expressway(km)	
一级公路（公里）	First Class(km)	
二级公路（公里）	Second Class(km)	
改建公路（公里）	Reconstructed Highways(km)	
新（扩）建客、货运站（个）	New(expanded)Passenger and Freight Stations(unit)	
新（扩）建公路客、货运站（平方米）	New(expanded)Road Passenger and Freight Station (square meter)	
飞机购置（驾）	Airplane Purchasing(set)	86
城市自来水供水能力（万吨/日）	Tap Water Supply Capacity in City(10 000 tons/day)	10
城市污水处理能力（万吨/日）	Waste Water Treated Capacity in City(10 000 tons/day)	11.5

5-14 分区县、开发区固定资产投资增长速度（2021年）

The Growth Rate of Total Investment in Fixed Assets by Region and Development Zone (2021)

单位：% (%)

区县、开发区	Region	固定资产投资 Investment in Fixed Assets	房地产开发投资 Real Estate Investment
全市	**Total**	**-11.6**	**-7.0**
新城区	Xincheng	20.8	44.1
碑林区	Beilin	-19.1	57.9
莲湖区	Lianhu	-23.2	-2.2
灞桥区	Baqiao	0.3	37.1
未央区	Weiyang	-12.5	-25.3
雁塔区	Yanta	-7.0	-9.4
阎良区	Yanliang	-34.5	-21.0
临潼区	Lintong	-23.1	-29.3
长安区	Chang'an	0.9	2.1
高陵区	Gaoling	-58.9	-51.7
鄠邑区	Huyi	9.1	49.3
蓝田县	Lantian	9.3	323.6
周至县	Zhouzhi	-8.8	11.1
西咸新区	Xixian New Area	-19.1	-17.0
# 开发区	**Development Zones**		
高新区	Hi-Tech Industries Development Zone	-1.5	32.2
经开区	Economic Development Zone	-36.2	-43.5
曲江新区	Qujiang New District	-19.3	-37.3
航空基地	National Aviation Hi-tech Industrial Base	-46.9	-33.0
航天基地	National Civil Aerospace Industrial Base	22.2	-4.4
浐灞生态区	Chan-ba Ecological District	-17.9	-26.8
国际港务区	International Trade & Logistics Park	21.5	165.8

5-15 分区县工业投资增长速度（2021年）

The Growth Rate of Industrial Investment by Region (2021)

单位：% (%)

区 县	Region	工业投资 Industrial Investment	工业企业技术改造 Technological Transformation of Industrial Enterprises
全 市	**Total**	**-15.8**	**40.6**
新城区	Xincheng	-31.7	-22.6
碑林区	Beilin	-69.6	-69.6
莲湖区	Lianhu	-82.4	-75.0
灞桥区	Baqiao	9.3	-67.7
未央区	Weiyang	-62.2	-22.2
雁塔区	Yanta	19.6	-13.5
阎良区	Yanliang	-56.4	-75.9
临潼区	Lintong	-30.1	-46.6
长安区	Chang'an	-0.7	69.6
高陵区	Gaoling	-42.0	20.0
鄠邑区	Huyi	75.2	400.6
蓝田县	Lantian	-33.1	-42.6
周至县	Zhouzhi	18.6	101.7
西咸新区	Xixian New Area	-25.5	-15.1

5–16 分区县、开发区新增固定资产及房屋施工、竣工面积增长速度（2021年）

单位：%

区县、开发区	Region	本年新增固定资产 Increased Fixed Assets this Year	房屋施工面积 Floor Space of Buildings Under Construction	住宅 Residential Buildings
区县	**Region**	**-57.7**	**-1.2**	**-0.7**
新城区	Xincheng	166.9	4.1	-1.6
碑林区	Beilin	-76.0	-19.2	-23.4
莲湖区	Lianhu	-24.5	-12.6	-14.2
灞桥区	Baqiao	-51.2	-0.7	-1.9
未央区	Weiyang	-64.3	-5.5	-5.5
雁塔区	Yanta	-12.3	12.6	20.9
阎良区	Yanliang	21.8	6.2	13.9
临潼区	Lintong	64.9	-26.8	-30.5
长安区	Chang'an	-81.2	-8.2	-9.6
高陵区	Gaoling	-84.7	-5.7	-1.9
鄠邑区	Huyi	-32.3	-4.9	0.3
蓝田县	Lantian	-13.6	21.4	31.8
周至县	Zhouzhi	-67.6	10.2	16.3
西咸新区	Xixian New Area	-32.0	16.9	10.3
开发区	**Development Zones**	**-62.3**	**5.3**	**7.0**
高新区	Hi-Tech Industries Development Zone	-71.9	23.1	42.0
经开区	Economic Development Zone	-63.3	-9.5	-10.7
曲江新区	Qujiang New District	-75.2	-7.0	-9.0
航空基地	National Aviation Hi-tech Industrial Base	16.3	4.9	19.0
航天基地	National Civil Aerospace Industrial Base	109.0	-4.4	-4.1
浐灞生态区	Chan-ba Ecological District	-25.8	-3.6	-3.9
国际港务区	International Trade & Logistics Park	-49.3	59.1	51.2

The Growth Rate of Newly Added Fixed Assets and Floor Space of Constructing and Completed Buildings by Region and Development Zone (2021)

(%)

本年房屋竣工面积 Floor Space of Buildings this Year Completed	住宅 Residential Buildings	本年房屋竣工价值 Value of Buildings Completed this Year	住宅 Residential Buildings	本年商品房销售面积 Floor Space of Houses Sales this year	本年商品房销售额 Sales Income of Commercial Houses this year
-45.9	**-42.4**	**-50.8**	**-49.5**	**-24.3**	**-16.4**
-100.0	-100.0	-100.0	-100.0	45.9	96.2
-100.0	-100.0	-100.0	-100.0	-93.1	-89.9
-9.0	-23.4	-43.2	-51.8	7.6	15.2
-87.1	-83.5	-85.7	-82.5	-2.2	5.2
-45.2	-47.2	-1.6	-13.6	-46.4	-36.7
-0.7	153.9	-36.0	16.7	-29.1	-24.5
-100.0	-100.0	-100.0	-100.0	-29.8	-27.8
				-66.5	-69.0
-47.6	-43.6	-42.9	-40.6	-14.9	1.2
529.8	585.2	365.0	393.0	-32.6	-28.5
48.7	116.2	43.4	164.9	-43.0	-37.3
113.9	36.1	109.8	31.3	173.6	205.8
-100.0	-100.0	-100.0	-100.0	-36.2	-36.8
-49.5	-39.5	-47.8	-42.4	-34.7	-31.4
-17.3	**11.8**	**-12.3**	**4.5**	**-27.4**	**-17.5**
-6.9		-11.5		5.8	16.3
6.7	-0.8	-6.5	-11.9	-66.2	-65.1
-100.0	-100.0	-100.0	-100.0	-59.6	-56.2
				-50.7	-50.3
259.9	694.9	516.8	1269.5	-59.4	-54.5
-83.4	-100.0	-72.8	-100.0	-36.5	-23.0
-27.5	3.4	-39.5	-24.4	24.2	42.5

5-17 主要年份房地产开发投资主要指标

单位：万平方米

指 标	Item	2000	2001	2002	2003	2004	2005
本年完成投资额（亿元）	Investment Completed This Year(100 million yuan)	51.85	67.42	79.37	124.82	169.67	225.23
本年房屋施工面积	Floor Space of Buildings Under Construction This Year	763.18	743.78	1172.58	1343.12	1633.68	2174.29
#住宅	Residential Buildings	619.85	580.43	964.68	943.61	1204.01	1783.36
本年房屋竣工面积	Floor Space of Buildings Completed This Year	321.10	316.24	329.71	339.67	380.84	361.62
#住宅	Residential Buildings	295.55	269.61	290.30	289.56	308.06	316.52
本年房屋竣工价值（亿元）	Value of Floor Space of Buildings Completed this Year(100million yuan)	26.94	37.20	36.93	54.73	73.75	80.58
#住宅	Residential Buildings	22.97	28.62	30.46	44.01	55.58	68.11
本年商品房销售面积	Floor Space of Commercialized Buildings Sold	212.92	225.35	252.90	252.74	305.47	497.34
#住宅	Residential Buildings	200.77	192.20	237.04	230.28	279.90	476.39
本年商品房销售额（亿元）	Total Sales of Commercialized Buildings (100 million yuan)	32.52	47.22	51.35	54.29	81.35	171.29
#住宅	Residential Buildings	29.46	35.53	45.46	44.25	71.27	158.03
本年批准预售面积	Approved Pre-sale Area of This Year	253.03	67.44	61.02	52.35	176.40	300.07
#住宅	Residential Buildings	253.03	65.20	55.73	49.12	159.10	287.13
待售面积	Area for Sale	36.41	50.82	57.14	63.85	108.52	123.59
#住宅	Residential Buildings	24.02	34.18	44.70	52.34	72.76	99.17
房屋出租面积	Rental Housing Area	1.17	9.19	15.75	10.56	11.18	17.32
#住宅	Residential Buildings	0.02	0.10	1.13	5.43	5.78	4.09
本年新增固定资产（亿元）	Newly Increased Fixed Assets This Year (100 million yuan)	38.38	50.77	48.43	62.13	83.36	92.78

Main Indicators of Investment in Real Estate Development in Representative Years

(10 000 sq.m)

2006	2007	2008	2009	2010	2011	2012	2013	2014	2015	2016	2017	2018	2019	2020	2021
285.76	387.33	540.26	696.34	842.34	996.81	1281.90	1595.64	1761.88	1831.67	1955.82	2333.34	2518.01	2464.78	2624.48	2428.63
2383.56	2915.95	3632.87	5708.63	6697.39	8247.69	9947.89	10454.27	12422.10	13392.94	14727.10	15843.92	16044.57	17475.02	16916.07	17119.50
1890.27	2376.82	3079.13	4901.59	5777.71	7108.27	8294.92	8461.71	9727.60	9777.23	10468.80	11134.28	11208.59	12450.59	11800.32	11816.05
399.64	483.30	443.96	542.81	463.65	631.03	1063.70	795.35	1533.70	976.64	1560.18	1634.63	977.28	1057.69	834.55	443.40
342.15	422.47	412.46	453.49	412.44	564.59	903.82	663.20	1307.64	766.58	1259.24	1281.71	623.40	761.59	623.39	360.40
82.02	101.13	106.50	168.08	145.62	213.29	310.57	279.63	442.74	301.86	456.48	571.96	330.61	372.11	316.10	156.64
65.80	77.13	96.02	137.42	128.69	185.31	260.04	222.64	368.25	236.66	351.46	448.02	208.68	231.24	245.62	126.85
621.50	833.92	760.72	1256.02	1587.81	1778.02	1538.91	1662.75	1707.71	1763.68	2047.67	2509.78	2713.46	2638.69	2559.79	1856.73
584.06	782.91	715.76	1202.12	1523.24	1674.85	1383.84	1522.50	1525.95	1584.08	1877.78	2147.67	2221.27	2155.46	2086.77	1579.46
206.15	281.79	296.44	488.55	707.00	1091.31	1017.74	1112.87	1100.71	1146.79	1347.08	2123.34	2753.13	2989.64	3294.01	2623.49
179.47	251.74	268.92	450.71	661.27	973.71	858.53	976.19	928.74	985.35	1194.41	1743.43	2214.18	2462.79	2734.58	2297.62
428.20	491.07	569.22	1125.44	1510.20	3105.76	2627.73	1787.89	842.98	751.15	717.54	634.50	1047.65			
408.11	457.54	541.20	1095.17	1452.20	2826.79	2340.69	1597.82	727.31	583.55	508.17	515.34	865.40			
112.49	45.42	55.40	40.68	34.32	59.76	102.58	74.59	187.13	296.50	378.24	379.66	240.04	202.71	149.51	144.50
85.89	38.62	35.40	28.73	26.23	45.41	83.78	61.24	143.21	185.96	215.40	176.90	59.98	55.57	29.45	36.41
8.53	10.84	34.94	38.23	28.60	8.01	15.16	15.57	7.15	19.64	48.67	57.12	51.95	26.97	25.48	3.75
3.74	5.36	4.53	6.55	0.70	3.25	4.03	0.73	0.07	1.47	1.47		2.37			0.58
100.22	143.17	124.02	195.71	168.20	25.53	358.03	334.41	531.44	335.91	574.54	807.26	409.04	498.31	389.93	186.33

5-18 分区县、开发区房地产开发主要指标（2021年）

单位：万元

区县、开发区	Region	企业（单位）个数（个） Number of Enterprises (unit)	本年完成投资 Investment Completed This Year	本年新增固定资产 Increased Fixed Assets This Year
全市	**Total**	**1092**	**24286345**	**1863295**
新城区	Xincheng	22	420545	
碑林区	Beilin	15	325370	
莲湖区	Lianhu	40	489723	402572
灞桥区	Baqiao	115	3510607	104415
未央区	Weiyang	172	2676545	250086
雁塔区	Yanta	249	5851102	193833
阎良区	Yanliang	38	230581	
临潼区	Lintong	19	324677	
长安区	Chang'an	118	2709658	220677
高陵区	Gaoling	38	209808	66790
鄠邑区	Huyi	31	179141	94650
蓝田县	Lantian	14	302670	51935
周至县	Zhouzhi	17	84429	
西咸新区	Xixian New Area	204	6971489	478337
# 开发区	**Development Zones**	**486**	**11636336**	**544909**
高新区	Hi-Tech Industries Development Zone	129	4013063	128101
经开区	Economic Development Zone	71	480137	69488
曲江新区	Qujiang New District	83	1607431	
航空基地	National Aviation Hi-tech Industrial Base	16	127969	
航天基地	National Civil Aerospace Industrial Base	60	1072517	198905
浐灞生态区	Chan-ba Ecological District	85	1837428	44000
国际港务区	International Trade & Logistics Park	42	2497791	104415

Main Indicators of Real Estate Development by Region and Development Zone (2021)

(10 000 yuan)

房屋施工面积（平方米）Floor Space of Buildings Under Construction(sq.m)	住宅 Residential Buildings	本年房屋竣工面积（平方米）Floor Space of Buildings Completed this Year(sq.m)	住宅 Residential Buildings	本年房屋竣工价值 Value of Buildings Completed this Year	住宅 Residential Buildings
171194981	**118160450**	**4434026**	**3604023**	**1566448**	**1268486**
4748648	3240478				
1818304	1267182				
9651147	7873439	1127192	850248	361377	274512
20210037	14936289	264482	264482	104415	104415
29251066	18583360	491739	387260	239864	183821
36324936	23069306	610791	432465	163296	110183
2144237	1873478				
2388261	1901497				
17264375	12661246	463063	360166	220677	167724
5468635	4830852	316671	316671	66790	66790
1631190	1245177	294604	237786	90900	79590
1815020	1478831	122767	78109	33722	21100
1118881	918047				
37360244	24281268	742717	676836	285407	260351
73302756	**49070243**	**1223169**	**929727**	**513432**	**383036**
14815490	9487165	302096	184212	104624	67244
10628545	5833303	179934	167273	69488	65425
11982541	7915122				
1035624	938922				
8775246	6350301	416657	313760	198905	145952
15696989	11379590	60000		36000	
10368321	7165840	264482	264482	104415	104415

5-19 房地产开发投资主要指标（2021年）

Main Indicators of Investment in Real Estate Development (2021)

单位：万元 (10 000 yuan)

指 标	Item	全市合计 Total	#国有 State-owned	#市区 Urban	#市属 Municipal
一、企业（单位）个数（个）	**Number of Enterprises(unit)**	**1092**	**65**	**897**	**1058**
二、本年完成投资	**Investment Completed This Year**	**24286345**	**2388272**	**18940133**	**22729276**
按工程用途分	Grouped by Function				
住宅	Residential Buildings	17439504	1574352	13885272	16279772
办公楼	Office Buildings	1671782	10341	1212903	1612958
商业营业用房	Houses for Business Use	2026591	78936	1631789	1910103
其他	Others	3148468	724643	2210169	2926443
三、本年新增固定资产	**Increased Fixed Assets This Year**	**1863295**	**232058**	**1339023**	**1758880**
四、房屋施工面积（平方米）	**Floor Space of Buildings Under Construction(sq.m)**	**171194981**	**10345129**	**140838293**	**164718721**
#住宅	Residential Buildings	118160450	8088513	97474560	113364803
五、本年房屋竣工面积（平方米）	**Floor Space of Buildings this Year Completed(sq.m)**	**4434026**	**491407**	**3577289**	**4169544**
#住宅	Residential Buildings	3604023	353665	2849078	3339541
六、本年房屋竣工价值	**Value of Buildings Completed this Year**	**1566448**	**220506**	**1253319**	**1462033**
#住宅	Residential Buildings	1268486	151787	987035	1164071
七、本年商品房屋销售面积（平方米）	**Floor Space of Commercialized Buildings Sold this Year(sq.m)**	**18567340**	**914287**	**14502563**	**17622007**
本年商品房销售额	Sales Income of Commercialized Buildings	26234874	1465630	21506861	25013517

5-20 商品房销售情况（2021年）

Sales of Commercial Houses (2021)

指 标	Item	全市合计 Total	#国有 State-owned	#市区 Urban	#市属 Municipal
本年商品房销售面积（平方米）	**Floor Space of Commercialized Buildings Sold(sq.m)**	**18567340**	**914287**	**14502563**	**17622007**
现房销售面积（平方米）	**Floor Space of Completed Apartment Sales(sq.m)**	**950727**	**3281**	**917876**	**939824**
期房销售面积（平方米）	**Floor Space of Forward Delivery Housing Sales(sq.m)**	**17616613**	**911006**	**13584687**	**16682183**
住宅	Residential Buildings	15794638	836279	11964261	15054726
办公楼	Office Buildings	758312	8792	707520	728097
商业营业用房	Houses for Business Use	892008	14717	718763	848294
其他	Others	1122382	54499	1112019	990890
本年商品房销售额（万元）	**Real estate sales this year(10 000Yuan)**	**26234874**	**1465630**	**21506861**	**25013517**
现房销售额（万元）	**Floor Space of Completed Apartment Sales(10 000Yuan)**	**1225649**	**2544**	**1187196**	**1215212**
期房销售额（万元）	**Floor Space of Forward Delivery Housing Sales(10 000Yuan)**	**25009225**	**1463086**	**20319665**	**23798305**
住宅	Residential Buildings	22976232	1407734	18480112	21911473
办公楼	Office Buildings	1182023	11865	1131987	1144097
商业营业用房	Houses for Business Use	1414656	15924	1236464	1359350
其他	Others	661963	30107	658298	598597
待售面积（平方米）	**Area for Sale(sq.m)**	**1444952**	**22730**	**1306852**	**1430401**
#待售一年以上（一到三年）	Being Idle for One Year	554910	1516	534989	543382
待售三年以上（含三年）	Being Idle for Three Years	382700	15349	326129	379677
住宅	Residence	364131	5447	283171	361108
办公楼	Office Buildings	266844		266844	266664
商业营业用房	Houses for Business Use	489558	17283	432418	478330
其他	Others	324419		324419	324299
房屋出租面积（平方米）	**Rental area(sq.m)**	**37464**	**2247**	**25670**	**37464**
住宅	Residential Buildings	5815		5815	5815
办公楼	Office Buildings	11794			11794
商业营业用房	Houses for Business Use	19855	2247	19855	19855
其他	Others				

5-21 房地产开发投资资金来源（2021年）

Source of Funds for Investment in Real Estate Development (2021)

单位：万元 (10 000 yuan)

指　标	Item	全市合计 Total	#国有 State-owned	#市区 Urban	#市属 Municipal
一、本年资金来源合计	**Total**	**44727174**	**3652778**	**36576312**	**41634279**
1. 上年末结余资金	Balance of Last Year	11446477	773233	10094977	10423025
2. 本年实际到位资金	Fully Funded Capital this Year	33280697	2879545	26481335	31211254
（1）国内贷款	Domestic Loans	2409464	120016	1905414	2191742
#银行贷款	Bank Loan	1792679	84794	1425329	1590179
#非银行金融机构贷款	Loans from financial Institutions except Bank	616785	35222	480085	601563
（2）自筹资金	Self-raising Funds	15806926	1583321	11981396	15024396
（3）定金及预收款	Earnest Money and Advance payment	10600783	561906	8939682	9635128
（4）个人按揭贷款	Personal Mortgage Loan	2895482	50843	2371031	2858534
（5）其他资金	Others	1568042	563459	1283812	1501454
二、本年各项应付款合计	**Total Sums of Money to be Paid This Year**	**8511550**	**1048594**	**7362577**	**7563521**
#工程款	Project Fund	4788872	437733	3992497	4207619

5-22 房地产开发经营情况（2021年）

Running of Real Estate Development (2021)

单位：万元 (10 000 yuan)

指 标	Item	全市合计 Total	#国有 State-owned	#市区 Urban	#市属 Municipal
一、资产负债情况	**Assets and Liabilities**				
1. 资产总计	Total Assets	189720543	30108701	160410240	179983210
2. 负债合计	Total Liabilities	164210760	22950510	139238376	155987613
3. 所有者权益合计	Total owners' equity	25509783	7158191	21171864	23995597
#实收资本	Held Capital	17982080	4054275	15241644	16684591
二、损益及分配情况	**Profit or Loss and the Distribution**				
1. 主营业务收入	Revenue from Principal Business	17157468	1519938	15069088	16145737
土地转让收入	Revenue of Land Transferred	4775		3649	4775
商品房屋销售收入	Revenue of Commercial Houses Sold	15511416	582557	13730584	14727881
自持物业收入	Self-owned Property Income	131443	8195	128830	127307
#房屋出租收入	Revenue of Houses Leased	111360	8195	108746	111360
其他收入	Other Revenue	1509834	929186	1206026	1285775
2. 主营业务成本	Cost of Principal Business	12191440	1084648	10668226	11630859
3. 主营业务税金及附加	Taxes and Other Charges on Principal Business	942715	27389	843922	902073
4. 其他业务利润	Other Business Profit	60104	3822	59749	56700
5. 销售费用	Sales Expenditures	890988	30693	757107	859848
6. 管理费用	Management Cost	708500	53440	650388	682308
7. 财务费用	Fiscal Expenditure	352601	175160	329277	343339
#利息支出	Interest Exchange	382264	173286	364446	353848
8. 营业利润	Operating Profit	2284277	188736	2010749	1968971
投资收益	Investment Revenue	349725	77867	264645	231703
营业外收入	Non-business Revenue	61117	11831	51995	60571
营业外支出	Non-business Expenditures	87480	8528	70826	86636
9. 利润总额	Total Profit	2199241	189794	1939138	1887486
10. 应付职工薪酬	Salary Payable	573547	64600	501358	531117
11. 应交增值税	Value-added Tax Payable	953986	87662	803604	895603
三、全部从业人员年平均人数（人）	**Average Number of Employed Persons(Person)**	**85323**			
四、本年应付工资总额	**Total Wages This Year**	**716474**			

注：因劳动工资统计制度改革，自2020年开始，取消登记注册类型分组数据和分区县数据，故相关分组数据暂缺。

主要统计指标解释

固定资产投资(不含农户) 指城镇和农村各种登记注册类型的企业、事业、行政单位及城镇个体户进行的计划总投资500万元及500万元以上的建设项目投资和房地产开发投资，包含原口径城镇固定资产投资加上农村企事业组织项目投资，该口径自2011年起开始使用。

房地产开发投资 指各种登记注册类型的房地产开发公司、商品房建设公司及其他房地产开发法人单位和附属于其他法人单位实际从事房地产开发或经营活动的单位统一开发的包括统代建、拆迁还建的住宅、厂房、仓库、饭店、宾馆、度假村、写字楼、办公楼等房屋建筑物和配套的服务设施，土地开发工程（如道路、给水、排水、供电、供热、通讯、平整场地等基础设施工程)的投资；不包括单纯的土地交易活动。

固定资产投资的资金来源 根据固定资产投资的资金来源不同，分为国家预算资金、国内贷款、利用外资、自筹资金和其他资金。

（1）国家预算资金：包括一般预算、政府性基金预算、国有资本经营预算和社保基金预算等资金。

（2）国内贷款：指报告期固定资产投资单位向银行及非银行金融机构借入的用于固定资产投资的各种国内借款，包括银行利用自有资金及吸收的存款发放的贷款、上级主管部门拨入的国内贷款、国家专项贷款、地方财政专项资金安排的贷款、国内储备贷款、周转贷款等。

（3）利用外资：指报告期收到的用于固定资产建造和购置的境外资金（包括设备、材料、技术在内）。包括对外借款（外国政府、国际金融组织贷款、出口信贷、外国银行商业贷款、对外发行债券和股票）、外商直接投资及外商其他投资。不包括我国自有外汇资金（国家外汇、地方外汇、留成外汇、调剂外汇和中国银行自有资金发行的外汇贷款等）。计算利用外资时，需要折算成人民币，折算中所使用的外汇汇率按现汇计算，即按使用外汇时的汇率计算。

（4）自筹资金：指固定资产投资单位报告期收到的，由各地区、各部门及企、事业单位筹集用于固定资产投资的预算外资金，包括中央各部门、各级地方和企、事业单位的自筹资金。

（5）其他资金：指在报告期收到的除以上各种资金之外其他用于固定资产投资的资金，包括企业或金融机构通过发行各种债券筹集到的资金、社会集资、个人资金、无偿捐赠的资金及其他单位拨人的资金等。

固定资产投资按国民经济行业分 根据现有企业、事业、行政单位和建设项目建成投产后的主要产品种类或主要用途及社会经济活动性质来确定国民经济行业。一般情况下，一个建设项目或一个企业、事业单位只能属于一种国民经济行业。

固定资产投资按隶属关系分 是按建设单位或企业、事业、行政单位的主管上级机关确定的。

（1）中央：是指中共中央、人大常委会和国务院各部、委、局、总公司以及直属机构直接领导的建设项目和企业、事业、行政单位。这些单位的固定资产投资计划由国务院各部门直接编制和下达，建设中所需物资、主要设备以及建设中的问题都由中央有关部门安排和解决。

（2）地方：是由省（自治区、直辖市）、地区（州、盟、省辖市）、县（旗、县级市）三级政府及业务主管部门直接领导和管理的建设项目、企业、事业、行政单位。地方项目还包括不隶属以上各级政府及主管部门的建设项目和企业、事业单位，如外商投资企业和无主管部门的企业等。

固定资产投资按建设性质分 根据整个建设项目情况来确定。建设项目的性质一般分为新建、扩建、改建和技术改造、单纯建造生活设施、迁建、恢复、单纯购置。房地产开发单位、农户投资不划分建设性质。

（1）新建：一般指从无到有开始建设的企业、事业和行政单位或建设项目。有的单位原有基础很小，经过建设后新增的固定资产价值超过该企、事业、行政单位原有固定资产价值（原值）三倍以上的也应作为新建。

（2）扩建：指在厂内或其他地点，为扩大原有产品的生产能力（或效益）或增加新的产品生产能力，而增建主要的生产车间（或主要工程）、分厂、独立的生产线。行政、事业单位在原单位增建业务用房（如学校增建教学用房、医院增建门诊部、病房等）也作为扩建。

现有企、事业单位为扩大原有主要产品生产能力或增加新的产品生产能力，增建一个或几个主要生产车间（或主要工程）、分厂，同时进行一些更新改造工程的，也应作为扩建。

（3）改建和技术改造：指现有企业、事业单位，对原有设施进行技术改造或更新（包括相应配套的辅助性生产、生活福利设施）的建设项目。现有企业、事业单位为适应市场变化的需要，而改变企业的主要产品种类（如军工企业转产民用品等）的建设项目，应作为改建。原有产品生产作业线由于各工序（车间）之间能力不平衡，为填平补齐充分发挥原有生产能力而增建不增加本企业主要产品设计能力的车间，也应作为改建。技术改造是指企业、事业单位在现有基础上，用先进的技术代替落后的技术，用先进的工艺和装备代替落后的工艺和装备，以改变企业落后的技术经济面貌，实现以内涵为主的扩大再生产，达到提高产品质量、促进产品更新换代、节约能源、降低消耗、扩大生产规模、全面提高社会经济效益的目的。技术改造具体包括以下内容：机器设备和工具的更新改造；生产工艺改革、节约能源和原材料的改造；厂房建筑和公共设施的改造；劳动条件和生产环境的改造等。

固定资产投资按构成分 固定资产投资活动按其工作内容和实现方式分为建筑安装工程，设备工具器具购置和其他费用三个部分。

（1）建筑安装工程（建筑安装工作量）：指各种房屋、建筑物的建造工程和各种设备、装置的安装工程。包括各种房屋建造工程；各种用途设备基础和各种工业窑炉的砌筑工程及金属结构工程；为施工而进行的各种准备工作和临时工程以及完工后的清理工作等；铁路、道路的铺设，矿井的开凿及石油管道的架设等；水利工程；防空地下建筑等特殊工程；列入房屋工程预算内的暖气、卫生、通风、照明、煤气等设备的价值及装设油饰工程；列入建筑工程预算内的各种管道（蒸汽、压缩空气、石油、给排水等管道）、电力、电讯电缆导线等的敷设工程；以及各种机械设备的安装下程；为测定安装工程质量，对设备进行的试运工作；房地产开发单位进行的商品房屋开发建设工程、土地开发工程。

在建筑安装工程中，不包括被安装设备本身的价值。

（2）设备工具器具购置：指建设单位或企、事业单位购置或自制的，达到固定资产标准的设备、工具、器具的价值。新建单位及扩建单位的新建车间，按照设计或计划要求购置或自制的全部设备、工具、器具，不论是否达到固定资产标准均计入“设备工具器具购置”中。

（3）其他费用：指在固定资产建造和购置过程中发生的，除上述几项内容以外的各种应分摊计入固定资产的费用。

施工项目 指报告期内所有施工的建设项目个数，包括本年新开工的项目和以前年度开工在本年继续施工的建设项目。凡是报告期内施过工的建设项目，不论施工时间长短，均作为施工项目统计。施工项目个数可以反映一定时期固定资产投资的实际规模，与同期全部建成投产项目个数相比，可以从建设速度的角度反映固定资产投资的效果。

全部建成投产项目 指报告期内按设计文件规定的全部生产能力（或效益）建成投产，经验收合格交付使用的建设项目。

新增生产能力（或工程效益） 指通过固定资产投资活动而增加的设计能力（或工程效益）。主要指标包括建设规模、本年施工规模、自开始建设累计新增生产能力（或工程效益）、 本年新增生产能力（或工程效益）等。

建设规模 指建设项目或工程设计文件中规定的全部设计能力（或工程效益）。包括已经建成投产和尚未建成投产的工程的生产能力（或工程效益）。

本年施工规模 指报告期内施工的单项工程的设计能力（或工程效益），即全部建设规模中在本年正式施工的部分。

自开始建设累计新增生产能力（或工程效益） 指自开始建设至本年底止建成投产的全部单项工程累计的新增生产能力（或工程效益）。

本年新增生产能力（或工程效益） 指在本年度内按照新增生产能力（或工程效益）的计算条件和标准，实际建成投入生产或交付使用的生产能力（或工程效益）。

房屋施工面积 指报告期内施工的全部房屋（包括地下室、半地下室以及配套房屋）建筑面积。包括本期新开工的面积和上期开工跨入本期继续施工的房屋面积，以及上期已停建在本期恢复施工的房屋面积。本期竣工和本期施工后又停缓建的房屋，其建筑面积仍计入本期房屋施工面积中。

房屋竣工面积 指在报告期内房屋建筑按照设计要求已经全部完工，达到住人和使用条件，经验收鉴定合格（或达到竣工验收标准），可正式移交使用的各栋房屋建筑面积的总和。

新增固定资产 指报告期内交付使用的固定资产价值。包括本年内建成投入生产或交付使用的工程投资和达到固定资产标准的设备、工具、器具的投资及有关应摊入的费用。该指标是表示固定资产投资成果的价值指标，也是反映建设进度，计算固定资产投资效果的重要指标。

项目建成投产率 指一定时期内全部建成投产项目个数与同期施工项目个数的比率。该指标是从建设单位建设速度的角度反映投资效果的指标。

固定资产交付使用率 指一定时期新增固定资产与同期完成投资额的比率。该指标是反映固定资产动用速度，衡量建设过程中宏观投资效果的综合指标。由于新增固定资产是较长时期内形成的结果，而投资额则是当年完成的，因此，该指标一般适宜于反映较长时期内固定资产的动用情况。

商品房销售面积 指报告期内出售商品房屋的合同总面积（即双方签署的正式买卖合同中所确定的建筑面积）。由现房销售建筑面积和期房销售建筑面积两部分组成。

商品房销售额 指报告期内出售商品房屋的合同总价款（即双方签署的正式买卖合同中所确定的合同总价）。该指标与商品房销售面积同口径，由现房销售额和期房销售额两部分组成。

Explanatory Notes on Main Statistical Indicators

Investment in Fixed Assets (Excluding Rural Households) refers to the investment in construction projects with a total planned investment of 5 million yuan and above by enterprises of various ownerships, public institutions, administrative units and urban self-employed individuals, and the investment in real estate development in both urban and rural areas. Since 2011, it has covered the urban investment in fixed assets of original statistical ranges and project investments by rural enterprises and public institutions.

Investment in Real Estate Development refers to investment by real estate development companies, commercialized buildings construction companies and other real estate development units of various types of ownership in the construction of buildings, such as residential buildings, factory buildings, warehouses, hotels, guesthouses, holiday villages, office buildings, and the complementary service facilities and land development projects, such as roads, water supply, water drainage, power supply,heating supply, telecommunications, land leveling and other infrastructural projects. It does not include activities in pure land transactions.

Sources of Funds for Investment in Fixed Assets are categorized as funds from the State budget, domestic loans, foreign investment, self-raised funds, and others, depending on the sources of investment.

(1) Fund from the State budget consists of budgetary appropriation and loans from the State budget. More specifically, it includes, from the budget of the central government, capital construction fund (operation fund and non-operational fund), special expenses, loans from repayment, discount fund, expenses on innovation and trial production of new products, expenses on urban construction, expenses on temporary construction from business departments, development fund for less developed areas, as well as local budgetary fund transferred from the central budget.

(2) Domestic loans refer to loans of various forms borrowed by investing units from banks and non-bank financial institutions during the reference period for the purpose of investment in fixed assets, including loans issued by banks from their self-owned funds and deposit, loans appropriated by higher authorities, special loans by government, loans arranged by local government from special funds, domestic reserve loan, and working loan.

(3) Foreign investment refers to overseas funds received during the reference period for the construction and purchase of investment in fixed assets (covering equipment, materials and technology), including foreign borrowings (loans from foreign governments and international financial institutions, export credit, commercial loans from foreign banks, issue of bonds and stocks overseas), foreign direct investment and other foreign investments. Excluded from this category is capital in foreign exchanges owned by China (foreign exchanges owned by the central and local governments, foreign exchanges retained by enterprises, foreign exchanges by enterprises through the regulating mechanism, loans in foreign exchanges issued by the Bank of China with its own fund, etc.). In calculating the utilization of foreign capital, foreign currencies are converted into the Chinese RMB applying the current exchange rate when the foreign capital are used.

(4) Self-raised funds refer to extra-budgetary funds for investment in fixed assets received during the reference period by investing units from central government ministries, local governments, enterprises and institutions, including their self-raised funds.

(5) Others refer to funds for investment in fixed assets received from sources other than those listed above, including capital raised through issuing bonds by enterprises or financial institutions, funds raised from individuals and through donations, and funds transferred from other units.

Investment in Fixed Assets by Sector The classification of construction projects by sector is determined by enterprises, institutions, administrative units and the major products or the purpose of the projects of existing enterprises, institutional and administrative units when they are put into production or use, and by the nature of their social economic activities. In general, one project or one enterprise or institution can only be classified into one sector.

Investment in Fixed Assets by Jurisdiction of Management refers to the classification of investment by the competent authorities under which investment is made by construction units, enterprises, institutions or administrative units.

(1) Central investment refers to the investment in projects or by enterprises, institutions or administrative

units which are under the direct leadership and management of the State Council and of the national commissions, ministries, agencies and State-owned large corporations. Various ministries and departments of the State Council prepare and implement plans for investment in fixed assets by those departments, and arrange and ensure the supply of materials and key equipment required for the projects.

(2) Local investment refers to the investment in projects or by enterprises, institutions or administrative units which are under the direct leadership and management of departments under the provincial, prefecture and county governments. Also included are projects by foreign-invested enterprises and enterprises without competent managing authorities.

Investment in Fixed Assets by Type of Construction

Construction projects in general can be classified, by the type of construction, into new construction, expansion, reconstruction and technical transformation, purely construction of living facilities, moving, restoration and purely purchasing. However, investment by type of construction is not applied to investment by real-estate development units and investment by rural households.

(1) New construction in general refers to construction projects, which start from scratch, of enterprises, institutions, administrative agencies. In case the size of the existing unit is quite small, and the value of newly added fixed assets is more than three times of the original value, the expansion will be considered as new construction.

(2) Expansion refers to construction of new major production workshop, branch factory or independent production line within a factory or in other locations, for the purpose of increasing the production capacity (or improving efficiency) or adding new production capacity. Newly constructed accommodations for the operation of institutions and administrative organizations (such as newly constructed buildings for teaching in schools, buildings for clinics or wards in hospitals, etc.) are also classified as expansion.Also included in expansion are investments by existing enterprises or institutions in building major production line(s) or branch factories along with some work on innovation, for the purpose of expanding the production capacity of original products or producing new products.

(3) Reconstruction and technological transformation refers to construction projects by existing enterprises or institutions in innovation or technological transformation of the old facilities (including auxiliary production equipment and welfare facilities). Also considered as reconstruction is the construction of new workshops by the existing enterprises or institutions to change the variety of products to meet the market demand (such as the production of civil products by defense industries), or to bring the designed production capacity into full play through a more balanced production process on production lines. Technological transformation refers to replacement of old technology or equipment with new technology or equipment, in order to expand the reproduction through improvement of technology contents in production, to improve product quality, to promote new products to save energy, to reduce consumption, to expand the production scale and to improve overall social- economic efficiency. Contents of technical transformation include: updating of machinery, equipment and tools; reforming production process by using energy or materials saving technology; construction of factory workshops and transformation of public facilities; improvement of working conditions and environment, etc.

Investment in Fixed Assets by Structure By their contents and the mode of implementation, investment activities are classified into three categories, i.e., construction and installation, purchase of equipment and instrument, and other expenses.

(1) Construction and installation (work volume of construction and installation) refers to the construction of houses and buildings and the installation of various kinds of equipment and instruments. They include construction of houses; equipment foundations, industrial kilns and stoves, and metal structure work; preparation works and temporary works for project construction, and clearing up works post project construction; pavement of railways and roads; drilling of mines and putting up of oil pipes; construction of water conservancy; construction of underground air-raid shelters and construction of other special projects; value of equipment for heating, sanitation, ventilation, lighting, gas, painting, etc. that are

covered by the budget of housing projects; laying out of various pipelines (for steam, compressed air, petroleum, tap water and sewage) and wiring and cabling for electric power and for communications; installation of various machinery and equipment; testing operation for pre-testing the quality of installation projects, and land and other development work conducted by real estate developers for commercialized housing.

The value of equipment installed is itself not included in the value of construction and installation projects.

(2) Purchase of equipment and instruments refers to the total value of equipment, tools, and instruments purchased or self-produced which come up to the cut-off point for fixed assets by the construction units or investing enterprises or institutions. Equipment, tools and instruments purchased or self-produced for new workshops by newly established or expanded units are categorized as "purchase of equipment and instruments" no matter whether they come up to the cut- off point for fixed assets.

(3) Other expenses refer to expenses arising during the construction or purchase of fixed assets other than those mentioned above.

Projects under Construction refer to number of all projects with construction activities newly started in current year or left-over from the previous year in the reference period. All projects that have construction activities undertaken during the reference period are reported as projects under construction irrespective of the length of construction work. The number of projects under construction can reflect the actual size of investment in fixed assets during a given period, and when compared with the number of projects completed and put into use during the same period, it demonstrates the results of investment in fixed assets from the angle of the speed of the construction.

Projects Completed and Put into Use refer to projects have been completed in accordance with the design documents, resulting in forming production capacity (efficiency) and have been checked and accepted after relevant tests, and have been formally delivered for use.

Newly Increased Production Capacity (or Project Efficiency) refers to the increase in design capacity (or project efficiency) through investment in fixed assets. The main indicators include: construction scale, scale of projects under construction in current year, the accumulated newly increased production capacity (project efficiency) since the start of the projects and the newly increased production capacity (project efficiency) of current year.

Construction Scale refers to the total designed production capacity (project efficiency) of the construction projects in accordance with the design document, including those have been put into operation and those that have not been completed.

Scale of Projects under Construction in Current Year refers to the designed production capacity (project efficiency) of a single project under construction in the reference period, i.e. the part of the total scale of project which is officially under construction in current year.

The Accumulated Newly Increased Production Capacity (project efficiency) since the Start of the Projects refers to the accumulated newly increased production capacity of all the single projects which have been put into use from the beginning of the projects till the end of current year.

The Newly Increased Production Capacity (project efficiency) of Current Year refers to the production capacity (project efficiency) that has been completed and put into operation in current year according to the calculation conditions and standards on newly increased production capacity (project efficiency).

Floor Space of Buildings under Construction refers to the total floor space of all the buildings (including basement, semi-basement and auxiliary buildings), including the effective area and the area occupied by the structure. This indicator is one of the important indicators in physical terms to reflect the scale and accomplishment of the construction industry and also an important basis for monitoring the progress, Calculating the cost, analyzing the efficiency and studying the supply of building materials in relation to the construction projects.

Floor Space Completed refers to the floor space of all buildings completed in the reference period, which have been appraised and accepted (or come up to the designed standards) and have been transferred to owner units.

Newly Increased Fixed Assets refer to the value of fixed that has been put into use, including investment in projects that have been completed and put into operation in current year and the investment in equipment, tools and appliances that meet the standard of fixed assets and fees that should be apportioned. This is an indicator that demonstrates the results of investment in fixed assets in monetary terms, and an important indicator to reflect the speed of construction and to calculate the efficiency of investment.

Rate of Construction Projects Completed and Put into Use refers to the ratio of the number of construction projects completed and put into use in a certain period of time to the number of projects under construction in the same period. This reflects the investment efficiency from the perspective of the speed of project construction.

6 财　政

GOVERNMENT FINANCE

资料整理：孟　刚
Data management: Meng Gang
数据审核：罗延庆
Data audit: Luo Yanqing

第六部分　财政

一、简要说明

本章资料主要包括地方财政收入、支出总额构成及分区县情况，由西安市统计局综合处根据西安市财政局提供资料整理。

二、主要指标

财政总收入（亿元）	1851.57	比上年增长	20.1%
一般公共预算收入（亿元）	856.00	比上年增长	18.2%
一般公共预算支出（亿元）	1474.62	比上年增长	9.4%

6　GOVERNMENT FINANCE

Ⅰ.Brief Introduction

This chapter consists of primarily data on regional revenue, expenditure of the municipal government, regional revenue and expenditure of the districts and the counties. The data are provided by the Xi'an Bureau of Finance and are compiled by Integration division of the Xi'an Bureau of Statistics.

Ⅱ.Major Indicators

		Increase over Preceding Year
Total Government Revenue(100 mil.yuan)	1851.57	20.1%
General Pubilc Budget Revenue(100 mil.yuan)	856.00	18.2%
General Pubilc Budget Expenditures(100 mil.yuan)	1474.62	9.4%

6-1 主要年份地方财政一般预算收入及支出

General Public Budget Revenue and Expenditure of Local Finance in Representative Years

单位：亿元 (100 million yuan)

年 份 Year	财政总收入 Fiscal Revenue	一般公共预算收入 General Public Budget Revenue	一般公共预算支出 General Public Budget Expenditure	收支差额 Balance of Payments	财政总收入比上年增长（%） Fiscal Revenue Increased over the Previous Year (%)	一般公共预算收入比上年增长（%） General Public Budget Revenue Growth over the Previous Year (%)	一般公共预算支出比上年增长（%） General Public Budget Expenditures Growth over the Previous Year (%)
2000	61.57	41.39	46.50	-5.11		14.4	
2001	75.79	51.45	54.21	-2.76	23.1	9.9	10.2
2002	99.84	54.49	63.80	-9.32	31.7	16.9	11.3
2003	120.64	64.80	72.37	-7.57	20.8	21.6	22.6
2004	133.52	75.31	84.20	-8.88	10.7	20.0	16.3
2005	163.87	73.05	97.82	-24.76	22.7	18.2	16.2
2006	195.96	85.89	119.22	-33.33	19.6	18.6	21.9
2007	260.70	112.92	161.25	-48.33	33.0	31.5	35.3
2008	324.49	145.61	226.99	-81.38	24.5	28.9	40.8
2009	399.53	181.40	276.85	-95.45	23.4	24.6	22.0
2010	510.69	241.86	371.62	-129.76	27.6	33.3	34.2
2011	649.88	318.55	494.58	-176.03	27.3	31.7	33.1
2012	753.08	396.96	597.49	-200.53	15.9	24.6	20.8
2013	902.76	501.98	729.81	-227.84	19.9	26.5	22.1
2014	1019.69	583.79	819.54	-235.75	13.0	16.3	12.3
2015	1114.98	650.99	917.24	-266.25	9.3	16.3	12.9
2016	1135.68	641.07	942.52	-301.46	8.5	11.1	2.8
2017	1364.71	654.50	1045.09	-390.59	12.6	9.8	7.1
2018	1460.39	684.70	1151.87	-467.17	13.6	10.8	10.2
2019	1533.89	702.56	1247.02	-544.45	5.0	2.6	8.3
2020	1541.50	724.14	1347.58	-623.44	0.5	3.1	8.1
2021	1851.57	856.00	1474.62	-618.62	20.1	18.2	9.4

注：本表数据来源于市财政局，对部分历史数据进行了修订。

6-2 财政收入（2021年）

Government Revenue (2021)

单位：万元 (10 000 yuan)

指　　标	Item	2021
财政总收入	**Total Government Revenue**	**18515744**
#一般公共预算收入	**General Public Budget Revenue**	**8559990**
一、税收收入	**Total Tax Revenue**	**6824732**
1. 增值税	Value-added Tax	2605377
2. 企业所得税	Corporate Income Tax	804489
3. 个人所得税	Individual Income Tax	329364
4. 城市建设维护税	City Maintenance and Construction Tax	570100
5. 房产税	House Property Tax	351420
6. 城镇土地使用税	Urban Land Use Tax	114444
7. 印花税	Stamp Tax	236580
8. 车船税	Tax on the Use of Vehicles and Ships	133026
9. 土地增值税	Land Appreciation Tax	557770
10. 资源税	Resource Tax	22547
11. 环境保护税	Environment Protection Tax	901
12. 耕地占用税	Farm Land Occupatian Tax	105840
13. 契税	Deed Tax	992783
14. 其他税收收入	Other Tax Revenue	91
二、非税收入	**Total Non-tax Revenue**	**1735258**
1. 行政事业性收费收入	Charge of Administrative and Institutional Units	239777
2. 罚没收入	Penalty Receipts	253382
3. 专项收入	Special Program Receipts	565329
4. 国有资本经营收入	State-owned Assets Profit	11878
5. 国有资源（资产）有偿使用收入	Revenue for the Use of State-owned Assets (Resources)	359732
6. 捐赠收入	Donation Income	226
7. 政府住房基金收入	Governmental Housing Fund Income	304080
8. 其他收入	Other Non-tax Revenue	854
政府性基金预算收入	**Government Fund Budget Revenue**	**14603853**

注：本表数据来源于市财政局。

6-3 财政支出（2021年）

Government Expenditure (2021)

单位：万元 (10 000 yuan)

指　标	Item	2021
一般公共预算支出	**General Public Budget Expenditure**	**14746219**
1. 一般公共服务支出	Expenditure for General Public Services	1413346
2. 国防支出	Expenditure for National Defense	15860
3. 公共安全支出	Expenditure for Public Security	868972
4. 教育支出	Expenditure for Education	2559436
5. 科学技术支出	Expenditure for Science and Technology	573530
6. 文化旅游体育与传媒支出	Expenditure for Culture,Tourism,Sport and Media	480690
7. 社会保障和就业支出	Expenditure for Social Safety Net and Employment Effort	1556139
8. 卫生健康支出	Expenditure for Health Care	1498789
9. 节能环保支出	Expenditure for Energy Conservation and Environment Protection	513272
10. 城乡社区支出	Expenditure for Urban and Rural Community Affairs	1834153
11. 农林水支出	Expenditure for Agriculture, Forestry and Water Conservancy	520077
12. 交通运输支出	Expenditure for Transportation	408243
13. 资源勘探工业信息等支出	Expenditure for Industry Exploration of the Power of Information	539922
14. 商业服务业等支出	Expenditure for Business Services	336173
15. 金融支出	Expenditure for Finance	181594
16. 自然资源海洋气象等支出	Expenditure for Nature Resources，Ocean and Weather	100391
17. 住房保障支出	Expenditure for Housing Security	786836
18. 粮油物资储备支出	Expenditure for Grain and Oil Stockpiles	28867
19. 灾害防治及应急管理支出	Expenditures for Disaster Prevention and Emergency Management	94952
20. 其他支出	Other Expenditure	116756
21. 债务付息支出	Debt Service Expenditure	315875
22. 债务发行费用支出	Debt Issuance Expenditure	2346
政府性基金预算支出	**Governmental Fund Budgetary Expenditure**	**14693637**

注：本表数据来源于市财政局。

6-4 各区县、开发区财政收入（2021年）

单位：万元

区县、开发区	Region	一般公共预算收入 General Public Budget Revenue	税收收入 Tax Revenue	增值税 Value Added Tax
合计	**Total**	**8559990**	**6824732**	**2605377**
市本级	City Level	1688132	831913	475773
新城区	Xincheng	226272	209026	65500
碑林区	Beilin	410933	379508	168951
莲湖区	Lianhu	400385	367814	158911
灞桥区	Baqiao	201166	175383	63790
未央区	Weiyang	341533	299439	112328
雁塔区	Yanta	492942	442414	179465
阎良区	Yanliang	88991	61494	23971
临潼区	Lintong	140817	81310	32505
长安区	Chang'an	239588	197979	71378
高陵区	Gaoling	141552	124594	50767
鄠邑区	Huyi	88595	66668	30504
蓝田县	Lantian	45132	36097	14945
周至县	Zhouzhi	26449	19988	7953
西咸新区	Xixian New Area	1064896	853606	248740
高新区	Hi-Tech Industries Development Zone	1386329	1290206	489102
经开区	Economic Development Zone	467588	437483	160088
曲江新区	Qujiang New District	418158	377502	94623
航空基地	National Aviation Hi-tech Industrial Base	24135	21604	7143
航天基地	National Civil Aerospace Industrial Base	127401	116951	30219
浐灞生态区	Chan-ba Ecological District	235587	201083	41242
国际港务区	International Trade & Logistics Park	303409	232670	77479

注：本表数据来源于市财政局。

Government Revenue by Region and Development Zone (2021)

(10 000 yuan)

一般公共预算收入 General Public Budgetary Revenue				
税收收入 Tax Revenue				
企业所得税 Corporate Income Tax	个人所得税 Individual Income Tax	城市维护建设税 City Maintenance and Construction Tax	房产税 House Property Tax	城镇土地使用税 Urban Land Use Tax
804489	**329364**	**570100**	**351420**	**114444**
54282	12389	118734	16073	2183
48768	16157	15779	15658	3589
71700	37752	31979	26399	2995
42315	30099	29328	17990	5714
27704	2978	14598	7793	4973
39608	9875	23768	17232	6750
41848	24780	36460	28989	5194
6021	5005	3327	4940	2716
7806	3003	6103	4113	2454
30580	5961	15693	7596	3243
8964	3674	11560	7077	6684
4082	1803	6207	3895	2198
1950	706	2132	1336	963
394	761	1041	588	440
75061	16006	53090	31607	20360
173352	107785	108817	94640	18546
58941	19198	38784	26500	10781
56894	15068	18685	19448	4593
1990	1666	3037	1163	1078
16611	8681	6761	4040	1172
13708	3692	7851	4472	3497
21910	2325	16366	9871	4321

6-4 续表1

单位：万元

区县、开发区	Region	一般公共预算收入 General Public Budget Revenue		
		税收收入 Tax Revenue		
		印花税 Stamp Tax	车船税 Tax on the Use of Vehicles and Ships	土地增值税 Land Appreciation Tax
合计	**Total**	**236580**	**133026**	**557770**
市本级	City Level	22473	108458	
新城区	Xincheng	6348		19862
碑林区	Beilin	13167		3876
莲湖区	Lianhu	13560		19348
灞桥区	Baqiao	5400		19122
未央区	Weiyang	9706		28171
雁塔区	Yanta	9400		38390
阎良区	Yanliang	1982	2497	2343
临潼区	Lintong	3375	2863	2239
长安区	Chang'an	7447	3543	8207
高陵区	Gaoling	6651	2446	5810
鄠邑区	Huyi	1412	2816	3461
蓝田县	Lantian	829	1416	3122
周至县	Zhouzhi	422	1890	1732
西咸新区	Xixian New Area	22557	7097	115474
高新区	Hi-Tech Industries Development Zone	49251		111471
经开区	Economic Development Zone	31870		18273
曲江新区	Qujiang New District	7202		46709
航空基地	National Aviation Hi-tech Industrial Base	558		2932
航天基地	National Civil Aerospace Industrial Base	4955		17388
浐灞生态区	Chan-ba Ecological District	4269		47222
国际港务区	International Trade & Logistics Park	13746		42618

continued 1

(10 000 yuan)

一般公共预算收入 General Public Budget Revenue					
税收收入 Tax Revenue					非税收入 Non-tax Revenue
资源税 Resource Tax	环境保护税 Environment Protection Tax	耕地占用税 Farm Land Occupation Tax	契税 Deed Tax	其他税收收入 Other Tax Revenue	
22547	**901**	**105840**	**992783**	**91**	**1735258**
20849	697			2	856219
			17354	11	17246
1			22641	47	31425
18			50505	26	32571
			29024	1	25783
3		187	51775	36	42094
11		1458	76283	136	50528
			8692		27497
210		622	16012	5	59507
112		1851	42360	8	41609
		1257	19704		16958
47		2086	8157		21927
39		1167	7492		9035
92		714	3961		6461
1111	204	91668	170180	451	211290
24		4830	132386	2	96123
12			73051	-15	30105
18			115140	-878	40656
			1983	54	2531
			27128	-4	10450
			74919	211	34504
			44036	-2	70739

6-4 续表2

单位：万元

区县、开发区	Region	一般公共预算收入 General Public Budget Revenue		
		非税收入 Non-tax Revenue		
		行政事业性收费收入 Charge of Adiministrative and Institutional Units	罚没收入 Penalty Receipts	专项收入 Special Program Receipts
合计	**Total**	**239777**	**253382**	**565329**
市本级	City Level	162848	123702	189468
新城区	Xincheng	2543	3936	8809
碑林区	Beilin	2520	4926	18040
莲湖区	Lianhu	4019	5277	17457
灞桥区	Baqiao	3312	3924	7603
未央区	Weiyang	1200	3458	26080
雁塔区	Yanta	6839	15940	19998
阎良区	Yanliang	3259	2341	7258
临潼区	Lintong	3088	11651	3472
长安区	Chang'an	6916	20448	7892
高陵区	Gaoling	2638	3044	5878
鄠邑区	Huyi	2701	4466	3525
蓝田县	Lantian	1342	2703	1808
周至县	Zhouzhi	2057	933	927
西咸新区	Xixian New Area	18663	24264	104827
高新区	Hi-Tech Industries Development Zone	7729	3961	62175
经开区	Economic Development Zone	1535	1138	23134
曲江新区	Qujiang New District	437	3259	15949
航空基地	National Aviation Hi-tech Industrial Base	218	389	1710
航天基地	National Civil Aerospace Industrial Base	2701	2114	4787
浐灞生态区	Chan-ba Ecological District	561	5860	5585
国际港务区	International Trade & Logistics Park	2651	5648	28947

continued 2

(10 000 yuan)

一般公共预算收入 General Public Budget Revenue					政府性基金预算收入
非税收入 Non-tax Revenue					
国有资本经营收入 State-owned Assets Profit	国有资源（资产）有偿使用收入 The Revenues of the Compensation for the Use of State-owned Resoures(Assants)	捐赠收入 Donation Income	政府住房基金收入 Government Housing Fund Income	其他收入 Other income	Government Fund Budget Revenue
11878	**359732**	**226**	**304080**	**854**	**14603853**
	107017	108	272279	797	798140
	1958				1128
	5939				3492
	5818				63370
	10906	38			82678
	11356				127608
3	7748				
	14639				62272
11801	29333		162		229199
	6046		250	57	167230
	5352		46		463282
	10778		457		71949
	3175		7		190971
	2544				47149
	56281	30	7225		6556712
	6081		16177		2169072
	541		3757		627824
74	18770		2167		685859
	168		46		37239
	593		255		295170
	21246		1252		817809
	33443	50			1105700

6-5 各区县、开发区财政支出（2021年）

单位：万元

区县、开发区	Region	一般公共预算支出 General Public Budget Expenditure	一般公共服务支出 Expenditure for General Public Services	国防支出 Expenditure for National Defense	公共安全支出 Expenditure for Public Safety
合计	**Total**	**14746219**	**1413346**	**15860**	**868972**
市本级	City Level	4773541	256463	10447	462056
新城区	Xincheng	342964	25246	169	28550
碑林区	Beilin	310000	32555		29477
莲湖区	Lianhu	394009	44094	108	28096
灞桥区	Baqiao	296719	47989	1398	28752
未央区	Weiyang	390285	35425		25670
雁塔区	Yanta	375501	48987	1486	39197
阎良区	Yanliang	237076	27887		14519
临潼区	Lintong	475822	47116		20519
长安区	Chang'an	518904	61313	67	20061
高陵区	Gaoling	345484	48590		15086
鄠邑区	Huyi	374032	32381		16360
蓝田县	Lantian	537650	48771	7	14215
周至县	Zhouzhi	435722	41519		15997
西咸新区	Xixian New Area	1506859	325192	600	60665
高新区	Hi-Tech Industries Development Zone	1404551	99329	1078	23704
经开区	Economic Development Zone	592036	44494	500	8646
曲江新区	Qujiang New District	440848	47657		3489
航空基地	National Aviation Hi-tech Industrial Base	37220	7259		
航天基地	National Civil Aerospace Industrial Base	149590	27786		3074
浐灞生态区	Chan-ba Ecological District	281535	25982		8936
国际港务区	International Trade & Logistics Park	525871	37311		1903

注：本表数据来源于市财政局。

Government Expenditure by Region and Development Zone (2021)

(10 000 yuan)

教育支出 Expenditure for Education	科学技术支出 Expenditure for Science and Technology	文化旅游体育与传媒支出 Expenditure for Culture,Tourism, Sport and Media	社会保障和就业支出 Expenditure for Social Safety Net and Employment Effort	卫生健康支出 Expenditure for Health Care	节能环保支出 Expenditure for Energy Conservation and Environment Protection
2559436	**573530**	**480690**	**1556139**	**1498789**	**513272**
166682	76612	144152	475526	811887	181983
68699	971	2763	82689	39070	2522
92772	378	1569	76527	29381	1408
128739	720	1030	68168	22487	3005
79240	130	1598	36518	26347	1847
119183	615	3518	48815	33591	5092
105772	1174	1483	51236	38009	2271
59690	142	2210	36753	23870	4684
122274	624	9960	106211	44712	11307
143505	96	5286	97390	48754	7906
91399	253	4651	37695	42311	4883
72157	155	3690	70288	32312	13181
112248	165	8182	102385	40383	16126
113355	344	6468	72827	30713	16793
323824	6822	44968	119232	147225	29243
208225	452631	10754	59072	39705	184249
178221	309	52311	2895	19207	15589
107882		147327	1542	10476	2845
8174	2660	504	147	600	907
67680	27010	22	556	2791	2724
79119	1419	21839	590	2196	2830
110596	300	6405	9077	12762	1877

6-5 续表1

单位：万元

区县、开发区	Region	一般公共预算支出 General Public Budget Expenditure			
		城乡社区支出 Expenditure for Urban and Rural Community Affairs	农林水支出 Expenditure for Agriculture, Foresty and Water Conservancy	交通运输支出 Expenditure for Transportation	资源勘探工业信息等支出 Expenditure for Industry Exploration of Information
合计	**Total**	**1834153**	**520077**	**408243**	**539922**
市本级	City Level	913117	93009	281747	46325
新城区	Xincheng	34408	922	1436	2477
碑林区	Beilin	20060	1081	378	412
莲湖区	Lianhu	36064	1448	485	6661
灞桥区	Baqiao	30261	10572	2843	6889
未央区	Weiyang	63984	8223	2587	1415
雁塔区	Yanta	19258	3424	1530	2422
阎良区	Yanliang	31549	17119	3689	4132
临潼区	Lintong	26002	44186	7337	2772
长安区	Chang'an	35330	48612	9469	521
高陵区	Gaoling	37728	28296	10653	2208
鄠邑区	Huyi	20360	44186	14654	1327
蓝田县	Lantian	73106	79939	17016	915
周至县	Zhouzhi	38192	69236	12518	29
西咸新区	Xixian New Area	95309	31903	31969	45946
高新区	Hi-Tech Industries Development Zone	49841	13121	3324	205379
经开区	Economic Development Zone	45084	133	1308	196077
曲江新区	Qujiang New District	79187	10984		2097
航空基地	National Aviation Hi-tech Industrial Base	12201	1		2612
航天基地	National Civil Aerospace Industrial Base	2106	501		7856
浐灞生态区	Chan-ba Ecological District	117830	3749		1021
国际港务区	International Trade & Logistics Park	53176	9432	5300	429

continued 1

(10 000 yuan)

商业服务业等支出 Expenditure for Business Services	金融支出 Expenditure for Finance	自然资源海洋气象等支出 Expenditure for Nature Resources，Ocean and Weather	住房保障支出 Expenditure for Housing Support	粮油物资储备支出 Expenditure for Grain and Oil Stockpiles	灾害防治及应急管理支出 Disaster Prevention and emergency management expenditure
336173	**181594**	**100391**	**786836**	**28867**	**94952**
15624	173011	27742	412473	18240	38855
956	10	609	49022	294	659
287		860	19977	132	1063
1500	41	774	43979	120	981
296		1602	5174	243	3560
608	400	2309	23033	238	972
1617	355	1851	53558	128	956
422	160	2057	3507	400	993
545		4403	19972	100	3431
1119	214	7459	27037	437	2368
779		4607	10227	87	2522
558	85	20101	27287	178	1740
671	92	4035	11810	119	4759
1101	114	8500	2847	225	2143
28442	208	4541	36233	62	19855
4358	996	1570	9127	40	1196
1013		95	15497	7824	1660
7354	5908	35	3237		1118
113					
231		1154	3000		2190
4863		1422	6417		730
263716		4665	3422		3201

6-5 续表2 continued 2

单位：万元 (10 000 yuan)

区县、开发区	Region	一般公共预算支出 General Public Budget Expenditure			政府性基金预算支出 Government Fund Budget Expenditure
		其他支出 Other Expenditure	债务付息支出 Debt Service Expenditure	债务发行费用支出 Debt Issuance Expenditure	
合计	**Total**	**116756**	**315875**	**2346**	**14693637**
市本级	City Level	1878	163560	2152	2355657
新城区	Xincheng		1492		47112
碑林区	Beilin		1683		66555
莲湖区	Lianhu	333	5176		108223
灞桥区	Baqiao	183	11277		118128
未央区	Weiyang	69	14538		54318
雁塔区	Yanta		787		16409
阎良区	Yanliang		3293		54134
临潼区	Lintong		4351		151251
长安区	Chang'an	123	1837		150087
高陵区	Gaoling		3509		373109
鄠邑区	Huyi		3032		108574
蓝田县	Lantian	250	2456		96737
周至县	Zhouzhi	470	2331		51031
西咸新区	Xixian New Area	113280	41146	194	6090620
高新区	Hi-Tech Industries Development Zone	150	36702		1956484
经开区	Economic Development Zone		1173		351998
曲江新区	Qujiang New District		9710		697642
航空基地	National Aviation Hi-tech Industrial Base		2042		108244
航天基地	National Civil Aerospace Industrial Base		909		154949
浐灞生态区	Chan-ba Ecological District		2592		694762
国际港务区	International Trade & Logistics Park	20	2279		887613

主要统计指标解释

财政收入 指国家财政参与社会产品分配所取得的收入，是实现国家职能的财力保证。主要包括：

（1）税收收入：包括增值税、消费税、企业所得税、企业所得税退税、个人所得税、资源税、城市维护建设税、房产税、印花税、城镇土地使用税、土地增值税、车船税、船舶吨税、车辆购置税、关税、耕地占用税、契税、烟叶税、环境保护税和其他税收收入。

（2）非税收入：包括专项收入、行政事业性收费收入、罚没收入、国有资本经营收入、国有资源（资产）有偿使用收入、捐赠收入、政府住房基金收入和其他收入。

财政支出 指国家财政将筹集起来的资金进行分配使用，以满足经济建设和各项事业的需要。主要包括：

（1）一般公共服务支出：指政府提供基本公共管理与服务的支出，包括人大事务、政协事务、政府办公厅（室）及相关机构事务、发展与改革事务、统计信息事务、财政事务、税收事务、审计事务、海关事务、人力资源事务、纪检监察事务、商贸事务、知识产权事务、民族事务、港澳台侨事务、档案事务、民主党派及工商联事务、群众团体事务、党委办公厅（室）及相关机构事务、组织事务、宣传事务、统战事务、对外联络事务、其他共产党事务支出、网信服务、市场监督管理实务和其他一般公共服务支出。

（2）外交支出：指政府外交事务支出，包括外交管理事务、驻外机构、对外援助、国际组织、对外合作与交流、对外宣传、边界勘界联检、国际发展合作等方面的支出。

（3）国防支出：指政府用于国防方面的支出，包括用于现役部队、国防科研事业、专项工程、国防动员等方面的支出。

（4）公共安全支出：指政府维护社会公共安全方面的支出，包括武装警察部队、公安、国家安全、检察、法院、司法、监狱、强制隔离戒毒、国家保密、缉私警察、海警等。

（5）教育支出：指政府教育事务支出，包括教育管理事务、普通教育、职业教育、成人教育、广播电视教育、留学教育、特殊教育、进修及培训、教育费附加安排的支出等。

（6）科学技术支出：指用于科学技术方面的支出，包括科学技术管理事务、基础研究、应用研究、技术研究与开发、科技条件与服务、社会科学、科学技术普及、科技交流与合作、科技重大项目等。

（7）文化旅游体育与传媒支出：指政府在文化和旅游、文物、体育、新闻出版电影、广播电视等方面的支出。

（8）社会保障和就业支出：指政府在社会保障与就业方面的支出，包括人力资源和社会保障管理事务、民政管理事务、补充全国社会保障基金、行政事业单位离退休、企业改革补助、就业补助、抚恤、退役安置、社会福利、残疾人事业、红十字事业、最低生活保障、临时救助、特困人员救助供养、补充道路交通事故社会救助基金、其他生活救助、财政对基本养老保险基金的补助、财政对其他社会保险基金的补助、退役军人管理实务等。

（9）卫生健康支出：指政府卫生健康方面的支出，包括卫生健康管理事务、公立医院、基层医疗卫生机构、公共卫生、中医药、计划生育事务、行政事业单位医疗、财政对基本医疗保险基金的补助、医疗救助、优抚对象医疗、医疗保障管理事务、老龄卫生健康事务等。

（10）节能环保支出：指政府节能环保支出，包括环境保护管理事务、环境监测与监察、污染防治、自然生态保护、天然林保护、退耕还林、风沙荒漠治理、退牧还草、已垦草原退耕还草、能源节约利用、污染减排、可再生能源、循环经济、能源管理事务等支出。

（11）城乡社区支出：指政府城乡社区事务支出，包括城乡社区管理事务、城乡社区规划与管理、城乡社区公共设施、城乡社区环境卫生、建设市场管理与监督等。

（12）农林水支出：指政府用于农林水事务支出，包括农业、林业和草原、水利、南水北调、扶贫、农业综合开发、农村综合改革、普惠金融发展支出、目标价格补贴等。

（13）交通运输支出：指政府交通运输和邮政业方面的支出，包括公路水路运输、铁路运输、民用航空运输、成品油价格改革对交通运输的补贴、邮政业支出、车辆购置税支出等。

（14）资源勘探信息等支出：指政府用于资源勘探、制造业、建筑业、工业信息等方面的支出，包括资源勘探开发、制造业、建筑业、工业和信息产业监管、国有资产监管、支持中小企业发展和管理等。

（15）商业服务业支出：指政府用于商业服务业方面的支出，包括商业流通事务、涉外发展服务等。

（16）金融支出：指政府用于金融方面的支出，包括金融部门行政支出、金融部门监管支出、金融发展、金融调控等。

（17）援助其他地区支出：指用于援助方政府安排并管理的对其他地区各类援助、捐赠等资金支出。包括一般公共服务、教育、文化体育与传媒、医疗卫生、节能环保、农业、交通运输、住房保障等支出

（18）自然资源海洋气象等支出：指政府用于自然资源、海洋管理、测绘、气象等公益服务事业方面的支出。

（19）住房保障支出：指政府用于住房方面的支出，包括保障性安居工程支出、住房改革支出、城乡社区住宅等。

（20）粮油物资储备支出：指政府用于粮油物资储备方面的支出，包括粮油事务、物资事务、能源储备、粮油储备、重要商品储备等。

（21）灾害防治及应急管理支出：指政府用于灾害防治及应急管理方面的支出，包括应急管理事务、消防事务、森林消防事务、煤矿安全、地震事务、自然灾害防治、自然灾害救灾及恢复重建支出等。

（22）债务付息支出：指政府用于归还债务利息等所发生的支出。

（23）债务发行费用支出：指政府用于债务发行兑付费用的支出。

（24）其他支出：指不能划分到上述功能科目的其他政府支出。

中央财政收入和地方财政收入 指按现行分税制财政体制划分的中央本级收入和地方本级收入。属于中央财政的收入包括关税，进口货物增值税和消费税，出口货物退增值税和消费税，消费税，铁道部门、各银行总行、各保险公司总公司等集中缴纳的城市维护建设税，增值税50%部分，纳入共享范围的企业所得税60%部分，未纳入共享范围的中央企业所得税、中央企业上交的利润，个人所得税60%部分，车辆购置税，船舶吨税，证券交易印花税，海洋石油资源税，中央非税收入等。属于地方财政的收入包括地方企业上交利润，城市维护建设税（不含铁道部门、各银行总行、各保险公司总公司集中缴纳的部分），房产税，城镇土地使用税，土地增值税，车船税，耕地占用税，契税，烟叶税，印花税（不含证券交易印花税），增值税50%部分，纳入共享范围的企业所得税40%部分，个人所得税40%部分，海洋石油资源税以外的其他资源税，地方非税收入等。

中央财政支出和地方财政支出 指根据政府在经济和社会活动中的不同职责，划分中央和地方政府的责权，按照政府的责权划分确定的支出。中央财政支出包括一般公共服务，外交支出，国防支出，公共安全支出，以及中央政府调整国民经济结构、协调地区发展、实施宏观调控的支出等。地方财政支出包括一般公共服务，公共安全支出，地方统筹的各项社会事业支出等。

Explanatory Notes on Main Statistical Indicators

Government Revenue refers to income for the government finance through participating in the distribution of social products. It is the financial guarantee to ensure government functioning. The contents of government revenue include the following main items:

(1) Tax revenue, including value added tax(VAT), consumption tax, business tax, corporate income tax, corporate income tax refund ,individual income tax, resource tax, city maintenance and construct tax, house property tax, stamp tax, urban land use tax, land appreciation tax, tax on vehicles and boat operation, ship tonnage tax, vehicle purchase tax, tariffs, farm land occupation tax, deed tax, and tobacco leaf tax, etc.

(2) Non-tax revenue, including special program receipts, charge of administrative and institutional units, penalty receipts, state-owned capital operating income, state-owned resources (assets) compensation for the use of income, donation income, government housing fund income and others non-tax receipts.

Government Expenditure refers to the distribution and use of the funds which the government finance has raised, so as to meet the needs of economic construction and various causes. It includes the following main items:

(1) Expenditure for general public services: It refers to the spending on the basic public management and services which provided by governments, including the expense on affairs of People's Congress, affairs of People's Political Consultative Conference, affairs of government general office and relative institutions, affairs of development and reform, affairs of statistics, affairs of finance, affairs of taxation, affairs of audit, affairs of customs, affairs of human resources and social security, affairs of discipline inspection and supervision, affairs of population and family planning, affairs of commerce and trade, affairs of intellectual property, affairs of administration for industry and commerce, affairs of land and resources, affairs of oceanic administration, affairs of surveying and mapping, affairs of earthquake, ethnic affairs, religious affairs, affairs of Hong Kong, Macao, Taiwan, and Overseas Chinese, affairs of archives administration, affairs of democratic parties and federation of industry and commerce, affairs of mass organization, and affairs of lottery, affairs of the general office of the Party Committee and related institutions, affairs of propaganda, affairs of united front, affairs of external liaison, affairs of expenditure on other Communist Party, other affairs of Chinese Communist Party, etc.

(2) Expenditure for foreign affairs: It refers to the spending of government on foreign affairs, including the expense on administration of foreign affairs, missions overseas, external assistance, international organizations, foreign cooperation and communication, surveying and joint inspection on borderline, etc.

(3) Expenditure for national defense: It refers to the spending of government on national defense, including the expense on active force, scientific research on national defense, special projects, mobilization of national defense, etc.

(4) Expenditure for public security: It refers to the spending of government on maintaining social and public security, including the expense on armed police force, public security, state security, prosecution, courts, justice, prison, compulsory isolation and drug treatment, state secrecy, anti-smuggling police, maritime police, etc.

(5) Expenditure for education: It refers to the spending of government on education, including the expense on the administration of education, general education, regular vocational school education, adult education, radio and television education, student abroad education, special education, education and training, education surtax arrangements spending, etc.

(6) Expenditure for science and technology: It refers to the spending of government on science and technology (S&T), including the expense on the administration of S&T, basic research, applied research, research and development, conditions and services of S&T, social science, popularization of science and technology, exchanges and cooperation of S&T, major project of S&T, etc.

(7) Expenditure for culture, sport and media: It refers to the spending of government on culture, sports, radio, film, television, press and publication, etc.

(8) Expenditure for social safety net and employment effort: It refers to the spending of government on social safety net and employment, including the expense on administration of social safety net and employment, civil affairs, subsidy on National Social Security Fund, retirees of administrative units and institutions, subsidy on enterprise reform, subsidy on employment effort, pension, placement of ex-serviceman, social welfare, the handicapped undertakings, living relief of natural disasters, affairs of Red Cross Society, minimum subsistence security, temporary assistance, relief and assistance for the residents living in extreme poverty, supplementary social assistance fund for road traffic accidents, other life assistance, financial subsidy for basic old-age insurance fund, financial subsidy for other social insurance funds, etc.

(9) Expenditure for medical health care and birth control planning: It refers to government spending on health care, including health management services, public hospitals, primary health care institutions, public health, the pharmaceutical, family planning affairs, food and drug supervision and administration affairs, medical treatment of administrative institutions, financial subsidies to basic medical insurance funds, medical assistance, preferential care for the target medical treatment, etc.

(10) Expenditure for energy saving: It refers to the government energy-saving and environmental protection expenditures, including environmental management services, environmental monitoring and surveillance, pollution control, ecological protection, natural forest protection project, forest, desert sand control, pasture, grassland of cultivated farmland, energy conservation and utilization expenditure pollution reduction, renewable energy and comprehensive utilization of resources, etc.

(11) Expenditure for urban and rural community affairs: It refers to the spending of government on urban and rural community affairs, including the expense on administration of urban and rural community, planning and management of urban and rural community, public facilities of urban and rural community, housing of urban and rural community, sanitation of urban and rural community, management and supervision on the construction market, etc.

(12) Expenditure for agriculture, forestry and water conservancy: It refers to the spending of government on agriculture, forestry and water conservancy, including the expense on agriculture, forestry, water conservancy, South-to-North Water Diversion Project, poverty alleviation, agricultural comprehensive development, comprehensive agricultural reform, inclusive financial development expenditure and target price subsidies, etc.

(13) Expenditure for transportation: It refers to the spending of government on transportation and postal services, including the expense on road transport, sea transport, rail transport, civil aviation transportation, oil price reform subsidies for transportation, postal services, vehicle purchase tax, etc.

(14) Expenditure for exploration of the power of information: It refers to the spending on exploration, manufacturing, construction, industry information and other aspects of information, including resource exploration and development, manufacturing, construction, industry and information industry regulation, safety supervision, the state-owned assets supervision and support of small and medium enterprise development and management, etc.

(15) Expenditure for business services: It refers to government spending on commercial aspects of services, including commercial distribution business, tourism management and services, foreign development services, etc.

(16) Expenditure for financial: It refers to government spending on financial aspects, including administrative of financial sector, financial sector supervision, financial development, financial control, etc.

(17) Expenditure for assistance to other parts: It refers to the various types of assistance to other regions, financial donations, donors, government expenditure and management arrangements, etc.

(18) Expenditure for Land and Marine Meteorology: It refers to government spending on land resources, marine, mapping, seismic, weather and other aspects of

public service undertakings, etc.

(19) Expenditure for housing security: It refers to government spending on housing, including affordable housing projects, housing reform, urban and rural communities housing, etc.

(20) Expenditure for Grain and Oil stockpiles: It refers to government spending on supplies of grain and oil reserves, including grain and oil services, supplies services, energy reserves, grain and oil reserves, reserves of other important commodities, etc.

(21) Expenditure on disaster prevention and emergency management: refers to the government expenditure on disaster prevention and emergency management, including expenditure on emergency management, fire control, forest fire control, coal mine safety, earthquake, natural disaster prevention and control, natural disaster relief and recovery and reconstruction, etc.

(22) Expenditure for debt interest payment: It refers to the government expenditure for repayment of interest on debts, etc.

(23) Expenditure for debt issuance: It refers to the Government expenditure on debt issuance and payment fees.

(24) Other expenditure: It refers to other government spending cannot be divided into the above functions subjects.

Revenue of the Central Government and Revenue of the Local Governments refers to the revenue collected by the Central Government and that by the local governments as defined by the decentralized taxation system. In accordance with this system, the revenue of the Central Government includes tariff, VAT and consumption tax from imports, VAT and consumption tax rebate for exports, consumption tax, city maintenance and construct tax from the Ministry of Railways, head offices of banks, head offices of insurance company, which are handed over to the government in a centralized way, 50% of the value added tax, 60% the share part of the corporate income tax, unshared part of corporate income tax of the central enterprises, profit handed in by the central enterprises, 60% of individual income tax, vehicle purchase tax, ship tonnage tax, stamp tax on securities transactions, resource tax on the offshore petroleum resources, Central Government non-tax revenue, etc. The revenue of the local governments includes profit handed in by the local enterprises, city maintenance and construct tax (excluding the part of the Ministry of Railways, head offices of banks, head offices of insurance company, which are handed over to the government in a centralized way), house property tax, urban land use tax, land appreciation tax, tax on vehicles and boat operation, farm land occupation tax, deed tax, and tobacco leaf tax, stamp tax, 50% of the value added tax, 40% the share part of the corporate income tax, 40% of individual income tax, resource tax other than the tax on offshore petroleum resources, local non-tax revenue, etc.

Expenditure of the Central Government and Expenditure of the Local Governments according to the different functions of the Central Government and local governments in economic and social activities, the rights of affairs administration are demarcated between those of the Central Government and those of local governments; and the classification of the expenditure between the Central Government and local governments are made on the basis of the classification of the rights of affairs administration between them. The expenditure of the Central Government includes the expenditure for general public services, expenditure for foreign affairs, expenditure for defense, expenditure for public security, and the expenditure of the Central Government for adjusting the national economic structure; coordinating the development among different regions; and exercising macroeconomic regulation. The expenditure of the local governments includes mainly the expenditure for general public services, expenditure for public security, and expenditures for social development which are planned by local governments, etc.

7 物价指数

PRICE INDICES

资料整理：张元园　乔兴录
Data management: Zhang Yuanyuan Qiao Xinglu
数据审核：景春玲　高小琴　贾海宇
Data audit：Jing Chunling Gao Xiaoqin Jia Haiyu

第七部分　物价指数

一、简要说明

1.本章资料主要反映生产、流通、消费、投资与房地产等环节价格变动趋势和变动幅度。主要包括居民消费价格指数、商品零售价格指数、工业生产者出厂价格指数、工业生产者购进价格指数、固定资产投资价格指数和住宅销售价格指数。

2.本章资料由国家统计局西安调查队提供。

3.居民消费价格指数、商品零售价格指数资料的获取，是通过抽样调查和重点调查相结合的方式。在西安市区域内选定经营规模大、商品种类多的大型商场、超市、农贸市场和服务网点作为调查点，选择具有代表性的商品和服务项目作为样本，对其市场价格进行定期调查，以样本推断总体。

4.工业生产者出厂价格指数、工业生产者购进价格指数、固定资产投资价格指数，采取抽样调查和重点调查的方法。工业生产者出厂、工业生产者购进价格指数通过西安工业企业网上直报获取。住宅销售价格指数通过西安市月度住宅销售网签数据获取。

二、主要指标

居民消费价格总指数（上年=100）	101.7	比上年下降	0.4个百分点
商品零售价格总指数（上年=100）	101.4	比上年下降	0.1个百分点

7 PRICE INDICES

Ⅰ.Brief Introduction

1.The data on price indices in this chapter show the changing trends and change rates in the price of production, circulation, consumption, investment and real estate, including mainly consumer price indices, retail price indices, producer price indices for industrial producers, purchasing price indices for industrial producers, price indices for investment in fixed assets, and selling price indices of residential buildings.

2.The data are provided by NBS Survey Office in Xi'an.

3.The data for the calculation of consumer price indices and retail prices and retail price indices in the province are collected through stratified random sampling. Large-scale shops, supermarkets, fairs and service outlets with wide variety of commodities in Xi'an are selected as survey points. Representative commodities and services are selected as sample commodities and services. Regular surveys are conducted to collect data on market prices. The data on the population are estimated on the basis of the sample.

4.The producer price indices for industrial producers, purchasing price indices for industrial producers and price indices for investment in fixed assetsare collected through stratified random sampling. The producer price indices for industrial producers and purchasing price indices for industrial producers are collected by online direct report of Xi'an industrial enterprises. Selling price indices of residential buildings are collected by monthly data of online residential sales record.

Ⅱ.Major Indicators

		Increase over Preceding Year
Consumer Price Index(the price of preceding year=100)	101.7	-0.4 percentage points
Retail Price Index(the price of preceding year=100)	101.4	-0.1 percentage points

7-1 主要年份各种价格指数

Price Indices in Representative Years

(以上年价格为100) (the price of preceding year=100)

年 份 Year	居民消费价格指数 Consumer Price Index	商品零售价格指数 Retail Price Index	工业生产者出厂价格指数 Producer Price Indices (PPI) for Industrial Producers	工业生产者购进价格指数 Industrial Purchasing Indices （IPI） for Industrial Producers	固定资产投资价格指数 Price Index for Investment in Fixed Assets
1980	108.7	109.3			
1983	102.6	102.0			
1984	104.7	104.8			
1985	109.7	109.3			
1986	108.5	107.4			
1987	110.6	111.4			
1988	122.8	123.2			
1989	118.3	117.8			
1990	102.5	100.9			
1991	109.4	108.3			
1992	112.2	112.4			
1993	117.2	112.8	102.5	104.3	
1994	128.5	126.2	132.2	115.0	
1995	117.0	114.6	110.8	113.1	
1996	110.9	107.9	100.7	103.8	
1997	106.0	101.5	98.6	102.5	
1998	97.9	95.5	94.4	97.5	
1999	96.8	97.4	97.5	96.9	100.8
2000	100.2	98.7	99.4	102.4	102.1
2001	99.9	98.9	99.3	101.0	101.3
2002	98.6	98.5	98.2	98.4	101.2
2003	100.5	100.0	101.5	105.3	102.4
2004	102.3	101.9	102.7	110.4	103.3
2005	100.3	99.7	103.9	109.6	102.4
2006	101.6	101.5	103.2	106.1	102.0
2007	104.7	103.7	101.9	106.2	103.5
2008	106.0	105.4	103.7	108.5	110.5
2009	99.7	99.5	99.9	100.7	97.9
2010	103.5	102.7	102.3	106.3	103.8
2011	105.6	104.4	102.5	108.8	105.4
2012	102.8	102.3	100.5	97.2	101.9
2013	102.7	101.7	99.5	97.2	100.8
2014	101.4	100.7	99.5	99.5	100.8
2015	100.7	99.7	98.5	94.5	97.9
2016	100.9	100.1	97.8	97.6	100.0
2017	102.0	101.7	100.3	104.7	105.4
2018	101.9	102.2	101.1	102.7	104.7
2019	102.7	102.1	101.6	100.0	
2020	102.1	101.5	100.2	100.4	
2021	101.7	101.4			

注：本表数据来源国家统计局西安调查队。

本表2017年数据为西安原口径数据。下同。

本表2018年起PPI、IPI包含西咸新区；2019年起住宅销售价格指数不含西咸地区；其他指标为西安原口径数据。下同。

2018年固定资产投资价格指数包含西咸地区，2019年固定资产投资价格调查方案变动，2019年不出价格指数。2020年固投调查暂停。

2021年起，PPI、IPI调查方案变动，西安市不出价格指数。

7-2 居民消费价格指数（2021年）

Residents Consumer Price Indices (2021)

(以上年价格为100)　　　　(the price of preceding year=100)

指　标	Item	2021
居民消费价格指数	**Consumer Price Index**	**101.7**
非食品烟酒价格指数	Non-Food,Tobacco and Liquor Price Index	101.6
服务价格指数	Price Index of Services	102.2
工业品价格指数	Industrial Price Index	100.9
鲜活食品价格指数	Price Index of Fresh Food	98.9
消费品价格指数	Price Index of Consumer Goods	101.4
能源价格指数	Energy Price Index	107.3
非食品价格指数	Non-foodstuff Price Index	101.9
扣除食品和能源价格指数	Price Index with Food And Energy Excluded	101.5
扣除鲜菜鲜果价格指数	Price Index with Fresh Vegetables Fruits Excluded	101.6
扣除自有住房价格指数	Price Index with Self-owned Housing Excluded	101.7
居住（扣自有住房）价格指数	Housing (Self-owned Housing Excluded) Price Index	102.6
一、食品和烟酒	**Food,Tobacco and Liquor**	**101.9**
1. 食品	Food	100.7
（1）粮食	Grain	105.6
（2）薯类	Potato	91.2
（3）豆类	Beans	103.6
（4）食用油	Cooking Oil	114.0
（5）菜及食用菌	Vegetables and Edible fungi	106.7
（6）畜肉类	Livestock Meat	85.6
（7）禽肉类	Poultry Meat	91.1
（8）水产品	Aquatic Products	110.9
（9）蛋类	Eggs	123.9
（10）奶类	Milk	101.2
（11）干鲜瓜果类	Dried Fresh Melons and Fruits	100.9
（12）糖果糕点类	Sweets and Cake	100.0
（13）调味品	Flavouring	99.5
（14）其他食品类	Other Foods	102.0
2. 茶及饮料	Tea and Drinks	100.8
3. 烟酒	Tobacco and Liquor	102.1
（1）卷烟	Tobacco	100.6
（2）酒类	Liquor	104.7
4. 在外餐饮	Dining Out	104.4
二、衣着	**Clothing**	**101.1**
1. 服装	Garments	101.3
2. 鞋类	Footwear	100.6
三、居住	**Residence**	**102.0**
1. 租赁房房租	Rental Housing	102.2
2. 住房保养维修及管理	Housing Maintenance And Management	102.5
3. 水电燃料	Water,Electricity,Fuels	102.9
4. 自有住房	Private Housing	101.5

注：本表数据来源国家统计局西安调查队。

7-2 续表 continued

(以上年价格为100) (the price of preceding year=100)

指　标	Item	2021
四、生活用品及服务	**Daily Necessities and Services**	**100.3**
1. 家具及室内装饰品	Furniture and Interior Decorations	103.2
2. 家用器具	Household Appliances	99.6
3. 家用纺织品	Home Textiles	100.8
4. 家庭日用杂品	Daily Use Household Articles	99.3
5. 个人护理用品	Personal Care Articles	99.3
6. 家庭服务	Home Services	100.3
五、交通和通信	**Transportation And Communication**	**102.8**
1. 交通	Transportation	102.8
（1）交通工具	Transportation Facility	97.9
（2）交通工具用燃料	Fuels For Vehicles	116.8
（3）交通工具使用和维修	Vehicles Use And Maintenance	101.3
（4）交通费	Traffic Fare	103.4
2. 通信	Communication	102.8
（1）通信工具	Telecommunication facility	109.2
（2）通信服务	Telecommunication Service	100.0
（3）邮递服务	Postal Service	98.3
六、教育文化和娱乐	**Education,Culture And Recreation**	**103.7**
1. 教育	Education	104.6
（1）教育用品	Educational Articles	100.9
（2）教育服务	Education Service	105.0
2. 文化娱乐	Culture And Recreation	102.1
（1）文娱耐用消费品	Durable Consumer Goods for Cultural and Recreational Use	99.4
（2）其他文娱用品	Other Cultural and Recreational Articles	100.6
（3）文化娱乐服务	Cultural And Recreational Services	99.8
（4）旅游	Touring	105.8
七、医疗保健	**Health Care**	**98.3**
1. 药品及医疗器具	Medicines and Medical Instruments	95.1
（1）中药	Traditional Chinese Medicine	99.9
（2）西药	Western Medicine	91.9
（3）滋补保健品	Health Care Articles	98.6
（4）医疗卫生器具	Medical Apparatus	94.9
（5）保健器具	Health Care Appliances	100.0
2. 医疗服务	Medical Service	100.0
八、其他用品及服务	**Other Supplies And Services**	**101.5**
1. 其他用品	Other Supplies	100.3
（1）首饰手表	Jewelry and Watches	100.9
（2）母婴用品	Maternal and Infant Supplies	97.8
（3）其他杂项用品	Other Miscellaneous Articles	100.9
2. 其他服务	Other Service	102.5

7-3 商品零售价格指数（2021年）

Retail Price Indices (2021)

(以上年价格为100) (the price of preceding year = 100)

指 标	Item	2021
商品零售价格指数	**Retail Price Indices**	**101.4**
一、食品	**Food**	**101.9**
1. 粮食	Grain	105.6
2. 薯类	Potato	91.2
3. 豆类	Beans	103.6
4. 食用油	Cooking Oil	114.0
5. 菜及食用菌	Vegetables and Edible fungi	106.7
6. 畜肉类	Livestock Meat	84.4
7. 禽肉类	Poultry Meat	91.1
8. 水产品	Aquatic Products	110.9
9. 蛋类	Eggs	123.9
10. 奶类	Milk	101.2
11. 干鲜瓜果类	Dried Fresh Melons and Fruits	100.9
12. 糖果糕点类	Sweets and Cake	100.0
13. 调味品	Flavouring	100.5
14. 其他食品类	Other Foods	102.0
15. 餐饮业零售	Dining Out	104.4
二、饮料、烟酒	**Drinks,Tobacco and Liquor**	**101.9**
1. 茶及饮料	Tea and Drinks	100.9
2. 卷烟	Cigarette	100.6
3. 酒类	Liquor	104.7
三、服装、鞋帽	**Garments,Shoes And Hats**	**101.2**
1. 服装	Garments	101.4
2. 鞋帽袜	Footwear and Hats	100.4
3. 其他衣着配件	Other Clothing Accessories	102.9
四、纺织品	**Textiles**	**100.8**
1. 服装材料	Clothing Material	100.0
2. 床上用品	Bedding	100.9
五、家用电器及音像器材	**Household Appliances,Music and Video Equipment**	**99.6**
1. 家庭设备	Household Facility	99.6
2. 文娱用耐用消费品	Durable Consumer Goods for Cultural and Recreational Use	97.4
3. 专业音响器材	Music and Video Equipment	107.6

注：本表数据来源国家统计局西安调查队。

7-3 续表 continued

(以上年价格为100) (the price of preceding year=100)

指　标	Item	2021
六、文化办公用品	**Cultural and Office Appliances**	**101.9**
七、日用品	**Articles for Daily Use**	**100.6**
1. 日用百货	General Merchandise for Daily Use	100.5
2. 厨具餐具茶具	Kitchenware,Tableware,Tea Set	98.3
3. 清洗用品	Daily Use Articles For Washing	102.0
4. 其他日用品	Other Daily Articles	100.6
八、体育娱乐用品	**Sports And Recreation Articles**	**100.9**
1. 体育户外用品	Sports Outdoor Articles	101.4
2. 娱乐用品	Recreation Articles	100.7
九、交通、通信用品	**Transportation And Communication Goods**	**100.0**
1. 交通运输机械	Transportation Machinery	98.2
2. 通信器材	Communication Equipment	109.7
十、家具	**Furniture**	**104.0**
十一、化妆品	**Cosmetics**	**98.9**
十二、金银饰品	**Gold ,Silver and Jewelry**	**99.1**
十三、中西药品及医疗保健用品	**Traditional Chinese And Western Medicines And Health Care Articles**	**95.1**
1. 医疗卫生器具	Medical Apparatus	94.9
2. 中药	Traditional Chinese Medicine	99.9
3. 西药	Western Medicine	91.9
4. 保健器具及用品	Health Care Apparatus and Article	98.9
十四、书报杂志及电子出版物	**Books,Newspapers,Magazines And Electronic Publications**	**100.5**
1. 教材及参考书	Teaching Materials and Reference Books	100.9
2. 书报杂志及音像制品	Books,Newspapers,Magazines	100.0
3. 计算机办公软件	Computer Office Software	100.0
十五、燃料	**Fuels**	**110.0**
1. 煤炭及制品	Coal and Its Products	113.9
2. 石油及制品	Oil and Its Products	109.5
十六、建筑材料及五金电料	**Building Materials And Hardware**	**99.4**
1. 建筑装潢材料	Building Decoration Materials	99.3
2. 五金水暖	Hardware Plumbing	99.6

7-4 主要年份工业生产者出厂价格指数

（上年价格=100）

类　别	Classify	1999	2000	2001	2002	2003	2004
工业生产者出厂价格指数	**Producer Price Index**	**97.5**	**99.4**	**99.3**	**98.2**	**101.5**	**102.7**
按轻重工业分	Grouped by Light Industry and Heavy Industry						
轻工业	Light Industry	95.9	97.8	99.6	98.4	101.3	103.4
以农产品为原料	Using Farm Products as Raw Materials	95.2	99.2	99.0	98.4	104.5	108.7
以非农产品为原料	Using Non-farm Products as Raw Materials	97.0	95.5	100.6	98.6	99.9	100.8
重工业	Heavy Industry	98.9	100.8	99.2	98.2	101.6	101.9
采掘	Mining & Excavating	101.5	97.5	94.8	101.3	103.4	. 140.5
原料	Raw Materials	102.3	107.7	101.1	101.3	111.2	109.0
加工	Processing	98.0	98.4	98.5	97.7	100.1	100.6
按生产生活资料分	by means of production and livelihood						
生产资料	Means of Production	98.3	100.5	99.1	98.0	101.8	102.7
采掘	Mining & Excavating	101.5	97.5	94.8	101.3	103.4	140.5
原料	Raw Materials	100.2	106.4	101.1	101.0	108.1	106.6
加工	Processing	97.6	98.7	98.5	97.4	100.9	102.0
生活资料	Consumer Goods	96.5	97.3	99.9	99.1	100.5	102.5
（1）食品	Food	95.8	94.4	99.6	101.2	101.0	103.6
（2）衣着	Dress	95.2	101.6	99.4	100.8	99.4	102.7
（3）一般日用品	Articles for Daily Use	97.6	96.9	101.9	97.9	101.2	101.2
（4）耐用消费品	Durable Consumer Goods	98.0	95.9	97.0	98.1	97.2	98.3
按工业部门分	Grouped by Industrial Sector						
1. 冶金工业	Metallurgical Industry	91.2	98.2	97.2	98.7	103.8	107.1
2. 电力工业	Power Industry	109.3	109.6	102.4	100.0	103.2	104.1
3. 煤炭及炼焦工业	Coal and Coking Industry	96.3	100.5	110.3	106.7	136.8	131.4
4. 石油工业	Petroleum Industry	107.1	134.2	96.6	100.7	118.6	110.5
5. 化学工业	Chemical Industry	96.6	96.7	100.5	99.2	100.2	100.8
6. 机械工业	Machine Manufacturing Industry	98.1	98.0	98.3	97.6	99.8	100.6
7. 建筑材料工业	Building Materials Industry	96.7	98.5	100.6	99.6	99.7	100.0
8. 森林工业	Timber Industry	97.9	98.9	98.1	98.9	100.1	100.2
9. 食品工业	Food Industry	95.5	94.3	99.8	101.1	102.8	107.5
10. 纺织工业	Textiles Industry	93.7	103.4	97.5	94.9	117.3	119.1
11. 缝纫工业	Tailoring Industry	99.1	103.5	100.0	101.1	100.2	103.6
12. 皮革工业	Leather Industry	98.0	99.2	101.0	101.8	98.7	99.6
13. 造纸工业	Paper Industry	95.3	96.7	102.3	95.0	96.9	100.2
14. 文教艺术用品工业	Cultural,Educational & Handicrafts Articles	96.7	96.4	101.1	103.4	97.5	96.5
15. 其他工业	Other Industry	98.9	104.8	107.1	99.4	103.3	105.0

注：本表数据来源国家统计局西安调查队。2021年工业生产者出厂价格调查方案变动，西安市不出价格指数。

Producer Price Indices (PPI) for Industrial Producers in Representative Years

(the price of preceding year = 100)

2005	2006	2007	2008	2009	2010	2011	2012	2013	2014	2015	2016	2017	2018	2019	2020
103.9	**103.2**	**101.9**	**103.7**	**99.9**	**102.3**	**102.5**	**100.5**	**99.5**	**99.5**	**98.5**	**97.8**	**100.3**	**101.1**	**101.6**	**100.2**
99.9	100.2	101.8	103.7	100.6	102.5	107.0	100.4	100.7	100.9	100.3	98.5	100.5	102.5	101.3	100.8
97.3	100.1	103.3	106.0	98.9	104.0	109.3	100.3	101.0	100.8	99.1	97.8	100.9	103.0	101.2	100.4
101.2	100.2	100.8	102.1	101.8	101.4	100.9	100.5	99.9	101.3	103.3	100.1	99.7	101.3	101.5	101.8
107.9	105.5	101.9	103.8	99.3	102.2	101.6	100.5	99.2	99.2	98.2	97.6	100.3	100.7	101.8	100.1
107.9	100.6	111.6	122.3	90.0	150.2	102.6	101.8	100.6	100.6	99.8	99.8	106.0	107.1	110.3	100.1
114.2	111.8	104.9	110.8	99.5	108.9	111.2	108.6	95.1	97.6	90.4	91.4	103.4	106.1	103.6	100.4
106.7	104.2	101.2	101.9	99.4	100.8	100.1	99.2	99.9	99.5	99.3	98.3	99.8	100.0	101.5	100.0
105.3	104.2	101.3	103.4	99.3	102.2	101.9	100.3	99.2	99.5	98.3	97.4	100.7	101.7	101.7	100.1
107.9	100.6	111.6	122.3	90.0	105.2	102.6	101.8	100.6	100.6	99.8	99.8	106.0	107.1	110.3	100.1
111.3	111.6	104.8	110.2	99.7	109.0	111.3	108.7	95.2	97.7	90.5	91.2	102.7	106.0	103.6	100.4
104.3	103.0	100.6	102.0	99.3	101.0	100.3	98.9	99.9	99.7	99.6	98.3	100.3	101.0	101.4	100.1
100.4	100.4	103.5	104.7	101.4	102.5	104.5	100.8	100.4	99.7	99.4	98.6	99.7	100.1	101.5	100.5
100.3	100.4	105.3	106.6	100.3	103.3	109.5	101.6	100.9	101.2	100.1	97.7	100.3	102.5	101.9	100.3
102.0	103.3	104.6	105.1	102.7	101.2	111.9	99.4	100.4	99.1	96.0	100.2	101.3	100.4	100.2	100.6
101.3	100.8	100.1	102.7	102.6	101.2	101.5	101.5	99.1	101.3	102.1	98.9	99.6	96.8	99.9	100.8
99.1	99.4	100.7	100.7	103.9	101.9	99.5	99.0	100.9	95.9	95.6	99.5	98.5	101.3	103.3	100.4
103.9	106.5	103.2	104.8	92.0	105.8	116.3	100.7	97.5	97.5	96.5	95.2	104.9	107.3	104.3	99.3
110.6	107.9	105.5	110.0	109.0	101.2	104.7	111.2	100.6	99.4	98.9	92.3	99.4	102.3	95.5	95.2
97.1	95.4	106.8	104.8	101.7	110.6	109.3	101.5	100.0	100.0	100.0					
121.7	117.6	104.8	115.6	96.7	114.2	108.4	108.2	89.7	97.2	81.0	95.4	102.5	107.3	107.1	101.2
103.2	100.8	101.1	104.1	102.6	100.8	104.2	100.3	99.6	100.9	100.6	96.8	100.6	97.9	99.6	99.6
104.9	103.4	101.0	101.7	99.9	100.9	99.5	99.0	100.0	99.4	99.5	98.6	99.5	100.1	101.4	100.5
98.6	98.9	98.9	101.8	101.9	99.9	100.6	99.6	99.3	99.1	99.5	98.0	106.1	118.8	114.5	95.5
101.6	101.6	101.1	101.1	101.1	101.7	105.2	103.2	103.4	101.6	91.7	99.9	100.0	102.0	102.0	100.6
98.3	99.0	106.1	109.3	98.3	104.3	110.1	101.7	101.0	101.3	99.8	97.0	99.9	102.6	101.8	100.6
89.9	102.4	98.4	99.7	97.5	108.9	107.2	88.7	103.9	99.3	96.0	93.7	103.5	102.8	100.4	96.0
100.8	103.5	104.6	105.1	102.6	101.3	113.4	99.4	100.4	99.0	93.4	100.5	102.7	100.7	100.4	101.1
101.2	100.0	99.0	99.6	99.7	99.6	98.0	99.9	99.9	100.0	118.9	99.8	99.6	100.0	100.0	100.0
101.2	100.0	100.1	104.5	98.4	100.4	103.4	99.2	98.4	98.1	98.1	100.9	109.7	106.3	97.8	99.8
98.1	100.1	99.1	99.2	102.2	99.9	100.7	106.0	97.5	100.0	102.6	98.0	99.0	100.9	99.9	100.3
103.4	105.7	111.4	104.3	99.7	100.5	104.3	101.2	99.6	100.0	100.0	99.7	96.2	93.6	101.9	105.2

7-5 主要年份工业生产者购进价格指数

Industrial Purchasing Indices (IPI) for Industrial Producers in Representative Years

(上年价格=100) (the price of preceding year =100)

指　标	Item	2000	2003	2004	2005	2006	2007	2008	2009	2010
工业生产者购进价格指数	**Industrial Producer Price Index**	**102.4**	**105.3**	**110.4**	**109.6**	**106.1**	**106.2**	**108.5**	**100.7**	**106.3**
（一）燃料、动力类	Fuel and Power	105.0	105.7	109.4	123.5	112.6	107.0	109.8	105.1	108.6
（二）黑色金属材料类	Ferrous Metals	102.7	107.4	117.4	107.6	99.2	104.8	111.3	99.2	103.1
#钢材	Steel	103.4	106.0	114.8	107.5	98.5	104.9	111.7	98.7	103.5
（三）有色金属材料和电线类	Non-Ferrous Metals and Electric Wires	105.2	105.8	114.1	107.8	116.5	110.7	99.1	93.9	113.6
（四）化工原料类	Chemical Materials	104.6	102.4	106.3	106.1	101.6	105.6	111.4	95.0	103.9
（五）木材及纸浆类	Timber and Paper Pulp	101.2	101.2	100.3	108.2	111.7	105.9	106.5	102.6	101.1
（六）建筑材料及非金属矿类	Building Materials and Non-metal ores	100.3	99.6	110.4	99.3	100.7	104.0	104.8	106.8	102.1
（七）其他工业原材料及半成品	Other Industrial Raw Materials and Semi-Products	98.8	102.5	111.2	106.1	104.3	108.8	110.6	101.4	108.1
（八）农副产品类	Agricultural and Sideline Products	100.4	113.7	112.7	100.9	107.2	107.2	108.9	99.6	106.5
（九）纺织原料类	Textile Raw Materials	98.0	103.4	103.9	97.6	101.5	100.5	99.8	97.6	104.6

注：本表数据来源国家统计局西安调查队。2021年工业生产者购进价格调查方案变动，西安市不出价格指数。

7-5 续表 continued

(上年价格=100) (the price of preceding year =100)

指　标	Item	2011	2012	2013	2014	2015	2016	2017	2018	2019	2020
工业生产者购进价格指数	**Industrial Producer Price Index**	**108.8**	**97.2**	**97.2**	**99.5**	**94.5**	**97.6**	**104.7**	**102.7**	**100.0**	**100.4**
（一）燃料、动力类	Fuel and Power	113.5	102.3	96.8	98.2	95.3	98.3	101.6	99.8	101.7	100.1
（二）黑色金属材料类	Ferrous Metals	102.9	93.4	98.0	97.9	91.6	96.0	109.0	104.1	99.4	100.0
#钢材	Steel	102.9	93.3	98.0	97.9	91.5	96.0	109.0	104.0	99.4	100.0
（三）有色金属材料和电线类	Non-Ferrous Metals and Electric Wires	118.9	93.0	94.5	96.6	96.3	99.3	117.7	115.1	104.0	103.3
（四）化工原料类	Chemical Materials	108.1	87.7	90.8	104.6	91.3	94.1	104.2	99.2	97.0	99.7
（五）木材及纸浆类	Timber and Paper Pulp	105.4	100.9	99.2	100.7	101.0	98.7	107.3	103.9	95.6	100.1
（六）建筑材料及非金属矿类	Building Materials and Non-metal ores	102.9	97.4	102.2	101.1	98.1	97.1	101.0	111.1	111.0	99.5
（七）其他工业原材料及半成品	Other Industrial Raw Materials and Semi-Products	109.4	100.3	98.9	100.9	99.1	98.9	100.8	100.4	99.7	100.2
（八）农副产品类	Agricultural and Sideline Products	107.4	103.4	100.5	98.8	92.8	100.4	101.0	102.3	101.2	101.4
（九）纺织原料类	Textile Raw Materials	107.0	89.1	97.6	99.3	89.7	94.1	102.7	99.4	99.3	98.5

7-6 住宅销售价格指数（2021年）

Selling Price Indices of Residential Buildings (2021)

(上年价格=100) (the price of preceding year=100)

指　标	Item	2021
新建商品住宅	**New commodity residential house**	**107.5**
90平方米及以下	90 square meters and less	108.0
90-144平方米	90-144 square meters	107.5
144平方米以上	144 square meters and more	107.2
二手住宅	**used/second hand residential buildings**	**106.3**
90平方米及以下	90 square meters and the following	106.2
90-144平方米	90-144 square meters	106.4
144平方米以上	144 square meters and more	106.3

注：本表数据来源国家统计局西安调查队。

主要统计指标解释

居民消费价格指数 是反映一定时期内城乡居民所购买的生活消费品和服务项目价格变动趋势和程度的相对数，是对城市居民消费价格指数和农村居民消费价格指数进行综合汇总计算的结果。通过该指数可以观察和分析消费品的零售价格和服务项目价格变动对城乡居民实际生活费支出的影响程度。

商品零售价格指数 是反映一定时期内城乡商品零售价格变动趋势和程度的相对数。商品零售价格的变动与国家的财政收入、市场供需的平衡、消费与积累的比例关系有关。因此，该指数可以从一个侧面对上述经济活动进行观察和分析。

工业生产者价格指数 是反映工业产品价格变化趋势和变动幅度的统计指标，是工业企业的产品价格在不同的时间和空间条件下平均变动的相对数。工业生产者价格包括工业品第一次出售时的出厂价格和企业作为中间投入的原材料、燃料、动力购进价格，简称工业生产者出厂价格和工业生产者购进价格。工业生产者价格指数是进行国民经济核算和经济管理的主要依据。

住宅销售价格指数 是综合反映商品住宅价格水平总体变化趋势和变化幅度的相对数。

固定资产投资价格指数 是反映一定时期内固定资产投资品和取费项目价格的变动趋势和变动幅度的相对数。固定资产投资额是由建筑安装工程投资完成额、设备工器具购置投资完成额和其他费用投资完成额三部分组成的。编制固定资产投资价格指数应首先分别编制上述三部分投资的价格指数，然后采用加权算术平均法求出固定资产投资价格总指数。

该指数可以准确地反映固定资产投资中涉及的各类投资品和取费项目价格变动趋势和变动幅度，消除按现价计算的固定资产投资指标中的价格变动因素，真实地反映固定资产投资的规模、速度、结构和效益，为国家科学地制定、检查固定资产投资计划和进行国民经济核算提供科学的、可靠的依据。

Explanatory Notes on Main Statistical Indicators

Consumer Price Indices reflect the trend and degree of changes in prices of consumer goods and services purchased by urban and rural households during a given period. They are obtained by combining Consumer Price Indices of Urban Household and Consumer Price Indices of Rural Household. The Indices enable the observation and analysis of the degree of impact of the changes in the prices of retailed goods and services on the actual living expenses of urban and rural residents.

Retail Price Indices reflect the trend and degree of change in retail prices of commodities during a given period. The change in retail prices of commodities is related to government revenue, the equilibrium of market supply and demand, and the ratio of consumption to accumulation. Therefore, the retail price indices are useful from an oblique perspective for observing and analyzing the changes of the above economic activities.

Industrial Producer Price Index refelct the trend and degree of changes of industrial product price, which is the relative number of average change prices of industrial enterprises products under different condition of time and space. Including the first time of sale prices of industrial products and the price of raw materials, fuel and power as intermediate inputs, be called for short of PPI and IPI.

Industrial producer price Index is an important basis for national accounts and economic manegement.

Price Indices for Investment in Fixed Assets reflect the trend and degree of changes in prices of investment goods and projects in fixed assets during a given period. The investment in fixed assets consists of three components, namely the investment in construction and installation, the investment in purchases of equipment and instrument, and the investment in other items. Price indices for investment in fixed assets are calculated as the weighted arithmetic mean of the price indices for the three components of investment in fixed assets.

Removing the factor of price change in the aggregates of investment at current prices, this indicator shows the changes in the prices of commodities and fees involved in the investment of fixed assets, and can be used to observe the actual size, growth, structure, and efficiency of investment in fixed assets and provides reliable and scientific data for government planning and further improving the current national accounting .

8 人民生活

PEOPLE´S LIVELIHOOD

资料整理：张 磊 孙婷婷 孟 刚
Data management: Zhang Lei Sun Tingting Meng Gang
数据审核：罗朝晖 罗延庆
Data audit: Luo Zaohui Luo Yanqing

第八部分　人民生活

一、简要说明

1.本章资料反映我市城乡居民生活现状和变化情况，主要包括居民家庭基本情况及生活状况、收入及支出、住房等。

2.本章资料来源于国家统计局西安调查队城乡一体化住户收支与生活状况抽样调查。

3.统计资料范围及口径变化：①2014年西安开始实施城乡住户一体化改革，新老口径存在差距。②因2018年是分市、分省数据衔接年的基数年，衔接后西安各区县新口径与老口径数据相比，绝对额有所下降。③自2018年起本章调查资料包含13区、县及西咸新区城乡住户调查数据。

4.统计调查方法：住户收支与生活状况以各市（区）为总体，采用分层、多阶段、与人口规模大小成比例的概率抽样方法，随机抽选调查住宅，确定调查户。在全市抽选出调查小区，对抽中小区中的住户进行全面摸底调查，在此基础上随机等距选出调查户参与记账调查。定期对调查小区和调查住宅进行轮换。

二、主要指标

全体居民人均可支配收入（元）	38701	比上年增长	8.2%
城镇常住居民人均可支配收入（元）	46931	比上年增长	7.4%
城镇常住居民人均消费支出（元）	28809.8	比上年增长	11.6%
农村常住居民人均可支配收入（元）	17389	比上年增长	10.4%
农村常住居民人均消费支出（元）	14520.8	比上年增长	12.1%

8 PEOPLE'S LIVELIHOOD

Ⅰ.Brief Introduction

1.The data in this chapter reflects the people's living conditions and their changes in Xi'an , consisting of the basic conditions of all households, income, expenditure, the inhabit situation and etc.

2.The data are provided by NBS Survey Office in Xi'an , collected though sample survey.

3.The field of investigation and statistics range have been changed. ①In 2014, reformed household survey programme was used in Xi'an in order to produce aggregates with the same concepts and definitions for the urban and rural population. ② Since 2018 is the base year for the data convergence of cities and provinces, the absolute amount of new caliber data of Xi'an districts and counties has declined compared with the old caliber data. ③Since 2018, the data in this chapter consists of 13 Districts (Counties) and Xi'an new area.

4. Methodology on household survey. The household survey is conducted by selecting sampled houses randomly, deciding surveyed households, with all households in the city (district) as the population, with stratified sampling, multi-stage sampling, probability sampling in proportion scale. The households in selected communities are surveyed comprehensively, and then on the basis, randomly select some households for keeping diaries. Communities and households surveyed rotate regularly.

Ⅱ.Major Indicators

		Increase over Preceding Year
Per capita disposable income of all residents(yuan)	38701	8.2%
Per capita annual disposable income of Urban residents (yuan)	46931	7.4%
Per capita consumption expenditure of Urban residents (yuan)	28809.8	11.6%
Per capita annual disposable income of Rural residents (yuan)	17389	10.4%
Per capita consumption expenditure of Rural residents(yuan)	14520.8	12.1%

8-1 主要年份城乡居民人均收入及恩格尔系数

Per Capita Annual Income and Engel's Coefficient of Urban and Rural Households in Representative Years

年 份 Year	城镇居民人均可支配收入 Per Capita Annual Disposable Income of Urban		农村居民人均纯收入（可支配收入） Per Capita Annual Net Income of Rural （Disposable Income）		城镇居民家庭恩格尔系数（%） Engel's Coefficient of Urban Households (%)	农村居民家庭恩格尔系数（%） Engel's Coefficient of Rural Households (%)
	绝对数(元) Value (yuan)	指数 1980年=100 Index year of 1980=100	绝对数(元) Value (yuan)	指数 1978年=100 Index year of 1978=100		
1978			140	100.0		
1979						
1980	414	100.0	190	135.7	53.3	53.3
1985	719	173.5	351	250.7	49.5	48.5
1990	1518	366.5	610	435.7	53.1	49.5
1991	1619	390.9	707	505.0	51.6	46.7
1992	1992	481.0	783	559.3	52.5	50.9
1993	2661	642.5	870	621.4	46.4	46.0
1994	3517	849.1	1078	770.0	45.2	50.1
1995	4153	1002.5	1353	966.4	44.7	50.3
1996	5023	1212.6	1586	1132.9	42.6	49.9
1997	5344	1290.1	1846	1318.6	40.7	49.2
1998	5670	1368.7	2052	1465.7	39.8	42.4
1999	5999	1448.3	2203	1573.6	36.3	39.1
2000	6364	1536.5	2344	1674.3	36.5	36.6
2001	6705	1618.8	2490	1778.6	34.8	33.9
2002	7184	1734.3	2641	1886.4	34.4	31.1
2003	7748	1870.7	2838	2027.1	34.8	37.6
2004	8544	2062.8	3143	2245.0	36.1	35.7
2005	9628	2324.5	3460	2471.4	37.0	36.3
2006	10905	2632.9	3808	2720.0	34.4	36.8
2007	12662	3057.0	4399	3142.1	36.6	38.2
2008	15207	3671.4	5212	3722.9	36.4	37.0
2009	18963	4578.2	6275	4482.3	32.4	35.8
2010	22244	5370.4	7750	5535.7	31.3	32.5
2011	25981	6272.6	9788	6991.4	31.3	31.9
2012	29982	7238.5	11442	8172.9	32.5	33.8
2013	33100	7991.3	12930	9235.7	32.5	33.0
2014	30715	8718.5	12898	10334.7	32.3	34.2
2015	33188	9422.0	14072	11270.0	32.7	32.2
2016	35630	10119.2	15191	12171.6	29.3	26.9
2017	35837	10948.9	12190	13242.7	29.4	27.3
2018	38729	11835.8	13286	14434.5	27.1	24.4
2019	41850	12794.5	14588	15849.1	26.8	25.4
2020	43713	13370.3	15749	17117.1	28.1	28.0
2021	46931	14359.7	17389	18897.2	27.0	28.9

注：2014年实施城乡住户一体化调查后，统计口径发生变化，新老口径存在差异。本表2014年开始为新口径数据，“农村居民人均纯收入”改为“农村居民人均可支配收入”。2014-2015年恩格尔系数按新口径进行了修订。

本表2018年起数据包含西咸新区数据。下同。

8-1表中2017年城镇、农村居民人均可支配收入已依据2018年口径进行衔接，其他年份不可比。

8-2 主要年份城乡居民人民币储蓄存款

Savings Deposit of Urban and Rural Households in Representative Years

单位：亿元 (100 million yuan)

年 份 Year	年末余额 Balance at Year-end	指数（上年=100） Index(preceding year=100)
1978	2.57	
1979	3.30	128.4
1980	4.22	127.8
1981	4.90	116.0
1982	5.97	121.9
1983	7.35	123.1
1984	10.73	146.0
1985	14.26	132.9
1986	19.45	136.4
1987	33.95	174.6
1988	40.77	120.1
1989	56.65	138.9
1990	77.09	136.1
1991	97.42	126.4
1992	120.27	123.5
1993	158.28	131.6
1994	218.74	138.2
1995	291.46	133.2
1996	394.02	135.2
1997	433.56	110.0
1998	499.68	115.3
1999	586.40	117.4
2000	675.83	115.3
2001	800.86	118.5
2002	988.04	123.4
2003	1210.56	122.5
2004	1432.86	118.4
2005	1716.76	119.8
2006	1950.53	113.6
2007	2002.38	102.7
2008	2513.70	125.5
2009	3084.20	122.7
2010	3641.09	118.1
2011	4155.65	114.1
2012	4787.03	115.2
2013	5357.05	111.9
2014	5698.15	106.4
2015	6571.18	115.3
2016	7035.81	107.1
2017	7497.30	106.6
2018	8360.33	111.5
2019	9553.29	114.3
2020	10913.05	114.2
2021	11996.54	109.9

注：1.本表数据来源于人民银行西安分行营管部，对部分历史年份数据进行了修订，为西安原口径数据。
2.2015年以后“储蓄存款”为“住户存款”。

8-3 各区县城乡居民人均可支配收入（2020-2021年）

Per Capita Income of Urban and Rural Households by Region (2020-2021)

区 县	Region	城镇居民人均可支配收入 Per Capita Disposable Income of Urban Households			农村居民人均可支配收入 Per Capita Disposable Income of Rural Households		
		绝对数（元） Value(yuan)		2021年比2020年增长% Growth of 2021 than 2020(%)	绝对数（元） Value(yuan)		2021年比2020年增长% Growth of 2021 than 2020(%)
		2020	2021		2020	2021	
全 市	**Total**	**43713**	**46931**	**7.4**	**15749**	**17389**	**10.4**
新城区	Xincheng	50233	54302	8.1			
碑林区	Beilin	50040	53643	7.2			
莲湖区	Lianhu	50155	53816	7.3			
灞桥区	Baqiao	42183	45389	7.6	19353	21385	10.5
未央区	Weiyang	46859	50655	8.1			
雁塔区	Yanta	51217	55109	7.6			
阎良区	Yanliang	42703	45863	7.4	17104	18746	9.6
临潼区	Lintong	32320	34744	7.5	15802	17588	11.3
长安区	Chang'an	44027	47197	7.2	17186	18956	10.3
高陵区	Gaoling	40579	43704	7.7	17696	19448	9.9
鄠邑区	Huyi	25854	27922	8.0	14723	16372	11.2
蓝田县	Lantian	24920	26739	7.3	15851	17309	9.2
周至县	Zhouzhi	23438	25266	7.8	14162	15691	10.8
西咸新区	Xixian New Area	26331	28358	7.7	15177	16725	10.2

8-4 全市居民家庭基本情况（2020-2021年）

Basic Conditions of All Households (2020-2021)

指标名称	Item	2020	2021
调查户数（户）	**Number of Households Surveyed(household)**	**2410**	**2410**
调查户人口（人）	**Residents Surveyed(person)**		
平均每户常住人口	Average Household Size	3.0	3.0
平均每户劳动力人数	Average Number of Employed Persons	2.2	2.2
平均每劳动力负担人口	Average Number of Persons Supported by a Laborer	1.4	1.4
人均可支配收入（元）	**Annual Per Capita Disposable Income(yuan)**	**35783**	**38701**
工资性收入	Income of Wages and Salaries	21346.9	23069.2
经营净收入	Net Business Income	2710.9	2765.4
财产净收入	Net Income from Property	3426.6	3962.2
转移净收入	Net Income from Transfer	8298.6	8904.2
人均消费支出（元）	**Annual Per Capita Consumption Expenditure(yuan)**	**22167.6**	**24828.9**
食品烟酒	Food,Tobacco and Liquor	6221.1	6778.1
衣着	Clothing and Footwear	1452.7	1473.9
居住	Housing	5367.4	6296.7
生活用品及服务	Household Equipments,Furnishings and Services	1538.3	1575.0
交通通信	Transport and Communication Services	2535.0	2653.7
教育文化娱乐	Recreation,Education and Culture Services	2379.7	2862.6
医疗保健	Health Care and Medical Services	2193.7	2599.6
其他用品和服务	Miscellaneous Goods and Services	479.7	589.3

8-5 全市居民人均可支配收入（2020-2021年）

Per Capita Annual Disposable Income of All Households (2020-2021)

单位：元 (yuan)

指标名称	Item	2020	2021
人均可支配收入	**Annual Per Capita Disposable income**	**35783**	**38701**
一、工资性收入	**Income of Wages and Salaries**	**21346.9**	**23069.2**
（一）工资	Wage	19935.8	21604.0
（二）实物福利	Benefits in kind	77.4	88.6
（三）其他	Others	1333.7	1376.6
二、经营净收入	**Net Business Income**	**2710.9**	**2765.4**
（一）第一产业经营净收入	Net Income from Primary Industry Business	385.2	406.6
（二）第二产业经营净收入	Net Income from Secondary Industry Business	195.5	210.1
（三）第三产业经营净收入	Net Income from Tertiary Industry Business	2130.2	2148.7
三、财产净收入	**Net Income from Property**	**3426.6**	**3962.0**
#利息净收入	Net interest	168.2	173.6
红利收入	Bonus	408.8	410.4
转让承包土地经营权租金净收入	Net Rental from Transfer of Contracted Land Management Rights	56.1	56.9
出租房屋财产性收入	The Property Income by Renting House	1131.0	1141.3
出租机械、专利、版权等资产的收入	The Income by Renting Assets like Mechanical, Patents,Copyright ect.	77.6	22.1
四、转移净收入	**Net Income from Transfer**	**8298.6**	**8904.2**
（一）转移性收入	Net Income from Transfer	10059.7	10745.0
（二）转移性支出	Transfer Expenditure	1761.1	1840.8

8-6 全市居民年人均消费支出（2020-2021年）

Per Capita Living Expenditure of All Households (2020-2021)

单位：元 (yuan)

指标名称	Item	2020	2021
消费支出	**Total Living Expenditure**	**22167.6**	**24828.9**
一、食品烟酒	**Food,Tobacco and Liquor**	**6221.1**	**6778.1**
1.食品	food	3958.0	3943.6
2.烟酒	Alcohol and tobacco	530.0	592.2
3.饮料	Drink	158.3	169.6
4.饮食服务	Catering Services	1574.8	2072.7
二、衣着	**Clothing and Footwear**	**1452.7**	**1473.9**
衣类	Garments	1158.0	1167.9
鞋类	Footwear	294.7	306.0
三、居住	**Housing**	**5367.4**	**6296.7**
#租赁房房租	Rental Housing Rent	337.3	245.8
住房维修及管理	Housing Repair and Management	694.3	812.9
水电燃料及其他	Water,Electric Power Fuel and Others	1089.7	1113.1
四、生活用品及服务	**Household Equipments,Furnishings and Services**	**1538.3**	**1575.0**
家具及室内装饰品	Furniture and External Decorations	268.2	313.3
家用器具	Household Appliances	314.3	320.3
家用纺织品	Household textile	108.3	121.7
家庭日用杂品	Household Articles of Daily Use	383.4	356.9
个人用品	Personal Items	375.5	361.4
家庭服务	Household Services	88.6	101.4
五、交通通信	**Transport and Communications**	**2535.0**	**2653.7**
交通	Transportation	1710.0	1803.6
通信	Communications	825.0	850.1
六、教育文化娱乐	**Recreation, Education and Culture Services**	**2379.7**	**2862.6**
教育	Education	1687.9	2189.8
文化娱乐	Recreation	691.8	672.8
七、医疗保健	**Health Care and Medical Services**	**2193.7**	**2599.6**
医疗器具及药品	Medical Instruments and Medicines	749.1	741.3
医疗服务	Medical Services	1444.6	1858.3
八、其他用品和服务	**Miscellaneous Goods and Services**	**479.7**	**589.3**

8-7 全市居民家庭人均购买主要商品数量（2020-2021年）

Per Capita Annual Purchases of Major Commodities of All Households (2020-2021)

单位：千克 (kg)

指标名称	Item	2020	2021
面粉	Flour	25.5	23.7
大米	Rice	16.0	17.9
薯类	Potato	19.2	18.8
豆类	Beans	12.4	12.9
食用植物油	Edible vegetable oil	10.3	10.4
鲜菜	Fresh vegetables	102.2	105.1
猪肉	Pork	9.5	13.3
牛肉	Beef	2.3	2.3
羊肉	Lamb	0.7	0.8
鸡	Chicken	3.3	3.2
鱼类	Fish	3.1	3.3
虾类	Shrimp	0.8	0.9
鲜蛋	Eggs	13.2	13.8
鲜奶	Milk	13.3	14.3
酸奶	Yogurt	6.6	5.3
奶粉	Milk	0.8	0.8
鲜瓜果	Fresh Melons and Fruit	64.3	64.8
糕点	Cake	5.1	5.6
茶叶	Tea	0.4	0.4
卷烟（盒）	Cigarettes(box)	30.1	31.2
啤酒	Beer	3.4	3.6
白酒	Liquor	1.1	1.4
果酒	Wine	0.3	0.2
鞋（双）	Footwear(pair)	2.5	2.6
水（吨）	Water (tons)	34.4	29.2
电（度）	Electricity(kWh)	803.6	806.6
煤炭	Coal	10.1	8.8
管道天然气（立方米）	Gas pipeline(cu.m)	87.7	87.7
罐装液化石油气	Bottled liquefied petroleum gas	3.0	2.4

8-8 全市居民家庭每百户年末耐用品拥有情况（2020-2021年）

Ownership of Major Durable Consumer Goods Every 100 Households (2020-2021)

指标名称	Item	2020	2021
家用汽车（辆）	Automobile(unit)	39.4	44.0
摩托车（辆）	Motorcycle(unit)	10.0	13.1
助力车（台）	Electric Bicycle(unit)	48.4	52.4
洗衣机（台）	washing machine(unit)	101.0	100.3
电冰箱（柜）	Refrigerator(unit)	98.3	99.3
微波炉（台）	Microwave Oven(unit)	45.8	46.8
彩色电视机（台）	Color TV Set(unit)	109.0	105.9
空调（台）	Air conditioning(unit)	165.3	181.3
热水器（台）	Water Heater(set)	91.2	86.2
洗碗机（台）	Dishwasher (unit)	1.5	1.9
排油烟机（台）	Kitchen Ventilator (set)	74.9	77.1
固定电话（部）	Ordinary Telephone (unit)	10.7	11.7
移动电话（部）	Mobile phone (set)	254.1	257.3
#接入互联网（部）	Access to the Internet(unit)	231.9	235.1
计算机（台）	Computer(a)	59.9	52.6
#接入互联网（台）	Access to the Internet(unit)	46.9	44.9
照相机（台）	Camera(set)	19.7	12.1
中高档乐器（架）	High-end Instruments(unit)	8.4	6.8
健身器材（台）	Setting-up Apparatus(unit)	8.2	4.3
空气净化器（台）	Air-cleaner(unit)	13.1	13.0
吸尘器（台）	Vacuum Cleaner(unit)	12.5	10.3

8-9 城镇常住居民家庭基本情况（2020-2021年）

Basic Conditions of Urban Households (2020-2021)

指标名称	Item	2020	2021
调查户数（户）	**Number of Households Surveyed(household)**	**1770**	**1770**
调查户人口（人）	**Residents Surveyed(person)**		
平均每户常住人口	Average Household Size	2.8	2.9
平均每户劳动力人数	Average Number of Employed Persons	2.2	2.2
平均每劳动力负担人口	Average Number of Persons Supported by a Laborer	1.3	1.3
人均可支配收入（元）	**Annual Per Capita Disposable Income(yuan)**	**43713**	**46931**
工资性收入	Income of Wages and Salaries	26145.0	27872.4
经营净收入	Net Business Income	2733.9	2789.8
财产净收入	Net Income from Property	4632.9	5343.8
转移净收入	Net Income from Transfer	10201.2	10925.0
人均消费支出（元）	**Annual Per Capita Consumption Expenditure(yuan)**	**25813.1**	**28809.8**
食品烟酒	Food,Tobacco and Liquor	7248.4	7772.8
衣着	Clothing and Footwear	1715.5	1724.6
居住	Housing	6248.3	7400.9
生活用品及服务	Household Equipments,Furnishings and Services	1849.3	1864.3
交通通信	Transport and Communication Services	2892.5	2973.3
教育文化娱乐	Recreation, Education and Culture Services	2736.4	3300.4
医疗保健	Health Care and Medical Services	2530.2	3052.9
其他用品和服务	Miscellaneous Goods and Services	592.5	720.6

8-10 城镇常住居民人均消费支出（2020-2021年）

Per Capita Living Expenditure of Urban Households (2020-2021)

单位：元 (yuan)

指标名称	Item	2020	2021
消费支出	**Total Living Expenditure**	**25813.1**	**28809.8**
一、食品烟酒	**Food,Tobacco and Liquor**	**7248.4**	**7772.8**
1.食品	food	4534.1	4437.1
2.烟酒	Alcohol and tobacco	563.3	616.1
3.饮料	Drink	188.0	202.9
4.饮食服务	Catering Services	1963.0	2516.7
二、衣着	**Clothing and Footwear**	**1715.5**	**1724.6**
衣类	Garments	1370.9	1371.6
鞋类	Footwear	344.6	353.0
三、居住	**Housing**	**6248.3**	**7400.9**
#租赁房房租	Rental Housing Rent	383.4	298.5
住房维修及管理	Housing Repair and Management	771.4	922.1
水电燃料及其他	Water,Electric Power Fuel and Others	1303.4	1323.1
四、生活用品及服务	**Household Equipments,Furnishings and Services**	**1849.3**	**1864.3**
家具及室内装饰品	Furniture and External Decorations	332.0	376.2
家用器具	Household Appliances	377.2	377.8
家用纺织品	Household textile	129.0	146.6
家庭日用杂品	Household Articles of Daily Use	440.0	397.4
个人用品	Personal Items	458.4	437.4
家庭服务	Household Services	112.7	128.9
五、交通通信	**Transportation and Communications**	**2892.5**	**2973.3**
交通	Transportation	1951.8	2025.0
通信	Communications	940.7	948.3
六、教育文化娱乐	**Recreation, Education and Culture Services**	**2736.4**	**3300.4**
教育	Education	1861.4	2461.4
文化娱乐	Recreation	875.0	839.0
七、医疗保健	**Health Care and Medical Services**	**2530.2**	**3052.9**
医疗器具及药品	Medical Instruments and Medicines	909.1	903.2
医疗服务	Medical Services	1621.1	2149.7
八、其他用品和服务	**Miscellaneous Goods and Services**	**592.5**	**720.6**

8-11 城镇常住居民家庭人均购买主要商品数量（2020-2021年）

Per Capita Annual Purchases of Major Commodities of Urban Households (2020-2021)

单位：千克 (kg)

指标名称	Item	2020	2021
面粉	Flour	22.6	22.2
大米	Rice	16.7	19.2
薯类	Potato	19.5	19.0
豆类	Beans	12.4	13.5
食用植物油	Edible vegetable oil	9.3	9.7
鲜菜	Fresh vegetables	110.5	113.9
猪肉	Pork	10.4	14.0
牛肉	Beef	3.0	2.9
羊肉	Lamb	0.8	0.9
鸡	Chicken	3.9	3.9
鱼类	Fish	3.9	4.2
虾类	Shrimp	1.1	1.1
鲜蛋	Eggs	14.3	14.6
鲜奶	Milk	15.1	15.3
酸奶	Yogurt	8.2	6.4
奶粉	Milk	0.8	0.8
鲜瓜果	Fresh Melons and Fruit	72.2	71.4
糕点	Cake	6.0	6.4
茶叶	Tea	0.5	0.4
卷烟（盒）	Cigarettes(box)	27.3	27.5
啤酒	Beer	3.5	3.8
白酒	Liquor	1.3	1.6
果酒	Wine	0.2	0.2
鞋（双）	Footwear (pair)	2.5	2.5
水（吨）	Water(tons)	40.6	34.7
电（度）	Electricity(kWh)	833.1	830.3
煤炭	Coal	4.0	2.5
管道天然气（立方米）	Gas pipeline(cu.m)	119.1	118.6
罐装液化石油气	Bottled liquefied petroleum gas	1.6	1.3

8-12 城镇常住居民家庭每百户耐用品拥有情况（2020-2021年）

Ownership of Major Durable Consumer Goods Every 100 Urban Households (2020-2021)

指标名称	Item	2020	2021
家用汽车（辆）	Automobile(unit)	40.6	45.5
摩托车（辆）	Motorcycle(unit)	3.0	6.5
助力车（台）	Electric Bicycle(unit)	36.7	39.1
洗衣机（台）	washing machine(unit)	101.4	100.3
电冰箱（柜）	Refrigerator(unit)	99.0	99.7
微波炉（台）	Microwave Oven(unit)	56.0	56.7
彩色电视机（台）	Color TV Set(unit)	106.1	105.3
空调（台）	Air conditioning(unit)	180.9	194.8
热水器（台）	Water Heater(set)	95.3	89.5
洗碗机（台）	Dishwasher (unit)	1.8	2.4
排油烟机（台）	Kitchen Ventilator (set)	88.1	87.8
固定电话（部）	Ordinary Telephone (unit)	12.6	13.7
移动电话（部）	Mobile phone (set)	238.6	241.9
#接入互联网（部）	Access to the Internet(unit)	222.1	222.7
计算机（台）	Computer(a)	69.2	60.9
#接入互联网（台）	Access to the Internet(unit)	55.7	53.8
照相机（台）	Camera(set)	24.9	15.5
中高档乐器（架）	High-end Instruments(unit)	10.5	8.7
健身器材（台）	Setting-up Apparatus(unit)	10.0	5.3
空气净化器（台）	Air-cleaner(unit)	16.9	16.8
吸尘器（台）	Vacuum Cleaner(unit)	16.0	13.2

8-13 城镇常住居民家庭居住情况（2020-2021年）

Housing Conditions of Urban Households (2020-2021)

指标名称	Item	2020	2021
调查户数（户）	**Number of Households Surveyed(household)**	**1770**	**1770**
平均每户居住人口（人）	**Average Number of Resident Population(person)**	**2.8**	**2.9**
人均现住房建筑面积（平方米/人）	**The Average Floor Area Per Person (sq.m / person)**	**34.9**	**35.2**
一、按居住空间样式分（%）	**by Living space style(%)**	**100.0**	**100.0**
单栋楼房	Single building Room	8.1	9.2
单栋平房	Single-storey House	4.6	4.4
单元房	Apartment	83.2	85.4
筒子楼或连片平房	Tube-shaped Apartment or Lace Single-storey Houses	4.1	1.0
其他	Other		
二、按主要建筑材料分（%）	**by main construction materials(%)**	**100.0**	**100.0**
钢筋混凝土	Reinforced concrete soil	65.6	73.6
砖混材料	Brick and concrete material	33.8	26.4
砖瓦砖土	Tile and brick earth	0.5	
其他	Others	0.1	
三、按房屋来源分（%）	**by Source of Housing(%)**	**100.0**	**100.0**
租赁住房	Rental housing	11.9	10.3
自建住房	Self-establish Housing	14.2	16.6
购买商品房	Commercial Residential Housing	36.2	42.3
购买房改住房	Private Housing through Housing Reform	19.4	15.9
购买保障性住房	Indemnificatory Housing	3.7	4.4
拆迁安置房	Resettlement Housing	9.7	8.6
继承或获赠住房	Inheriting and Donation Housing	1.3	0.6
其他	Others	3.6	1.3
四、按住户主要饮水来源情况分（%）	**By Source of main Drinking Water(%)**	**100.0**	**100.0**
经过净化处理的自来水	Purified Tap Water	92.0	96.9
受保护的井水和泉水	Protected Wells and Springs	5.6	2.6
不受保护的井水和泉水	Unprotected Wells and Springs	0.9	
江河湖泊水	Rivers and Lakes Water	0.6	
其他饮用水来源	Others	0.9	0.5
五、按住宅内厕所类型分（%）	**By Household Lavatory Type(%)**	**100.0**	**100.0**
水冲式卫生厕所	Sanitary Water Closet	97.6	99.2
水冲式非卫生厕所	Insanitary Water Closet	1.0	0.1
卫生旱厕	Sanitary Latrine	1.3	0.7
普通旱厕	Latrine	0.1	
无厕所	No Lavatory		
六、按主要炊用能源状况分（%）	**By Cooking Fuel Condition(%)**	**100.0**	**100.0**
天然气、煤气、液化石油气	Pipeline Natural Gas,Pipeline Gas, Pipeline Liquified Petroleum Gas	87.3	88.6
煤炭	Coal		0.1
电	Electricity	11.8	10.8
沼气	Methane		
其他	Others	0.9	0.5

8-14 农村常住居民家庭基本情况（2020-2021年）

Basic Conditions of Rural Households (2020-2021)

指标名称	Item	2020	2021
调查户数（户）	**Number of Households Surveyed(household)**	**640**	**640**
调查户人口（人）	**Residents Surveyed(person)**		
平均每户常住人口	Average Household Size	3.5	3.4
平均每户劳动力人数	Average Number of Employed Persons	2.4	2.4
平均每劳动力负担人口	Average Number of Persons Supported by a Laborer	1.5	1.4
人均可支配收入（元）	**Annual Per Capita Disposable Income(yuan)**	**15749**	**17389**
工资性收入	Income of Wages and Salaries	9225.8	10631.8
经营净收入	Net Business Income	2652.5	2702.1
财产净收入	Net Income from Property	378.8	384.0
转移净收入	Net Income from Transfer	3491.9	3671.1
人均消费支出（元）	**Annual Per Capita Consumption Expenditure(yuan)**	**12958.3**	**14520.8**
食品烟酒	Food,Tobacco and Liquor	3625.8	4202.4
衣着	Clothing and Footwear	788.8	824.9
居住	Housing	3141.9	3437.3
生活用品及服务	Household Equipments,Furnishings and Services	752.7	826.1
交通通信	Transport and Communication Services	1632.0	1826.3
教育文化娱乐	Recreation, Education and Culture Services	1478.4	1729.0
医疗保健	Health Care and Medical Services	1343.6	1425.7
其他用品和服务	Miscellaneous Goods and Services	195.1	249.1

8-15 农村常住居民人均消费支出（2020-2021年）

Per Capita Living Expenditure of Rural Households (2020-2021)

单位：元 (yuan)

指标名称	Item	2020	2021
消费支出	**Total Living Expenditure**	**12958.3**	**14520.8**
一、食品烟酒	**Food,Tobacco and Liquor**	**3625.8**	**4202.4**
1.食品	food	2502.7	2665.6
2.烟酒	Alcohol and tobacco	445.7	530.2
3.饮料	Drink	83.1	83.3
4.饮食服务	Catering Services	594.3	923.3
二、衣着	**Clothing and Footwear**	**788.8**	**824.9**
衣类	Garments	620.2	640.5
鞋类	Footwear	168.6	184.4
三、居住	**Housing**	**3141.9**	**3437.3**
#租赁房房租	Rental Housing Rent	220.8	109.3
住房维修及管理	Housing Repair and Management	499.3	530.2
水电燃料及其他	Water,Electric Power Fuel and Others	549.7	569.3
四、生活用品及服务	**Household Equipments,Furnishings and Services**	**752.7**	**826.1**
家具及室内装饰品	Furniture and External Decorations	106.8	150.4
家用器具	Household Appliances	155.6	171.5
家用纺织品	Household textile	56.1	57.4
家庭日用杂品	Household Articles of Daily Use	240.4	252.1
个人用品	Personal Items	166.2	164.6
家庭服务	Household Services	27.6	30.1
五、交通通信	**Transportation and Communications**	**1632.0**	**1826.3**
交通	Transportation	1099.1	1230.2
通信	Communications	532.9	596.1
六、教育文化娱乐	**Recreation, Education and Culture Services**	**1478.4**	**1729.0**
教育	Education	1249.6	1486.4
文化娱乐	Recreation	228.8	242.6
七、医疗保健	**Health Care and Medical Services**	**1343.6**	**1425.7**
医疗器具及药品	Medical Instruments and Medicines	344.9	322.1
医疗服务	Medical Services	998.7	1103.6
八、其他用品和服务	**Miscellaneous Goods and Services**	**195.1**	**249.1**

8-16 农村常住居民家庭人均购买主要商品数量（2020-2021年）

Per Capita Annual Purchases of Major Commodities of Rural Households (2020-2021)

单位：千克 (kg)

指标名称	Item	2020	2021
面粉	Flour	32.9	27.5
大米	Rice	14.4	14.3
薯类	Potato	18.7	18.4
豆类	Beans	12.4	11.3
食用植物油	Edible vegetable oil	13.0	12.4
鲜菜	Fresh vegetables	81.3	82.4
猪肉	Pork	7.3	11.4
牛肉	Beef	0.6	0.8
羊肉	Lamb	0.3	0.4
鸡	Chicken	1.7	1.6
鱼类	Fish	0.9	1.0
虾类	Shrimp	0.1	0.3
鲜蛋	Eggs	10.2	11.5
鲜奶	Milk	8.9	11.5
酸奶	Yogurt	2.6	2.3
奶粉	Milk	0.9	0.9
鲜瓜果	Fresh Melons and Fruit	44.5	47.8
糕点	Cake	2.9	3.8
茶叶	Tea	0.3	0.2
卷烟（盒）	Cigarettes (box)	37.1	40.9
啤酒	Beer	2.9	3.1
白酒	Liquor	0.7	0.8
果酒	Wine	0.3	0.2
鞋（双）	Footwear(pair)	2.6	2.7
水（吨）	Water (tons)	18.6	15.0
电（度）	Electricity(kWh)	729.2	745.4
煤炭	Coal	25.4	24.8
管道天然气（立方米）	Gas pipeline(cu.m)	8.5	7.9
罐装液化石油气	Bottled liquefied petroleum gas	6.6	5.1

8-17 农村常住居民家庭平均每百户耐用品拥有情况（2020-2021年）

Ownership of Major Durable Consumer Goods Every 100 Rural Households (2020-2021)

指标名称	Item	2020	2021
家用汽车（辆）	Automobile(unit)	35.9	39.4
摩托车（辆）	Motorcycle(unit)	32.0	32.9
助力车（台）	Electric Bicycle(unit)	85.1	92.6
洗衣机（台）	washing machine(unit)	99.8	100.4
电冰箱（柜）	Refrigerator(unit)	96.2	97.9
微波炉（台）	Microwave Oven (unit)	13.8	16.7
彩色电视机（台）	Color TV Set (unit)	118.0	107.5
空调（台）	Air conditioning(unit)	116.0	140.2
热水器（台）	Water Heater(set)	78.5	76.1
洗碗机（台）	Dishwasher(unit)	0.3	0.3
排油烟机（台）	Kitchen Ventilator(set)	33.4	44.6
固定电话（部）	Ordinary Telephone(unit)	4.7	5.6
移动电话（部）	Mobile phone(set)	302.6	304.1
#接入互联网（部）	Access to the Internet(unit)	262.6	272.3
计算机（台）	Computer(a)	30.7	27.5
#接入互联网（台）	Access to the Internet(unit)	19.1	18.0
照相机（台）	Camera(set)	3.2	1.7
中高档乐器（架）	High-end Instruments(unit)	1.8	1.1
健身器材（台）	Setting-up Apparatus(unit)	2.6	1.3
空气净化器（台）	Air-cleaner(unit)	1.0	1.4
吸尘器（台）	Vacuum Cleaner(unit)	1.1	1.5

8-18 农村常住居民家庭居住情况（2020-2021年）

Housing Conditions of Rural Households (2020-2021)

指标名称	Item	2020	2021
调查户数（户）	**Number of Households Surveyed(household)**	**640**	**640**
平均每户居住人口（人）	**Average Number of Resident Population(person)**	**3.5**	**3.4**
人均现住房建筑面积（平方米/人）	**The Average Floor Area Per Person (sq.m / person)**	**50.2**	**46.8**
一、按居住空间样式分（%）	**by Living space style(%)**	**100.0**	**100.0**
单栋楼房	Single building Room	53.7	57.3
单栋平房	Single-storey House	43.7	40.5
单元房	Apartment	2.0	2.2
筒子楼或连片平房	Tube-shaped Apartment or Lace Single-storey Houses		
其他	Other	0.6	
二、按主要建筑材料分（%）	**by main construction materials(%)**	**100.0**	**100.0**
钢筋混凝土	Reinforced concrete soil	19.6	23.0
砖混材料	Brick and concrete material	75.1	73.2
砖瓦砖土	Tile and brick earth	5.2	3.8
竹草土坯	Bamboo grass mud		
其他	Others	0.1	
三、按房屋来源分（%）	**by Source of Housing(%)**	**100.0**	**100.0**
租赁住房	Rental housing	3.1	3.0
自建住房	Self-establish Housing	95.0	95.3
购买商品房	Commercial Residential Housing	0.4	0.2
购买房改住房	Private Housing through Housing Reform		0.1
购买保障性住房	Indemnificatory Housing		
拆迁安置房	Resettlement Housing	0.8	1.4
继承或获赠住房	Inheriting and Donation Housing		
其他	Others	0.7	
四、按住户主要饮水来源情况分（%）	**By Source of main Drinking Water(%)**	**100.0**	**100.0**
经过净化处理的自来水	Purified Tap Water	55.4	68.4
受保护的井水和泉水	Protected Wells and Springs	38.8	31.6
不受保护的井水和泉水	Unprotected Wells and Springs	4.5	
江河湖泊水	Rivers and Lakes Water	0.7	
其他饮用水来源	Others	0.6	
五、按住宅内厕所类型分（%）	**By Household Lavatory Type(%)**	**100.0**	**100.0**
水冲式卫生厕所	Sanitary Water Closet	70.0	85.9
水冲式非卫生厕所	Insanitary Water Closet	18.1	5.2
卫生旱厕	Sanitary Latrine	9.9	8.4
普通旱厕	Latrine	2.0	0.5
无厕所	No Lavatory		
六、按主要炊用能源状况分（%）	**By Cooking Fuel Condition(%)**	**100.0**	**100.0**
天然气、煤气、液化石油气	Pipeline Natural Gas,Pipeline Gas, Pipeline Liquified Petroleum Gas	23.0	24.1
煤炭	Coal	0.1	1.3
电	Electricity	66.8	59.9
沼气	Methane		
其他	Others	10.1	14.7

主要统计指标解释

住户 指居住在一个住宅内，共同分享生活开支或收入的一群人。居住在同一房间内、不共同分享生活开支的人群，每个人都视为一个住户。住家保姆、住家家庭帮工视为单独的住户。

常住成员指住户成员中，经常在家居住、或者调查期内居住时间超过一半的人员，以及本住户供养的学生。

可支配收入 指调查户在调查期内获得的、可用于最终消费支出和储蓄的总和，即调查户可以用来自由支配的收入。可支配收入既包括现金，也包括实物收入。按照收入的来源，可支配收入包含四项，分别为：工资性收入、经营净收入、财产净收入和转移净收入。计算公式为：

可支配收入 = 工资性收入 + 经营净收入 + 财产净收入 + 转移净收入

工资性收入 指就业人员通过各种途径得到的全部劳动报酬和各种福利，包括受雇于单位或个人、从事各种自由职业、兼职和零星劳动得到的全部劳动报酬和福利。

经营净收入 指住户或住户成员从事生产经营活动所获得的净收入，是全部经营收入中扣除经营费用、生产性固定资产折旧和生产税之后得到的净收入。计算公式具体为：

经营净收入 = 经营收入 – 经营费用–生产性固定资产折旧–生产税

财产净收入 指住户或住户成员将其所拥有的金融资产、住房等非金融资产和自然资源交由其他机构单位、住户或个人支配而获得的回报并扣除相关的费用之后得到的净收入。

财产性净收入=财产性收入– 财产性支出

转移性收入 指国家、单位、社会团体对住户的各种经常性转移支付和住户之间的经常性收入转移。包括养老金或退休金、社会救济和补助、政策性生产补贴、政策性生活补贴、经常性捐赠和赔偿、报销医疗费、住户之间的赡养收入，以及本住户非常住成员寄回带回的收入等。计算公式为：

转移净收入 = 转移性收入–转移性支出

消费支出 指住户用于满足家庭日常生活消费需要的全部支出，包括用于消费品的支出和用于服务性消费的支出。根据用途不同，消费支出可划分为食品烟酒、衣着、居住、生活用品及服务、交通通信、教育文化娱乐、医疗保健、其他用品及服务八大类。

农村居民人均纯收入（老口径） 指农村住户当年从各个来源得到的家庭总收入扣除相关费用性支出后，最终归农村居民所有的收入总和，按照农村住户人口平均的纯收入水平。计算公式为：

纯收入=总收入 –家庭经费费用支出–税费支出–生产性固定资产折旧–赠送农村内部亲友

Explanatory Notes on Main Statistical Indicators

Households refer to persons living and sharing economically together in one house. When people don`t share living expenses, every single person are deemed to be one household. Live-in Nanny and family helpers are deemed to be one household.

Usual Resident Population refers to persons staying at home regularly or for over half of time in survey period and students provided by the by the household.

Disposable Income of Households refers to the actual income of households for purpose of final expenditure and savings in survey period, households can use that at their disposable. It includes income both in cash and in kind. By sources of income, disposable income includes four categories: income from wages and salaries, net business income, net income from properties and net income from transfer. The formula is:

Disposable Income of Households = Income from Wages and Salaries + Net Business Income + Net Income from Properties + Net Income from Transfer

Income from Wages and Salaries refers to remuneration of labour and salaries from all kinds of sources, including those employed by other units or individuals, freelance work, part-time jobs, and sporadic labour.

Net Business Income refers to net income earned by households and their members engaged in production and business activities. It refers to the operating revenue minus operating costs, depreciation of productive fixed assets, and production tax. The formula is:

Net Business Income = Operating Revenue - Operating Costs - Depreciation of Productive Fixed Assets - Production Tax

Net Income from Properties refers to net income received as returns by households or members of financial assets, non-financial assets such as housing, to other institutions, households and individuals, and minus relevant costs. The formula is:

Net Income from Properties = Property Income – Property Expenditure

Income from Transfer refers to the regular transfer from country, institutions, social communities to households and between households. It includes old-age and retirement pension, regular donation and compensation, applying for medical fees, supporting income between households, income from non-usual-residing members of households, etc.

Net Income from Transfer The formula is:

Net Income from Transfer = Income from Transfer – Expenditure from Transfer

Consumption Expenditure of Households refers to all expenditure of households for living expenditure to satisfy family daily living. It includesexpenditureon eight categories: food tobacco and liquor; clothing; residence; household facilities, articles and services; transport and communications; education, cultural and recreational activities; health care and medical services, and miscellaneous goods and services.

The Average Per Capita Net Income of Rural Residents (the old range) refers to the total income of rural households from all sources minus all corresponding expenses. The formula is:

Net Income = Total Income –Household Operation Expenses – Taxes and Fees Paid – Taxes and Fees Depreciation of Fixed Assets for Production – Gifts to Non-rural Relatives

9 城市公用事业

URBAN PUBLIC UTILITIES

资料整理：陈超毅
Data management：Chen Chaoyi
数据审核：刘栋婷
Data audit：Liu Dongting

第九部分　城市公用事业

一、简要说明

本章资料主要包括城市供水、供燃气、供热、公共交通、市政设施、市政设施水平、城市规模及用地状况、园林绿地、环境卫生等情况，由西安市统计局服务业与社会科技处根据西安市住房和城乡建设局、市交通局、市轨道交通集团有限公司及市水务局等提供的数据整理。

二、主要指标

人均公园绿地面积（平方米）	11.80	比上年增加	0.01
人均城市道路面积（平方米）	19.57	比上年增加	1.44
供水普及率（%）	99.40	比上年提高	0.73个百分点
燃气普及率（%）	99.95	比上年提高	0.08个百分点

9　URBAN PUBLIC UTILITIES

Ⅰ.Brief Introduction

Data in this chapter reflects basic condition of urban public utilities of Xi'an City. Data on public utilities primarily consists of urban water supply, gas sales, urban heating, public transportation, municipal facilities, level of municipal construction, scale of the city, condition of land utilization, parks, greenbelt and environmental sanitation. Data in this chapter is compiled by Tertiary Industry and Social Science & Technology Division of Xi'an Bureau of Statistics according to the data provided by Housing and Urban Planning Construction of Xi'an , Xi'an Rail Transit Group Company Limited and Xi'an Metro Office.

Ⅱ.Major Indicators

		Increase over Preceding Year
Per Capita Public Green Areas (sq.m)	11.80	0.01
Per Captia Area of Roads (sq.m)	19.57	1.44
Water–Consuming Popularization (%)	99.40	0.73 percenage points
Gas–Consuming Popularization (%)	99.95	0.08 percenage points

9-1 主要年份城市（县城）供水

Urban (County) Water Supply in Representative Years

指　标	Item	2010	2016	2017	2018	2019	2020	2021
年末水厂个数（个）	Number of Water Factory at Year-end(units)	9	22	24	22	28	28	30
供水综合生产能力（万立方米/日）	Total Volume of Water Supply (10 000 cu.m/day)	197.40	219.38	206.47	215.10	287.22	300.41	362.28
#地下水	Groundwater	55.80	64.61	65.11	89.86	86.64	113.37	118.99
年末供水管道总长度（公里）	Length of Water Supply Pipelines at Year-end(kms)	2416.00	4522.46	4899.56	4959.94	4977.08	5991.32	6364.49
全年供水总量（万立方米）	Total Annual Volume of Water Supply (10 000 cu.m)	41089.00	59953.03	89215.62	90394.45	75392.33	76943.51	82379.37
#生产运营用水	For Productive Use	6267.00	16567.21	43095.31	39453.60	22675.54	21173.30	23069.09
居民家庭用水	For Residential Use	20944.00	32182.87	34896.60	39078.56	39962.46	41774.05	46185.81
用水人口（万人）	Population with Access to Tap Water (10 000 persons)	410.90	475.00	506.26	589.90	642.91	672.05	752.95

注：本表数据来源于市住房和城乡建设局、市水务局。
本表2017年及以后年份数据含西咸新区。

9-2 主要年份城市（县城）供燃气

Urban (County) Gas Supply in Representative Years

指　标	Item	2010	2016	2017	2018	2019	2020	2021
一、天然气	**Natural Gas**							
供气管道长度（公里）	Total Length of Gas Pipelines(km)	4488	8199.80	9174.87	10659.68	11928.62	12636.49	16873.99
供气总量（万立方米）	Total Gas Supply(10 000 cu.m)	109052	206068.05	231168.38	285215.47	320847.29	329150.02	366538.95
#销售气量	Volume of Gas Sales	104055	201078.36	224419.93	279030.23	311544.57	320566.43	358843.55
#家庭用量	Residential Households	20989	67024.75	105249.81	100959.64	103357.70	121623.10	106230.99
用气人口（万人）	Population with Access to Gas (10 000 persons)	333	452.11	477.01	588.40	646.89	671.05	715.00
二、液化石油气	**Liquefied Petroleum Gas**							
供气总量（吨）	Total Gas Supply(tons)	11469	4955.50	7607.20	31023.54	9965.79	12449.70	56095.78
#销售气量	Volume of Gas Sales	11441	4875.20	7478.90	30397.32	9865.50	12286.60	55906.37
#家庭用量	Residential Households	7376	4056.00	6081.47	8881.82	7241.36	6936.00	28652.33
用气人口（万人）	Population with Access to Gas (10 000 persons)	31.20	17.60	13.02	13.65	7.11	9.16	41.90

注：本表数据来源于市住房和城乡建设局。
本表2017年及以后年份数据含西咸新区。
本表2021年液化石油气相关指标统计口径调整。

9-3 主要年份城市（县城）集中供热

Urban (County) Heating in Representative Years

指 标	Item	2010	2016	2017	2018	2019	2020	2021
供热能力	Heating Capacity							
蒸汽（吨/小时）	Steam(tons/hour)	2235	3013	6200	4325	4425	3690	3909
热水（兆瓦）	Hot Water(megawatts)	3531	17765.90	14477.00	14465.47	15414.44	17226.21	22302.13
供热总量（万吉焦）	Volume Supplied(10 000 gigajoules)							
蒸汽	Steam	1674	1789.13	2813.00	1972.08	2042.18	1709.25	1402.74
热水	Hot Water	2570	5032.84	6338.00	6532.89	7538.46	8596.49	7068.00
集中供热管道长度（公里）	Length of Centralized Heating Pipelines(km)	541	1141.24	1842.00	1516.83	1739.61	1826.96	2182.41
集中供热面积（万平方米）	Heated Area(10 000sq.m)	6094	19566.81	29118.90	24922.93	27615.69	29153.07	34535.58
#住宅	Residential Buildings	5009	17282.39	17541.10	20751.73	22778.29	24473.31	28375.15

注：本表数据来源于市住房和城乡建设局。
本表2017年及以后年份数据含西咸新区。

9-4 主要年份城市公共交通

Urban Public Traffic in Representative Years

指 标	Item	2010	2016	2017	2018	2019	2020	2021
运营车辆（辆）	Operating Vehicles(units)	7107	7829	7780	8743	10566	9363	9318
标准运营车辆（标台）	Standard Vehicles(units)	8139	9140	9243	10712	13092	11710	10961
公交客运总量（万人次）	Total of Bus Passenger (10 000 person-times)	162400	147089	133465	135919	145280	73927	83581
公交客运收入（万元）	Bus Passenger Transport Income (10 000 yuan)	129397	129132	165072	126590	159040	85016	82201
出租汽车数（辆）	Number of Taxis(units)	12786	14459	14509	14609	16832	16923	15329
地铁运营线路长度（公里）	Length of Subway Lines in Operation(km)		88.97	88.97	126.70	132.41	244.27	259.00
地铁客运量（万人次）	Total of Subway Passenger (10 000 person-times)		40815.75	60534.01	74624.64	94383.62	72528.87	102302.09

注：本表数据来源于市交通局和市轨道交通集团有限公司。

9-5 主要年份市政设施

Municipal Facilities in Representative Years

指　标	Item	2010	2016	2017	2018	2019	2020	2021
一、道路长度（公里）	**Length of Roads(km)**	**2662**	**3683.14**	**4398.83**	**4712.47**	**5141.85**	**5283.95**	**5876.75**
二、道路面积（万平方米）	**Area of Roads(10 000 sq.m)**	**5965**	**8618.93**	**10063.55**	**10834.70**	**11998.06**	**12345.21**	**14825.72**
三、人行道面积（万平方米）	**Area of Sidewalks(10 000 sq.m)**	**1834**	**2423.70**	**2814.31**	**2886.16**	**3105.42**		**3371.88**
四、桥梁数（座）	**Number of Bridges(units)**	**347**	**449**	**491**	**502**	**439**	**454**	**467**
#立交桥	Overpasses	71	107	127	126	99	103	115
五、路灯盏数（盏）	**Number of Street Lights(units)**	**291754**	**349808**	**382979**	**383174**	**461408**	**464069**	**466795**
六、排水管道长度（公里）	**Length of Drainage Pipelines(km)**	**3765**	**5161.83**	**5802.36**	**6126.11**	**6445.80**	**6959.60**	**7807.62**
七、污水年排放量（万立方米）	**Annual Discharge Volume of Sewage (10 000 cu.m)**	**34706**	**56578**	**58303**	**70374**	**74617**	**78629**	**111452**
八、污水处理厂处理能力（万立方米/日）	**Daily Disposal Capacity of Sewage (10 000 cu.m/day)**	**106.5**	**212.1**	**147.6**	**225.1**	**229.7**	**242.4**	**355.6**
九、污水年处理量（万立方米）	**Yearly Disposal Capacity of Sewage Disposal Plant(10 000 cu.m)**	**25088**	**52011**	**54279**	**66048**	**71917**	**75881**	**107961**

注：本表数据来源于市住房和城乡建设局。
本表2017年及以后年份数据含西咸新区。
2020年立交桥数、路灯盏数来源于市城市管理和综合执法局。
2020年人行道面积数据暂缺。
2021年污水处理相关指标统计口径调整。

9-6 主要年份城市（县城）设施水平

Urban (County) Municipal Facilities in Representative Years

指　标	Item	2010	2016	2017	2018	2019	2020	2021
一、人均日生活用水量（升）	**Per Capita Daily Consumption of Tap Water For Residential Use(liters)**	**186.20**	**191.35**	**199.09**	**189.56**	**176.07**	**176.38**	**173.04**
二、供水普及率（%）	**Water-Consuming Popularization(%)**	**98.8**	**100.00**	**99.25**	**97.85**	**98.27**	**98.67**	**99.40**
三、燃气普及率（%）	**Gas-Consuming Popularization(%)**	**97.0**	**98.89**	**96.07**	**99.90**	**99.96**	**99.87**	**99.95**
四、人均城市道路面积（平方米）	**Per Captia Area of Roads(sq.m)**	**15.4**	**18.15**	**19.73**	**17.97**	**18.34**	**18.13**	**19.57**
五、建成区排水管道密度（公里/平方公里）	**Density of Drainage Pipelines in Developed Areas(km/sq.km)**	**9.5**	**9.12**	**1.46**	**7.88**	**7.96**	**8.58**	**9.32**
六、污水处理率（%）	**Rate of Sewerage Disposal(%)**	**84.0**	**91.93**	**93.10**	**93.85**	**96.38**	**96.51**	**96.87**
七、园林绿化	**Afforestation and Parks and Gardens**							
人均公园绿地面积（平方米）	Per Capita Public Green Areas(sq.m)	9.1	11.61	12.04	9.97	9.97	11.79	11.80
建城区绿地率（%）	Rate of Green Areas in Developed Areas(%)	29.2	34.95	36.78	35.23	36.02	38.11	38.33
八、生活垃圾无害化处理率（%）	**Rate of No Harm Disposal of Garbage(%)**	**93.9**	**96.70**	**98.11**	**98.97**	**98.87**	**98.75**	**99.98**

注：本表数据来源于市住房和城乡建设局。
本表2017年及以后年份数据含西咸新区。
本表供水普及率指标2016年及以前年份数据为用水普及率。

9–7 主要年份城市（县城）园林绿化

Urban (County) landscaping in Representative Years

指　标	Item	2010	2016	2017	2018	2019	2020	2021
一、公园个数（个）	**Number of Parks(units)**	**68**	**95**	**103**	**104**	**117**	**149**	**160**
二、公园面积（公顷）	**Area of Parks(hectares)**	**1335**	**2647.40**	**3259.70**	**3272.70**	**3490.53**	**4803.83**	**5958.76**
三、绿地面积（公顷）	**Total Area of Parks,Gardens and Green Areas(hectares)**	**12140**	**22502.87**	**30703.66**	**31680.89**	**32586.46**	**36034.00**	**43838.75**
#公园绿地面积	Public Green Areas	3526	5517.08	6142.98	6010.08	6522.65	8027.79	8936.54
四、年末绿化覆盖面积（公顷）	**Coverage Space of Green Areas at year-end(hectares)**	**15646**	**27617.83**	**35936.49**	**35939.67**	**36885.61**	**40560.79**	**46466.30**
五、建成区绿化覆盖率（%）	**Coverage of Green Areas in Developed Areas(%)**	**37.50**	**42.57**	**40.79**	**38.53**	**39.32**	**41.54**	**42.72**

注：本表数据来源于市住房和城乡建设局。
本表2017年及以后年份数据含西咸新区。

9–8 主要年份城市（县城）环境卫生

Urban (County) Environment Sanitation in Representative Years

指　标	Item	2010	2016	2017	2018	2019	2020	2021
清扫面积（万平方米）	Area Under Cleaning Program(10 000 sq.m)	6290	9137	12241	7790	10527	12552	13625
生活垃圾清运量（万吨）	Volume of Residential Garbage Disposal (10 000 tons)	237	371.51	422.25	430.68	396.78	301.45	401.16
公共厕所（座）	Number of Public Lavatories(units)	1257	2314	3274	4030	3551	3612	3609
市容环卫专用车辆设备总数（辆）	Special Vehicles of Environmental Sanitation(units)	1042	2000	2571	3305	2491	3133	3197

注：本表数据来源于市住房和城乡建设局。
本表2017年及以后年份数据含西咸新区。

9-9 市区及县供水（2021年）

Urban and County Water Supply (2021)

指　标	Item	西安 Xi'an	市区 Urban	蓝田 Lantian	周至 ZhouZhi
年末水厂个数（个）	Number of Water Factory at Year-end(units)	30	27	1	2
供水综合生产能力	Total Volume of Water Supply	362.28	354.53	3.74	4.01
（万立方米/日）	(10 000 cu.m/day)				
#地下水	Groundwater	118.99	112.45	3.74	2.80
年末供水管道总长度	Length of Water Supply Pipelines	6364.49	6076.36	128.46	159.67
（公里）	at Year-end (km)				
全年供水总量	Total Annual Volume of Water Supply	82379.37	81084.56	715.22	579.59
（万立方米）	(10 000 cu.m)				
#生产运营用水	For Productive Use	23069.09	22682.19	312.60	74.30
居民家庭用水	For Residential Use	46185.81	45628.33	247.54	309.94
用水人口（万人）	Population with Access to Tap Water	752.95	735.99	9.26	7.70
	(10 000 persons)				

注：本表数据来源于市住房和城乡建设局、市水务局。
本表数据含西咸新区。

9-10 市区及县供燃气（2021年）

Urban and County Gas Supply (2021)

指　标	Item	西安 Xi'an	市区 Urban	蓝田 Lantian	周至 ZhouZhi
一、天然气	**Natural Gas**				
管道长度（公里）	Total Length of Gas Pipelines(km)	16873.99	16233.39	169.02	471.58
供气总量（万立方米）	Total Gas Supply(10 000 cu.m)	366538.95	359901.33	2974.62	3663.00
#销售气量	Volume of Gas Sales	358843.55	352297.18	2885.37	3661.00
#家庭用量	Residential Households	106230.99	102583.48	2194.51	1453.00
用气人口（万人）	Population with Access to Gas(10 000 persons)	715.00	700.00	8.00	7.00
二、液化石油气	**Liquefied Petroleum Gas**				
供气总量（吨）	Total Gas Supply(tons)	56095.78	52681.28	1092.50	2322.00
#销售气量	Volume of Gas Sales	55906.37	52544.37	1059.00	2303.00
#家庭用量	Residential Households	28652.33	25374.33	975.00	2303.00
用气人口（万人）	Population with Access to Gas(10 000 persons)	41.90	40.22	0.98	0.70

注：本表数据来源于市住房和城乡建设局。
本表数据含西咸新区。
本表2021年液化石油气相关指标统计口径调整。

9-11 市区及县集中供热（2021年）

Urban and County Heating (2021)

指　标	Item	西安 Xi'an	市区 Urban	蓝田 Lantian	周至 ZhouZhi
供热能力	Heating Capacity				
蒸汽（吨/小时）	Steam(tons/hour)	3909.40	3909.40		
热水（兆瓦）	Hot Water(megawatts)	22302.13	22288.72		13.41
供热总量(万吉焦）	Volume Supplied(10 000 gigajoules)				
蒸汽	Steam	1402.74	1402.74		
热水	Hot Water	7068.00	7061.17		6.83
集中供热管道长度（公里）	Length of Centralized Heating Pipelines(km)	2182.41	2173.61		8.80
供热面积（万平方米）	Heated Area(10 000sq.m)	34535.58	34515.82		19.76
#住宅	Residential Buildings	28375.15	28356.94		18.21

注：本表数据来源于市住房和城乡建设局。
本表数据含西咸新区。

9-12 市区及县市政设施（2021年）

Urban and County Municipal Facilities (2021)

指 标	Item	西安 Xi'an	市区 Urban	蓝田 Lantian	周至 ZhouZhi
一、道路长度（公里）	**Length of Roads(km)**	**5876.75**	**5733.19**	**95.20**	**48.36**
二、道路面积（万平方米）	**Area of Roads(10 000 sq.m)**	**14825.72**	**14532.64**	**194.00**	**99.08**
三、人行道面积（万平方米）	**Area of Sidewalks(10 000 sq.m)**	**3371.88**	**3268.10**	**68.84**	**34.94**
四、桥梁数（座）	**Number of Bridges(units)**	**467**	**453**	**8**	**6**
#立交桥	Crossroads	115	115		
五、路灯盏数（盏）	**Number of Street Lights(units)**	**466795**	**457822**	**3236**	**5737**
六、排水管道长度（公里）	**Length of Drainage Pipelines(km)**	**7807.62**	**7610.05**	**122.67**	**74.90**
七、污水年排放量（万立方米）	**Annual Discharge Volume of Sewage (10 000 cu.m)**	**111452**	**110412**	**553**	**487**
八、污水处理厂处理能力（万立方米/日）	**Daily Disposal Capacity of Sewage (10 000 cu.m/day)**	**355.6**	**350.0**	**3.0**	**2.6**
九、污水年处理量（万立方米）	**Yearly Disposal Capacity of Sewage Disposal Plant (10 000 cu.m)**	**107961**	**107033**	**498**	**430**

注：本表数据来源于市住房和城乡建设局。
本表数据含西咸新区。

9-13 市区及县市政设施水平（2021年）

Urban and County Municipal Facilities Level (2021)

指 标	Item	西安 Xi'an	市区 Urban	蓝田 Lantian	周至 ZhouZhi
一、人均日生活用水量（升）	**Per Capita Daily Consumption of Tap Water For Residential Use(liter)**	**173.04**	**173.99**	**103.30**	**165.51**
二、供水普及率（%）	**Water-Consuming Popularization(%)**	**99.40**	**99.40**	**98.83**	**100.00**
三、燃气普及率（%）	**Gas-Consuming Popularization(%)**	**99.95**	**99.99**	**100.00**	**96.10**
四、人均城市道路面积（平方米）	**Per Captia Area of Roads(sq.m)**	**19.57**	**19.63**	**20.70**	**12.87**
五、建成区排水管道密度（公里/平方公里）	**Density of Drainage Pipelines (km/sq.km)**	**9.32**	**9.45**	**4.12**	**5.07**
六、污水处理率（%）	**Rate of Sewerage Disposal(%)**	**96.87**	**96.94**	**90.00**	**88.30**
七、园林绿化	**Afforestation and Parks and Gardens**				
人均公园绿地面积（平方米）	Per Capita Public Green Areas(sq.m)	11.80	11.85	8.59	10.69
建城区绿地率（%）	Rate of Green Areas in Developed Areas(%)	38.33	38.67	33.29	17.04
八、生活垃圾无害化处理率（%）	**Rate of No Harm Disposal of Garbage(%)**	**99.98**	**100.00**	**98.07**	**99.98**

注：本表数据来源于市住房和城乡建设局。
本表数据含西咸新区。

主要统计指标解释

供水综合生产能力 指按供水设施取水、净化、送水、出厂输水干管等环节设计能力计算的综合生产能力。包括在原设计能力的基础上，经挖、革、改增加的生产能力。计算时，以四个环节中最薄弱的环节为主确定能力。

供水管道长度 指从送水泵至用户水表之间所有管道的长度。不包括新安装尚未使用、水厂内以及用户建筑物内的管道。在同一条街道埋设两条或两条以上管道时，应按每条管道的长度计算。

供水总量 指报告期供水企业（单位）供出的全部水量。包括有效供水量和漏损水量。

供水普及率 指报告期末城区内用水人口与总人口的比率。计算公式:

$$供水普及率=\frac{用水人口（含暂住人口）}{人口+暂住人口}\times 100\%$$

供气管道长度 指报告期末从气源厂压缩机的出口或门站出口至各类用户引入管之间的全部已经通气投入使用的管道长度。不包括煤气生产厂、输配站、液化气储存站、灌瓶站、储配站、气化站、混气站、供应站等厂（站）内的管道。

供气总量 指报告期燃气企业（单位）向用户供应的燃气数量。包括销售量和损失量。

燃气普及率 指报告期末城区内使用燃气的人口与总人口的比率。计算公式：

$$燃气普及率=\frac{用气人口（含暂住人口）}{人口+暂住人口}\times 100\%$$

供热能力 指供热企业（单位）向城市热用户输送热能的设计能力。不是热电厂的生产能力。

供热总量 指在报告期供热企业（单位）向城市热用户输送全部蒸汽和热水的总热量。

供热管道长度 指从各类热源到热用户建筑物接入口之间的全部蒸汽和热水的管道长度。不包括各类热源厂内部的管道长度。

供热面积 指供热企业（单位）向城市各类房屋建筑物、构筑物及其附属设施供热的全部建筑面积。

道路长度 指道路长度和与道路相通的桥梁、隧道的长度，按车行道中心线计算。

道路面积 指道路实际铺装面积和与道路相通的广场、桥梁、隧道的铺装面积（统计时，将人行道面积单独统计）。

人行道面积按道路两侧面积相加计算，包括步行街和广场，不含人车混行的道路。

排水管道长度 指所有排水总管、干管、支管、检查井及连接井进出口等长度之和。计算时按单管计算，即在同一条街道上如有两条或两条以上并排的排水管道时，应按每条排水管道的长度相加计算。

绿化覆盖面积 指城市中的乔木、灌木、草坪等所有植被的垂直投影面积。包括公园绿地、防护绿地、生产绿地、附属绿地、其他绿地的绿化种植覆盖面积、屋顶绿化覆盖面积以及零散树木的覆盖面积，不含各类绿地中的水域面积以及没有被植被覆盖的面积（硬化道路、无屋顶绿化的建筑物等）。乔木树冠下重迭的灌木和草本植物不重复计算。

人均城市道路面积 指报告期末城区内平均每人拥有的城市道路面积。计算公式：

$$人均城市道路面积=\frac{城区道路面积}{城区人口+城区暂住人口}$$

建成区排水管道密度 指报告期末建成区排水管道分布的疏密程度，计算公式：

$$排水管道密度=\frac{排水管道长度}{建成区面积}$$

污水处理率 指报告期内污水处理总量与污水排放总量的比率。计算公式：

$$污水处理率=\frac{污水处理总量}{污水排放总量}\times 100\%$$

人均公园绿地面积 指报告期末城区内平均每人拥有的公园绿地面积。计算公式：

$$人均公园绿地面积=\frac{城区公园绿地面积}{城区人口+城区暂住人口}$$

建成区绿地率 指报告期末建成区内绿地面积与建成区面积的比率。计算公式：

$$建成区绿地率=\frac{建成区绿地面积}{建成区面积}\times 100\%$$

Explanatory Notes on Main Statistical Indicators

Production Capacity of Water Supply refers to the designed overall production capacity of water facilities, covering the four segments of water collection, purification, conveyance, and out flow through trunk pipelines. Increased capacity through transformation and innovation projects is included as well. The capacity is determined mainly on the weakest of the above-mentioned four segments.

Length of Water Supply Pipelines at Year–end refers to the total length of all the pipelines between the water pumps and the user water meters, excluding pipelines newly installed but not used yet, pipeline in the water factory, and pipeline in the user's buildings.

Volume of Water Supply refers to the total volume of water supplied by water-works(units) during the reference period, including both the effective water supply and loss during the water supply.

Popularity of Water Supply refers to the ratio of the urban population with access to tap water to the total urban population. The formula is:

$$\text{Popularity of Water Supply} = \frac{\text{Water users (including temporary residents)}}{\text{Population + temporary resident population}} \times 100\%$$

Length of Gas Pipeline refers to the total length of pipelines in use between the outlet of the compressor of gas-work of outlet gas stations and the leading pipe of users , excluding pipelines within gasworks , delivery stations ,LPG storage stations ,refilling stations, gas-mixing stations and supply stations.

Volume of Gas Supply refers to the total volume of gas provided to users by gas-producing enterprises (units) in a year , including the volume sold and the volume lost .

Coverage Rate of Urban Population with Access to Gas refers to the ratio of the urban population with access to gas to the total urban population at the end of the reference period. The formula is :

$$\text{Coverage rate of urbanpopulation with access to gas} = \frac{\text{Gas users (including temporary residents)}}{\text{Population + temporary resident population}} \times 100\%$$

City Heating capacity in Urban Areas refers to the designed capacity of heating enterprises (units) in supplying heating energy to urban users during the reference period .

City Quantity of Heat Supplied in Urban Areas refers to the total quantity of heat from steam and hot water urban users by heating enterprises (units) during the reference period .

City Length of Urban Heating Pipelines refers to the total length of steam or hot water pipelines for sources of heat to the leading pipelines of the building of the users, excluding internal pipelines in heat generating enterprises.

Heated Area refers to the total structure area of heat supplied to urban constructions, structures and ancillary facilities by heating enterprises (units) during the reference period .

Length of Paved Roads refers to the length of roads with paved surface including bridges and tunnels connected with roads. Length of the roads is measured by the central lines .

Area of Paved Roads refers to the actual pavement area of roads and the actual pavement area of squares, bridges and tunnels connecting to the roads (the area of sidewalk pavements is calculated separately).

The area of sidewalk pavements is the sum of area of roads on sides of road, including pedestrian streets and squares, excluding roads for both pedestrians and vehicles .

Length of exhaust pipelines refers to the total length of all main drain piles, trunk pipes ,branch pipes, access manholes , and connector well entrances and exits, and so on . The whole length is calculated as of single pipes. Namely, if there are two or more drain pipes parallel on a street , the length of every pipe shall be summed .

Total area of green land refers to vertical projection area of all vegetation including trees, shrubs, lawns. Including parks, protective green space, production green space, green subsidiaries, green plants covering area, covering an area other green spaces, green roofs and covering area of scattered trees, excluding kinds of water area in kinds of green area and the area not covered by vegetation(hardened road, building of no green roof). shrubs and herbaceous plants overlap under the canopy of trees do not double counting.

Per Capita Area of Paved Roads refers to the area of urban roads per capita at the end of the reporting period. The formula is :

$$\text{Per capita area of paved roads} = \frac{\text{Area of urban roads}}{\text{Urban population+temporary resident population}}$$

Density of Drainage Pipelines refers to density of drainage pipelines in developed areas at the end of the reporting period .The formula is :

$$\text{Density of drainage pipelines} = \frac{\text{Length of drainage pipelines}}{\text{Area of developed areas}}$$

Rate of Sewerage Disposal refers to the ratio of waste water disposed with the total discharge of waste water in the reporting period .The formula is:

$$\text{Rate of Sewerage Disposal} = \frac{\text{Waste Water Disposed}}{\text{Total Discharge of Waste Water}} \times 100\%$$

Per Capita Area of Public Green refers to the area of public green areas per capita at end of the reporting period .The formula is :

$$\text{Per capita area of public green} = \frac{\text{Area of public green areas}}{\text{Urban population+temporary resident population}}$$

Coverage of Green Areas in Developed Areas refers to the ratio of green areas in built-up areas with the area of developed areas at the end of reporting period . The formula is:

$$\text{Coverage of green land in developed areas} = \frac{\text{Area of green land in developed areas}}{\text{Area of developed areas}} \times 100\%$$

10 环境保护

ENVIRONMENT PROTECTION

资料整理：张　育
Data management: Zhang Yu
数据审核：马建华
Data audit: Ma Jianhua

第十部分　环境保护

一、简要说明

本章资料反映环境保护、工业污染排放及处理利用情况、危险废物集中处置情况、生活及其他污染情况和工业污染治理项目建设情况，由西安市统计局能源与环境统计处根据西安市生态环境局提供的数据资料整理。本章数据不包含西咸新区。

二、主要指标

全年环境空气质量达标天数（天）	265	比上年增加	15

10 ENVIRONMENT PROTECTION

Ⅰ.Brief Introduction

This chapter contains information that reflect environment protection, discharge and treatment of industrial pollutant, centralized treatment of dangerous wastes, domestic pollution and other pollution, construction of projects of industrial pollution treatment. Data in this chapter is compiled by General Division of the Xi'an Bureau of Statistics according to the reported data from Xi'an Ecology and Environment Bureau. Data from Xixian is not contained in this chapter .

Ⅱ.Major Indicators

		Increase over Preceding Year
Days of Air Quality up to the Standards（days）	265	15

10-1 城市环境保护（2021年）

Urban Environmental Protection (2021)

指　标	Item	2021
一、饮用水环境	**Potable Water Environment**	
全市饮用水水质达标率(%)	Compliance Rate of the City's Potable Water Quality (%)	100
二、大气环境	**Atmospheric Environment**	
颗粒物（PM_{10}）年平均浓度（微克/立方米）	Particulate matter (PM_{10}) Annual average concentration (μg / m^3)	82
颗粒物（$PM_{2.5}$）年平均浓度（微克/立方米）	Particulate matter ($PM_{2.5}$) Annual average concentration (μg / m^3)	41
二氧化硫浓度年平均值（微克/立方米）	Annual Average Concentration of Sulphur Dioxide (μg / m^3)	8
二氧化氮浓度年平均值（微克/立方米）	Annual Average Concentration of Nitrogen Dioxide (μg / m^3)	40
一氧化碳第95百分位数（微克/立方米）	The 95th percentile of carbon monoxide (μg / m^3)	1.3
臭氧八小时第90百分位数（微克/立方米）	Ozone eight hours 90th percentile (μg / m^3)	154
全年环境空气质量达标天数(天)	Days of Air Quality up to the Standards(days)	265
全年环境空气质量达标率(%)	Annual compliance rate of Ambient Air Quality(%)	72.6
三、声环境	**Voice**	
1.功能区噪声平均值(昼/夜)	Average Noise Value of Functional Districts（day/night)	
0类区(dB(A)/dB(A))	Class 0(dB(A)/dB(A))	49/44
1类区(dB(A)/dB(A))	Class 1(dB(A)/dB(A))	54/48
2类区(dB(A)/dB(A))	Class 2(dB(A)/dB(A))	55/50
3类区(dB(A)/dB(A))	Class 3(dB(A)/dB(A))	58/52
4类区(dB(A)/dB(A))	Class 4(dB(A)/dB(A))	67/62
2.道路交通噪声平均值(dB(A))	Average Noise Value of Road Traffic(dB(A))	68.7
3.区域噪声平均值(dB(A))	Average Noise Value of Region(dB(A))	56.2
四、环境污染治理	**Environmental pollution treatment**	
当年完成环保验收项目环境保护投资（亿元）	Year Completed Investment in Environmental Protection Projects of Environmental acceptance(100 million yuan)	11.48

注：本表数据来源于市生态环境局。表中当年完成环保验收项目环境保护投资额包含市本级及区县、开发区。2017年起数据为不含西咸新区口径。下同。

10-2 主要年份工业“三废”排放及处理利用情况

指 标	Item	2000	2010
一、工业废水排放量（万吨）	**Volume of Waste Water Discharge (10 000 tons)**	**9145**	**13840**
工业废水处理量（万吨）	Volume of Industrial Wastewater Disposal (10 000 tons)		10673.52
废水治理设施数（套）	Number of Facilities for Treatment of Waste Water (sets)		267
二、工业废气排放量（亿立方米）	**Total Volume of Industrial Waste Gas Emission (100 million cu.m)**	**275.97**	**791.56**
废气治理设施数（套）	Number of Facilities for Treatment of Waste Gas(sets)		816
三、工业固体废物产生量（万吨）	**Volume of Industrial Solid Wastes Produced (10 000 tons)**	**107**	**267.29**
工业固体废物处置量（万吨）	Volume of Industrial Solid Wastes Treated (10 000 tons)	20	3.56
工业固体废物综合利用量（万吨）	Volume of Industrial Solid Waste Utilized (10 000 tons) in a Comprehensive Way	63	262
工业固体废物综合利用率（%）	Percentage of Volume of Industrial Solid Waste Utilized in a Comprehensive Way(%)	58.88	98.05
四、工业锅炉（台/蒸吨）	**Industrial Boilers (units/tons)**		

注：1.本表数据来源于市生态环境局。
2.2010年全国统一进行了污染源普查动态更新调查工作，“十二五”的环境统计体系与污染源普查体系相衔接，与“十一五”环境统计口径不同。
3.工业固体废物综合利用率依据环境统计口径计算。

Discharge and Treatment of Waste Gas, Water & Solid Wastes in Representative Years

2011	2012	2013	2014	2015	2016	2017	2018	2019	2020	2021
13148	**10223.73**	**8972.97**	**6339.85**	**5203.56**	**4029.83**	**4247.57**	**4163.40**	**3913.70**	**2998.24**	**3812.82**
12632.38	9089.04	6798.71	5818.27	4783.60	4264.99	4448.08	4091.10	3955.70	3384.43	4356.43
314	312	295	305	315	266	275	299	311	311	305
1018.46	**1043.31**	**844.11**	**901.23**	**1108.48**	**1034.46**	**1444.60**	**1040.40**	**1067.30**	**1194.32**	**1372.78**
745	649	661	740	801	834	1048	1225	1641	1271	1189
279	**259.14**	**255.78**	**252.66**	**238.53**	**195.99**	**190.30**	**198.70**	**206.66**	**183.07**	**178.12**
6	9.24	9.68	17.54	20.95	28.66	28.00	78.10	22.70	27.09	23.65
271	248.58	244.08	233.52	216.64	167.20	159.80	118.30	182.98	156.00	154.49
97.30	95.92	95.43	92.43	90.82	85.31	83.97	59.50	87.50	85.21	86.73
	503/8785	**576/13466**	**520/14177**	**501/18278**	**480/12791.8**	**457/14682.3**	**466/17078.2**	**478/16955.3**	**455/17065.5**	**411/10799.0**

10-3 工业污染排放及处理利用情况（2021年）

Discharge and Treatment of Industrial Pollution (2021)

指　标	Item	2021
一、被调查企业基本情况	**Basic condition of Enterprises investigated**	
1. 企业数（个）	Number of Enterprises (units)	554
2. 工业总产值（亿元）	Gross Industry Output Value (100 million yuan)	5382.13
3. 工业锅炉数（台/蒸吨）	Industrial Boilers (units/tons)	411/10799.0
4. 工业炉窑数（座）	Number of Industrial Grates (items)	383
二、工业废水	**Industrial Waste Water**	
1. 工业取水量（万吨）	Industrial water intake (10000 tons)	7884.09
2. 工业废水排放量（万吨）	Volume of Industrial Waste Water Discharged (10 000 tons)	3812.82
3. 工业废水处理量（万吨）	Volume of Industrial Wastewater Disposal (10 000 tons)	4356.43
4. 废水治理设施数（套）	Number of Facilities for Treatment of Waste Water (sets)	250
5. 废水治理设施处理能力（万吨/日）	Disposal Capacity of Facilities for Treatment of Waste Water (10 000 tons/day)	28.67
6. 废水治理设施运行费用（万元）	Operating Expense of Facilities for Treatment of Waste Water (10 000 yuan)	38973.74
三、工业废气	**Industrial Waste Gas**	
1. 煤炭消费量（万吨）	Total Coal Consumption (10 000 tons)	381.99
2. 燃料油消费量（不含车船用）（万吨）	Fuel Oil Consumption (10 000 tons)	0.22
3. 天然气消费量（亿立方米）	Natural Gas Consumption (100 million cu.m)	12.15
4. 工业废气排放总量（亿立方米）	Total Volume of Industrial Waste Gas Emission (100 million cu.m)	1372.78
5. 废气治理设施数（套）	Number of Facilities for Treatment of Waste Gas (sets)	1189
6. 废气治理设施处理能力（万立方米/时）	Disposal Capacity of Facilities for Treatment of Waste Gas (10 000 cu.m./h)	10775.59
7. 废气治理设施设备运行费用（万元）	Operating Expense of Facilities for Treatment of Waste gas(10 000 yuan)	22475.94
8. 二氧化硫产生量（吨）	Sulfur dioxide production (tons)	81313.21
9. 二氧化硫排放量（吨）	Volume of Sulphur Dioxide Emission (tons)	1154.29
10. 氮氧化物产生量（吨）	Production of nitrogen oxides(tons)	18367.09
11. 氮氧化物排放量（吨）	Nitrogen oxide emissions(tons)	2595.05
12. 烟（粉）尘产生量（吨）	Tobacco (powder) dust production(tons)	8404.57
13. 烟（粉）尘排放量（吨）	The smoke (powder) dust emissions(tons)	801.54
四、工业固体废物	**Industrial Solid Waste**	
1. 工业固体废物产生量（万吨）	Volume of Industrial Solid Waste Produced (10 000tons)	178.12
2. 工业固体废物综合利用量（万吨）	Volume of Industrial Solid Waste Utilized (10 000tons)	154.49
3. 工业固体废物综合利用率（%）	Percentage of Industrial Solid Waste Utilized（%）	86.73
4. 工业固体废物贮存量（万吨）	Volume of Industrial Solid Waste Accumulated (10 000tons)	0.06
5. 工业固体废物处置量（万吨）	Volume of Industrial Solid Waste Treated (10 000tons)	23.65
6. 工业固体废物倾倒丢弃量（吨）	Volume of Industrial Solid Waste Discharged (tons)	93.50

注：本表数据来源于市生态环境局。

10-4 城市污水处理情况（2021年）

Urban Sewage Treatment(2021)

指 标	Item	2021
一、污水处理厂数（座）	**Number of Sewage Treatment Works(units)**	**48**
污水处理厂处理能力（万吨/日）	Daily Disposal Capacity of Sewage(10 000 tons/day)	326.14
二、污水处理	**Sewgae Disposal**	
污水实际处理量（万吨）	Volume of Sewgae Disposal(10 000 tons)	102416.83
生活污水处理量	Volume of Domestic Sewgae Disposal	98787.46
工业污水处理量	Volume of Industrial Sewage Disposal	3559.62
三、再生水（万吨）	**Utilization(10 000 tons)**	
生产量	Production	7126.11
利用量	Utilization	6068.94
四、化学需氧量去除量（吨）	**Volume of COD Removed (tons)**	**331285.61**
五、氨氮去除量（吨）	**Volume of Ammonia and Nitrogen Removed(tons)**	**31655.55**
六、总磷去除量（吨）	**Volume of Total Phosphorus Removed(tons)**	**5012.38**
七、污泥生产量（万吨）	**Volume of Sludge Produced(10 000 tons)**	**45.82**
八、污泥处置量（万吨）	**Volume of Sludge Disposal(10 000 tons)**	**45.82**
九、污泥倾倒丢弃量（吨）	**Dumping sludge discards (tons)**	
十、本年运行费用（万元）	**Operating Expense(10 000 yuan)**	**115123.09**

注：本表数据来源于市生态环境局。

10-5 危险废物（医疗废物）集中处理情况（2021年）

Condition of Concentrated Disposal of Dangerous Wastes (Medical Wastes)(2021)

指 标	Item	2021
一、危险废物集中处理（置）厂数（个）	**Number of Collected Dangerous Wastes Treated Plants(items)**	**4**
二、医疗废物集中处理（置）厂数（个）	**The number of Manufacturing Plants of Medical waste treatment (units)**	**1**
三、危险废物设计处置能力（吨/日）	**Design hazardous waste disposal capacity (tons / day)**	**84**
四、实际处置危险废物量（吨）	**The actual amount of hazardous waste disposal (tons)**	**23426.0**
五、危险废物综合利用量（吨）	**Volume of Dangerous Wastes Utilized in a Comprehensive Way (tons)**	**2445.2**
六、焚烧残渣流向（千克）	**Flow Direction of Residuum after Burning (kg)**	
1. 焚烧残渣量	Volume of Residuum after Burning	3712.0
2. 焚烧残渣安全填埋处置量	Secure landfill disposal incineration residues	2912.0
3. 焚烧飞灰产生量	Fly ash production	181.7
4. 焚烧飞灰安全填埋处置量	Fly ash landfill disposal safety	178.3
七、当年运行费用（万元）	**Operating Expenses in Current year(10 000 yuan)**	**6909.1**

注：本表数据来源于市生态环境局。

10-6 生活及其他污染情况（2021年）

Domestic Pollution and Other Conditions(2021)

指 标	Item	2021
一、基本情况	**Basic Condition**	
1. 生活天然气消费量（万立方米）	Volume of Living natural gas consumption (10 000 cu.m)	365300
2. 生活用水总量（万吨）	Volume of Living water (10 000 tons)	76944
二、污染排放情况	**Discharge of Pollutant**	
1. 城镇生活污水排放量（万吨）	Volume of Urban Domestic Sewage Discharged(10 000 tons)	63367
2. 生活污水处理量（万吨）	Volume of Domestic Sewgae Disposal(10 000 tons)	98787
3. 生活CDD产生量（吨）	Volume of Life CDD production (tons)	337126
4. 生活CDD排放量（吨）	Volume of Life CDD emissions (tons)	41289
5. 生活氨氮产生量（吨）	Volume of Ammonia and Nitrogen in Urban Domestic Sewage Produced (tons)	36045
6. 生活氨氮排放量（吨）	Volume of Ammonia and Nitrogen in Urban Domestic Sewage Discharged (tons)	5317
7. 二氧化硫排放量（吨）	Volume of Domestic and Other Sulphur Dioxide Emission (tons)	3726
8. 氮氧化物排放量（吨）	Volume of Ammonia and Nitrogen in Urban Domestic Sewage Discharged (tons)	5554
9. 烟尘排放量（吨）	Volume of Soot Emission (tons)	11043

注：本表数据来源于市生态环境局。

10-7 工业污染治理项目建设情况（2021年）

Condition of Anti-Industrial-Pollution Projects (2021)

指　标	Item	2021
一、工业企业数（个）	**Number of Industrial Enterprises (units)**	**6**
二、老工业污染源项目治理本年施工总数（个）	**The total number of construction projects of Old industrial pollution sources control this year(units)**	**5**
#工业废水治理项目	Treatment of Waste Water	
工业废气治理项目	Treatment of Waste Gas	2
工业固体废物治理项目	Treatmen of Solid Wastes	
三、老工业污染源项目治理本年竣工总数（个）	**The Total Number of Old Industrial Pollution Control Projects Completed this year(units)**	**2**
#工业废水治理项目	Treatment of Waste Water	
工业废气治理项目	Treatment of Waste Gas	2
工业固体废物治理项目	Treatmen of Solid Wastes	
四、老工业污染源治理项目本年完成投资（万元）	**Investment completed in Old industrial pollution control projects this Year(10 000 yuan)**	**26092**
#废水治理项目	Treatment of Waste Water	
废气治理项目	Treatment of Waste Gas	27
固体废物治理项目	Treatmen of Solid Wastes	
五、老工业污染源治理项目本年投资来源（万元）	**Source of Investment in Old industrial pollution control projects this Year(10 000 yuan)**	**26092**
#政府其他补助	Other Government Subsidies	
企业自筹	Self-raising Funds	26092
银行贷款	Lonans	

注：本表数据来源于市生态环境局。

10-8 各区县、开发区环境保护基本情况（2021年）

区县、开发区	Region	本年完成环保验收项目环保投资额（万元）Investment Completed in accepted Environmental projects this year (10 000 yuan)	工业二氧化硫排放量（吨）Volume of Industrial Sulphur Dioxide Discharged (tons)
全 市	**Total**	**114788.2**	**1154.3**
新城区	Xincheng	8555.8	1.4
碑林区	Beilin	267.2	
莲湖区	Lianhu	18166.6	7.0
灞桥区	Baqiao	4307.6	246.9
未央区	Weiyang	1711.2	1.2
雁塔区	Yanta	34397.8	60.0
阎良区	Yanliang	2438.0	1.4
临潼区	Lintong	20479.0	59.2
长安区	Chang'an		194.4
高陵区	Gaoling	403.5	107.6
鄠邑区	Huyi		471.6
蓝田县	Lantian	736.3	0.6
周至县	Zhouzhi	2399.5	0.2
高新区	Hi-Tech Industries Development Zone		0.9
经开区	Economic Development Zone		0.8
曲江新区	Qujiang New District		
航空基地	National Aviation Hi-tech Industrial Base		
航天基地	National Civil Aerospace Industrial Base	19980.7	0.4
浐灞生态区	Chan-ba Ecological District		
国际港务区	International Trade & Logistics Park	945.2	0.6

注：本表数据来源于市生态环境局。
环境统计中污水处理厂个数包含部分大学园区及部分大型小区的污水处理厂。
区县、开发区环保验收项目环保投资额未包括市本级完成数。

Condition of Environment Protection by Regions (2021)

工业化学需氧量排放量 （吨） Volume of COD Removed (tons)	垃圾处理站数 （座） Number of Rubbish Disposal Works (units)	污水处理厂数 （个） Number of Sewage Treatment Works (units)
904.0	**4**	**48**
11.7		
81.5		2
1.6		4
41.8		6
40.8		3
30.5	1	3
127.7	1	4
16.2		7
26.3		1
64.1		3
6.5	1	4
5.5	1	2
318.7		6
104.1		2
27.3		
		1

主要统计指标解释

工业用水 指工矿企业在生产过程中用于制造、加工、冷却、空调、净化、洗涤等方面的用水，按新水取用量计，不包括企业内部的重复利用水量。

工业废水排放量 指经过企业厂区所有排放口排到企业外部的工业废水量。包括生产废水、外排的直接冷却水、超标排放的矿井地下水和与工业废水混排的厂区生活污水，不包括外排的间接冷却水（清污不分流的间接冷却水应计算在内）。

直接排入海的 指经企业位于海边的排放口，直接排入海的废水量。直接排放指废水经过工厂的排污口直接排入海，而未经过城市下水道或其他中间体，也不受其他水体的影响。

工业废水排放达标量 指报告期内废水中各项污染物指标都达到国家或地方排放标准的外排工业废水量，包括未经处理外排达标的，经废水处理设施处理后达标排放的，以及经污水处理厂处理后达标排放的。

生活污水排放量 指城镇居民每年排放的生活污水。用人均系数法测算。测算公式为：

$$\frac{\text{生活污水}}{\text{排放量}} = \frac{\text{城镇生活污水}}{\text{排放系数}} \times \frac{\text{市镇非}}{\text{农业人口}} \times 365$$

生活污水中化学需氧量（COD）排放量 指城镇居民每年排放的生活污水中的COD的量。用人均系数法测算。测算公式为：

$$\frac{\text{城镇生活污水中}}{\text{COD产生系数}} = \frac{\text{城镇生活污水}}{\text{中COD排放量}} \times \frac{\text{市镇非}}{\text{农业人口}} \times 365$$

化学需氧量（COD） 指用化学氧化剂氧化水中有机污染物时所需的氧量。COD值越高，表示水中有机污染物污染越重。

工业废气排放量 指报告期内企业厂区内燃料燃烧和生产工艺过程中产生的各种排入大气的含有污染物的气体的总量，以标准状态（273K，101325Pa）计算。测算公式为：

$$\frac{\text{工业废气}}{\text{排放量}} = \frac{\text{燃料燃烧过程}}{\text{中废气排放量}} + \frac{\text{生产工艺过程}}{\text{中废气排放量}}$$

生活及其他SO_2排放量 以生活及其他煤炭消费量和其含硫量为基础，根据以下公式计算：

$$\frac{\text{生活及其他}}{SO_2\text{排放量}} = \frac{\text{生活及其他}}{\text{煤炭消费量}} \times \text{含硫量} \times 0.8 \times 2$$

工业SO_2排放量 指报告期内企业在燃料燃烧和生产工艺过程中排入大气的SO_2总量，计算公式为：

$$\frac{\text{工业}SO_2}{\text{排放量}} = \frac{\text{燃料燃烧过程}}{\text{中}SO_2\text{排放量}} + \frac{\text{生产工艺过程}}{\text{中}SO_2\text{排放量}}$$

工业烟尘排放量 指企业厂区内燃料燃烧过程中产生的烟气中夹带的颗粒物排放量。

生活及其他烟尘排放量 指除工业生产活动以外的所有社会、经济活动及公共设施的经营活动中燃烧所排放的烟尘纯重量。以生活及其他煤炭消费量为基础进行测算。

工业粉尘排放量 指企业在生产工艺过程中排放的能在空气中悬浮一定时间的固体颗粒物排放量。如钢铁企业的耐火材料粉尘、焦化企业的筛焦系统粉尘、烧结机的粉尘、石灰窑的粉尘、建材企业的水泥粉尘等。不包括电厂排入大气的烟尘。

工业固体废物产生量 指报告期内企业在生产过程中产生的固体状、半固体状和高浓度液体状废弃物的总量，包括危险废物、冶炼废渣、粉煤灰、炉渣、煤矸石、尾矿、放射性废物和其他废物等；不包括矿山开采的剥离废石和掘进废石（煤矸石和呈酸性或碱性的废石除外）。酸性或碱性废石指采掘的废石其流经水、雨淋水的pH值小于4或pH值大于10.5者。

危险废物 指列入国家危险废物名录或根据国家规定的危险废物鉴别标准和鉴别方法认定的，具有爆炸性、易燃性、易氧化性、毒性、腐蚀性、易传染疾病等危险特性之一的废物。

工业固体废物综合利用量 指报告期内企业通过回收、加工、循环、交换等方式，从固体废物中提取或者使其转化为可以利用的资源、能源和其他原材料的固体废物量（包括当年利用往年的工业固体废物贮存量），如用作农业肥料、生产建筑材料、筑路等。综合利用量由原产生固体废物的单位统计。

工业固体废物综合利用率 指工业固体废物综合利用量占工业固体废物产生量（包括综合利用往年贮存量）的百分率。计算公式为：

$$\text{工业固体废物综合利用率} = \frac{\text{工业固体废物综合利用量}}{\text{工业固体废物产生量} + \text{综合利用往年贮存量}} \times 100\%$$

工业固体废物贮存量 指报告期内企业以综合利用或处置为目的，将固体废物暂时贮存或堆存在专设的贮存设施或专设的集中堆存场所内的数量。专设的固体废物贮存场所或贮存设施必须有防扩散、防流失、防渗漏、防止污染大气、水体的措施。

工业固体废物处置量 指报告期内企业将固体废物焚烧或者最终置于符合环境保护规定要求的场所，并不再回取的工业固体废物量（包括当年处置往年的工业固体废物贮存量）。处置方式有填埋（其中危险废物应安全填埋）、焚烧、专业贮存场（库）封场处理、深层灌注、回填矿井及海洋处置（经海洋管理部门同意投海处置）等。

工业固体废物排放量 指报告期内企业将所产生的固体废物排到固体废物污染防治设施、场所以外的数量，不包括矿山开采的剥离废石和掘进废石（煤矸石和呈酸性或碱性的废石除外）。

“三废”综合利用产品产值 指报告期内利用“三废”作为主要原料生产的产品价值（现行价）；已经销售或准备销售的应计算产品价值，留作生产自用的不应计算产品价值。

生活垃圾清运量 指报告期内收集和运送到各生活垃圾处理厂（场）和生活垃圾最终消纳点的生活垃圾数量。生活垃圾指城市日常生活或为城市日常生活提供服务的活动中产生的固体废物以及法律行政规定的视为城市生活垃圾的固体废物。包括：居民生活垃圾、商业垃圾、集市贸易市场垃圾、街道清扫垃圾、公共场所垃圾和机关、学校、厂矿等单位的生活垃圾。

生活垃圾无害化处理率 指报告期生活垃圾无害化处理量与生活垃圾产生量的比率。在统计上，由于生活垃圾产生量不易取得，可用清运量代替。计算公式为：

$$\text{生活垃圾无害化处理率} = \frac{\text{生活垃圾无害化处理量}}{\text{生活垃圾产生量}} \times 100\%$$

Explanatory Notes on Main Statistical Indicators

Water Used by Industry refers to new withdrawals of water, excluding reuse of water within enterprises.

Waste Water Discharged by Industry refers to the volume of waste water discharged by industrial enterprises through all their outlets, including waste water from production process, directly cooled water, groundwater from mining wells which does not meet discharge standards and sewage from households mixed with waste water produced by industrial activities, but excluding indirectly cooled water discharged (It should be included if the discharge is not separated from waste water).

Waste Water Directly Discharged into Sea refers to the volume of waste water directly discharged into sea through outlets of enterprises situated by sea without going through municipal sewerage networks or any other intermediates or being affected by any other water bodies.

Industrial Waste Water Meeting Discharge Standards refers to volume of industrial waste water discharge which, with or without treatment, reaches national or local standards with regard to all pollutants.

Urban Non-industrial Waste Water Discharge refers to annual discharge of non-industrial waste water by urban households. It is estimated by per capita coefficient using the formula:

$$\text{Urban non-industrial waste water discharge} = \text{urban non-industrial waste water discharge coefficient} \times \text{urban non-alagricultur population} \times 365$$

Volume of Chemical Oxygen Demand (COD) Generated by Urban Non-industrial Waster Water refers to chemical oxygen demand generated through the annual discharge of non-industrial waste water by urban households. It is estimated as:

$$\text{Volume of chemical oxygen demand (cod) generated by urban non-industrial waster water} = \text{Coefficient of COD generated through urban non-industrial waste water} \times \text{urban non-agricultural population} \times 365$$

Chemical Oxygen Demand (COD) refers to the amount of oxygen required when chemical oxidants are used to oxidize organic pollutants in water. A higher value of COD corresponds to more serious pollution by organic pollutants.

Industrial Waste Air Emission refers to the discharge into atmosphere of waste air containing pollutants generated from fuel burning and production processes in enterprises within a given period of time. It is calculated at standard status (273K, 101325Pa) as:

$$\text{Industrial waste air emission} = \text{tnoissimehrough fuel burning} + \text{tnoissimehrough production process}$$

SO_2 Emission through Non-industrial and Other Activities is calculated on the basis of consumption of coal by households and other activities and the sulphur content of coal with the following formula:

$$SO_2 \text{ emission through non-industrial and other activities} = \text{of coalby households andother activities} \times \text{sulphur content} \times 0.8 \times 2$$

SO_2 Emission through Industrial Activities refers to volume of sulphur dioxide emission from fuel burning and production process by enterprises during a given period of time. It is calculated as:

$$SO_2 \text{ emission through industrial activities} = SO_2 \text{emission from fuel burning} + SO_2 \text{ emission from production process}$$

Industrial Soot Emission refers to the volume of soot in smoke emitted in the process of fuel burning in the premises of enterprises.

Soot Emission by Consumption and Others refers to the net volume of soot emitted by fuel burning from all social and economic activities and operations of public facilities other than industrial activities. It is calculated on the basis of coal consumption by households and others.

Industrial Dust Emission refers to volume of dust emitted by production process of enterprises and suspended in the air for a given period of time, including dust from refractory material of iron and steel works, dust from coke-screening systems and sintering machines of coke plants, dust from lime kilns and dust from cement production in building material enterprises, but excluding soot and dust emitted from power plants.

Industrial Solid Wastes Produced refers to total volume of solid, semi-solid and high concentration liquid residues produced by industrial enterprises from production process in a given period of time, including hazardous wastes, slag, coal ash, gangue, tailings, radioactive residues and other wastes, but excluding stones stripped or dug out in mining - gangue and acid or alkaline stones not included (a stone is acid or alkaline according to the pH value of the water being below 4 or above 10.5 when the stone is in, or soaked by water).

Hazardous Wastes refers to those included in the national hazardous wastes catalogue or specified as any one of the following properties in the national hazardous wastes identification standards: explosive, ignitable, oxidizable, toxic, corrosive or liable to cause infectious diseases or lead to other dangers.

Industrial Solid Wastes Utilized refers to volume of solid wastes from which useful materials can be extracted or which can be converted into usable resources, energy or other materials by means of reclamation, processing, recycling and exchange (including utilizing in the year the stocks of industrial solid wastes of the previous year). Examples of such utilizations include fertilizers, building materials and road materials. The information shall be collected by the producing units of the wastes.

Rate of Utilization of Industrial Solid Wastes refers to the percentage of industrial solid wastes utilized over industrial solid wastes produced (including stocks of the previous years). It is calculated as:

$$\text{Rate of utilization of industrial solid wastes} = \frac{\text{volume of industrial solid wastes utilized}}{\text{industrial solid wastesproduced+ stock of previous years}} \times 100\%$$

Stock of Industrial Solid Wastes refers to the volume of solid wastes placed in special facilities or special sites for purposes of utilization or disposal. The sites or facilities should take measures against dispersion, loss, seepage, and air and water contamination.

Industrial Solid Wastes Disposed refers to the quantity of industrial solid wastes which are burnt or placed ultimately in the sites meeting the requirements for environmental protection and not salvaged or recycled (including disposition in the year of those wastes of previous years). The disposition includes landfill (Safe landfills should be conducted for hazardous wastes), incineration, containment spaces, deep underground disposal, backfill in mining pits and disposal at sea.

Industrial Solid Wastes Discharged refers to the volume of industrial solid wastes discharged by producing enterprises to disposal facilities or to other sites. The wastes exclude stones stripped or dug from mining (gangue and acid or alkaline waste stones not included).

Output Value of Products Made from Waste Gas, Waste Water and Solid Wastes refers to the current value of products with waste gas, waste water and solid wastes as main materials of production. Products sold and ready to sell shall be included while those produced for own use shall not be included.

Consumption Wastes Transported refers to volume of consumption wastes collected and transported to disposal factories or sites. Consumption wastes are solid wastes produced from urban households or from service activities for urban households, and solid wastes regarded by laws and regulations as urban consumption wastes, including those from households, commercial activities, markets, cleaning of streets, public sites, offices, schools, factories, mining units and other sources.

Ratio of Consumption Wastes Treated refers to consumption wastes treated over that produced. In practical statistics, as it is difficult to estimate, the volume of consumption wastes produced is replaced with that transported. It is calculated as:

$$\text{Ratio of consumption wastes treated} = \frac{\text{consumption wastes treated}}{\text{consumption wastes produced}} \times 100\%$$

11 农 业

AGRICULTURE

资料整理：薛　丰　张喜兰　马秋娟　吴光卫　刘　琪　罗文毅

Data management：Xue Feng　Zhang Xilan　Ma Qiujuan　Wu Guangwei　Liu Qi　Luo Wenyi

数据审核：马　琰　赵明正

Data audit：Ma Yan　Zhao Mingzheng

第十一部分　农业

一、简要说明

1.本章资料反映西安农业生产和农村经济的基本情况。内容主要包括农林牧渔业产值、主要农产品产量、造林、水利水保、农业机械拥有量、农村经济效益主要指标、区县农业生产情况等方面统计资料。粮食、畜牧业相关指标数据表由国家统计局西安调查队负责完成。

2.农业统计范围包括主要涉农区县的农业生产经营活动。

3.涉及主要年份数据资料，按照《陕西省根据第三次全国农业普查结果核定和修订常规年报相关数据方案》要求，对2007–2017年数据进行了修订。其中，畜牧业中猪牛羊禽修订了2013–2017年数据。11–1、11–3、11–5、11–7表不做修订。

4.西安市及西咸新区2021年数据均不包含西安（西咸新区）—咸阳共管区。

二、主要指标

农林牧渔业总产值（亿元）	560.59	比上年增长	6.6%
农作物播种面积（万亩）	514.88	比上年下降	0.9%
粮食产量（万吨）	141.92	比上年增长	1.3%

11 AGRICULTURE

Ⅰ.Brief Introduction

1. Data in this chapter reflects basic condition of agriculture production of Xi'an city. The mainly including output of agriculture, forestry, animal husbandry and fishery, output of major products, forestation, water conservancy and protection, quantity of agricultural machinery and agricultural base county. The data table of grain and animal husbandry indicators is completed by XI'AN Investigation Team of National Bureau of Statistics.

2. Rural social and economic statistics cover social and economic activities in all townships except county towns.

3. Data related to major years, revised the data from 2007 to 2017 by Shaanxi Province in accordance with the results of the third national agricultural census approved and revised the regular annual report data programmed. Among them, animal husbandry such as hog, cattle, sheep are revised the data from 2013 to 2017.

4. The data in 2021 exclude areas mutually controlled by Xi'an (Xixian New Area)–Xianyang.

Ⅱ.Major Indicators

		Increase over Preceding Year
Gross Output Value of Farming, Forestry, Animal Husbandry and Fishery (100 mil. Yuan)	560.59	6.6%
Sown Area of Crops(10 000 mu)	514.88	–0.9%
Grain Output(10 000 tons)	141.92	1.3%

11-1 主要年份乡村从业人员及基础设施情况

Rural Employees and Basic Facilities in Representative Years

指 标	Item	2000	2005	2009	2010	2011	2012	2013
一、乡村从业人员数	**Number of Rural Workers**	**212.65**	**223.30**	**223.13**	**225.04**	**230.56**	**226.92**	**222.67**
（万人）	**(10000 persons)**							
#女性	Female	99.07	103.22	102.76	103.25	109.61	107.63	106.70
#农林牧渔业	Forestry Animal Husbandry and Fishery	146.07	137.69	121.78	116.58	116.15	113.29	108.48
二、自来水受益村数（个）	**The Number of Tap Water Villages (unit)**	**1527**	**1756**	**2058**	**2184**	**2400**	**2545**	**2650**
三、通有线电视村数（个）	**The Number of Villages connected**							
	with cable TV (unit)							
四、通宽带村数（个）	**The Number of Villages connected**							
	to broadband (unit)							

注：本表基础设施数据2021年农业统计报表制度取消。

11-1 续表 continued

指 标	Item	2014	2015	2016	2017	2018	2019	2020	2021
一、乡村从业人员数（万人）	**Number of Rural Workers (10000 persons)**	**216.33**	**200.38**	**204.11**	**225.88**	**222.99**	**224.11**	**221.16**	**213.47**
#女性	Female	104.03	96.46	98.10	107.16	105.88	105.89	103.57	100.60
#农林牧渔业	Forestry Animal Husbandry and Fishery	110.30	105.10	102.32	110.38	97.65	97.83	98.42	97.07
二、自来水受益村数（个）	**The Number of Tap Water Villages (unit)**	**2765**	**2718**	**2507**	**2706**	**2027**	**1966**	**1944**	
三、通有线电视村数（个）	**The Number of Villages connected with cable TV (unit)**			**2338**	**2328**	**1750**	**1637**	**1645**	
四、通宽带村数（个）	**The Number of Villages connected to broadband (unit)**			**2720**	**2694**	**2070**	**1964**	**1950**	

11-2 各区县乡村从业人员数（2021年）

Number of Rural Employees by Region (2021)

单位：万人 (10 000 persons)

区 县	Region	乡村从业人员数 Total number of employees in rural areas	女性 Female employees	农林牧渔业 Forestry Animal Husbandry and Fishery
全 市	**Total**	**213.47**	**100.60**	**97.07**
新城区	Xincheng			
碑林区	Beilin			
莲湖区	Lianhu			
灞桥区	Baqiao	14.01	5.49	3.73
未央区	Weiyang	0.08	0.01	0.02
雁塔区	Yanta			
阎良区	Yanliang	10.26	4.80	6.69
临潼区	Lintong	32.59	14.88	22.87
长安区	Chang'an	36.84	16.78	9.95
高陵区	Gaoling	8.56	3.73	2.52
鄠邑区	Huyi	26.89	12.44	12.04
蓝田县	Lantian	28.93	18.28	12.17
周至县	Zhouzhi	33.31	14.04	18.19
西咸新区	Xixian New Area	22.00	10.15	8.89

11-3 主要年份农业机械年末拥有量

指　标	Item	2005	2009	2010	2011
农业机械总动力（千瓦）	Total Power of Agricultural Machinery(kW)	2239001	2616053	2677334	2890247
大中型拖拉机（台）	Large and Medium Tractors(unit)	8415	11479	14675	12585
小型拖拉机（台）	Mini-tractors(unit)	26326	18406	14194	13008
拖拉机配套农具（台）	Number of Tactor Towing Farm Machinery(unit)	67217	55614	53608	65833
农用水泵（台）	Agricultural Water Pump(unit)	77567	80174	77367	75426
节水灌溉类机械（套）	Equipment in Water-saving Irrigation(set)	1290	1799	1710	1733
联合收割机（台）	Combine Harvesters(unit)	4802	6155	6718	7854
机动脱粒机（台）	Motorized Huller (unit)	13870	11960	13231	13407

注：1.本表数据来源于市农业农村局，2017年西咸新区由西安代管，2017年、2018年数据不含西咸新区，2019年及以后含西咸新区。
2.2017年以前大中型拖拉机动力标准为14.7千瓦及以上，小型拖拉机动力标准为2.2-14.7千瓦（含2.2千瓦）。2018年及以后大中型拖拉机动力标准为22.1千瓦以上，小型拖拉机动力标准为22.1千瓦及以下。
3.表中“农用水泵”“节水灌溉类机械”和“机动脱粒机”三项指标由于部门报表制度发生变化，2020年暂无数据。

Possession of Agricultural Machinery year end in Representative Years

2012	2013	2014	2015	2016	2017	2018	2019	2020	2021
2983979	3108354	3203302	3253733	2615435	2543023	2429137	2456028	2478420	2485307
12987	12927	9946	9652	10177	9275	8580	8938	9357	8587
11471	8971	7538	8447	9175	8501	8226	6009	6264	5771
60035	58515	53257	54120	59805	50559	47582	45635	47677	47591
80982	80575	79849	79695	79681	76916	70533	62397		52597
2106	2218	2562	2517	2476	2366	2135	1869		1884
8502	9114	7815	8144	8458	7656	7390	7685	7947	7811
14493	14700	14749	14504	14272	14169	14074	12813		12665

11-4 各区县农业机械年末拥有量（2021年）

指 标	Item	西安市 Xi' an	新城区 Xincheng	碑林区 Beilin	莲湖区 Lianhu	灞桥区 Baqiao
农业机械总动力（千瓦）	Total Power of Agricultural Machinery(kW)	2485307				117043
大中型拖拉机（台）	Large and Medium Tractors(unit)	8587				66
小型拖拉机（台）	Mini-tractors(unit)	5771				17
拖拉机配套农具（台）	Number of Tactor Towing Farm Machinery(unit)	47591				277
农用水泵（台）	Agricultural Water Pump(unit)	52597				1330
节水灌溉类机械（套）	Equipment in Water-saving Irrigation(set)	1884				45
联合收割机（台）	Combine Harvesters(unit)	7811				47
机动脱粒机（台）	Motorized Huller (unit)	12665				35

注：本表数据来源于市农业农村局。

Possession of Agricultural Machinery year end in Representative Years (2021)

未央区 Weiyang	雁塔区 Yanta	阎良区 Yanliang	临潼区 Lintong	长安区 Chang'an	高陵区 Gaoling	鄠邑区 Huyi	蓝田县 Lantian	周至县 Zhouzhi	西咸新区 Xixian New Area
29093	22467	122526	479249	369460	205843	522550	248811	324748	43517
6	12	519	1341	1364	1426	1944	936	730	243
	8	241		720	74	1664	833	2012	202
40	40	2254	9834	4841	6300	10300	6284	6637	784
380	307	4212	16460	9718	3760	12744	2486	1200	
80		225	142	936		193	63	200	
3	7	499	2238	929	614	2575	396	261	242
4		1064	4948	792	540	2240	1815	1227	

11-5 主要年份农业机械化、化肥、水利情况

指 标	Item	2000	2005	2008	2009
一、农业机械化水平（万亩）	**Statistics on Agricultural Machinery (10 000 mu)**				
当年机械耕地面积（实际）	Area Ploughed by Tractors	366.81	360.68	404.42	413.70
当年机械播种面积（作业）	Seeded Area by Tractors	482.74	485.62	539.81	544.86
当年机械收获面积（作业）	Harvest Area by Tractors	272.83	271.77	313.11	342.82
二、农用化肥施用量（吨）	**Use of Agricultural Fertilizers and Insecticides(ton)**				
按折纯法计算合计	Standard Consumption	196343	211790	225949	230299
氮肥	Nitrogenous Fertilizer	102982	107645	112000	112275
磷肥	Phosphate Fertilizer	18658	19368	18855	18457
钾肥	Potash Fertilizer	15921	17055	17077	16534
复合肥	Compound Fertilizer	39313	57009	66247	71042
三、农用塑料薄膜使用量（公斤）	**Plastic Sheet for Agricultural Use(kg)**	**1622198**	**1855383**	**2122310**	**2141969**
四、农用柴油使用量（吨）	**Diesel Oil for Agricultural Use (ton)**	**52706**	**50832**	**51097**	**51346**
五、农药使用量（公斤）	**Pesticide (kg)**	**1559333**	**1427879**	**1465819**	**1325459**
六、农村水利化情况（万亩）	**Irrigation and Water Conservancy (10 000 mu)**				
有效灌溉面积	Effective Irrigation Area	335.97	280.10	274.48	273.17
旱涝保收面积	Stable-Harvesting Arable Land	294.06	255.37	249.31	247.60

注：1.本表第一部分数据来源于市农业农村局，第六部分数据来源于市水务局。
2.2017年西咸新区由西安代管，2017年、2018年第一部分和第六部分数据不含西咸新区，2019年及以后第六部分不含西咸新区。

Agricultural Machinery,Chemical Fertilizers,Water Conservancy, in Representative Years

2010	2011	2012	2013	2014	2015	2016	2017	2018	2019	2020	2021
367.32	427.03	425.40	425.21	549.07	533.21	518.07	498.57	465.25	417.01	409.26	420.19
548.28	507.55	529.99	523.15	509.58	492.90	499.36	532.61	501.27	469.46	451.77	458.00
403.50	413.93	428.28	443.57	466.21	474.10	488.85	470.66	456.27	393.97	406.26	387.42
235532	239497	243281	239701	251217	246284	242871	255267	252662	243916	251814	252739
108868	110412	113662	109497	116055	108833	111150	115631	113745	103059	103218	98349
18315	18026	18061	18023	18505	18584	18033	19072	18456	16797	16551	16528
17997	18095	21267	18973	20110	21986	21779	21486	21228	20969	20753	20748
78811	81764	90291	93208	96547	96881	91909	99078	99233	103091	111292	117114
2450496	**2533372**	**2683201**	**2678745**	**2657870**	**2770750**	**2880480**	**3157710**	**3380130**	**3350070**	**3241783**	**3317016**
61917	**61637**	**57451**	**62563**	**74935**	**59360**	**55982**	**67510**	**67091**	**61141**	**57954**	**49312**
1243105	**1242773**	**1252490**	**1210060**	**1220638**	**1174883**	**1126305**	**1703736**	**1506859**	**1367993**	**1346652**	**1304319**
281.28	262.32	267.84	240.22	248.34	244.72	259.78	256.13	282.83	245.72	228.01	229.68
234.15	214.62	211.31	196.96	189.69	188.50	201.70	184.91	184.78	193.44	195.00	220.35

11-6 各区县农业机械化、化肥、水利情况（2021年）

指 标	Item	西安市 Xi' an	新城区 Xincheng	碑林区 Beilin	莲湖区 Lianhu
一、农业机械化水平（万亩）	**Statistics on Agricultural Machinery (10 000 mu)**				
当年机械耕地面积（实际）	Area Ploughed by Tractors	420.19			
当年机械播种面积（作业）	Seeded Area by Tractors	458.00			
当年机械收获面积（作业）	Harvest Area by Tractors	387.42			
二、农用化肥施用量（吨）	**Use of Agricultural Fertilizers and Insecticides(ton)**				
按折纯法计算合计	Standard Consumption	252739			
氮肥	Nitrogenous Fertilizer	98349			
磷肥	Phosphate Fertilizer	16528			
钾肥	Potash Fertilizer	20748			
复合肥	Compound Fertilizer	117114			
三、农用塑料薄膜使用量（公斤）	**Plastic Sheet for Agricultural Use(kg)**	**3317016**			
四、农用柴油使用量（吨）	**Diesel Oil for Agricultural Use (ton)**	**49312**			
五、农药使用量（公斤）	**Pesticide (kg)**	**1304319**			
六、农村水利化情况（万亩）	**Irrigation and Water Conservancy (10 000 mu)**				
有效灌溉面积	Effective Irrigation Area	229.68			
旱涝保收面积	Stable-Harvesting Arable Land	220.35			

注：本表第一部分数据来源于市农业农村局，第六部分数据来源于市水务局。

Agricultural Machinery,Chemical Fertilizers,
Water Conservancy by Region (2021)

灞桥区 Baqiao	未央区 Weiyang	雁塔区 Yanta	阎良区 Yanliang	临潼区 Lintong	长安区 Chang'an	高陵区 Gaoling	鄠邑区 Huyi	蓝田县 Lantian	周至县 Zhouzhi	西咸新区 Xixian New Area
8.69			43.86	102.59	45.67	31.49	54.41	50.25	38.08	45.15
8.28			31.14	112.13	49.19	25.94	56.06	64.50	52.10	58.66
7.59			33.22	100.88	47.46	16.57	54.92	55.20	36.75	34.83
2750	215		32224	43727	15292	12669	36371	46147	51262	12082
832	75		13763	11581	6230	4002	16117	28410	14518	2821
55	27		1674	4873	968	1792	1954	2610	1819	756
360	62		3068	2235	2782	1487	2394	3622	4268	470
1503	51		13719	25038	5312	5388	15906	11505	30657	8035
7971	**10015**		**1645733**	**277083**	**159937**	**34088**	**514154**	**373958**	**103027**	**191050**
197	**200**		**3389**	**5755**	**7220**	**1800**	**11015**	**9005**	**3342**	**7389**
4751	**280**		**182820**	**197632**	**60914**	**155745**	**57725**	**68700**	**165295**	**410457**
4.07	0.94		21.59	47.25	34.33	20.30	39.63	7.45	54.12	
	0.94		22.56	47.25	24.93	20.67	42.92	19.71	41.37	

11-7 主要年份农林牧渔业总产值及指数

Gross Output Value of Farming,Forestry,Animal Husbandry,Fishery and Related Indices in Representative Years

单位：万元 (10 000 yuan)

年份 Year	农林牧渔业总产值（现价） Gross Output Value (At current prices)	农业 Farming	林业 Forestry	牧业 Animal Husbandry	渔业 Fishery	农林牧渔专业及辅助性活动 Farming, Forestry, Animal Husbandry, Fishery and Auxiliary Activities	指数（上年=100）（可比价） Indices(preceding year = 100) (At constant prices)
1970	40617	35965	713	3896	43		111.2
1975	55322	47378	1509	6403	32		93.9
1978	65423	56519	1444	7427	33		104.7
1980	65322	54004	1177	10106	35		85.0
1985	134933	105888	2559	26186	300		106.4
1990	262073	191088	3134	65840	2011		102.5
1991	295620	208324	3362	81070	2864		108.6
1992	321155	219160	4225	94045	3725		108.6
1993	387068	261959	5031	115810	4268		112.8
1994	565056	359609	7819	192140	5488		102.4
1995	754597	513348	7185	228598	5466		106.8
1996	786003	552726	7573	219214	6490		102.1
1997	836201	585973	9226	233623	7379		110.3
1998	853279	625465	8146	212045	7623		107.5
1999	739905	530029	8883	194552	6441		100.7
2000	743712	514845	8482	212612	7773		104.3
2001	767511	527160	8427	223861	8063		102.8
2002	797444	539978	11378	238761	7327		103.0
2003	837857	551398	10550	269610	6299		101.5
2004	967946	580798	12773	314517	6728	53130	108.4
2005	1065437	657262	13086	329856	7340	57893	107.7
2006	1141484	686748	15188	346626	7017	85905	107.2
2007	1317442	790316	15845	395003	9147	107131	105.3
2008	1629892	943261	23365	521950	11348	129968	107.8
2009	1695468	1034208	22663	486142	11830	140625	106.5
2010	2124191	1389118	26787	538396	12830	157060	107.4
2011	2501236	1651250	34453	616943	14856	183734	106.6
2012	2785682	1827705	62291	643347	19877	232462	106.0
2013	3057732	2038346	80199	648800	22773	267614	104.9
2014	3232984	2196966	86889	633519	24030	291580	105.1
2015	3308141	2251512	97776	613417	19519	325917	105.1
2016	3467506	2357901	102222	621737	19640	366006	104.2
2017	4373298	3009278	135570	729219	22700	476531	104.8
2018	4612088	3230380	169157	679813	26268	506470	103.5
2019	4993219	3493828	184739	727047	21867	565738	104.3
2020	5644139	3924251	236065	849948	18895	614980	103.2
2021	5605906	3904610	193903	837389	25576	644428	106.6

注：本表2007-2017年数根据第三次全国农业普查结果进行了修订。

11-8 主要年份农林牧渔业总产值指数

Related Indices of Gross Output Value of Farming,Forestry,Animal Husbandry and Fishery in Representative Years

年 份 Year	农林牧渔业总产值指数（上年=100）（可比价） Gross Output Value Index of Farming, Forestry, Animal Husbandry and Fishery (preceding year = 100) (At constant prices)	农业 Farming	林业 Forestry	牧业 Animal Husbandry	渔业 Fishery	农林牧渔专业及辅助性活动 Farming, Forestry, Animal Husbandry, Fishery and Auxiliary Activities
2005	107.7	108.0	98.7	107.3	112.6	108.0
2006	107.2	106.0	102.5	109.3	104.5	109.0
2007	105.3	106.4	101.3	102.4	106.3	109.0
2008	107.8	107.9	112.2	106.0	100.5	114.0
2009	106.5	105.4	121.3	106.8	107.4	110.2
2010	107.4	108.7	115.2	104.3	92.7	108.9
2011	106.6	108.2	105.7	102.9	102.1	107.8
2012	106.0	105.6	143.0	104.8	113.4	108.5
2013	104.9	104.3	131.3	104.0	110.1	105.9
2014	105.1	105.8	105.7	103.2	106.0	105.9
2015	105.1	106.7	113.8	100.2	71.2	106.2
2016	104.2	104.8	114.7	100.6	100.1	106.6
2017	104.8	105.0	111.0	103.0	104.3	106.2
2018	103.5	102.8	131.0	100.1	111.4	105.1
2019	104.3	104.7	120.1	98.0	86.4	105.5
2020	103.2	101.6	144.5	100.1	90.7	103.4
2021	106.6	102.4	118.0	123.3	119.2	105.1

11-9 主要年份农林牧渔业总产值构成

Gross Output Value and Its Composition of Farming, Forestry, Animal Husbandry and Fishery at Current Price in Representative Years

单位：%　　(%)

年 份 Year	农林牧渔业总产值（现价） Gross Output Value (At current prices)	农业 Farming	林业 Forestry	牧业 Animal Husbandry	渔业 Fishery	农林牧渔专业及辅助性活动 Farming, Forestry, Animal Husbandry, Fishery and Auxiliary Activities
2005	100.0	61.7	1.2	31.0	0.7	5.4
2006	100.0	60.9	1.3	31.5	0.6	5.7
2007	100.0	60.0	1.2	30.0	0.7	8.1
2008	100.0	57.9	1.4	32.0	0.7	8.0
2009	100.0	61.0	1.3	28.7	0.7	8.3
2010	100.0	65.4	1.3	25.3	0.6	7.4
2011	100.0	66.0	1.4	24.7	0.6	7.3
2012	100.0	65.6	2.2	23.1	0.7	8.4
2013	100.0	66.7	2.6	21.2	0.7	8.8
2014	100.0	68.0	2.7	19.6	0.7	9.0
2015	100.0	68.1	3.0	18.5	0.6	9.8
2016	100.0	68.0	2.9	17.9	0.6	10.6
2017	100.0	68.8	3.1	16.7	0.5	10.9
2018	100.0	70.0	3.7	14.7	0.6	11.0
2019	100.0	70.0	3.7	14.6	0.4	11.3
2020	100.0	69.5	4.2	15.1	0.3	10.9
2021	100.0	69.7	3.5	14.9	0.5	11.4

11-10 各区县农林牧渔业总产值（2021年）

Gross Output Value of Farming, Forestry, Animal Husbandry and Fishery by Region (2021)

单位：万元 (10 000 yuan)

区 县	Region	农林牧渔业总产值（现价）Gross Output Value (At current prices)	农业 Farming	林业 Forestry	牧业 Animal Husbandry	渔业 Fishery	农林牧渔专业及辅助性活动 Farming, Forestry, Animal Husbandry, Fishery and Auxiliary Activities
全 市	**Total**	**5605906**	**3904610**	**193903**	**837389**	**25576**	**644428**
新城区	Xincheng						
碑林区	Beilin						
莲湖区	Lianhu						
灞桥区	Baqiao	333120	245167	7775	28801	369	51008
未央区	Weiyang	22050	16168	3141	145	600	1996
雁塔区	Yanta						
阎良区	Yanliang	566427	429817	3011	74405	239	58955
临潼区	Lintong	804561	509128	9131	188295	9280	88727
长安区	Chang'an	590455	408378	13078	87105	6459	75435
高陵区	Gaoling	627125	403021	14217	104333	2952	102602
鄠邑区	Huyi	564710	377765	19900	106428	1569	59048
蓝田县	Lantian	608535	383188	36181	125118	3120	60928
周至县	Zhouzhi	753511	521571	59155	91785	511	80489
西咸新区	Xixian New Area	735412	610407	28314	30974	477	65240

11-11 各区县农林牧渔业总产值指数和构成（2021年）

Gross Output Value and Its Composition of Farming, Forestry, Animal Husbandry and Fishery at Current Price by Region（2021）

单位：% (%)

区 县	Region	农林牧渔业总产值 Gross Output Value	农业 Farming	林业 Forestry	牧业 Animal Husbandry	渔业 Fishery	农林牧渔专业及辅助性活动 Farming, Forestry, Animal Husbandry, Fishery and Auxiliary Activities
全市指数	**Total**	**106.6**	**102.4**	**118.0**	**123.3**	**119.2**	**105.1**
新城区	Xincheng						
碑林区	Beilin						
莲湖区	Lianhu						
灞桥区	Baqiao	98.2	93.8	128.9	125.5	280.0	100.2
未央区	Weiyang	79.3	106.2	39.2	56.5	150.6	80.1
雁塔区	Yanta						
阎良区	Yanliang	102.6	98.8	57.8	127.4	115.8	105.0
临潼区	Lintong	108.7	104.3	87.3	122.4	171.3	104.2
长安区	Chang'an	107.4	103.0	204.3	115.9	137.2	106.4
高陵区	Gaoling	106.7	101.8	115.5	125.7	85.0	106.6
鄠邑区	Huyi	107.8	102.4	114.4	126.4	87.1	106.4
蓝田县	Lantian	109.1	103.2	128.8	121.5	86.4	105.8
周至县	Zhouzhi	108.9	105.0	120.0	124.0	87.0	106.3
西咸新区	Xixian New Area	106.3	104.6	125.8	125.7	47.5	103.9
全市构成	**Total**	**100.0**	**69.7**	**3.5**	**14.9**	**0.5**	**11.4**
新城区	Xincheng						
碑林区	Beilin						
莲湖区	Lianhu						
灞桥区	Baqiao	100.0	73.6	2.3	8.6	0.1	15.4
未央区	Weiyang	100.0	73.3	14.2	0.7	2.7	9.1
雁塔区	Yanta						
阎良区	Yanliang	100.0	75.9	0.5	13.1	0.0	10.5
临潼区	Lintong	100.0	63.3	1.1	23.4	1.2	11.0
长安区	Chang'an	100.0	69.2	2.2	14.8	1.1	12.7
高陵区	Gaoling	100.0	64.3	2.3	16.6	0.5	16.3
鄠邑区	Huyi	100.0	66.9	3.5	18.8	0.3	10.5
蓝田县	Lantian	100.0	63.0	5.9	20.6	0.5	10.0
周至县	Zhouzhi	100.0	69.2	7.9	12.2	0.1	10.6
西咸新区	Xixian New Area	100.0	83.0	3.9	4.2	0.1	8.8

注：1.总产值指数按可比价计算，上年=100。
2.总产值构成按现价计算。

11–12 主要年份农林牧渔业增加值

Value-Added of Farming, Forestry, Animal Husbandry and Fishery in Representative Years

单位：万元 (10 000 yuan)

年 份 Year	农林牧渔业增加值（现价） Value-Added of Farming,Forestry,Animal Husbandry and Fishery (At current prices)	农业 Farming	林业 Forestry	牧业 Animal Husbandry	渔业 Fishery	农林牧渔专业及辅助性活动 Farming, Forestry, Animal Husbandry, Fishery and Auxiliary Activities
2017	2708351	1953733	78658	406750	11740	257470
2018	2861844	2097265	98148	379191	13586	273654
2019	3096776	2267013	107115	405837	11310	305501
2020	3461645	2511807	141282	463791	10587	334178
2021	3437031	2501890	116713	455032	14609	348787

注：本表2017年数根据第三次全国农业普查结果进行了修订。

11–13 主要年份农林牧渔业增加值指数

Indices of Value-Added of Farming, Forestry, Animal Husbandry and Fishery in Representative Years

年 份 Year	农林牧渔业增加值指数（上年=100）（可比价） Value-Added Index of Farming, Forestry, Animal Husbandry and Fishery (preceding year = 100) (At constant prices)	农业 Farming	林业 Forestry	牧业 Animal Husbandry	渔业 Fishery	农林牧渔专业及辅助性活动 Farming, Forestry, Animal Husbandry, Fishery and Auxiliary Activities
2008	107.6	107.6	112.0	105.8	100.0	114.0
2009	106.3	103.6	114.6	111.2	106.3	108.8
2010	106.9	107.9	108.7	104.3	94.0	108.9
2011	106.7	108.1	106.1	102.8	102.7	108.1
2012	106.0	105.6	142.8	104.8	113.4	108.5
2013	104.8	104.3	131.3	104.0	110.1	105.9
2014	105.2	105.8	104.1	103.2	106.0	105.9
2015	105.1	106.5	114.0	100.5	71.3	106.2
2016	104.1	104.5	112.6	100.5	100.3	106.9
2017	104.8	105.1	111.0	102.3	104.3	106.2
2018	103.5	102.8	131.0	100.1	111.4	105.1
2019	104.4	104.8	120.1	98.1	86.4	105.5
2020	103.1	101.6	144.7	100.1	90.8	103.4
2021	106.0	103.1	118.1	118.1	120.8	104.6

11-14 各区县农林牧渔业增加值（2021年）

Value-Added of Farming, Forestry, Animal Husbandry, and Fishery by Region (2021)

单位：万元 (10 000 yuan)

区 县	Region	农林牧渔业增加值（现价）Value-Added of Farming,Forestry,Animal Husbandry and Fishery (At current prices)	农业 Farming	林业 Forestry	牧业 Animal Husbandry	渔业 Fishery	农林牧渔专业及辅助性活动 Farming, Forestry, Animal Husbandry, Fishery and Auxiliary Activities
全 市	**Total**	**3437031**	**2501890**	**116713**	**455032**	**14609**	**348787**
新城区	Xincheng						
碑林区	Beilin						
莲湖区	Lianhu						
灞桥区	Baqiao	208297	158705	5141	16124	182	28145
未央区	Weiyang	14077	10870	1614	78	300	1215
雁塔区	Yanta						
阎良区	Yanliang	363197	285675	1743	43239	134	32406
临潼区	Lintong	479317	323252	5377	95776	4515	50397
长安区	Chang'an	381993	291728	7759	37929	4785	39792
高陵区	Gaoling	382111	248414	9024	59219	1372	64082
鄠邑区	Huyi	346622	243737	11802	63108	1155	26820
蓝田县	Lantian	362402	234343	23005	71939	1588	31527
周至县	Zhouzhi	462432	337113	33482	51497	304	40036
西咸新区	Xixian New Area	436583	368053	17766	16123	274	34367

11-15 各区县农林牧渔业增加值指数（2021年）

Indices of Value-Added of Farming, Forestry, Animal Husbandry and Fishery by Region (2021)

区县	Region	农林牧渔业增加值指数（上年=100）（可比价）Value-Added Index of Farming, Forestry, Animal Husbandry and Fishery (preceding year = 100) (At constant prices)	农业 Farming	林业 Forestry	牧业 Animal Husbandry	渔业 Fishery	农林牧渔专业及辅助性活动 Farming, Forestry, Animal Husbandry, Fishery and Auxiliary Activities
全市	**Total**	**106.0**	**103.1**	**118.1**	**118.1**	**120.8**	**104.6**
新城区	Xincheng						
碑林区	Beilin						
莲湖区	Lianhu						
灞桥区	Baqiao	96.8	93.2	126.6	118.6	291.2	100.1
未央区	Weiyang	81.6	106.5	36.8	63.4	162.2	80.1
雁塔区	Yanta						
阎良区	Yanliang	103.2	100.3	57.7	126.1	115.5	104.7
临潼区	Lintong	107.3	104.7	86.8	117.4	174.9	104.4
长安区	Chang'an	106.4	103.7	188.3	111.3	140.3	106.0
高陵区	Gaoling	106.2	102.9	112.3	120.3	82.7	105.9
鄠邑区	Huyi	107.5	103.7	115.2	121.4	99.7	105.2
蓝田县	Lantian	108.1	103.4	130.2	116.4	83.2	105.3
周至县	Zhouzhi	108.5	106.5	121.2	113.4	110.3	105.7
西咸新区	Xixian New Area	106.3	104.9	126.7	121.3	42.0	103.1

11-16 主要年份粮食生产情况

Statistics on Food Production in Representative Years

单位：万亩、万吨　　　　(10 000 mu,10 000 ton)

年 份 Year	粮食播种面积 Grain Sowing Area	小麦 Wheat	玉米 Corn	粮食产量 Grain Crops	夏粮 Summer Grain	小麦 Wheat	秋粮 Autumn Grain	稻谷 Rice	玉米 Corn
1980	706.35	324.17	273.14	114.40	56.60	52.20	57.80	4.70	47.70
1985	704.36	378.20	271.14	150.10	76.10	74.80	74.00	5.10	65.10
1990	731.42	387.20	282.14	172.40	91.70	89.70	80.70	5.50	70.40
1991	731.37	389.19	283.14	178.80	91.10	89.20	87.70	5.00	77.50
1992	715.50	384.60	273.60	183.40	101.70	99.60	81.70	4.70	72.30
1993	713.49	380.40	273.69	190.00	101.10	99.00	88.90	4.90	78.60
1994	719.00	375.90	272.40	157.40	86.90	84.90	70.50	4.50	61.40
1995	690.63	370.41	259.55	175.30	99.80	97.40	75.50	3.40	67.80
1996	709.00	366.30	286.80	187.50	80.10	78.40	107.40	3.40	95.60
1997	670.83	367.71	248.79	190.50	114.30	112.30	76.20	3.50	69.40
1998	705.03	370.17	285.45	212.70	104.40	104.00	108.30	3.20	99.10
1999	709.95	371.94	294.00	204.40	95.50	94.40	108.90	2.90	99.70
2000	697.55	369.89	283.70	201.90	92.60	91.60	109.30	3.10	100.50
2001	678.05	359.19	278.57	197.10	98.10	97.20	98.90	2.70	91.30
2002	655.59	350.64	271.95	192.40	94.50	93.50	97.90	2.10	91.60
2003	632.55	336.05	261.89	176.30	98.20	96.70	78.10	1.60	72.30
2004	630.63	311.52	286.50	195.80	97.80	96.00	98.00	1.70	91.60
2005	642.75	325.10	287.87	205.50	100.00	99.10	105.50	1.60	99.30
2006	648.00	313.23	307.89	193.50	86.00	85.40	107.40	1.40	101.20
2007	646.06	296.48	327.93	192.52	73.97	71.97	118.55	1.51	113.83
2008	605.57	294.42	292.34	185.48	87.95	87.36	97.53	0.80	94.02
2009	578.01	285.73	273.35	177.91	81.90	81.03	96.01	0.78	92.49
2010	559.09	277.34	264.07	174.51	81.29	80.71	93.22	0.56	89.47
2011	525.12	259.98	240.74	167.05	78.35	76.66	88.70	0.54	84.37
2012	508.16	256.22	233.84	167.67	79.69	79.02	87.98	0.44	84.18
2013	465.64	236.98	211.66	151.68	67.73	67.05	83.95	0.29	80.04
2014	437.10	224.27	200.39	140.77	68.72	68.15	72.05	0.16	69.99
2015	413.31	215.61	189.60	141.42	72.34	71.95	69.08	0.00	67.71
2016	401.95	209.78	180.80	135.39	68.86	68.45	66.53	0.07	64.09
2017	424.14	228.89	180.39	139.89	75.26	74.90	64.63	0.05	60.96
2018	419.56	227.84	177.58	142.14	74.28	73.86	67.86	0.06	64.36
2019	409.71	221.62	174.43	139.89	70.62	70.22	69.27	0.06	65.85
2020	408.15	218.75	176.22	144.58	72.58	72.21	72.00	0.06	68.64
2021	386.44	210.35	166.20	141.92	72.34	71.82	69.58	0.11	67.56

注：1.本表2007-2017年数根据第三次全国农业普查结果进行了修订。
　　2.本表数据自2020年起来源于国家统计局西安调查队。

11-17 各区县粮食生产情况（2021年）

Statistics on Food Production by Region (2021)

单位：万亩、万吨 (10 000 mu,10 000 ton)

区 县	Region	粮食播种面积 Grain Sowing Area	小麦 Wheat	玉米 Corn	粮食产量 Grain Crops	夏粮 Summer Grain	小麦 Wheat	秋粮 Autumn Grain	稻谷 Rice	玉米 Corn
全 市	**Total**	**386.43**	**210.35**	**166.20**	**141.92**	**72.32**	**71.84**	**69.57**	**0.11**	**67.56**
新城区	Xincheng									
碑林区	Beilin									
莲湖区	Lianhu									
灞桥区	Baqiao	5.73	4.07	1.53	2.07	1.41	1.41	0.66		0.64
未央区	Weiyang	0.01								
雁塔区	Yanta									
阎良区	Yanliang	26.70	13.72	12.92	11.98	5.99	5.99	5.99		5.98
临潼区	Lintong	101.24	53.50	46.75	36.60	17.66	17.60	18.94		18.55
长安区	Chang'an	49.41	29.10	20.02	17.87	9.76	9.75	8.11	0.10	8.01
高陵区	Gaoling	25.96	13.12	12.29	12.41	5.85	5.85	6.56		6.33
鄠邑区	Huyi	53.46	27.45	24.70	20.17	10.00	9.75	10.16		10.08
蓝田县	Lantian	59.55	35.76	19.25	18.12	10.14	10.01	7.97	0.01	7.17
周至县	Zhouzhi	31.39	17.70	12.95	10.78	5.92	5.86	4.86		4.71
西咸新区	Xixian New Area	32.98	15.93	15.78	11.92	5.59	5.59	6.32		6.09

注：本表数据来源于国家统计局西安调查队。

11-18 主要年份粮食单位面积产量

Grain Output Per Unit Area in Representative Years

单位：公斤/亩 (kg/mu)

年 份 Year	粮食作物 Grain Crops	夏粮 Summer Grain	小麦 Wheat	秋粮 Autumn Grain	玉米 Corn
1990	236	232	232	241	249
1991	245	229	229	264	274
1992	256	259	259	253	264
1993	266	260	260	274	287
1994	219	226	226	211	225
1995	254	263	263	243	261
1996	265	214	214	321	333
1997	284	305	306	257	279
1998	302	278	279	328	347
1999	288	253	254	327	339
2000	289	247	248	338	354
2001	291	270	271	314	328
2002	293	266	267	326	337
2003	279	287	288	269	276
2004	310	308	308	313	320
2005	320	304	305	336	345
2006	299	273	273	323	329
2007	298	247	246	342	347
2008	306	297	297	315	322
2009	308	284	284	331	338
2010	312	292	291	333	339
2011	318	297	295	340	350
2012	330	309	308	352	360
2013	326	284	283	370	378
2014	322	304	304	342	349
2015	342	333	334	352	357
2016	337	326	326	349	354
2017	330	325	327	333	338
2018	339	324	324	357	362
2019	341	317	317	371	378
2020	354	330	330	383	389
2021	367	341	341	400	407

注：1.本表2007-2017年数据根据第三次全国农业普查结果进行了修订。
2.本表数据自2020年起来源于国家统计局西安调查队。

11-19 各区县粮食单位面积产量(2021年)

Grain Output Per Unit Area by Region(2021)

单位：公斤/亩 (kg/mu)

区 县	Region	粮食作物 Grain Crops	夏粮 Summer Grain	小麦 Wheat	秋粮 Autumn Grain	玉米 Corn
全 市	**Total**	**367**	**341**	**341**	**400**	**407**
新城区	Xincheng					
碑林区	Beilin					
莲湖区	Lianhu					
灞桥区	Baqiao	361	346	346	398	420
未央区	Weiyang	365	371	371	359	359
雁塔区	Yanta					
阎良区	Yanliang	449	437	437	462	463
临潼区	Lintong	361	329	329	399	397
长安区	Chang'an	362	335	335	400	400
高陵区	Gaoling	478	446	446	511	515
鄠邑区	Huyi	377	351	355	407	408
蓝田县	Lantian	304	281	280	341	372
周至县	Zhouzhi	343	330	331	362	364
西咸新区	Xixian New Area	361	351	351	371	386

注：本表数据来源于国家统计局西安调查队。

11-20 主要年份主要经济作物生产情况

Production of Main Cash Crop in Representative Years

单位：万亩、万吨 (10 000 mu,10 000 ton)

年份 Year	经济作物播种面积 Sown Area of Cash Crops	油料 Oil-bearing	蔬菜 Vegetables	经济作物产量 Economic Crop Yield 油料 Oil-bearing	油菜籽 Rapeseeds	蔬菜 Vegetables
1980	129.08	10.01	24.02	0.54	0.50	40.13
1985	91.05	8.01	45.03	0.75	0.39	86.44
1990	84.99	12.00	51.03	1.35	0.94	119.32
1991	89.04	13.01	47.03	1.20	0.74	117.41
1992	105.15	16.20	54.60	1.49	0.87	128.12
1993	108.14	14.84	63.90	1.40	1.00	145.80
1994	102.10	13.80	59.90	1.08	0.78	135.26
1995	94.11	18.57	57.59	2.17	1.90	133.60
1996	88.40	18.80	55.50	1.83	1.55	138.01
1997	84.95	15.53	59.36	1.86	1.65	142.11
1998	84.96	14.69	60.95	1.67	1.36	148.87
1999	83.13	12.74	60.68	1.30	1.00	153.24
2000	87.39	13.46	64.35	1.34	0.95	162.14
2001	85.11	11.87	61.77	1.23	0.90	152.80
2002	95.51	11.40	67.71	1.22	0.84	169.74
2003	104.51	11.04	69.44	1.13	0.70	169.67
2004	123.20	9.74	77.55	1.14	0.84	180.96
2005	115.16	9.51	83.33	1.16	0.89	195.70
2006	121.49	8.58	87.03	1.08	0.87	189.30
2007	107.48	7.18	75.31	0.93	0.74	168.98
2008	104.91	8.04	75.86	1.08	0.86	180.60
2009	106.55	7.75	77.23	1.04	0.84	195.07
2010	106.80	7.77	78.06	1.01	0.84	207.11
2011	106.33	7.40	78.98	1.00	0.84	214.13
2012	104.74	6.25	79.54	0.83	0.74	227.96
2013	104.31	5.93	80.82	0.77	0.71	243.92
2014	106.09	5.21	81.72	0.71	0.59	257.86
2015	107.47	4.86	82.50	0.68	0.57	267.91
2016	100.68	4.13	81.43	0.58	0.50	268.87
2017	124.36	4.28	104.64	0.62	0.55	354.74
2018	127.90	4.61	107.74	0.67	0.57	373.69
2019	128.19	4.66	107.72	0.67	0.59	378.58
2020	130.25	5.20	109.45	0.74	0.71	381.31
2021	128.44	5.47	106.60	0.79	0.76	362.80

注：本表2007-2017年数根据第三次全国农业普查结果进行了修订。

11-21 各区县主要经济作物生产情况（2021年）

Production of Main Cash Crop by Region(2021)

单位：万亩、万吨 (10 000 mu,10 000 ton)

区 县	Region	经济作物播种面积 Sown Area of Cash Crops	油料 Oil-bearing	蔬菜 Vegetables	瓜果 Fruits Class
全 市	**Total**	**128.44**	**5.47**	**106.60**	**14.47**
新城区	Xincheng				
碑林区	Beilin				
莲湖区	Lianhu				
灞桥区	Baqiao	2.92	0.11	2.61	0.19
未央区	Weiyang	0.74		0.70	0.04
雁塔区	Yanta				
阎良区	Yanliang	22.63	0.07	15.96	6.59
临潼区	Lintong	20.42	1.18	17.21	1.42
长安区	Chang'an	12.64	0.65	10.15	1.83
高陵区	Gaoling	14.58		14.32	0.26
鄠邑区	Huyi	10.76	0.25	8.98	1.49
蓝田县	Lantian	10.38	2.40	6.55	1.20
周至县	Zhouzhi	9.69	0.28	8.55	0.05
西咸新区	Xixian New Area	23.68	0.53	21.58	1.40

11-21 续表 continued

单位：万亩、万吨 (10 000 mu,10 000 ton)

区 县	Region	经济作物产量 Economic Crop Yield			
		油料 Oil-bearing	油菜籽 Rapeseeds	蔬菜 Vegetables	瓜果 Fruits Class
全 市	**Total**	**0.79**	**0.76**	**362.79**	**44.00**
新城区	Xincheng				
碑林区	Beilin				
莲湖区	Lianhu				
灞桥区	Baqiao	0.02	0.02	7.15	0.17
未央区	Weiyang			0.91	0.04
雁塔区	Yanta				
阎良区	Yanliang	0.01	0.01	74.83	22.76
临潼区	Lintong	0.16	0.15	55.07	5.41
长安区	Chang'an	0.09	0.09	20.24	3.28
高陵区	Gaoling			63.09	1.04
鄠邑区	Huyi	0.04	0.02	30.50	4.63
蓝田县	Lantian	0.34	0.34	12.94	2.91
周至县	Zhouzhi	0.04	0.04	22.80	0.08
西咸新区	Xixian New Area	0.09	0.09	75.26	3.68

11-22 主要年份主要经济作物单位面积产量

Main Cash Crop of Per Unit Area in Representative Years

单位：公斤/亩　　(kg/mu)

年 份 Year	油料 Oil-bearing	油菜籽 Rapeseeds	蔬菜 Vegetables
1990	103	101	2349
1991	94	89	2332
1992	92	101	2344
1993	94	107	2282
1994	79	84	2260
1995	117	128	2320
1996	86	100	2489
1997	76	129	2395
1998	114	121	2443
1999	102	106	2526
2000	102	112	2520
2001	104	113	2474
2002	107	115	2507
2003	102	110	2444
2004	117	129	2333
2005	121	132	2349
2006	125	135	2175
2007	130	131	2244
2008	134	137	2381
2009	134	130	2526
2010	130	130	2653
2011	135	133	2711
2012	133	129	2866
2013	129	122	3018
2014	136	129	3155
2015	139	132	3247
2016	141	132	3302
2017	144	138	3390
2018	146	137	3468
2019	144	135	3514
2020	142	139	3484
2021	144	142	3403

注：本表2007－2017年数根据第三次全国农业普查结果进行了修订。

11-23 各区县主要经济作物单位面积产量（2021年）

Main Cash Crop of Per Unit Area by Region (2021)

单位：公斤/亩 (kg/mu)

区县	Region	油料 Oil-bearing	油菜籽 Rapeseeds	蔬菜 Vegetables	瓜果 Fruits Class
全市	**Total**	**144**	**142**	**3403**	**3039**
新城区	Xincheng				
碑林区	Beilin				
莲湖区	Lianhu				
灞桥区	Baqiao	152	149	2738	885
未央区	Weiyang			1301	842
雁塔区	Yanta				
阎良区	Yanliang	148	148	4688	3453
临潼区	Lintong	138	132	3201	3818
长安区	Chang'an	143	143	1995	1786
高陵区	Gaoling			4407	4005
鄠邑区	Huyi	167	130	3396	3101
蓝田县	Lantian	141	141	1976	2423
周至县	Zhouzhi	149	143	2667	1569
西咸新区	Xixian New Area	164	166	3488	2639

11–24 设施农业生产情况（2021年）

Agricultural Production Facilities(2021)

指　标	Item	面积（亩）Seeded Area (mu)	产量（吨）output (ton)
一、蔬菜	**Vegetables**	**269878**	**1129147**
芹菜	Celery	75354	354158
油菜	Rape	11003	31873
菠菜	Spinach	21347	61778
黄瓜	Cucumber	22585	102900
西红柿	Tomato	22606	93045
生姜	Ginger	1	2
辣椒	Chilli	15116	60714
其他蔬菜	Other Vegetables	101866	424677
二、瓜果类	**Fruits class**	**100305**	**330652**
其中：草莓	Strawberry	17553	33583
三、花卉苗木	**Flower seedling wood**	**5302**	
四、食用菌	**Edible Fungi**		**8447**
干品	Dry Product		796
鲜品	Fresh Product		7651
其中：蘑菇	Mushroom		5955
五、其他作物	**Others**	**6880**	
补充资料：设施数量（个）	Number of Facilities (unit)		138173
设施占地面积（亩）	Area of Facilities(mu)	245691	
设施实际使用面积（亩）	Actual use area of the facility(mu)	227666	

注：2020年起，其他作物面积含设施园林水果面积。

11–25 主要年份林业生产情况

Statistics on Forestry in Representative Years

指　标	Item	2000	2005	2010	2014	2015	2016	2017	2018	2019	2020	2021
一、营林情况	**Afforestation**											
当年造林面积合计(万亩)	Build Forestry Areas(10 000 mu)	27.47	16.56	16.10	14.70	8.28	4.51	4.07	3.56	3.83	3.40	0.75
封山育林面积（万亩）	Hill-closeure for Afforestation Areas(10 000 mu)	18.78	18.65	55.10	42.99	44.00	43.80	28.80	28.8			
零星（四旁）植树（万株）	Planting(10 000 plants)	731	1064	509	621	516	462	687	656			
育苗面积（万亩）	Raise Seedlings Areas(10 000 mu)	2.05	5.99	11.95	17.73	19.84	22.78	48.24	61.02	68.63	76.66	75.45
二、主要林产品产量（吨）	**Main Forestry Product(ton)**											
核桃	Walnuts	997	3351	7875	16531	24344	24097	36639	36970	38732	34580	33318
板栗	Chinese Chestnut	744	2076	7736	6922	8225	8223	8970	9282	9042	9137	7929
花椒	Pepper	140	525	1420	371	204	402	293	1044	937	826	719
三、村及村以下采伐木材（万立方米）	**Timber Harvested at or below Village Level(10 000 cu.m)**	1.62	1.87	3.30		0.07	0.28		0.37			

注：本表数据第一、三部分来源于市自然资源和规划局。

11–26 各区县林业生产情况（2021年）

Statistics On Forestry by Region (2021)

区 县	Region	当年造林面积（亩） Build Forestry Areasin in The Year(mu)	零星植树（万株） Planting (10 000 plants)	育苗面积（亩） Raise Seedlings Areas(mu)	核桃产量（吨） Output of Walnuts (ton)	板栗产量（吨） Output of Chinese Chestnut (ton)
全 市	**Total**	**7500**		**754545**	**33318**	**7929**
新城区	Xincheng					
碑林区	Beilin					
莲湖区	Lianhu					
灞桥区	Baqiao			540	2233	112
未央区	Weiyang					
雁塔区	Yanta					
阎良区	Yanliang			4350	6	
临潼区	Lintong	1500		82530	6123	167
长安区	Chang'an	1000		63180	4339	942
高陵区	Gaoling			54000	18	
鄠邑区	Huyi			81285	633	21
蓝田县	Lantian	3000		173265	16010	5965
周至县	Zhouzhi	2000		194040	3306	722
西咸新区	Xixian New Area			101355	650	

注：本表前三项指标数据来源于市自然资源和规划局。

11–27 主要年份果业生产情况

Statistics on Fruits in Representative Years

指 标	Item	2000	2005	2010	2014	2015	2016	2017	2018	2019	2020	2021
果园面积合计（万亩）	**Areas of Orchards (10 000 mu)**	**47.86**	**55.55**	**63.26**	**63.44**	**61.00**	**62.73**	**72.72**	**74.28**	**74.53**	**75.93**	**73.85**
苹果园	Apple Orchards	12.15	5.96	3.07	0.91	1.04	0.99	6.03	6.08	6.07	5.95	1.99
梨园	Pears Orchards	5.79	3.01	1.64	0.84	0.74	1.06	0.95	0.97	1.10	1.11	0.81
葡萄园	Grapes Orchards	1.89	3.02	6.42	10.78	10.94	11.65	12.55	12.61	11.98	12.04	11.85
桃园	Peach Orchards	3.47	8.66	7.68	5.85	5.33	5.82	5.99	6.19	5.96	6.43	6.06
猕猴桃园	Kiwi Orchards	16.83	4.33	20.36	27.88	27.69	27.97	28.19	29.32	30.09	30.90	33.88
杏园	Apricot Orchards	0.62	2.50	2.21	1.49	1.31	1.25	1.63	1.74	1.95	1.87	1.93
柿子园	Presimmons Orchards	1.96	2.69	2.08	0.35	0.21	0.22	0.19	0.27	0.36	0.46	0.48
石榴园	Pomegranate Orchards			3.31	3.30	2.93	2.93	3.33	3.24	3.24	3.56	3.40
水果产量（万吨）	**Output of Fruits (10 000ton)**	**34.36**	**51.29**	**66.11**	**73.11**	**73.33**	**75.53**	**89.80**	**89.15**	**97.18**	**100.93**	**101.01**
苹果	Apple	8.94	5.34	2.96	1.49	1.71	1.70	6.93	6.91	7.07	6.97	4.08
梨	Pears	6.55	5.71	3.61	2.09	2.11	2.20	2.28	2.27	2.03	2.20	1.66
葡萄	Grapes	1.66	3.10	6.20	10.81	11.48	13.07	16.45	16.62	16.86	18.31	18.63
桃	Peach	2.70	8.98	9.85	7.52	7.76	8.61	9.92	10.51	11.02	10.75	10.38
猕猴桃	Kiwi	9.66	13.79	24.87	35.10	35.30	35.47	36.84	35.83	42.45	45.10	50.23
杏	Apricot			3.71	3.02	2.57	2.53	2.57	2.45	2.61	2.63	2.57
柿子	Persimmon			3.01	1.11	0.81	0.26	0.33	0.40	0.41	0.43	0.52
石榴	Pomegranate			2.93	2.66	2.54	2.44	3.20	3.32	3.51	4.01	3.66

注：本表2007–2017年数据根据第三次全国农业普查结果进行了修订。

11–28 各区县果业生产情况（2021年）

Area and Output of Fruits by Region (2021)

区 县	Region	果园面积（亩） Orchard (mu)	水果产量（吨） Output of Fruits(ton)
全 市	**Total**	**738509**	**1010078**
新城区	Xincheng		
碑林区	Beilin		
莲湖区	Lianhu		
灞桥区	Baqiao	61974	60896
未央区	Weiyang	199	293
雁塔区	Yanta		
阎良区	Yanliang	16539	30017
临潼区	Lintong	75325	86296
长安区	Chang'an	37018	56283
高陵区	Gaoling	11463	16564
鄠邑区	Huyi	81460	114474
蓝田县	Lantian	65495	71166
周至县	Zhouzhi	341540	493350
西咸新区	Xixian New Area	47496	80739

11-29 果品加工、销售及生产服务情况（2021年）

指　标	Item	西安市 Xi' an	灞桥区 Baqiao
一、果品加工企业数（个）	**Number of Fruit Processing Enterprises(unit)**	**34**	
其中：苹果加工企业数	Number of Apple Processing Enterprises		
猕猴桃加工企业数	Number of Kiwi Processing Enterprises	25	
二、果品加工企业果汁加工能力（吨）	**Processing Ability of Fruit Juice in Fruit Processing Enterprises(ton)**	**3890**	
其中：苹果汁加工能力	Processing Ability of Apple Juice		
三、当年果品加工企业鲜果消耗量（吨）	**Fresh Fruit Consumption of Fruit Processing Enterprise in the Year(ton)**	**95340**	
其中：加工消耗苹果数量	Number of Fresh Apple Consumption		
加工消耗猕猴桃数量	Number of Fresh Kiwi Consumption	80000	
四、仓储能力（吨）	**Storage Capacity(ton)**	**395768**	**200**
其中：气调库	Gas Reservoir	59848	200
机械库	Machine Shop	335920	
五、果业合作（个）	**Fruit Industry Cooperation(unit)**	**1322**	**68**
六、果苗木繁育中心（个）	**Fruit Seedling Breeding Center(unit)**	**16**	
七、果业服务投入（万元）	**Service Investment in Fruit Industry(10000 yuan)**	**1140**	**75**
1. 技术培训投入	Technical Training Investment	181	25
2. 科研投入	Scientific Research Investment	205.5	
3. 生产技术指导投入	Production Technology Guidance Investment	753.5	50
八、果品销售方式（吨）	**Fruit Sales Mode(ton)**	**1101840**	**79546**
1. 产地批发市场	Product Wholesale Market	554693	50346
2. 采供商	Supplier	89640	
3. 专卖、直销店	Franchised and Direct Outlets	12461	
4. 超级市场	Supermarket	47935	1560
5. 电子商务	Electronic Commerce	197985	2200
6. 农产品加工厂	Agricultural Product Processing Plant	88460	
7. 其他	Others	110666	25440
九、按销售区域分（吨）	**By the Sales Area(ton)**	**1101840**	**79546**
1. 国内市场	Domestic market	1071840	79546
2. 国际市场	International Market	30000	
附记：累计建成绿色果园面积（亩）	Cumulative Green Orchard Area(mu)	6750	1200
建成有机果园面积（亩）	Construction of Organic Orchard Area(mu)	1452	

The Situation of Fruit Processing, Sales and Production Service (2021)

未央区 Weiyang	阎良区 Yanliang	临潼区 Lintong	长安区 Chang'an	高陵区 Gaoling	鄠邑区 Huyi	蓝田县 Lantian	周至县 Zhouzhi	西咸新区 Xixian New Area
		4			**2**	**3**	**25**	
							25	
		2640			**1000**	**250**		
		2640			**12350**	**350**	**80000**	
							80000	
	17143	**4985**	**1040**	**2005**	**10945**	**200**	**359250**	
	16793	2650	1000	2005	2050		35150	
	350	2335	40		8895	200	324100	
	18	**81**	**18**	**4**	**62**	**29**	**1024**	**18**
	11				**3**		**2**	
	11	**485**	**7**	**15**	**430**	**25**	**5**	**87**
	6	98	5	5	10	15	5	12
		119			80	5		1.5
	5	268	2	10	340	5		73.5
	29919	**62650**	**58100**	**15798**	**112760**	**73900**	**581200**	**87967**
	4100	12000	40260	5000	66270	60190	303040	13487
	16910	11000	10610	7000	23310	4500	5120	11190
	26	300	800		3450		7560	325
	355		480		4000		41540	
	2083	13000	4830	3798	11420	6260	140360	14034
		2100	640		3320	350	82050	
	6445	24250	480		990	2600	1530	48931
	29919	**62650**	**58100**	**15798**	**112760**	**73900**	**581200**	**87967**
	29919	62650	58100	15798	112760	73900	551200	87967
							30000	
					3320	850	1380	
						650	802	

11-30 主要年份畜牧业生产情况

Statistics on Livestock Husbandry in Representative Years

指 标	Item	2013	2014	2015	2016	2017	2018	2019	2020	2021
一、活牲畜年末存栏（头）	**Live Animals in Stock at Year-end (head)**	**55619**	**58737**	**56100**	**61179**	**51075**	**50705**	**51704**	**52595**	**52639**
1.牛	Cattle	54900	58100	55900	61000	50900	50556	51567	52505	52563
#肉牛	Farm Cattle	15673	17317	18465	23736	21509	21325	23258	27594	31557
奶牛	Dairy Cattle	31479	33887	30705	31061	28819	28681	27895	24884	21006
2.马（匹）	Horses	220	219	200	176	175	149	137	90	76
3.驴	Donkeys	52	59							
4.骡	Mules	447	359		3					
二、猪年末存栏（头）	**Hogs in Stock at Year-end(head)**	**377300**	**377100**	**366800**	**363000**	**335700**	**312882**	**296612**	**301322**	**320018**
#能繁殖的母猪	Sow of Reproductive Ability	60900	58700	56300	55600	51800	44304	41317	42202	38253
三、羊年末存栏（只）	**Sheep and Goats in Stock at Year-end(head)**	**84100**	**101700**	**107600**	**109800**	**75200**	**74200**	**71900**	**72625**	**74822**
1.山羊	Goats	82145	98974	104033	107260	73769	72942	71198	67978	68252
#奶山羊	Milch Goats	68370	69093	65180	66388	62120	60619	69052		
2.绵羊	Sheep	1955	2726	3567	2540	1431	1258	702	4647	6570
四、家禽年末存栏（万只）	**Poultry in Stock at Year-end (10 000 heads)**	**663.37**	**663.05**	**702.69**	**702.42**	**642.73**	**625.83**	**643.67**	**641.63**	**572.22**
五、年末养蜂箱数（箱）	**Honey (box)**	**23346**	**22485**	**19536**	**21420**	**20377**	**19129**	**23033**		

注：1.本表2013-2017年数根据第三次全国农业普查结果进行了修订。
2.本表数据自2020年起来源于国家统计局西安调查队。
3.2020年起“奶山羊”和“养蜂箱数”数据国家统计局陕西调查总队不反馈。
4.2021年畜牧业生产数据不含西咸新区“共管区”部分。

11-31 各区县畜牧业生产情况（2021年）

Statistics On Livestock, Animal Husbandry by Region (2021)

区 县	Region	活牲畜年末存栏（头）Live Animals In Stock at Year-end (head)	牛 Cattle	肉牛 Farm Cattle	奶牛 Dairy Cattle	马（匹）Horses (head)	驴 Donkeys	骡 Mutes
全 市	Total	**52639**	**52563**	**31557**	**21006**	**76**		
新城区	Xincheng							
碑林区	Beilin							
莲湖区	Lianhu							
灞桥区	Baqiao	1007	942	258	684	65		
未央区	Weiyang	4	4		4			
雁塔区	Yanta							
阎良区	Yanliang	5393	5393	1776	3617			
临潼区	Lintong	19335	19335	8363	10972			
长安区	Chang'an	2375	2375	1243	1132			
高陵区	Gaoling	3765	3765	2481	1284			
鄠邑区	Huyi	3899	3899	2902	997			
蓝田县	Lantian	10443	10443	9441	1002			
周至县	Zhouzhi	6003	5992	4929	1063	11		
西咸新区	Xixian New Area	415	415	164	251			

注：1.本表数据来源于国家统计局西安调查队。
2.2021年畜牧业生产数据不含西咸新区“共管区”部分。

11-31 续表 continued

区 县	Region	猪年末存栏（头）Hogs (head)	能繁殖的母猪 sow of reproductive ability	羊年末存栏（只）Sheep and Goats (head)	山羊 Goats	家禽年末存栏（万只）Poultry (10 000 head)	年末养蜂箱数（箱）Honey (box)
全 市	Total	**320018**	**38253**	**74822**	**68252**	**572.22**	
新城区	Xincheng						
碑林区	Beilin						
莲湖区	Lianhu						
灞桥区	Baqiao	7319	1099	2117	2115	3.16	
未央区	Weiyang			518	518	0.06	
雁塔区	Yanta						
阎良区	Yanliang	16987	2654	10626	8256	21.62	
临潼区	Lintong	62349	5979	23012	19249	164.09	
长安区	Chang'an	20725	3095	3874	3874	56.29	
高陵区	Gaoling	25099	3800	5182	5047	36.50	
鄠邑区	Huyi	64666	8130	5838	5838	80.81	
蓝田县	Lantian	40011	6262	20292	20292	106.00	
周至县	Zhouzhi	70082	5856	2036	1982	75.81	
西咸新区	Xixian New Area	12780	1378	1327	1081	27.88	

11-32 主要年份畜禽产品产量

Production of animal products in Representative Years

单位：吨 (ton)

年 份 Year	肉类总产量 Output of Meat	猪 肉 Pork	牛 肉 Beef	羊 肉 Mutton	禽 肉 Poultry	奶类产量 Output of Milk	牛 奶 Cow Milk	禽 蛋 Poultry Eggs	蜂蜜（公斤） Honey(kg)
2013	66100	43900	4000	3300	13100	73834	41700	48700	380000
2014	70900	47400	4400	3700	13400	80961	42200	47900	376800
2015	72100	47100	4400	4100	14500	76779	40800	51000	351582
2016	68700	44200	3700	4400	14600	79281	43100	62900	371409
2017	58708	36900	4600	3300	12300	116491	83300	52785	404337
2018	54496	35932	3439	989	12473	115200	80446	52610	308015
2019	51437	33531	3329	927	12257	123711	80060	53874	322965
2020	45596	28482	3354	1001	12292	140291	85255	52242	391867
2021	49255	34004	3321	1100	10548	138637	82665	47693	318588

注：1.本表2013—2017年数据根据第三次全国农业普查结果进行了修订。
2.本表数据自2020年起来源于国家统计局西安调查队。
3.2021年畜牧业生产数据不含西咸新区“共管区”部分。

11-33 各区县主要畜禽产品产量（2021年）

Production of animal products by Region (2021)

单位：吨 (ton)

区县	Region	肉类总产量 Output of Meat	猪肉 Pork	牛肉 Beef	羊肉 Mutton	禽肉 Poultry	奶类产量 Output of Milk	牛奶 Cow Milk	禽蛋 Poultry Eggs	蜂蜜（公斤） Honey(kg)
全市	**Total**	**49255**	**34003**	**3321**	**1099**	**10548**	**138637**	**82666**	**47693**	**318588**
新城区	Xincheng									
碑林区	Beilin									
莲湖区	Lianhu									
灞桥区	Baqiao	843	662	73	29	74	3551	2069	240	12000
未央区	Weiyang	2			1	1	237	7	4	
雁塔区	Yanta									
阎良区	Yanliang	2756	1417	311	161	867	21307	12228	2995	500
临潼区	Lintong	12893	8889	890	310	2588	63717	47821	13011	13000
长安区	Chang'an	4066	2683	208	93	1062	7316	4433	7026	54588
高陵区	Gaoling	4303	3188	177	111	786	9044	4014	4608	
鄠邑区	Huyi	6931	4961	382	94	1493	7412	3209	7424	63600
蓝田县	Lantian	7373	4492	766	228	1886	18661	4194	5714	171000
周至县	Zhouzhi	8447	6478	470	34	1464	5269	3683	4984	2800
西咸新区	Xixian New Area	1642	1233	44	38	328	2123	1008	1687	1100

注：1.本表数据来源于国家统计局西安调查队。
　　2.2021年畜牧业生产数据不含西咸新区“共管区”部分。

11-34 主要年份水产品养殖面积和产量

Output of Aquatic Products and Aquaculture Area in Representative Years

单位：万亩、吨 (10 000 mu,ton)

年 份 Year	水产品养殖面积 Aquaculture Area of Aquatic Products	水产品产量 Output of Aquatic Products
1990	2.55	4258
1991	2.63	4949
1992	2.80	6015
1993	2.97	7132
1994	3.10	7900
1995	3.21	8517
1996	3.51	8910
1997	3.46	10054
1998	3.40	10480
1999	3.38	11061
2000	3.35	11384
2001	3.17	12480
2002	3.31	12017
2003	2.48	9967
2004	2.46	9721
2005	2.38	9370
2006	1.60	11937
2007	1.38	12402
2008	1.40	12487
2009	1.52	13044
2010	2.24	11850
2011	2.20	11800
2012	2.95	14010
2013	2.19	14200
2014	2.31	14218
2015	2.26	14190
2016	1.96	13449
2017	2.24	13832
2018	2.23	13528
2019	1.82	13614
2020	1.54	11302
2021	1.44	13164

注：本表数据2010年起来源于市水务局，2019年起来源于市农业农村局。

11-35 各区县水产品养殖面积和产量（2021年）

Output of Aquatic Products and Aquaculture Area by Region(2021)

单位：亩、吨 (mu,ton)

区 县	Region	水产品养殖面积 Aquaculture Area of Aquatic Products	水产品产量 Output of Aquatic Products
全 市	**Total**	**14445**	**13164**
新城区	Xincheng		
碑林区	Beilin		
莲湖区	Lianhu		
灞桥区	Baqiao	1005	261
未央区	Weiyang	240	360
雁塔区	Yanta		
阎良区	Yanliang	180	230
临潼区	Lintong	4965	4460
长安区	Chang'an	2956	4195
高陵区	Gaoling	180	230
鄠邑区	Huyi	301	746
蓝田县	Lantian	3165	1860
周至县	Zhouzhi	1258	522
西咸新区	Xixian New Area	195	300

注：本表数据来源于市农业农村局。

11-36 农业科技、教育情况（2021年）

Agricultural Science and Technology Education (2021)

指 标	Item	2021
农业研究开发机构（个）	Agricultural research and development institutions (unit)	185
农业科技人员（人）	Agricultural scientific and technical personnel(persons)	2285
农业科研成果（个）	Agricultural scientific research achievements (unit)	
农民技能培训人数（万人）	The number of peasants skills training(10000 persons)	11.22
良种推广面积（万亩）	Thoroughbred promotion area (10000 mu)	506.7
农业信息站（个）	Information station of Agricultural (unit)	2024

注：本表数据来源于市农业农村局。

11-37 主要年份农产品人均占有量

Per Capita Output of Major Farm Products in Representative Years

单位：公斤/人 (kg/ person)

年 份 Year	粮食 Grain	油料 Oil-bearing Crops	猪牛羊肉 Pork Beef and Mutton	禽蛋 Poultry Eggs	奶类 Milk	水果 Fruits	蔬菜 Vegetables
1978	266.7	0.2	5.4	0.9	3.3	6.8	91.7
1979	288.6	0.6	6.7	1.0	4.0	5.1	97.3
1980	223.5	1.1	5.9	1.2	4.1	6.9	78.4
1985	271.4	1.4	6.8	5.7	10.2	7.6	156.3
1990	298.7	2.1	9.4	9.2	14.2	11.5	196.0
1995	270.4	3.4	15.7	21.8	20.5	37.5	206.1
2000	293.5	1.9	17.9	20.1	35.7	49.9	235.7
2005	277.1	1.6	21.1	15.9	56.9	69.1	263.8
2010	206.4	1.2	13.8	14.6	74.8	78.2	245.0
2011	192.7	1.2	13.9	14.5	74.7	74.5	247.0
2012	186.2	0.9	14.0	14.4	74.0	74.8	253.1
2013	164.0	0.8	5.5	5.3	8.0	77.8	263.7
2014	148.5	0.7	5.9	5.1	8.5	77.1	272.0
2015	145.2	0.7	5.7	5.2	7.9	75.3	275.1
2016	134.2	0.6	5.2	6.2	7.9	74.9	266.5
2017	129.3	0.6	4.1	4.9	10.8	83.0	327.9
2018	122.3	0.6	3.5	4.5	9.9	76.7	321.5
2019	115.3	0.6	3.1	4.4	10.2	80.1	312.1
2020	114.2	0.6	2.6	4.1	11.1	79.8	301.3
2021	109.9	0.6	3.8	3.7	10.7	78.2	280.9

注：1.本表2013—2017年数据根据第三次全国农业普查结果进行了修订。
2.本表2011—2020年数据根据第七次全国人口普查结果进行了修订。

11-38 主要年份农村经济效益指标

Main Indicators of Rural Economic Benefit in Representative Years

年份 Year	每一劳动力创造的 Average Labor Force Production			每百元物耗生产的总产值（元） Output per 100-Yuan of Material Consumed(yuan)
	农林牧渔业总产值（元） Gross Output Value of Farming,Forestry, Animal Husbandry, Fishery (yuan)	粮食（公斤） Grain Crops(kg)	油料（公斤） Oil-bearing Crops(kg)	
1978	504.7	1024.6	0.7	
1979	549.0	1096.5	2.3	
1980	483.1	846.1	4.0	
1981	502.8	840.5	5.5	
1982	631.5	1058.9	3.6	
1983	606.5	1053.2	2.6	
1984	850.7	1154.2	3.4	
1985	1020.1	1134.6	5.6	
1986	1132.2	1236.4	9.5	
1987	1280.3	1277.2	11.7	
1988	1558.4	1148.0	6.5	
1989	1605.3	1231.9	9.5	
1990	1766.3	1279.1	10.0	233.3
1991	1958.8	1326.6	8.9	238.4
1992	2093.7	1360.7	11.1	241.8
1993	2528.9	1409.7	10.4	240.1
1994	3705.0	1167.8	8.0	227.6
1995	4953.0	1300.6	16.1	225.9
1996	5154.8	1391.2	13.6	234.5
1997	5493.0	1413.4	13.8	239.2
1998	5615.9	1578.1	12.4	247.0
1999	4826.5	1516.6	9.7	251.7
2000	5091.5	1498.0	9.9	250.2
2001	5328.5	1462.4	9.1	248.6
2002	5617.4	1427.5	9.1	265.9
2003	5761.2	1308.1	8.4	254.3
2004	6885.4	1452.7	8.5	261.7
2005	7737.9	1524.7	8.6	262.9
2006	8415.5	1435.7	8.0	263.1
2007	9983.6	1458.9	7.0	259.6
2008	12888.6	1466.7	8.5	257.7
2009	13922.4	1460.9	8.5	259.7
2010	18220.9	1496.9	8.7	258.7
2011	21534.5	1438.2	8.6	271.0
2012	24588.9	1480.0	7.3	269.8
2013	28187.1	1398.2	7.1	269.9
2014	29310.8	1276.2	6.4	270.3
2015	31476.1	1345.6	6.5	268.3
2016	33888.8	1323.2	5.7	265.9
2017	39620.4	1267.3	5.6	262.7
2018	47231.8	1455.6	6.9	263.5
2019	51037.4	1429.9	6.8	263.3
2020	57346.4	1469.0	7.5	258.6
2021	57748.3	1462.0	8.1	258.5

主要统计指标解释

农林牧渔业总产值 指以货币表现的农、林、牧、渔业全部产品和对农林牧渔业生产活动进行的各种支持性服务活动的价值总量，它反映一定时期内农林牧渔业生产总规模和总成果。1957年以前的农林牧渔业总产值中包括了厩肥和农民自给性手工业（如农民自制衣服、鞋、袜，自己从事粮食初步加工等）。1958年及以后，林业中增加了村及村以下竹木采伐产值；牧业中取消了厩肥产值；副业中取消了农民自给性手工业产值，增加了村及村以下办的工业产值；渔业中增加了海洋捕捞水产品产值。1980年及以后，在副业中增加了农民家庭兼营工业商品部分的产值。从1984年起村及村以下工业产值划归工业。从1993年起取消副业，将野生动物的捕猎划入牧业，野生植物采集和农民家庭兼营商品性工业划归农业。从2003年起，执行新的国民经济行业分类标准，农林牧渔业总产值中包括了农林牧渔服务业产值。林业中增加了森林采运业产值。农业中取消了家庭兼营商品性工业产值，将野生林产品的采集划归林业。第三次农业普查以后，由于主要农产品年报数据与普查数据之间存在一定的差距，根据农业普查结果对主要农产品年报数据进行了修正，并对产值进行了相应修正。

农林牧渔业总产值的计算方法通常是按农、林、牧、渔业产品及其副产品的产量分别乘以各自单位产品价格求得；少数生产周期较长，当年没有产品或产品产量不易统计的，则采用间接方法匡算其产值；然后将四业产品产值及农林牧渔服务业产值相加即为农林牧渔业总产值。

粮食产量 指全社会的产量。包括国有经济经营的、集体统一经营的和农民家庭经营的粮食产量，还包括工矿企业办的农场和其他生产单位的产量。粮食除包括稻谷、小麦、玉米、高粱、谷子及其他杂粮外，还包括薯类和豆类。其产量计算方法，豆类按去豆荚后的干豆计算；薯类（包括甘薯和马铃薯，不包括芋头和木薯）1963年以前按每4公斤鲜薯折1公斤粮食计算，从 1964年开始改为按5公斤鲜薯折1公斤粮食计算。城市郊区作为蔬菜的薯类（如马铃薯等）按鲜品计算，并且不作粮食统计。其他粮食一律按脱粒后的原粮计算。1989年以前全国粮食产量数据主要靠全面报表取得，1989年开始使用抽样调查数据。

油料产量 指全部油料作物的生产量。包括花生、油菜籽、芝麻、向日葵籽、胡麻籽（亚麻籽）和其他油料。不包括大豆、木本油料和野生油料。花生以带壳干花生计算。

水产品产量 指人工养殖的水产品和天然生长的水产品的捕捞量。包括海水的鱼类、虾蟹类、贝类和藻类以及内陆水域的鱼类、虾蟹类和贝类，不包括淡水生植物。水产品产量是通过各级水产和统计部门逐级上报取得数据。1995年及以前，贝类中牡蛎按鲜肉计算；蚶、蛤、蛙按5斤鲜品折1斤计算。1996年以后则统一按鲜品计算。

猪、牛、羊肉产量 指当年出栏并已屠宰、除去头蹄下水后带骨肉（即胴体重）的重量。包括全社会范围内的产量。1996年前为各级逐级上报数据。1996年第一次农业普查以后，由于畜牧业产品年报数据与普查数据之间存在一定的差距，根据普查结果对畜牧业年报数据进行了修正。1999年以后，国家统计局在部分地区开展了猪、牛、羊、禽等主要畜禽品种的抽样调查，并用抽样数据作为国家定案数据使用。未开展抽样调查的地区和品种，仍使用各级统计部门逐级上报数据。2008年,根据第二次农业普查结果,对2006年、2007年畜牧业年报数据进行了修正。2019年，根据第三次农业普查结果,对2013—2017年畜牧业年报数据进行了修正。

畜禽存栏头（只）数 指报告期末农村各种合作经济组织和国营农场、农民个人、机关、团体、学校、工矿企业、部队等单位以及城镇居民饲养的大牲畜、猪、羊、家禽等畜禽的存栏数。

农作物播种面积 指实际播种或移植有农作物的面积。凡是实际种植有农作物的面积，不论种植在耕地上还是种植在非耕地上，均包括在农作物播种面积中。在播种季节基本结束后，因遭灾而重新改种和补种的农作物面积，也包括在内。它是反映我国耕地面积利用情况的一个重要指标。目前，农作物播种面积主要包括粮食、棉花、油料、糖料、麻类、烟叶、蔬菜和瓜类、药材和其他农作物九大类。

有效灌溉面积 指具有一定的水源，地块比较平整，灌溉工程或设备已经配套，在一般年景下，当年能够进行正常灌溉的耕地面积。在一般情况下，有效灌溉面积应等于灌溉工程或设备已经配备，能够进行正常灌溉的水田和水浇地面积之和。它是反映我国耕地抗旱能力的一个重要指标。

农用化肥施用量 指本年内实际用于农业生产的化肥数量，包括氮肥、磷肥、钾肥和复合肥。化肥施用量要求按折纯量计算数量。折纯量是指把氮肥、磷肥、钾肥分别按含氮、含五氧化二磷、含氧化钾的百分之百成份进行折算后的数量。复合肥按其所含主要成分折算。公式为：

折纯量=实物量×某种化肥有效成份含量的百分比

农业机械总动力 指主要用于农、林、牧、渔业的各种动力机械的动力总和。包括耕作机械、排灌机械、收获机械、农用运输机械、植物保护机械、牧业机械、林业机械、渔业机械和其他农业机械【内燃机按引擎马力折成瓦（特）计算、电动机按功率折成瓦（特）计算】。不包括专门用于乡、镇、村、组办工业、基本建设、非农业运输、科学试验和教学等非农业生产方面用的动力机械与作业机械。这个指标的统计数据主要来源于农机部门。

Explanatory Notes on Main Statistical Indicators

Gross Output Value of Agriculture, Forestry, Animal Husbandry and Fishery refers to the total value of products of agriculture, forestry, animal husbandry and fishery, and total value of services in support of agriculture, forestry, animal husbandry and fishery activities. It reflects the total scale and results of agricultural production during a given period. Prior to 1957, China's gross agricultural output value included barnyard manure and handicraft products for self- consumption (clothes, shoes, stockings, and initial grain processing undertaken by peasants). Since 1958, cutting and felling of bamboo and trees by villages and other cooperative organizations under villages have been included in forestry; value of barnyard manure has been excluded from animal husbandry; self consumed handicrafts have not been included from sideline occupations, while the output value of industries run by villages and cooperative organizations under village has been included in sideline occupations; and the output value of fish catches by motor fishing boats has been added to fishery. Since 1980, the value of handicraft products made for sale by individuals in households has been added to sideline occupations. Since 1984, industries run by villages and under villages have been included in the sector of industry. Since 1993, the subdivision of sideline occupations has been cancelled, and the hunting of wild animals has been classified into animal husbandry, and the gathering of wild plants and commodity industry run by rural household have been included in farming. A new industrial classification of economic activities was introduced in 2003. Under the new classification, value of services to agriculture, forestry, animal husbandry and fishery is included in the gross output value of agriculture, value of wood felling and transport is included in forestry, value of industrial output by rural households is not included in agriculture, and the collection of wild forest products is taken from agriculture and included in forestry. The third Agriculture Census of China revealed some discrepancy between the main agricultural products from the annual reports and that from the census. According to the result of the First Agriculture census, efforts were made to adjust the output value of main agricultural to make the figures from the annual reports consistent with the census data.

Gross output value of Agriculture,Forestry,Animal Husbandry and Fishery is obtained by multiplying the output of each product or by-product by its price, resulting in the output value of each single item. For a small number of products, annual output of which is not available or difficult to get due to the long production (growing) process involved, the output value is estimated through an indirect approach. The sum of output values of all products of agriculture, forestry, animal husbandry and fishery and services in support to those industries is then equal to the gross output value of agriculture.

Grain Output refers to the total output in the whole country including grains produced by State farms, collective units, rural households, as well as by farms affiliated to industrial and mining enterprises and other production units. Grain includes rice, wheat, corn, sorghum, millet and other miscellaneous grains as well as tubers and beans. Output of beans refers to dry beans without pods. The output of tubers (sweet potatoes and potatoes, not including taros and cassava) are converted into that of grain at the ratio 4:1, i.e. 4 kilograms of fresh tubers were equivalent to 1 kilogram of grain up to 1963. Since 1964 the ratio for conversion has been 5:1. Tubers supplied as vegetables (such as potatoes) in cities and suburbs are calculated as fresh vegetables and their output is not included in the output of grain. Output of all other grains refers to husked grain. Data on grain production before 1989 were obtained through the Comprehensive Statistical Reporting System. Since 1989, data from sample surveys are used.

Output of Oil–bearing Crops refers to the total production of oil-bearing crops of various kinds, including peanuts (dry, in shell), rapeseeds, sesame, sunflower seeds, flax seeds, and other oil-bearing crops. Soybeans, oil-bearing woody plants, and wild oil-bearing crops are not included.

Output of Aquatic Products refers to catches of both artificially cultured and naturally grown aquatic products, including fish, shrimps, crabs and shellfish in sea and inland water as well as seaweed. Freshwater plants are not included. Data on output of aquatic products are reported by aquatic product and statistical agencies level by level. Before 1995, among the shellfish, oyster was counted as fresh meat; 5 kilograms of ark shell, clams and frogs are equivalent to 1 kilogram of fresh aquatic products; they have all been counted as flesh aquatic products since 1996.

Output of Pork, Beef, and Mutton refers to the meat of slaughtered hogs, cattle, sheep and goats with head, feet, and offal taken away. Data refers to the production of the whole country. The First Agricultural Census of China in 1996 revealed some discrepancy between the production of animal products from the annual reports and that from the census. Efforts were made to adjust the output value of animal husbandry to make the figures from the annual reports consistent with the census data. Since 1999, the NBS conducted sample surveys for the major animal husbandry products, such as hogs, cattle, sheep and goats and fowls, and the data from sample surveys are used as national finalized data. Those products, which are not covered by the sample survey, are still reported by statistical agencies level by level. In 2007. the data on animal husbandry from 2000 to 2006 were revised according to the results of the Second Agriculture Census of China. In 2008, A Monitoring and Survey Program was set up on main livestock, the data on the main livestock such as hog, cattle, sheep and poultry became the official data based on the sampling survey. In 2019, data from the annual husbandry report 2013 to 2017were revised based on the results of the third agricatural census.

Number of Livestock or Poultry in Stock at Beginning (or End) of Period refers to the total number of large animals, pigs, sheep, fowls, etc. raised by rural cooperative organizations, State farms, rural individuals, government agencies, schools, industrial and mining enterprises, army, and urban residents at the beginning (or end) of the reference period.

Sown Area of Crops refers to area of transplanted with crops regardless of being land sown or in cultivated area or non-cultivated area. Area of land re-sown due to disasters is also included. This is an important indicator that can reflect the utilization condition of the cultivated land in China. At present, the sown area of crops mainly include the following 9 categories of crops: grain, cotton, oil-bearing crops, sugar crops, flax crops, tobacco, vegetables and melons, medicinal materials and other farm crops.

Irrigated Area refers to area of land that are effectively irrigated, i.e. relatively level land, where there are water sources or complete sets of irrigation facilities to lift and move adequate water for irrigation purpose under normal conditions. Under normal situations, irrigated area is the sum of watered fields and irrigated fields where irrigation systems or equipment have been installed for regular irrigation purpose. This important indicator reflects drought resistance capacity of the cultivated land in China.

Consumption of Chemical Fertilizers in Agriculture refers to the quantity of chemical fertilizers applied in agriculture in the year, including nitrogenous fertilizer, phosphate fertilizer, potash fertilizer, and compound fertilizer. The consumption of chemical fertilizers is calculated in terms of volume of effective components by means of converting the gross weight of the respective fertilizers into weight containing effective component (e.g. nitrogen content in nitrogenous fertilizer, phosphorous pentoxide contents in phosphate fertilizer, and potassium oxide contents in potash fertilizer). Compound fertilizer is converted in regard to its major components. The formula is:

Volume of effective component= physical quantity × effective component of certain chemical fertilizer (%)

Total Power of Agricultural Machinery refers to total mechanical power of machinery used in agriculture, forestry, animal husbandry and fishery, including machinery for ploughing, irrigation and drainage, harvesting, transport, plant protection, animal husbandry, forestry and fishery and other agricultural machineries. (For the power of internal combustion engines, it is converted from its horsepower into watts while for electric motors the output power is converted into watts.) Machinery employed for non-agricultural purposes, such as the machines used in township-run and village-run industry, construction, non-agricultural transport, scientific experiments and teaching, are not included. Data are mainly from agricultural machinery agencies.

12 工　业

INDUSTRY

资料整理:陈小兵　左　宇　沈佳慧　张思敏　张宇涵　王　玥
Data management: Chen Xiaobing Zuo Yu Shen Jiahui Zhang Simin Zhang Yuhan Wang Yue
数据审核: 刘　婷
Data audit: Liu Ting

第十二部分　工业

一、简要说明

1.本章资料反映西安市工业经济方面的基本情况。

2.本章资料包括规模以上工业企业按企业登记类型、轻重工业、企业规模、工业行业大类分组的主要经济指标和经济效益指标，主要工业产品产量，主要产品生产能力。

3.规模以上工业企业统计范围。

1998年至2006年为全部国有及年主营业务收入在500万元及以上非国有工业企业。

2007年至2010年为年主营业务收入在500万元及以上工业企业。

2011年起提高到年主营业务收入在2000万元及以上工业企业。

4.2021年数据不含西安（西咸新区）—咸阳共管区。

5.数据来源。

根据国家统计局制定的《企业一套表统计调查制度》和《工业统计报表制度》，对规模以上工业法人单位采用全面调查的方法，从国家一套表平台采集。

二、主要指标

规模以上工业企业单位数（个）	1731	比上年增长	4.0%
规模以上工业增加值（快报数）	–	比上年增长	5.7%
规模以上工业出口交货值（亿元）（快报数）	946.91	比上年增长	20.0%

12 INDUSTRY

Ⅰ.Brief Introduction

1. This chapter reflects the basic conditions of the industrial sector.

2. This chapter mainly including economic indicators of industrial enterprises above designated size; as well as their economic indicators, efficiency indicators, output and production capacity of key industrial products classified by type of registration by light and heavy industries, by size of enterprise, by branch of industry.

3. The Scopes of Industrial Statistics.

The scopes of industrial statistics are all State-owned industrial enterprises and non-State-owned industrial enterprises with revenue from principal business over 5 million yuan from 1998 to 2006.

The scopes of industrial statistics are all industrial enterprises with revenue from principal business over 5 million yuan from 2007 to 2010.

The scopes of industrial statistics are raised to all industrial enterprises with revenue from principal business over 20 million yuan from 2011.

4.The data in 2021 excludes ares mutually controlled by Xi'an (Xixian New Area) – Xianyang.

5.Sources of Data.

According to the A set of table survey system for enterprises and System of industrial statistical report forms by the National Bureau of Statistics, the method of comprehensive investigation shall be adopted for industrial legal entities above the designated size, collected from a set of table platforms by the National Bureau of Statistics.

Ⅱ.Major Indicators

		Increase over Preceding Year
Number of industrial Enterprises Gross Output Above Designated Size(item)	1731	4.0%
Industrial added value above designated size	–	5.7%
Export delivery value above designated size (100million yuan)	946.91	20.0%

12-1 主要年份规模以上工业企业主要经济指标

Major Economic Indicators of Industrial Enterprises above Designated Size in Representative Years

单位：亿元 (100 million yuan)

年 份 Year	企业单位数（个） Number of Enterprises (unit)	平均用工人数（万人） Average Number of Employed Persons (10 000person)	资产总计 Total Assets	负债合计 Total Liabilites	所有者权益合计 Owners' Equities	主营业务收入 Revenue from Principal Business	利润总额 Total Profits	利税总额 Total Pre-tax Profits
1998	793	51.71	810.56	548.68	261.88	346.84	-1.26	14.82
1999	770	45.64	853.90	577.94	275.96	346.26	8.26	27.30
2000	816	43.25	958.05	622.46	323.72	420.42	16.11	36.29
2001	785	40.12	1054.36	657.88	384.65	451.62	17.97	40.84
2002	771	38.48	1065.76	643.78	412.27	541.64	25.43	51.31
2003	735	36.55	1195.69	733.04	460.97	645.53	33.82	64.99
2004	1066	38.08	1333.91	869.30	464.60	812.46	38.57	74.23
2005	902	37.92	1503.85	977.42	508.82	980.97	28.72	67.25
2006	904	37.94	1651.67	1062.11	578.33	1183.51	61.46	110.23
2007	937	38.55	1940.52	1254.01	686.51	1561.25	106.22	168.54
2008	1032	40.17	2426.13	1518.86	907.27	1928.05	84.89	168.63
2009	1131	43.42	2913.56	1779.38	1130.76	2384.52	177.20	280.68
2010	1126	47.11	3592.13	2069.29	1515.65	3011.19	245.37	373.56
2011	891	50.42	3975.38	2295.49	1678.19	3381.27	172.94	312.78
2012	970	49.23	4775.92	2835.55	1926.72	3758.56	167.77	320.57
2013	1056	48.36	5127.69	3049.36	2071.72	4171.21	211.26	392.14
2014	1146	49.65	6048.34	3607.62	2436.06	4566.20	226.17	401.20
2015	1150	50.59	6740.26	3860.55	2926.55	4374.11	206.88	341.40
2016	1220	49.54	7473.07	4158.75	3302.36	5028.28	290.96	438.59
2017	1403	51.11	7862.59	4162.97	3595.73	5710.70	367.77	532.35
2018	1474	51.87	8409.16	4603.87	3805.29	6055.58	399.52	573.30
2019	1631	49.75	9449.95	5096.70	4349.39	6483.80	325.60	465.42
2020	1667	50.16	10638.17	5871.38	4736.91	6650.76	466.63	610.93
2021	1731	53.70	11999.61	6882.22	5117.39	7895.23	444.48	620.97

注：2013年数据为第三次全国经济普查数据。2018年数据为全国第四次经济普查数据。下同。

12-2 各区县规模以上工业企业主要经济指标（2021年）

单位：亿元

区 县	Region	企业单位数（个）Number of Enterprises (unit)	平均用工人数（万人）Average Number of Employed Persons (10 000 persons)	资产合计 Total Assets
新城区	Xincheng	9	4.14	464.54
碑林区	Beilin	8	0.21	24.68
莲湖区	Lianhu	33	3.08	613.26
灞桥区	Baqiao	83	1.99	311.01
未央区	Weiyang	172	8.20	1597.37
雁塔区	Yanta	275	7.02	1567.36
阎良区	Yanliang	117	3.30	884.49
临潼区	Lintong	95	1.61	454.64
长安区	Chang'an	246	9.73	3393.74
高陵区	Gaoling	213	5.17	1172.79
鄠邑区	Huyi	144	3.91	632.37
蓝田县	Lantian	58	0.57	110.26
周至县	Zhouzhi	32	0.64	31.10
西咸新区	Xixian New Area	246	4.12	742.02

Major Economic Indicators of Industrial Enterprises above Designated Size by Region (2021)

(100 million yuan)

负债合计 Total Liabilites	所有者权益合计 Total Owners' Equities	营业收入 Revenue	利润总额 Total Profits	利税总额 Total Pre-tax Profits
297.92	166.62	334.43	6.17	12.86
10.41	14.27	15.55	1.72	2.39
365.94	247.32	340.22	13.18	21.81
205.34	105.67	192.73	10.56	15.02
982.31	615.06	1257.67	39.74	64.49
786.23	781.13	726.58	70.94	93.18
563.15	321.34	359.29	15.22	19.37
300.64	154.00	288.54	19.36	27.21
1560.32	1833.42	2365.18	198.87	239.87
796.75	376.04	1137.89	28.60	46.40
430.65	201.72	606.11	20.16	43.14
76.03	34.23	64.41	3.14	4.83
15.35	15.75	25.24	0.91	1.66
491.18	250.84	443.62	15.90	28.75

12-3 规模以上工业企业主要工业产品产量（2021年）

Major Output of Industrial Enterprises above Designated Size (2021)

产品名称	Name of Products	2021	比上年增长(%) Increase over Preceding Year (%)
自来水生产量（亿立方米）	Tap Water Production (100 million cu.m)	7.76	4.8
大米（万吨）	Rice (10 000 ton)	1.11	5.3
小麦粉（万吨）	Wheat Flour (10 000 ton)	23.80	-63.1
精制食用植物油（万吨）	Edible Vegetable Oil (10 000 ton)	19.62	6.1
鲜、冷藏肉（万吨）	Fresh/Frozen Meat(10 000 ton)	4.87	13.5
饲料（万吨）	Mixed Feed(10 000 ton)	77.75	-17.2
#配合饲料	Compound feed	22.17	-0.5
混合饲料	Mixed feed	55.54	-20.1
方便面（万吨）	Instant Noodle(10 000 ton)	16.47	-2.1
乳制品（万吨）	Dairy Products (10 000 ton)	54.45	-6.6
液体乳	Milk	52.35	-5.4
固体及半固体乳制品	Solid and semi-solid dairy products	2.10	-29.0
饮料酒（万千升）	Beverage Wine (10 000 kiloliter)	31.49	-8.4
#白酒（折65度，商品量）	Liquor (as 65 degree, amount of goods)		
啤酒	Beer	31.34	-0.6
葡萄酒	Wine	0.14	-36.8
饮料（万吨）	Beverage (10 000 ton)	201.88	24.3
#碳酸饮料类（汽水）	Carbonated Beverage	52.37	27.4
果汁和蔬菜汁饮料	Juice and Fruit Beverage	19.78	118.9
包装饮用水类	Canned Drinking Water	80.97	18.9
纱（万吨）	Yarn (10 000 ton)	2.18	4.0
棉纱	Cotton Yarn	1.22	16.6
棉混纺纱	Blend Fabric	0.45	1.7
化学纤维纱	Pure Chemical-Fibre Yarn	0.51	-15.9
布（亿米）	Cloth (100 million m)	1.13	4.2

12-3 续表1 continued 1

产品名称	Name of Products	2021	比上年增长(%) Increase over Preceding Year (%)
棉布	Cotton Cloth	0.63	10.2
棉混纺布	Blend Fabric	0.26	3.2
化学纤维短纤布	Chemical Fiber short fiber Cloth	0.24	-7.9
人造板（万立方米）	Artificial Board (10 000 cu.m)	4.02	-71.0
纤维板	Fibre Board	4.02	-71.0
家具（万件）	Furniture (10 000unit)	19.15	-33.6
#木质家具	Wooden Furniture	13.11	-30.8
软体家具	Soft Furniture (inc.: Sofa ,Mattress etc.)	3.67	-7.5
机制纸及纸板（外购原纸加工除外）（万吨）	Machine Made Paper(not including processing of procured base paper)(10 000 ton)	3.52	-12.3
纸制品（万吨）	Paper-Made Products (10 000 ton)	10.94	1.4
#瓦楞纸箱	Corrugated Paper	9.14	2.5
单色印刷品（万令）	Monochrom Printed products(10 000 ream)	52.13	-14.9
多色印刷品（万对开色令）	Colored Printed products(10 000 ream)	822.15	46.5
化学农药原药(折有效成分100%)(万吨)	Chemical Pesticide(100% effective content)(10 000 ton)	0.09	-5.0
涂料（万吨）	Construction Paint(10 000 ton)	1.41	24.5
合成洗涤剂（万吨）	Synthetic Detergents (10 000 ton)	1.80	-56.3
#合成洗衣粉	Washing Power	1.04	-13.4
液体洗涤剂	Liquid detergent	0.14	-93.4
化学原料药（万吨）	Chemical Medicine (10 000 ton)	1.15	1.1
中成药（万吨）	Traditional Chinese Medicine (10 000 ton)	1.22	2.7
化学纤维（万吨）	Chemical Fiber(10 000 ton)	3.49	-6.1
人造纤维（纤维素纤维）	Man-made Fiber	3.49	-6.1
塑料制品（万吨）	Plastic Product (10 000 ton)	23.99	-7.5
水泥（万吨）	Cement (10 000 ton)	202.07	-8.9

12-3 续表2 continued 2

产品名称	Name of Products	2021	比上年增长(%) Increase over Preceding Year (%)
硅酸盐水泥熟料（万吨）	Portland Cement Clinker (10 000 ton)	33.74	-56.8
水泥混凝土电杆（万根）	Cement Pole(10 000 unit)	2.16	-12.0
商品混凝土(万平方米)	Ready-mixed Concrete (10 000 cu.m)	5387.59	5.3
沥青和改性沥青防水卷材（万平方米）	Asphalt and Modified Bitumen Membrane(10 000 sq.m)	1825.19	-31.8
钢化玻璃（万平方米）	Toughened Glass(10 000 sq.m)	54.75	-8.8
日用玻璃制品（万吨）	Glassware(10 000 ton)		
钢材（万吨）	Rolled-steel Final Products (10 000 ton)	37.88	-5.0
#线材（盘条）	Wire Rod	20.31	0.0
其他钢材	Other steel	11.09	-8.4
铝材(万吨)	Aluminum Material (10 000 ton)	2.27	-1.7
单晶硅（万千克）	Monocrystalline Silicon (10 000kg)	165.13	0.8
多晶硅（万千克）	Polycrystalline Silicon(10 000kg)	272.00	83.7
工业锅炉（蒸发量吨）	Industrial Boiler steam(ton)	679.80	-34.4
发动机（万千瓦）	Engine (10 000 kW)	804.13	35.0
#汽车发动机（万千瓦）	Motor Engine(10 000 kW)	804.13	35.0
金属切削机床（万台）	Metal-cutting Machines (10 000 unit)	0.60	36.8
泵（万台）	Pump (Liquid pump)(10 000 unit)	0.59	30.9
风机（万台）	Fan(10 000 unit)	0.77	41.7
气体压缩机（万台）	Gas Compressor(10 000 unit)	98.40	18.1
阀门（万吨）	Valves (10 000 ton)	0.38	-23.3
铸铁件（万吨）	Iron Castings (10 000 ton)	1.68	8.3
铸钢件（万吨）	Steel Castings (10 000 ton)		
锻件（万吨）	Forgings (10 000 ton)	1.38	0.9
矿山专用设备（万吨）	Mining Equipment (10 000 ton)	2.12	15.2
炼油、化工生产专用设备（万吨）	Oil Refining and Chemical industry Machine(10 000 ton)	0.29	-9.5

12-3 续表3 continued 3

产品名称	Name of Products	2021	比上年增长(%) Increase over Preceding Year (%)
金属冶炼设备（万吨）	Metal Smelting Equipments(10 000 ton)	0.79	38.6
金属轧制设备（万吨）	Metal-rolling Machine(10 000 ton)	0.89	61.1
印刷专用设备（吨）	Printing Equipment(ton)		
环境污染防治专用设备（万台/套）	Special Equipment for Environment Protection(10 000 unit)	0.28	35.6
#大气污染防治设备	Equipment for Preventing Atmospheric Pollution	0.07	29.8
汽车（万辆）	Motor Vehicle(10 000unit)	63.87	28.2
其中：基本型乘用车（轿车）	Basic Type Passenger Vehicles(car)	20.88	106.6
#轿车（排量≤1升）	Car0L-1.0L Gas Displacement(1.0L included)	7.85	91.4
轿车（1升＜排量≤1.6升）	Car1.0L-1.6L Gas Displacement(1.6L included)	13.03	117.0
运动型多用途乘用车（SUV）	Sports Utility Vehicle (SUV)	25.85	68.6
载货汽车	Trucks	17.14	-29.7
其中：新能源汽车	New Energy Vehicles	26.88	351.6
改装汽车（万辆）	Refit Trucks (10 000 unit)	1.23	-17.7
铁路货车（万辆）	Freight(10 000 unit)	0.26	-2.9
电动机（万千瓦）	Electric motor (10 000 kW)	313.77	9.0
#直流电动机	DC motors	12.53	-31.1
交流电动机	Alternating Current Motor	277.19	14.9
变压器（亿千伏安）	Transformer(100 million KVA)	0.67	-13.8
高压开关板（万面）	High-voltage Switch Panel(10 000 unit)	0.52	12.7
低压开关板（万面）	Low-voltage Switch Panel(10 000 unit)	0.58	2.2
电力电缆(万千米)	Electric Power Cables(10 000 km)	23.34	21.9
通信及电子网络用电缆（万对千米）	Communication Cables(10 000 pair km)	6.71	67.2
光缆（万芯千米）	Optical Cable (10 000 Core.km)	986.69	8.1
绝缘制品（万吨）	Insulating Products (10 000 ton)	1.88	0.3
电子元件（亿只）	Electronic Components(100 million unit)	52.52	16.5
工业自动化调节仪表与控制系统（万台/套）	Automatization Meter and System (10 000 unit)	12.28	34.3

12-3 续表4 continued 4

产品名称	Name of Products	2021	比上年增长(%) Increase over Preceding Year (%)
分析仪器及装置（万台/套）	Analysis Instruments and Apparatus(10 000 set)	0.14	25.8
化学试剂（万吨）	Chemicals Reagents(10 000 ton)	20.60	10.1
起重机（万吨）	Crane (10 000 ton)	0.21	-14.9
减速机（万台）	Reducer (10 000 unit)	5.36	43.4
模具（万套）	Molds (10 000 set)	5.46	42.9
电动自行车（万辆）	Electric Bicycle (10 000 car)	0.26	-79.9
电力电容器（万千乏）	Power Capacitors (10 000 kvar)	6511.57	5.6
高压开关设备（11万伏以上）（万台）	High Voltage Switchgear (above 110,000 volt) (10 000a)	2.83	10.1
灯具及照明装置（万套/台/个）	Lamps and lighting Equipment (10 000set /a)	1.60	-71.2
半导体分立器件（亿只）	Discrete Semiconductor Devices (100million unit)	26.55	-36.3
工业仪表（万台/个）	Industrial Instrumentation (10 000a)	64.39	26.1
环境监测专用仪器仪表（万台）	Special Equipment for Prevention and Control of Environmental Pollution(10 000 unit)	0.89	-11.7
集成电路圆片（万片）	Integrated Circuit Wafer (10 000 pieces)	286.60	39.2
锂离子电池（万只）	Lithium Ion Battery (10 000 unit)	2179.58	5.2
太阳能电池（万千瓦）	Solar Cell (10 000 kW)	1542.47	306.2
智能手机（万台）	Smart Phones (10 000 sets)	4916.63	37.6
光纤（万千米）	Optical Fiber(10 000 km)	809.39	10.6
3D打印设备（台）	3D Printing Equipment(unit)	218	44.4
移动通信基站设备（万射频模块）	Mobile Communication Base Station Equipment (10 000 RF modules)	50.64	-87.1
民用无人机（架）	Civilian Drone(unit)	75	7.1
发电量（亿千瓦小时）	Electricity(100 million kWh)	167.67	6.1
火力发电量	Thermal Power	167.03	6.5
水力发电量	Hydro Power	0.18	-75.9
太阳能发电量	Solar Power	0.46	3.2

12-4 主要年份规模以上工业企业经济效益指标

Indicators of Economic Performance of Industrial Enterprises above Designated Size in Representative Years

年份 Year	总资产贡献率 (%) Ratio of Total Assets to Industrial Output Value (%)	资产负债率 (%) Assets-Liability Ratio (%)	流动资产周转次数 (次/年) Rate of Annual Turnover Working Capitals (times/year)	成本费用利润率 (%) Ratio of Profits to Cost (%)	产品销售率 (%) Proportion of Industrial Products Sold (%)
1998		67.7	0.9	-266.1	95.3
1999		67.7	0.9	2.5	95.9
2000		65.0	1.0	4.2	97.1
2001	5.8	62.4	0.9	4.1	96.7
2002	6.2	60.4	1.1	5.1	96.7
2003	7.0	61.3	1.1	5.7	96.3
2004	6.9	65.2	1.2	5.0	97.9
2005	8.4	65.0	1.3	3.1	97.5
2006	7.8	64.3	1.4	5.5	98.2
2007	10.2	64.6	1.6	7.3	96.8
2008	8.6	62.6	1.5	4.6	96.1
2009	11.3	61.1	1.7	8.1	97.6
2010	12.2	57.6	1.7	8.8	97.1
2011	8.6	57.7	1.5	5.2	97.4
2012	7.7	59.4	1.5	4.5	96.7
2013	8.5	59.5	1.5	5.2	95.7
2014	7.4	59.7	1.4	5.2	94.9
2015	5.7	57.3	1.3	4.8	94.5
2016	6.4	55.7	1.3	6.0	96.0
2017	7.2	53.0	1.4	6.6	97.3
2018	7.3	54.5	1.3	6.8	96.2
2019	5.4	53.9	1.2	5.1	94.0
2020	6.1	55.2	1.1	7.1	93.0
2021	5.4	57.4	1.1	5.7	92.4

注：2019年及以后年份产品销售率为快报数。

12-5 规模以上工业企业主要经济指标（2021年）

单位：万元

分　组	Classify	企业单位数（个） Number of Enterprises (unit)	亏损企业 Loss Making Enterprises
总计	**Total**	**1731**	**368**
#亏损企业	Deficit Enterprises	368	368
按隶属关系分	**Grouped by Jurisdiction of Management**		
#中央企业	Central Enterprises	111	16
地方企业	Provincial Enterprises	249	55
按登记注册类型分	**Grouped by Registration Type**		
内资企业	Domestic Investment Enterprises	1606	338
国有	State-owned Enterprises	36	5
集体	Collective-owned Enterprises	2	
股份合作	Share-holding Cooperative	4	
联营	Joint Ownership Enterprises		
有限责任公司	Limited Liability Corporations	462	102
股份有限公司	Share-holding Corporation Ltd.	101	23
私营	Private Enterprises	1001	208
其他	Other Domestic Funded Enterprises		
港澳台商投资	Enterprises with Funds from Hong Kong,Macao and Taiwan	26	7
外商投资	Foreign Funded Enterprises	99	23
按轻重工业分	**Grouped by Light Industry and Heavy Industry**		
轻工业	Light Industry	350	93
重工业	Heavy Industry	1381	275
按企业规模分	**Grouped by Size of Enterprises**		
大型企业	Large-size	67	13
中型企业	Medium-size	198	34
小型企业	Small-size	1344	277
微型企业	Microenterprise	122	44
按控股情况分	**Grouped by Cast strand**		
国有控股	State owned shares	360	71

Major Economic Indicators of Industrial Enterprises above Designated Size (2021)

(10 000 yuan)

平均用工人数（人） Average Number of Employed Persons (person)	资产总计 Total Assets	流动资产合计 Total Working Capitals	固定资产原价 Origing Value of Fixed Assets	累计折旧 Accumulative Total Depreciation
536973	**119996090**	**71861532**	**53835807**	**25122395**
111159	25148794	15003007	9370852	3497517
144407	25311234	16178248	12283982	6755462
117470	31588956	19758239	10765674	4455092
464626	97246380	62721635	31366031	13832932
60522	8640185	4104249	6365382	3117358
266	8379	7173	1202	611
510	102612	83827	13417	7104
209825	39540836	24751558	15321341	7025862
59474	26080972	17099374	4287329	2036359
134029	22873395	16675454	5377360	1645639
8350	1416493	717240	621043	239091
63997	21333217	8422657	21848732	11050372
80834	12793916	7870064	4434472	1840245
456139	107202174	63991468	49401335	23282151
292220	70151973	39445046	39417289	19657422
102395	21552045	14108624	5513696	2347338
133078	24765469	16245046	7431232	3042573
9280	3526604	2062816	1473590	75062
261877	56900190	35936487	23049656	11210554

12-5 续表1

单位：万元

分组	Classify	负债合计 Total Liabilites	流动负债合计 Total Working Liabilities
总计	**Total**	**68822203**	**57435991**
#亏损企业	Deficit Enterprises	17778525	14608913
按隶属关系分	**Grouped by Jurisdiction of Management**		
#中央企业	Central Enterprises	15070497	12917912
地方企业	Provincial Enterprises	19702800	14245669
按登记注册类型分	**Grouped by Registration Type**		
内资企业	Domestic Investment Enterprises	58421716	48168858
国有	State-owned Enterprises	5706245	3108745
集体	Collective-owned Enterprises	4658	4614
股份合作	Share-holding Cooperative	79548	71984
联营	Joint Ownership Enterprises		
有限责任公司	Limited Liability Corporations	23560622	18943785
股份有限公司	Share-holding Corporation Ltd.	13812777	12331586
私营	Private Enterprises	15257866	13708143
其他	Other Domestic Funded Enterprises		
港澳台商投资	Enterprises with Funds from Hong Kong,Macao and Taiwan	979689	810922
外商投资	Foreign Funded Enterprises	9420799	8456211
按轻重工业分	**Grouped by Light Industry and Heavy Industry**		
轻工业	Light Industry	7632224	5341424
重工业	Heavy Industry	61189979	52094567
按企业规模分	**Grouped by Size of Enterprises**		
大型企业	Large-size	40306476	36039927
中型企业	Medium-size	10858778	8903912
小型企业	Small-size	14932232	12165418
微型企业	Microenterprise	2724718	326732
按控股情况分	**Grouped by Cast strand**		
国有控股	State owned shares	34773297	27163581

continued 1

(10 000 yuan)

所有者权益合计 Total Owners' Equities	实收资本 Total Capital Hold	营业收入 Total Revenue	主营业务收入 Revenue from Principal Business	营业成本 Total Cost	税金及附加 Taxs and Other Changes
51173866	**20292523**	**81574513**	**78952279**	**70856213**	**474288**
7370266	4403051	17695284	16475734	17006179	67149
10240737	5109906	14603730	14355128	13065863	63165
11886155	4591313	18671040	17102983	16827172	88875
38824643	14874267	65509006	63255949	57382234	283292
2933940	1499424	4695272	4406237	4356140	17558
3721	1894	11065	11065	9883	13
23064	8011	56317	56313	48719	1188
15980212	7422867	28436957	26963585	25046592	140880
12268194	2763054	11427417	11250159	9905101	40511
7615513	3179016	20881977	20568589	18015800	83142
436804	267232	1089915	1031195	951783	5608
11912418	5151024	14975591	14665135	12522196	185388
5161687	1932892	8986195	8505585	6516035	64192
46012179	18359630	72588318	70446694	64340179	410096
29845497	11103649	51064871	49469329	46331921	299421
10693266	3690138	13843712	13559426	11031886	82275
9833217	5291701	15710570	15386302	12625544	88685
801886	207034	955361	537222	866863	3907
22126892	9701219	33274770	31458110	29893035	152040

12-5 续表2

单位：万元

分　组	Classify	销售费用 Expenses for Sales	管理费用 Expenses for Management	研发费用 R&D Expenses
总计	**Total**	**2318801**	**2684713**	**1958863**
#亏损企业	Deficit Enterprises	423046	512485	326123
按隶属关系分	**Grouped by Jurisdiction of Management**			
#中央企业	Central Enterprises	148102	586165	368601
地方企业	Provincial Enterprises	327927	550046	411312
按登记注册类型分	**Grouped by Registration Type**			
内资企业	Domestic Investment Enterprises	1680642	2134031	1570103
国有	State-owned Enterprises	13942	170624	71695
集体	Collective-owned Enterprises	329	416	1
股份合作	Share-holding Cooperative	2887	1057	206
联营	Joint Ownership Enterprises			
有限责任公司	Limited Liability Corporations	699812	970862	688061
股份有限公司	Share-holding Corporation Ltd.	260952	348103	240444
私营	Private Enterprises	702720	642968	569695
其他	Other Domestic Funded Enterprises			
港澳台商投资	Enterprises with Funds from Hong Kong,Macao and Taiwan	67273	51956	17174
外商投资	Foreign Funded Enterprises	570887	498727	371586
按轻重工业分	**Grouped by Light Industry and Heavy Industry**			
轻工业	Light Industry	1096859	507624	130179
重工业	Heavy Industry	1221943	2177089	1828685
按企业规模分	**Grouped by Size of Enterprises**			
大型企业	Large-size	1012910	1256305	929590
中型企业	Medium-size	649037	547200	515720
小型企业	Small-size	641793	838442	500678
微型企业	Microenterprise	15062	42766	12876
按控股情况分	**Grouped by Cast strand**			
国有控股	State owned shares	476029	1136211	779914

continued 2

(10 000 yuan)

财务费用 Financial cost	营业利润 Operating Profit	利润总额 Total Profits	亏损企业亏损总额 Total Loss of Deficit Enterprises	利税总额 Total Pre-tax Profits	应付职工薪酬 Salary Payable	本年应交增值税 Value Added Tax Payable
469616	**4374117**	**4444844**	**870559**	**6209660**	**6781184**	**1290529**
184229	-873208	-870559	870559	-668084	1294551	135326
53541	434396	453626	102417	773145	2330747	256354
84800	584327	589533	303135	955890	1393923	277481
392422	2775810	2853729	751698	4212068	5591747	1075046
24345	67678	79497	22696	218555	677407	121500
37	386	605		895	902	277
1482	1316	1501		3273	2909	584
134671	1030144	1055840	345108	1664842	2718560	468122
62672	900119	907941	113108	1087706	1028483	139255
169216	776167	808346	270787	1236797	1163486	345309
4102	79355	78150	51745	97232	111533	13474
73092	1518951	1512964	67116	1900361	1077905	202009
83260	812415	836176	95055	1143237	832455	242870
386356	3561702	3608668	775505	5066423	5948730	1047659
153095	2220432	2203484	416984	3055169	4176977	552263
79565	1253806	1279664	177896	1707336	1305945	345397
216029	898476	958133	241178	1425926	1282868	379109
20926	1403	3563	34501	21229	15395	13759
138341	1018723	1043159	405552	1729034	3724670	533836

12-5 续表3

单位：万元

分 组	Classify	企业单位数（个）Number of Enterprises (unit)	亏损企业 Loss Making Enterprises
集体控股	Collective shares	8	4
私人控股	Private holdings	1275	275
港澳台控股	Hong Kong, Macao and Taiwan Holdings	18	4
外商投资	Foreign Investment	70	14
其他	Others		
按工业行业大类分	**Grouped by Sector**		
煤炭开采和洗选业	Mining and Washing of Coal		
石油和天然气开采业	Extraction of Petroleum and Natural Gas		
黑色金属矿采选业	Mining and Processing of Ferrous Metal Ores		
有色金属矿采选业	Mining and Processing of Non-ferrous Metal Ores		
非金属矿采选业	Mining and Processing of Nonmetal Ores		
开采专业及辅助性活动	Mining Professional and Auxiliary Activity	15	3
其他采矿业	Mining of other Ores		
农副食品加工业	Processing of Food from Agricultural Porducts	43	9
食品制造业	Manufacture of Foods	47	14
酒、饮料和精制茶制造业	Manufacture of Alcohol,Beverages and Tea	16	6
烟草制品业	Manufacture of Tobacco	2	0
纺织业	Manufacture of Textile	14	3
纺织服装、服饰业	Textile, apparel industry	3	1
皮革、毛皮、羽毛及其制品和制鞋业	Manufacture of Leather, Fur, Feather and Related Products, and Shoes	2	1
木材加工和木、竹、藤、棕、草制品业	Processing of Timber, Manufacture of Wood,Plam and Straw Products	3	2
家具制造业	Manufacture of Furniture	12	4
造纸和纸制品业	Manufacture of Paper and Paper Products	22	5
印刷和记录媒介复制业	Printing,Reproduction of Recording Media	29	8

continued 3

(10 000 yuan)

平均用工人数（人） Average Number of Employed Persons (person)	资产总计 Total Assets	流动资产合计 Total Working Capitals	固定资产原价 Origing Value of Fixed Assets	累计折旧 Accumulative Total Depreciation
1444	144854	92108	67275	29056
235680	46469123	30882714	10133642	3437613
4715	706449	394566	256446	163203
33257	15775474	4555657	20328787	10281970
15129	1650192	1074233	1292051	929625
4940	984959	699594	293252	74019
13868	909741	509296	478800	242849
6351	1087582	473300	519091	264138
652	67733	37437	51477	25402
4739	297931	120059	204061	87019
410	61663	37147	13993	5788
732	72310	48408	9480	6767
355	97978	44238	32149	13031
1465	90842	48788	35188	8812
1789	165664	92774	58718	23119
5823	707405	410215	494966	349639

12-5 续表4

单位：万元

分　组	Classify	负债合计 Total Liabilites	流动负债合计 Total Working Liabilities
集体控股	Collective shares	64670	63103
私人控股	Private holdings	28007226	25065524
港澳台控股	Hong Kong, Macao and Taiwan Holdings	333157	247588
外商投资	Foreign Investment	5643853	4896195
其他	Others		
按工业行业大类分	**Grouped by Sector**		
煤炭开采和洗选业	Mining and Washing of Coal		
石油和天然气开采业	Extraction of Petroleum and Natural Gas		
黑色金属矿采选业	Mining and Processing of Ferrous Metal Ores		
有色金属矿采选业	Mining and Processing of Non-ferrous Metal Ores		
非金属矿采选业	Mining and Processing of Nonmetal Ores		
开采专业及辅助性活动	Mining Professional and Auxiliary Activity	748809	631807
其他采矿业	Mining of other Ores		
农副食品加工业	Processing of Food from Agricultural Porducts	615896	529790
食品制造业	Manufacture of Foods	532266	492284
酒、饮料和精制茶制造业	Manufacture of Alcohol,Beverages and Tea	577034	484374
烟草制品业	Manufacture of Tobacco	11588	8588
纺织业	Manufacture of Textile	182098	73099
纺织服装、服饰业	Textile, apparel industry	36634	35394
皮革、毛皮、羽毛及其制品和制鞋业	Manufacture of Leather, Fur, Feather and Related Products, and Shoes	23826	22058
木材加工和木、竹、藤、棕、草制品业	Processing of Timber, Manufacture of Wood,Plam and Straw Products	44543	10543
家具制造业	Manufacture of Furniture	54078	49231
造纸和纸制品业	Manufacture of Paper and Paper Products	107510	90479
印刷和记录媒介复制业	Printing,Reproduction of Recording Media	250695	219584

continued 4

(10 000 yuan)

所有者权益合计 Total Owners' Equities	实收资本 Total Capital Hold	营业收入 Total Revenue	主营业务收入 Revenue from Principal Business	营业成本 Total Cost	税金及附加 Taxs and Other Changes
80184	45502	86160	78758	67241	587
18461877	6058492	38457167	37773927	33217076	251813
373292	171437	530403	522586	347756	3626
10131621	4315873	9226013	9118897	7331105	66222
901382	590875	1237491	1218631	1132698	6243
369062	96349	1130244	1055693	1023970	2328
377473	203273	1005024	980729	788587	7811
510548	165125	766929	750574	566412	12485
56146	35471	28242	27872	17712	667
115833	44185	201926	187833	187524	1640
25029	19000	30187	29991	25589	182
48484	41000	24293	23796	20211	391
53435	13720	9531	7951	7594	42
36764	21015	67085	66689	53883	378
58154	31189	173319	166397	155843	652
456709	250406	471762	461499	373595	4064

12-5 续表5

单位：万元

分　组	Classify	销售费用 Expenses for Sales	管理费用 Expenses for Management	研发费用 R&D Expenses
集体控股	Collective shares	5575	7236	1513
私人控股	Private holdings	1327489	1149903	845890
港澳台控股	Hong Kong, Macao and Taiwan Holdings	50372	31146	14922
外商投资	Foreign Investment	459338	360216	316625
其他	Others			
按工业行业大类分	**Grouped by Sector**			
煤炭开采和洗选业	Mining and Washing of Coal			
石油和天然气开采业	Extraction of Petroleum and Natural Gas			
黑色金属矿采选业	Mining and Processing of Ferrous Metal Ores			
有色金属矿采选业	Mining and Processing of Non-ferrous Metal Ores			
非金属矿采选业	Mining and Processing of Nonmetal Ores			
开采专业及辅助性活动	Mining Professional and Auxiliary Activity	1132	39754	52861
其他采矿业	Mining of other Ores			
农副食品加工业	Processing of Food from Agricultural Porducts	28650	33512	6170
食品制造业	Manufacture of Foods	110945	47276	7653
酒、饮料和精制茶制造业	Manufacture of Alcohol,Beverages and Tea	110132	27883	2040
烟草制品业	Manufacture of Tobacco	1102	6512	
纺织业	Manufacture of Textile	4649	9274	2886
纺织服装、服饰业	Textile, apparel industry	1461	1640	917
皮革、毛皮、羽毛及其制品和制鞋业	Manufacture of Leather, Fur, Feather and Related Products, and Shoes	1268	1659	887
木材加工和木、竹、藤、棕、草制品业	Processing of Timber, Manufacture of Wood,Plam and Straw Products	212	2491	
家具制造业	Manufacture of Furniture	2857	8674	276
造纸和纸制品业	Manufacture of Paper and Paper Products	4661	5666	398
印刷和记录媒介复制业	Printing,Reproduction of Recording Media	10031	43411	9452

continued 5

(10 000 yuan)

财务费用 Financial cost	营业利润 Operating Profit	利润总额 Total Profits	亏损企业亏损总额 Total Loss of Deficit Enterprises	利税总额 Total Pre-tax Profits	应付职工薪酬 Salary Payable	本年应交增值税 Value Added Tax Payable
138	3577	8035	3279	11545	14039	2923
261092	1857592	1906232	402869	2778761	2320488	620716
5622	126388	125342	2954	136116	57486	7148
64422	1367838	1362077	55906	1554203	664501	125905
-14204	-7809	-9978	15044	63579	355186	67314
8157	26500	37634	8672	45262	36159	5300
3309	45953	47324	13085	83514	105249	28379
232	53689	60834	12708	90204	53241	16885
-310	2602	2534		5130	8093	1929
312	-3978	-2614	10333	2508	34887	3482
285	112	93	867	1239	2436	964
100	-717	-716	828	-709	4275	-383
1309	-2117	-2033	2060	-1673	1251	319
1188	973	942	609	2811	9455	1492
1846	6981	7639	706	11400	10519	3109
3888	31416	31966	4852	53529	94207	17500

12-5 续表6

单位：万元

分 组	Classify	企业单位数（个） Number of Enterprises (unit)	亏损企业 Loss Making Enterprises
文教、工美、体育和娱乐用品制造业	Manufacture of Articles For Cultural,Educational and Sports Activities	7	2
石油、煤炭及其他燃料加工业	Petroleum, coal and other fuel processing industries	7	2
化学原料和化学制品制造业	Manufacture of Raw Chemical Materials and Chemical Products	79	12
医药制造业	Manufacture of Medicines	68	20
化学纤维制造业	Manufacture of Chemical Fibers	3	
橡胶和塑料制品业	Manufacture of Rubber and Plastics	40	6
非金属矿物制品业	Manufacture of Non-metallic Mineral Products	198	50
黑色金属冶炼和压延加工业	Smelting and Pressing of Ferrous Metals	16	4
有色金属冶炼和压延加工业	Smelting and Pressing of Non-ferrous Metals	51	13
金属制品业	Manufacture of Metal Products	114	24
通用设备制造业	Manufacture of General Purpose Machinery	96	23
专用设备制造业	Manufacture of Special Equipment	146	25
汽车制造业	Manufacture of Motor Vehicle	81	25
铁路、船舶、航空航天和其他运输设备制造业	Railways,Shipbuilding,Aerospace and Other Transportation Equipment Manufacturing Industry	97	8
电气机械和器材制造业	Manufacture of Electric Equipment and Machinery	183	33
计算机、通讯和其他电子设备制造业	Manufacture of Communication Equipment, Computers and other Electronic Equipment	150	17
仪器仪表制造业	Manufacture of Measuring Instruments and Machinery	86	14
其他制造业	Manufacture of Other Manufacturing	7	3
废弃资源综合利用业	Recycling and Disposal of Waste	7	
金属制品、机械和设备修理业	Metal Products,Machinery and Equipment Repair Industry	16	3
电力、热力生产和供应业	Production and Supply of Electric Power and Heat Power	32	13
燃气生产和供应业	Gas Mining and Supplying Industry	20	8
水的生产和供应业	Production and Supply of Water	19	7

continued 6

(10 000 yuan)

平均用工人数（人）Average Number of Employed Persons (person)	资产总计 Total Assets	流动资产合计 Total Working Capitals	固定资产原价 Origing Value of Fixed Assets	累计折旧 Accumulative Total Depreciation
540	31608	17599	7204	2054
790	276797	232553	27515	15255
13521	3231010	2011355	1244276	593435
18921	3133002	2047727	872761	299344
726	166821	95220	163993	96913
9834	2605364	1628616	730042	139464
21400	4854405	3786145	1254066	584822
1240	194595	136552	57326	24768
9617	3323561	1802907	764301	303115
21578	3017082	1990554	1109104	500335
18712	4614925	3838512	718650	356038
29437	6582430	4766763	1210626	511653
60063	13085870	9550615	3056732	1456005
63657	15213613	11091895	3548395	1766749
60846	14521757	10463695	3240790	1060569
71133	25362342	9839661	20775682	9995067
12023	1848909	1492766	277217	124973
998	82667	56550	35889	15674
411	108890	53282	33930	7997
2091	276132	144263	69009	26597
50900	7288636	2119363	8200217	4155316
7741	2693779	786868	2038844	749748
4541	1287896	312585	916011	306298

12-5 续表7

单位：万元

分　组	Classify	负债合计 Total Liabilites	流动负债合计 Total Working Liabilities
文教、工美、体育和娱乐用品制造业	Manufacture of Articles For Cultural,Educational and Sports Activities	10178	5554
石油、煤炭及其他燃料加工业	Petroleum, coal and other fuel processing industries	229105	227900
化学原料和化学制品制造业	Manufacture of Raw Chemical Materials and Chemical Products	1682065	1277382
医药制造业	Manufacture of Medicines	1531759	1300782
化学纤维制造业	Manufacture of Chemical Fibers	49353	48355
橡胶和塑料制品业	Manufacture of Rubber and Plastics	1884037	468005
非金属矿物制品业	Manufacture of Non-metallic Mineral Products	3587077	3313834
黑色金属冶炼和压延加工业	Smelting and Pressing of Ferrous Metals	133282	107289
有色金属冶炼和压延加工业	Smelting and Pressing of Non-ferrous Metals	1216742	961547
金属制品业	Manufacture of Metal Products	2229687	1641945
通用设备制造业	Manufacture of General Purpose Machinery	2920405	2634638
专用设备制造业	Manufacture of Special Equipment	3538858	2936738
汽车制造业	Manufacture of Motor Vehicle	8847581	8271325
铁路、船舶、航空航天和其他运输设备制造业	Railways,Shipbuilding,Aerospace and Other Transportation Equipment Manufacturing Industry	8528420	7848048
电气机械和器材制造业	Manufacture of Electric Equipment and Machinery	10405153	9535514
计算机、通讯和其他电子设备制造业	Manufacture of Communication Equipment, Computers and other Electronic Equipment	9550114	7986873
仪器仪表制造业	Manufacture of Measuring Instruments and Machinery	936747	888244
其他制造业	Manufacture of Other Manufacturing	46906	44127
废弃资源综合利用业	Recycling and Disposal of Waste	77215	65625
金属制品、机械和设备修理业	Metal Products,Machinery and Equipment Repair Industry	99698	71488
电力、热力生产和供应业	Production and Supply of Electric Power and Heat Power	5556176	3225914
燃气生产和供应业	Gas Mining and Supplying Industry	1577083	1245582
水的生产和供应业	Production and Supply of Water	999584	682052

continued 7

(10 000 yuan)

所有者权益合计 Total Owners' Equities	实收资本 Total Capital Hold	营业收入 Total Revenue	主营业务收入 Revenue from Principal Business	营业成本 Total Cost	税金及附加 Taxs and Other Changes
21430	7865	14057	13375	10124	234
47692	55003	415405	409288	386728	1699
1548945	530076	1972806	1889214	1506977	10813
1601242	372093	2309164	2272409	1136096	22285
117468	95052	215940	215211	176075	1709
721326	423505	744908	501654	648849	3939
1267323	675680	3624718	3529738	3125279	20447
61314	46540	533570	522520	513154	1142
2106818	620273	1310231	1266899	1040300	7901
787392	583371	2061631	2020233	1779102	7559
1694519	634070	2015319	1988603	1678268	12057
3043570	1036542	3155225	3130184	2308339	21355
4238288	1450551	15128966	13945120	14085614	148451
6685193	2225546	6219826	6135351	5287106	21904
4116601	2281246	12342271	12089634	11225641	38084
15812227	5107288	16877165	16775967	14699684	78826
912161	338586	1107682	1097815	816326	6479
35760	18308	39175	38340	27616	409
31675	23762	141275	140867	130017	1850
176434	175371	135555	121412	109171	865
1732460	1400541	3985763	3869417	3872093	18964
1116696	426803	1820221	1760954	1732256	6670
288312	252845	257609	240421	207781	3766

12-5 续表8

单位：万元

分　组	Classify	销售费用 Expenses for Sales	管理费用 Expenses for Management	研发费用 R&D Expenses
文教、工美、体育和娱乐用品制造业	Manufacture of Articles For Cultural,Educational and Sports Activities	478	1661	300
石油、煤炭及其他燃料加工业	Petroleum, coal and other fuel processing industries	3210	7718	2212
化学原料和化学制品制造业	Manufacture of Raw Chemical Materials and Chemical Products	49515	95365	66874
医药制造业	Manufacture of Medicines	671165	236443	47815
化学纤维制造业	Manufacture of Chemical Fibers	1143	6523	1512
橡胶和塑料制品业	Manufacture of Rubber and Plastics	27574	26952	19381
非金属矿物制品业	Manufacture of Non-metallic Mineral Products	100931	128777	56548
黑色金属冶炼和压延加工业	Smelting and Pressing of Ferrous Metals	2030	6443	2824
有色金属冶炼和压延加工业	Smelting and Pressing of Non-ferrous Metals	18757	61707	67742
金属制品业	Manufacture of Metal Products	26972	101867	54836
通用设备制造业	Manufacture of General Purpose Machinery	62490	109901	80879
专用设备制造业	Manufacture of Special Equipment	163635	185463	138386
汽车制造业	Manufacture of Motor Vehicle	248436	253168	229347
铁路、船舶、航空航天和其他运输设备制造业	Railways,Shipbuilding,Aerospace and Other Transportation Equipment Manufacturing Industry	102143	281559	162907
电气机械和器材制造业	Manufacture of Electric Equipment and Machinery	326813	306489	219467
计算机、通讯和其他电子设备制造业	Manufacture of Communication Equipment, Computers and other Electronic Equipment	116575	382248	639780
仪器仪表制造业	Manufacture of Measuring Instruments and Machinery	55232	68072	62028
其他制造业	Manufacture of Other Manufacturing	2972	3868	3986
废弃资源综合利用业	Recycling and Disposal of Waste	1557	2773	1809
金属制品、机械和设备修理业	Metal Products,Machinery and Equipment Repair Industry	1353	15575	3764
电力、热力生产和供应业	Production and Supply of Electric Power and Heat Power	7039	96239	9265
燃气生产和供应业	Gas Mining and Supplying Industry	41457	54140	2439
水的生产和供应业	Production and Supply of Water	10226	24014	1225

continued 8

(10 000 yuan)

财务费用 Financial cost	营业利润 Operating Profit	利润总额 Total Profits	亏损企业亏损总额 Total Loss of Deficit Enterprises	利税总额 Total Pre-tax Profits	应付职工薪酬 Salary Payable	本年应交增值税 Value Added Tax Payable
258	1142	1492	302	2743	3930	1017
37	15416	15477	600	51331	5289	34155
36617	275040	276150	23906	322303	190498	35340
14330	198888	201795	11295	349773	270789	125694
-236	28438	28352		37020	13905	6960
18903	23082	21192	9082	36683	46418	11552
42350	145392	150058	28442	275868	182099	105363
1949	6271	6574	824	10502	9465	2787
15583	120558	122674	21194	157509	132327	26934
17633	129745	134606	10782	167340	270482	25175
-13592	102598	112792	46029	177115	236105	52267
18185	369475	377028	35640	488133	400542	89750
-22819	377681	380976	102152	713017	741319	183590
26237	394632	401724	3838	485950	1064665	62323
106225	131269	133344	240287	260596	732176	89168
82172	1825976	1818590	84131	2057060	972209	159644
7152	115542	120879	6055	159769	167249	32411
1196	-562	-454	1859	1525	9883	1570
3116	3469	3612		20405	3316	14942
857	4329	4586	6615	11141	33396	5690
72849	-65428	-60918	98785	17999	400244	59954
15561	22683	23911	51316	41812	116667	11231
18944	-5122	-3216	17662	7272	63257	6722

12-6 规模以上国有及国有控股工业企业主要经济指标（2021年）

单位：万元

分组	Classify	企业单位数（个）Number of Enterprises (unit)	亏损企业 Loss Making Enterprises
总计	**Total**	**360**	**71**
#亏损企业	Deficit Enterprises	71	71
按隶属关系分	**Grouped by Jurisdiction of Management**		
#中央企业	Central Enterprises	111	16
地方企业	Provincial Enterprises	249	55
按轻重工业分	**Grouped by Light Industry and Heavy Industry**		
轻工业	Light Industry	36	10
重工业	Heavy Industry	324	61
按企业规模分	**Grouped by Size of Enterprises**		
大型企业	Large-size	42	8
中型企业	Medium-size	95	14
小型企业	Small-size	203	42
微型企业	Microenterprise	20	7
按工业行业大类分	**Grouped by Sector**		
煤炭开采和洗选业	Mining and Washing of Coal		
石油和天然气开采业	Extraction of Petroleum and Natural Gas		
黑色金属矿采选业	Mining and Processing of Ferrous Metal Ores		
有色金属矿采选业	Mining and Processing of Non-ferrous Metal Ores		
非金属矿采选业	Mining and Processing of Nonmetal Ores		
开采专业及辅助性活动	Mining Professional and Auxiliary Activity	2	1
其他采矿业	Mining of Other Ores		
农副食品加工业	Processing of Food from Agricultural Porducts		
食品制造业	Manufacture of Foods	8	2
酒、饮料和精制茶制造业	Manufacture of Alcohol,Beverages and Tea	2	
烟草制品业	Manufacture of Tobacco	1	
纺织业	Manufacture of Textile	4	1
纺织服装、服饰业	Textile, apparel industry		
皮革、毛皮、羽毛及其制品和制鞋业	Manufacture of Leather, Fur, Feather and Related Products, and Shoes	1	1
木材加工和木、竹、藤、棕、草制品业	Processing of Timber, Manufacture of Wood,Plato and Straw Products		

Major Economic Indicators of State-owned and State-holding Share Industrial Enterprises above Designated Size (2021)

(10 000 yuan)

平均用工人数（人） Average Number of Employed Persons (person)	资产总计 Total Assets	流动资产合计 Total Working Capitals	固定资产原价 Origing Value of Fixed Assets	累计折旧 Accumulative Total Depreciation
261877	**56900190**	**35936487**	**23049656**	**11210554**
45072	11205412	6247285	5369023	2466066
144407	25311234	16178248	12283982	6755462
117470	31588956	19758239	10765674	4455092
20056	3447108	2156359	1313391	565913
241821	53453083	33780128	21736266	10644641
176623	35602355	22899651	16201134	8794069
52671	11160303	7009307	3067250	1368122
26268	7533502	4580002	2661809	997362
6315	2604031	1447527	1119464	51000
13981	1489422	951856	1221180	895255
2765	160396	105661	79276	44206
1606	294214	156947	68259	9098
523	42943	26297	31621	18233
3798	243661	76391	192152	81143
585	63528	39751	8780	6249

12-6 续表1

单位：万元

分　组	Classify	负债合计 Total Liabilites	流动负债合计 Total Working Liabilities
总计	**Total**	**34773297**	**27163581**
#亏损企业	Deficit Enterprises	7328916	5429803
按隶属关系分	**Grouped by Jurisdiction of Management**		
#中央企业	Central Enterprises	15070497	12917912
地方企业	Provincial Enterprises	19702800	14245669
按轻重工业分	**Grouped by Light Industry and Heavy Industry**		
轻工业	Light Industry	2090158	574095
重工业	Heavy Industry	32683139	26589486
按企业规模分	**Grouped by Size of Enterprises**		
大型企业	Large-size	21207143	18563833
中型企业	Medium-size	6216402	4624170
小型企业	Small-size	5140694	3823254
微型企业	Microenterprise	2209058	152325
按工业行业大类分	**Grouped by Sector**		
煤炭开采和洗选业	Mining and Washing of Coal		
石油和天然气开采业	Extraction of Petroleum and Natural Gas		
黑色金属矿采选业	Mining and Processing of Ferrous Metal Ores		
有色金属矿采选业	Mining and Processing of Non-ferrous Metal Ores		
非金属矿采选业	Mining and Processing of Nonmetal Ores		
开采专业及辅助性活动	Mining Professional and Auxiliary Activity	660176	558650
其他采矿业	Mining of Other Ores		
农副食品加工业	Processing of Food from Agricultural Porducts		
食品制造业	Manufacture of Foods	48035	46801
酒、饮料和精制茶制造业	Manufacture of Alcohol,Beverages and Tea	149647	99282
烟草制品业	Manufacture of Tobacco	4957	4957
纺织业	Manufacture of Textile	154004	45955
纺织服装、服饰业	Textile, apparel industry		
皮革、毛皮、羽毛及其制品和制鞋业	Manufacture of Leather, Fur, Feather and Related Products, and Shoes	21189	19421
木材加工和木、竹、藤、棕、草制品业	Processing of Timber, Manufacture of Wood,Plato and Straw Products		

continued 1

(10 000 yuan)

所有者权益合计 Total Owners' Equities	实收资本 Total Capital Hold	营业收入 Total Revenue	主营业务收入 Revenue from Principal Business	营业成本 Total Cost	税金及附加 Taxs and Other Changes
22126892	**9701219**	**33274770**	**31458110**	**29893035**	**152040**
3876496	2667447	8358619	7339944	8271636	32396
10240737	5109906	14603730	14355128	13065863	63165
11886155	4591313	18671040	17102983	16827172	88875
1356949	581481	1648016	1387969	1352041	18335
20769943	9119739	31626754	30070141	28540994	133705
14395212	5701765	22107904	20870881	20191454	93080
4943901	2231526	6525098	6344090	5647920	33497
2392806	1648308	4216918	4081782	3663238	23600
394973	119620	424850	161357	390423	1863
829246	576917	1151475	1135762	1063142	5648
112360	54869	257307	253244	217837	1294
144567	46790	314981	314393	231591	8530
37986	27400	11494	11399	5258	365
89656	22581	128437	117235	124997	1355
42339	34500	20772	20275	17726	366

12-6 续表2

单位：万元

分 组	Classify	销售费用 Expenses for Sales	管理费用 Expenses for Management	研发费用 R&D Expenses
总计	**Total**	**476029**	**1136211**	**779914**
#亏损企业	Deficit Enterprises	96876	192603	153151
按隶属关系分	**Grouped by Jurisdiction of Management**			
#中央企业	Central Enterprises	148102	586165	368601
地方企业	Provincial Enterprises	327927	550046	411312
按轻重工业分	**Grouped by Light Industry and Heavy Industry**			
轻工业	Light Industry	63495	86211	20845
重工业	Heavy Industry	412534	1050001	759069
按企业规模分	**Grouped by Size of Enterprises**			
大型企业	Large-size	287184	688703	471726
中型企业	Medium-size	112493	259982	187661
小型企业	Small-size	72087	167059	116101
微型企业	Microenterprise	4265	20467	4425
按工业行业大类分	**Grouped by Sector**			
煤炭开采和洗选业	Mining and Washing of Coal			
石油和天然气开采业	Extraction of Petroleum and Natural Gas			
黑色金属矿采选业	Mining and Processing of Ferrous Metal Ores			
有色金属矿采选业	Mining and Processing of Non-ferrous Metal Ores			
非金属矿采选业	Mining and Processing of Nonmetal Ores			
开采专业及辅助性活动	Mining Professional and Auxiliary Activity	570	30312	51385
其他采矿业	Mining of Other Ores			
农副食品加工业	Processing of Food from Agricultural Porducts			
食品制造业	Manufacture of Foods	11566	14271	715
酒、饮料和精制茶制造业	Manufacture of Alcohol,Beverages and Tea	22562	6602	1274
烟草制品业	Manufacture of Tobacco	909	2989	
纺织业	Manufacture of Textile	1357	6359	1194
纺织服装、服饰业	Textile, apparel industry			
皮革、毛皮、羽毛及其制品和制鞋业	Manufacture of Leather, Fur, Feather and Related Products, and Shoes	974	1339	663
木材加工和木、竹、藤、棕、草制品业	Processing of Timber, Manufacture of Wood,Plato and Straw Products			

continued 2

(10 000 yuan)

财务费用 Financial cost	营业利润 Operating Profit	利润总额 Total Profits	亏损企业亏损总额 Total Loss of Deficit Enterprises	利税总额 Total Pre-tax Profits	应付职工薪酬 Salary Payable	本年应交增值税 Value Added Tax Payable
138341	**1018723**	**1043159**	**405552**	**1729034**	**3724670**	**533836**
19610	-407156	-405552	405552	-286997	688000	86159
53541	434396	453626	102417	773145	2330747	256354
84800	584327	589533	303135	955890	1393923	277481
7307	133460	133609	21890	189669	180572	37725
131034	885262	909550	383662	1539365	3544098	496111
13914	546303	562020	206190	975604	2632952	320504
49545	341417	350044	83536	508618	737365	125077
58325	139074	138717	91205	244944	348242	82628
16558	-8072	-7622	24622	-132	6111	5626
-15449	-11164	-13415	14981	57031	345581	64798
-83	11970	11960	3682	17954	26110	4700
-3575	54799	56294		68476	2515	3652
-338	2352	2290		3689	4417	1034
108	-6542	-5282	9614	-1712	29723	2215
38	-828	-828	828	-944	3558	-482

12－6 续表3

单位：万元

分 组	Classify	企业单位数（个）Number of Enterprises (unit)	亏损企业 Loss Making Enterprises
家具制造业	Manufacture of Furniture		
造纸和纸制品业	Manufacture of Paper and Paper Products		
印刷和记录媒介复制业	Printing,Reproduction of Recording Media	7	3
文教、工美、体育和娱乐用品制造业	Manufacture of Articles For Cultural,Educational and Sports Activities	1	
石油、煤炭和其他燃料加工业	Petroleum, coal and other fuel processing industries		
化学原料及化学制品制造业	Manufacture of Raw Chemical Materials and Chemical Products	17	4
医药制造业	Manufacture of Medicines	3	2
化学纤维制造业	Manufacture of Chemical Fibers	2	
橡胶和塑料制品业	Manufacture of Rubber and Plastics	5	1
非金属矿物制品业	Manufacture of Non-metallic Mineral Products	18	3
黑色金属冶炼和压延加工业	Smelting and Pressing of Ferrous Metals	3	1
有色金属冶炼和压延加工业	Smelting and Pressing of Non-ferrous Metals	19	6
金属制品业	Manufacture of Metal Products	19	2
通用设备制造业	Manufacture of General Purpose Machinery	23	5
专用设备制造业	Manufacture of Special Equipment	36	2
汽车制造业	Manufacture of Motor Vehicle	19	3
铁路、船舶、航空航天和其他运输设备制造业	Railways,Shipbuilding,Aerospace and Other Transportation Equipment Manufacturing Industry	35	
电气机械和器材制造业	Manufacture of Electric Equipment and Machinery	33	5
计算机、通讯和其他电子设备制造业	Manufacture of Communication Equipment, Computers and other Electronic Equipment	34	4
仪器仪表制造业	Manufacture of Measuring Instruments and Machinery	14	1
其他制造业	Manufacture of Other Manufacturing		
废弃资源综合利用业	Recycling and Disposal of Waste	2	
金属制品、机械和设备修理业	Metal Products,Machinery and Equipment Repair Industry	7	2
电力、热力的生产和供应业	Production and Supply of Electric Power and Heat Power	23	11
燃气生产和供应业	Gas Mining and Supplying Industry	8	4
水的生产和供应业	Production and Supply of Water	14	7

continued 3

(10 000 yuan)

平均用工人数（人） Average Number of Employed Persons (person)	资产总计 Total Assets	流动资产合计 Total Working Capitals	固定资产原价 Origing Value of Fixed Assets	累计折旧 Accumulative Total Depreciation
3289	506900	295480	386791	291997
114	4335	3978	461	237
8099	1123499	607280	582797	292718
835	104783	47847	63930	16586
521	94326	63233	86041	56266
7323	2384588	1505024	609995	92178
4057	1403483	1062234	329678	128889
266	90593	65169	32069	16029
5562	2887630	1497424	643745	258165
13654	2320633	1503118	880033	411218
8481	3583204	3111809	409572	200385
14165	3791874	2809290	654725	308459
24909	6093088	4931651	1140689	703336
54157	13243600	9663284	3152079	1634509
12290	3403608	2456707	772732	384729
14462	2875671	1656038	1040110	281186
4559	918611	716039	155760	69484
195	39065	14915	24042	5334
1309	163792	92822	32710	7695
50019	6230769	1626545	7741467	4022227
6233	2173292	576075	1801049	668964
4120	1168687	273624	907915	305780

12-6 续表4

单位：万元

分组	Classify	负债合计 Total Liabilites	流动负债合计 Total Working Liabilities
家具制造业	Manufacture of Furniture		
造纸和纸制品业	Manufacture of Paper and Paper Products		
印刷和记录媒介复制业	Printing,Reproduction of Recording Media	114834	109378
文教、工美、体育和娱乐用品制造业	Manufacture of Articles For Cultural,Educational and Sports Activities	1352	1352
石油、煤炭和其他燃料加工业	Petroleum, coal and other fuel processing industries		
化学原料及化学制品制造业	Manufacture of Raw Chemical Materials and Chemical Products	686577	559828
医药制造业	Manufacture of Medicines	55249	27015
化学纤维制造业	Manufacture of Chemical Fibers	11711	10713
橡胶和塑料制品业	Manufacture of Rubber and Plastics	1740577	348735
非金属矿物制品业	Manufacture of Non-metallic Mineral Products	1064265	942021
黑色金属冶炼和压延加工业	Smelting and Pressing of Ferrous Metals	68813	54356
有色金属冶炼和压延加工业	Smelting and Pressing of Non-ferrous Metals	994628	761206
金属制品业	Manufacture of Metal Products	1771190	1212740
通用设备制造业	Manufacture of General Purpose Machinery	2443210	2229465
专用设备制造业	Manufacture of Special Equipment	2140656	1790649
汽车制造业	Manufacture of Motor Vehicle	3691676	3405991
铁路、船舶、航空航天和其他运输设备制造业	Railways,Shipbuilding,Aerospace and Other Transportation Equipment Manufacturing Industry	7734445	7179220
电气机械和器材制造业	Manufacture of Electric Equipment and Machinery	1959182	1734242
计算机、通讯和其他电子设备制造业	Manufacture of Communication Equipment, Computers and other Electronic Equipment	1750147	1023059
仪器仪表制造业	Manufacture of Measuring Instruments and Machinery	495546	480267
其他制造业	Manufacture of Other Manufacturing		
废弃资源综合利用业	Recycling and Disposal of Waste	30463	27463
金属制品、机械和设备修理业	Metal Products,Machinery and Equipment Repair Industry	57638	43859
电力、热力的生产和供应业	Production and Supply of Electric Power and Heat Power	4711908	2797382
燃气生产和供应业	Gas Mining and Supplying Industry	1288125	986095
水的生产和供应业	Production and Supply of Water	923097	663481

continued 4

(10 000 yuan)

所有者权益合计 Total Owners' Equities	实收资本 Total Capital Hold	营业收入 Total Revenue	主营业务收入 Revenue from Principal Business	营业成本 Total Cost	税金及附加 Taxs and Other Changes
392066	205481	316034	310974	240780	3155
2982	200	3263	3263	2009	31
436923	137343	805164	784048	679593	4039
49534	29490	58537	58416	42306	496
82615	74052	139094	139094	116106	1072
644011	356317	525731	287431	468943	2866
339217	241320	965302	962582	850368	5561
21779	20500	374640	373593	366999	779
1893001	512965	781533	754693	587693	5889
549443	414745	1424551	1397553	1233673	4354
1139994	342742	1380611	1368065	1194926	7783
1651218	673224	1590127	1573421	1339036	10675
2401411	721422	7897777	6960206	7462839	24361
5509155	1853446	5200090	5125821	4564815	15309
1444426	787262	2541222	2344394	2205757	12075
1125524	435515	1228206	1205424	959931	5579
423064	167584	564097	558503	472094	2820
8602	5500	13427	13197	8375	223
106154	124905	84905	70889	76125	558
1518861	1279128	3764368	3648719	3698904	17698
885167	336805	1503218	1451834	1473108	5503
245590	218217	228408	213684	188105	3660

12-6 续表5

单位：万元

分　组	Classify	销售费用 Expenses for Sales	管理费用 Expenses for Management	研发费用 R&D Expenses
家具制造业	Manufacture of Furniture			
造纸和纸制品业	Manufacture of Paper and Paper Products			
印刷和记录媒介复制业	Printing,Reproduction of Recording Media	5005	33654	5049
文教、工美、体育和娱乐用品制造业	Manufacture of Articles For Cultural,Educational and Sports Activities		510	48
石油、煤炭和其他燃料加工业	Petroleum, coal and other fuel processing industries			
化学原料及化学制品制造业	Manufacture of Raw Chemical Materials and Chemical Products	7541	49220	31670
医药制造业	Manufacture of Medicines	6933	4425	189
化学纤维制造业	Manufacture of Chemical Fibers	483	4340	1512
橡胶和塑料制品业	Manufacture of Rubber and Plastics	19678	14765	13710
非金属矿物制品业	Manufacture of Non-metallic Mineral Products	8325	23942	19920
黑色金属冶炼和压延加工业	Smelting and Pressing of Ferrous Metals	727	1724	15
有色金属冶炼和压延加工业	Smelting and Pressing of Non-ferrous Metals	10737	45445	48423
金属制品业	Manufacture of Metal Products	9671	61639	44646
通用设备制造业	Manufacture of General Purpose Machinery	29811	63388	50959
专用设备制造业	Manufacture of Special Equipment	39230	73749	60431
汽车制造业	Manufacture of Motor Vehicle	121317	91507	144194
铁路、船舶、航空航天和其他运输设备制造业	Railways,Shipbuilding,Aerospace and Other Transportation Equipment Manufacturing Industry	62122	224234	121768
电气机械和器材制造业	Manufacture of Electric Equipment and Machinery	52596	109507	78019
计算机、通讯和其他电子设备制造业	Manufacture of Communication Equipment, Computers and other Electronic Equipment	20632	88091	65225
仪器仪表制造业	Manufacture of Measuring Instruments and Machinery	8598	29202	26075
其他制造业	Manufacture of Other Manufacturing			
废弃资源综合利用业	Recycling and Disposal of Waste	526	1595	787
金属制品、机械和设备修理业	Metal Products,Machinery and Equipment Repair Industry	450	9064	1638
电力、热力的生产和供应业	Production and Supply of Electric Power and Heat Power	1278	87093	7970
燃气生产和供应业	Gas Mining and Supplying Industry	22538	34705	2439
水的生产和供应业	Production and Supply of Water	9893	22541	

continued 5

(10 000 yuan)

财务费用 Financial cost	营业利润 Operating Profit	利润总额 Total Profits	亏损企业亏损总额 Total Loss of Deficit Enterprises	利税总额 Total Pre-tax Profits	应付职工薪酬 Salary Payable	本年应交增值税 Value Added Tax Payable
1553	29133	28981	3691	46860	76716	14725
-1	667	887		1163	930	246
4796	39006	42380	13046	61150	129355	14731
1228	3546	3778	2998	6556	7280	2281
-261	15941	15920		20609	10354	3617
14752	15061	12284	6226	22181	30809	7030
17017	35819	36233	3951	69904	59663	28111
730	3990	4025	94	6351	3244	1547
10929	91575	92097	19170	116276	96056	18289
11916	115482	118653	3435	135986	214008	12979
-20597	71073	72496	34677	112524	137168	32245
9002	93972	96474	18309	148976	226839	41828
-31372	127267	127860	62315	245448	301633	93227
24894	238118	241375		289553	957386	32869
16051	43001	50282	31433	97039	196586	34682
19290	77984	79489	13616	106382	202854	21314
-1402	45722	46935	576	64804	86404	15050
750	1174	1033		2219	1957	962
512	-2949	-3070	5396	2045	22449	4557
50767	-70743	-71915	91426	9664	390275	63881
9715	3759	4592	48429	16924	99985	6829
17371	-10462	-8653	17662	1927	60816	6920

12-7 规模以上外商及港澳台商投资工业企业主要经济指标（2021年）

单位：万元

分组	Classify	企业单位数（个）Number of Enterprises (unit)	亏损企业 Loss Making Enterprises
总计	**Total**	**125**	**30**
#亏损企业	Deficit Enterprises	30	30
按登记注册类型分	**Grouped by Type of Registration**		
港澳台商投资	Enterprises with Funds from Hong Kong, Macao &Taiwan	26	7
与港澳台商合资经营	Joint-venture Enterprises	13	3
与港澳台商合作经营	Cooperative Enterprises	2	1
港澳台商独资	Enterprises with Sole Investment	10	3
港澳台商投资股份有限公司	Share-holding Corporations Ltd. With their Investment	1	
其他港澳台投资	Other		
外商投资	Foreign Funded Enterprises	99	23
中外合资经营	Joint-venture Enterprises	49	12
中外合作经营	Cooperation Enterprises		
外资企业	Foreign Capital Enterprise	46	9
外商投资股份有限公司	Share-holding Corporations Ltd. With Foreign Funds	4	2
其他外商投资	Other		
按轻重工业分	**Grouped by Light Industry and Heavy Industry**		
轻工业	Light Industry	35	11
重工业	Heavy Industry	90	19
按企业规模分	**Grouped by Size of Enterprises**		
大型企业	Large-size	11	2
中型企业	Medium-size	32	6
小型企业	Small-size	76	18
微型企业	Microenterprise	6	4
按工业行业大类分	**Grouped by Sector**		
煤炭开采和洗选业	Mining and Washing of Coal		
石油和天然气开采业	Extraction of Petroleum and Natural Gas		
黑色金属矿采选业	Mining and Processing of Ferrous Metal Ores		
有色金属矿采选业	Mining and Processing of Non-ferrous Metal Ores		
非金属矿采选业	Mining and Processing of Nonmetal Ores		
开采专业及辅助性活动	Mining Professional and Auxiliary Activity		
其他采矿业	Mining of Other Ores		

Major Economic Indicators of Foreign,Hong Kong,Macao and Taiwan Invested Industrial Enterprises above Designated Size(2021)

(10 000 yuan)

平均用工人数（人） Average Number of Employed Persons (person)	资产总计 Total Assets			
		流动资产合计 Total Working Capitals	固定资产原价 Origing Value of Fixed Assets	
				累计折旧 Accumulative Total Depreciation
72347	**22749710**	**9139897**	**22469776**	**11289463**
9861	1595085	753127	829763	338702
8350	1416493	717240	621043	239091
4662	1007520	464570	426072	127872
113	8959	7729	1198	852
3231	258412	173200	168426	104260
344	141602	71740	25348	6106
63997	21333217	8422657	21848732	11050372
40614	8186917	5649184	2585856	1264287
22303	12671829	2564312	19143052	9725078
1080	474471	209161	119824	61007
16645	3054364	1646773.9	1552118	742647
55702	19695347	7493122.9	20917658	10546816
47143	17747499	5892148	20384210	10205749
16764	2871825	1967923	1001175	513110
8105	2021469	1195916	1060487	564524
335	108917	83910	23903	6081

12-7 续表1

单位：万元

分 组	Classify	负债合计 Total Liabilites	流动负债合计 Total Working Liabilities
总计	**Total**	**10400487**	**9267133**
#亏损企业	Deficit Enterprises	1211536	1045767
按登记注册类型分	**Grouped by Type of Registration**		
港澳台商投资	Enterprises with Funds from Hong Kong, Macao &Taiwan	979689	810922
与港澳台商合资经营	Joint-venture Enterprises	768162	609734
与港澳台商合作经营	Cooperative Enterprises	2665	2665
港澳台商独资	Enterprises with Sole Investment	114322	106083
港澳台商投资股份有限公司	Share-holding Corporations Ltd. With their Investment	94539	92439
其他港澳台投资	Other		
外商投资	Foreign Funded Enterprises	9420799	8456211
中外合资经营	Joint-venture Enterprises	5246209	4860189
中外合作经营	Cooperation Enterprises		
外资企业	Foreign Capital Enterprise	3947590	3400698
外商投资股份有限公司	Share-holding Corporations Ltd. With Foreign Funds	227000	195324
其他外商投资	Other		
按轻重工业分	**Grouped by Light Industry and Heavy Industry**		
轻工业	Light Industry	1760426	1547751
重工业	Heavy Industry	8640062	7719381
按企业规模分	**Grouped by Size of Enterprises**		
大型企业	Large-size	7880451	7124960
中型企业	Medium-size	1533848	1417402
小型企业	Small-size	929950	685057
微型企业	Microenterprise	56238	39713
按工业行业大类分	**Grouped by Sector**		
煤炭开采和洗选业	Mining and Washing of Coal		
石油和天然气开采业	Extraction of Petroleum and Natural Gas		
黑色金属矿采选业	Mining and Processing of Ferrous Metal Ores		
有色金属矿采选业	Mining and Processing of Non-ferrous Metal Ores		
非金属矿采选业	Mining and Processing of Nonmetal Ores		
开采专业及辅助性活动	Mining Professional and Auxiliary Activity		
其他采矿业	Mining of Other Ores		

continued 1

(10 000 yuan)

所有者权益合计 Total Owners' Equities	实收资本 Total Capital Hold	营业收入 Total Revenue	主营业务收入 Revenue from Principal Business	营业成本 Total Cost	税金及附加 Taxs and Other Changes
12349222	**5418256**	**16065507**	**15696330**	**13473979**	**190996**
383548	427528	1015298	942517	989494	4902
436804	267232	1089915	1031195	951783	5608
239358	179681	657842	607059	658974	2782
6294	1281	6028	5764	3914	26
144090	83487	348383	341184	276001	1844
47063	2784	77662	77189	12894	956
11912418	5151024	14975591	14665135	12522196	185388
2940708	1234140	8557648	8276452	7275451	132313
8724239	3859436	6345634	6319687	5194604	52212
247471	57448	72309	68996	52142	862
1293938	536558	2895431	2833258	2036425	17684
11055285	4881698	13170076	12863072	11437555	173311
9867047	4108689	12247884	11963579	10492986	168633
1337977	560866	2298499	2260373	1810422	13771
1091519	715314	1447852	1430193	1103907	8352
52679	33387	71272	42186	66663	241

12-7 续表2

单位：万元

分　组	Classify	销售费用 Expenses for Sales	管理费用 Expenses for Management	研发费用 R&D Expenses
总计	**Total**	**638160**	**550683**	**388760**
#亏损企业	Deficit Enterprises	83318	70666	17054
按登记注册类型分	**Grouped by Type of Registration**			
港澳台商投资	Enterprises with Funds from Hong Kong, Macao &Taiwan	67273	51956	17174
与港澳台商合资经营	Joint-venture Enterprises	19407	33307	8410
与港澳台商合作经营	Cooperative Enterprises	239	327	1283
港澳台商独资	Enterprises with Sole Investment	38950	14623	5140
港澳台商投资股份有限公司	Share-holding Corporations Ltd. With their Investment	8676	3698	2341
其他港澳台投资	Other			
外商投资	Foreign Funded Enterprises	570887	498727	371586
中外合资经营	Joint-venture Enterprises	432295	313716	74638
中外合作经营	Cooperation Enterprises			
外资企业	Foreign Capital Enterprise	134660	174874	292895
外商投资股份有限公司	Share-holding Corporations Ltd. With Foreign Funds	3932	10137	4053
其他外商投资	Other			
按轻重工业分	**Grouped by Light Industry and Heavy Industry**			
轻工业	Light Industry	431622	192882	18781
重工业	Heavy Industry	206538	357800	369979
按企业规模分	**Grouped by Size of Enterprises**			
大型企业	Large-size	471661	349612	307405
中型企业	Medium-size	102839	112324	45702
小型企业	Small-size	63331	85942	35224
微型企业	Microenterprise	329	2804	429
按工业行业大类分	**Grouped by Sector**			
煤炭开采和洗选业	Mining and Washing of Coal			
石油和天然气开采业	Extraction of Petroleum and Natural Gas			
黑色金属矿采选业	Mining and Processing of Ferrous Metal Ores			
有色金属矿采选业	Mining and Processing of Non-ferrous Metal Ores			
非金属矿采选业	Mining and Processing of Nonmetal Ores			
开采专业及辅助性活动	Mining Professional and Auxiliary Activity			
其他采矿业	Mining of Other Ores			

continued 2

(10 000 yuan)

财务费用 Financial cost	营业利润 Operating Profit	利润总额 Total Profits	亏损企业亏损总额 Total Loss of Deficit Enterprises	利税总额 Total Pre-tax Profits	应付职工薪酬 Salary Payable	本年应交增值税 Value Added Tax Payable
77194	**1598306**	**1591115**	**118861**	**1997593**	**1189437**	**215482**
9816	-122286	-118861	118861	-102731	115419	11228
4102	79355	78150	51745	97232	111533	13474
2127	-30614	-30657	48791	-25060	66630	2815
14	148	227	282	463	1250	209
1967	10035	10894	2671	19827	39675	7089
-6	99785	97686		102003	3978	3361
73092	1518951	1512964	67116	1900361	1077905	202009
17332	365405	364493	39276	660827	665792	164020
50950	1156732	1147655	18311	1235917	404690	36049
4810	-3186	816	9529	3617	7422	1940
17481	267076	266919	22892	363949	299927	79346
59712	1331231	1324196	95969	1633644	889510	136136
48961	1186468	1170143	51556	1456056	868780	117280
12681	267068	275726	26523	361899	200539	72403
14120	145371	146175	34510	177937	117146	23410
1431	-600	-928	6273	1701	2972	2389

12-7 续表3

单位：万元

分组	Classify	企业单位数（个） Number of Enterprises (unit)	亏损企业 Loss Making Enterprises
农副食品加工业	Processing of Food from Agricultural Porducts	1	
食品制造业	Manufacture of Foods	6	2
酒、饮料和精制茶制造业	Manufacture of Alcohol,Beverages and Tea	7	3
烟草制品业	Manufacture of Tobacco		
纺织业	Manufacture of Textile		
纺织服装、服饰业	Textile, apparel industry		
皮革、毛皮、羽毛及其制品和制鞋业	Manufacture of Leather, Fur, Feather and Related Products, and Shoes		
木材加工和木、竹、藤、棕、草制品业	Processing of Timber,Manufacture of Wood,Plam and Straw Products		
家具制造业	Manufacture of Furniture		
造纸和纸制品业	Manufacture of Paper and Paper Products	2	
印刷和记录媒介复制业	Printing,Reproduction of Recording Media	1	
文教、工美、体育和娱乐用品制造业	Manufacture of Articles For Cultural,Educational and Sports Activities	1	
石油、煤炭和其他燃料加工业	Petroleum, coal and other fuel processing industries	1	
化学原料及化学制品制造业	Manufacture of Raw Chemical Materials and Chemical Products	9	3
医药制造业	Manufacture of Medicines	5	2
化学纤维制造业	Manufacture of Chemical Fibers	2	
橡胶和塑料制品业	Manufacture of Rubber and Plastics	1	
非金属矿物制品业	Manufacture of Non-metallic Mineral Products	7	1
黑色金属冶炼和压延加工业	Smelting and Pressing of Ferrous Metals		
有色金属冶炼和压延加工业	Smelting and Pressing of Non-ferrous Metals	3	2
金属制品业	Manufacture of Metal Products	5	
通用设备制造业	Manufacture of General Purpose Machinery	6	3
专用设备制造业	Manufacture of Special Equipment	12	3
汽车制造业	Manufacture of Motor Vehicle	11	
铁路、船舶、航空航天和其他运输设备制造业	Railways,Shipbuilding,Aerospace and Other Transportation Equipment Manufacturing Industry	4	
电气机械和器材制造业	Manufacture of Electric Equipment and Machinery	11	3
计算机、通讯和其他电子设备制造业	Manufacture of Communication Equipment, Computers and other Electronic Equipment	14	1
仪器仪表制造业	Manufacture of Measuring Instruments and Machinery	3	1
其他制造业	Manufacture of Other Manufacturing	1	1
废弃资源综合利用业	Recycling and Disposal of Waste		
金属制品、机械和设备修理业	Metal Products,Machinery and Equipment Repair Industry	8	3
电力、热力生产和供应业	Production and Supply of Electric Power and Heat Power	1	
燃气生产和供应业	Gas Mining and Supplying Industry	2	2
水的生产和供应业	Production and Supply of Water	1	

continued 3

(10 000 yuan)

平均用工人数（人） Average Number of Employed Persons (person)	资产总计 Total Assets	流动资产合计 Total Working Capitals	固定资产原价 Origing Value of Fixed Assets	累计折旧 Accumulative Total Depreciation
32	1513	1337	234	81
4579	277995	149715	202653	111653
3873	638223	272185	381532	232764
303	42449	18154	19810	9849
35	2933	2537	419	131
160	6785	6242	656	329
413	217990	187284	2203	1123
963	562610	251917	468519	228068
4650	1057632	686069	378017	104213
394	115563	64685	138953	92430
44	15790	9012	5857	678
1274	385364	252152	226000	111094
269	44998	21588	27327	7946
689	92023	55208	68440	34758
1672	167041	113848	85687	47536
2404	488653	384515	113990	61746
29963	5240392	3674341	1416607	708377
1093	223691	202122	25245	18720
3194	1024123	578444	488240	231704
12084	11038927	1674645	17943038	9137568
692	121426	113382	21114	13916
45	1369	1141	1015	788
681	127065	67224	46981	16587
54	122113	29641	582	209
2763	707588	317039	406599	117143
24	25457	5471	60	52

12-7 续表4

单位：万元

分组	Classify	负债合计 Total Liabilites	流动负债合计 Total Working Liabilities
农副食品加工业	Processing of Food from Agricultural Porducts	674	674
食品制造业	Manufacture of Foods	182237	172955
酒、饮料和精制茶制造业	Manufacture of Alcohol,Beverages and Tea	373334	346118
烟草制品业	Manufacture of Tobacco		
纺织业	Manufacture of Textile		
纺织服装、服饰业	Textile, apparel industry		
皮革、毛皮、羽毛及其制品和制鞋业	Manufacture of Leather, Fur, Feather and Related Products, and Shoes		
木材加工和木、竹、藤、棕、草制品业	Processing of Timber,Manufacture of Wood,Plam and Straw Products		
家具制造业	Manufacture of Furniture		
造纸和纸制品业	Manufacture of Paper and Paper Products	24706	15249
印刷和记录媒介复制业	Printing,Reproduction of Recording Media	1022	1022
文教、工美、体育和娱乐用品制造业	Manufacture of Articles For Cultural,Educational and Sports Activities	176	125
石油、煤炭和其他燃料加工业	Petroleum, coal and other fuel processing industries	186439	186408
化学原料及化学制品制造业	Manufacture of Raw Chemical Materials and Chemical Products	273839	161055
医药制造业	Manufacture of Medicines	603605	516404
化学纤维制造业	Manufacture of Chemical Fibers	44587	44587
橡胶和塑料制品业	Manufacture of Rubber and Plastics	7869	7165
非金属矿物制品业	Manufacture of Non-metallic Mineral Products	208705	188870
黑色金属冶炼和压延加工业	Smelting and Pressing of Ferrous Metals		
有色金属冶炼和压延加工业	Smelting and Pressing of Non-ferrous Metals	37992	32898
金属制品业	Manufacture of Metal Products	61094	56768
通用设备制造业	Manufacture of General Purpose Machinery	78360	65705
专用设备制造业	Manufacture of Special Equipment	215766	205639
汽车制造业	Manufacture of Motor Vehicle	3700812	3490903
铁路、船舶、航空航天和其他运输设备制造业	Railways,Shipbuilding,Aerospace and Other Transportation Equipment Manufacturing Industry	51383	47628
电气机械和器材制造业	Manufacture of Electric Equipment and Machinery	613421	529050
计算机、通讯和其他电子设备制造业	Manufacture of Communication Equipment, Computers and other Electronic Equipment	2932291	2584197
仪器仪表制造业	Manufacture of Measuring Instruments and Machinery	31156	29316
其他制造业	Manufacture of Other Manufacturing	144	144
废弃资源综合利用业	Recycling and Disposal of Waste		
金属制品、机械和设备修理业	Metal Products,Machinery and Equipment Repair Industry	60928	37123
电力、热力生产和供应业	Production and Supply of Electric Power and Heat Power	65482	602
燃气生产和供应业	Gas Mining and Supplying Industry	629816	542205
水的生产和供应业	Production and Supply of Water	14649	4324

continued 4

(10 000 yuan)

所有者权益合计 Total Owners' Equities	实收资本 Total Capital Hold	营业收入 Total Revenue	主营业务收入 Revenue from Principal Business	营业成本 Total Cost	税金及附加 Taxs and Other Changes
839	20	3513	3488	2755	15
95758	58838	399250	391663	304621	3250
264889	95153	425098	411195	315343	2746
17744	7397	65598	61744	56813	182
1911	120	3096	3096	2625	8
6609	2465	3500	3351	2941	36
31551	33660	361642	361575	344197	1349
288772	182918	353470	351490	226138	2139
454026	80632	1096279	1061419	682749	8516
70975	45800	132408	131679	101393	1084
7920	8000	9429	9049	8199	86
176658	48700	221329	204011	162564	1484
7007	18482	19482	16575	16613	193
30930	29103	125640	124348	112143	700
88680	85267	146000	145643	130454	697
272887	91135	409925	409050	316687	1876
1539579	599135	5707461	5504761	5140113	118815
172308	35152	114482	113676	83288	797
410701	389043	988749	985530	801231	2488
8106637	3360650	4772566	4759204	3968007	41420
90270	10128	84804	84804	52544	705
1224	714	979	955	981	5
66137	87440	71168	57026	61785	266
56631	40398	21883	21874	7657	293
77772	100420	524006	475470	570982	1820
10808	7489	3753	3655	1158	29

12-7 续表5

单位：万元

分组	Classify	销售费用 Expenses for Sales	管理费用 Expenses for Management	研发费用 R&D Expenses
农副食品加工业	Processing of Food from Agricultural Porducts	33	156	
食品制造业	Manufacture of Foods	60742	16741	1837
酒、饮料和精制茶制造业	Manufacture of Alcohol,Beverages and Tea	84620	16521	482
烟草制品业	Manufacture of Tobacco			
纺织业	Manufacture of Textile			
纺织服装、服饰业	Textile, apparel industry			
皮革、毛皮、羽毛及其制品和制鞋业	Manufacture of Leather, Fur, Feather and Related Products, and Shoes			
木材加工和木、竹、藤、棕、草制品业	Processing of Timber,Manufacture of Wood,Plam and Straw Products			
家具制造业	Manufacture of Furniture			
造纸和纸制品业	Manufacture of Paper and Paper Products	2662	1127	
印刷和记录媒介复制业	Printing,Reproduction of Recording Media	166	74	
文教、工美、体育和娱乐用品制造业	Manufacture of Articles For Cultural,Educational and Sports Activities		117	
石油、煤炭和其他燃料加工业	Petroleum, coal and other fuel processing industries		2614	
化学原料及化学制品制造业	Manufacture of Raw Chemical Materials and Chemical Products	18262	12309	4050
医药制造业	Manufacture of Medicines	220421	129055	3110
化学纤维制造业	Manufacture of Chemical Fibers	929	4742	
橡胶和塑料制品业	Manufacture of Rubber and Plastics	411	561	
非金属矿物制品业	Manufacture of Non-metallic Mineral Products	1538	9736	4733
黑色金属冶炼和压延加工业	Smelting and Pressing of Ferrous Metals			
有色金属冶炼和压延加工业	Smelting and Pressing of Non-ferrous Metals	421	1331	1069
金属制品业	Manufacture of Metal Products	2066	5281	924
通用设备制造业	Manufacture of General Purpose Machinery	7134	7293	2337
专用设备制造业	Manufacture of Special Equipment	12975	25720	13705
汽车制造业	Manufacture of Motor Vehicle	116204	129289	49071
铁路、船舶、航空航天和其他运输设备制造业	Railways,Shipbuilding,Aerospace and Other Transportation Equipment Manufacturing Industry	4928	5183	6340
电气机械和器材制造业	Manufacture of Electric Equipment and Machinery	74868	34563	10265
计算机、通讯和其他电子设备制造业	Manufacture of Communication Equipment, Computers and other Electronic Equipment	5937	117311	287947
仪器仪表制造业	Manufacture of Measuring Instruments and Machinery	6493	2049	1599
其他制造业	Manufacture of Other Manufacturing	111	100	
废弃资源综合利用业	Recycling and Disposal of Waste			
金属制品、机械和设备修理业	Metal Products,Machinery and Equipment Repair Industry	257	8009	1291
电力、热力生产和供应业	Production and Supply of Electric Power and Heat Power		1168	
燃气生产和供应业	Gas Mining and Supplying Industry	16983	19528	
水的生产和供应业	Production and Supply of Water		106	

continued 5

(10 000 yuan)

财务费用 Financial cost	营业利润 Operating Profit	利润总额 Total Profits	亏损企业亏损总额 Total Loss of Deficit Enterprises	利税总额 Total Pre-tax Profits	应付职工薪酬 Salary Payable	本年应交增值税 Value Added Tax Payable
4	550	558		675	288	101
313	14427	14511	8916	33227	43738	15466
3218	1173	5659	9661	21045	46099	12639
875	6764	6872		8411	2852	1357
18	206	208		265	197	49
9	537	537		1026	1523	453
-311	15226	15224		49172	2238	32600
5032	137596	135316	2380	142342	15040	4887
4802	62237	59099	560	113270	156604	45655
-194	23511	23408		30458	7240	5966
35	85	156		242	565	
2949	40599	41390	2577	48537	12092	5663
402	-455	-472	1156	786	3889	1065
1354	3144	3135		5110	8916	1276
1021	-3579	-3413	7702	-3015	20855	-299
2310	38831	39151	2861	46776	37428	5749
4063	173697	174202		369707	399147	76690
-176	15041	15171		20239	22861	4271
8224	77513	83103	8368	85121	55802	-469
39975	1003907	989894	21234	1033422	285890	2108
542	22746	22914	182	24273	9612	654
-4	-283	-282	282	-244	356	33
556	-914	-885	6615	1222	12416	1842
2825	9941	9946		5299	1078	-4940
-1024	-46277	-46368	46368	-41574	42425	2974
377	2083	2083		1804	286	-308

12-8 规模以上大中型工业企业主要经济指标（2021年）

单位：万元

分 组	Classify	企业单位数（个） Number of Enterprises (unit)	亏损企业 Loss Making Enterprises
总计	**Total**	**265**	**47**
#亏损企业	Deficit Enterprises	47	47
按隶属关系分	**Grouped by Jurisdiction of Management**		
#中央企业	Central Enterprises	62	7
地方企业	Provincial Enterprises	75	15
按登记注册类型分	**Grouped by Registration Type**		
内资企业	Domestic Investment Enterprises	222	39
国有	State-owned Enterprises	13	1
集体	Collective-owned Enterprises		
股份合作	Share-holding Cooperative	1	
联营	Joint Ownership Enterprises		
有限责任公司	Limited Liability Corporations	122	19
股份有限公司	Share-holding Corporation Ltd.	41	9
私营	Private Enterprises	45	10
其他	Other Domestic Funded Enterprises		
港澳台商投资	Enterprises with Funds from Hong Kong,Macao and Taiwan	9	2
外商投资	Foreign Funded Enterprises	34	6
按轻重工业分	**Grouped by Light Industry and Heavy Industry**		
轻工业	Light Industry	56	12
重工业	Heavy Industry	209	35
按企业规模分	**Grouped by Size of Enterprises**		
大型企业	Large-size	67	13
中型企业	Medium-size	198	34

Major Economic Indicators of Large and Medium-sized Industrial Enterprises above Designated Size (2021)

(10 000 yuan)

平均用工人数（人）Average Number of Employed Persons (person)	资产总计 Total Assets	流动资产合计 Total Working Capitals	固定资产原价 Origing Value of Fixed Assets	累计折旧 Accumulative Total Depreciation
394615	**91704018**	**53553670**	**44930985**	**22004760**
80719	18420818	11481603	6435086	2696876
137450	23803692	15092666	11706578	6529548
91844	22958966	14816292	7561805	3632643
330708	71084694	45693599	23545600	11285901
53271	6066625	2511188	5700399	2992993
322	84108	67871	8774	3908
172106	30148168	19246113	11710844	5946279
50460	22861455	14988440	3703768	1831737
54549	11924338	8879988	2421815	510984
7100	1129497	571058	581330	219828
56807	19489827	7289013	20804055	10499031
46647	6959247	4003824	2658632	1236796
347968	84744771	49549846	42272353	20767964
292220	70151973	39445046	39417289	19657422
102395	21552045	14108624	5513696	2347338

12-8 续表1

单位：万元

分组	Classify	负债合计 Total Liabilites	流动负债合计 Total Working Liabilities
总计	**Total**	**51165254**	**44943840**
#亏损企业	Deficit Enterprises	12657856	11032075
按隶属关系分	**Grouped by Jurisdiction of Management**		
#中央企业	Central Enterprises	14154519	12154627
地方企业	Provincial Enterprises	13269026	11033376
按登记注册类型分	**Grouped by Registration Type**		
内资企业	Domestic Investment Enterprises	41750955	36401477
国有	State-owned Enterprises	3850959	2835827
集体	Collective-owned Enterprises		
股份合作	Share-holding Cooperative	75308	67744
联营	Joint Ownership Enterprises		
有限责任公司	Limited Liability Corporations	16969546	14294081
股份有限公司	Share-holding Corporation Ltd.	12204803	11205646
私营	Private Enterprises	8650339	7998179
其他	Other Domestic Funded Enterprises		
港澳台商投资	Enterprises with Funds from Hong Kong,Macao and Taiwan	833358	740647
外商投资	Foreign Funded Enterprises	8580941	7801716
按轻重工业分	**Grouped by Light Industry and Heavy Industry**		
轻工业	Light Industry	3759158	3173011
重工业	Heavy Industry	47406096	41770829
按企业规模分	**Grouped by Size of Enterprises**		
大型企业	Large-size	40306476	36039927
中型企业	Medium-size	10858778	8903912

continued 1

(10 000 yuan)

所有者权益合计 Total Owners' Equities	实收资本 Total Capital Hold	营业收入 Total Revenue	主营业务收入 Revenue from Principal Business	营业成本 Total Cost	税金及附加 Taxs and Other Changes
40538763	**14793788**	**64908582**	**63028755**	**57363807**	**381696**
5762961	3006700	15201672	14115874	14782797	51185
9649174	4671741	13020046	12810484	11642533	55863
9689940	3261551	15612957	14404487	14196841	70715
29333738	10124233	50362199	48804803	45060398	199292
2215666	1187514	4230053	4176676	3950582	14894
8800	1572	46422	46422	40384	1102
13178622	5747610	23098026	21780804	20486088	110973
10656652	2207019	10048774	9953098	8913173	33382
3273999	980518	12938924	12847803	11670171	38942
296139	173544	914021	858037	810810	4846
10908886	4496012	13632363	13365915	11492599	177557
3200089	1061812	5841094	5731413	4085246	45073
37338674	13731975	59067488	57297341	53278561	336622
29845497	11103649	51064871	49469329	46331921	299421
10693266	3690138	13843712	13559426	11031886	82275

12-8 续表2

单位：万元

分　组	Classify	销售费用 Expenses for Sales	管理费用 Expenses for Management	研发费用 R&D Expenses
总计	**Total**	**1661946**	**1803506**	**1445310**
#亏损企业	Deficit Enterprises	299652	309252	255660
按隶属关系分	**Grouped by Jurisdiction of Management**			
#中央企业	Central Enterprises	129467	545365	333330
地方企业	Provincial Enterprises	270209	403320	326057
按登记注册类型分	**Grouped by Registration Type**			
内资企业	Domestic Investment Enterprises	1087446	1341570	1092203
国有	State-owned Enterprises	6966	151141	60607
集体	Collective-owned Enterprises			
股份合作	Share-holding Cooperative	2623	458	
联营	Joint Ownership Enterprises			
有限责任公司	Limited Liability Corporations	563688	730290	540682
股份有限公司	Share-holding Corporation Ltd.	195785	279998	180742
私营	Private Enterprises	318385	179683	310172
其他	Other Domestic Funded Enterprises			
港澳台商投资	Enterprises with Funds from Hong Kong,Macao and Taiwan	63859	44957	13696
外商投资	Foreign Funded Enterprises	510642	416979	339411
按轻重工业分	**Grouped by Light Industry and Heavy Industry**			
轻工业	Light Industry	846743	333845	64681
重工业	Heavy Industry	815203	1469661	1380629
按企业规模分	**Grouped by Size of Enterprises**			
大型企业	Large-size	1012910	1256305	929590
中型企业	Medium-size	649037	547200	515720

continued 2

(10 000 yuan)

财务费用 Financial cost	营业利润 Operating Profit	利润总额 Total Profits	亏损企业亏损总额 Total Loss of Deficit Enterprises	利税总额 Total Pre-tax Profits	应付职工薪酬 Salary Payable	本年应交增值税 Value Added Tax Payable
232661	**3474238**	**3483149**	**594880**	**4762505**	**5482922**	**897661**
80352	-588679	-594880	594880	-454784	1062260	88912
46882	380541	397621	87984	684869	2233554	231385
16577	507180	514442	201742	799353	1136763	214196
171018	2020702	2037280	516802	2944550	4413603	707977
19206	51288	61645	19173	191045	638116	114507
1469	862	905		2217	1948	211
46052	818892	839540	212983	1310143	2300349	359630
19014	752339	753530	96727	896336	923127	109425
85278	397322	381662	187920	544809	550064	124205
27	63076	61711	48536	82333	99302	15776
61616	1390460	1384157	29542	1735622	970017	173908
19148	594659	599853	47877	814814	606761	169887
213513	2879580	2883295	547003	3947691	4876161	727774
153095	2220432	2203484	416984	3055169	4176977	552263
79565	1253806	1279664	177896	1707336	1305945	345397

12-8 续表3

单位：万元

分组	Classify	企业单位数（个） Number of Enterprises (unit)	亏损企业 Loss Making Enterprises
按控股情况分	**Grouped by Cast strand**		
国有控股	State owned shares	137	22
集体控股	Collective shares	2	1
私人控股	Private holdings	91	18
港澳台控股	Hong Kong, Macao and Taiwan Holdings	7	
外商投资	Foreign Investment	28	6
其他	Others		
按工业行业大类分	**Grouped by Sector**		
煤炭开采和洗选业	Mining and Washing of Coal		
石油和天然气开采业	Extraction of Petroleum and Natural Gas		
黑色金属矿采选业	Mining and Processing of Ferrous Metal Ores		
有色金属矿采选业	Mining and Processing of Non-ferrous Metal Ores		
非金属矿采选业	Mining and Processing of Nonmetal Ores		
开采专业及辅助性活动	Mining Professional and Auxiliary Activity	2	1
其他采矿业	Mining of other Ores		
农副食品加工业	Processing of Food from Agricultural Porducts	4	
食品制造业	Manufacture of Foods	14	4
酒、饮料和精制茶制造业	Manufacture of Alcohol,Beverages and Tea	6	2
烟草制品业	Manufacture of Tobacco	1	
纺织业	Manufacture of Textile	3	1
纺织服装、服饰业	Textile, apparel industry		
皮革、毛皮、羽毛及其制品和制鞋业	Manufacture of Leather, Fur, Feather and Related Products, and Shoes	1	1
木材加工和木、竹、藤、棕、草制品业	Processing of Timber, Manufacture of Wood,Plam and Straw Products		
家具制造业	Manufacture of Furniture	1	
造纸和纸制品业	Manufacture of Paper and Paper Products		
印刷和记录媒介复制业	Printing,Reproduction of Recording Media	4	2

continued 3

(10 000 yuan)

平均用工人数（人） Average Number of Employed Persons (person)	资产总计 Total Assets	流动资产合计 Total Working Capitals	固定资产原价 Origing Value of Fixed Assets	累计折旧 Accumulative Total Depreciation
229294	46762658	29908958	19268383	10162191
816	82320	58548	29557	14632
131952	29861301	19470049	5924096	1844236
3965	460661	280663	230168	149844
28588	14537078	3835451	19478781	9833857
14492	1549516	1004828	1243208	913122
1452	148119	84157	17703	8037
10226	605501	349460	336736	182963
5270	835209	378564	399601	222045
523	42943	26297	31621	18233
3589	211770	49929	189547	79023
585	63528	39751	8780	6249
251	24059	17521	6577	264
3145	461934	267321	345916	263432

12-8 续表4

单位：万元

分 组	Classify	负债合计 Total Liabilites	流动负债合计 Total Working Liabilities
按控股情况分	**Grouped by Cast strand**		
国有控股	State owned shares	27423545	23188002
集体控股	Collective shares	41089	40737
私人控股	Private holdings	18443195	17049696
港澳台控股	Hong Kong, Macao and Taiwan Holdings	204758	194627
外商投资	Foreign Investment	5052668	4470778
其他	Others		
按工业行业大类分	**Grouped by Sector**		
煤炭开采和洗选业	Mining and Washing of Coal		
石油和天然气开采业	Extraction of Petroleum and Natural Gas		
黑色金属矿采选业	Mining and Processing of Ferrous Metal Ores		
有色金属矿采选业	Mining and Processing of Non-ferrous Metal Ores		
非金属矿采选业	Mining and Processing of Nonmetal Ores		
开采专业及辅助性活动	Mining Professional and Auxiliary Activity	671018	569381
其他采矿业	Mining of other Ores		
农副食品加工业	Processing of Food from Agricultural Porducts	44312	43312
食品制造业	Manufacture of Foods	400084	376287
酒、饮料和精制茶制造业	Manufacture of Alcohol,Beverages and Tea	452201	374994
烟草制品业	Manufacture of Tobacco	4957	4957
纺织业	Manufacture of Textile	139433	31708
纺织服装、服饰业	Textile, apparel industry		
皮革、毛皮、羽毛及其制品和制鞋业	Manufacture of Leather, Fur, Feather and Related Products, and Shoes	21189	19421
木材加工和木、竹、藤、棕、草制品业	Processing of Timber, Manufacture of Wood,Plam and Straw Products		
家具制造业	Manufacture of Furniture	20045	20045
造纸和纸制品业	Manufacture of Paper and Paper Products		
印刷和记录媒介复制业	Printing,Reproduction of Recording Media	106370	99205

continued 4

(10 000 yuan)

所有者权益合计 Total Owners' Equities	实收资本 Total Capital Hold	营业收入 Total Revenue	主营业务收入 Revenue from Principal Business	营业成本 Total Cost	税金及附加 Taxs and Other Changes
19339113	7933292	28633002	27214971	25839374	126578
41231	22000	46602	41393	33814	462
11418105	2801871	27555536	27190046	24632207	191047
255903	93389	406292	398844	249597	3072
9484410	3943236	8267150	8183501	6608814	60537
878498	578027	1173652	1157049	1081025	5980
103807	15500	258210	257446	222553	499
205417	122407	808215	790734	630384	6033
383007	121161	700465	686761	513129	10800
37986	27400	11494	11399	5258	365
72336	18024	111360	100183	111137	1302
42339	34500	20772	20275	17726	366
4014	3800	10050	10050	8046	39
355564	184152	301422	297553	228590	2882

12-8 续表5

单位：万元

分　组	Classify	销售费用 Expenses for Sales	管理费用 Expenses for Management	研发费用 R&D Expenses
按控股情况分	**Grouped by Cast strand**			
国有控股	State owned shares	399676	948686	659387
集体控股	Collective shares	3701	4630	1476
私人控股	Private holdings	796067	522776	472299
港澳台控股	Hong Kong, Macao and Taiwan Holdings	48849	26143	13696
外商投资	Foreign Investment	413654	301272	298452
其他	Others			
按工业行业大类分	**Grouped by Sector**			
煤炭开采和洗选业	Mining and Washing of Coal			
石油和天然气开采业	Extraction of Petroleum and Natural Gas			
黑色金属矿采选业	Mining and Processing of Ferrous Metal Ores			
有色金属矿采选业	Mining and Processing of Non-ferrous Metal Ores			
非金属矿采选业	Mining and Processing of Nonmetal Ores			
开采专业及辅助性活动	Mining Professional and Auxiliary Activity	683	32903	51385
其他采矿业	Mining of other Ores			
农副食品加工业	Processing of Food from Agricultural Porducts	7157	3963	2388
食品制造业	Manufacture of Foods	97640	32982	4504
酒、饮料和精制茶制造业	Manufacture of Alcohol,Beverages and Tea	105838	20381	1756
烟草制品业	Manufacture of Tobacco	909	2989	
纺织业	Manufacture of Textile	562	5547	
纺织服装、服饰业	Textile, apparel industry			
皮革、毛皮、羽毛及其制品和制鞋业	Manufacture of Leather, Fur, Feather and Related Products, and Shoes	974	1339	663
木材加工和木、竹、藤、棕、草制品业	Processing of Timber, Manufacture of Wood,Plam and Straw Products			
家具制造业	Manufacture of Furniture	42	1637	
造纸和纸制品业	Manufacture of Paper and Paper Products			
印刷和记录媒介复制业	Printing,Reproduction of Recording Media	4754	31639	4726

continued 5

(10 000 yuan)

财务费用 Financial cost	营业利润 Operating Profit	利润总额 Total Profits	亏损企业亏损总额 Total Loss of Deficit Enterprises	利税总额 Total Pre-tax Profits	应付职工薪酬 Salary Payable	本年应交增值税 Value Added Tax Payable
63458	887721	912064	289726	1484222	3370317	445581
235	2431	6544	1048	9310	10188	2303
111520	1209621	1197522	274565	1719660	1461821	331091
1666	112742	111598		126203	50043	11533
55782	1261724	1255420	29542	1423110	590554	107153
-15912	-9479	-11709	14981	59961	350465	65690
-336	22430	22615		26273	14619	3158
1106	39576	40113	10759	69343	83221	23198
-152	54102	59857	9406	86094	46150	15438
-338	2352	2290		3689	4417	1034
87	-7130	-6430	9614	-2930	27767	2199
38	-828	-828	828	-944	3558	-482
	286	285		558	2292	233
2134	30027	29871	1978	47027	72860	14274

12-8 续表6

单位：万元

分组	Classify	企业单位数（个）Number of Enterprises (unit)	亏损企业 Loss Making Enterprises
文教、工美、体育和娱乐用品制造业	Manufacture of Articles For Cultural,Educational and Sports Activities		
石油、煤炭和其他燃料加工业	Petroleum, coal and other fuel processing industries	1	
化学原料及化学制品制造业	Manufacture of Raw Chemical Materials and Chemical Products	8	1
医药制造业	Manufacture of Medicines	13	
化学纤维制造业	Manufacture of Chemical Fibers	1	
橡胶和塑料制品业	Manufacture of Rubber and Plastics	3	1
非金属矿物制品业	Manufacture of Non-metallic Mineral Products	11	
黑色金属冶炼和压延加工业	Smelting and Pressing of Ferrous Metals		
有色金属冶炼和压延加工业	Smelting and Pressing of Non-ferrous Metals	8	3
金属制品业	Manufacture of Metal Products	9	1
通用设备制造业	Manufacture of General Purpose Machinery	12	5
专用设备制造业	Manufacture of Special Equipment	26	4
汽车制造业	Manufacture of Motor Vehicle	22	4
铁路、船舶、航空航天和其他运输设备制造业	Railways,Shipbuilding,Aerospace and Other Transportation Equipment Manufacturing Industry	24	1
电气机械和器材制造业	Manufacture of Electric Equipment and Machinery	28	7
计算机、通讯和其他电子设备制造业	Manufacture of Communication Equipment, Computers and other Electronic Equipment	39	1
仪器仪表制造业	Manufacture of Measuring Instruments and Machinery	8	1
其他制造业	Manufacture of Other Manufacturing		
废弃资源综合利用业	Recycling and Disposal of Waste		
金属制品、机械和设备修理业	Metal Products,Machinery and Equipment Repair Industry	1	
电力、热力生产和供应业	Production and Supply of Electric Power and Heat Power	7	4
燃气生产和供应业	Gas Mining and Supplying Industry	6	2
水的生产和供应业	Production and Supply of Water	2	1

continued 6

(10 000 yuan)

平均用工人数（人）Average Number of Employed Persons (person)	资产总计 Total Assets	流动资产合计 Total Working Capitals	固定资产原价 Origing Value of Fixed Assets	累计折旧 Accumulative Total Depreciation
413	217990	187284	2203	1123
8074	1486454	899712	504080	236495
12551	2315792	1520404	617949	192583
332	51259	30535	25040	4484
2725	629845	258519	301449	86773
5308	1375784	1026765	396304	180135
5725	2637768	1336780	554640	229791
13240	2072183	1325565	831296	381968
10071	3406579	2934854	451949	252545
17438	4399593	3194343	840815	373330
53962	12383440	9032373	2898632	1389921
54579	13581158	9990513	3104761	1593547
48195	12164795	8747567	2696442	853138
59122	22935708	8475733	19982501	9885868
5071	835273	669050	152836	74069
757	18381	16240	1472	430
48290	4322530	827660	6614155	3667817
6482	2362708	679967	1889077	686846
2747	564203	181978	485698	220531

12-8 续表7

单位：万元

分组	Classify	负债合计 Total Liabilites	流动负债合计 Total Working Liabilities
文教、工美、体育和娱乐用品制造业	Manufacture of Articles For Cultural,Educational and Sports Activities		
石油、煤炭和其他燃料加工业	Petroleum, coal and other fuel processing industries	186439	186408
化学原料及化学制品制造业	Manufacture of Raw Chemical Materials and Chemical Products	732035	606631
医药制造业	Manufacture of Medicines	1048593	886916
化学纤维制造业	Manufacture of Chemical Fibers	4766	3768
橡胶和塑料制品业	Manufacture of Rubber and Plastics	336647	257004
非金属矿物制品业	Manufacture of Non-metallic Mineral Products	978098	877281
黑色金属冶炼和压延加工业	Smelting and Pressing of Ferrous Metals		
有色金属冶炼和压延加工业	Smelting and Pressing of Non-ferrous Metals	800032	597616
金属制品业	Manufacture of Metal Products	1615029	1077669
通用设备制造业	Manufacture of General Purpose Machinery	2253794	2177012
专用设备制造业	Manufacture of Special Equipment	2251754	1830086
汽车制造业	Manufacture of Motor Vehicle	8380867	7838107
铁路、船舶、航空航天和其他运输设备制造业	Railways,Shipbuilding,Aerospace and Other Transportation Equipment Manufacturing Industry	7874423	7310064
电气机械和器材制造业	Manufacture of Electric Equipment and Machinery	9189977	8479905
计算机、通讯和其他电子设备制造业	Manufacture of Communication Equipment, Computers and other Electronic Equipment	8396910	7419116
仪器仪表制造业	Manufacture of Measuring Instruments and Machinery	395337	384456
其他制造业	Manufacture of Other Manufacturing		
废弃资源综合利用业	Recycling and Disposal of Waste		
金属制品、机械和设备修理业	Metal Products,Machinery and Equipment Repair Industry	8966	6469
电力、热力生产和供应业	Production and Supply of Electric Power and Heat Power	3013770	2070433
燃气生产和供应业	Gas Mining and Supplying Industry	1404887	1095991
水的生产和供应业	Production and Supply of Water	433322	299598

continued 7

(10 000 yuan)

所有者权益合计 Total Owners' Equities	实收资本 Total Capital Hold	营业收入 Total Revenue	主营业务收入 Revenue from Principal Business	营业成本 Total Cost	税金及附加 Taxs and Other Changes
31551	33660	361642	361575	344197	1349
754419	94127	724334	690148	501456	5583
1267198	172396	1887610	1852752	946539	17312
46493	49252	83532	83532	74682	625
293198	309317	244610	236567	209681	1961
397686	165348	915307	912148	758419	5471
1837736	493139	716482	684323	539562	5506
457154	339485	1240056	1215091	1066108	3306
1152785	386670	1266969	1252198	1084717	7748
2147839	680821	1813428	1799126	1330704	13973
4002572	1319406	14424615	13247540	13472105	145546
5706735	1889957	5481099	5414864	4788384	16025
2974818	1520844	10794571	10584893	9955663	30319
14538798	4617819	15792374	15721052	13931021	72594
439936	153176	538829	535349	425625	2820
9415	10000	24312	24312	21142	291
1308760	1069286	3423502	3366177	3398331	15214
957820	343243	1636549	1585052	1578058	5872
130882	40871	143123	130608	119566	1916

12-8 续表8

单位：万元

分　组	Classify	销售费用 Expenses for Sales	管理费用 Expenses for Management	研发费用 R&D Expenses
文教、工美、体育和娱乐用品制造业	Manufacture of Articles For Cultural,Educational and Sports Activities			
石油、煤炭和其他燃料加工业	Petroleum, coal and other fuel processing industries		2614	
化学原料及化学制品制造业	Manufacture of Raw Chemical Materials and Chemical Products	20411	52229	29889
医药制造业	Manufacture of Medicines	545773	195498	24539
化学纤维制造业	Manufacture of Chemical Fibers	214	1782	1512
橡胶和塑料制品业	Manufacture of Rubber and Plastics	10444	9906	8639
非金属矿物制品业	Manufacture of Non-metallic Mineral Products	21959	28376	24224
黑色金属冶炼和压延加工业	Smelting and Pressing of Ferrous Metals			
有色金属冶炼和压延加工业	Smelting and Pressing of Non-ferrous Metals	10205	37040	38466
金属制品业	Manufacture of Metal Products	9419	57304	42915
通用设备制造业	Manufacture of General Purpose Machinery	34934	66911	43373
专用设备制造业	Manufacture of Special Equipment	76572	111965	78877
汽车制造业	Manufacture of Motor Vehicle	227029	221246	216089
铁路、船舶、航空航天和其他运输设备制造业	Railways,Shipbuilding,Aerospace and Other Transportation Equipment Manufacturing Industry	77548	223642	124575
电气机械和器材制造业	Manufacture of Electric Equipment and Machinery	267208	229622	164337
计算机、通讯和其他电子设备制造业	Manufacture of Communication Equipment, Computers and other Electronic Equipment	83675	281381	547037
仪器仪表制造业	Manufacture of Measuring Instruments and Machinery	17886	23499	25457
其他制造业	Manufacture of Other Manufacturing			
废弃资源综合利用业	Recycling and Disposal of Waste			
金属制品、机械和设备修理业	Metal Products,Machinery and Equipment Repair Industry		2560	324
电力、热力生产和供应业	Production and Supply of Electric Power and Heat Power	428	69921	7196
燃气生产和供应业	Gas Mining and Supplying Industry	30805	41239	2439
水的生产和供应业	Production and Supply of Water	8879	13391	

continued 8

(10 000 yuan)

财务费用 Financial cost	营业利润 Operating Profit	利润总额 Total Profits	亏损企业亏损总额 Total Loss of Deficit Enterprises	利税总额 Total Pre-tax Profits	应付职工薪酬 Salary Payable	本年应交增值税 Value Added Tax Payable
-311	15226	15224		49172	2238	32600
-505	183540	180895	1078	202426	129074	15948
8431	166488	166002		281468	222531	98154
-41	4927	4944		6562	6665	994
7592	-2795	-2796	6226	2065	26016	2900
10867	63871	65593		99005	65316	27942
9844	92470	92647	14900	117845	86456	19692
9296	109429	112867	2600	123539	208584	7365
-19104	65714	70538	36009	108311	155717	30025
7852	237382	239485	26612	307020	274330	53562
-26815	355390	356221	96402	670521	693559	168755
24261	276033	279017	1668	330412	962830	35370
92857	44076	37929	198177	121104	607701	52856
73029	1737775	1724487	33850	1934537	830951	137456
-531	54769	56489	1459	71473	78060	12164
94	34	36		2409	14033	2082
35886	-80354	-73313	80237	2779	364407	60878
10298	20583	20727	47339	35362	105787	8764
3035	-1655	93	760	7424	43320	5415

12-9 规模以上高技术产业工业企业主要经济指标（2021年）

单位：万元

行 业	Sector	企业单位数（个） Number of Enterprises (unit)	亏损企业 Loss Making Enterprises
总计	**Total**	**412**	**65**
一、医药制造业	**Pharmaceutical Manufacturing**	**68**	**20**
（一）化学药品制造	Chemical manufacturing	26	7
化学药品原料药制造	Chemical raw materials Medicine manufacturing	11	4
化学药品制剂制造	Chemical preparations manufacturing	15	3
（二）中药饮片加工	Chinese medicine Pieces processing	3	2
（三）中成药生产	Chinese medicine production	23	8
（四）兽用药品制造	Veterinary pharmaceutical manufacturing	4	1
（五）生物药品制造	Biopharmaceutical manufacturing	5	1
（六）卫生材料及医药用品制造	Sanitary materials and medical supplies manufacturing	1	
（七）药用辅料及包装材料	Pharmaceutical Excipients and Packaging Materials	6	1
二、航空、航天及设备制造业	**Aviation, Aerospace and Equipment Manufacturing Industry**	**76**	**7**
（一）飞机制造	Aircraft Manufacturing	19	1
（二）航天器及运载火箭制造	Spacecraft and Launch Vehicles Manufacturing	2	
（三）航空、航天相关设备制造	Aviation and aerospace-related equipment manufacturing	38	3
（四）其他航空航天器制造	Other aerospace manufacturing	9	
（五）航空航天器修理	Aerospace vehicle repair	8	3
三、电子及通讯设备制造业	**Electronic and communication equipment manufacturing**	**159**	**19**
（一）电子工业专用设备制造	Electronic equipment manufacturing	12	
（二）光纤、光缆及锂离子电池制造	Optical Fiber, Cable and Lithium-ion Battery Manufacturing	4	3
（三）通信设备、雷达及配套设备制造	Communications Equipment, Radar and Ancillary Equipments	38	5
（四）广播电视设备制造	Broadcasting and TV Equipment	2	2
（五）非专业视听设备制造	Non-professional audiovisual equipment manufacturing	2	
（六）电子器件制造	Electronic device manufacturing	44	5
（七）电子元件及电子专用材料制造	Electronic components and electronic materials manufacturing	41	2
（八）智能消费设备制造	Smart consumer device manufacturing	3	
（九）其他电子设备制造	Other electronic equipment manufacturing	13	2
四、计算机及办公设备制造业	**Computer and office equipment manufacturing**	**7**	**1**
（一）计算机整机制造	Computer machine manufacturing	1	
（二）计算机零部件制造	Computer parts manufacturing	1	
（三）计算机外围设备制造	Computer peripheral equipment manufacturing	1	
（四）工业控制计算机及系统制造	Industrial Control Computer and System Manufacturing	4	1
（五）信息安全设备制造	Information Security Equipment Manufacturing		
（六）其他计算机制造	Other computer manufacturing		
（七）办公设备制造	Office Equipment manufacturing		
五、医疗设备及仪器仪表制造业	**Medical equipment and instrumentation manufacturing**	**101**	**17**
（一）医疗仪器设备及器械制造	Medical equipment and device manufacturing	18	4
（二）通用仪器仪表制造	General Measuring Instruments and Machinery Manufacturing	49	9
（三）专用仪器仪表制造	Special Measuring Instruments and Machinery Manufacturing	23	3
（四）光学仪器制造	Optical Instruments Manufacturing	6	
（五）其他仪器仪表制造业	Other instrumentation manufacturing	5	1
六、信息化学品制造业	**Information chemicals manufacturing**	**1**	**1**
信息化学品制造	Information Chemical Manufacturing	1	1

Major Economic Indicators of High Technology Industry

Industrial Enterprises above Designated Size(2021)

(10 000 yuan)

平均用工人数（人）Average Number of Employed Persons (person)	资产总计 Total Assets	流动资产合计 Total Working Capitals	固定资产原价 Origing Value of Fixed Assets	累计折旧 Accumulative Total Depreciation
167730	**46535572**	**24900841**	**25855975**	**12317044**
18921	**3133002**	**2047727**	**872761**	**299344**
8829	1810619	1260059	573917	186363
1276	295269	237438	45102	19029
7553	1515350	1022621	528815	167333
306	71452	22679	42814	3254
7724	914669	572238	196765	80914
337	28771	14272	6913	2332
991	228495	120021	34515	17918
66	4463	2371	2719	690
668	74533	56087	15118	7874
54894	**13651526**	**9926621**	**3234424**	**1615346**
41272	10339629	7970082	2203491	1215879
4022	1528719	734177	544308	206858
7584	1351357	959555	389596	160741
1379	295695	203989	50206	16322
637	136127	58817	46823	15546
78295	**27065892**	**10775991**	**21382624**	**10237479**
1266	288482	247970	32281	10150
6609	1570159	802690	593631	236449
26447	3293526	2528633	820614	431117
230	35037	30916	3739	2125
102	41763	38648	6307	793
27593	13665566	3267155	18799187	9366727
14124	7916347	3656253	1099424	178574
556	67885	55055	7177	3324
1368	187128	148669	20264	8221
713	**155090**	**114331**	**18970**	**4187**
30	2963	2961	8	6
85	6351	5595	1039	342
310	111851	74028	15140	2941
288	33925	31746	2783	899
14772	**2463080**	**2000103**	**321401**	**144722**
3051	662536	537848	67644	23565
5716	676404	566421	70305	33712
3188	667029	553713	61761	34226
2311	389027	301034	114837	49885
506	68084	41087	6855	3333
135	**66982**	**36070**	**25796**	**15967**
135	66982	36070	25796	15967

12-9 续表1

单位：万元

行 业	Sector	负债合计 Total Liabilites	流动负债合计 Total Working Liabilities
总计	**Total**	**21685123**	**18962294**
一、医药制造业	**Pharmaceutical Manufacturing**	**1531759**	**1300782**
（一）化学药品制造	Chemical manufacturing	795115	695426
化学药品原料药制造	Chemical raw materials Medicine manufacturing	63091	54702
化学药品制剂制造	Chemical preparations manufacturing	732024	640724
（二）中药饮片加工	Chinese medicine Pieces processing	55317	27029
（三）中成药生产	Chinese medicine production	598630	514750
（四）兽用药品制造	Veterinary pharmaceutical manufacturing	26440	9927
（五）生物药品制造	Biopharmaceutical manufacturing	34035	32864
（六）卫生材料及医药用品制造	Sanitary materials and medical supplies manufacturing	910	910
（七）药用辅料及包装材料	Pharmaceutical Excipients and Packaging Materials	21312	19876
二、航空、航天及设备制造业	**Aviation, Aerospace and Equipment Manufacturing Industry**	**7891834**	**7228077**
（一）飞机制造	Aircraft Manufacturing	6319601	5936163
（二）航天器及运载火箭制造	Spacecraft and Launch Vehicles Manufacturing	831074	675932
（三）航空、航天相关设备制造	Aviation and aerospace-related equipment manufacturing	606751	511787
（四）其他航空航天器制造	Other aerospace manufacturing	81703	76268
（五）航空航天器修理	Aerospace vehicle repair	52706	27927
三、电子及通讯设备制造业	**Electronic and communication equipment manufacturing**	**10957457**	**9194768**
（一）电子工业专用设备制造	Electronic equipment manufacturing	219075	209160
（二）光纤、光缆及锂离子电池制造	Optical Fiber, Cable and Lithium-ion Battery Manufacturing	1252860	1061139
（三）通信设备、雷达及配套设备制造	Communications Equipment, Radar and Ancillary Equipments	1812585	1483688
（四）广播电视设备制造	Broadcasting and TV Equipment	14036	13973
（五）非专业视听设备制造	Non-professional audiovisual equipment manufacturing	36508	36508
（六）电子器件制造	Electronic device manufacturing	3908115	3208118
（七）电子元件及电子专用材料制造	Electronic components and electronic materials manufacturing	3633286	3110043
（八）智能消费设备制造	Smart consumer device manufacturing	12011	11847
（九）其他电子设备制造	Other electronic equipment manufacturing	68982	60292
四、计算机及办公设备制造业	**Computer and office equipment manufacturing**	**64591**	**62404**
（一）计算机整机制造	Computer machine manufacturing	2193	2193
（二）计算机零部件制造	Computer parts manufacturing	4810	4500
（三）计算机外围设备制造	Computer peripheral equipment manufacturing	39981	39054
（四）工业控制计算机及系统制造	Industrial Control Computer and System Manufacturing	17608	16656
（五）信息安全设备制造	Information Security Equipment Manufacturing		
（六）其他计算机制造	Other computer manufacturing		
（七）办公设备制造	Office Equipment manufacturing		
五、医疗设备及仪器仪表制造业	**Medical equipment and instrumentation manufacturing**	**1155825**	**1092608**
（一）医疗仪器设备及器械制造	Medical equipment and device manufacturing	238227	218456
（二）通用仪器仪表制造	General Measuring Instruments and Machinery Manufacturing	376944	351569
（三）专用仪器仪表制造	Special Measuring Instruments and Machinery Manufacturing	294015	281108
（四）光学仪器制造	Optical Instruments Manufacturing	215801	212737
（五）其他仪器仪表制造业	Other instrumentation manufacturing	30839	28739
六、信息化学品制造业	**Information chemicals manufacturing**	**83656**	**83656**
信息化学品制造	Information Chemical Manufacturing	83656	83656

continued 1

(10 000 yuan)

所有者权益合计 Total Owners' Equities	实收资本 Total Capital Hold	营业收入 Total Revenue	主营业务收入 Revenue from Principal Business	营业成本 Total Cost	税金及附加 Taxs and Other Changes
24850444	**8095916**	**27354091**	**27105701**	**22621040**	**127763**
1601242	**372093**	**2309164**	**2272409**	**1136096**	**22285**
1015503	196327	1617556	1582075	917893	13153
232178	59365	233120	232953	152695	921
783326	136962	1384436	1349123	765198	12232
16135	21000	20547	20542	19058	123
316039	85684	524622	523662	150455	7146
2331	4314	7591	7526	4934	93
194460	47647	81727	81547	16355	1031
3553	500	6767	6767	2563	76
53221	16620	50354	50289	24839	664
5759691	**1917477**	**5186450**	**5109196**	**4482487**	**14584**
4020027	1444604	3956501	3921258	3588575	9404
697645	70000	503736	480722	388711	612
744606	249809	580697	575842	399868	3466
213992	57474	95303	95303	62168	771
83421	95590	50212	36070	43164	331
16108434	**5387934**	**18198270**	**18083637**	**15966377**	**80016**
69407	31401	144732	140775	114120	781
317299	282825	1247635	1227785	1201331	937
1480940	402807	5629194	5605732	5366935	12610
21001	4356	45187	44654	35120	167
5255	1290	54862	54862	53186	21
9757450	3885766	6601377	6565429	5192183	52918
4283061	718507	4343892	4315843	3922041	11748
55874	4443	34286	34286	20942	76
118146	56538	97106	94272	60520	760
90499	**33581**	**71261**	**60890**	**48758**	**527**
770	500	2597	2597	2013	16
1541	1338	8001		6478	4
71870	27600	38483	36143	24821	381
16318	4143	22180	22150	15446	127
1307253	**380832**	**1578914**	**1569539**	**969265**	**10224**
424309	57000	494033	493744	168162	4057
299460	137180	446874	441996	317539	2666
373014	95026	324057	321663	217461	3049
173226	75274	288258	286567	250852	282
37245	16352	25693	25569	15251	171
-16674	**4000**	**10031**	**10031**	**18057**	**127**
-16674	4000	10031	10031	18057	127

12-9 续表2

单位：万元

行 业	Sector	销售费用 Expenses for Sales	管理费用 Expenses for Management
总计	**Total**	**1022311**	**958198**
一、医药制造业	**Pharmaceutical Manufacturing**	**671165**	**236443**
（一）化学药品制造	Chemical manufacturing	370724	163722
化学药品原料药制造	Chemical raw materials Medicine manufacturing	12901	8396
化学药品制剂制造	Chemical preparations manufacturing	357823	155326
（二）中药饮片加工	Chinese medicine Pieces processing	472	2654
（三）中成药生产	Chinese medicine production	244660	57118
（四）兽用药品制造	Veterinary pharmaceutical manufacturing	1095	1010
（五）生物药品制造	Biopharmaceutical manufacturing	48372	7429
（六）卫生材料及医药用品制造	Sanitary materials and medical supplies manufacturing	1384	806
（七）药用辅料及包装材料	Pharmaceutical Excipients and Packaging Materials	4459	3705
二、航空、航天及设备制造业	**Aviation, Aerospace and Equipment Manufacturing Industry**	**59207**	**227516**
（一）飞机制造	Aircraft Manufacturing	44817	147417
（二）航天器及运载火箭制造	Spacecraft and Launch Vehicles Manufacturing	166	25836
（三）航空、航天相关设备制造	Aviation and aerospace-related equipment manufacturing	10006	40493
（四）其他航空航天器制造	Other aerospace manufacturing	3464	8105
（五）航空航天器修理	Aerospace vehicle repair	754	5666
三、电子及通讯设备制造业	**Electronic and communication equipment manufacturing**	**169567**	**397717**
（一）电子工业专用设备制造	Electronic equipment manufacturing	4628	6098
（二）光纤、光缆及锂离子电池制造	Optical Fiber, Cable and Lithium-ion Battery Manufacturing	50142	16445
（三）通信设备、雷达及配套设备制造	Communications Equipment, Radar and Ancillary Equipments	12725	72671
（四）广播电视设备制造	Broadcasting and TV Equipment	2494	6975
（五）非专业视听设备制造	Non-professional audiovisual equipment manufacturing	424	452
（六）电子器件制造	Electronic device manufacturing	62587	168139
（七）电子元件及电子专用材料制造	Electronic components and electronic materials manufacturing	28641	113578
（八）智能消费设备制造	Smart consumer device manufacturing	1680	4202
（九）其他电子设备制造	Other electronic equipment manufacturing	6247	9157
四、计算机及办公设备制造业	**Computer and office equipment manufacturing**	**1778**	**7075**
（一）计算机整机制造	Computer machine manufacturing		118
（二）计算机零部件制造	Computer parts manufacturing	159	202
（三）计算机外围设备制造	Computer peripheral equipment manufacturing	700	4308
（四）工业控制计算机及系统制造	Industrial Control Computer and System Manufacturing	919	2447
（五）信息安全设备制造	Information Security Equipment Manufacturing		
（六）其他计算机制造	Other computer manufacturing		
（七）办公设备制造	Office Equipment manufacturing		
五、医疗设备及仪器仪表制造业	**Medical equipment and instrumentation manufacturing**	**120538**	**88675**
（一）医疗仪器设备及器械制造	Medical equipment and device manufacturing	66026	23063
（二）通用仪器仪表制造	General Measuring Instruments and Machinery Manufacturing	31284	31073
（三）专用仪器仪表制造	Special Measuring Instruments and Machinery Manufacturing	20150	19050
（四）光学仪器制造	Optical Instruments Manufacturing	809	13633
（五）其他仪器仪表制造业	Other instrumentation manufacturing	2270	1856
六、信息化学品制造业	**Information chemicals manufacturing**	**56**	**772**
信息化学品制造	Information Chemical Manufacturing	56	772

continued 2

(10 000 yuan)

研发费用 R&D Expenses	财务费用 Financial cost	营业利润 Operating Profit	利润总额 Total Profits	亏损企业亏损总额 Total Loss of Deficit Enterprises	利税总额 Total Pre-tax Profits	应付职工薪酬 Salary Payable	本年应交增值税 Value Added Tax Payable
918532	**141813**	**2677750**	**2686031**	**143255**	**3182719**	**2489830**	**368925**
47815	**14330**	**198888**	**201795**	**11295**	**349773**	**270789**	**125694**
27741	8235	129646	127062	3849	213069	196857	72854
10972	2906	41880	42303	1273	45980	12333	2756
16769	5329	87766	84759	2576	167089	184525	70098
185	1583	-3008	-2971	2977	-2650	2136	199
13090	3606	51305	55043	2939	105719	51247	43530
158	415	-73	133	30	458	1511	232
3174	325	5892	6215	273	13171	11595	5925
493	8	1490	1423		1994	882	496
2974	159	13636	14890	1227	18013	6562	2459
130702	**28253**	**296365**	**301224**	**8399**	**350415**	**934691**	**34607**
46514	22548	139494	140424	769	163907	681859	14080
43726	2328	48506	48615		49785	122908	558
30144	2274	98108	100722	1015	116618	104325	12431
7887	310	12883	13849		19506	17922	4886
2431	793	-2626	-2384	6615	599	7677	2652
645386	**90180**	**1856948**	**1850646**	**105435**	**2086507**	**1058082**	**155845**
8330	1883	9539	9820		13770	12427	3170
3761	7337	34844	35749	21351	31943	83869	-4743
51779	14776	116791	120520	8878	205330	296682	72200
3050	20	-2676	-2692	2692	-2152	4647	373
38	44	698	698		719	713	
516039	49715	1259419	1246217	24960	1359832	477212	60697
49352	16121	421577	422863	44505	454878	161767	20268
3276	-88	3946	4606		4934	4721	252
9761	371	12809	12865	3050	17253	16044	3628
6484	**1212**	**13411**	**13513**	**47**	**16266**	**10422**	**2226**
303	1	147	146		294	128	132
	196	863	913		916	933	
3745	763	10947	10919		12454	5551	1154
2436	253	1455	1534	47	2602	3811	941
87435	**7735**	**321807**	**328494**	**8439**	**389086**	**214404**	**50369**
27271	656	208808	210169	2385	233126	52866	18901
28000	2988	46662	48225	5229	65639	65292	14748
15226	4718	55844	58441	798	76205	49999	14716
14278	-1271	9438	10090		11552	41447	1181
2660	645	1056	1569	27	2564	4800	824
710	**103**	**-9670**	**-9640**	**9640**	**-9329**	**1443**	**184**
710	103	-9670	-9640	9640	-9329	1443	184

12-10 规模以上工业企业主要经济效益指标（2021年）

行 业	Sector	总资产贡献率 (%) Ratio of Total Assets to Industrial Output Value (%)	资产负债率 (%) Assets-Liability Ratio (%)
总计	**Total**	**5.4**	**57.4**
按工业行业大类分	**Grouped by Sector**		
煤炭开采和洗选业	Mining and Washing of Coal		
石油和天然气开采业	Extraction of Petroleum and Natural Gas		
黑色金属矿采选业	Mining and Processing of Ferrous Metal Ores		
有色金属矿采选业	Mining and Processing of Non-ferrous Metal Ores		
非金属矿采选业	Mining and Processing of Nonmetal Ores		
开采专业及辅助性活动	Mining Professional and Auxiliary Activity	3.4	45.4
其他采矿业	Mining of Other Ores		
农副食品加工业	Processing of Food from Agricultural Porducts	5.2	62.5
食品制造业	Manufacture of Foods	9.4	58.5
酒、饮料和精制茶制造业	Manufacture of Alcohol,Beverages and Tea	8.7	53.1
烟草制品业	Manufacture of Tobacco	8.1	17.1
纺织业	Manufacture of Textile	0.9	61.1
纺织服装、服饰业	Textile, Garments industry	2.5	59.4
皮革、毛皮、羽毛及其制品和制鞋业	Manufacture of Leather, Fur, Feather and Related Products	-0.8	33.0
木材加工和木、竹、藤、棕、草制品业	Processing of Timber, Manufacture of Wood,Plam and Straw Products	-0.4	45.5
家具制造业	Manufacture of Furniture	4.4	59.5
造纸和纸制品业	Manufacture of Paper and Paper Products	8.0	64.9
印刷和记录媒介复制业	Printing,Reproduction of Recording Media	8.1	35.4
文教、工美、体育和娱乐用品制造业	Manufacture of Articles For Cultural,Educational and Sports Activities	8.8	32.2

Major Indicators of Economic Performance of Industrial Enterprises above Designated Size(2021)

流动资产周转率（次/年） Rate of Annual Turnover Working Capitals (times/year)	成本费用利润率 (%) Ratio of Profits to Cost (%)	营业收入利润率 (%) Profit Margin of Operating Income (%)	每百元资产实现营业收入（元） Operating Income per 100 yuan of Assets (yuan)
1.1	**5.7**	**5.5**	**68.0**
1.2	-0.8	-0.8	75.0
1.6	3.4	3.3	114.8
2.0	4.9	4.7	110.5
1.6	8.6	7.9	70.5
0.8	10.1	9.0	41.7
1.7	-1.3	-1.3	67.8
0.8	0.3	0.3	49.0
0.5	-3.0	-3.0	33.6
0.2	-17.5	-21.3	9.7
1.4	1.4	1.4	73.9
1.9	4.5	4.4	104.6
1.2	7.3	6.8	66.7
0.8	11.6	10.6	44.5

12-10 续表

行　业	Sector	总资产贡献率 (%) Ratio of Total Assets to Industrial Output Value (%)	资产负债率 (%) Assets-Liability Ratio (%)
石油、煤炭和其他燃料加工业	Petroleum, coal and other fuel processing industries	18.5	82.8
化学原料及化学制品制造业	Manufacture of Raw Chemical Materials and Chemical Products	10.4	52.1
医药制造业	Manufacture of Medicines	11.4	48.9
化学纤维制造业	Manufacture of Chemical Fibers	22.0	29.6
橡胶和塑料制品业	Manufacture of Rubber and Plastics	1.9	72.3
非金属矿物制品业	Manufacture of Non-metallic Mineral Products	6.3	73.9
黑色金属冶炼和压延加工业	Smelting and Pressing of Ferrous Metals	6.1	68.5
有色金属冶炼和压延加工业	Smelting and Pressing of Non-ferrous Metals	5.0	36.6
金属制品业	Manufacture of Metal Products	6.1	73.9
通用设备制造业	Manufacture of General Purpose Machinery	3.4	63.3
专用设备制造业	Manufacture of Special Equipment	7.7	53.8
汽车制造业	Manufacture of Motor Vehicle	5.3	67.6
铁路、船舶、航空航天和其他运输设备制造业	Railways, Shipbuilding,Aerospace and Other Transportation Equipment Manufacturing Industry	3.4	56.1
电气机械和器材制造业	Manufacture of Electric Equipment and Machinery	1.9	71.7
计算机、通讯和其他电子设备制造业	Manufacture of Communication Equipment, Computers and other Electronic Equipment	8.5	37.7
仪器仪表制造业	Manufacture of Measuring Instruments and Machinery	8.7	50.7
其他制造业	Manufacture of Other Manufacturing	2.8	56.7
废弃资源综合利用业	Recycling and Disposal of Waste	19.4	70.9
金属制品、机械和设备修理业	Metal Products,Machinery and Equipment Repair Industry	4.2	36.1
电力、热力生产和供应业	Production and Supply of Electric Power and Heat Power	1.1	76.2
燃气生产和供应业	Gas Mining and Supplying Industry	2.3	58.6
水的生产和供应业	Production and Supply of Water	2.1	77.6

continued

流动资产周转率（次/年）Rate of Annual Turnover Working Capitals (times/year)	成本费用利润率 (%) Ratio of Profits to Cost (%)	营业收入利润率 (%) Profit Margin of Operating Income (%)	每百元资产实现营业收入（元）Operating Income per 100 yuan of Assets (yuan)
1.8	3.9	3.7	150.1
1.0	15.7	14.0	61.1
1.1	9.6	8.7	73.7
2.3	15.3	13.1	129.4
0.5	2.9	2.8	28.6
1.0	4.3	4.1	74.7
3.9	1.3	1.2	274.2
0.7	10.2	9.4	39.4
1.0	6.8	6.5	68.3
0.5	5.9	5.6	43.7
0.7	13.4	12.0	47.9
1.6	2.6	2.5	115.6
0.6	6.9	6.5	40.9
1.2	1.1	1.1	85.0
1.7	11.4	10.8	66.5
0.7	12.0	10.9	59.9
0.7	-1.2	-1.2	47.4
2.7	2.6	2.6	129.7
0.9	3.5	3.4	49.1
1.9	-1.5	-1.5	54.7
2.3	1.3	1.3	67.6
0.8	-1.2	-1.3	20.0

12-11 规模以上大中型工业企业主要经济效益指标（2021年）

行 业	Sector	总资产贡献率 (%) Ratio of Total Assets to Industrial Output Value (%)	资产负债率 (%) Assets-Liability Ratio (%)
总计	**Total**	**5.4**	**55.8**
按工业行业大类分	**Grouped by Sector**		
煤炭开采和洗选业	Mining and Washing of Coal		
石油和天然气开采业	Extraction of Petroleum and Natural Gas		
黑色金属矿采选业	Mining and Processing of Ferrous Metal Ores		
有色金属矿采选业	Mining and Processing of Non-ferrous Metal Ores		
非金属矿采选业	Mining and Processing of Nonmetal Ores		
开采专业及辅助性活动	Mining Professional and Auxiliary Activity	3.4	43.3
其他采矿业	Mining of other Ores		
农副食品加工业	Processing of Food from Agricultural Porducts	17.5	29.9
食品制造业	Manufacture of Foods	11.6	66.1
酒、饮料和精制茶制造业	Manufacture of Alcohol,Beverages and Tea	10.7	54.1
烟草制品业	Manufacture of Tobacco	9.4	11.5
纺织业	Manufacture of Textile	-1.4	65.8
纺织服装、服饰业	Textile, apparel industry		
皮革、毛皮、羽毛及其制品和制鞋业	Manufacture of Leather, Fur, Feather and Related Products,and Shoes	-1.4	33.4
木材加工和木、竹、藤、棕、草制品业	Processing of Timber,Manufacture of Wood,Plam and Straw Products		
家具制造业	Manufacture of Furniture	2.3	83.3
造纸和纸制品业	Manufacture of Paper and Paper Products		
印刷和记录媒介复制业	Printing,Reproduction of Recording Media	10.7	23.0
文教、工美、体育和娱乐用品制造业	Manufacture of Articles For Cultural,Educational and Sports Activities		

Major Economic Indicators of Large and Medium-sized Industrial Enterprises above Designated Size (2021)

流动资产周转率（次/年）Rate of Annual Turnover Working Capitals (times/year)	成本费用利润率 (%) Ratio of Profits to Cost (%)	营业收入利润率 (%) Profit Margin of Operating Income (%)	每百元资产实现营业收入（元）Operating Income per 100 yuan of Assets (yuan)
1.2	**5.6**	**5.4**	**70.8**
1.2	-1.0	-1.0	75.7
3.1	9.6	8.8	174.3
2.3	5.2	5.0	133.5
1.9	9.3	8.6	83.9
0.4	26.0	19.9	26.8
2.2	-5.5	-5.8	52.6
0.5	-4.0	-4.0	32.7
0.6	2.9	2.8	41.8
1.1	11.0	9.9	65.3

12-11 续表

行 业	Sector	总资产贡献率 (%) Ratio of Total Assets to Industrial Output Value (%)	资产负债率 (%) Assets-Liability Ratio (%)
石油、煤炭和其他燃料加工业	Petroleum, coal and other fuel processing industries	22.4	85.5
化学原料及化学制品制造业	Manufacture of Raw Chemical Materials and Chemical Products	14.2	49.3
医药制造业	Manufacture of Medicines	12.3	45.3
化学纤维制造业	Manufacture of Chemical Fibers	12.6	9.3
橡胶和塑料制品业	Manufacture of Rubber and Plastics	1.3	53.5
非金属矿物制品业	Manufacture of Non-metallic Mineral Products	8.0	71.1
黑色金属冶炼和压延加工业	Smelting and Pressing of Ferrous Metals		
有色金属冶炼和压延加工业	Smelting and Pressing of Non-ferrous Metals	4.7	30.3
金属制品业	Manufacture of Metal Products	6.4	77.9
通用设备制造业	Manufacture of General Purpose Machinery	2.5	66.2
专用设备制造业	Manufacture of Special Equipment	7.2	51.2
汽车制造业	Manufacture of Motor Vehicle	5.2	67.7
铁路、船舶、航空航天和其他运输设备制造业	Railways,Shipbuilding,Aerospace and Other Transportation Equipment Manufacturing Industry	2.6	58.0
电气机械和器材制造业	Manufacture of Electric Equipment and Machinery	1.1	75.6
计算机、通信和其他电子设备制造业	Manufacture of Communication Equipment, Computers and other Electronic Equipment	8.8	36.6
仪器仪表制造业	Manufacture of Measuring Instruments and Machinery	8.2	47.3
其他制造业	Manufacture of Other Manufacturing		
废弃资源综合利用	Recycling and Disposal of Waste		
金属制品、机械和设备修理业	Metal Products,Machinery and Equipment Repair Industry	13.5	48.8
电力、热力生产和供应业	Production and Supply of Electric Power and Heat Power	0.8	69.7
燃气生产和供应业	Gas Mining and Supplying Industry	2.1	59.5
水的生产和供应业	Production and Supply of Water	1.9	76.8

continued

流动资产周转率 （次/年） Rate of Annual Turnover Working Capitals (times/year)	成本费用利润率 (%) Ratio of Profits to Cost (%)	营业收入利润率 (%) Profit Margin of Operating Income (%)	每百元资产实现营业收入（元） Operating Income per 100 yuan of Assets (yuan)
1.9	4.4	4.2	165.9
0.8	30.0	25.0	48.7
1.2	9.7	8.8	81.5
2.7	6.3	5.9	163.0
1.0	-1.1	-1.1	38.8
0.9	7.8	7.2	66.5
0.5	14.6	12.9	27.2
0.9	9.5	9.1	59.8
0.4	5.8	5.6	37.2
0.6	14.9	13.2	41.2
1.6	2.5	2.5	116.5
0.6	5.3	5.1	40.4
1.2	0.4	0.4	88.7
1.9	11.6	10.9	68.9
0.8	11.5	10.5	64.5
1.5	0.2	0.2	132.3
4.1	-2.1	-2.1	79.2
2.4	1.3	1.3	69.3
0.8	0.1	0.1	25.4

12-12 规模以上工业主要产品生产能力（2021年）

Production Capacity of Major Products of Industrial Enterprises above Designated Size (2021)

指　标	Item	2021
棉纺锭/纺纱量（锭/吨）	Cotton Spindles / Spinning Volume (ingot/ton)	200831
气流纺锭/纺纱量（头/吨）	Rotor Spinning / Spinning Volume (head/ton)	1056
棉布织机（台）	Cotton Loom (unit)	3799
原油加工能力（吨）	Crude Oil Processing Capacity (ton)	150000
烧碱(折100%)（吨）	Caustic Soda (ton)	77000
农用氮、磷、钾化学肥料总计(折纯)（吨）	Chemical Fertilizers (ton)	80000
初级形态塑料（吨）	Primary Plastic (ton)	123100
化学纤维（吨）	Chemical Fibre (ton)	40000
硅酸盐水泥熟料（吨）	Portland Cement Clinker (ton)	350000
水泥（吨）	Cement (ton)	3808528
平板玻璃（重量箱）	Plate Glass (weight case)	4715839
钢材（吨）	Rolled Steel (ton)	667393
金属切削机床（台）	Metal-cutting Machine Tools (set)	7716
挖掘机（台）	Excavator (set)	80
汽车（辆）	Motor Vehicles (unit)	540000
其中：乘用车	Passenger Vehicle (unit)	400000
其中：新能源乘用车	New Energy Passenger Car (unit)	130000
商用车	Commercial Vehicle (unit)	140000
太阳能电池（千瓦）	Solar Cell (kW)	20300000
家用电冰箱（台）	Household Refrigerators (set)	31600
移动通信手持机（台）	Mobile Telephones (set)	65092113
彩色电视机（台）	Color TV Set (set)	100000
发电设备容量总计（万千瓦）	Total Capacity of Power Generation Equipment (10 000 kW)	361
其中：火电设备容量	Thermal Power	335
水电设备容量	Hydro Power	3

主要统计指标解释

工业 指从事自然资源的开采，对采掘品和农产品进行加工和再加工的物质生产部门。具体包括：（1）对自然资源的开采，如采矿、晒盐等（但不包括禽兽捕猎和水产捕捞）；（2）对农副产品的加工、再加工，如粮油加工、食品加工、缫丝、纺织、制革等；（3）对采掘品的加工、再加工，如炼铁、炼钢、化工生产、石油加工、机器制造、木材加工等，以及电力、自来水、煤气的生产和供应等；（4）对工业品的修理、翻新，如机器设备的修理、交通运输工具（如汽车）的修理等。

工业统计调查单位为独立核算法人工业企业。

独立核算法人工业企业指从事工业生产经营活动的单位。独立核算法人工业企业应同时具备以下条件：①依法成立，有自己的名称、组织机构和场所，能够承担民事责任；②独立拥有和使用资产，承担负债，有权与其他单位签订合同；③独立核算盈亏，并能够编制资产负债表。

国有及国有控股企业 指国有企业加上国有控股企业。国有企业（即原全民所有制工业或国营工业）指企业全部资产归国家所有，并按《中华人民共和国企业法人登记管理条例》规定登记注册的非公司制的经济组织。包括国有企业、国有独资公司和国有联营企业。1957年以前的公私合营和私营工业，后均改造为国营工业，1992年改为国有工业，这部分工业的资料不单独分列时，均包括在国有企业内。国有控股企业是对混合所有制经济的企业进行的“国有控股”分类。它是指这些企业的全部资产中国有资产（股份）相对其他所有者中的任何一个所有者占资（股）最多的企业。该分组反映了国有经济控股情况。

本篇涉及的其他企业登记注册类型的解释详见综合篇。

轻工业 指主要提供生活消费品和制作手工工具的工业。按其所使用的原料不同，可分为两大类：（1）以农产品为原料的轻工业，是指直接或间接以农产品为基本原料的轻工业。主要包括食品制造、饮料制造、烟草加工、纺织、缝纫、皮革和毛皮制作、造纸以及印刷等工业；（2）以非农产品为原料的轻工业，是指以工业品为原料的轻工业。主要包括文教体育用品、化学药品制造、合成纤维制造、日用化学制品、日用玻璃制品、日用金属制品、手工工具制造、医疗器械制造、文化和办公用机械制造等工业。

重工业 指为国民经济各部门提供物质技术基础的主要生产资料的工业。按其生产性质和产品用途，可以分为下列三类：（1）采掘（伐）工业，是指对自然资源的开采，包括石油开采、煤炭开采、金属矿开采、非金属矿开采等工业；（2）原材料工业，指向国民经济各部门提供基本材料、动力和燃料的工业。包括金属冶炼及加工、炼焦及焦炭、化学、化工、原料、水泥、人造板以及电力、石油和煤炭加工等工业；（3）加工工业，是指对工业原材料进行再加工制造的工业。包括装备国民经济各部门的机械设备制造工业、金属结构、水泥制品等工业，以及为农业提供的生产资料如化肥、农药等工业。

根据上述划分原则，修理业中以重工业产品为修理作业对象的划为重工业，反之划为轻工业。

资产总计 指企业过去的交易或者事项形成的、由企业拥有或者控制的、预期会给企业带来经济利益的资源。包括企业拥有的土地、办公楼、厂房、机器、运输工具、存货等实物资产和现金、存款、应收账款和预付账款等金融资产。资产一般按流动性（资产的变现或耗用时间长短）分为流动资产和非流动资产。其中流动资产可分为货币资金、交易性金融资产、应收票据、应收账款、预付款项、其他应收款、存货等；非流动资产可分为长期股权投资、固定资产、无形资产及其他非流动资产等。根据会计“资产负债表”中“资产总计”项目的期末余额数填报。

流动资产合计 资产满足以下条件之一应归为流动资产：（1）预计在一个正常营业周期中变现、出售或耗用，主要包括存货、应收账款等；（2）主要为交易目的而持有；（3）预计在资产负债表日起一年内（含一年）变现；（4）自资产负债表日起一年内，交换其他资产或清偿负债的能力不受限制的现金或现金等价物。包括货币资金、应收票据、应收账款、存货等项目。根据会计“资产负债表”中“流动资产合计”项目的期末余额数填报。

固定资产原价 指固定资产的成本，包括企业在购置、自行建造、安装、改建、扩建、技术改造某项固定资产时所发生的全部支出总额。根据会计“固定资产”科目的期末借方余额填报。

固定资产净额 指固定资产原价减去累计折旧、固定资产减值准备后的金额。根据会计“资产负债表”中“固定资产”或“固定资产净额”项目的期末余额填报。

负债合计 指企业过去的交易或者事项形成的，预期会导致经济利益流出企业的现时义务。包括银行贷款、借款、应付账款、应付职工工资、应付职工福利费、应交税金等企业负有偿还责任的债务。根据会计“资产负债表”中“负债合计”项目的期末余额数填报。

所有者权益合计 指企业资产扣除负债后由所有者享有的剩余权益。公司的所有者权益又称股东权益。包括实收资本、资本公积、盈余公积、未分配利润等。根据会计“资产负债表”中“所有者权益合计”项目的期末余额数填报。

营业收入 指企业从事销售商品、提供劳务和让渡资产使用权等生产经营活动形成的经济利益流入。包括“主营业务收入”和“其他业务收入”。根据会计“利润表”中“营业收入”项目的本年累计数填报。

主营业务收入 指企业经营主要业务所实现的收入。如果会计“利润表”列示“主营业务收入”项目，则根据其本年累计数填报；或者，根据会计“主营业务收入”科目的本年各月贷方余额（结转前）之和填报，如未设置该科目，以“营业收入”代替填报。

营业成本 指企业从事销售商品、提供劳务和让渡资产使用权等生产经营活动发生的实际成本。“营业成本”应当与“营业收入”进行配比。包括“主营业务成本”和“其他业务成本”。根据会计“利润表”中“营业成本”项目的本年累计数填报。

税金及附加 指企业因从事生产经营活动按税法规定应缴纳的消费税、城市维护建设税、资源税、环境保护税、教育费附加、房产税、城镇土地使用税、车船税、印花税等相关税费。根据会计“利润表”中“税金及附加”项目的本年累计数填报。

销售费用 指企业在销售商品和材料、提供劳务的过程中发生的各种费用，包括保险费、包装费、展览费和广告费、商品维修费、预计产品质量保证损失、运输费、装卸费等以及为销售本企业商品而专设的销售机构（含销售网点、售后服务网点等）的职工薪酬、业务费、折旧费等经营费用。

管理费用 指企业为组织和管理企业生产经营所发生的费用，包括企业在筹建期间内发生的开办费、董事会和行政管理部门在企业经营管理中发生的，或者应当由企业统一负担的公司经费等，不包含“研发费用”。执行企业会计准则的企业，根据会计“利润表”中“管理费用”项目的本年累计数填报。执行《小企业会计准则》的企业，应将会计“利润表”中“管理费用”项目本年累计数减“研发费用”项目本年累计数后填报。执行其他企业会计制度的企业以及未执行财政部《关于修订印发2019年度一般企业财务报表格式的通知》（财会[2019]6号）的企业，在会计“利润表”中“管理费用”项目的本年累计数的基础上，根据会计“管理费用”科目下的“研究费用”明细科目，将“研发费用”剔除后填报。

研发费用 指企业在新知识、新技术、新产品、新工艺等的研究与开发过程中发生的费用化支出，以及计入“管理费用”会计科目的企业自行开发无形资产的摊销。费用化支出主要包括研发活动的人工费用、直接投入费用、用于研发活动的仪器、设备的折旧费、用于研发活动的软件、专利权、非专利技术的摊销费用、新产品设计费、新工艺规程制定费以及其他研发活动相关费用。执行企业会计准则的企业，根据会计“利润表”中“研发费用”项目的本年累计数填报。执行《小企业会计准则》的企业，根据会计“利润表”中“研发费用”项目的本年累计数填报。执行其他企业会计制度的企业以及会计“利润表”未列示“研发费用”或“研究费用”的企业，根据会计“管理费用”科目下“研究费用”明细科目的本期发生额，以及“管理费用”科目下“无形资产摊销”明细科目的本期发生额分析填报。

财务费用 指企业为筹集生产经营所需资金等而发生的筹资费用，包括企业生产经营期间发生的利息支出（减利息收入）、汇兑损失（减汇兑收益）以及相关的手续费等。根据会计“利润表”中“财务费用”项目的本年累计数填报。

利润总额 指企业在一定会计期间的经营成果，是生产经营过程中各种收入扣除各种耗费后的盈余，反映企业在报告期内实现的盈亏总额。利润总额为营业利润加上营业外收入，减去营业外支出后的金额，根据会计“利润表”中“利润总额”项目的本年累计数填报。

应交增值税 指按照税法规定，以销售货物、服务、无形资产、不动产或提供加工、修理修配劳务的增值额和货物进口金额为计税依据而课征的一种流转税。填报本指标时，应按权责发生制核算企业本期应负担的增值税，有两种计算方法，可选其一，一旦确定，原则上不得更改。

计算方法一：

根据本期会计科目（1）“销项税额”、“进项税额转出”、“出口退税”年初至期末贷方累计发生额（一般与期末贷方余额相等，因为年初贷方余额为零），（2）“进项税额”年初至期末借方累计发生额，即期末借方余额—年初借方余额，（3）“出口抵减内销产品应纳税额”、“减免税款”年初至期末借方累计发生额（一般与期末借方余额相等，因为年初借方余额为零），取值后按照下述公式计算填报：

应交增值税= 销项税额—（进项税额—进项税额转出）—出口抵减内销产品应纳税额—减免税款+ 出口退税

计算方法二：

根据本期《增值税纳税申报表（一般纳税人适用）》（以“国家税务总局公告2019 年第15 号”版式为例）“销项税额”（第11 栏）、“进项税额”（第12 栏）、“进项税额转出”（第14 栏）、“免、抵、退应退税额”（第15 栏）、“简易计税办法计算的应纳税额”（第21 栏）、“按简易计税办法计算的纳税检查应补缴税额”（第22 栏）、“应纳税额减征额”（第23 栏）栏目“一般项目”列中“本年累计”列，按照下述公式计算填报：

应交增值税= 销项税额—（进项税额—进项税额转出—免、抵、退应退税额）+ 简易计税办法计算的应纳税额+ 按简易计税办法计算的纳税检查应补缴税额—应纳税额减征额

计算方法说明及填报要求：

（1）计算公式均体现权责发生制，本期发生的进项税额全部参与计算，相当于不设置留抵，同时也不抵扣会计账簿或增值税纳税申报表中上年年末留抵的进项税额，公式计算结果可以为负数。

（2）按照公式计算本指标后，不应再加增值税减免税额，因为这部分价值不再形成企业缴纳义务。

本年进项税额 指工业企业在报告期内购入货物或接受应税劳务而支付的、准予从销项税额中抵扣的增值税额。

本年销项税额 指工业企业在报告期内销售货物或提供应税劳务应收取的增值税额。

总资产贡献率 反映企业全部资产的获利能力，是企业经营业绩和管理水平的集中体现，是评价和考核企业盈利能力的核心指标。计算公式为：

总资产贡献率（%）=（利润总额+税金总额+利息支出）/ 平均资产总额 × 100%

公式中：税金总额为产品销售税金及附加与应交增值税之和；平均资产总额为期初期末资产之和的算术平均值。

资产负债率 该指标既反映企业经营风险的大小，也反映企业利用债权人提供的资金从事经营活动的能力。计算公式为：

资产负债率（%）=负债总额 / 资产总额 × 100%

资产与负债均为报告期期末数。

流动资产周转次数 指一定时期内流动资产完成的周转次数，反映投入工业企业流动资金的周转速度。计算公式为：

流动资产周转次数 = 产品销售收入 / 全部流动资产平均余额

公式中：全部流动资产平均余额为期初和期末的流动资产之和的算术平均值。

成本费用利润率 反映企业投入的生产成本及费用的经济效益，同时也反映企业降低成本所取得的经济效益。计算公式为：

成本费用利润率（%）=利润总额 / 成本费用总额 × 100%

公式中：成本费用总额为产品销售成本、销售费用、管理费用、财务费用之和。

产品销售率 该指标反映工业产品已实现销售的程度，是分析工业产销衔接情况，研究工业产品满足社会需求的指标。计算公式为：

产品销售率（%）=工业销售产值 / 工业总产值（现价）× 100%

Explanatory Notes on Main Statistical Indicators

Industry refers to the material production sector which is engaged in the extraction of natural resources and processing and reprocessing of minerals and agricultural products, including (1) extraction of natural resources, such as mining, salt production (but not including hunting and fishing); (2) processing and reprocessing of farm and sideline produces, such as rice husking, flour milling, wine making, oil pressing, silk reeling, spinning and weaving, and leather making; (3) manufacture of industrial products, such as steel making, iron smelting, chemicals manufacturing, petroleum processing, machine building, timber processing; water and gas production and electricity generation and supply; (4)repairing of industrial products such as the repairing of machinery and means of transport (including cars).

In industrial statistics surveys, the units of enquiry are corporate industrial enterprises with independent accounting systems.

Corporate industrial enterprises with independent accounting systems refer to enterprises engaging in industrial production activities, which meet the following requirements: (1) They are established legally, having their own names, organizations, location and able to take civil liability; (2) They possess and use their assets independently, assume liabilities and are entitled to sign contracts with other units; (3) They are financially independent and compile their own balance sheets.

State-owned and State-holding Enterprises refer to state-owned enterprises plus State-holding enterprises. State-owned enterprises (originally known as State-run enterprises with ownership by the whole society) are non-corporate economic entities registered in accordance with the Regulation of the People's Republic of China on the Management of Registration of Legal Enterprises, where all assets are owned by the State. Included in this category are State-owned enterprises, State-funded corporations and State-owned joint-operation enterprises. Joint State- private industries and private industries, which existed before 1957, were transformed into state-run industries since 1957, and into State-owned industries after 1992. Statistics on those enterprises are included in the State- owned industries instead of being grouped them separately. State-holding enterprises are a sub- classification of enterprises with mixed ownership, referring to enterprises where the percentage of State assets (or shares by the State) is larger than any other single share holder of the same enterprise. This sub- classification illustrates the control of the State over a particular industry.

For explanation of enterprises of other types of registration covered in this chapter, please refer to General Survey.

Light Industry refers to the industry that produces consumer goods and hand tools. It consists of two categories, depending on the materials used:

(1) Industries using farm products as raw materials. These are the branches of light industry which directly or indirectly use farm products as basic raw materials, including the manufacture of food and beverages, tobacco processing, textile, clothing, fur and leather manufacturing, paper making, printing, etc.

(2) Industries using non-farm products as raw materials. These are the branches of light industry which use manufactured goods as raw materials, including the manufacture of cultural, educational articles and sports goods, chemicals, synthetic fibre, chemical products for daily use, glass products for daily use, metal products for daily use, hand tools, medical apparatus and instruments, and the manufacture of cultural and office machinery.

Heavy Industry refers to the industry which produces capital goods, and provides various sectors of the national economy with necessary material and technical basis for production. It consists of the following three branches according to the purpose of production or the use of products:

(1) Mining, quarrying and logging industry, which refers to the industry that extracts natural resources, including extraction of petroleum, coal, metal and non-metal ores.

(2) Raw materials industry refers to the industry that provides various sectors of the national economy with raw materials, fuels and power. It includes smelting and processing of metals, coking and coke chemistry, chemical materials and building materials such as cement, plywood, and power, petroleum refining and coal dressing.

(3) Manufacturing industry which refers to the industry that processes raw materials. It includes machine-building industries which equip sectors of the national economy; industries producing metal structure and cement products; and industries producing means of agricultural production, such as chemical fertilizers and pesticides.

In accordance with the above principles of classification, the repairing trades, which are engaged primarily in repairing products of heavy industry, are classified as heavy industry while those which are engaged in repairing products of light industry are classified as light industry.

Total Assetsrefer to all resources that are owned or controlled by enterprises through previous trades or transactions, with expectation of making economic profits to enterprises. Included are all assets owned by enterprises such as land, office buildings, factories, machines, vehicles, inventories and other physical assets as well as cash, deposits, accounts receivable, prepayments and other financial assets. Classified by the degree of liquidity (the time of realization or consumption of assets), total assets include current assets and non-current assets. Current assets can be classified into monetary capital, trading financial assets, notes receivable, accounts receivable, advanced payments, other receivables and inventories. Non-current assets can be divided into long-term equity investment, fixed assets, intangible assets and other non-current assets. Filling in according to the ending balance of "Total Assets" in the "Balance Sheet" of the accounting.

Current Assets refer to the assets that meet one of the following requirements: (1) expected to be cashed, sold or used in a normal operation cycle, mainly including inventory and accounts receivable; (2) owned for transaction purpose mainly; (3) expected to be cashed within one year (including one year) from the day of the Balance Sheet; (4) unlimited cash or cash equivalents that can be exchanged with other assets or capable of settling debts during one year since the day of the Balance Sheet. Included are monetary capital, notes receivable, accounts receivable and inventories. Data on this indicator can be obtained from the year-end figures of total current assets in the Balance Sheet of accounting records.Filling in according to the ending balance of "Total Current Assets" in the "Balance Sheet".

Fixed Assets Original Costrefer to the cost of fixed assets, including the total amount of all expenditures incurred by an enterprise when purchasing, self constructing, installing, rebuilding, expanding, or technically reforming a fixed asset. Filling in according to the ending debit balance of the accounting "fixed assets" account.

Net Fixed Assetsrefer to the amount of the original price of fixed assets minus accumulated depreciation and fixed assets depreciation reserves. Filling in according to the ending balance of "fixed assets" or "net fixed assets" in the accounting "Balance Sheet".

Total Liabilities refer to payable liabilities of enterprises that are accumulated from earlier transactions with expectation of leaking out of economic profits. Included are debts that enterprises are responsible for repaying such as bank loans, borrowings, accounts payable, wages payable, employee benefits payable, taxes payable, etc. In terms of payment, it can be divided into liquid liabilities and long-term liabilities. Filling in according to the ending balance of the "Total liabilities" item in the "Balance Sheet".

Total Investors Equity refer to the residual equity enjoyed by the owner after deducting the liabilities from the assets of the enterprise. The owner's equity of a company is also called shareholders' equity. Including paid in capital, capital reserve, surplus reserve, undistributed profits, etc. Filling in according to the ending balance of the item "Total owner's equity" in the accounting "Balance Sheet".

Operating Income It refers to the inflow of economic interests generated by an enterprise's production and operation activities such as selling goods, providing labor services and transferring the right to use assets. Operating income includes "main business income" and "other business income". The current year's cumulative counting is reported according to the item of "Operating income" in the accounting "income statement".

The Main Business Incomerefer to the income from the main business of the enterprise. If the "main business income" item is listed in the "income statement", it should be filled in according to the accumulated amount of the current year; Or, fill in according to the sum of the credit balance of each month of the current year (before carry forward) of the "main business income" account. If the account is not set, fill in with "operating income" instead.

Operating Cost It refers to the actual cost incurred by an enterprise in such production and operation activities as selling goods, providing labor services and transferring the right to use assets. "Operating cost" shall be matched with "operating revenue". Include "main business cost" and "other business cost". The current year's cumulative counting is reported according to the operating cost item in the accounting "income statement".

Taxes and surcharges refer to the consumption tax, urban maintenance and construction tax, resource tax, environmental protection tax, education surcharges, property tax, urban land use tax, vehicle and vessel tax, stamp tax and other relevant taxes payable by enterprises in accordance with the provisions of the tax law for production and operation activities. Filling in according to the accumulated amount of the current year of the item "taxes and surcharges" in the accounting "income statement".

Sales Cost It refers to the enterprises in the process of selling goods and materials to provide services of all kinds of costs, including insurance premium package exhibition and advertising goods maintenance product quality assurance is expected loss freight handling charge and so on and designed for sales of the enterprise products sales organizations (including sales outlets after-sales service network, etc.) of business expenses such as depreciation of employee compensation fees.

Cost management It refers to the enterprise for the cost of production in which the enterprise organization and management, including enterprise organization expenses the board of directors in the preparation period and the administrative departments in the enterprise management, or shall be borne by the enterprise unified company funds, etc., does not include the development costs, perform the enterprise accounting standard for business enterprises according to the management of project cost accounting profit statement this year accumulative fill in the implementation of accounting standards for small business enterprises, should be to reduce the management cost accounting profit statement project this year accumulative R&D projects this year accumulative after fill in Perform other enterprise accounting system of enterprises and not issued by the Ministry of Finance on revising the 2019 annual general enterprise financial report format to inform (finance and accounting) [2019] 6 enterprises, management of project cost in accounting profit this year accumulative frequency, on the basis of administrative subjects and research expenses according to the accounting detail course, will cost out the development is allowed.

R & D Expenses It refer to the expenses incurred by enterprises in the research and development process of new knowledge, new technology, new products and new processes. It mainly includes the labor cost of research and development activities, direct input cost, depreciation cost of instruments and equipment used in research and development activities, amortization cost of software, patent right and non-patent technology used in research and development activities, new product design fee, new process procedure formulation fee and other related costs of research and development activities. An enterprise implementing the accounting standards for business enterprises shall fill in the current year's cumulative count of the items of "Research and development expenses" in the accounting "income statement". The enterprises implementing the Accounting Standards for Small Enterprises shall fill in the current year's accumulations according to the items of "research expenses" in the accounting "income statement". Enterprises implementing accounting systems of other enterprises and enterprises that do not list "RESEARCH and development expenses" or "research expenses" in the accounting "income statement" shall fill in the amount incurred in the current period according to the relevant items of "Research expenses" under the accounting "administrative expenses".

Total Profits refer to the operational results in a certain accounting period, and it is the balance of various incomes minus various spendings in the course of operation, reflecting the total profits and losses of enterprises in reference period, filling in according to the accumulated amount of the current year of the item "Total profit" in the accounting "Profit Statement".

Value Added Tax Payablerefer to a turnover tax levied on the basis of sales of goods, services, intangible assets, real estate or the value added of processing, repair and replacement services and the amount of goods imported according to the tax law. When filling in this indicator, the VAT payable by the enterprise in the current period should be calculated on the accrual basis. There are two calculation methods, one of which can be selected. Once determined, it should not be changed in principle.

Calculation Method I:

According to the account items of the current period (1) "Output Tax", "Input Tax Transfer out", "Export Tax Refund", the cumulative credit amount from the beginning of the year to the end of the period (generally equal to the credit balance at the end of the period, because the credit balance at the beginning of the year is zero), (2) "Input Tax", the cumulative debit amount from the beginning of the year to the end of the period, that is, the debit balance at the end of the period – the debit balance at the beginning of the year, (3) "Export minus the tax payable on domestic products" The cumulative debit amount of "tax deduction" from the beginning of the year to the end of the period (generally equal to the debit balance at the end of the period, because the debit balance at the beginning of the year is zero) is calculated and reported according to the following formula after taking the value:

Value Added Tax Payable=Output VAT – (Input VAT – Input Tax Amount Transferred Out) – Export Offset Against Domestic Product Tax Payable – Tax Deduction+Export Tax Refund

Calculation method II:

According to the current VAT Tax Return (applicable to general taxpayers) (taking the format of "Announcement of the State Administration of Taxation No. 15 in 2019" as an example), "output tax" (column 11), "input tax" (column 12), "input tax transfer out" (column 14), "tax exemption, – 250 – industrial statistical statement system credit, refundable tax" (column 15), "tax payable calculated by simple tax calculation method" (column 21) The "tax payable for tax inspection calculated according to the simple tax calculation method" (column 22), the "tax payable reduction" (column 23), the "accumulated amount of this year" column in the "general items" column, shall be calculated and reported according to the following formula:

Value Added Tax Payable=Output VAT – (Input VAT– Input Tax Amount Transferred Out – Tax Exempt, Offset and Refundable)+Tax Payable Calculated By Simple Tax Calculation Method+Tax Payable For Tax Inspection Calculated By Simple Tax Calculation Method – Tax Payable Reduction

Description of calculation method and filling requirements:

(1) The calculation formulas all reflect the accrual system. All the input tax incurred in the current period is involved in the calculation, which is equivalent to that no allowance is set, and the input tax retained at the end of the previous year in the accounting book or VAT return is not offset. The formula calculation result can be negative.

(2) After this indicator is calculated according to the formula, no VAT reduction or exemption should be added, because this part of value no longer forms the enterprise's payment obligation.

Tax on Purchase in Current Year refers to goods purchased by industrial enterprises or value added tax that should be paid but being granted the right to deduct from the tax on sales.

Tax on Sales in Current Year refers to value added tax on industrial enterprises from sales of goods or taxable services that should be charged value added tax.

Ratio of Profits, Taxes and Interests to Average Assets reflects the profit-making capability of all assets of the enterprise and is a key indicator manifesting the performance and management and evaluating the profit-making potential of the enterprise. It is calculated as

$$\text{Ratio of Profits, Taxes and Interests to Average Assets(\%)} = \frac{\text{total profits} + \text{total taxes} + \text{interest payment}}{\text{average assets}} \times 100\%$$

In the above formula, total taxes is the sum of tax and extra charges on the sales of products and value-added tax payable; and average assets is the arithmetic mean of the sum of beginning assets and ending assets.

Ratio of Debts to Assets reflects both the operation risk and the capability of the enterprise in making use of the capital from the creditors. It is calculated as follows:

$$\text{Ratio of Debts to Assets(\%)} = \frac{\text{total debts}}{\text{total assets}} \times 100\%$$

Both assets and debts are figures at the end of the reference period.

Turnover of Working Capital refers to the number of times of turnover of working capital in a given period of time, which reflects the speed of the turnover of working capital of industrial enterprises, and is calculated as follows:

$$\text{Turnover of Working Capital} = \frac{\text{sales revenue of products}}{\text{average balance of total working capital}}$$

In the above formula, average balance of total working capital refers to the arithmetic mean of the sum of working capital at the beginning and at the end of the reference period.

Ratio of Profits to Total Industrial Costs refers to the ratio of profits realized in a given period to the total costs in the same period, which reflects the economic efficiency of input cost and is calculated as follows:

$$\text{Ratio of Profits to Total Industrial Cost (\%)} = \frac{\text{total profits}}{\text{total costs}} \times 100\%$$

Total costs in the above formula are the sum of cost of products sold, marketing cost, management cost and financial cost.

Sales Ratio of Products is an indicator reflecting the actual sale of industrial products, analyzing the production-selling and supply-demand relations. It is calculated as:

$$\text{Sales Ratio of Products (\%)} = \frac{\text{value of industrial sales}}{\text{gross industrial output value (current prices)}} \times 100\%$$

13 能　源

ENERGY

资料整理：于元英　张　育　李　婷
Data management：Yu Yuanying　Zhang Yu　Li Ting
数据审核：马建华
Data audit：Ma Jianhua

第十三部分　能源

一、简要说明

本章资料包括规模以上工业能源购消存情况、全市单位GDP能耗、规模以上工业企业用水情况等，由西安市统计局能源与环境处提供。

二、主要指标

规模以上工业综合能源消费量（万吨标准煤）	584.77	比上年下降	2.3%
单位GDP能耗（吨标准煤/万元）	0.269	比上年增长	0.94%

13　ENERGY

Ⅰ.Brief Introduction

Data in this chapter reflects energy purchases consumption and inventory of industrial enterprises above designated size,energy consumption per unit of GDP in whole city, and statistics on water use of industrial enterprises above designated size. data in this chapter are provided and compiled by Energy and Environment Division of the Xi'an Bureau of Statistics.

Ⅱ.Major Indicators

		Increase over Preceding Year
Comprehensive Energy Consumption Above Designated Size(10 000 Tons of Standard Coal)	584.77	-2.3%
Energy Consumption of GDP per Unit (Tons of Standard Coal /10 000 yuan)	0.269	0.94%

13-1 主要年份全市及各区县单位GDP能耗增长率

Growth Rates of Energy Consumption per Unit of GDP by Region in Representative Years

单位：% (%)

区 县	Region	2010	2011	2012	2013	2014	2015	2016	2017	2018	2019	2020	2021
西安市	**Xi'an**	**-2.06**	**-3.56**	**-3.51**	**-3.57**	**-5.89**	**-3.20**	**-3.83**	**-4.61**	**-5.99**	**-4.78**	**-7.52**	**0.94**
新城区	Xincheng	-1.15	-3.51	-3.50	-3.50	-5.39	-3.27	-3.58	-3.27	-4.72	-4.19	-9.92	1.22
碑林区	Beilin	-0.91	-3.89	-3.50	-3.50	-6.06	-3.20	-3.66	-3.65	-5.42	-4.37	-10.98	2.66
莲湖区	Lianhu	-3.58	-3.84	-3.60	-3.61	-7.76	-3.14	-3.58	-5.93	-6.12	-3.50	-11.01	3.58
灞桥区	Baqiao	-4.20	-3.81	-3.62	-3.64	-5.20	-3.30	-3.75	-6.95	-8.25	-3.98	-10.41	2.51
未央区	Weiyang	-1.31	-3.60	-3.60	-3.60	-7.60	-4.16	-3.86	-4.49	-4.48	-2.95	-2.80	1.83
雁塔区	Yanta	-4.18	-3.61	-3.61	-3.60	-3.89	-3.58	-3.55	-6.36	-6.54	-5.86	-9.09	-0.23
阎良区	Yanliang	-0.61	-3.38	-3.50	-3.50	-7.59	-3.00	-3.46	-3.99	-4.32	-2.91	-2.74	-0.39
临潼区	Lintong	-4.81	-3.52	-3.51	-3.51	-8.07	-3.00	-3.46	-6.29	-5.71	-5.18	-1.64	1.20
长安区	Chang'an	-2.08	-3.60	-3.63	-3.63	-3.40	-4.10	-3.56	-5.10	-4.56	-2.95	-4.26	7.00
高陵区	Gaoling	-3.82	-3.93	-3.52	-3.54	-7.32	-3.00	-3.52	-4.00	-5.88	-2.90	-2.05	5.19
鄠邑区	Huyi	-2.99	-3.85	-3.60	-3.62	-3.40	-3.82	-3.84	-3.89	-5.86	-4.13	-6.35	-13.65
蓝田县	Lantian	-2.06	-3.39	-3.40	-3.30	-5.48	-3.17	-3.84	-3.27	-5.21	-3.35	5.47	-4.94
周至县	Zhouzhi	-2.06	-3.30	-3.30	-3.30	-7.63	-2.90	-3.50	-3.64	-5.59	-2.96	-11.62	-3.46
西咸新区	Xixian New Area									-12.51	-12.31	-26.33	-3.27

注：单位GDP能耗中GDP按可比价计算。

13-2 主要年份全社会用电量

单位：万千瓦时

指 标	Sector	2000	2007	2008	2009	2010
总 计	**Total**	**732373**	**1482896**	**1605089**	**1724067**	**1993751**
A、全行业用电量合计	Total of Industry of Electricity	599855	1215799	1293574	1358483	1499903
1. 第一产业	Primary Industry	77579	120134	127054	99083	108720
2. 第二产业	Secondary Industry	354245	700026	724852	766029	883259
3. 第三产业	Tertiary Industry	168031	395639	441668	493371	507924
B、城乡居民生活用电	Electricity Consumption for Urban and Rural Residents	132518	267097	311515	365585	493848
1. 乡村	Rural	31281	38395	63072	99941	142059
2. 城市	City	101237	228702	248443	265644	351789
一、农、林、牧、渔业	Agriculture,Forestry,Animal Husbandry and Fishery	77579	120134	127054	99083	108720
二、工业	Industry	345175	674990	696291	724920	838317
三、建筑业	Construction	9070	25036	28561	41108	44942
四、交通运输、仓储及邮政业	Traffic,Transport, Storage and Post	22904	53825	56614	62031	58509
五、信息传输、软件和信息技术服务业	Information Transmission,Computer Services and Software		21938	26680	29328	30760
六、批发和零售业	Wholesale and Retail Trades		107343	111676	122203	148418
七、住宿和餐饮业	Hotels and Catering Services					
八、金融业	Financial Intermediation		67674	81674	102400	116163
九、房地产业	Real Estate					
十、租赁和商务服务业	Leasing and Business Services					
十一、公共事业及管理组织	Public Utilities and Management Organization		144859	165024	177409	154074

注：1.本表数据来源于国网陕西省供电公司西安供电公司和国网陕西电力公司西咸供电公司。
2.2017年及以后为包含西咸新区数据。
3.2018年采用新行业分类标准，所以2017年及之前的农、林、牧、渔业、批发和零售业、住宿和餐饮业、金融业、房地产业、租赁和商务服务业无法分类，故2017年及之前农、林、牧、渔业为农、林、牧、渔、水利业合计，批发和零售业为商业、住宿和餐饮业合计，金融业为金融、房地产、商务及居民服务业合计。

Electricity Consumption of the Whole Society in Representative Years

(10 000 kWh)

2011	2012	2013	2014	2015	2016	2017	2018	2019	2020	2021
2167453	**2352571**	**2554679**	**2753213**	**2844836**	**3120582**	**3613693**	**3967465**	**4184997**	**4150188**	**4893749**
1590486	1706859	1854696	2002503	2049492	2216797	2586468	2821250	3031213	3043246	3595717
117984	109086	110405	95997	89970	87825	102033	28998	26057	31941	28170
910360	932622	991202	1086105	1088866	1147294	1388903	1430389	1470195	1487484	1693777
562142	665151	753089	820401	870656	981678	1095531	1361863	1534962	1523821	1873770
576966	645713	699982	750710	795344	903785	1027226	1146216	1153784	1106942	1298032
169898	197937	216148	235938	241920	263871	288571	321715	347306	333809	373268
407068	447776	483834	514773	553424	639914	738655	824501	806478	773134	924764
117984	109086	110405	95997	89970	87825	102033	100432	75902	70414	68089
859796	875018	920024	998132	997115	1062188	1287836	1326060	1345516	1361355	1537472
50564	57605	71179	87973	91750	85106	101068	110600	131824	129172	159222
66684	69633	78722	88805	90914	109911	128970	149353	174658	191568	247882
33191	37444	39551	42662	46203	61950	77104	90433	105752	124898	147946
166558	199970	228117	253199	277248	301414	334387	302014	371987	387667	479077
							94270	98522	85667	103761
131236	150832	165833	180824	185329	212666	232317	13599	13908	13891	14866
							180942	214133	202529	265561
							25860	30222	36738	40936
164473	207271	240866	254911	270962	295737	322753	427688	468790	439347	530903

13-3　规模以上工业企业能源购进、消费及库存（2021年）

能源名称	Name	年初库存量 Stock (year-beginning)	购进量 Purchases	其中： 购自省外 Wherein: purchased from outside the province
原煤(吨)	Raw Coal(ton)	474360	8390903	63910
洗精煤（用于炼焦）（吨）	Washed Coal(Coking Coal)(ton)			
其他洗煤(吨)	Other Washed Coals(ton)	46010	85581	
煤制品（吨）	Briquettes(ton)			
焦炭(吨)	Coke(ton)		360	360
其他焦化产品(吨)	Other Coking Products(ton)			
焦炉煤气(万立方米)	Coke Oven Gas(10000 cu.m)			
高炉煤气(万立方米)	Blast Furnace Gas(10000 cu.m)			
转炉煤气(万立方米)	Converter Gas(10000 cu.m)			
其他煤气(万立方米)	Other Gas(10000 cu.m)			
天然气（万立方米）	Natural Gas(10 000cu.m)	201	153569	
液化天然气（吨）	Liquefied Natural Gas (ton)	53	5974	
氢气（万立方米）	hydrogen(10000cu.m)		449	
原油(吨)	Crude Oil(ton)			
汽油(吨)	Gasoline(ton)	35	13358	115
煤油(吨)	Kerosene(ton)	33	179	
柴油(吨)	Diesel Oil(ton)	1623	87645	603
燃料油(吨)	Fuel Oil(ton)	111	3191	
液化石油气(吨)	LPG(ton)		20575	
炼厂干气(吨)	Refinery Gas(ton)			
石脑油(吨)	Naphtha(ton)			
润滑油（吨）	Lubricating Oil(ton)	158	3878	2634
石蜡(吨)	Paraffin(ton)			
溶剂油（吨）	Solvent Oil(ton)			
石油焦(吨)	Petrol Coke(ton)			
石油沥青(吨)	Petroleum Asphalt(ton)	949	30698	
其他石油制品(吨)	Other Petroleum Products(ton)	1	1310	
热力(百万千焦)	Heat(1 million kilo-joule)		11300197	
电力(万千瓦时)	Electricity(10 000kWh)		1069037	
煤矸石(用于燃料)(吨)	Coal Gangue(used for fuel)(ton)			
城市生活垃圾(用于燃料)(吨)	City Domestic Waste(used for fuel)(ton)	37862		
生物燃料（吨标准煤）	Biofuel(tons of SCE)	652	8445	2732
余热余压（百万千焦）	Residual Heat and Pressure(million of KJ)			
工业废料(用于燃料)(吨)	Industrial Waste(used for fuel)(ton)			
其他燃料（吨标准煤）	Other Fuels(ton of SCE)		137	
能源合计(吨标准煤)	Total Energy(ton of SCE)			

Energy Purchases, Consumption and Inventory of Industrial Enterprises above Designated Size (2021)

购进金额（千元） Purchase amount (Thousand Dollars)	工业 生产消费量 Industrial Production Consume	用于原材料 as Raw Material	运输工具消费 Means of transport Consume	期末库存量 Stock (year-end)
5383440	8280946			566921
78536	101828			14044
1080	360			
3703367	151453	6118	191	1365
28786	6012		1112	8
24811	899			
109625	12580		8996	54
1037	180			32
593785	87514		49922	1112
12482	3195			107
91862	20574	20260		
23728	3632	3140		190
83787	27162	27162		4485
15716	1310			
633334	3918518			
5873336	1216173		11983	
	2311126			35433
5396	7444			496
	123724			
325	137			
16664433	9967858	148398		

13-4 规模以上工业企业分行业主要能源品种消费量（2021年）

Major Energy Consumption above Designated Size by Industry (2021)

行 业	Sector	原煤（吨）Raw Coal (ton)	天然气（万立方米）Natural Gas(10 000 cu.m)
总 计	**Total**	**8280946**	**151453**
煤炭开采和洗选业	Mining and Washing of Coal		
石油和天然气开采业	Extraction of Petroleum and Natural Gas		
黑色金属矿采选业	Mining and Processing of Ferrous Metal Ores		
有色金属矿采选业	Mining and Processing of Non-ferrous Metal Ores		
非金属矿采选业	Mining and Processing of Nonmetal Ores		
开采专业及辅助性活动	Mining Professional and Auxiliary Activity		321
其他采矿业	Mining of other Ores		
农副食品加工业	Processing of Food from Agricultural Products	36606	1866
食品制造业	Manufacture of Foods		2696
酒、饮料和精制茶制造业	Manufacture of Alcohol,Beverages and Tea		2087
烟草制品业	Manufacture of Tobacco		61
纺织业	Manufacture of Textile		385
纺织服装、服饰业	Textile, apparel industry		
皮革、毛皮、羽毛及其制品和制鞋业	Manufacture of Leather, Fur, Feather and Related Products, and Shoes		
木材加工和木、竹、藤、棕、草制品业	Processing of Timber, Manufacture of Wood,Bamboo, Rattan,palm and Straw Products		
家具制造业	Manufacture of Furniture		82
造纸和纸制品业	Manufacture of Paper and Paper Products		1181
印刷和记录媒介复制业	Printing,Reproduction of Recording Media		388
文教、工美、体育和娱乐用品制造业	Manufacture of Articles For Cultural,Educational and Sports Activities		
石油、煤炭及其他燃料加工业	Processing of Petroleum, Coal and Other Fuel		278
化学原料和化学制品制造业	Manufacture of Raw Chemical Materials and Chemical		8040
医药制造业	Manufacture of Medicines		2450
化学纤维制造业	Manufacture of Chemical Fibers		
橡胶和塑料制品业	Manufacture of Rubber and Plastics	32168	10486
非金属矿物制品业	Manufacture of Non-metallic Mineral Products	50059	5075
黑色金属冶炼和压延加工业	Smelting and Pressing of Ferrous Metals		1191
有色金属冶炼和压延加工业	Smelting and Pressing of Non-ferrous Metals		940
金属制品业	Manufacture of Metal Products		390
通用设备制造业	Manufacture of General Purpose Machinery		282
专用设备制造业	Manufacture of Special Equipment		173
汽车制造业	Manufacture of Motor Vehicle		5078
铁路、船舶、航空航天和其他运输设备制造业	Railways,Shipbuilding,Aerospace and Other Transportation Equipment Manufacturing Industry		204
电气机械和器材制造业	Manufacture of Electric Equipment and Machinery		1987
计算机、通讯和其他电子设备制造业	Manufacture of Communication Equipment, Computers and other Electronic Equipment		5789
仪器仪表制造业	Manufacture of Measuring Instruments and Machinery		28
其他制造业	Manufacture of Other Manufacturing		14
废弃资源综合利用业	Recycling and Disposal of Waste		
金属制品、机械和设备修理业	Metal Products,Machinery and Equipment Repair Industry		5
电力、热力生产和供应业	Production and Supply of Electric Power and Heat Power	8162114	97034
燃气生产和供应业	Gas Mining and Supplying Industry		2942
水的生产和供应业	Production and Supply of Water		1

13-4 续表 continued

行 业	Sector	汽油(吨) Gasoline (ton)	柴油(吨) Diesel Oil (ton)	热力(百万千焦) Heat (million kilo joule)	电力(万千瓦时) Electricity (10 000 kWh)
总 计	**Total**	**12580**	**87514**	**3918518**	**1216173**
煤炭开采和洗选业	Mining and Washing of Coal				
石油和天然气开采业	Extraction of Petroleum and Natural Gas				
黑色金属矿采选业	Mining and Processing of Ferrous Metal Ores				
有色金属矿采选业	Mining and Processing of Non-ferrous Metal Ores				
非金属矿采选业	Mining and Processing of Nonmetal Ores				
开采专业及辅助性活动	Mining Professional and Auxiliary Activity	1018	13068		3465
其他采矿业	Mining of other Ores				
农副食品加工业	Processing of Food from Agricultural Products	272	261	356392	9999
食品制造业	Manufacture of Foods	386	1174	450447	16467
酒、饮料和精制茶制造业	Manufacture of Alcohol,Beverages and Tea	50	56	753	12795
烟草制品业	Manufacture of Tobacco	11	27	40397	654
纺织业	Manufacture of Textile	70	41	27177	17718
纺织服装、服饰业	Textile, apparel industry	24	15		45
皮革、毛皮、羽毛及其制品和制鞋业	Manufacture of Leather, Fur, Feather and Related Products, and Shoes	24		5870	108
木材加工和木、竹、藤、棕、草制品业	Processing of Timber, Manufacture of Wood,Bamboo, Rattan,palm and Straw Products	38			1093
家具制造业	Manufacture of Furniture	91	246		1881
造纸和纸制品业	Manufacture of Paper and Paper Products	60	116	43947	3992
印刷和记录媒介复制业	Printing,Reproduction of Recording Media	186	147	52186	9372
文教、工美、体育和娱乐用品制造业	Manufacture of Articles For Cultural,Educational and Sports Activities	24	6		404
石油、煤炭及其他燃料加工业	Processing of Petroleum, Coal and Other Fuel	447	33		1187
化学原料和化学制品制造业	Manufacture of Raw Chemical Materials and Chemical	324	707	394255	84898
医药制造业	Manufacture of Medicines	504	62	208789	15024
化学纤维制造业	Manufacture of Chemical Fibers			1163772	6160
橡胶和塑料制品业	Manufacture of Rubber and Plastics	90	1390	99137	29545
非金属矿物制品业	Manufacture of Non-metallic Mineral Products	466	60887	36213	47687
黑色金属冶炼和压延加工业	Smelting and Pressing of Ferrous Metals	24	40		5598
有色金属冶炼和压延加工业	Smelting and Pressing of Non-ferrous Metals	191	151	9355	39934
金属制品业	Manufacture of Metal Products	530	397	12234	19232
通用设备制造业	Manufacture of General Purpose Machinery	440	152	5500	14598
专用设备制造业	Manufacture of Special Equipment	1159	1125	17569	14884
汽车制造业	Manufacture of Motor Vehicle	2661	5189	210998	112910
铁路、船舶、航空航天和其他运输设备制造业	Railways,Shipbuilding,Aerospace and Other Transportation Equipment Manufacturing Industry	453	140	99494	18674
电气机械和器材制造业	Manufacture of Electric Equipment and Machinery	882	402	312795	139508
计算机、通讯和其他电子设备制造业	Manufacture of Communication Equipment, Computers and other Electronic Equipment	484	35	365074	376751
仪器仪表制造业	Manufacture of Measuring Instruments and Machinery	423	27	3486	2204
其他制造业	Manufacture of Other Manufacturing	44			524
废弃资源综合利用业	Recycling and Disposal of Waste		110		1023
金属制品、机械和设备修理业	Metal Products,Machinery and Equipment Repair Industry	59	1		1374
电力、热力生产和供应业	Production and Supply of Electric Power and Heat Power	180	1402	1906	176516
燃气生产和供应业	Gas Mining and Supplying Industry	744	66	772	5134
水的生产和供应业	Production and Supply of Water	219	42		24816

13-5 规模以上工业企业分行业综合能源消费量（2021年）

Comprehensive Energy Consumption by Sector above Designated Size (2021)

单位：吨标准煤 (ton of SCE)

行 业	Scetor	2021	比上年增长(%) Increase over Preceding Year (%)
总 计	**Total**	**5847670**	**-2.3**
煤炭开采和洗选业	Mining and Washing of Coal		-100.0
石油和天然气开采业	Extraction of Petroleum and Natural Gas		-100.0
黑色金属矿采选业	Mining and Processing of Ferrous Metal Ores		-100.0
有色金属矿采选业	Mining and Processing of Non-ferrous Metal Ores		-100.0
非金属矿采选业	Mining and Processing of Nonmetal Ores		-100.0
开采专业及辅助性活动	Mining Professional and Auxiliary Activity	29215	2.7
其他采矿业	Mining of other Ores		-100.0
农副食品加工业	Processing of Food from Agricultural Products	59645	-65.9
食品制造业	Manufacture of Foods	72315	-3.9
酒、饮料和精制茶制造业	Manufacture of Alcohol,Beverages and Tea	40359	-0.2
烟草制品业	Manufacture of Tobacco	3045	-28.8
纺织业	Manufacture of Textile	27919	15.5
纺织服装、服饰业	Textile, apparel industry	112	-84.5
皮革、毛皮、羽毛及其制品和制鞋业	Manufacture of Leather, Fur,Feather and Related Products, and Shoes	368	-18.7
木材加工和木、竹、藤、棕、草制品业	Processing of Timber, Manufacture of Wood,Bamboo, Rattan,palm and Straw Products	3513	-38.4
家具制造业	Manufacture of Furniture	3871	19.4
造纸和纸制品业	Manufacture of Paper and Paper Products	21256	8.3
印刷和记录媒介复制业	Printing,Reproduction of Recording Media	18667	-13.4
文教、工美、体育和娱乐用品制造业	Manufacture of Articles For Cultural,Educational and Sports Activities	632	113.5
石油、煤炭及其他燃料加工业	Processing of Petroleum, Coal and Other Fuel	10096	33.8
化学原料和化学制品制造业	Manufacture of Raw Chemical Materials and Chemical Products	249432	-46.6
医药制造业	Manufacture of Medicines	56777	4.8
化学纤维制造业	Manufacture of Chemical Fibers	47255	-6.7
橡胶和塑料制品业	Manufacture of Rubber and Plastics	76187	-23.9
非金属矿物制品业	Manufacture of Non-metallic Mineral Products	341847	-7.1
黑色金属冶炼和压延加工业	Smelting and Pressing of Ferrous Metals	22233	2.0
有色金属冶炼和压延加工业	Smelting and Pressing of Non-ferrous Metals	62898	19.9
金属制品业	Manufacture of Metal Products	31298	13.0
通用设备制造业	Manufacture of General Purpose Machinery	22754	17.4
专用设备制造业	Manufacture of Special Equipment	24750	9.0
汽车制造业	Manufacture of Motor Vehicle	206005	-3.0
铁路、船舶、航空航天和其他运输设备制造业	Railways,Shipbuilding,Aerospace and Other Transportation Equipment Manufacturing Industry	30100	13.9
电气机械和器材制造业	Manufacture of Electric Equipment and Machinery	209500	83.3
计算机、通信和其他电子设备制造业	Manufacture of Communication Equipment,Computers and other Electronic Equipment	554661	23.7
仪器仪表制造业	Manufacture of Measuring Instruments and Machinery	3857	5.4
其他制造业	Manufacture of Other Manufacturing	893	-10.7
废弃资源综合利用业	Recycling and Disposal of Waste	1418	-2.0
金属制品、机械和设备修理业	Metal Products,Machinery and Equipment Repair Industry	1837	12.3
电力、热力生产和供应业	Production and Supply of Electric Power and Heat Power	3546123	0.8
燃气生产和供应业	Gas Mining and Supplying Industry	35928	-11.9
水的生产和供应业	Production and Supply of Water	30905	8.4

13-6 规模以上工业企业用水情况（2021年）

Statistics on Water Use of Industrial Enterprises above Designated Size (2021)

指　标	Item	取水量（万立方米）Water Use (10 000 cu.m)	外供水量（万立方米）Outward Water Supply (10 000 cu.m)
合　计	**Total**	**93386.06**	**80605.54**
地表淡水	Surface fresh water	61774.38	1694.63
地下淡水	Underground fresh water	14508.62	1295.77
自来水	Tap Water	15923.17	77560.74
陆地苦咸水	Land lake Salt water		
矿井水	Mine Water	3.92	
雨水	Rain Water	2.66	
再生水	Reclaimed Water	1171.46	
其他水	Other Water	1.85	54.40
外排水量	Efflux capacity	30458.32	
重复用水量	Repeated water consumption	161632.11	

13-7 规模以上工业企业分行业用水情况（2021年）

Volume of Water Use of Industrial Enterprises above Designated Size by Industry (2021)

行 业	Sector	取水量（万立方米） Water Use (10 000 cu.m)
总 计	**Total**	**93386.06**
煤炭开采和洗选业	Mining and Washing of Coal	
石油和天然气开采业	Extraction of Petroleum and Natural Gas	
黑色金属矿采选业	Mining and Processing of Ferrous Metal Ores	
有色金属矿采选业	Mining and Processing of Non-ferrous Metal Ores	
非金属矿采选业	Mining and Processing of Nonmetal Ores	
开采专业及辅助性活动	Mining Professional and Auxiliary Activity	147.47
其他采矿业	Mining of other Ores	
农副食品加工业	Processing of Food from Agricultural Products	86.02
食品制造业	Manufacture of Foods	600.68
酒、饮料和精制茶制造业	Manufacture of Alcohol,Beverages and Tea	605.02
烟草制品业	Manufacture of Tobacco	8.72
纺织业	Manufacture of Textile	108.56
纺织服装、服饰业	Textile, apparel industry	0.58
皮革、毛皮、羽毛及其制品和制鞋业	Manufacture of Leather, Fur, Feather and Related Products, and Shoes	0.95
木材加工和木、竹、藤、棕、草制品业	Processing of Timber, Manufacture of Wood,Bamboo, Rattan,palm and Straw Products	2.48
家具制造业	Manufacture of Furniture	10.78
造纸和纸制品业	Manufacture of Paper and Paper Products	12.76
印刷和记录媒介复制业	Printing,Reproduction of Recording Media	51.57
文教、工美、体育和娱乐用品制造业	Manufacture of Articles For Cultural,Educational and Sports Activities	1.48
石油、煤炭及其他燃料加工业	Processing of Petroleum, Coal and Other Fuel	2.82
化学原料和化学制品制造业	Manufacture of Raw Chemical Materials and Chemical Products	268.79
医药制造业	Manufacture of Medicines	320.11
化学纤维制造业	Manufacture of Chemical Fibers	44.89
橡胶和塑料制品业	Manufacture of Rubber and Plastics	109.22
非金属矿物制品业	Manufacture of Non-metallic Mineral Products	586.15
黑色金属冶炼和压延加工业	Smelting and Pressing of Ferrous Metals	5.30
有色金属冶炼和压延加工业	Smelting and Pressing of Non-ferrous Metals	167.34
金属制品业	Manufacture of Metal Products	74.11
通用设备制造业	Manufacture of General Purpose Machinery	73.80
专用设备制造业	Manufacture of Special Equipment	131.20
汽车制造业	Manufacture of Motor Vehicle	804.53
铁路、船舶、航空航天和其他运输设备制造业	Railways,Shipbuilding,Aerospace and Other Transportation Equipment Manufacturing Industry	104.70
电气机械和器材制造业	Manufacture of Electric Equipment and Machinery	648.99
计算机、通讯和其他电子设备制造业	Manufacture of Communication Equipment, Computers and other Electronic Equipment	2202.24
仪器仪表制造业	Manufacture of Measuring Instruments and Machinery	28.17
其他制造业	Manufacture of Other Manufacturing	3.47
废弃资源综合利用业	Recycling and Disposal of Waste	6.67
金属制品、机械和设备修理业	Metal Products,Machinery and Equipment Repair Industry	14.99
电力、热力的生产和供应业	Production and Supply of Electric Power and Heat Power	4267.01
燃气生产和供应业	Gas Mining and Supplying Industry	29.05
水的生产和供应业	Production and Supply of Water	81855.44

13-7 续表 continued

行 业	Sector	外供水量（万立方米）Outward Water Supply (10 000 cu.m)
总 计	**Total**	**80605.54**
煤炭开采和洗选业	Mining and Washing of Coal	
石油和天然气开采业	Extraction of Petroleum and Natural Gas	
黑色金属矿采选业	Mining and Processing of Ferrous Metal Ores	
有色金属矿采选业	Mining and Processing of Non-ferrous Metal Ores	
非金属矿采选业	Mining and Processing of Nonmetal Ores	
开采专业及辅助性活动	Mining Professional and Auxiliary Activity	
其他采矿业	Mining of other Ores	
农副食品加工业	Processing of Food from Agricultural Products	
食品制造业	Manufacture of Foods	
酒、饮料和精制茶制造业	Manufacture of Alcohol,Beverages and Tea	79.90
烟草制品业	Manufacture of Tobacco	
纺织业	Manufacture of Textile	
纺织服装、服饰业	Textile, apparel industry	
皮革、毛皮、羽毛及其制品和制鞋业	Manufacture of Leather, Fur, Feather and Related Products, and Shoes	
木材加工和木、竹、藤、棕、草制品业	Processing of Timber, Manufacture of Wood,Bamboo, Rattan,palm and Straw Products	
家具制造业	Manufacture of Furniture	0.03
造纸和纸制品业	Manufacture of Paper and Paper Products	
印刷和记录媒介复制业	Printing,Reproduction of Recording Media	
文教、工美、体育和娱乐用品制造业	Manufacture of Articles For Cultural,Educational and Sports Activities	
石油、煤炭及其他燃料加工业	Processing of Petroleum, Coal and Other Fuel	
化学原料和化学制品制造业	Manufacture of Raw Chemical Materials and Chemical Products	
医药制造业	Manufacture of Medicines	
化学纤维制造业	Manufacture of Chemical Fibers	
橡胶和塑料制品业	Manufacture of Rubber and Plastics	
非金属矿物制品业	Manufacture of Non-metallic Mineral Products	
黑色金属冶炼和压延加工业	Smelting and Pressing of Ferrous Metals	
有色金属冶炼和压延加工业	Smelting and Pressing of Non-ferrous Metals	
金属制品业	Manufacture of Metal Products	
通用设备制造业	Manufacture of General Purpose Machinery	1.84
专用设备制造业	Manufacture of Special Equipment	1.93
汽车制造业	Manufacture of Motor Vehicle	
铁路、船舶、航空航天和其他运输设备制造业	Railways,Shipbuilding,Aerospace and Other Transportation Equipment Manufacturing Industry	
电气机械和器材制造业	Manufacture of Electric Equipment and Machinery	
计算机、通讯和其他电子设备制造业	Manufacture of Communication Equipment, Computers and other Electronic Equipment	30.74
仪器仪表制造业	Manufacture of Measuring Instruments and Machinery	
其他制造业	Manufacture of Other Manufacturing	
废弃资源综合利用业	Recycling and Disposal of Waste	
金属制品、机械和设备修理业	Metal Products,Machinery and Equipment Repair Industry	
电力、热力的生产和供应业	Production and Supply of Electric Power and Heat Power	147.25
燃气生产和供应业	Gas Mining and Supplying Industry	
水的生产和供应业	Production and Supply of Water	80343.85

主要统计指标解释

单位生产总值能耗 指一定时期内，一个国家或地区每生产一个单位的生产总值所消耗的能源。计算公式为：

单位生产总值能耗=能源消费总量/生产总值

工业企业能源消费量 指工业企业在工业生产活动和非工业生产活动中消费的能源，包括工业生产活动中作为燃料、动力、原料、辅助材料使用的能源，生产工艺中使用的能源，用于能源加工转换的能源；非工业生产活动中使用的能源。具体包括：

（1）用于本企业产品生产、工业性作业和其他生产性活动的能源；

（2）用于技术更新改造措施、新技术研究和新产品试制以及科学试验等方面的能源；

（3）用于经营维修、建筑及设备大修理、机电设备和交通运输工具等方面的能源；

（4）用于劳动保护的能源；

（5）生产交通运输工具的企业（如造船厂、汽车制造厂），向成品轮船、汽车中添加动力用油，应算作企业的能源消费，但不作为工业生产消费，应作为非工业生产消费和交通运输工具消费。

（6）其他非生产消费的能源。

工业生产能源消费量 指工业企业为进行工业生产活动所消费的能源。主要包括：

（1）用于本企业产品生产、工业性作业的能源，包括用作原料、材料、燃料、动力的能源；作为能源加工转换企业，还包括用作加工转换的能源（这部分能源不能理解为用作原材料，用作原材料的概念见后面的解释）；

（2）产品生产过程中作为辅助材料使用的能源；

（3）生产工艺过程使用的能源；

（4）新技术研究、新产品试制、科学试验使用的能源；

（5）为了工业生产活动而在进行的各种修理过程中使用的能源；

（6）生产区内的劳动保护用能等。

用于原材料的能源消费量 指能源产品不作能源使用，即不作燃料、动力使用，而作为生产另外一种产品（非能源产品）的原料或作为辅助材料使用，作原料使用时通常构成这种产品的实体。它与用作加工转换的区别是：用作加工转换，投入的是能源，产出的主要产品还是能源（或产出的产品属于加工转换过程中产生的不作能源使用的其他副产品和联产品）。而用作原材料时，投入的是能源，产出的主要产品是能源范畴以外的产品，包括产出的某种产品在广义上可以用作能源（比如可以燃烧以提供热量），但通常意义上不作能源使用的产品。

非工业生产能源消费量 指在工业企业能源消费中，除“工业生产能源消费”以外的能源消费，即非工业生产用能和工业企业附属的不从事工业生产活动的非独立核算单位用能。比如本企业施工单位进行技术更新改造、维修等过程用能，非生产区的劳动保护用能，科研单位、农场、车队、学校、医院、食堂、托儿所等单位用能。但是必须注意，上述单位如果是独立核算的，其用能既不能包括在“工业企业能源消费”中，亦不能包括在“非工业生产能源消费”中。

生产交通运输工具的企业（如造船厂、汽车制造厂），向成品轮船、汽车中添加动力用油，应算作企业的非工业生产消费。

综合能源消费量 指企业（单位）在报告期内工业生产实际消费的各种能源（扣除能源加工转换和能源回收利用等重复因素）的总和。计算综合能源消费量时，需要将各种能源品种的消费量换算成按照标准计量单位（如：吨标准煤）计量的消费量。

取水量 指企业从各种水源直接提取或者从市场购买的用于厂区、办公区内工业生产活动的水量，以实际获得的新水量为准。

外供水量 指企业外供给其他单位的水或水产品的量，以离厂水量为准。包括外供给其他企业或市场的原水、自来水、海水淡化水、矿泉水、纯净水等。不包括直流冷却水量、再生水（中水）、未利用直接排放的矿井水和雨水量、北方地区供暖企业供给城镇热力网内循环的热水量、进入城镇污水管网和直接排到自然环境中的水量。

Explanatory Notes on Main Statistical Indicators

Energy Consumption per Unit of GDP refers to the energy consumption per unit of Gross Domestic Product in a country or the Gross Regional Product in a region in the same reference period. The formula is:

Energy Consumption per Unit of GDP= Total Energy Consumption/Gross Domestic Product

Energy Consumption of Industrial Enterprises refers to the energy consumed by industrial enterprises in industrial production activities and non-industrial production activities, including energy used as fuel, power, raw materials and auxiliary materials in industrial production activities, energy used in production processes, energy for processing and conversion, and energy in the course of use of non-industrial production activities. Specifically, it includes:

(1)Energy used for the production, industrial operation and other productive activities of the enterprise;

(2)Energy for technological upgrading, new technology research and trial production of new products and scientific experiments.

(3) Energy for maintenance, construction and equipment repair, electrical and mechanical equipment and transportation.

(4) Energy for labor protection;

(5)Enterprises manufactured means of conveyance (such as making shipyards and automobile manufacturers), adding power oil to the finished product ships and cars, should be used as the energy consumption of the enterprises, but not as industrial production and consumption, it should be included in the consumption of non-industrial production and transportation means.

(6)Other non-productive energy sources.

Energy Consumption of Industrial Production refers to the energy consumed by industrial enterprises in industrial production activities. It mainly includes:

(1)Energy for the production and industrial operation of the products of the enterprise, including energy for raw materials, materials, fuel and power; as energy processing and conversion enterprises, including energy for processing and conversion (this part of the energy cannot be understood as raw materials, the concept of raw material is explained later)

(2)Energy used as auxiliary material during the production of products;

(3)Energy used in the production process;

(4)Energy for new technology research, trial production of new products and scientific test;

(5)Energy used in various repair processes for industrial production activities;

(6)Labor protection energy in the production area.

Energy Consumption for Raw Materials refers the energy products are not used for energy use, that is, not to be used as fuel and power, but as raw materials for the production of another product (non-energy products) or as auxiliary materials, which usually constitute the entity of this product when used as a raw material. The difference between it and the conversion of processing is that it is used as a process conversion, which is invested in energy, the main product of the output still is energy (or the produced product belongs to other by-products and associated products that are not used for energy use in the process of processing and conversion). When used as raw materials, energy is invested, and the main product is beyond the energy category, including a product that can be used as a source of energy in the broad sense (for example, to be burned to provide heat), but in general, it is not used for energy use.

Non–industry Consumption Energy refers to the energy consumed by industrial enterprises except for industrial production activities, means that energy consumed by non-industry production and it is not independent accounting units which was engaged in industrial production activities affiliated to industrial enterprises. For example, the energy consumption of technical renovation, maintenance and other processes carried out by construction units of this enterprise, labor protection for non-production areas, energy consumption of scientific research units, farms, motorcade, schools, hospitals, canteens, nursery schools and other units. However, it must be noted that if the above-mentioned units are independently accounted, their use can neither be included in the "industrial energy consumption" nor in the "non-industrial production energy consumption".

Enterprises manufactured means of conveyance(such as making shipyards and automobile manufacturers) adding power oil to finished ships and cars, should be regarded as non-industrial production and consumption of enterprises.

Comprehensive Energy Consumption refers to the sum of the various energy sources for the actual consumption of industrial production during the reporting period (the repeating factors of the conversion of energy processing and energy recovery and utilization have been deducted). When calculating the comprehensive energy consumption, it is necessary to convert the consumption of various types of energy into the consumption measured in accordance with the standard unit of measurement (e.g. tons of standard coal).

Water Intake refers to the amount of water directly extracted from a variety of water sources or purchased from the market for industrial production activities in the factory and office areas, which is based on the actual new amount of water.

External Water Supply refers to the quantity of water or aquatic products supplied to other units by the enterprises, taking the quantity of water away from the plant as the criterion. It includes raw water, tap water, desalination water, mineral water, purified water, etc., which are supplied to other enterprises or markets. Direct current cooling water, reclaimed water (water), unused mine water and rain water, the hot water in the urban heat network supplied by the heating enterprises in the north are not included.

14 建筑业

CONSTRUCTION

资料整理：杨雪峰
Data management: Yang Xuefeng
数据审核：席锋旭
Data audit: Xi Fengxu

第十四部分　建筑业

一、简要说明

1.本章资料反映我市建筑业概况和发展情况。包括建筑业企业基本情况和生产经营情况。主要指标有企业个数、签订合同额、本年新签合同额、建筑业总产值、从事建筑业活动的平均人数、房屋施工面积、营业利润、应交增值税、劳动生产率等。

2.本章资料统计范围，根据建筑业发展的实际情况，建筑业统计范围从2002年年报起由原具有建筑业资质等级四级及四级以上的独立核算的建筑业企业调整为具有建筑业资质的独立核算建筑业企业。

3.本章建筑业企业统计数据是根据国家统计局制定的《建筑业统计报表制度》整理汇总的。资质以内建筑业统计报表由国家统计局根据企业实际情况采取全面调查的方法布置、收集，2011年年报开始由资质内建筑业企业通过联网直报系统上报。

4.2019年年报取消劳务分包建筑业企业生产经营情况表。

二、主要指标

企业个数（个）	1402	比上年增长	3.0%
#国有及国有控股企业	217	比上年增长	12.4%
建筑业总产值（亿元）	5404.47	比上年增长	5.6%
#国有及国有控股企业	4272.50	比上年增长	6.8%
房屋建筑竣工面积（万平方米）	3319.74	比上年下降	4.5%
房屋建筑面积竣工率（%）	14.8	比上年回落	2.4个百分点

14 CONSTRUCTION

I .Brief Introduction

1 .Main Contents:Data in this chapter show the general situation and the development of the construction industry in Xi'an. They cover the situation of production and management of the construction enterprises, including the number of enterprises; total contract value; newly signed contract value; gross output value of the construction industry; the average number of employed persons engaging in the activities of construction enterprises; floor space of building completed in construction enterprises; profits of construction enterprises; value-added tax payable; labor productivity, etc.

2.Scope of Statistics:In view of the development of the construction industry, starting from 2002, the scope of construction statistics has been adjusted to include all the construction enterprises of various types of ownership with qualification certificates and independent accounting systems, replacing the previous criteria that required construction enterprises of various types of ownership to have qualification certificates at or above Class 4 with independent accounting systems.

3.Sources of Data and Methods of Survey:Data on construction enterprises are collected in accordance with the Statistical Reporting System of Construction by the National Bureau of Statistics. The construction statistical reports are deployed and collected through comprehensive surveys by the National Bureau of Statistics in accordance with the real conditions of the enterprises. Since 2011,construction enterprises with qualification certificates reported through internet.

4.The annual report cancels the production and operation table of labor subcontracting construction enterprises in 2019.

II. Major Indicators

		Increase over Preceding Year
Number of Enterprises(item)	1402	3.0%
#State-owned or State-Holding Majority Shares	217	12.4%
Total Output Value of Construction(100 mil. yuan)	5404.47	5.6%
State-owned or State-Holding Majority Shares	4272.50	6.8%
Floor Space of Buildings Completed(10000 sq.m)	3319.74	-4.5%
Rate of Floor Space of Buildings Completed(%)	14.8	-2.4 percentage points

14-1 主要年份建筑业总产值

Total Output Value of Construction in Representative Years

单位：亿元 (100 million yuan)

年 份 Year	单位数（个） Number of Enterprises (unit)	建筑业总产值 Total Output Value of Construction	国有及国有控股 State-owned or State Holding Majority Shares	集体企业 Collective-owned Enterprises
2000	184	105.93	78.87	14.87
2001	205	114.81	91.82	15.47
2002	223	133.47	85.03	15.35
2003	204	177.11	119.99	13.40
2004	244	244.42	201.68	16.59
2005	235	326.65	276.68	19.61
2006	217	416.48	348.20	23.65
2007	279	604.75	432.63	32.67
2008	328	915.12	676.12	460.14
2009	326	1074.55	875.19	47.15
2010	324	1334.00	1034.04	58.39
2011	336	1619.09	1278.33	79.42
2012	396	1874.23	1364.70	96.83
2013	420	2228.41	1702.08	154.87
2014	539	2586.33	1981.24	95.02
2015	706	2650.41	2044.05	69.73
2016	893	2897.55	2288.23	63.35
2017	1055	3304.54	2588.18	70.56
2018	1209	3925.72	3083.48	52.99
2019	1288	4514.38	3467.90	47.48
2020	1361	5124.37	4002.19	24.67
2021	1402	5404.47	4272.50	19.56

注：1.1996年以后建筑业年报统计范围由往年的县及县以上（含县级建制镇）各种经济类型的建筑企业，改为具有建筑业资质等级三级及三级以上的各种经济类型的建筑施工企业；2002年改为具有建筑业资质等级的各种经济类型的建筑施工企业。
2.本表资料含劳务分包企业。
3.由于统计口径变化，对部分年份建筑业总产值相关数据进行了修订。

14-2 全市建筑施工总承包企业基本情况（2021年）

Basic Situation of Construction General Contracting Contractors in Whole City (2021)

指 标	Item	合计 Total	国有及国有控股 State-owned or State Holding Majority Shares
企业单位数（个）	Number of Enterprises (unit)	929	169
#二级以上企业	Special and First and Second Class Enterprise	704	149
计算劳动生产率的平均人数（万人）	Average Number of Employed Persons in Calculation of Labor Productivity (10 000 persons)	91.29	69.43
#二级以上企业	Special and First and Second Class Enterprise	87.81	67.91
建筑业总产值（亿元）	Total Output Value of Construction(100 million yuan)	5025.16	4130.06
#二级以上企业	Special and First and Second Class Enterprise	4870.65	4050.45
全员劳动生产率	Overall Labor Productivity	55.05	59.49
按总产值计算（万元/人）	Calculated by Total Output Value(10 000yuan/person)		

14-3 施工总承包和专业承包建筑企业生产情况（2021年）

分 组	Classify	签订的合同额（万元） Contract Value (10 000 yuan)	上年结转合同额（万元） Contract Value Carried Over from last year (10 000 yuan)	本年新签合同额（万元） Contract Value Signed in this year (10 000 yuan)
总计	**Total**	**151511806**	**69669298**	**81842509**
#国有及国有控股	State-owned and State Holding Majority Shares	128729517	57486506	71243011
一、按登记注册类型分	**Grouped by Registraion Status**			
内资	Domestic Investment Enterprises	150959132	69236420	81722713
国有企业	State-owned Enterprises	3558241	1734110	1824131
集体企业	Collective-owned Enterprises	375319	130975	244344
股份合作企业	Share-holding Cooperative Enterprises	19188		19188
联营企业	Joint Ownership Enterprises	65328	22103	43225
国有独资公司	State-owned Company	25947555	13092075	12855480
其他有限责任公司	Limited Liability Corporations	103713369	44465728	59247641
股份有限公司	Share-holding Corporation Ltd.	148756	41064	107692
私营企业	Private Enterprises	17131378	9750365	7381013
其他企业	Others			
港澳台商投资企业	Enterprises with Funds from Hong Kong,Macao and Taiwan	193918	110476	83442
外商投资企业	Enterprises with Foreign Investment	358756	322402	36353
二、按国民经济行业分	**Grouped by Sector**			
房屋建筑业	Building Engineering Construction	57335127	26808499	30526629
土木工程建筑业	Civil Engineering Construction	86915014	40929493	45985520
建筑安装业	Installation of Construction	5295086	1249076	4046010
建筑装饰和其他建筑业	Architectural Decoration and Other Construction	1966579	682230	1284350
三、按隶属关系分	**Grouped by Administrative Relationship**			
中央	Central	79783636	39155687	40627949
地方	Region	40032227	13640344	26391883
其他	Others	31695944	16873267	14822676
四、按企业资质等级分	**Grouped by Class of Enterprises**			
1. 施工总承包	Overall Contractor for Construction	145279795	67399196	77880599
#特级	Special Class	88891127	39499541	49391586
一级	First Class	43602722	21511313	22091410
二级	Second Class	11156772	5559013	5597759
2. 专业承包	Special Contractor	6232011	2270102	3961910
#一级	First Class	3909115	1161203	2747912
二级	Second Class	1201970	487711	714259

Main Indicators on General Constructing Contractors and Professional Contractors (2021)

建筑业总产值（万元） Total Output Value of Construction (10 000 yuan)	在外省完成的产值 Output Value in Other Provinces	建筑工程产值 Output Value of Construction	安装工程产值 Output Value of Installation	其他产值 Others	竣工产值（万元） Completed Output Value (10 000 yuan)	房屋建筑施工面积（平方米） Number of Projects under Construction (sq.m)	新开工面积 Beginning Projects in This Year
54044702	**26857849**	**47965722**	**4235433**	**1843547**	**17442464**	**224521105**	**54512695**
42724954	24123929	39166758	2153879	1404317	14897220	185518332	44466450
53811623	26783602	47772227	4195849	1843547	17397233	223087100	54345833
1659521	322980	1513497	55203	90821	399211	4012249	117904
195614	1683	164547	24439	6628	70845	1367225	277062
22102		22102			19588		
7425		7425			1242	12424	
9626796	5929701	9117580	165077	344139	4668598	35277587	7251027
33752745	18227434	29988340	2765640	998765	10419347	156664104	38175368
99055	64194	83635	15420		20690		
8448364	2237609	6875101	1170069	403194	1797711	25753511	8524472
118325	72436	97590	20735		27322	996834	161684
114754	1812	95904	18850		17910	437171	5178
20098353	6801874	18609896	1059529	428929	8320174	185257412	43264714
29827356	18601415	26932309	1819318	1075729	8427679	32449290	8930762
2629370	1017970	1183926	1231123	214321	365488	4447694	1067599
1489622	436591	1239591	125463	124568	329124	2366709	1249620
25834650	19955378	24301020	1151404	382226	8388277	72668748	15911142
13989523	3037199	12459161	979723	550640	5704029	97439724	25238474
14220528	3865272	11205541	2104307	910681	3350159	54412633	13363079
50251601	25799988	45084422	3486296	1680883	16524879	221680594	53492002
26161929	15383337	24846487	1127117	188324	8335176	150765110	34315489
16063719	8115304	14061330	1281115	721274	6609307	57533475	15374869
6480874	1596843	5198250	945627	336997	1317889	12620813	3659275
3793101	1057861	2881300	749137	162664	917585	2840511	1020693
2431955	780243	1814043	547819	70094	653306	1688890	872960
849403	181436	639186	129014	81204	218771	305099	57613

14-3 续表

分　组	Classify	房屋竣工面积（平方米）Floor Space of Buildings Completed (sq.m)	房屋竣工价值（万元）Housing Completion Value (10 000 yuan)
总计	**Total**	**33197354**	**7451603**
#国有及国有控股	State-owned and State Holding Majority Shares	25688181	6169623
一、按登记注册类型分	**Grouped by Registraion Status**		
内资	Domestic Investment Enterprises	33050465	7424282
国有企业	State-owned Enterprises	433350	82815
集体企业	Collective-owned Enterprises	280409	49336
股份合作企业	Share-holding Cooperative Enterprises		
联营企业	Joint Ownership Enterprises	12420	1042
国有独资公司	State-owned Company	4111884	1167552
其他有限责任公司	Limited Liability Corporations	23597197	5305468
股份有限公司	Share-holding Corporation Ltd.		
私营企业	Private Enterprises	4615205	818069
其他企业	Others		
港澳台商投资企业	Enterprises with Funds from Hong Kong,Macao and Taiwan	146889	27322
外商投资企业	Enterprises with Foreign Investment		
二、按国民经济行业分	**Grouped by Sector**		
房屋建筑业	Building Engineering Construction	30198513	6844873
土木工程建筑业	Civil Engineering Construction	1934480	504867
建筑安装业	Installation of Construction	290915	53077
建筑装饰和其他建筑业	Architectural Decoration and Other Construction	773446	48786
三、按隶属关系分	**Grouped by Administrative Relationship**		
中央	Central	6723202	1641885
地方	Region	17029877	4119573
其他	Others	9444275	1690146
四、按企业资质等级分	**Grouped by Class of Enterprises**		
1. 施工总承包	Overall Contractor for Construction	32259026	7367515
#特级	Special Class	21056619	4908814
一级	First Class	8472159	1879216
二级	Second Class	2548333	539337
2. 专业承包	Special Contractor	938328	84089
#一级	First Class	379736	36206
二级	Second Class	165953	26312

continued

从事建筑业活动的平均人数（人）Average Number of Employed Persons in Construction Enterprises Productivity(person)	建筑业企业期末从业人员数（人）The Number of Employees in Construction Enterprises at the end of Period (person)	工程技术人员 Technical Personnel	自有机械设备年末净值（万元）The Net Value of Machinery and Equipment Owned at the end of the Year (10 000 yuan)	自有机械设备年末总台数（台）The Total Number of Machinery and Equipment Owned owned (stand)	自有机械设备年末总功率（千瓦）Total Power of Machinery and Equipment Owned at the end of the Year (kW)	企业总产值（万元）Gross Output Value of Enterprises (10 000 yuan)
1000689	**751733**	**122467**	**535050**	**48424**	**3542961**	**67148972**
726255	543099	85282	422794	37747	3152923	56227006
995939	748908	121708	535050	48424	3542961	66851083
52885	42109	7048	11700	4378	144156	1616045
5515	4242	892	1116	662	8460	163663
384	349	75				22102
1097	1042	208	3352	3	18	2625
180948	125547	21813	90794	8120	738756	10827026
535278	392717	60457	335636	26183	2325701	46113526
3304	3202	177				30011
216528	179700	31038	92452	9078	325870	8076085
2221	1870	222				118325
2529	955	537				179564
410512	297679	40102	67885	10602	311658	30141649
506958	393847	69771	448252	33786	3146813	33261237
50825	31314	6868	3647	2480	31424	2549897
32394	28893	5726	15265	1556	53066	1196189
434007	354615	51630	384950	28627	2897390	39735061
236736	143455	25285	30894	8449	235996	13593771
329946	253663	45552	119205	11348	409575	13820140
912898	687151	110016	511056	46012	3486120	63830381
418067	294367	41387	268558	24351	2096819	39016920
327683	262383	40289	160699	13966	1038863	17039488
132396	100304	22051	57018	6478	277942	6274602
87791	64582	12451	23993	2412	56841	3318591
53372	36022	7750	11258	1552	31309	2040095
19172	14991	2937	11041	524	11250	797175

14-4 施工总承包和专业承包建筑业企业主要指标（2021年）

指　　标	Item	企业数（个）Number of Enterprises (unit)	总产值（万元）Total Output Value (10 000 yuan)	从事建筑业活动的平均人数（人）Average Number of Employed Persons in Construction Enterprises (person)
总计	**Total**	**1402**	**54044702**	**1000689**
#国有及国有控股	State-owned and State Holding Majority Shares	217	42724954	726255
一、按登记注册类型分	**Grouped by Registraion Status**			
内资	Domestic Investment Enterprises	1394	53811623	995939
国有企业	State-owned Enterprises	27	1659521	52885
集体企业	Collective-owned Enterprises	29	195614	5515
股份合作企业	Share-holding Cooperative Enterprises	2	22102	384
联营企业	Joint Ownership Enterprises	2	7425	1097
国有独资公司	State-owned Company	65	9626796	180948
其他有限责任公司	Limited Liability Corporations	180	33752745	535278
股份有限公司	Share-holding Corporation Ltd.	8	99055	3304
私营企业	Private Enterprises	1081	8448364	216528
其他企业	Others			
港澳台商投资企业	Enterprises with Funds from Hong Kong,Macao and Taiwan	2	118325	2221
外商投资企业	Enterprises with Foreign Investment	6	114754	2529
二、按国民经济行业分	**Grouped by Sector**			
房屋建筑业	Building Engineering Construction	472	20098353	410512
土木工程建筑业	Civil Engineering Construction	496	29827356	506958
建筑安装业	Installation of Construction	203	2629370	50825
建筑装饰和其他建筑业	Architectural Decoration and Other Construction	231	1489622	32394
三、按隶属关系分	**Grouped by Administrative Relationship**			
中央	Central	61	25834650	434007
地方	Region	130	13989523	236736
其他	Others	1211	14220528	329946
四、按企业资质等级分	**Grouped by Class of Enterprises**			
1. 施工总承包	Overall Contractor for Construction	929	50251601	912898
#特级	Special Class	27	26161929	418067
一级	First Class	187	16063719	327683
二级	Second Class	490	6480874	132396
2. 专业承包	Special Contractor	473	3793101	87791
#一级	First Class	203	2431955	53372
二级	Second Class	194	849403	19172

Major Indicators of General Construction Contractors and Professional Contractors(2021)

建筑业企业期末人数（人） The Number of Employees in Construction Enterprises at the End of Period (person)	利润总额（万元） Total Profit (10000 yuan)	利税总额（万元） Total Profits and Taxes (10000 yuan)	按总产值计算劳动生产率（万元/人） Productivity by Gross Output Value (10000 yuan/person)	产值利润率(%) Profit Rate of Output Value (%)	产值利税率(%) Profit and Tax Rate of Output Value (%)	资产总计（万元） Total Assets (10000 yuan)	负债总计（万元） Total Liabilities (10000 yuan)	资产负债率(%) Asset Liability Ratio (%)
751733	**1811308**	**2811089**	**54.01**	**3.4**	**5.2**	**81467904**	**64832286**	**79.6**
543099	1508620	2106270	58.83	3.5	4.9	65058545	53137699	81.7
748908	1763510	2743049	54.03	3.3	5.1	81111841	64598088	79.6
42109	73179	107115	31.38	4.4	6.5	2230896	1848728	82.9
4242	143	9538	35.47	0.1	4.9	318218	251452	79.0
349	124	783	57.56	0.6	3.5	16038	13022	81.2
1042	313	2109	6.77	4.2	28.4	62664	34455	55.0
125547	368112	543596	53.20	3.8	5.6	16638931	13594170	81.7
392717	1131853	1575020	63.06	3.4	4.7	49435718	40385532	81.7
3202	-2824	1850	29.98	-2.9	1.9	174426	127262	73.0
179700	192609	503038	39.02	2.3	6.0	12234951	8343467	68.2
1870	20706	24521	53.28	17.5	20.7	109584	84832	77.4
955	27093	43519	45.38	23.6	37.9	246479	149366	60.6
297679	597598	1015148	48.96	3.0	5.1	31258606	26383166	84.4
393847	1022047	1467864	58.84	3.4	4.9	44104575	34060796	77.2
31314	163421	254545	51.73	6.2	9.7	4489539	3221813	71.8
28893	28242	73532	45.98	1.9	4.9	1615185	1166510	72.2
354615	774686	1058480	59.53	3.0	4.1	31278898	24816822	79.3
143455	605817	879720	59.09	4.3	6.3	26875741	22493491	83.7
253663	430805	872889	43.10	3.0	6.1	23313265	17521972	75.2
687151	1704080	2566061	55.05	3.4	5.1	76048504	60918210	80.1
294367	1055447	1397016	62.58	4.0	5.3	42718467	35404167	82.9
262383	362527	640639	49.02	2.3	4.0	20818561	16484534	79.2
100304	199645	388346	48.95	3.1	6.0	9833253	7273235	74.0
64582	107229	245028	43.21	2.8	6.5	5419401	3914076	72.2
36022	88833	175537	45.57	3.7	7.2	3339948	2409944	72.2
14991	13201	41826	44.30	1.6	4.9	1182862	766284	64.8

14–5 施工总承包和专业承包建筑业企业财务状况（2021年）

单位：万元

指　标	Item	资产总计 Total Assets	流动资产合计 Total Current Assets
总计	**Total**	**81467904**	**67633687**
#国有及国有控股	State-Owned and State Holding Majority Shares	64993857	52805716
一、按登记注册类型分	**Grouped by Registraion Status**		
内资	Domestic Investment Enterprises	81111841	67278726
国有企业	State-owned Enterprises	2230896	2059784
集体企业	Collective-owned Enterprises	318218	284894
股份合作企业	Share-holding Cooperative Enterprises	16038	14486
联营企业	Joint Ownership Enterprises	62664	58317
国有独资公司	State-owned Company	16638931	13163645
其他有限责任公司	Limited Liability Corporations	49435718	40510748
股份有限公司	Share-holding Corporation Ltd.	174426	140877
私营企业	Private Enterprises	12234951	11045976
其他企业	Others		
港澳台商投资企业	Enterprises with Funds from Hong Kong, Macao and Taiwan	109584	109507
外商投资企业	Enterprises with Foreign Investment	246479	245454
二、按国民经济行业分	**Grouped by Sector**		
房屋建筑业	Building Engineering Construction	31258606	28516068
土木工程建筑业	Civil Engineering Construction	44104575	33657931
建筑安装业	Installation of Construction	4489539	4005086
建筑装饰和其他建筑业	Architectural decoration and other Construction	1615185	1454602
三、按隶属关系分	**Grouped by Administrative Relationship**		
中央	Central	31278898	23052579
地方	Region	26875741	23608485
其他	Others	23313265	20972623
四、按企业资质等级分	**Grouped by Class of Enterprises**		
1. 施工总承包	Overall Contractor for Construction	76048504	62848895
#特级	Special Class	42718467	33929751
一级	First Class	20818561	18685346
二级	Second Class	9833253	8466225
2. 专业承包	Special Contractor	5419401	4784792
#一级	First Class	3339948	3005335
二级	Second Class	1182862	1025417

Financial Status of General Constructing Contractors and Professional Contractors (2021)

(10 000 yuan)

固定资产原价 Original Value of Fixed Assets	累计折旧 Accumulated Depreciation	本年折旧 Depreciation of This Year	负债合计 Total Liabilities	流动负债合计 Total Current Liabilities	非流动负债合计 Total Non Current Liabilities	所有者权益合计 Total Owners' Equity	实收资本 Paid in Capital
4198721	**2350485**	**248587**	**64832286**	**61807399**	**2918030**	**16635619**	**9947202**
3058163	1796591	171549	53088903	50403547	2680460	11904954	6423153
4196759	2348925	248094	64598088	61574437	2918030	16513753	9936802
111021	54066	5520	1848728	1779373	69354	382168	242683
29367	10546	1120	251452	249459	1343	66766	58060
1897	529	407	13022	12961	61	3016	3447
5917	2129	19	34455	20377	14078	28209	14200
981804	696351	66387	13594170	12799829	794160	3044761	1803920
2081842	1109678	105516	40385532	38523900	1855089	9050185	4702770
15454	6477	580	127262	126494	739	47163	31116
969458	469150	68545	8343467	8062044	183207	3891484	3080606
133	55	29	84832	84832		24752	5500
1830	1505	465	149366	148130		97113	4900
745955	343633	39422	26383166	25259305	1062638	4875440	3012844
3120724	1853513	188993	34060796	32352379	1680427	10043779	5810950
202379	94113	11975	3221813	3059069	160486	1267726	758578
129663	59227	8196	1166510	1136646	14480	448675	364830
2525917	1550086	142572	24816822	23507897	1308866	6462076	3461981
481570	220345	25090	22493491	21371321	1117586	4382250	2274153
1191234	580054	80925	17521972	16928181	491578	5791293	4211068
3819711	2166926	223864	60918210	58025627	2827820	15130294	8915716
1743323	977451	102130	35404167	33549204	1854963	7314300	3238925
1326302	831985	70380	16484534	15920284	550855	4334027	3163706
609055	282263	41006	7273235	6856861	380582	2560018	2049723
379010	183559	24723	3914076	3781772	90210	1505325	1031486
205836	110024	12647	2409944	2345918	49188	930004	593029
95948	44382	6416	766284	734868	26282	416578	310201

14-5 续表

单位：万元

指 标	Item	营业收入 Total Revenue	主营业务收入 Main Business Income
总计	**Total**	**60703020**	**59620801**
#国有及国有控股	State-Owned and State Holding Majority Shares	47620122	47178557
一、按登记注册类型分	**Grouped by Registraion Status**		
内资	Domestic Investment Enterprises	60367831	59374897
国有企业	State-owned Enterprises	1814328	1809637
集体企业	Collective-owned Enterprises	257789	257178
股份合作企业	Share-holding Cooperative Enterprises	22963	22401
联营企业	Joint Ownership Enterprises	52695	52695
国有独资公司	State-owned Company	11060683	10814114
其他有限责任公司	Limited Liability Corporations	37088015	36477482
股份有限公司	Share-holding Corporation Ltd.	130083	129757
私营企业	Private Enterprises	9941275	9811633
其他企业	Others		
港澳台商投资企业	Enterprises with Funds from Hong Kong, Macao and Taiwan	116513	116513
外商投资企业	Enterprises with Foreign Investment	218676	129392
二、按国民经济行业分	**Grouped by Sector**		
房屋建筑业	Building Engineering Construction	21433795	21233619
土木工程建筑业	Civil Engineering Construction	34328761	33613712
建筑安装业	Installation of Construction	3267938	3105743
建筑装饰和其他建筑业	Architectural decoration and other Construction	1672526	1667727
三、按隶属关系分	**Grouped by Administrative Relationship**		
中央	Central	27997027	27699634
地方	Region	16400161	16274582
其他	Others	16305832	15646585
四、按企业资质等级分	**Grouped by Class of Enterprises**		
1. 施工总承包	Overall Contractor for Construction	56182757	55240200
#特级	Special Class	32587915	32469486
一级	First Class	14599645	14447088
二级	Second Class	7439238	6872621
2. 专业承包	Special Contractor	4520263	4380601
#一级	First Class	2931564	2924876
二级	Second Class	1001669	999049

continued

(10 000 yuan)

营业成本 Total Cost	主营业务成本 Main Business Costs	税金及附加 Taxes and Other Charges	主营业务税金及附加 The Main Business Tax and Surcharges	管理费用 Management Costs	营业利润 Operating Profit	利润总额 Total Profit	应付职工薪酬 Payable to Employees	应交增值税 Value Added Tax Payable
56911454	**55459618**	**155962**	**148993**	**1360922**	**1805602**	**1811308**	**3420157**	**843818**
44634437	43909006	96669	92414	817077	1503020	1508619	2461338	500932
56626788	55260145	153757	147490	1355066	1758955	1763510	3391825	825782
1666494	1658603	6082	6082	35874	70588	73179	115118	27854
245229	244303	1528	1458	12026	271	143	18992	7867
22440	21899	80	80	314	124	124	671	579
50533	50533	337	322	1088	304	313	1453	1459
10372103	10022597	27851	26523	242148	365873	368112	664484	147633
34763254	34053589	69865	66254	635948	1130964	1131853	1849729	373303
123724	123426	897	896	5670	-2951	-2824	7968	3777
9383011	9085194	47118	45876	421999	193781	192609	733410	263311
94924	92633	611	611	1189	20696	20706	1173	3204
189742	106841	1595	892	4667	25951	27093	27160	14832
20217307	19760691	66302	63184	397677	600556	597598	991117	351249
32230280	31393763	71977	69339	755336	1013917	1022047	2057486	373840
2918464	2767143	10773	10159	129570	161638	163421	270431	80351
1545403	1538022	6911	6312	78340	29492	28242	101123	38379
26534502	26038399	45451	43340	418867	766819	774686	1588478	238343
15085266	14879481	46682	44807	342845	608921	605817	721183	227221
15291687	14541738	63829	60846	599211	429862	430805	1110496	378255
52780536	51485707	139098	133032	1144598	1699137	1704080	3026974	722883
30691480	30322820	60687	58419	473501	1052103	1055447	1350026	280883
13815984	13496176	41551	41036	301553	360892	362527	1043591	236562
6863104	6366438	29241	27092	306699	200529	199645	487875	159460
4130918	3973911	16864	15962	216325	106465	107229	393183	120935
2677642	2653208	10958	10374	126454	87609	88833	189612	75746
918318	910071	3595	3525	58073	13881	13201	81173	25030

14-6 各区县建筑业主要经济指标（2021年）

Major Indicators of Construction Enterprises by Region (2021)

区 县 Region	企业个数（个）Number of Enterprises (unit)	总产值（亿元）Total Output Value (100 million yuan)	从事建筑业活动的平均人数（万人）Average Number of Employed Persons in Construction Enterprises Labor Productivity(10 000person)	全员劳动生产率（万元/人）Overall Labor Productivity (10 000 yuan/person)	利税总额（亿元）Total Pre-tax Profits (100 million yuan)
全 市 Total	**1402**	**5404.47**	**100.07**	**54.01**	**281.11**
新城区 Xincheng	69	381.33	3.74	101.96	13.56
碑林区 Beilin	157	983.55	17.63	55.79	55.71
莲湖区 Lianhu	88	346.54	8.46	40.96	27.48
灞桥区 Baqiao	57	426.45	5.51	77.40	17.37
未央区 Weiyang	270	1178.64	25.01	47.13	51.49
雁塔区 Yanta	428	1345.16	25.08	53.63	75.31
阎良区 Yanliang	35	20.26	0.61	33.21	1.20
临潼区 Lintong	37	12.63	0.35	36.09	0.94
长安区 Chang'an	87	297.34	6.12	48.58	14.53
高陵区 Gaoling	21	20.26	1.12	18.09	1.48
鄠邑区 Huyi	19	16.29	0.39	41.77	1.14
蓝田县 Lantian	16	6.42	0.25	25.68	0.42
周至县 Zhouzhi	18	5.17	0.20	25.85	0.21
西咸新区 Xixian New Area	100	364.43	5.59	65.19	20.25

注：本表数据依据施工总承包和专业承包企业数据加工整理。

14-7 各区县建筑业房屋施工及竣工面积（2021年）

Floor Space of Buildings under Construction & Completed by Region (2021)

区 县	Region	房屋建筑施工面积（万平方米）Floor Space under Construction (10 000sq.m)	本年新开工面积 Newly Started This Year	房屋建筑竣工面积（万平方米）Floor Space of Buildings Completed (10 000sq.m)	竣工房屋价值（亿元）Value of Buildings Completed (100 million yuan)
全 市	**Total**	**22452.11**	**5451.27**	**3319.74**	**745.16**
新城区	Xincheng	777.41	239.55	46.43	10.86
碑林区	Beilin	6628.91	1327.20	1072.81	271.13
莲湖区	Lianhu	3310.31	736.75	466.11	146.36
灞桥区	Baqiao	526.90	99.81	4.31	1.08
未央区	Weiyang	5918.46	1273.34	805.07	134.90
雁塔区	Yanta	3077.44	1114.01	652.68	136.32
阎良区	Yanliang	65.75	43.35	43.25	1.71
临潼区	Lintong	61.68	19.54	11.52	2.98
长安区	Chang'an	645.08	122.84	42.00	3.99
高陵区	Gaoling	57.23	15.62	29.21	5.17
鄠邑区	Huyi	84.17	38.14	22.01	5.55
蓝田县	Lantian	18.03	9.35	9.79	1.76
周至县	Zhouzhi	4.15	3.03	1.46	0.42
西咸新区	Xixian New Area	1276.58	408.75	113.10	22.92

14-8 各区县建筑业企业主要经济效益指标（2021年）

Major Economic Performance Indicators on Construction Enterprises by Region (2021)

区 县	Region	人均利润总额（元/人）Per Profit (yuan/person)	人均利税（元/人）Per Pre-Tax Profits (yuan/person)	人均竣工产值（元/人）Per Output Value of Buildings Completed (yuan/person)	人均施工面积（平方米/人）Per Floor Space of Buildings Under Construction (sq.m/person)	人均竣工面积（平方米/人）Per Floor Space of Buildings Completed (sq.m/person)
全 市	**Total**	**18101**	**28092**	**174305**	**224**	**33**
新城区	Xincheng	23623	36271	905744	208	12
碑林区	Beilin	22026	31597	234960	376	61
莲湖区	Lianhu	22376	32482	258468	391	55
灞桥区	Baqiao	23370	31511	126155	96	1
未央区	Weiyang	13202	20586	91908	237	32
雁塔区	Yanta	18787	30030	149299	123	26
阎良区	Yanliang	5349	19486	161894	107	70
临潼区	Lintong	6117	26741	109228	175	33
长安区	Chang'an	13771	23748	33131	105	7
高陵区	Gaoling	3452	13260	54557	51	26
鄠邑区	Huyi	13634	29092	177983	214	56
蓝田县	Lantian	8563	17117	91018	73	39
周至县	Zhouzhi	177	10539	105351	21	7
西咸新区	Xixian New Area	20413	36247	84858	229	20

14-8 续表 continued

区 县	Region	产值利润率（%）Ratio of Profits to Output Value (%)	产值利税率（%）Ratio of Pre-tax Profits to Output Value (%)	资产利润率（%）Ratio of Profits to Assets (%)	资产利税率（%）Ratio of Pre-tax Profits to Assets (%)	资产负债率（%）Ratio of Debts to Assets (%)
全 市	**Total**	**3.4**	**5.2**	**2.2**	**3.5**	**79.6**
新城区	Xincheng	2.3	3.6	1.9	2.8	85.8
碑林区	Beilin	3.9	5.7	2.4	3.4	84.0
莲湖区	Lianhu	5.5	7.9	1.8	2.7	87.4
灞桥区	Baqiao	3.0	4.1	3.4	4.6	66.2
未央区	Weiyang	2.8	4.4	2.3	3.5	78.6
雁塔区	Yanta	3.5	5.6	2.1	3.3	76.1
阎良区	Yanliang	1.6	5.9	1.1	4.1	74.9
临潼区	Lintong	1.7	7.5	0.6	2.5	67.0
长安区	Chang'an	2.8	4.9	2.5	4.4	78.5
高陵区	Gaoling	1.9	7.3	1.3	4.8	76.3
鄠邑区	Huyi	3.3	7.0	2.8	6.1	72.5
蓝田县	Lantian	3.3	6.6	3.0	6.0	64.7
周至县	Zhouzhi	0.1	4.1		2.3	74.0
西咸新区	Xixian New Area	3.1	5.6	2.6	4.6	74.2

主要统计指标解释

建筑业统计单位 指从事房屋、构筑物建造和设备安装活动的法人企业。建筑业法人企业应具有建筑业资质并能够独立核算，同时其应具备以下条件：①依法成立，有自己的名称、组织机构和场所，能够承担民事责任；②独立拥有和使用资产，承担负债，有权与其他单位签订合同；③独立核算盈亏，能够编制资产负债表。

建筑业总产值 是以货币形式表现的建筑业企业在一定时期内生产的建筑业产品和提供的服务的总和。建筑业总产值包括：

（1）建筑工程产值：指列入建筑工程预算内的各种工程价值。

（2）安装工程产值：指设备安装工程价值，不包括被安装设备本身的价值。

（3）其他产值：建筑业总产值中除建筑工程、安装工程以外的产值。包括房屋构筑物修理产值、非标准设备制造产值、总包企业向分包企业收取的管理费以及不能明确划分的施工活动所完成的产值。

a. 房屋构筑物修理产值：指房屋和构筑物修理所完成的产值，但不包括被修理房屋、构筑物本身价值和生产设备的修理价值。

b. 非标准设备制造产值：指加工制造没有定型的非标准生产设备的加工费和原材料价值（如化工厂、炼油厂用的各种罐、槽，矿井生产统一使用的各种漏斗、三角槽、阀门等）以及附属加工厂为本企业承建工程制作的非标准设备的价值。

建筑业增加值 指建筑业企业在报告期内以货币形式表现的建筑业生产经营活动的最终成果。

从2004年第一次全国经济普查开始，建筑业现价增加值按生产法和分配法（收入法）两种方法计算，以收入法的计算结果为准，即从收入的角度出发，根据生产要素在生产过程中应得的收入份额计算。具体计算方法：经济普查年度建筑业增加值按照《经济普查年度GDP核算方案》计算，非经济普查年度建筑业增加值按照《非经济普查年度GDP核算方案》计算。

房屋建筑施工面积 指在报告期内施过工的全部房屋建筑面积，包括本期新开工的房屋面积、上期施工跨入本期继续施工的房屋面积、上期停缓建在本期恢复施工的房屋面积、本期竣工的房屋面积及本期施工后又停缓建的房屋面积。

房屋建筑竣工面积 指在报告期内房屋建筑按照设计要求全部完工，达到了使用条件，经验收鉴定合格，正式移交使用单位的房屋建筑面积。

Explanatory Notes on Main Statistical Indicators

Statistical Unit in the Construction Industry refers to a corporate enterprise engaged in the construction of buildings and structures and in the installation of equipment. A corporate construction enterprise should have qualification certificates with the independent accounting system. It should meet the following three requirements: a) being set up in line with relevant legal basis, having its full name, organization and location, and being capable of taking civil liabilities; b) independently possessing and using its assets and assuming its liabilities, and entitled to sign contracts with other institutions; c) making independent accounts of its profits and losses, and capable of compiling its balance sheet.

Gross Output Value of Construction refers to total of construction products and services, expressed in monetary terms, produced or rendered by construction and installation enterprises during a given period of time. It includes:

(1)Output value of construction projects: the value of projects covered by the project budgets;

(2) Output value of installation projects: the value of the installation of equipment, (excluding the value of the equipment to be installed);

(3)Other output values: the output value of the construction industry apart from that of construction projects and installation projects. It includes: output value of repair of buildings and structures; output value of non-standard equipment manufacturing, overhead expenses received by contracted enterprises from the sub-contracted enterprises and the completed output value of construction activities for which there is no clear definition.

a. Output value of repair of buildings and structures: the value created through the repairs of buildings or structures. It does not include the value of buildings or structures being repaired and the value of the repair of production equipment;

b. Output value of non-standard manufactured equipment: the value of non-standard production equipment, including raw materials and manufacturing cost, made for the construction project (i.e., chemical plant; kettles or tanks used by refineries; various fillers, triangle tanks, valves used by mines). It also includes the output value of equipment manufactured by subsidiary workshops.

Value-added of Construction refers to the final result of the activities of production and operation of enterprises of the construction industry in monetary terms during the reference period. Starting from the 2004 economic census, the value-added of construction is calculated by both production approach and income approach, with the figures from the income approach as the final figures. Under the income approach, calculation starts from the perspective of income and is based on the share of income derived from the production process by the relevant factors of production. Specifically, value-added of construction for the Census years is calculated in accordance with the Programme of Compilation of GDP and National Accounts for the Year of Economic Census, and value- added of construction for other years is calculated in accordance with the Programme of Compilation of GDP and National Accounts for the Non-Economic Census Years.

Floor Space of Buildings Under Construction refers to floor space of buildings under construction during the reference period, including the floor space of buildings for which construction has newly started, buildings for which construction has started earlier and is continuing during the reference period, and buildings for which construction has been suspended earlier but has restarted during the reference period; buildings completed during the reference period; and buildings under construction but construction has subsequently been during the reference period.

Floor Space of Buildings Completed refers to the floor space of buildings that are completed in the reference period in accordance with the requirements of the design, up to the standard for being put into use, and having been checked and accepted by departments concerned as qualified ones.

15 运输邮电和信息化

TRANSPORT,POSTAL TELECOMMUNICATION SERVICE AND INFORMATIZATION

资料整理：陈春光　刘志杰
Data management: Chen Chunguang　Liu Zhijie
数据审核：刘栋婷
Data audit: Liu Dongting

第十五部分　运输邮电和信息化

一、简要说明

本章资料包括交通运输业和邮电通信业的基本情况，主要是交通运输工具、货物和旅客运输量、邮电业务、邮政局所及服务点等基本情况，以及一套表单位信息化情况。运输邮电资料由西安市统计局服务业和社会科技统计处根据有关部门提供资料整理。信息化资料主要根据国家统计联网直报平台一套表单位的信息化统计数据整理。2017年起运输邮电数据为西安原口径数据，信息化数据为包含西咸新区数据。

二、主要指标

邮电业务总量（亿元）	2039.02	比上年增长	18.4%
全社会车辆数（万辆）	445.38	比上年增长	11.9%
#民用小轿车	237.78	比上年增长	7.9%

15　TRANSPORT,POSTAL TELECOMMUNICATION SERVICES AND INFORMATIZATION

Ⅰ.Brief Introduction

Data in this chapter consists of primarily basic condition of transportation, postal service and communication, mainly including transportation facility amount of goods and passenger transportation, basic data of postal service, post offices and service establishments of Xi'an City. Data on transportation industry in this chapter is compiled by Tertiary Industry and Social&Science and Technology Division of the Xi'an Bureau of Statistics according to the data provided by department concerned of the municipal government. Data on informationization are obtained from data in "Five Top" Units of National Statistical Networking Platrform. Since 2017, the range of data on transportation, post and communication industry is the original range in Xi'an and data on informationization includes data in XiXian.

Ⅱ.Major Indicators

		Increase over Preceding Year
Amount of Postal and Telecommunication Service(100 mil. yuan)	2039.02	18.4%
Number of Vehicles in the whole Society(10000 unit)	445.38	11.9%
Civil Car	237.78	7.9%

15-1 主要年份各种交通线路和桥梁

Transportation Routes and Bridges in Representative Years

年 份 Year	公路里程 （公里） Length of Highways (km)	桥 梁 （座） Bridges (seat)	桥梁长度 （米） Length of Bridge (m)
1989	2563		
1990	2586		
1991	2785		
1992	2786		
1993	2801		
1994	2830		
1995	2852		
1996	2877		
1997	3026		
1998	3047		
1999	2789		
2000	3010		
2001	3298		
2002	7862	629	29799
2003	8360	629	29799
2004	8360	629	29799
2005	8500	634	46973
2006	9530	634	46973
2007	9672	1319	91412
2008	11895	1710	151996
2009	12378	1856	154866
2010	12378	1856	154866
2011	12599	1863	149743
2012	13127	2190	214978
2013	13135	2213	224962
2014	13251	2213	224949
2015	13328	2323	250910
2016	13356	2423	256058
2017	13383	2435	286841
2018	14722	2413	292710
2019	13386	2436	300939
2020	13755	2447	321458
2021	13640	3374	427421

注：1.本表数据来自市交通局。
2.民航通航里程2013年统计口径发生较大变化,从2018年起此数据不再统计。
3.2018年桥梁数和桥梁长度重新进行了修订。
4.本表数据为西安原口径数据。

15-1 续表 continued

年 份 Year	永久式桥梁 （座） Permanent Bridges (seat)	永久式桥梁长度 （米） Length of Permanent Bridges(m)	民航通航里程 （重复航线）（公里） Length of Total Civil Aviation Routes(km)
1989			
1990			
1991			
1992			65007
1993			83215
1994			100800
1995			119753
1996			126433
1997			173010
1998			180000
1999			141284
2000			139764
2001			154614
2002	629	29799	211000
2003	629	29799	381800
2004	629	29799	386953
2005	632	46915	485749
2006	632	46915	418852
2007	1275	90716	553355
2008	1657	150980	515524
2009	1803	153850	587904
2010	1803	153850	742375
2011	1811	148810	898628
2012	2138	213985	981450
2013	2161	223970	70643568
2014	2171	224165	78626210
2015	2286	250175	93375419
2016	2386	255322	92561215
2017	2399	286164	113501600
2018	2438	292960	
2019	2414	300416	
2020	2431	321044	
2021	3359	427018	

15-2 各种交通线路里程和桥梁数（2021年）

Length of Transportation Routes and Number of Bridges (2021)

指　标	Item	2021
公路里程（公里）	**Length of Highways(km)**	**13640**
等级公路	Expressways and Class I to IV Highways	13450
高速	Expressway	652
一级	First Class	430
二级	Second Class	1284
三级	Third Class	1081
四级	Fourth Class	10003
等外公路	Highways below Class IV	190
桥梁	**Bridges**	
永久式桥梁	Permanent	
座（座）	Seat(seat)	3359
长度（米）	Length(m)	427018
民航航线条数（条）	**Length of Civil Aviation routes(Article)**	**321**
国际航线（条）	International routes(Article)	28

注：1.本表数据来自市交通局，为西安原口径数据。
2.自2021年起，国际航线为在营航线数。

15-3 主要年份全社会车辆数

Possession of Civil Vehicles in Representative Years

单位：辆、台 (unit)

年 份 Year	合计 Total	汽车 Motor	载客汽车 Passenger vehicles	载货汽车 Ordinary Trucks	摩托车 Motorcycles	拖拉机 Tractors
1999	**279335**	133192	63772	44348		38023
2000	**310252**	138318	89783	44974		37177
2001	**369988**	172436	110744	55453		31355
2002	**454998**	206653	134527	64623	176960	36083
2003	**516719**	242599	163872	70781	191834	34733
2004	**512802**	276012	195524	74557	156709	34755
2005	**544586**	377628	240923	82463	131440	34741
2006	**608155**	393778	296078	89772	131449	33236
2007	**840376**	522616	360081	97614	284594	32028
2008	**875005**	595735	430472	89093	247079	30176
2009	**1012937**	754803	567326	113430	224121	31347
2010	**1253461**	961283	739038	145740	259239	29151
2011	**1445811**	1174874	928669	171649	241132	25600
2012	**1633257**	1380125	1123105	186412	224279	24458
2013	**1862063**	1634885	1372371	207058	200419	21898
2014	**2139024**	1926012	1658714	224409	190625	17484
2015	**2394052**	2191023	1929195	224322	179619	18099
2016	**2588479**	2444000	2191862	226915	119771	19352
2017	**2885557**	2716361	2451906	243998	145207	17776
2018	**3256344**	3098008	2804240	272474	134264	16808
2019	**3594233**	3427557	3137323	269155	158203	
2020	**3980103**	3734527	3424924	290062	235573	
2021	**4453781**	4090847	3747797	320941	351273	

注：本表数据来自市车管所，为西安原口径数据。

15-4 全社会车辆数（2021年）

Possession of Civil Vehicles (2021)

单位：辆 (unit)

指 标	Item	2021
合计	**Total**	**4453781**
民用汽车	Motor	4090847
#私人汽车拥有量	Possession of Private Vehicles	3690627
载客汽车	Passenger Vehicles	3747797
#大 型	Large	20067
轿 车	Car	2377777
普通载货汽车	Ordinary Trucks	320941
#重、中型	Heavy and Medium	78904
#三轮汽车	Three Wheelers Cars	1508
摩托车	Motorcycle	351273
普通摩托车	Bicycle Motor	298027
挂车	Articulated Trailers	11661
其他类型车	Others	

注：本表数据来自市车管所，为西安原口径数据。

15-5 主要年份交通运输量及周转量

Passenger Traffic and Kilometers and Freight Traffic and Ton-kilometers in Representative Years

年 份 Year	客运量 （万人次） Passenger Traffic (10 000 person-times)	旅客周转量 （万人公里） Passenger-Km (10 000 person-Km)	货运量 （万吨） Freight Traffic (10 000 tons)	货物周转量 （万吨公里） Freight Ton-Km (10 000 ton-Km)
1978	1334		3723	
1979	1420		3919	
1980	1508		3655	
1981	1839		3379	
1982	2340		4067	
1983	3054		4225	
1984	2899		4966	
1985	2404		5681	
1986	2186		5409	
1987	3781		6294	
1988	5721		6968	
1989	6092		8742	
1990	5748		6980	
1991	4193		3389	
1992	4368		8233	
1993	8036		8406	
1994	8321		8754	
1995	9069		9590	
1996	9854		10577	
1997	8922		9358	
1998	9223		9429	
1999	10311	2130383	9766	3452383
2000	8068	2507896	6999	3691963
2001	9078	2658037	7728	4229430
2002	12399	2524444	9482	4544040
2003	11413	2596402	9392	5037684
2004	10832	3112374	14845	5850029
2005	10479	1607568	12051	1249525
2006	11245	1721217	11832	1354318
2007	12466	1753464	15124	1473182
2008	26501	2529007	27560	3490707
2009	28693	2582025	30606	3766806
2010	30294	2942957	34323	4301680
2011	33375	3223544	39239	5212010
2012	36154	3387448	44924	5958742
2013	38289	3634915	50119	6471497
2014	25719	3091147	42039	6234128
2015	26904	3241463	46270	6430083
2016	23671	2909172	23888	5521252
2017	24287	3267158	25497	5979131
2018	26057	3624193	26219	5188953
2019	26315	3875080	27426	5190086
2020	14338	2314604	25713	5026965
2021	10632	2204462	27048	5054835

注：1.本表数据由市交通局、西安铁路局、咸阳机场、长安航空公司、东方航空公司西北分公司提供，2018年起铁路数据为西铁局西安辖区数据，与以前年度不可比。

2.2016年陕西省公路运输统计计算系数变化，因此与往年数据不可比。

3.本表数据为西安原口径数据。

15-6 交通运输量及运输周转量（2020-2021年）

Passenger Traffic and Kilometers and Freight Traffic and Ton-kilometers (2020-2021)

指　标	Item	2020	2021
一、客运量合计（万人次）	**Passenger Traffic(10 000 person-times)**	**14338**	**10632**
铁路	Railways	3745	4283
公路	Highways	7486	3332
民航	Civil Aviation	3107	3017
二、旅客周转量合计（万人公里）	**Passenger-Km(10 000 person-Km)**	**2314604**	**2204462**
铁路	Railways	480108	522624
公路	Highways	465858	308396
民航	Civil Aviation	1368638	1373441
三、货运量合计（万吨）	**Freight Traffic(10 000 tons)**	**25713**	**27048**
铁路	Railways	471	481
公路	Highways	25204	26527
民航	Civil Aviation	38	40
四、货物周转量合计（万吨公里）	**Freight Ton-Kin(10 000 ton-Km)**	**5026965**	**5054835**
铁路	Railways	1279281	1338517
公路	Highways	3736745	3705345
民航	Civil Aviation	10939	10973

注：1.本表数据由市交通局、西安铁路局、咸阳机场、长安航空公司、东方航空公司西北分公司提供，2018年起铁路数据为西铁局西安辖区数据。
2.本表数据为西安原口径数据。

15-7 主要年份邮政电信情况

年 份 Year	邮电业务总量（万元） Business Volume of Postal and Telecommunication Services(10 000 yuan)	电信业务总量 Business Volume of Telecommunication Services	邮政业务总量 Business Volume of Postal Services
1978	1420		
1979	1616		
1980	1640		
1981	1713		
1982	2154		
1983	2250		
1984	2484		
1985	2972		
1986	3244		
1987	3911		
1988	5327		
1989	5973		
1990	7843		
1991	5700		
1992	6610		
1993	36581		
1994	54034		
1995	76450		
1996	104566		
1997	124601		
1998	204927		
1999	306457		
2000	461628		
2001	367620		
2002	515259	470492	44767
2003	820943	770673	50270
2004	1027415	975045	52370
2005	1320447	1261033	59414
2006	1867560	1796533	71027
2007	2267633	2191250	76383
2008	2646662	2564524	82138
2009	2989246	2900836	88410
2010	3231059	3167750	63309
2011	2005025	1944329	60696
2012	2162035	2098273	63762
2013	2479430	2313630	165800
2014	2922011	2695332	226679
2015	3315324	2983024	332300
2016	3831119	3299859	531260
2017	4398547	3728783	669764
2018	7395253	6621776	773477
2019	14217000	13096111	1120889
2020	17215477	15810239	1405238
2021	20390158	19502959	887199

注：1.2002年及以后，邮政电信机构分离；2001－2010年邮电业务总量按2000年不变价格计算；2011－2021年邮电业务总量按2010年不变价格计算，故与以往年份不可比。
2.本表数据为西安原口径数据。
3.本表数据由市邮政管理局，中国联通、中国电信、中国移动等西安分公司提供。

Basic Statistic on Postal and Telecommunication Service in Representative Years

固定电话年末用户数（户） Number of Immobile Telephone at Year-end (subscriber)	农村电话用户数 Number of Telephone in Rural Areas at Year-end	移动电话用户年末数（户） Number of Mobile Phone at Year-end (subscriber)	互联网年末宽带用户数（户） Number of Broad Band Net User (subscriber)
12828	1062		
13487	1052		
14024	1086		
14497	1125		
15357	1129		
16922	1156		
18611	1203		
21624	1239		
26373	1235		
30200	1290		
34265	1357		
39506	1498		
45267	1668		
49516	2479		
60727	2613		
101327	2671		
197398	5067		
299485	8386		
430270	13654		
573244	21202		
736998	37863		
874586	74761		
1242637	170199		
1711500	259374	1277400	17183
2095230	358803	1964200	35230
2538393	415593	2412392	160900
2934424	480276	3500900	243448
3214806	500847	4199570	339280
3159639	467526	5510720	508775
3145819	419446	6645863	586213
3068807	383869	7377575	813987
2891009	358238	11200566	1167916
2617691	335048	14230800	1461804
2703640	320189	16141463	1841027
3110176	335864	18035397	2023059
3191112	330602	21606662	2670473
3066575	372823	20253157	2779458
2920773	306336	17669953	2899714
2843336	314457	17395026	3358343
2732174	294055	18542137	3467859
2622787	244984	18580879	3924786
2500807	206246	17113569	4386532
2389480	191674	17044663	4792399
2403150	214041	17589986	6158669

15-8　主要年份邮政业务及服务网点

Postal Service and Branch Post Office in Representative Years

指　标	Item	2014	2015	2016	2017	2018	2019	2020	2021
一、邮政业务总量（万元）	**Business Volume of Postal Services (10 000 yuan)**	**226679**	**332300**	**531260**	**669764**	**773477**	**1120889**	**1405238**	**887199**
二、邮政业务收入（万元）	**Gross Income of Post Services (10 000 yuan)**	**213893**	**307008**	**439867**	**544555**	**616823**	**794417**	**912500**	**1015100**
其中：快递业务收入	Express Delivery Business Income	134306	207451	331605	413699	475783	624260	757100	841800
三、函件（万件）	**Number of Letters(10 000 pcs)**	**2112**	**1707**	**1367**	**1360**	**1081**	**1028**	**902**	**810**
四、包件（万件）	**Parcels(10 000 pcs)**	**71**	**69**	**51**	**48**	**49**	**31**	**26**	**26**
五、汇票（万张）	**Money Order(10 000 pcs)**	**81**	**48**	**17**	**15**	**11**	**16**	**12**	**8**
六、报纸订销累计份数（万份）	**Accumulated Newspaper Prescribing and Sales Volume(10 000 pcs)**	**14338**	**14457**	**14395**	**14744**	**14915**	**14749**	**14462**	**15855**
七、杂志订销累计份数（万份）	**Accumulated Magazine Prescribing and Sales Volume(10 000 pcs)**	**1572**	**1285**	**1155**	**956**	**1059**	**760**	**656**	**622**
八、特快专递类业务（万件）	**Express Mail Service Volume(10 000 pcs)**	**22289**	**23724**	**43941**	**64961**	**86995**	**63110**	**69815**	**21733**
九、集邮业务量（万枚）	**Stamps For Collection(10 000 pcs)**	**1477**	**1920**	**1607**	**1687**	**1135**	**51**	**54**	**16**
十、邮政营销网点（处）	**Number of Post Office Branch Establishments(unit)**	**280**	**299**	**297**	**297**	**297**	**297**	**308**	**316**
#设在农村的局所	In it: Number of Post Offices in Rural Area	123	140	149	149	148	148	148	149
十一、邮政信筒信箱（个）	**Number of Mailboxes(unit)**	**1170**	**1170**	**422**	**422**	**290**	**417**	**246**	**914**

注：1.本表数据来自市邮政管理局，2013年邮政数据统计口径变化，对部分历史数据进行了修订。
2.本表数据为西安原口径数据。

15–9 主要年份电信业务情况

Telecommunication Service in Representative Years

指　标	Item	2014	2015	2016	2017	2018	2019	2020	2021
一、电信业务总量（万元）	**Business Volume of Telecommunication Services(10 000 yuan)**	**2695332**	**2983024**	**3299859**	**3728783**	**6621776**	**13096111**	**15810239**	**19502959**
二、电信业务总收入（万元）	**Gross Income of Telecommunication Services(10 000 yuan)**	**1356705**	**1338203**	**1420708**	**1451625**	**1495207**	**1465283**	**1547138**	**1681870**
三、固定电话年末用户数（万户）	**Number of Immobile Telephone at Year-end(10 000 subscribers)**	**306.66**	**292.08**	**284.33**	**273.22**	**262.28**	**250.08**	**238.95**	**240.32**
#农村电话年末户数（万户）	Number of Telephone in Rural Areas at Year-end(10 000 subscribers)	37.28	30.63	31.45	29.41	24.50	20.62	19.17	21.40
四、电话交换机总容量（万门）	**Capacity (number) of Telephone Switchboard(10 000 lines)**	**230.01**	**145.08**	**75.92**					
五、移动电话用户年末数（万户）	**Number of Mobile Phone at Year-end (10 000 subscribers)**	**2025.32**	**1767.00**	**1739.50**	**1854.21**	**1858.09**	**1711.36**	**1704.47**	**1759.00**
#5G（4G）电话用户数	5G(4G)Mobile Phone Subscribers			1113.03	1369.00	1499.18	1439.45	1353.40	756.51
六、互联网年末用户数（万户）	**Number of Broad Band Net User (10 000 subscribers)**	**277.95**	**289.97**	**335.83**	**346.79**	**392.48**	**438.65**	**479.24**	**615.87**

注：1.本表数据由中国联通、中国电信、中国移动等西安分公司提供，为西安原口径数据。
　　2.2020年及以前，5G（4G）电话用户数为4G电话用户数，2021年为5G电话用户数。

15-10 一套表单位信息化基本情况（2021年）

单位：个

指　标	Item	企业数 Number of Enterprises
总计	**Total**	**9293**
按国民经济门类分	**According To the Categories of National Economy**	
采矿业	Mining Industry	14
制造业	Manufacturing Industry	1567
电力、热力、燃气及水生产和供应业	Electricity,Heat,Gas and Water Production and Supply	69
建筑业	Construction Business	1277
批发和零售业	Wholesale and Retail Trade	2299
交通运输、仓储和邮政业	Transportation, Warehousing and Postal Services	232
住宿和餐饮业	Accommodation and Catering Industry	747
信息传输、软件和信息技术服务业	Information Transmission,Software and Information Technology	362
房地产业	Estate	1307
租赁和商务服务业	Leasing and Business Services	462
科学研究和技术服务业	Scientific Eesearch and Eechnical Services	444
水利、环境和公共设施管理业	Management of Water Wonservancy, Environment and Public Facilities	64
居民服务、修理和其他服务业	Services of Households,Repairs and Other Services	70
教育	Education	26
卫生和社会工作	Health and Social Service	74
文化、体育和娱乐业	Culture,Sports and Entertainment	279

注：一套表单位包括规模以上工业企业、限额以上批零住餐企业、资质以内建筑业企业、规模以上服务业企业、房地产开发经营企业。

Basic Statistics on Informatization of "One Sheet" Units (2021)

(unit)

使用计算机的企业 Computer-used Enterprise	有信息技术人员的企业 Enterprises with Information Technology Personnel	有局域网的企业 LAN Enterprises	使用信息化管理的企业 Enterprises Managed by Information Technology	有信息化投入的企业 Enterprises with Informatization Input
9288	**6910**	**7015**	**8839**	**7254**
14	10	8	12	9
1567	1421	1367	1535	1414
69	60	53	69	63
1277	980	918	1213	1048
2299	1459	1624	2142	1627
231	156	170	216	161
746	528	548	705	561
362	348	321	354	340
1304	867	936	1236	970
462	332	326	436	311
444	375	361	433	378
64	46	50	60	48
70	54	52	69	53
26	24	22	26	20
74	68	63	72	70
279	182	196	261	181

15-11 一套表单位信息化设施及投入情况（2021年）

指 标	Item	期末使用计算机数量（台）Computers Used at the End of Period (unit)
总计	**Total**	**790262**
按国民经济门类分	**According To the Categories of National Economy**	
采矿业	Mining Industry	9047
制造业	Manufacturing Industry	185165
电力、热力、燃气及水生产和供应业	Electricity,Heat,Gas and Water Production and Supply	8817
建筑业	Construction Business	90981
批发和零售业	Wholesale and Retail Trade	78508
交通运输、仓储和邮政业	Transportation, Warehousing and Postal Services	33612
住宿和餐饮业	Accommodation and Catering Industry	18544
信息传输、软件和信息技术服务业	Information Transmission,Software and Information Technology	180874
房地产业	Estate	42135
租赁和商务服务业	Leasing and Business Services	24497
科学研究和技术服务业	Scientific Eesearch and Eechnical Services	76173
水利、环境和公共设施管理业	Management of Water Wonservancy, Environment and Public Facilities	4261
居民服务、修理和其他服务业	Services of Households,Repairs and Other Services	1475
教育	Education	10080
卫生和社会工作	Health and Social Service	15836
文化、体育和娱乐业	Culture,Sports and Entertainment	10257

注：一套表单位包括规模以上工业企业、限额以上批零住餐企业、资质以内建筑业企业、规模以上服务业企业、房地产开发经营企业。

Information Technology Facilities and Investment of "One Sheet" Units (2021)

信息技术人员 （人） Information Technology Personnel (Person)	拥有网站个数 （个） Number of Websites Owned (unit)
55844	**5757**
66	7
9473	1346
451	37
4735	743
4477	1039
1053	116
1278	348
23746	363
2212	710
2343	322
4185	396
221	33
188	30
274	27
261	79
881	161

15-12 一套表单位信息化管理情况（2021年）

单位：个

指 标	Item	企业数 Number of Enterprises	使用信息化管理的企业 Number of Enterprises Managed by Information Technology
总计	**Total**	**9293**	**8839**
按国民经济门类分	**According To the Categories of National Economy**		
采矿业	Mining Industry	14	12
制造业	Manufacturing Industry	1567	1535
电力、燃气及水的生产供应业	Electricity,Heat,Gas and Water Production and Supply	69	69
建筑业	Construction Business	1277	1213
批发和零售业	Wholesale and Retail Trade	2299	2142
交通运输、仓储和邮政业	Transportation,Warehousing and Postal Services	232	216
住宿和餐饮业	Accommodation and Catering Industry	747	705
信息传输、软件和信息技术服务业	Information Transmission,Software and Information Technology	362	354
房地产业	Estate	1307	1236
租赁和商务服务业	Leasing and Business Services	462	436
科学研究和技术服务业	Scientific Eesearch and Eechnical Services	444	433
水利、环境和公共设施管理业	Management of Water Wonservancy, Environment and Public Facilities	64	60
居民服务、修理和其他服务业	Services of Households,Repairs and Other Services	70	69
教育	Education	26	26
卫生和社会工作	Health and Social Service	74	72
文化、体育和娱乐业	Culture,Sports and Entertainment	279	261

注：一套表单位包括规模以上工业企业、限额以上批零住餐企业、资质以内建筑业企业、规模以上服务业企业、房地产开发经营企业。

Information Management Situation of "One Sheet" Units (2021)

(unit)

财务管理 Financial Management	购销存管理 Purchase and Sale Management	生产制造管理 Manufacturing Management	物流配送管理 Logistics Distribution Management	客户关系管理 Customer Relationship Management	人力资源管理 Human Resource Management	产品研发管理 Product Research and Development Management	其他 Others
8098	**4040**	**1277**	**954**	**2566**	**3230**	**659**	**1218**
11	5	2	1	3	4	2	
1437	1055	810	272	432	539	300	138
61	32	26	4	15	25		8
1145	249	93	42	272	495	34	209
1869	1482	77	426	680	548	41	228
197	51	18	80	47	76	4	32
618	372	30	38	218	205	10	127
331	120	32	28	132	197	121	46
1164	322	93	21	388	559	56	189
411	65	8	12	143	185	20	73
411	108	61	8	120	214	62	82
53	16	2		4	25		11
57	28	4	3	17	22	1	9
25	5			8	11	1	3
64	47	9	2	21	30	1	16
244	83	12	17	66	95	6	47

15-13 一套表单位电子商务交易情况（2021年）

指　标	Item	企业数（个）Number of Enterprises (unit)
总计	**Total**	**9293**
按国民经济门类分	**According To the Categories of National Economy**	
采矿业	Mining Industry	14
制造业	Manufacturing Industry	1567
电力、燃气及水的生产供应业	Electricity,Heat,Gas and Water Production and Supply	69
建筑业	Construction Business	1277
批发和零售业	Wholesale and Retail Trade	2299
交通运输、仓储和邮政业	Transportation,Warehousing and Postal Services	232
住宿和餐饮业	Accommodation and Catering Industry	747
信息传输、软件和信息技术服务业	Information Transmission,Software and Information Technology	362
房地产业	Estate	1307
租赁和商务服务业	Leasing and Business Services	462
科学研究和技术服务业	Scientific Eesearch and Eechnical Services	444
水利、环境和公共设施管理业	Management of Water Wonservancy, Environment and Public Facilities	64
居民服务、修理和其他服务业	Services of Households,Repairs and Other Services	70
教育	Education	26
卫生和社会工作	Health and Social Service	74
文化、体育和娱乐业	Culture,Sports and Entertainment	279

注：一套表单位包括规模以上工业企业、限额以上批零住餐企业、资质以内建筑业企业、规模以上服务业企业、房地产开发经营企业。

E-commerce Transactions of "One Sheet" Units (2021)

有电子商务交易的企业（个）Enterprises with Ecommerce Transactions(unit)	有电子商务销售的企业 Ecommerce Sales Enterprises	有电子商务采购的企业 E-Commerce Purchases Enterprises	拥有电子商务交易平台的企业（个）With Ecommerce Trading Platform Enterprises(unit)	全年电子商务销售金额（万元）Sales of Ecommerce (10 000 yuan)	全年电子商务采购金额（万元）Purchases of Ecommerce (10 000 yuan)
1245	**1039**	**454**	**109**	**18948342**	**12837376**
140	85	79	8	281008	778129
4	1	3	1	24410	824
65	5	62	3	252	3117521
411	396	158	49	17481807	8693177
17	10	9	4	281261	14206
398	395	44	6	317723	2351
54	36	28	13	340352	170184
23	8	17	5	5377	1355
41	34	13	9	114907	52217
28	12	21	3	16184	4004
6	6			5090	
8	6	5		1513	72
4	3	4		42556	3028
6	5	2		6361	61
40	37	9	8	29540	245

主要统计指标解释

公路里程 指报告期末公路的实际长度。统计范围：包括城间、城乡间、乡（村）间能行驶汽车的公共道路，公路通过城镇街道的里程，公路桥梁长度、隧道长度、渡口宽度。不包括城市街道里程，断头路里程，农（林）业生产用道路里程，工（矿）企业等内部道路里程。统计原则：按已竣工验收或交付使用的实际里程计算；两条或多条公路共同经由同一路段的重复里程，只计算一次。

货（客）运量 指在一定时期内，各种运输工具实际运送的货物重量（旅客数量）。货运按吨计算，客运按人计算。货物不论运输距离长短、货物类别，均按实际重量统计。旅客不论行程远近或票价多少，均按一人一次客运量统计；半价票、儿童票也按一人统计。

货物（旅客）周转量 指在一定时期内，由各种运输工具运送的货物（旅客）数量与其相应运输距离的乘积之总和。该指标可以反映运输业生产的总成果，也是编制和检查运输生产计划，计算运输效率、劳动生产率以及核算运输单位成本的主要基础资料。计算货物周转量通常按发出站与到达站之间的最短距离，也就是计费距离计算。计算公式为：

货物（旅客）周转量=∑（货物（旅客）运输量×运输距离）

邮政、电信业务总量 指以货币形式表示的邮政、电信通信企业为社会提供各类邮政、电信通信服务的总数量。计算方法为各类业务的实物量分别乘以相应的不变单价，求出各类业务的货币量加总求得。没有不变单价的业务按其业务收入直接相加。

移动电话用户 指在电信运营企业营业网点办理开户登记手续，通过移动电话交换机进入移动电话网，占用移动电话号码的各类电话用户。包括各类签约用户、智能网预付费用户、无线上网卡用户。

局用交换机容量 指安装在电信企业内用于接续本地固定电话的电话交换机容量，包括接入网设备容量（安装在电信运营企业用于连接语音用户的远端节点的设备容量）。

计算机数 指报告期末企业（单位）使用的计算机数量，包括台式机、笔记本电脑和平板电脑。

信息技术人员 指专职从事信息技术系统的制定、设计、开发、安装、操作、维护、管理和评估的人员。

信息化投入 包括企业（单位）一次性投入和运营维护投入。

一次性投入 包括企业（单位）购置各类硬件和软件的实际支出。

运营维护投入 包括企业（单位）更新维护各类信息通信硬件和软件的实际支出。

互联网 指在世界范围内的公共计算机网络。它提供一系列通信服务（包括万维网）的接入，并传送电子邮件、新闻、娱乐和数据文件等。

全年电子商务销售金额 指报告期内企业（单位）借助网络订单而销售的商品和服务总额。借助网络订单指通过网络接受订单，付款和配送可以不借助于网络。

全年电子商务采购金额 指报告期内企业（单位）借助网络订单而采购的商品和服务总额。借助网络订单指通过网络发送订单，付款和配送可以不借助于网络。

Explanatory Notes on Main Statistical Indicators

Length of highways refers to the actual length of highways at the end of the reporting period. It includes highways between cities, between cities and rural areas, and between rural areas that cars can run on, highways passing through streets of towns, and the length of bridges, tunnels, and ferries. It does not include the length of streets in cities or dead-end highways, or highways built for production purposes in agricultural and forest areas, or highways inside factories and mining companies. According to the statistical principles, the actual length should be calculated after the highway is completed or ready to be put into practice. If two or more highways go the same section of the way, the length of the section is only calculated once.

Freight (Passenger) traffic refers to the volume of freight (passenger) transported by various means in a designated period. Freight transport is calculated in tons and passenger traffic in the number of persons. Despite the type of freight and traveling distance, the freight transport is calculated in the actual weight of the goods: and despite the traveling distance and ticket price, the passenger traffic is calculated by the principle that one person can be counted only once in one travel. The passenger who travels with a half-price ticket or a child ticket is also calculated as one person.

Freight Ton-kilometers (Passenger-kilometers) refer to the added sum of the volume of freight (passengers) transported by various means multiplied by the corresponding transport distance in a designated period. This is an important indicator to show the total results of the transport industry, to prepare and examine the transport plan, and to measure the efficiency, the labor productivity, and the unit cost of transport. Normally, the shortest distance between the departure station and the destination station (i.e., the payable distance) is the basis to calculate the freight ton-kilometers. The formula is as follows:

Freight Ton-kilometers (Passenger-kilometers) = Freight (Passenger) Traffic×Distance of Transportation)

Business volume of postal and telecommunications refers to the total monetary amount of postal and telecommunications services provided by postal and telecommunications enterprises for the society. The calculating approach is to multiply the physical volume of all types of business with the corresponding constant price, and then add up all the monetary results thereof. Businesses without constant unit prices are directly added according to their business revenue

Mobile telephone subscribers refer to people who own mobile telephone numbers, have completed registration at mobile communication business outlets, and are connected to the mobile telephone communication network through the mobile telephone switchboards, including all kinds of contracted users, prepaid users of intelligent network, and wireless network card users.

Capacity of office telephone exchanges refers to the capacity of telephone exchanges installed in telecommunication enterprises for communication between fixed local telephones, including the capacity of access network equipment (the remote nodes installed in telecommunication operating enterprises to interconnect voice users).

The number of computer refers to the number of computers used in an enterprise or a company at the end of the reporting period, including desktops, laptops, and tablet computers.

Information technology personnel refers topeople who is engaged in the formulation, design, development, installation, operation, maintenance, management and evaluation of an information technology system.

Informatization Input includes the One-time investment input and operation maintenance investment of an enterprise or a company.

One-time Investment Input includes the actual expenditure in purchasing all kinds of hardware and software of an enterprise or a company.

Operation and Maintenance Input includesthe actual expenditure inupdating and maintenance of all kinds of information communication hardware and software of an enterprise or a company.

The Internet refers to the public computer network around the world. It provides access to a range of communications services including the world wide web, and transmits e-mail, news, entertainment, and data files,etc.

The amount of E-commerce sales during the whole year the total amount of goods and services sold by means of network orders of an enterprise or a company during the reporting period.By means of network orders means that the orders are received over the network, but the payment and distribution can be made without the network.

The amount of E-commerce purchases during the whole year refers to the total amount of goods and services purchased by means of network orders of an enterprise or a company during the reporting period.

By means of network orders means that the orders are sent over the network, but the payment and distribution can be made without the network.

16 国内贸易

DOMESTIC TRADE

资料整理：王　峰　宣耀华　赵琳瑛　李鹏涛　闫小溪　刘琼之
Data management: Wang Feng Xuan Yaohua Zhao Linying Li Pengtao Yan Xiaoxi Liu Qiongzhi
数据审核：赵　晖
Data audit: Zhao Hui

第十六部分　国内贸易

一、简要说明

1.本章资料反映西安市批发和零售业、住宿和餐饮业的发展与经营状况，主要内容包括：社会消费品零售总额，限额以上批发和零售业、住宿和餐饮业基本情况，连锁经营情况，重点交易市场情况等。

2.2021年数据不含西安（西咸新区）—咸阳共管区。

3.限额以上企业指年主营业务收入2000万元及以上的批发企业（单位）；500万元及以上的零售业企业（单位）；200万元及以上的住宿和餐饮业企业（单位）。

4.批发业、零售业、住宿业、餐饮业大中小微型企业划分按照《统计上大中小微型企业划分办法（2017）》标准执行。

二、主要指标

社会消费品零售总额（亿元）	4963.42	比上年增长	0.8%

16 DOMESTIC TRADE

I.Brief Introduction

1.This chapter reflects the management and development of wholesale and retail trades, hotels and catering services in Xi'an , mainly including: total retail sales of consumer goods, the basic conditions enterprises above designated size in wholesale and retail trades, hotels and catering services, the conditions of chain stores,focus on transaction markets, etc.

2.The data in 2021 exclude areas mutually controlled by Xi'an (Xixian New Area) – Xianyang.

3.Enterprises above designated size cover wholesale enterprises with revenue from principal business over 20 million yuan, retail enterprises with revenue from principal business over 5 million yuan, hotel and catering services enterprises with revenue from principal business over 2 million yuan.

4.The division standard of large/medium/small/mini sized enterprises of wholesale, retail trades,hotels and catering services is based on the Division Standard of Large/Medium/Small/Mini Sized Enterprises in 2017.

Ⅱ. Maior Indicators

		Increase over Preceding Year
Total Retail Sales of Consumer Goods (100 mil. yuan)	4963.42	0.8%

16-1 主要年份社会消费品零售总额

Total Retail Sales of Consumer Goods in Representative Years

单位：亿元 (100 million yuan)

年　份 Year	社会消费品零售总额 Total Retail Sales of Consumer Goods	城镇 Urban	乡村 Village	批发和零售贸易业 Wholesale Trades and Retail Trades	住宿餐饮业 Accommodation and Catering Trade	其他行业 Others
1978	12.70	8.82	3.88	11.01	0.53	0.21
1980	15.88	11.53	4.35	13.05	0.80	0.20
1985	32.92	26.09	6.83	25.04	1.69	0.48
1986	37.50	29.25	8.25	28.88	1.97	0.64
1987	43.86	34.62	9.24	33.32	2.50	0.49
1988	59.65	47.74	11.91	44.84	2.97	0.78
1989	68.05	54.60	13.45	54.41	2.98	0.76
1990	72.77	59.42	13.35	57.46	3.79	0.90
1991	81.04	66.93	14.11	60.35	4.43	1.26
1992	100.84	89.17	11.67	71.86	6.13	2.30
1993	117.10	105.97	11.13	77.12	7.60	2.75
1994	148.95	135.48	13.47	92.46	9.39	3.53
1995	188.35	167.54	20.81	116.54	12.08	3.76
1996	225.71	200.65	25.06	146.85	16.03	4.07
1997	268.49	241.79	26.70	171.65	22.46	4.23
1998	296.71	262.04	34.67	186.74	31.53	4.35
1999	330.13	289.24	40.89	212.31	35.51	4.95
2000	368.96	324.63	44.33	238.41	42.40	5.56
2001	416.95	368.46	48.49	272.26	50.16	6.01
2002	473.12	421.77	51.35	318.35	52.91	6.64
2003	518.67	463.95	54.72	454.32	55.00	9.36
2004	601.12	541.21	59.91	529.43	59.09	12.60
2005	698.37	629.71	68.66	617.36	66.23	14.79
2006	819.32	739.33	80.00	724.42	78.04	16.86
2007	979.18	884.40	94.78	866.67	93.42	19.10
2008	1233.44	1115.35	118.09	1082.92	128.84	21.68
2009	1469.37	1404.26	65.11	1313.89	155.47	
2010	1765.42	1694.79	70.63	1575.73	189.69	
2011	2146.43	2071.87	74.55	1921.76	224.67	
2012	2530.95	2453.11	77.84	2273.52	257.43	

年　份 Year	社会消费品零售总额 Total Retail Sales of Consumer Goods	按销售单位所在地分 By Location of Establishments			按消费形态分By Consumption Patterns	
		城镇零售额 Urban Areas	城区 Urban District	乡村零售额 Rural Areas	商品零售 Retail Sales	餐饮收入 Catering income
2013	2898.62	2808.37	2245.35	90.25	2669.52	229.10
2014	3277.33	3174.09	2749.92	103.24	3034.94	242.39
2015	3620.90	3501.23	3011.94	119.67	3345.59	275.32
2016	4012.44	3876.23	3479.35	136.20	3713.16	299.28
2017	4422.72	4264.73	3667.72	157.99	4075.53	347.18
2018	4854.70	4759.97	4067.48	94.73	4476.48	378.22
2019	5140.93	5039.17	4280.42	101.76	4733.65	407.28
2020	4989.33	4881.52	4145.45	107.81	4636.57	352.77
2021	4963.42	4806.07	4135.92	157.35	4555.98	407.45

注：本表1993-2017年数据根据第四次全国经济普查结果进行了修订，2018年为经普数。

16-2 社会消费品零售总额

Total Retail Sales of Consumer Goods

单位：亿元 (100 million yuan)

分 类	Classify	2020	2021
社会消费品零售总额	**Total Retail Sales of Consumer Goods**	**4989.33**	**4963.42**
（一）按销售单位所在地分	Grouped by Region		
（1）城镇	Urban Areas	4881.52	4806.07
#城区	Urban District	4145.45	4135.92
（2）乡村	Rural Areas	107.81	157.35
（二）按消费形态分	Grouped by Consumption Patterns		
（1）商品零售	Retail Sales	4636.57	4555.98
（2）餐饮收入	Catering Income	352.77	407.45

16-3 主要年份各区县社会消费品零售总额

Total Retail Sales of Consumer Goods by Region in Representative Years

单位：亿元 (100 million yuan)

区 县	Region	2005	2010	2011	2012	2013	2014	2015	2016	2017	2018	2019	2020	2021
全 市	**Total**	**698.37**	**1765.42**	**2146.43**	**2530.95**	**2898.62**	**3277.33**	**3620.90**	**4012.44**	**4422.72**	**4854.70**	**5140.93**	**4989.33**	**4963.42**
新城区	Xincheng	58.12	121.94	145.61	167.61	187.08	209.82	235.49	255.50	259.80	292.82	293.11	252.50	253.36
碑林区	Beilin	130.35	269.18	321.45	368.06	412.03	468.74	523.35	566.28	568.99	584.86	622.29	556.00	592.05
莲湖区	Lianhu	124.47	238.27	284.80	326.71	367.14	411.75	453.14	490.72	493.16	507.10	553.76	482.37	518.55
灞桥区	Baqiao	32.63	86.80	117.08	163.08	224.57	262.22	296.24	341.66	366.32	417.48	448.66	516.66	530.32
未央区	Weiyang	103.08	372.62	454.94	542.65	631.55	717.33	773.27	875.42	772.86	865.32	904.20	909.49	827.04
雁塔区	Yanta	156.02	462.69	563.77	659.18	739.97	826.95	915.51	991.33	1006.54	1107.71	1162.36	1144.40	1139.20
阎良区	Yanliang	6.55	14.80	17.90	20.72	23.17	25.83	28.19	30.51	31.27	34.81	38.33	37.22	31.59
临潼区	Lintong	13.25	25.26	30.52	35.19	38.80	44.02	47.55	51.36	54.25	61.57	64.77	55.09	63.09
长安区	Chang'an	39.55	92.22	111.30	129.03	142.84	161.78	181.97	199.95	211.78	240.51	251.33	232.46	229.38
高陵区	Gaoling	11.68	32.86	40.68	51.68	57.26	65.08	73.15	102.17	110.09	127.80	142.11	177.86	180.68
鄠邑区	Huyi	8.21	17.92	21.52	24.67	27.47	31.03	34.58	37.79	38.91	44.05	46.78	41.25	46.11
蓝田县	Lantian	8.15	16.96	20.26	23.24	25.64	28.94	31.84	34.88	36.67	42.91	47.63	39.20	41.82
周至县	Zhouzhi	6.31	13.91	16.61	19.15	21.11	23.83	26.63	34.88	36.44	40.77	40.85	34.33	38.03
西咸新区	Xixian New Area									435.65	487.00	524.74	510.51	472.21

注：本表2017年及之前年份数据根据第四次全国经济普查结果进行了修订。

16-4 限额以上批发和零售贸易企业财务状况（2021年）

单位：万元

分 组	Classify	单位数（个） Number (unit)	资产总计 Total Assets	流动资产合 计 Circulating Funds
总计	**Total**	**2375**	**50309764.1**	**41624761.6**
一、批发企业	**Wholesale Enterprises**	**1485**	**38422456.9**	**33972456.7**
1. 按登记注册类型分组	Grouped by Category of Commodities			
内资	Domestic Funded Enterprises	1452	31267042.0	27471518.4
国有	State-owned Enterprises	37	6746443.0	5878637.6
集体	Collective-owned Enterprises	4	31115.0	15705.7
股份合作	Cooperative Enterprises	1	38171.4	28056.5
联营	Joint Ownership Enterprises			
国有联营	State Joint Ownership Enterprises			
集体联营	Collective Joint Ownership Enterprises			
国有与集体联营	Joint State-collective Enterprises			
其他联营	Others Joint Ownership Enterprises			
有限责任公司	Limited Liability Corporations	298	14277323.8	12358815.7
国有独资公司	State Funded Corporations	27	2915236.7	2364256.1
其他有限责任公司	Other Limited Liability Corporations	271	11362087.1	9994559.6
股份有限公司	Share-holding Corporations Ltd.	20	1951577.3	1565320.7
私营	Private Enterprises	1091	8219066.4	7621646.9
私营独资	Private-funded Enterprises	5	11625.5	9625.7
私营合伙	Private Partnership Enterprises	1	1765.4	1624.7
私营有限责任公司	Private Limited Liability Corporations	1078	8099708.3	7522440.9
私营股份有限公司	Private Share-holding Corporations Ltd.	7	105967.2	87955.6
其他	Other Enterprises	1	3345.1	3335.3
港澳台商投资	Enterprises with Funds from Hong Kong, Macao &Taiwan	10	614721.0	544295.5
外商投资	Foreign Funded Enterprises	23	6540693.9	5956642.8
2. 按国民经济行业分组	Grouped by Sector			

Financial Status of Wholesale and Retail Enterprises above Designated Size (2021)

(10 000 yuan)

固定资产原价 Original Value of Fixed Assets	累计折旧 Accumulated Depreciation	负债合计 Total Liabilities	流动负债合计 Circulating Liabilities	所有者权益合计 Total Owners' Equities	实收资本 Paid in Capital	营业收入 Total Revenue	主营业务收入 Revenue from Principal Business
3232202.5	**1254477.0**	**38535940.2**	**36163059.5**	**10582774.5**	**6824746.4**	**121439937.2**	**120390434.5**
1202868.9	**482188.5**	**29752099.3**	**28578973.9**	**7688277.2**	**4823489.8**	**100545503.5**	**99862839.8**
1167846.5	467914.9	23387231.2	22325590.4	6902039.1	4441353.1	86769254.4	86103274.7
143654.5	77319.7	4859303.4	4279884.0	1887139.6	1264908.1	21793827.3	21780713.1
12166.6	3191.5	16592.4	17925.2	13075.8	11415.0	10204.5	9764.5
15.7	0.3	27802.0	27760.9	10369.4	10000.0	49034.2	49034.2
473371.9	146771.3	10226389.0	9975409.9	3096118.9	1919535.9	35086341.5	34567497.4
38059.5	19015.9	2147223.5	2075654.2	768013.2	419314.7	11120449.2	10678518.0
435312.4	127755.4	8079165.5	7899755.7	2328105.7	1500221.2	23965892.3	23888979.4
126458.2	55725.6	1648108.3	1641484.3	303469.0	141695.4	6879718.0	6820725.6
412166.8	184903.5	6605753.1	6379843.1	1591804.3	1093748.7	22942422.6	22867833.6
735.9	402.0	9472.4	7272.2	2153.1	1650.0	19388.2	19388.2
158.6	18.0	1398.7	1398.7	366.7		13721.0	13721.0
402547.3	178710.1	6542538.2	6325729.4	1535661.1	1050948.7	22762394.9	22687820.8
8725.0	5773.4	52343.8	45442.8	53623.4	41150.0	146918.5	146903.6
12.8	3.0	3283.0	3283.0	62.1	50.0	7706.3	7706.3
13697.9	6424.0	306783.3	293648.2	307937.7	104029.7	901460.8	899210.1
21324.5	7849.6	6058084.8	5959735.3	478300.4	278107.0	12874788.3	12860355.0

16-4 续表1

单位：万元

分　组	Classify	营业成本 Total Cost	税金及附加 Taxes and Other Changes
总计	**Total**	**115891541.8**	**344892.8**
一、批发企业	**Wholesale Enterprises**	**97410257.5**	**271987.2**
1. 按登记注册类型分组	Grouped by Category of Commodities		
内资	Domestic Funded Enterprises	83920836.0	264962.5
国有	State-owned Enterprises	21221295.9	206770.9
集体	Collective-owned Enterprises	9059.7	35.1
股份合作	Cooperative Enterprises	48541.7	38.1
联营	Joint Ownership Enterprises		
国有联营	State Joint Ownership Enterprises		
集体联营	Collective Joint Ownership Enterprises		
国有与集体联营	Joint State-collective Enterprises		
其他联营	Others Joint Ownership Enterprises		
有限责任公司	Limited Liability Corporations	34160121.7	30469.9
国有独资公司	State Funded Corporations	10988132.6	8486.7
其他有限责任公司	Other Limited Liability Corporations	23171989.1	21983.2
股份有限公司	Share-holding Corporations Ltd.	6749458.2	4874.0
私营	Private Enterprises	21725067.8	22769.2
私营独资	Private-funded Enterprises	18275.7	19.6
私营合伙	Private Partnership Enterprises	13184.9	6.8
私营有限责任公司	Private Limited Liability Corporations	21560318.7	22625.2
私营股份有限公司	Private Share-holding Corporations Ltd.	133288.5	117.6
其他	Other Enterprises	7291.0	5.3
港澳台商投资	Enterprises with Funds from Hong Kong, Macao &Taiwan	759944.7	2607.6
外商投资	Foreign Funded Enterprises	12729476.8	4417.1
2. 按国民经济行业分组	Grouped by Sector		

continued 1

(10 000 yuan)

销售费用 Sale Expenses	管理费用 Management Expenses	财务费用 Financial Expenses	营业利润 Business Profits	利润总额 Total Profits	应付职工薪酬 Salary Payable	所得税费用 Income Tax Expenses	应交增值税 Value Added Tax Payable
2952100.2	**1179442.1**	**422765.6**	**795396.3**	**850773.1**	**1373227.8**	**211823.6**	**688981.3**
1360996.4	**630590.5**	**296340.5**	**655883.8**	**673776.5**	**655604.0**	**145898.5**	**413152.8**
1244460.0	584204.1	266429.8	533670.4	550426.6	596705.6	118968.8	386726.0
86750.8	72496.7	46556.8	159696.4	162759.0	91239.5	59869.7	76716.6
454.2	839.4	217.2	-369.4	-339.6	680.2	4.5	53.3
0.1	35.4	65.5	492.5	492.5	5.7	123.1	25.4
368729.5	212276.6	138224.4	222242.5	222441.7	240494.5	19245.5	118392.9
39280.1	36321.3	20526.9	50991.0	51215.8	51655.6	2904.8	16497.6
329449.4	175955.3	117697.5	171251.5	171225.9	188838.9	16340.7	101895.3
130619.1	17042.0	8835.0	-13914.9	-9780.5	49503.4	4187.9	18432.4
657664.2	281404.4	72519.1	165476.9	174807.2	214732.6	35537.8	173105.4
96.8	714.4	54.2	176.0	173.3	224.4	14.5	95.2
226.8	104.4	27.6	170.2	171.2	38.8	2.5	44.2
648628.8	277176.8	71882.5	164554.0	173925.1	212772.8	35393.1	172109.8
8711.8	3408.8	554.8	576.7	537.6	1696.6	127.7	856.2
242.1	109.6	11.8	46.4	46.3	49.7	0.3	
77696.6	25730.6	512.6	67686.6	69324.0	40252.6	10505.0	17407.5
38839.8	20655.8	29398.1	54526.8	54025.9	18645.8	16424.7	9019.3

16-4 续表2

单位：万元

分 组	Classify	单位数（个）Number (unit)	资产总计 Total Assets	流动资产合 计 Circulating Funds
农、林、牧、渔产品批发	Wholesale of Agricultural,Forestry,Livestock and Fishery Products	14	122510.6	97907.6
食品、饮料及烟草制品批发	Wholesale of food Beverages and Tobaccos	154	2618935.6	2273109.9
纺织、服装及家庭用品批发	Wholesale of Textiles, Garments and Daily Articles	79	1132028.0	1028617.0
文化、体育用品及器材批发	Wholesale of Culture, Sports Appliances and Equipment	50	641418.1	496894.1
医药及医疗器材批发	Wholesale of Medicines and Medical Appliances	202	4346174.9	4073017.9
矿产品、建材及化工产品批发	Wholesale of Mineral Products, Building Materials and Chemical Products	642	24821536.7	22021946.5
机械设备、五金产品及电子产品批发	Wholesale of Machinery, Hardware, and Electronic Equipment	302	4183538.7	3645622.7
贸易经纪与代理	Trade Broker and Agency	5	94848.0	89597.1
其他批发业	Other wholesale not Classified Elsewhere	37	461466.3	245743.9
二、零售企业	**Retail Trade**	**890**	**11887307.2**	**7652304.9**
1. 按登记注册类型分组	Grouped by Category of Commodities			
内资	Domestic Funded Enterprises	825	8058982.0	5696988.3
国有	State-owned Enterprises	14	483313.9	418471.4
集体	Collective-owned Enterprises	7	8076.7	6407.5
股份合作	Cooperative Enterprises			
联营	Joint Ownership Enterprises			
国有联营	State Joint Ownership Enterprises			
集体联营	Collective Joint Ownership Enterprises			
国有与集体联营	Joint State-collective Enterprises			
其他联营	Others Joint Ownership Enterprises			
有限责任公司	Limited Liability Corporations	190	2888747.1	1734033.1
国有独资公司	State Funded Corporations	11	358260.6	233030.1

continued 2

(10 000 yuan)

固定资产原价 Original Value of Fixed Assets	累计折旧 Accumulated Depreciation	负债合计 Total Liabilities	流动负债合计 Circulating Liabilities	所有者权益合计 Total Owners' Equities	实收资本 Paid in Capital	营业收入 Total Revenue	主营业务收入 Revenue from Principal Business
15298.5	5431.1	82565.2	77727.2	39945.4	28011.0	168551.7	166477.2
174951.9	86821.3	1124920.4	1335525.7	985797.5	217182.9	3447247.7	3413909.8
33606.8	21249.8	738878.9	732281.0	393149.1	149107.9	1847374.8	1836737.0
40191.7	14885.6	435179.2	403944.3	206238.9	115804.0	1190929.1	1184903.6
187109.7	77917.4	3621923.9	3551051.1	724251.0	428954.9	5852882.0	5834565.3
495869.1	186702.4	20165183.7	19115883.2	4208496.6	3146430.4	79555899.8	79376079.3
151137.7	68747.9	3147467.1	3079390.4	1027090.5	621454.3	7527767.6	7101200.7
4586.2	518.1	85864.4	82927.5	8983.6	5643.8	199583.7	198980.7
100117.3	19914.9	350116.5	200243.5	94324.6	110900.6	755267.1	749986.2
2029333.6	**772288.5**	**8783840.9**	**7584085.6**	**2894497.3**	**2001256.6**	**20894433.7**	**20527594.7**
1222754.3	422100.1	5998121.9	5357202.6	1862029.4	1457826.4	10958846.2	10756161.7
52325.7	18088.6	190599.5	276479.2	290999.4	16649.7	520375.6	513989.0
705.5	457.9	5372.7	4131.5	2704.0	433.8	21351.2	21044.8
614674.3	191004.1	2314169.4	1871982.3	570719.8	568300.0	4003395.4	3927676.9
107701.0	18188.0	263849.4	190386.8	94411.2	74802.4	428110.3	420414.6

16-4 续表3

单位：万元

分 组	Classify	营业成本 Total Cost	税金及附加 Taxs and Other Changes
农、林、牧、渔产品批发	Wholesale of Agricultural,Forestry,Livestock and Fishery Products	160703.4	107.3
食品、饮料及烟草制品批发	Wholesale of food Beverages and Tobaccos	2787565.1	200302.5
纺织、服装及家庭用品批发	Wholesale of Textiles, Garments and Daily Articles	1633613.0	3626.2
文化、体育用品及器材批发	Wholesale of Culture, Sports Appliances and Equipment	1097224.9	1233.1
医药及医疗器材批发	Wholesale of Medicines and Medical Appliances	5360324.7	12372.8
矿产品、建材及化工产品批发	Wholesale of Mineral Products, Building Materials and Chemical Products	78322475.1	45099.4
机械设备、五金产品及电子产品批发	Wholesale of Machinery, Hardware, and Electronic Equipment	7132148.0	8311.7
贸易经纪与代理	Trade Broker and Agency	188452.7	90.0
其他批发业	Other wholesale not Classified Elsewhere	727750.6	844.2
二、零售企业	**Retail Trade**	**18481284.3**	**72905.6**
1. 按登记注册类型分组	Grouped by Category of Commodities		
内资	Domestic Funded Enterprises	9682416.2	40784.1
国有	State-owned Enterprises	442641.9	2125.1
集体	Collective-owned Enterprises	16786.2	84.2
股份合作	Cooperative Enterprises		
联营	Joint Ownership Enterprises		
国有联营	State Joint Ownership Enterprises		
集体联营	Collective Joint Ownership Enterprises		
国有与集体联营	Joint State-collective Enterprises		
其他联营	Others Joint Ownership Enterprises		
有限责任公司	Limited Liability Corporations	3573702.5	23178.7
国有独资公司	State Funded Corporations	388909.4	955.0

continued 3

(10 000 yuan)

销售费用 Sale Expenses	管理费用 Management Expenses	财务费用 Financial Expenses	营业利润 Business Profits	利润总额 Total Profits	应付职工薪酬 Salary Payable	所得税费用 Income Tax Expenses	应交增值税 Value Added Tax Payable
4262.8	2402.1	1592.8	-2734.2	-2490.4	3277.5	30.7	636.8
156246.3	82090.5	-637.9	238452.2	240884.6	113677.9	66730.4	81532.8
148875.9	45656.6	48.8	15802.6	17022.1	64688.3	4382.8	24984.3
31481.5	38696.8	550.4	19998.4	19914.6	26271.9	2481.3	2809.0
234455.2	123294.1	69437.9	79499.0	83794.5	120608.7	16395.2	79055.6
587662.7	228090.3	205783.4	210493.3	216245.0	214542.1	53794.5	169293.4
176573.1	96969.2	9853.8	101220.8	105106.1	103131.1	1102.3	52116.0
6839.1	2948.2	456.2	816.9	748.7	1739.7	273.2	430.1
14599.8	10442.7	9255.1	-7665.2	-7448.7	7666.8	708.1	2294.8
1591103.8	**548851.6**	**126425.1**	**139512.5**	**176996.6**	**717623.8**	**65925.1**	**275828.5**
794330.0	380450.6	79467.2	32488.8	50615.4	485093.6	31837.5	162637.0
25915.1	26115.0	-295.5	24526.2	25400.2	52287.6	6124.2	11971.1
2889.0	1205.4	21.5	364.5	358.0	1877.9	35.6	613.1
275297.4	126140.6	35210.5	-9382.8	-5932.1	155174.5	12688.7	60714.0
22418.9	11293.1	2840.6	2504.7	2627.4	19490.1	493.4	1302.8

16-4 续表4

单位：万元

分 组	Classify	单位数（个） Number (unit)	资产总计 Total Assets	流动资产合 计 Circulating Funds
其他有限责任公司	Other Limited Liability Corporations	179	2530486.5	1501003.0
股份有限公司	Share-holding Corporations Ltd.	5	550024.4	301634.7
私营	Private Enterprises	606	4125814.1	3235404.4
私营独资	Private-funded Enterprises	20	17640.4	13453.6
私营合伙	Private Partnership Enterprises	1	401.5	318.1
私营有限责任公司	Private Limited Liability Corporations	582	4071886.4	3190605.9
私营股份有限公司	Private Share-holding Corporations Ltd.	3	35885.8	31026.8
其他	Other Enterprises	3	3005.8	1037.2
港澳台商投资	Enterprises with Funds from Hong Kong, Macao &Taiwan	27	1800910.8	1109864.1
外商投资	Foreign Funded Enterprises	38	2027414.4	845452.5
2. 按国民经济行业分组	Grouped by Sector			
综合零售	Integrated Retail	102	3684606.6	1951251.9
食品、饮料及烟草制品专门零售	Special Retail of Food, Beverages and Tobaccos	66	248793.8	206302.3
纺织、服装及日用品专门零售	Special Retail of Textiles,Garments and Daily Consumer Articles	51	549468.7	289729.2
文化、体育用品及器材专门零售	Special Retail of Culture,Sports Appliances and Equipment	59	374757.2	244366.0
医药及医疗器材专门零售	Special Retail of Medicines and Medical Appliances	45	458578.6	349910.0
汽车、摩托车、零配件和燃料及其他动力销售	Special Retail of Automobiles, Motorcycles, Spare Parts and Fuel and Other Power	331	4580885.3	2977511.1
家用电器及电子产品专门零售	Special Retail of Household Electric Appliances and Electronic Products	94	651185.9	596097.1
五金、家具及室内装饰材料专门零售	Special Retail of Hardware,Furniture and Decoration Materials	26	369370.7	253558.7
货摊、无店铺及其他零售业	Non-shop and Other Retail	116	969660.4	783578.6

continued 4

(10 000 yuan)

固定资产原价 Original Value of Fixed Assets	累计折旧 Accumulated Depreciation	负债合计 Total Liabilities	流动负债合计 Circulating Liabilities	所有者权益合计 Total Owners' Equities	实收资本 Paid in Capital	营业收入 Total Revenue	主营业务收入 Revenue from Principal Business
506973.3	172816.1	2050320.0	1681595.5	476308.6	493497.6	3575285.1	3507262.3
39276.8	30150.1	110476.2	166806.4	275535.1	289487.4	37004.5	36758.2
513521.1	181889.2	3376710.0	3036989.1	719859.4	580772.5	6371024.7	6250998.0
4946.4	2212.9	14422.5	13768.8	3217.9	2479.4	59216.6	59182.5
104.1	3.9	251.0	248.1	150.5	100.0	3218.9	3218.9
502108.8	175679.0	3343402.8	3004338.5	699238.9	573193.1	6223776.4	6103783.8
6361.8	3993.4	18633.7	18633.7	17252.1	5000.0	84812.8	84812.8
2250.9	510.2	794.1	814.1	2211.7	2183.0	5694.8	5694.8
227541.2	111506.9	1463612.1	1203871.1	327088.7	169056.5	5223037.7	5125088.7
579038.1	238681.5	1322106.9	1023011.9	705379.2	374373.7	4712549.8	4646344.3
981315.0	373663.1	2856028.6	2248465.9	806408.1	742143.8	3634135.9	3471175.5
22821.1	8067.1	211745.9	184565.8	34750.1	66604.7	315107.4	310870.2
135517.9	51505.9	352296.2	263165.1	197172.5	111567.2	619755.2	597718.5
101877.3	18483.0	280923.9	258558.1	93672.4	100836.7	252734.7	245316.3
29723.2	11710.2	344082.7	299122.0	114495.9	34129.4	669251.4	666663.9
657906.0	271867.1	3208654.4	2820906.8	1357452.7	719562.2	9123177.0	8980408.2
13990.0	7176.5	475376.4	436721.9	175760.5	120215.0	855330.5	839391.7
51648.4	17570.4	340200.4	319794.0	25027.8	47545.2	163224.3	159650.1
34534.7	12245.2	714532.4	752786.0	89757.3	58652.4	5261717.3	5256400.3

16-4 续表5

单位：万元

分 组	Classify	营业成本 Total Cost	税金及附加 Taxs and Other Changes
其他有限责任公司	Other Limited Liability Corporations	3184793.1	22223.7
股份有限公司	Share-holding Corporations Ltd.	24644.5	192.6
私营	Private Enterprises	5619316.8	15199.9
私营独资	Private-funded Enterprises	54156.4	153.9
私营合伙	Private Partnership Enterprises	2230.8	29.6
私营有限责任公司	Private Limited Liability Corporations	5491893.9	14725.8
私营股份有限公司	Private Share-holding Corporations Ltd.	71035.7	290.6
其他	Other Enterprises	5324.3	3.6
港澳台商投资	Enterprises with Funds from Hong Kong, Macao &Taiwan	4667175.0	16138.5
外商投资	Foreign Funded Enterprises	4131693.1	15983.0
2. 按国民经济行业分组	Grouped by Sector		
综合零售	Integrated Retail	2975288.9	23914.1
食品、饮料及烟草制品专门零售	Special Retail of Food, Beverages and Tobaccos	256576.8	759.0
纺织、服装及日用品专门零售	Special Retail of Textiles,Garments and Daily Consumer Articles	445127.5	3640.5
文化、体育用品及器材专门零售	Special Retail of Culture,Sports Appliances and Equipment	199349.0	1177.4
医药及医疗器材专门零售	Special Retail of Medicines and Medical Appliances	523356.7	2510.9
汽车、摩托车、零配件和燃料及其他动力销售	Special Retail of Automobiles, Motorcycles, Spare Parts and Fuel and Other Power	8391293.8	29006.9
家用电器及电子产品专门零售	Special Retail of Household Electric Appliances and Electronic Products	773789.2	1118.0
五金、家具及室内装饰材料专门零售	Special Retail of Hardware,Furniture and Decoration Materials	117935.7	2073.8
货摊、无店铺及其他零售业	Non-shop and Other Retail	4798566.7	8705.0

continued 5

(10 000 yuan)

销售费用 Sale Expenses	管理费用 Management Expenses	财务费用 Financial Expenses	营业利润 Business Profits	利润总额 Total Profits	应付职工薪酬 Salary Payable	所得税费用 Income Tax Expenses	应交增值税 Value Added Tax Payable
252878.5	114847.5	32369.9	-11887.5	-8559.5	135684.4	12195.3	59411.2
6576.7	15312.7	1654.7	11213.8	18226.3	14801.2	1960.8	820.9
483477.6	211518.2	42875.3	5733.8	12529.7	260803.5	11028.1	88517.1
3313.8	2073.1	92.1	-1.2	2.1	1818.1	22.6	233.2
519.2	421.5	0.2	17.7	18.0	247.5	0.6	10.6
469476.4	206774.4	42605.4	4803.9	11654.4	250625.8	10995.3	86804.2
10168.2	2249.2	177.6	913.4	855.2	8112.1	9.6	1469.1
174.2	158.7	0.7	33.3	33.3	148.9	0.1	0.8
425245.7	71916.2	25483.1	14634.3	32122.2	137650.1	11306.7	53106.8
371528.1	96484.8	21474.8	92389.4	94259.0	94880.1	22780.9	60084.7
439797.4	180934.6	50595.0	-13257.8	7535.8	231644.7	8475.5	34269.7
35090.8	17408.3	2011.4	3704.9	3959.4	23239.7	2452.8	4751.1
108982.7	49761.9	6241.2	5851.7	6845.0	65268.0	3483.7	13696.9
32435.9	23251.7	1816.1	-4354.8	-1397.5	24334.9	558.5	3131.7
105835.8	21907.6	6122.5	10558.1	11386.2	65098.8	2909.5	13127.6
392537.4	152075.2	45149.5	146641.9	152918.0	230794.1	41471.5	139001.2
86345.5	22514.8	5630.2	-32205.2	-30890.0	30701.3	397.2	12320.9
14059.6	20133.6	6442.6	7996.8	9093.0	10108.6	2521.9	7208.7
376018.7	60863.9	2416.6	14576.9	17546.7	36433.7	3654.5	48320.7

16-5 限额以上住宿和餐饮企业财务状况（2021年）

单位：万元

分　组	Classify	单位数（个） Number (unit)	资产总计 Total Assets	流动资产合　计 Circulating Funds
总计	**Total**	**799**	**4179608.2**	**1706112.6**
一、住宿业	**Hotel Services**	**447**	**3300260.2**	**1250065.5**
1.按登记注册类型分组	Grouped by Type of Registration			
内资	Domestic Funded Enterprises	433	2676097.0	1015730.7
国有	State-owned Enterprises	13	177524.6	29687.2
集体	Collective-owned Enterprises			
股份合作	Cooperative Enterprises			
联营	Joint Ownership Enterprises			
国有联营	State Joint Ownership Enterprises			
集体联营	Collective Joint Ownership Enterprises			
国有与集体联营	Joint State-collective Enterprises			
其他联营	Others Joint Ownership Enterprises			
有限责任公司	Limited Liability Corporations	106	1681631.9	534654.2
国有独资公司	State Sole Funded Corporations	11	111699.3	21007.8
其他有限责任公司	Other Limited Liability Corporations	95	1569932.6	513646.4
股份有限公司	Share-holding Corporations Ltd.			
私营	Private Enterprises	314	816940.5	451389.3
私营独资	Private-funded Enterprises	7	4238.9	2973.3
私营合伙	Private Partnership Enterprises			
私营有限责任公司	Private Limited Liability Corporations	306	802284.5	441741.0
私营股份有限公司	Private Share-holding Corporations Ltd.	1	10417.1	6675.0
其他	Other Enterprises			
港澳台商投资	Enterprises with Funds from Hong Kong, Macao &Taiwan	6	180921.6	73452.1
外商投资	Foreign Funded Enterprises	8	443241.6	160882.7
2.按国民经济行业分组	Grouped by Sector			
旅游饭店	Tourist Hotel	180	2631902.4	883026.4
一般旅馆	Normal Hotel	250	602261.2	351955.2
民宿服务	Home and Lodging Services	4	2831.2	1955.1
露营地服务	Campsite Services	1	9191.8	606.8
其他住宿业	Others	12	54073.6	12522.0

注：本表统计范围为法人单位。

Financial Status of Hotels and Catering Enterprises above Designated Size (2021)

(10 000 yuan)

固定资产原价 Original Value of Fixed Assets	累计折旧 Accumulated Depreciation	负债合计 Total Liabilities	流动负债合计 Circulating Liabilities	所有者权益合计 Total Owners' Equities	实收资本 Paid in Capital	营业收入 Total Revenue	主营业务收入 Revenue from Principal Business
2495649.4	**1051777.0**	**3749834.4**	**3115161.8**	**452568.8**	**1227018.0**	**1636718.1**	**1587307.7**
2281777.2	**932503.2**	**3051164.2**	**2531086.4**	**269814.6**	**987442.9**	**661818.9**	**642964.1**
1847068.4	775926.1	2406160.2	1963563.0	274341.8	871820.9	586773.9	569071.5
155677.4	73379.0	144525.0	86772.3	32999.6	61215.7	32142.4	31753.4
1336330.2	546523.5	1431231.5	1177920.0	252121.0	612906.1	258861.6	248952.0
147769.4	67780.8	42438.4	40525.1	69260.9	134776.8	31044.0	29117.2
1188560.8	478742.7	1388793.1	1137394.9	182860.1	478129.3	227817.6	219834.8
355060.8	156023.6	830403.7	698870.7	-10778.8	197699.1	295769.9	288366.1
1292.3	481.4	5075.0	4933.4	-960.7	230.0	3870.8	3850.7
344021.3	149526.3	800876.0	681084.2	4217.5	192469.1	290823.6	283439.9
9747.2	6015.9	24452.7	12853.1	-14035.6	5000.0	1075.5	1075.5
181152.8	103204.7	168372.2	92576.2	28863.0	86322.0	27421.7	26466.2
253556.0	53372.4	476631.8	474947.2	-33390.2	29300.0	47623.3	47426.4
2076994.2	838648.3	2475681.1	2056819.8	171056.8	792923.5	430536.5	418755.8
163431.3	81748.4	535108.8	439481.1	72939.6	183437.4	210017.6	203158.6
168.7	120.4	3539.9	3533.4	-708.7	150.0	2535.4	2535.4
7281.4	840.4	5348.5	539.6	3843.3	5000.0	1095.7	1095.7
33901.6	11145.7	31485.9	30712.5	22683.6	5932.0	17633.7	17418.6

16-5 续表1

单位：万元

分 组	Classify	营业成本 Total Cost	税金及附加 Taxs and Other Changes
总计	**Total**	**847512.3**	**16482.6**
一、住宿业	**Hotel Services**	**306057.1**	**14212.5**
1.按登记注册类型分组	Grouped by Type of Registration		
内资	Domestic Funded Enterprises	274068.7	10257.4
国有	State-owned Enterprises	10815.2	1462.6
集体	Collective-owned Enterprises		
股份合作	Cooperative Enterprises		
联营	Joint Ownership Enterprises		
国有联营	State Joint Ownership Enterprises		
集体联营	Collective Joint Ownership Enterprises		
国有与集体联营	Joint State-collective Enterprises		
其他联营	Others Joint Ownership Enterprises		
有限责任公司	Limited Liability Corporations	139983.0	6581.2
国有独资公司	State Sole Funded Corporations	18243.1	685.7
其他有限责任公司	Other Limited Liability Corporations	121739.9	5895.5
股份有限公司	Share-holding Corporations Ltd.		
私营	Private Enterprises	123270.5	2213.6
私营独资	Private-funded Enterprises	2391.4	15.7
私营合伙	Private Partnership Enterprises		
私营有限责任公司	Private Limited Liability Corporations	120785.4	2195.4
私营股份有限公司	Private Share-holding Corporations Ltd.	93.7	2.5
其他	Other Enterprises		
港澳台商投资	Enterprises with Funds from Hong Kong, Macao &Taiwan	13831.7	1567.0
外商投资	Foreign Funded Enterprises	18156.7	2388.1
2.按国民经济行业分组	Grouped by Sector		
旅游饭店	Tourist Hotel	205639.7	12825.9
一般旅馆	Normal Hotel	92797.7	1014.0
民宿服务	Home and Lodging Services	1164.4	93.5
露营地服务	Campsite Services	420.7	0.1
其他住宿业	Others	6034.6	279.0

continued 1

(10 000 yuan)

销售费用 Sale Expenses	管理费用 Management Expenses	财务费用 Financial Expenses	营业利润 Business Profits	利润总额 Total Profits	应付职工薪酬 Salary Payable	所得税费用 Income Tax Expenses	应交增值税 Value Added Tax Payable
518126.5	**342696.4**	**70665.5**	**-147454.4**	**-139922.7**	**416988.6**	**9915.3**	**23034.8**
193371.0	**239568.6**	**60744.8**	**-143925.6**	**-138360.5**	**186180.8**	**1652.1**	**11723.8**
178343.4	219113.6	38652.1	-124821.5	-119551.4	169296.2	974.4	11165.8
15143.8	16215.0	5723.4	-15942.4	-16836.6	15777.1	25.7	1076.2
71174.0	103041.9	26444.5	-77623.9	-74962.4	85968.8	217.7	5007.5
8722.9	10135.6	781.0	-7073.2	-6962.3	12693.6	-145.5	704.8
62451.1	92906.3	25663.5	-70550.7	-68000.1	73275.2	363.2	4302.7
92025.6	99856.7	6484.2	-31255.2	-27752.4	67550.3	731.0	5082.1
878.0	1444.6	10.0	-869.0	-863.0	667.5	2.2	124.4
90790.6	97779.2	6473.7	-30375.1	-26879.3	66680.8	728.8	4927.2
357.0	632.9	0.5	-11.1	-10.1	202.0		30.5
6862.2	10240.9	2011.2	-6764.9	-6917.5	10152.3	321.7	415.9
8165.4	10214.1	20081.5	-12339.2	-11891.6	6732.3	356.0	142.1
112645.3	166660.2	55468.9	-115259.7	-111988.7	134298.2	934.0	9086.5
68296.3	65221.8	4442.5	-21498.1	-19254.7	45823.5	702.7	2536.6
406.8	782.9	6.7	122.4	132.6	615.6	0.9	-90.6
407.1	587.7	159.0	-100.3	-100.2	436.2		-55.6
11615.5	6316.0	667.7	-7189.9	-7149.5	5007.3	14.5	246.9

16-5 续表2

单位：万元

分组	Classify	单位数（个） Number (unit)	资产总计 Total Assets	流动资产合计 Circulating Funds
二、餐饮业	**Catering Trade**	**352**	**879348.0**	**456047.1**
1.按登记注册类型分组	Grouped by Type of Registration			
内资	Domestic Funded Enterprises	337	686168.6	383188.2
国有	State-owned Enterprises	3	8669.4	4426.1
集体	Collective-owned Enterprises			
股份合作	Cooperative Enterprises			
联营	Joint Ownership Enterprises			
国有联营	State Joint Ownership Enterprises			
集体联营	Collective Joint Ownership Enterprises			
国有与集体联营	Joint State-collective Enterprises			
其他联营	Others Joint Ownership Enterprises			
有限责任公司	Limited Liability Corporations	78	189976.4	110896.1
国有独资公司	State Sole Funded Corporations	3	13066.0	4854.4
其他有限责任公司	Other Limited Liability Corporations	75	176910.4	106041.7
股份有限公司	Share-holding Corporations Ltd.	3	210011.6	64032.7
私营	Private Enterprises	253	277511.2	203833.3
私营独资	Private-funded Enterprises	6	1814.8	886.4
私营合伙	Private Partnership Enterprises			
私营有限责任公司	Private Limited Liability Corporations	245	272204.1	200474.0
私营股份有限公司	Private Share-holding Corporations Ltd.	2	3492.3	2472.9
其他	Other Enterprises			
港澳台商投资	Enterprises with Funds from Hong Kong, Macao &Taiwan	5	86690.7	44878.5
外商投资	Foreign Funded Enterprises	10	106488.7	27980.4
2.按国民经济行业分组	Grouped by Sector			
正餐服务	Dinner	320	653707.5	362515.3
快餐服务	Fast Food	14	140807.0	35433.4
饮料及冷饮服务	Beverages and Cold Drinks	11	75495.1	52315.7
餐饮配送及外卖送餐服务	Catering Distribution and Delivery Services	3	2817.9	2686.2
其他餐饮业	Other Catering Services	4	6520.5	3096.5

continued 2

(10 000 yuan)

固定资产原价 Original Value of Fixed Assets	累计折旧 Accumulated Depreciation	负债合计 Total Liabilities	流动负债合计 Circulating Liabilities	所有者权益合计 Total Owners' Equities	实收资本 Paid in Capital	营业收入 Total Revenue	主营业务收入 Revenue from Principal Business
213872.2	**119273.8**	**698670.2**	**584075.4**	**182754.2**	**239575.1**	**974899.2**	**944343.6**
161014.2	92012.6	585820.6	515858.8	102424.4	221101.2	722825.8	699222.9
5165.0	2853.8	2951.5	2456.6	5717.9	5404.1	4495.2	4495.2
64606.5	38825.6	199300.8	178203.8	-9324.4	45203.4	214593.3	196566.6
15894.2	8660.7	11499.9	10708.3	1566.1	6141.2	6242.1	6239.6
48712.3	30164.9	187800.9	167495.5	-10890.5	39062.2	208351.2	190327.0
22675.0	13867.4	113197.7	88250.8	96813.9	61505.6	77900.7	77493.8
68567.7	36465.8	270370.6	246947.6	9217.0	108988.1	425836.6	420667.3
1072.8	243.2	2011.9	885.4	613.6	151.4	2233.1	2021.0
66525.0	35744.5	267470.7	245174.2	5999.1	105834.9	420384.6	415427.4
969.9	478.1	888.0	888.0	2604.3	3001.8	3218.9	3218.9
23477.9	12371.2	33849.1	25242.8	52841.6	3595.4	82546.2	82546.2
29380.1	14890.0	79000.5	42973.8	27488.2	14878.5	169527.2	162574.5
150062.2	88127.6	555254.8	485414.7	100529.1	214144.7	652509.2	630504.9
46369.7	22770.4	100451.4	56274.5	40355.6	21085.7	205913.9	199534.2
12205.7	6133.7	30912.6	30507.3	44582.5	2894.7	104061.2	103987.6
389.1	270.0	1760.1	1764.2	1057.8	500.0	7847.5	5749.9
4845.5	1972.1	10291.3	10114.7	-3770.8	950.0	4567.4	4567.0

16-5　续表3

单位：万元

分　组	Classify	营业成本 Total Cost	税金及附加 Taxs and Other Changes
二、餐饮业	**Catering Trade**	**541455.2**	**2270.1**
1.按登记注册类型分组	Grouped by Type of Registration		
内资	Domestic Funded Enterprises	418635.3	2060.7
国有	State-owned Enterprises	3804.2	123.0
集体	Collective-owned Enterprises		
股份合作	Cooperative Enterprises		
联营	Joint Ownership Enterprises		
国有联营	State Joint Ownership Enterprises		
集体联营	Collective Joint Ownership Enterprises		
国有与集体联营	Joint State-collective Enterprises		
其他联营	Others Joint Ownership Enterprises		
有限责任公司	Limited Liability Corporations	132731.0	822.2
国有独资公司	State Sole Funded Corporations	6039.5	130.3
其他有限责任公司	Other Limited Liability Corporations	126691.5	691.9
股份有限公司	Share-holding Corporations Ltd.	46266.1	391.9
私营	Private Enterprises	235834.0	723.6
私营独资	Private-funded Enterprises	1464.7	12.7
私营合伙	Private Partnership Enterprises		
私营有限责任公司	Private Limited Liability Corporations	233061.6	710.8
私营股份有限公司	Private Share-holding Corporations Ltd.	1307.7	0.1
其他	Other Enterprises		
港澳台商投资	Enterprises with Funds from Hong Kong, Macao &Taiwan	23601.7	79.9
外商投资	Foreign Funded Enterprises	99218.2	129.5
2.按国民经济行业分组	Grouped by Sector		
正餐服务	Dinner	381510.1	1934.6
快餐服务	Fast Food	110533.2	175.9
饮料及冷饮服务	Beverages and Cold Drinks	40468.4	93.1
餐饮配送及外卖送餐服务	Catering Distribution and Delivery Services	6132.0	3.7
其他餐饮业	Other Catering Services	2811.5	62.8

continued 3

(10 000 yuan)

销售费用 Sale Expenses	管理费用 Management Expenses	财务费用 Financial Expenses	营业利润 Business Profits	利润总额 Total Profits	应付职工薪酬 Salary Payable	所得税费用 Income Tax Expenses	应交增值税 Value Added Tax Payable
324755.5	**103127.8**	**9920.7**	**-3528.8**	**-1562.2**	**230807.8**	**8263.2**	**11311.0**
240636.2	82771.6	7943.4	-27334.6	-24791.0	178697.3	2878.9	10200.4
1166.6	578.0	24.3	-1208.5	-1099.3	1951.8	38.3	268.1
64014.0	26213.7	1767.5	-9527.7	-9060.4	48654.3	595.3	2519.1
325.1	1284.7	56.0	-1550.0	-1536.2	2673.9	1.4	220.2
63688.9	24929.0	1711.5	-7977.7	-7524.2	45980.4	593.9	2298.9
33566.9	7316.6	2679.8	-11375.4	-10750.3	35104.2	132.7	2911.4
141888.7	48663.3	3471.8	-5223.0	-3881.0	92987.0	2112.6	4501.8
522.7	260.4	47.8	39.6	36.3	609.5	2.3	17.9
139488.4	48323.9	3410.5	-5203.7	-3881.1	91803.3	2110.2	4474.4
1877.6	79.0	13.5	-58.9	-36.2	574.2	0.1	9.5
45275.8	3066.7	453.0	10829.8	11022.0	22491.2	2789.9	492.0
38843.5	17289.5	1524.3	12976.0	12206.8	29619.3	2594.4	618.6
214603.8	75148.5	6642.5	-24980.9	-22363.9	166474.4	2845.7	10094.5
62480.1	20448.8	2317.3	10197.6	9387.8	41198.2	2613.6	463.8
45724.3	6160.3	-276.4	12405.5	12405.0	21604.6	2716.5	649.1
1407.7	49.7	51.7	201.7	302.6	1087.8	87.4	15.5
539.6	1320.5	1185.6	-1352.7	-1293.7	442.8		88.1

16-6 限额以上批发和零售贸易业商品购进、销售、库存总额（2021年）

单位：万元

分组	Classify	单位数（个）Number (unit)	商品购进额 Total Purchases	进口 Imports
总计	**Total**	**2375**	**128740934.0**	**4315144.3**
一、批发企业	**Wholesale Enterprises**	**1485**	**112337414.3**	**3789827.7**
1.按登记注册类型分组	Grouped by Type of Registration			
内资	Domestic Funded Enterprise	1452	98258920.4	1276242.3
国有	State-owned Enterprises	37	23587009.5	886021.2
集体	Collective-owned Enterprises	4	17309.8	
有限责任公司	Limited Liability Corporations	299	38270543.5	171491.3
国有独资公司	State Sole Funded Corporations	27	12336248.1	1252.9
其他有限责任公司	Other Limited Liability Corporations	272	25934295.4	170238.4
股份有限公司	Share-holding Corporations Ltd.	20	12548130.9	277.7
私营	Private Enterprises	1091	23828333.1	218452.1
私营独资	Private-funded Enterprises	5	19952.4	
私营合伙	Private Partnership Enterprises	1	14813.7	
私营有限责任公司	Private Limited Liability Corporations	1078	23643309.4	218452.1
私营股份有限公司	Private Share-holding Corporations Ltd.	7	150257.6	
其他	Other Enterprises	1	7593.6	
港澳台商投资	Enterprises with Funds from Hong Kong, Macao &Taiwan	10	799968.4	
外商投资	Foreign Funded Enterprises	23	13278525.5	2513585.4
2.按国民经济行业分组	Grouped by Sector			
农、林、牧、渔产品批发	Wholesale of Agricultural,Forestry and Animal Husbandry Products	14	177277.0	2858.0
食品、饮料及烟草制品批发	Wholesale of Food,Beverages and Tobacco Products	154	3079489.5	7812.9
纺织、服装及家庭用品批发	Wholesale of Textiles,Garments and Daily Articles	79	1776479.3	44658.4
文化、体育用品及器材批发	Wholesale of Culture,Sports Articles and Equipment	50	1182441.9	12236.4
医药及医疗器材批发	Wholesale of Medicines and Medical Appliances	202	6058111.4	35532.0
矿产品、建材及化工产品批发	Wholesale of Mineral Products,Building Materials and Chemical Products	642	91448481.9	991165.2

Total Purchases,Sales and Inventories of Wholesale and Retail Enterprises above Designated Size (2021)

(10 000 yuan)

商品销售额		批发额		零售额	期末商品库存额
	公共网络商品销售额		出口		Value of
Sales Value	Public Network Sales	Wholesale Trade	Exports	Retail Trade	Stock at Final goods
139439843.8	**16372374.9**	**116387368.8**	**2746052.1**	**23006865.0**	**5634407.6**
116655978.9	**9507451.9**	**115521937.4**	**2745588.2**	**1088893.7**	**3771308.2**
102007277.3	9506024.6	101005581.5	844168.5	960680.2	3399394.5
24231596.9	1964103.4	24227838.0	10607.4	3758.9	722553.9
31218.5		30587.7			107.6
39321143.9	1780112.9	39179928.5	519238.4	130320.4	1500707.9
12548081.0	3350.5	12538782.7	40323.4	9298.3	180594.7
26773062.9	1776762.4	26641145.8	478915.0	121022.1	1320113.2
12894926.8	5156126.6	12269224.5	20455.4	625693.6	44149.1
25520684.9	605681.7	25290296.5	293867.3	200907.3	1131621.1
21547.2		21257.2		290.0	425.9
15503.4		15503.4	3250.2		
25320909.9	605681.7	25090811.5	290617.1	200617.3	1120187.8
162724.4		162724.4			11007.4
7706.3		7706.3			254.9
1004612.6	1409.0	915388.9	29450.6	89223.7	146884.1
13644089.0	18.3	13600967.0	1871969.1	38989.8	225029.6
200008.7	94.3	199853.3	345.2	155.4	30550.8
3820249.8	1669696.0	3756946.5	26509.3	62683.6	320815.6
2039585.7	102778.1	1912400.4	202008.6	127185.3	407360.3
1300922.3	8621.3	1285185.8	14096.3	15736.5	67380.2
6539126.5	329778.4	6492064.3	22693.4	46112.4	604587.8
93731521.6	7257362.7	92977875.6	259800.0	721947.6	1747300.3

16-6 续表1

单位：万元

分　组	Classify	单位数（个）Number (unit)	商品购进额 Total Purchases	进口 Imports
机械设备、五金产品及电子产品批发	Wholesale of Machinery,Hardwares and Electronic Products	302	7575569.3	2611580.8
贸易经纪与代理	Trade Manage and Agent	5	195708.6	12031.6
其他批发业	Other Wholesales	37	843855.4	71952.4
3.按经营形式分组	Grouped by Means of Operation			
独立门店	Independent Shop	674	43922354.4	2677935.1
连锁总店（总部）	Headquarter of Chain Store	4	136035.7	
连锁门店	Chain Store	1	11260.7	
其他	Other	806	68267763.5	1111892.6
二、零售企业	**Retail Trade**	**890**	**16403519.7**	**525316.6**
1.按登记注册类型分组	Grouped by Registration Status			
内资	Domestic Funded Enterprises	825	10622394.8	293633.3
国有	State-owned Enterprises	14	455798.1	
集体	Collective-owned Enterprises	7	17427.5	
有限责任公司	Limited Liability Corporations	190	3802882.7	138039.4
国有独资公司	State Sole Funded Corporations	11	421163.8	15183.5
其他有限责任公司	Other Limited Liability Corporations	179	3381718.9	122855.9
股份有限公司	Share-holding Corporations Ltd.	5	25081.5	
私营	Private Enterprises	606	6315809.9	155593.9
私营独资	Private-funded Enterprises	20	63730.2	
私营合伙	Private Partnership Enterprises	1	2491.9	
私营有限责任公司	Private Limited Liability Corporations	582	6165138.1	155593.9
私营股份有限公司	Private Share-holding Corporations Ltd.	3	84449.7	
其他	Other Enterprises	3	5395.1	
港澳台商投资	Enterprises with Funds from Hong Kong, Macao &Taiwan	27	1807291.5	32174.3
外商投资	Foreign Funded Enterprises	38	3973833.4	199509.0
2.按国民经济行业分组	Grouped by Sector			
综合零售	General Retail Sales Trade	102	2480851.8	19.8
食品、饮料及烟草制品专门零售	Retail of Food,Beverage and Tobaccos	66	255661.5	430.7
纺织、服装及日用品专门零售	Retail of Textiles,Garments and Daily Articles	51	395232.0	4054.8
文化、体育用品及器材专门零售	Retail of Culture,Sports Articles and Equipment	59	232150.5	15183.5

continued 1

(10 000 yuan)

商品销售额 Sales Value	公共网络商品销售额 Public Network Sales	批发额 Wholesale Trade	出口 Exports	零售额 Retail Trade	期末商品库存额 Value of Stock at Final goods
7984685.1	51108.3	7879300.6	2093405.6	101718.5	306458.6
210431.0	700.0	210430.0	121583.8	1.0	11979.9
829448.2	87312.8	807880.9	5146.0	13353.4	274874.7
45558749.7	267827.7	44620589.5	2531073.1	921276.0	1318292.3
189668.0	44.5	187908.1		1759.9	6188.5
12740.2		12740.2			4594.6
70894821.0	9239579.7	70700699.6	214515.1	165857.8	2442232.8
22783864.9	**6864923.0**	**865431.4**	**463.9**	**21917971.3**	**1863099.4**
11982796.3	1590702.5	783267.2	463.9	11199066.9	1520210.9
571682.3	43845.6	31448.3		540234.0	210876.5
22376.2	5.8			22376.2	765.2
4406007.5	308591.5	226612.9	18.1	4179394.6	550488.6
422024.2	1097.1	19390.8	18.1	402633.4	58140.9
3983983.3	307494.4	207222.1		3776761.2	492347.7
92857.4	10015.8			92857.4	4642.9
6884173.0	1228243.8	525201.0	445.8	6358509.8	753385.4
66277.6	2947.5	590.1		65687.5	8442.2
3628.0				3628.0	234.7
6724904.5	1225296.3	524610.9	445.8	6199831.4	732709.2
89362.9				89362.9	11999.3
5699.9		5.0		5694.9	52.3
5607865.1	3867331.4	16660.5		5591204.6	202065.1
5193203.5	1406889.1	65503.7		5127699.8	140823.4
3897076.8	341017.8	16590.0		3880486.8	500428.4
340940.3	53202.7	68733.7		271744.4	32539.1
698709.6	25999.3	11228.2		687481.4	124540.6
257968.1	17331.4	28342.0	18.1	229626.1	84531.6

16-6 续表2

单位：万元

分 组	Classify	单位数（个）Number (unit)	商品购进额 Total Purchases	进口 Imports
医药及医疗器材专门零售	Retail of Medicines and Medical Appliances	45	573035.3	98.1
汽车、摩托车、零配件和燃料及其他动力销售	Sales of automobiles,motorcycles,spare parts and fuel and other power	331	9433882.1	465829.1
家用电器及电子产品专门零售	Retail of Household Electronic Equipment and Products	94	861040.6	28419.5
五金、家具及室内装饰材料专门零售	Retail of Hardwares,Furniture and Room Decorative Building	26	151793.3	
货摊、无店铺及其他零售业	No Fixed Stores and Other Retails	116	2019872.6	11281.1
3.按经营形式分组	Grouped by Means of Operation			
独立门店	Independent Shop	634	11926606.4	510093.4
连锁总店（总部）	Headquarter of Chain Store	36	659930.6	4054.8
连锁门店	Chain Store	26	636309.9	19.8
其他	Other	194	3180672.8	11148.6
4.按零售业态分组	Grouped by Retail Size			
有店铺	Retail of Shop	730	14228838.1	498852.0
食杂店	Grocery Store	4	4904.7	
便利店	Convenience Store	19	163801.4	19.8
折扣店	Dime Store	1	1815.5	
超市	Supermarket	51	182145.4	
大型超市	Large Supermarket	11	1627137.0	
仓储会员店	Warehouse Club	1	288.4	
百货店	Department Store	42	592785.0	
专业店	Special Store	265	5285817.6	154550.5
专卖店	Monopoly Store	308	6219026.8	344281.7
家居建材商店	Home-building Material Store	10	106815.1	
购物中心	Shopping Center	9	22662.4	
厂家直销中心	Factory Outlet Center	9	21638.8	
无店铺零售	Retail of No-shop	160	2174681.6	26464.6
电视购物	TV Shopping			
邮购	Mail Order	1	9440.6	
网上商店	Online Stores	109	1981031.0	11281.1
自动售货亭	Vending Machine			
电话购物	Tele Shopping	1	824.7	
其他	Others	49	183385.3	15183.5

continued 2

(10 000 yuan)

商品销售额 Sales Value	公共网络商品销售额 Public Network Sales	批发额 Wholesale Trade	出口 Exports	零售额 Retail Trade	期末商品库存额 Value of Stock at Final goods
707130.7	38625.6	23640.7		683490.0	112130.2
9899248.3	533219.0	296814.0		9602434.3	847922.7
942716.7	156956.7	144599.5		798117.2	98093.7
209384.5	13157.1	30715.7	230.4	178668.8	11329.9
5830689.9	5685413.4	244767.6	215.4	5585922.3	51583.2
14113031.4	787355.1	357819.3	18.1	13754749.9	1547033.4
854940.6	69229.9	18791.5		836149.1	108415.7
712213.0	117789.9	53164.7		659048.3	31405.6
7103679.9	5890548.1	435655.9	445.8	6668024.0	176244.7
16778830.5	1143964.4	576394.0		16201974.3	1785707.4
12921.5	122.1			12921.5	1315.1
217103.1	27235.3	27164.1		189476.8	10411.7
1748.4				1748.4	287.8
199164.2	3657.1	2393.0		196771.2	23593.0
1469859.5	279202.5	9731.1		1460128.4	162195.4
1120.5				1120.5	14.9
2025487.9	54787.3	772.6		2024715.3	316243.1
5637787.8	217828.8	227291.2		5410496.6	499277.8
6725167.5	551117.9	288057.2		6437110.3	759586.1
159136.4	7012.7	15629.3		143507.1	6059.8
304678.4				304678.4	5262.6
24655.3	3000.7	5355.5		19299.8	1460.1
6005034.4	5720958.6	289037.4	463.9	5715997.0	77392.0
9324.7	9324.7	4110.6		5214.1	1701.9
5784383.2	5692081.3	223424.3	215.4	5560958.9	51625.6
1065.8				1065.8	101.9
210260.7	19552.6	61502.5	248.5	148758.2	23962.6

16-7 限额以上住宿和餐饮业经营情况（2021年）

单位：万元

分　组	Classify	单位数（个）Number (unit)	营业额 Business Revenue
总计	**Total**	**799**	**1667522.0**
一、住宿业	**Lodging Services**	**447**	**658780.5**
1. 按国民经济行业分组	Grouped by Economic Sector		
旅游饭店	Tour Restaurant	180	421398.8
一般旅馆	Common Hotel	250	215152.1
民宿服务	Home and Lodging Services	4	2644.8
露营地服务	Campsite Services	1	1095.7
其他住宿业	Others	12	18489.1
2. 按登记注册类型分组	Grouped by Registration Status		
内资	Domestic Funded Enterprises	433	598450.4
国有	State-owned Enterprises	13	32645.3
集体	Collective-owned Enterprises		
股份合作	Cooperative Enterprises		
联营	Joint Ownership Enterprises		
有限责任公司	Limited Liability Corporations	106	264615.3
国有独资公司	State-funded Corporations	11	29307.3
其他有限责任公司	Other Limited Liability Corporations	95	235308.0
股份有限公司	Stock Limited Corporation		
私营	Private Enterprises	314	301189.8
私营独资	Private-funded Enterprises	7	4011.9
私营合伙	Private Partnership Enterprises		
私营有限责任公司	Private Limited Liability Corporations	306	296284.9
私营股份有限公司	Private Share Holding Corporations	1	893.0
其他	Others		
港澳台商投资	Enterprises Funded by Hong Kong, Macao and Taiwan	6	29018.5

注：本表统计范围为法人单位。

Statistic on Hotel Services and Catering Services above Designed Size (2021)

(10 000 yuan)

客房收入 From Hotel Room	公共网络客房收入 Public Network Room Revenue	餐费收入 From Meals	公共网络餐费收入 Public Network Catering Revenue	商品销售额 Merchandise sales
413192.1	**82756.2**	**1112900.3**	**127422.8**	**45874.8**
400129.7	**82046.6**	**195827.1**	**8851.6**	**6924.2**
217974.4	37180.9	150955.4	8128.8	5163.2
169298.3	44651.3	36648.4	718.5	1559.7
2041.7	98.4	554.6		
774.9		156.9		22.0
10040.4	116.0	7511.8	4.3	179.3
369221.5	78094.4	173598.2	6117.9	6405.2
11702.0	2500.1	11051.0		463.3
138220.8	21640.9	92711.7	3587.2	3396.7
13832.8	3032.3	10852.8	2119.3	925.7
124388.0	18608.6	81858.9	1467.9	2471.0
219298.7	53953.4	69835.5	2530.7	2545.2
3084.6	737.7	700.8		44.1
215403.9	53151.6	69051.9	2530.7	2501.1
810.2	64.1	82.8		
13198.3	1299.5	10397.9	68.2	190.7

16-7 续表

单位：万元

分　组	Classify	单位数（个）Number (unit)	营业额 Business Revenue
外商投资	Foreign Funded Enterprises	8	31311.6
二、餐饮业	**Catering Trade**	**352**	**1008741.5**
1. 按国民经济行业分组	Grouped by Economic Sector		
正餐服务	Dinner Services	320	666973.1
快餐服务	Fast Food Services	14	218155.6
饮料及冷饮服务	Beverages and Cold Drinks	11	110403.1
餐饮配送及外卖送餐服务	Catering Distribution and Delivery Services	3	8365.6
其他餐饮业	Other Catering Services	4	4844.1
2. 按登记注册类型分组	Grouped by Registration Status		
内资	Domestic Funded Enterprises	337	740231.2
国有	State-owned Enterprises	3	4591.3
集体	Collective-owned Enterprises		
股份合作	Cooperative Enterprises		
联营	Joint Ownership Enterprises		
有限责任公司	Limited Liability Corporations	78	211523.1
国有独资公司	State-funded Corporations	3	6635.0
其他有限责任公司	Other Limited Liability Corporations	75	204888.1
股份有限公司	Stock Limited Corporation	3	81828.7
私营	Private Enterprises	253	442288.1
私营独资	Private-funded Enterprises	6	2351.8
私营合伙	Private Partnership Enterprises		
私营有限责任公司	Private Limited Liability Corporations	245	436534.1
私营股份有限公司	Private Share Holding Corporations	2	3402.2
其他	Others		
港澳台商投资	Enterprises Funded by Hong Kong, Macao and Taiwan	5	87633.3
外商投资	Foreign Funded Enterprises	10	180877.0

continued

(10 000 yuan)

客房收入 From Hotel Room	公共网络客房收入 Public Network Room Revenue	餐费收入 From Meals	公共网络餐费收入 Public Network Catering Revenue	商品销售额 Merchandise sales
17709.9	2652.7	11831.0	2665.5	328.3
13062.4	**709.6**	**917073.2**	**118571.2**	**38950.6**
12825.3	538.9	596870.1	39330.4	27865.6
		209296.5	29497.7	920.3
		101426.2	48722.4	7372.7
		5958.0		2407.6
237.1	170.7	3522.4	1020.7	384.4
12822.7	695.5	668391.3	76742.2	29543.9
872.7	0.9	3188.3	161.0	448.8
7135.1	99.0	183435.0	33906.6	13768.5
539.8		4381.9	141.3	1284.3
6595.3	99.0	179053.1	33765.3	12484.2
652.9		62279.0	9560.0	5543.1
4162.0	595.6	419489.0	33114.6	9783.5
127.1		2098.2	32.5	126.5
4034.9	595.6	413994.1	31503.1	9657.0
		3396.7	1579.0	
		78360.5	36238.1	7409.3
239.7	14.1	170321.4	5590.9	1997.4

16-8 限额以上批发和零售业主要商品分类销售额（2021年）

Sale Values of Wholesale and Retail Enterprises above Designated Size by Category of Main Commodities (2021)

单位：万元 (10 000 yuan)

分组	Classify	销售合计 Total Sales Value	批发 Wholesale Value	零售 Retail Value
总计	**Total**	**124715233.9**	**101869240.2**	**22845993.7**
其中：通过公共网络实现的商品销售	Sales Achieved through the Public Network	14999788.5	8392462.4	6607326.1
粮油、食品类	Cereals, Oils and Foodstuffs	3045868.4	1214126.7	1831741.7
#粮油类	Grain and Oil	1204555.2	724170.2	480385.0
肉禽蛋类	Meat, Poultry and Eggs	424723.3	150770.4	273952.9
水产品类	Aquatic Products	123884.2	19611.5	104272.7
蔬菜类	Vegetables	133570.9	22722.7	110848.2
干鲜果品类	Fresh and Dried Fruit Category	401629.7	121660.4	279969.3
饮料类	Beverages	657211.0	244500.3	412710.7
烟酒类	Tobacco and Liquor	2873153.0	2356864.9	516288.1
服装、鞋帽、针纺织品类	Clothing, Shoes, Hats and Textiles	2811341.3	168630.8	2642710.5
服装类	Clothing	2140868.5	41474.3	2099394.2
鞋帽类	Shoes and Hats	467200.1	25896.0	441304.1
针纺织品类	Knitwear and Textiles	203272.7	101260.5	102012.2
化妆品类	Cosmetics	837408.4	65811.4	771597.0
金银珠宝类	Gold,Silver and Jewelry	992979.0	327063.7	665915.3
日用品类	Articles for Daily Use	1258853.9	168196.7	1090657.2
#可穿戴智能设备	Wearable intelligent device	5247.2	46.3	5200.9
五金、电料类	Hardware and Electrical Materials	315627.1	290358.8	25268.3
体育、娱乐用品类	Sports and Recreation Articles	383006.3	28826.0	354180.3
#照相器材类	Photography Equipment	148160.2	1.0	148159.2
书报杂志类	Newspapers and Magazines	479009.2	277963.1	201046.1
电子出版物及音像制品类	E-journal and Video Products	422.6	29.0	393.6
家用电器和音像器材类	Household Appliances and Video Products	2192908.5	570672.4	1622236.1
中西药品类	Traditional Chinese and Western Medicine	6017773.0	5302202.7	715570.3
#西药类	Western Medicine	4698724.9	4189416.5	509308.4
中草药及中成药类	Chinese Herbal Medicine and Traditional Chinese Medicine	292041.3	181827.3	110214.0
文化办公用品类	Cultural and Official Goods	1520347.2	566548.4	953798.8
#计算机及其配套产品	Computers and Ancillary Products	1221303.8	285050.6	936253.2
家具类	Furniture	247784.5	47584.1	200200.4
通讯器材类	Communication Appliances	1248925.4	389649.1	859276.3
煤炭及制品类	Coal and Related Products	13849810.0	13849810.0	
木材及制品类	Wood and Wooden Products	58749.0	58749.0	
石油及制品类	Petroleum and Related Products	18660771.5	16392102.9	2268668.6
化工材料及制品类	Raw Chemical Materials	6098070.8	6082595.0	15475.8
#化肥类	Chemical Fertilizers	264594.5	264594.5	
金属材料类	Metal Materials	42297196.4	42275573.8	21622.6
建筑及装潢材料类	Buildings and Decoration Materials	1331988.7	1259229.7	72759.0
机电产品及设备类	Mechanical and Electrical Products	5218627.6	5158176.1	60451.5
#农机类	Agricultural Machinery	47246.3	47246.3	
汽车类	Automobile	8426084.4	1107791.7	7318292.7
种子饲料类	Seeds and Feedstuff	57325.3	57325.3	
棉麻类	Cotton,Hemp	254.2	254.2	
其他类	Others	3833737.2	3608604.4	225132.8

注：本表为定期季度报表数据。

16-9 亿元以上商品交易市场成交情况（2021年）

Basic Statistics on Commodity Exchange Markets of Transaction Value over 100 Million Yuan (2021)

分 组	Classify	年末出租摊位数（个）Number of Rental Booths at Year-end (unit)	成交额（万元）Turnover (10 000 yuan)
粮油、食品类	Cereals, Oils and Foodstuffs	11522	4124310
#粮油类	Grain and Oil	1080	368305
肉禽蛋类	Meat, Poultry and Eggs	1295	408817
水产品类	Aquatic Products	1128	407325
蔬菜类	Vegetables	3750	749046
干鲜果品类	Fresh and Dried Fruit Category	4268	2190607
饮料类	Beverages	83	64103
烟酒类	Tobacco and Liquor	251	43175
服装、鞋帽、针纺织品类	Clothing, Shoes, Hats and Textiles	5380	280499
服装类	Clothing	3605	108411
鞋帽类	Shoes and Hats	957	115507
针纺织品类	Knitwear and Textiles	818	56581
化妆品类	Cosmetics	141	6427
金银珠宝类	Gold,Silver and Jewelry	8	1320
日用品类	Articles for Daily Use	337	25788
#可穿戴智能设备	Wearable intelligent device	43	645
五金、电料类	Hardware and Electrical Materials	4341	364056
体育、娱乐用品类	Sports and Recreation Articles	163	16430
书报杂志类	Newspapers and Magazines	5	50
电子出版物及音像制品类	E-journal and Video Products		
家用电器和音像器材类	Household Appliances and Video Products	96	16396
中西药品类	Traditional Chinese and Western Medicine	1	90
#西药类	Western Medicine	1	90
中草药及中成药类	Chinese Herbal Medicine and Traditional Chinese Medicine		
文化办公用品类	Cultural and Official Goods	1660	162717
#计算机及其配套产品	Computer and Related Products	1447	140566
家具类	Furniture	2001	349738
通讯器材类	Communication Appliances	353	33649
煤炭及制品类	Coal and Related Products		
木材及制品类	Wood and Wooden Products		
石油及制品类	Petroleum and Related Products		
化工材料及制品类	Raw Chemical Materials	147	173965
#化肥类	Chemical Fertilizers		
金属材料类	Metal Materials	83	233600
建筑及装潢材料类	Buildings and Decoration Materials	5553	2740112
机电产品及设备类	Mechanical and Electrical Products	1605	214695
#农机类	Agricultural Machinery		
汽车类	Automobile	1459	166946
种子饲料类	Seeds and Feedstuff		
棉麻类	Cotton,Hemp		
其他类	Others	1234	34848

16-10 批发和零售业连锁经营情况（2021年）

Basic Statistics on Chain Business of Wholesale and Retail Trades(2021)

指 标	Item	本年合计 Total	上年合计 Total Last Year	本年直营店 Regular Chain
一、门店总数（个）	**Number of Stores(unit)**	**3880**	**3726**	**3264**
二、年末从业人员数（人）	**Employees at Year-end(person)**	**39146**	**41284**	**36309**
三、年末零售营业面积（平方米）	**Operating Area of Retail at Year-end(sq.m)**	**2867027**	**2977507**	**2790081**
四、连锁门店商品购进额（万元）	**Purchases Value of Chain Stores(10 000 yuan)**	**3885253**	**3877924**	**3797223**
其中：统一配送商品购进额	Centralized Purchases and Delivery	2401989	2326638	2355602
其中：自有配送中心配送商品购进额	Self Centralized Purchases and Delivery	1911954	1762920	1908878
非自有配送中心配送商品购进额	Non-self Centralized Purchases and Delivery	341442	444429	316818
五、连锁门店商品销售额（万元）	**Total Sale of General Chain Stores(10 000yuan)**	**4281800**	**4280256**	**4153543**
其中：零售额	Retail Value	3574098	3771542	3474271

注：上年同期数为本年在库企业加报数据。

16-10 续表 continued

指 标	Item	上年直营店 Regular Chain Last Year	本年加盟店 Franchise Chain	上年加盟店 Franchise Chain Last Year
一、门店总数（个）	**Number of Stores(unit)**	**3260**	**616**	**466**
二、年末从业人员数（人）	**Employees at Year-end(person)**	**38883**	**2837**	**2401**
三、年末零售营业面积（平方米）	**Operating Area of Retail at Year-end(sq.m)**	**2909751**	**76946**	**67756**
四、连锁门店商品购进额（万元）	**Purchases Value of Chain Stores(10 000 yuan)**	**3818580**	**88030**	**59344**
其中：统一配送商品购进额	Centralized Purchases and Delivery	2270960	46387	55678
其中：自有配送中心配送商品购进额	Self Centralized Purchases and Delivery	1729765	3077	33155
非自有配送中心配送商品购进额	Non-self Centralized Purchases and Delivery	429561	24624	14869
五、连锁门店商品销售额（万元）	**Total Sale of General Chain Stores(10 000yuan)**	**4214618**	**128257**	**65639**
其中：零售额	Retail Value	3723897	99827	47645

16-11 住宿和餐饮业连锁经营情况（2021年）

Basic Statistics on Chain Business of Hotels and Catering Services(2021)

指　标	Item	本年合计 Total	上年合计 Total Last Year
一、门店总数（个）	**Number of Stores(unit)**	**834**	**738**
二、年末从业人员数（人）	**Employees at Year-end(person)**	**17451**	**16681**
三、年末餐饮营业面积（平方米）	**Operating Area of Catering Enterprises at Year-end(sq.m)**	**226998**	**213377**
四、客房数（间）	**Guest Rooms(room)**	**532**	**532**
五、床位数（张）	**Guest Beds(bed)**	**886**	**886**
六、餐位数（位）	**Dining Seats(set)**	**87831**	**85522**
七、连锁门店商品购进（采购）额（万元）	**Purchases Value of Chain Stores(10 000 yuan)**	**162229**	**139017**
其中：统一配送商品购进（采购）额	Centralized Purchases and Delivery	144447	123801
其中：自有配送中心配送商品购进（采购）额	Self Centralized Purchases and Delivery	81796	73719
非自有配送中心配送商品购进（采购）额	Non-self Centralized Purchases and Delivery	44700	35884
八、连锁门店商品营业额（万元）	**Business Revenue of General Chain Stores (10 000 yuan)**	**403796**	**337953**
其中：餐费收入	Catering Revenues	388266	325478
商品销售额	Total Sales of Commodities	10772	9446

注：上年同期数为本年在库企业加报数据。

16-11 续表 continued

指　标	Item	本年直营店 Regular Chain	上年直营店 Regular Chain Last Year
一、门店总数（个）	**Number of Stores(unit)**	**834**	**738**
二、年末从业人员数（人）	**Employees at Year-end(person)**	**17451**	**16681**
三、年末餐饮营业面积（平方米）	**Operating Area of Catering Enterprises at Year-end(sq.m)**	**226998**	**213377**
四、客房数（间）	**Guest Rooms(room)**	**532**	**532**
五、床位数（张）	**Guest Beds(bed)**	**886**	**886**
六、餐位数（位）	**Dining Seats(set)**	**87831**	**85522**
七、连锁门店商品购进（采购）额（万元）	**Purchases Value of Chain Stores(10 000 yuan)**	**162229**	**139017**
其中：统一配送商品购进（采购）额	Centralized Purchases and Delivery	144447	123801
其中：自有配送中心配送商品购进（采购）额	Self Centralized Purchases and Delivery	81796	73719
非自有配送中心配送商品购进（采购）额	Non-self Centralized Purchases and Delivery	44700	35884
八、连锁门店商品营业额（万元）	**Business Revenue of General Chain Stores (10 000 yuan)**	**403796**	**337953**
其中：餐费收入	Catering Revenues	388266	325478
商品销售额	Total Sales of Commodities	10772	9446

16-12 近年限额以上住宿和餐饮业经营情况

单位：个、亿元

分 组	Classify	2017	
		单位数 Number of Enterprises	营业额 Business Revenue
总计	**Total**	**716**	**142.38**
一、住宿业	**Lodging Services**	**319**	**68.04**
1. 按登记注册类型分组	Grouped by Registration Status		
内资	Domestic Funded Enterprises	301	57.61
国有	State-owned Enterprises	25	5.77
集体	Collective-owned Enterprises	1	0.04
股份合作	Cooperative Enterprises		
联营	Joint Ownership Enterprises		
国有联营	State Joint Ownership Enterprises		
集体联营	Collective Joint Ownership Enterprises		
国有与集体联营	Joint State-collective Ownership Enterprises		
其他联营	Other Joint Ownership Enterprises		
有限责任公司	Limited Liability Corporations	138	35.02
国有独资公司	State-funded Corporations	8	3.87
其他有限责任公司	Other Limited Liability Corporations	130	31.15
股份有限公司	Stock Limited Corporation	4	1.92
私营	Private Enterprises	133	14.86
私营独资	Private-funded Enterprises	2	0.10
私营合伙	Private Partnership Enterprises		
私营有限责任公司	Private Limited Liability Corporations	129	14.68
私营股份有限公司	Private Share Holding Corporations	2	0.08
其他	Others		
港澳台商投资	Enterprises Funded by Hong Kong, Macao and Taiwan	7	5.21
外商投资	Foreign Funded Enterprises	9	5.14
个体经营	Individual Enterprises	2	0.08
2. 按国民经济行业分组	Grouped by Economic Sector		
旅游饭店	Tour Restaurant	193	54.26
一般旅馆	Common Hotel	116	11.61
民宿服务	Home and Lodging Services		
露营地服务	Campsite Services		
其他住宿业	Others	10	2.17

注：本表统计范围2017－2020年为法人、个体及产业活动单位，2021年统计范围为法人单位。

Statistic on Hotel Services and Catering Services above Designed Size

(unit，100 million yuan)

2018		2019		2020		2021	
单位数 Number of Enterprises	营业额 Business Revenue	单位数 Number of Enterprises	营业额 Business Revenue	单位数 Number of Enterprises	营业额 Business Revenue	单位数 Number of Enterprises	营业额 Business Revenue
742	**166.64**	**873**	**192.26**	**908**	**153.22**	**799**	**166.75**
353	**81.53**	**436**	**92.15**	**467**	**71.48**	**447**	**65.88**
337	70.84	420	81.07	449	63.41	433	59.85
21	5.07	21	5.04	24	5.46	13	3.26
1	0.03	2	0.06	1	0.01		
134	40.03	150	45.26	108	30.02	106	26.46
6	3.01	9	3.49	7	1.53	11	2.93
128	37.02	141	41.77	101	28.49	95	23.53
5	2.24	4	2.31	3	2.06		
175	23.30	242	28.27	311	24.94	314	30.12
4	0.13	5	0.23	6	0.16	7	0.40
168	22.53	234	27.69	304	24.68	306	29.63
3	0.64	3	0.36	1	0.10	1	0.09
1	0.17	1	0.14	2	0.93		
7	5.62	8	6.83	7	4.87	6	2.90
8	5.05	7	4.20	10	3.16	8	3.13
1	0.02	1	0.05	1	0.03		
184	61.97	189	67.94	193	51.55	180	42.14
154	16.78	227	21.26	255	17.95	250	21.52
2	0.10	5	0.13	4	0.06	4	0.26
		1	0.12	1	0.13	1	0.11
13	2.68	14	2.69	14	1.78	12	1.85

16-12 续表

单位：个、亿元

分 组	Classify	2017 单位数 Number of Enterprises	2017 营业额 Business Revenue
二、餐饮业	**Catering Trade**	**397**	**74.34**
1. 按登记注册类型分组	Grouped by Registration Status		
内资	Domestic Funded Enterprises	364	56.40
国有	State-owned Enterprises	4	1.03
集体	Collective-owned Enterprises		
股份合作	Cooperative Enterprises		
联营	Joint Ownership Enterprises		
国有联营	State Joint Ownership Enterprises		
集体联营	Collective Joint Ownership Enterprises		
国有与集体联营	Joint State-collective Ownership Enterprises		
其他联营	Other Joint Ownership Enterprises		
有限责任公司	Limited Liability Corporations	144	22.36
国有独资公司	State-funded Corporations	2	0.67
其他有限责任公司	Other Limited Liability Corporations	142	21.69
股份有限公司	Stock Limited Corporation	5	8.58
私营	Private Enterprises	208	23.31
私营独资	Private-funded Enterprises	13	0.65
私营合伙	Private Partnership Enterprises		
私营有限责任公司	Private Limited Liability Corporations	192	22.49
私营股份有限公司	Private Share Holding Corporations	3	0.17
其他	Others	3	1.12
港澳台商投资	Enterprises Funded by Hong Kong, Macao and Taiwan	7	3.97
外商投资	Foreign Funded Enterprises	5	11.66
个体经营	Individual Enterprises	21	2.31
2. 按国民经济行业分组	Grouped by Economic Sector		
正餐服务	Dinner Services	384	58.74
快餐服务	Fast Food Services	10	15.25
饮料及冷饮服务	Beverage and Cold Beverage Services		
餐饮配送及外卖送餐服务	Catering Distribution and Delivery Services		
其他餐饮业	Other Catering Services	3	0.35

continued

(unit，100 million yuan)

2018		2019		2020		2021	
单位数 Number of Enterprises	营业额 Business Revenue	单位数 Number of Enterprises	营业额 Business Revenue	单位数 Number of Enterprises	营业额 Business Revenue	单位数 Number of Enterprises	营业额 Business Revenue
389	**85.11**	**437**	**100.11**	**441**	**81.74**	**352**	**100.87**
360	61.16	375	72.91	351	55.83	337	74.02
6	1.31	6	1.50	5	0.99	3	0.46
136	22.48	121	22.32	81	13.98	78	21.15
4	1.32	3	1.40	3	0.59	3	0.66
132	21.16	118	20.92	78	13.40	75	20.49
4	9.48	3	10.07	4	6.66	3	8.18
213	26.67	244	37.81	261	34.20	253	44.23
11	0.64	11	0.58	11	0.43	6	0.24
201	25.97	231	37.15	249	33.49	245	43.65
1	0.06	2	0.08	1	0.28	2	0.34
1	1.22	1	1.21				
6	7.65	6	8.79	5	7.83	5	8.76
6	13.93	6	15.52	7	16.07	10	18.09
17	2.37	50	2.89	78	2.01		
369	63.17	412	71.43	415	53.96	320	66.70
11	17.43	11	19.68	12	19.28	14	21.82
4	3.83	9	8.14	7	7.80	11	11.04
1	0.26	1	0.24	1	0.23	3	0.84
4	0.42	4	0.63	6	0.47	4	0.48

主要统计指标解释

批发业 指向其他批发或零售单位（含个体经营者）及其他企事业单位、机关团体等批量销售生活用品、生产资料的活动，以及从事进出口贸易和贸易经纪与代理的活动，包括拥有货物所有权，并以本单位（公司）的名义进行交易活动，也包括不拥有货物的所有权，收取佣金的商品代理、商品代售活动；还包括各类商品批发市场中固定摊位的批发活动，以及以销售为目的的收购活动。

零售业 指百货商店、超级市场、专门零售商店、品牌专卖店、售货摊等主要面向最终消费者（如居民等）的销售活动，以互联网、邮政、电话、售货机等方式的销售活动，还包括在同一地点，后面加工生产，前面销售的店铺（如面包房）；谷物、种子、饲料、牲畜、矿产品、生产用原料、化工原料、农用化工产品、机械设备（乘用车、计算机及通信设备除外）等生产资料的销售不作为零售活动；多数零售商对其销售的货物拥有所有权，但有些则是充当委托人的代理人，进行委托销售或以收取佣金的方式进行销售。

住宿业 指为旅行者提供短期留宿场所的活动，有些单位只提供住宿，也有些单位提供住宿、饮食、商务、娱乐一体的服务，不包括主要按月或按年长期出租房屋住所的活动。

餐饮业 指通过即时制作加工、商业销售和服务性劳动等，向消费者提供食品和消费场所及设施的服务。

社会消费品零售总额 指企业（单位、个体户）通过交易直接售给个人、社会集团非生产、非经营用的实物商品金额，以及提供餐饮服务所取得的收入金额。

批发和零售业商品购进、销售、库存总额 指各种登记注册类型的批发和零售业企业（单位）以本企业（单位）为总体的，从国内、国外市场购进的商品总量，销售和出口的商品总量、库存的商品总量等情况。该指标可以反映商品流转过程中商品的购进、销售、库存之间的比例关系和存在的问题。

商品购进额 指从本企业以外的单位和个人购进（包括从国外直接进口）作为转卖或加工后转卖的商品金额（含增值税）。商品购进包括：（1）从工农业生产者、批发和零售业、住宿和餐饮业、出版社或报社的出版发行部门和其他服务业等企事业单位和个体经营户购进的商品；（2）从机关、社会团体购进的商品；（3）从海关、市场管理部门购进的缉私和没收的商品；（4）从居民收购的废旧商品等。不包括：（1）企业为本单位自身经营用，不是作为转卖而购进的商品，如材料物资、包装物、低值易耗品、办公用品等；（2）未通过买卖行为而收入的商品，如接受其他部门移交的商品、借入的商品、收入代其他单位保管的商品、其他单位赠送的样品、加工回收的成品等；（3）经本单位介绍，由买卖双方直接结算，本单位只收取手续费的业务；（4）销售退回和买方拒付货款的商品；（5）商品溢余；（6）期货交易商品。

进口 指直接从国外进口或委托外贸企业代理进口的商品金额，不包括从国内有关单位购进的进口商品。对外贸易企业只统计自主经营进口的商品，不统计受托代理进口的商品。

商品销售额 指对本单位以外的单位和个人出售的商品金额（包括售给本单位消费用的商品，含增值税）。商品销售包括：（1）售给个人和社会集团消费用的商品；（2）售给农业、工业、建筑业、服务业等国民经济各行业用于生产、经营用的商品，包括售予批发和零售业作为转卖或加工后转卖的商品；（3）对国（境）外直接出口的商品。不包括：（1）未通过买卖行为付出的商品，如因机构变动移交给其他企业单位的商品、借出的商品、归还受其他单位委托代保管的商品、付出的加工原料和赠送给其他单位的样品等；（2）促销返券所销售的、不计入营业收入的商品；（3）经本单位介绍，由买卖双方直接结算，本单位只收取手续费的业务；（4）未发生所有权转移的商品预付卡销售，如加油卡；（5）汽车维修、电话卡销售等服务性经济活动；（6）购货退回的商品；（7）商品损耗和损失；（8）出售本单位自用的废旧物资；（9）期货交易商品；（10）自来水供应企业、电力企业、天然气供应企业提供的水、电、气。

出口 指直接向国（境）外出口商品和委托外贸企业代理出口的商品金额，商品出口不包括售给外贸企业出口或加工后出口的商品，以及在国内市场以外币销售的商品。外贸企业只统计自主经营出口的商品，不包括受托代理出口的商品。

期末商品库存额 对于批发和零售业法人单位和个体经营户，是指报告期末取得所有权的全部商品金额（含增值税）；对于批发和零售业产业活动单位，是指报告期末实际在库且归属法人具有所有权的全部商品金额（含增值税）。库存商品包括：（1）存放在本单位（如门市部、批发站、采购站、经营处）的仓库、货场、货柜和货架中的商品；（2）挑选、整理、包装中的商品；（3）已记入购进而尚未运到本单位的商品，即发货单或银行承兑凭证已到而货未到的商品；（4）寄放他处的商品，如因购货方拒绝付款而暂时存在购货方的商品；（5）委托其他单位代销（未作销售或调出）尚未售出的商品；（6）代其他单位购进尚未交付的商品。不包括：（1）所有权不属于本单位的商品，如商品已作销售但买方尚未取走的商品，代替他人保管、运输、加工的商品，代其他单位销售（未做购进或调入）而未售出的商品；（2）委托外单位加工的商品（包括本单位所属加工厂和其他生产单位加工生产尚未收回成品的商品）；（3）外贸企业代理其他单位从国外进口，尚未付给订货单位的商品；（4）代国家储备部门保管的商品。

营业额 指住宿和餐饮业单位在经营活动中，因提供服务或销售商品等取得的全部收入（含增值税），收入主要来源于提供客房、餐费服务、商品销售和其他服务，如商务服务。不包括多产业法人企业附营的其他行业产业活动单位的餐费收入、商品销售收入等各项收入。其中，客房收入指住宿和餐饮业单位在经营活动中因提供住宿服务取得的收入（含增值税）。不包括多产业法人企业附营的其他行业产业活动单位的客房收入。餐费收入指本单位为顾客提供就餐服务取得的收入（含增值税）。包括：经烹饪、调制加工后出售的各种食品，如主食、炒菜、凉拌菜等的收入。不包括多产业法人企业附营的其他行业产业活动单位的餐费收入。

连锁总店（总部） 指负责连锁企业资源（商号、商誉、经营模式、服务标准、管理模式等）的开发、配置、控制或使用等功能的企业核心管理机构。连锁经营是指经营同类商品或服务，使用统一商号的若干店铺，在同一总店（总部）的管理下，采取统一采购或特许经营等方式，实现规模效益的组织形式，包括直营连锁、特许连锁和自愿连锁三种形式。其中，直营连锁是指连锁店铺由连锁公司全资或控股开设，在总部的直接控制下，开展统一经营的连锁经营形式；特许连锁是指拥有注册商标、企业标志、专利、专有技术等经营资源的企业（特许人），以合同形式将其拥有的经营资源许可其他经营者（被特许人）使用，被特许人按合同约定在统一的经营模式下开展经营，并向特许人支付特许经营费用的连锁经营形式；自愿连锁是指若干个店铺或企业自愿组合起来，在不改变各自资产所有权关系的情况下，以同一个品牌形象面对消费者，以共同进货为纽带开展的连锁经营形式。

Explanatory Notes on Main Statistical Indicators

Wholesale Trade refers to the activities of selling wholesale commodities for daily use and capital goods to enterprises of wholesale and retail trades (including self-employed individuals) and other enterprises, institutions and government organs and organizations, and the activities of engaging in import and export and acting as a trade agent. The wholesaler may have the ownership of the commodities for wholesale and trade in the name of its own (a company), and the wholesaler can act as commission agent or commodity broker without the ownership of commodities. Also included are the wholesale activities at the fixed stalls in wholesale market and the acquisition for sales purpose.

Retail Trade refers to the activities of department store, supermarket, franchised store, brand store, retail stall and on-the-spot-making-selling store selling commodities to the final consumers (residents) by any means including internet, post, telephone, sales machine. It also includes shops with sales and production located in the same places (such as bakeries). Retail trade excludes the activities of sales of capital goods such as grain, seed, feed, livestock, mineral products, raw material for production, industrial chemicals, chemical products for agricultural use, machine and equipment (excluding vehicles, computers and communication equipment). Most retailers have the ownership of commodities to sell, but some are acting as agents or brokers to make transactions for a commission.

Hotel Services refer to the accommodation services provided to visitors. Some units may provide only accommodation while others provide a combination of accommodation, meals, business services and/or recreational facilities. It excludes activities related to the provision of long-term primary residences in facilities such as apartments typically leased on a monthly or annual basis.

Catering Services refer to the activities of providing foods, serving locations and facilities to customers through instant processing, commercial sales and service-type labor.

Total Retail Sales of Consumer Goods refer to the amount obtained by enterprises (units, self-employed individuals) through direct sales of non-production and non-business physical commodity to individuals, social institutions, and revenue from providing catering services.

Purchase, Sales and Stock of Commodities by Wholesale and Retail Trades refer to the total volume of commodities purchased, total volume of sales and exports, and the stock of commodities by wholesale and retail enterprises (establishments) of different status of registration from domestic and overseas markets. This indicator reflects the relationship among purchase, sales and stock of commodities in the circulation of goods and reveals the existing problems.

Total Purchases of Commodities refer to the total value of purchases of commodities by enterprises (establishments) from other establishments or individuals (including direct import from abroad) for the purpose of re-selling, either with or without further processing of the commodities purchased. The commodities include: (1) commodities purchased from agricultural and industrial producer, wholesaler, retailer, publishing house and other enterprises, institutions and individual operators of service business; (2) commodities purchased from institutions and government departments; (3) confiscated goods purchased from the customs authorities or market management agencies; (4) second-hand goods and wastes purchased from residents; The commodities exclude (1) commodities purchased by enterprises (establishments) for use in their own business operation, commodities obtained without buying or selling procedures such as materials, consumable goods of low value, office appliance, etc. (2) received goods without trading, such as goods handed over from others, borrowed goods, preserved goods for others, donated goods from others, processed and retrieved goods, etc. (3) goods of direct settlement between buyer and seller with handling fees introduced by others, (4) goods returned or refused to pay by the buyer, (5) excessive goods, (6) futures trading commodities.

Import refers to the amount of goods imported

directly from abroad or imported entrusted to foreign trade enterprises as agents, excluding imports purchased from relevant domestic units. Foreign trade enterprises only count imported goods independently, not imported goods entrusted by agents.

Total Sales of Commodities refer to value of commodities sold by the establishments to other establishments and individuals (including goods sold for self consumption, including the value-added tax). The commodities include: (1) commodities sold to individuals and social groups for their consumption; (2) commodities sold to establishments in all industries for their production and operation, including agriculture, industry, construction, and catering services including commodities sold to wholesale and retail establishments for re-selling, with or without further processing; and (3) commodities for direct export to abroad. Excluded are (1) extended commodities without trading, such as goods handed over to other enterprises and institutions because of the change of organizations, lent goods, returned goods preserved for others, extended processing materials and samples donated to others, (2) goods sold by coupon rebates that are not included in business income, (3) goods of direct settlement between buyer and seller with handling fees introduced by others, (4) prepaid cards for goods without transfer of ownership, such as gas cards, (5) Service-oriented economic activities such as automobile maintenance and telephone card sales, (6) goods returned after purchase, (7) damaged and spoiled goods, (8) waste and used goods of self use, (9) futures trading commodities, (10) water, electricity and gas supplied by water supply enterprises, electric power enterprises and natural gas supply enterprises.

Export refers to the amount of goods exported directly to foreign countries (borders) or exported entrusted to foreign trade enterprises as agents. Commodity export does not include goods sold to foreign trade enterprises for export or exported after processing, as well as goods sold in foreign currencies in the domestic market. Foreign trade enterprises only count the goods they export independently, excluding those exported by trusted agents.

Total Stock of Commodities at End of Period For corporate units and self-employed individuals engaged in wholesale and retail trade, it refers to total value (including VAT) of commodities possessed at the end of the reference period; and for wholesale and retail establishments, it refers to the value (including VAT) of all commodities actually in stock and owned by their corporate units at the end of reference period. The commodities in stock includes: (1) commodities located in storage, garages, counters, and shelves of operating places of wholesale and retail trades (such as sale stores, wholesale centres, procurement stations and operating offices); (2) commodities in the process of being selected, sorted, and packed; (3) commodities not arrived but recorded as purchased in the account, i.e. commodities not arrived but payment receipts for the commodities from the sellers or the banks arrived; (4) commodities deposited in other places rather than places mentioned above, for instance: commodities in the hold of purchasers temporarily due to the refusal of payment; (5) commodities entrusted to other units to sell but not sold yet; (6) commodities purchased for other units but not delivered yet. Commodities not included as stock are those not owned by the enterprises (units), commodities on commission for processing, imported commodities of agency of foreign trade enterprise but not yet delivered to ordering units and finally those put in stock on behalf of the state reserves units.

Business Revenue of Hotels and Catering Services refers to total revenue (including VAT) of hotels and catering services received from providing services or selling commodities through business activities, income comes mainly from providing hotels, catering services, selling of commodities and other services, such as commodity services. It does not include revenue such as meal fees, selling of commodities of other industrial units affiliated with multi industrial legal entities. Income from hotels refers to income (including VAT) of hotels and catering services by providing lodging services through business activities. Income from catering services refers to income (including VAT) from providing catering services, including selling of cooked or prepared foods, such as staple food, cooked dishes, or cold dishes. It does not include meal fees of other industrial units affiliated with multi industrial legal entities.

Chain Head Stores (headquarter) refer to the core leading stores responsible for development, allocation, administration and utilization of resources (name of stores, brand of stores, operation model, service standard, management way, etc.) of chain stores. Chain stores refers to the stores engaged in providing homogeneous commodities or services, with the central leadership of head store (headquarters) and guided by common policies, conduct centralized purchase and distributed selling of commodities, in order to gain better efficiency through standardized operation. The chain stores include regular chain stores, franchise chain stores and voluntary chain stores.

Regular Chain store refers to chain stores that are invested or controlled by the headquarters. They operate under direct and unified management from the headquarters.

Franchise chain store refers to the chain stores (franchisees) which are franchised with operation resources such as trade marks, names, patent and operation know–how by the franchisors in form of contract and pay the operation fees to the franchisors.

Voluntary chain store refers to the stores operate jointly on the voluntary bases while maintaining their status of independent legal entities with full ownership of their assets. They sell goods of same brand from same channel of resource to the consumers.

17 对外经济贸易和旅游

FOREIGN TRADE AND ECONOMIC COOPERATION TOURISM

资料整理：李鹏涛
Data management: Li Pengtao
数据审核：赵　晖
Data audit：Zhao Hui

第十七部分　对外经济贸易和旅游

一、简要说明

本章资料包括对外经济贸易、利用外资和旅游等方面资料，由西安市统计局贸易外经处根据西安市商务局、投资合作局、文化和旅游局、关中海关提供资料整理。

二、主要指标

进出口总值（亿元）	4399.96	比上年增长	26.5%
#出　口	2361.92	比上年增长	33.0%
实际利用外资（亿美元）	87.14	比上年增长	13.5%

17 FOREIGN TRADE AND ECONOMIC COOPERATION,TOURISM

Ⅰ.Brief Introduction

Data in this chapter consists of data on foreign trade, using of foreign capital and fund and tourism. Data on foreign economy and trade and tourism are compiled and provided by Foreign Economy Division of the Xi'an Bureau of Statistics according to the data from Xi'an Municipal Bureau of Commerce, Xi'an Municipal Bureau of Investment Cooperation. Guanzhong Customs District and Xi'an Municipal Administration of Culture and Tourism Committee.

Ⅱ.Major Indicators

		Increase over Preceding Year
Total Imports and Exports (100 mil.yuan)	4399.96	26.5%
#Exports	2361.92	33.0%
Actual Utilized Foreign Investments (USD 100 mil.)	87.14	13.5%

17–1 主要年份外资、外贸基本情况

Main Indicators on Foreign Investments and International Trading in Representative Years

指 标	Item	2000	2005	2010	2015*	2016*
一、新设立外商投资企业（个）	**Number of New Foreign-Invested Enterprises (unit)**	**135**	**157**	**82**	**73**	**72**
合同外资（万美元）	Contracted Foreign Investments (USD 10 000)	54123	121499	119689	193684	102103
实际利用外资（万美元）	Actual Utilized Foreign Investments (USD 10 000)	15633	57113	156653	400833	450466
二、进出口总值（万美元）	**Total Imports and Exports (USD 10 000)**	**173696**	**390146**	**1039273**	**17616896**	**18299476**
进口总值	Total Imports	67634	126705	507544	9418142	8826392
出口总值	Total Exports	106062	263441	531729	8198754	9473084
进出口差额(出口-进口)	Balance of Imports and Exports	38428	136736	24185	-1219388	646692
三、国际旅游人数总计（万人次）	**Total Number of International Tourists (10 000 person-times)**	**65.03**	**77.56**	**84.18**		
外国人	Foreigners	54.65	65.86	73.21		
港、澳、台同胞	Chinese Compatriot From Hong Kong, Macao and Taiwan	10.38	11.70	10.97		
四、国际旅游者人天数总计（万人天）	**Total Number of Days of International Tourists (10 000 person days)**	**162.69**	**224.93**	**241.67**		
外国人	Foreigners	131.44	190.99	211.48		
港、澳、台同胞	Chinese Compatriot From Hong Kong, Macao and Taiwan	31.15	33.94	30.19		
五、国际旅游收入（亿元）	**Earning of International Tourism (100 millon yuan)**	**22.41**	**33.54**	**42.40**		
商品收入	Income from Mercantile	7.71	11.25	11.87		
劳务收入	Income from Labour Service	14.70	22.29	30.53		
六、国际旅游者在西安人均停留天数（天）	**Number of Days of Average Tourists Staying in Xi'an (day)**	**2.5**	**2.9**	**2.9**		

注：1.2014年起市文化和旅游局未发布国际旅游统计数据。
2.本表“新设立外商投资企业”2018年前名称为“利用外资签定协议项目”，“合同外资”2016年前名称为“利用外资签订协议金额”，“实际利用外资”2016年前名称为“外商实际直接投资额”。
3.本表数据来源于市商务局、关中海关、市文化和旅游局、市投资合作局。2018年起利用外资部分数据包含西咸新区。进出口总额数据为西安原口径数据。
4.*号表示2014年起进出口数据计量单位由“万美元”更改为“万元”。

17-1 续表 continued

指 标	Item	2017*	2018*	2019*	2020*	2021*
一、新设立外商投资企业（个）	**Number of New Foreign-Invested Enterprises (unit)**	**143**	**219**	**237**	**212**	**221**
合同外资（万美元）	Contracted Foreign Investments (USD 10 000)	464954	475508	196410	735596	84579
实际利用外资（万美元）	Actual Utilized Foreign Investments (USD 10 000)	530680	635370	705738	767702	871421
二、进出口总值（万美元）	**Total Imports and Exports (USD 10 000)**	**25450843**	**33032389**	**32425181**	**34738438**	**43999596**
进口总值	Total Imports	9928641	13460734	15122342	16978644	20380386
出口总值	Total Exports	15522202	19571655	17302839	17759794	23619210
进出口差额(出口-进口)	Balance of Imports and Exports	5593561	6110921	2180497	781150	3238824
三、国际旅游人数总计（万人次）	**Total Number of International Tourists (10 000 person-times)**					
外国人	Foreigners					
港、澳、台同胞	Chinese Compatriot From Hong Kong, Macao and Taiwan					
四、国际旅游者人天数总计（万人天）	**Total Number of Days of International Tourists (10 000 person days)**					
外国人	Foreigners					
港、澳、台同胞	Chinese Compatriot From Hong Kong, Macao and Taiwan					
五、国际旅游收入（亿元）	**Earning of International Tourism (100 millon yuan)**					
商品收入	Income from Mercantile					
劳务收入	Income from Labour Service					
六、国际旅游者在西安人均停留天数（天）	**Number of Days of Average Tourists Staying in Xi'an (day)**					

17-2 主要年份利用外资情况

Utilization of Foreign Capital in Representative Years

单位：万美元 (USD 10 000)

年 份 Year	合同外资 Contracted Foreign Investments	实际利用外资 Actual Utilized Foreign Investments
1983	3500	800
1985	8361	1106
1987	3218	5552
1988	2423	6758
1989	1645	11632
1990	415	1154
1991	591	1094
1992	24165	5200
1993	57289	8996
1994	20321	15240
1995	28956	18653
1996	35978	20510
1997	27214	22057
1998	40034	22286
1999	40390	13801
2000	54123	15633
2001	60736	17687
2002	70692	20281
2003	96380	25557
2004	78312	27595
2005	121499	57113
2006	182525	82463
2007	143978	111567
2008	118230	114738
2009	60027	121872
2010	119689	156653
2011	120083	200522
2012	360264	247800
2013	251874	312994
2014	255321	370310
2015	193684	400833
2016	102103	450466
2017	464954	530680
2018	475508	635370
2019	196410	705738
2020	735596	767702
2021	84579	871421

注：本表数据来源于市投资合作局。2018年及以后数据包含西咸新区。

17-3 外国和港澳台地区在西安投资情况（2021年）

Foreign, Hong Kong, Macao and Taiwan Investment Situation in Xi'an (2021)

单位：万美元　　(USD 10 000)

指　标	Item	新设立外商投资企业（个） Number of New Foreign-Invested Enterprises(unit)	合同外资 Contracted Foreign Investments	实际利用外资 Actual Utilized Foreign Investments
合计数	**Total**	**221**	**84579**	**871421**
一、按国民经济行业分组	**By Sector**			
（一）农、林、牧、渔业	Agriculture, Forestry, Animal Husbandry and Fishery	2	-20532	
（二）采矿业	Mining	1	141	
（三）制造业	Manufacturing	15	7860	479846
（四）电力、热力、燃气及水生产供应业	Generation and Supply of Electricity, Production and Supply of Gas and Water	4	26639	18190
（五）建筑业	Construction	6	879	48308
（六）批发和零售业	Wholesale and Retail Trades	54	24020	82586
（七）交通运输、仓储和邮政业	Transportation, Storage and Post	2	1919	7532
（八）住宿和餐饮业	Hotels and Catering Services	11	1238	1189
（九）信息传输、软件和信息技术服务业	Information Transmission, Computer Service and Software	19	6999	8191
（十）金融业	Financial Intermediation		273	7468
（十一）房地产业	Real Estate	7	-18830	45088
（十二）租赁和商务服务业	Leasing and Business Services	42	25131	163429
（十三）科学研究和技术服务业	Scientific Research and Technical Service	42	17608	4901
（十四）水利、环境和公共设施管理业	Management of Water Conservancy, Environment and Public Facilities		938	87
（十五）居民服务、修理和其他服务业	Services to Households, repairs and other services	5	860	
（十六）教育	Education	2	93	
（十七）卫生和社会工作	Health and social work			506

注：本表数据来源于市投资合作局。本表数据包含西咸新区。

17-3 续表 continued

单位：万美元 (USD 10 000)

指 标	Item	新设立外商投资企业（个） Number of New Foreign-Invested Enterprises(unit)	合同外资 Contracted Foreign Investments	实际利用外资 Actual Utilized Foreign Investments
（十八）文化、体育和娱乐业	Culture, Sports and Entertainment	9	9343	4100
（十九）公共管理、社会保障和社会组织	Public administration, social security and social organizations			
（二十）国际组织	International Organizations			
二、按投资国别、地区分组	**By Country(Region)**			
中国香港	Hong Kong,China	57	47043	356029
中国澳门	Macao,China	1	153	31736
中国台湾	Taiwan,China	18	279	211506
日本	Japan	1	26	36506
马来西亚	Malaysia	2	26	
新加坡	Singapore	9	-12422	64065
韩国	Korea Rep.	18	1101	115632
德国	Germany	3	139	6114
意大利	Italy			
法国	France	2	6	1286
英国	United Kingdom	1	-189	4956
瑞士	Switzerland		56	178
丹麦	Denmark			
加拿大	Canada		939	5291
美国	United States	10	17141	7173
澳大利亚	Australia	1	108	1549
维尔京群岛	Virgin Is.(E)	2	4000	1048
其他	Others	96	26173	28352

17-4 主要年份各区县、开发区实际利用外资

Actual Utilized Investment by Foreign Entrepreneurs by Region and Development Zone in Representative Years

单位：万美元 (USD 10 000)

区县及开发区	Region and Development Zone	2011	2013	2014	2015	2016	2017	2018	2019	2020	2021
区县合计	**Sum of Region**	**49726**	**45164**	**51423**	**59765**	**67874**	**72527**	**119635**	**129183**	**124666**	**155017**
新城区	Xincheng	6765	5012	6500	7775	8768	10340	11947	11609	12097	12667
碑林区	Beilin	6273	5103	5871	6873	9360	9941	10570	11450	12127	12550
莲湖区	Lianhu	7405	5100	5843	6873	7532	8656	9392	9820	10398	10849
灞桥区	Baqiao	6001	6124	6933	8148	9056	9601	10570	11450	9200	9630
未央区	Weiyang	6202	6000	6834	7870	8614	9433	10380	11260	9420	9750
雁塔区	Yanta	6912	6179	6847	8074	8907	9843	10772	11450	9077	9631
阎良区	Yanliang	2070	2200	2346	2555	2801	3000	3200	3360	3460	3500
临潼区	Lintong	2000	2400	2504	2765	3031	1102	4094	3680	3855	3900
长安区	Chang'an	2300	3003	3360	3961	4440	4762	5200	5620	4476	4580
高陵区	Gaoling	1089	1100	1182	1478	1621	1740	1860	1960	2020	2040
鄠邑区	Huyi	1060	1173	1288	1339	1479	1700	1666	1600	1180	1190
蓝田县	Lantian	600	660	707	1283	1401	1490	1862	3185	1530	1540
周至县	Zhouzhi	1050	1110	1210	773	864	920	920			900
西咸新区	Xixian New Area							37202	42739	45826	72290
开发区合计	**Sum of Development Zones**	**150797**	**267830**	**318887**	**311265**	**381023**	**458153**	**515513**	**576495**	**643037**	**716404**
高新区	Hi-Tech Industries Development Zone	64935	132632	149387	167112	203870	260293	287000	321383	356615	396990
经开区	Economic Development Zone	54201	81423	103009	114538	129186	145000	167000	186900	206800	226379
曲江新区	Qujiang New District	21002	33870	41436		20588	24212	26500	29600	32488	36021
航空基地	National Aviation Hi-tech Industrial Base	3856	7266	8453	9800	10833	12402	13600	15000	8931	18702
航天基地	National Civil Aerospace Industrial Base	1701	2640	3082	3636	4186	2045	5250	6000	9853	10300
浐灞生态区	Chan-ba Ecological District	2030	3000	3501	3980	4567	5117	6100	6599	16460	14120
国际港务区	International Trade & Logistics Park	1571	3469	5050	6429	7793	9083	10063	11013	11890	13892
其他	**Others**				**29803**	**1569**		**222**	**60**		

注：本表数据来源于市投资合作局。2011–2015年开发区合计包含沣东新城。2018年起数据包含西咸新区。

17-5 主要年份进出口总值

Total Imports and Exports in Representative Years

单位：万美元 (USD 10 000)

年 份 Year	进出口总值 Total Imports and Exports	出口总值 Total Exports	进口总值 Total Imports
1987	13596	7540	6056
1990	38229	28290	9939
1993	93330	62393	30937
1994	104752	76897	27855
1995	137510	110163	27347
1996	143187	91745	51442
1997	150668	107753	42915
1998	180589	100492	80097
1999	172919	94495	78424
2000	173696	106062	67634
2001	169914	87948	81966
2002	186966	112479	74487
2003	230932	140327	90605
2004	309295	203539	105756
2005	390146	263441	126705
2006	415403	272862	142541
2007	536162	347133	189029
2008	704029	447113	256916
2009	724618	333114	391504
2010	1039273	531729	507544
2011	1260179	582662	677517
2012	1301446	729878	571568
2013	1798534	847819	950715
2014*	15321514	7346822	7974693
2015*	17616896	8198754	9418142
2016*	18299476	9473084	8826392
2017*	25450843	15522202	9928641
2018*	33032389	19571655	13460734
2019*	32425181	17302839	15122342
2020*	34738438	17759794	16978644
2021*	43999596	23619210	20380386

注：本表数据来源于关中海关。2014年起数据计量单位由“万美元”更改为“万元”。本表数据为西安原口径数据。

17-6 外贸商品进出口总值分国别和地区（2021年）

Total Value of Imports and Exports by Country and Region (2021)

单位：万元 (10 000 yuan)

国别和地区	Country and Region	进出口总值 Total Imports and Exports	出口 Exports
亚洲	**Asia**	**31062000**	**15930389**
#中国香港	Hong Kong,China	3527981	3524464
中国台湾	Taiwan,China	8273188	2511881
日本	Japan	3012817	468251
菲律宾	Philippines	189784	131142
马来西亚	Malaysia	1645133	1170030
韩国	Korea	9974769	55055642
非洲	**Africa**	**604131**	**345463**
#埃及	Egypt	60172	59526
突尼斯	Tunisia	7131	6719
埃塞俄比亚	Ethiopia	11576	11576
博茨瓦纳	Botswana	120	120
南非	South Africa	248866	248866
欧洲	**Europe**	**6333039**	**4519170**
#德国	Germany	1392531	931771
法国	France	536221	400777
意大利	Italy	240786	130810
荷兰	Netherland	1536249	1306256
英国	England	349204	293365
瑞士	Switzerland	67031	12183
西班牙	Spain	213183	187592
俄罗斯	Russia	400459	203502
拉丁美洲	**Latin America**	**1529556**	**738978**
#哥伦比亚	Colombia	30898	30892
巴西	Brazil	536778	244657
阿根廷	Argentina	10024	8930
北美洲	**North America**	**3681096**	**1931451**
#加拿大	Canada	154601	77028
美国	America	3526495	1854423
大洋洲及太平洋岛屿	**Oceanic and Pacific Islands**	**785059**	**153759**
#澳大利亚	Australia	764111	139746
新西兰	New Zealand	17762	11723

注：本表数据来源于关中海关，为西安原口径数据

17-7 主要年份主要商品分大类出口金额

Export Value of Major Merchandise by Type in Representative Years

单位：万美元 (USD 10 000)

商品分类	HS Section and Division	2000	2005
食用蔬菜、根及块茎	Edible Vegetables, Certain,Roots and Tubers	1095	1190
蔬菜、水果、坚果或植物其他部分的制品	Vegetables, Fruits, Nuts, or Products Made of Other Parts of Plants	2076	10531
矿砂、矿渣及矿灰	Ores,Slags and Ash	4083	63247
无机化学品；贵金属、稀土金属、放射性元素及其同位素的有机及无机化合物	Inorganic Chemicals,Organic or Inorganic Compounds of Precious Metals,of Rare Earth Metals,of Radioactive Elements or of Isotopes	3714	10997
有机化学品	Organic Chemicals	2367	8569
羊毛、动物细毛或粗毛、马毛纱线及机织物	Wool ,Fine or Coarse Animal Hair; Horsehair Yarn and Woven Fabric	810	903
棉花	Cotton	3197	3240
化学纤维短纤	Short Staple Chemical Fibers	5061	1471
针织或钩编的服装及衣着附件	Articles of Apparel and Clothing Accessories, Knitted or Crocheted	6753	5736
非针织或非钩编的服装及衣着附件	Articles of Apparel and Clothing Accessories, not Knitted or Crocheted	7269	5068
其他纺织制成品；成套物品；旧衣着及旧纺织品	Other Made Up Textile Articles;Sets;Worn Clothing and Worn Textile Articles;Rags Articles	1649	3000
鞋靴、护膝和类似品及其零件	Footwear,Gaiters and The Like;Parts of Such Articles Headgear and Parts Thereof	1347	1368
玻璃及其制品	Glass and Glassware	3376	8576
钢铁	Iron and Steel	3534	5314
钢铁制品	Articles of Iron or Steel	5535	13959
铅及制品	Lead Articles Thereof	1371	12
锌及制品	Zinc Articles Thereof	4031	135
其他贱金属、金属陶瓷及其制品	Other Base Metals,Cermets;Articles Thereof	1066	11233
贱金属工具、器具、利口器、餐匙、餐叉及其零件	Tools,Implements,Cutlery,Spoons and Forks, of Base Metal;Parts Thereof of Base Metal	2933	3052
核反应堆、锅炉、机器、机械器具及其零件	Nuclear Reactors ,Boilers, Machinery and Mechanical Appliances; and Parts Thereof	10915	30832
电机、电气设备及其零件；录音机及放声机、电视图像、声音的录制和重放设备及其零件、附件	Electrical Machinery and Equipment and Parts Thereof;Sound Recorders and Reproducers, Television Image and Sound Recorders and Reproducers, and Parts and Accessories of Such Articles	8339	23605
光学、照相、电影、计量、检验、医疗或外科仪器及设备、精密仪器及设备；上述物品的零配件、附件	Optical,Photographic,Cinematographic,Measuring, Checking,Precision Medical or Surgical Instruments and Apparatus;Parts and Accessories Thereof	2020	2341
家具、寝具、褥垫、弹簧床垫、软床垫及类似的填充制品；未列名灯具及照明装置；发光标志、发光铭牌及类似品；活动房屋	Furniture,Bedding,Mattresses,Mattress Supports,Cushions and Similar Stuffed Furnishings;Lamps and Lighting Fittings, not Elsewhere Specified or Included;Illuminated Signs,Illuminated	2587	4773

注：本表数据来源于关中海关。2014年起数据计量单位由“万美元”更改为“万元”。本表数据为西安原口径数据。

17-7 续表

单位：万美元

商品分类	HS Section and Division	2008	2009
食用蔬菜、根及块茎	Edible Vegetables, Certain,Roots and Tubers	1374	803
蔬菜、水果、坚果或植物其他部分的制品	Vegetables, Fruits, Nuts, or Products Made of Other Parts of Plants	29270	21920
矿砂、矿渣及矿灰	Ores,Slags and Ash	40502	6141
无机化学品；贵金属、稀土金属、放射性元素及其同位素的有机及无机化合物	Inorganic Chemicals,Organic or Inorganic Compounds of Precious Metals,of Rare Earth Metals,of Radioactive Elements or of Isotopes	15882	9774
有机化学品	Organic Chemicals	13954	16294
羊毛、动物细毛或粗毛、马毛纱线及机织物	Wool ,Fine or Coarse Animal Hair; Horsehair Yarn and Woven Fabric	720	460
棉花	Cotton	3213	2346
化学纤维短纤	Short Staple Chemical Fibers	1181	2217
针织或钩编的服装及衣着附件	Articles of Apparel and Clothing Accessories, Knitted or Crocheted	4371	3617
非针织或非钩编的服装及衣着附件	Articles of Apparel and Clothing Accessories, not Knitted or Crocheted	3623	2919
其他纺织制成品；成套物品；旧衣着及旧纺织品	Other Made Up Textile Articles;Sets;Worn Clothing and Worn Textile Articles;Rags Articles	3187	2813
鞋靴、护膝和类似品及其零件	Footwear,Gaiters and The Like;Parts of Such Articles Headgear and Parts Thereof	380	367
玻璃及其制品	Glass and Glassware	6538	5574
钢铁	Iron and Steel	11966	4254
钢铁制品	Articles of Iron or Steel	26568	11943
铅及制品	Lead Articles Thereof	2	1
锌及制品	Zinc Articles Thereof	46	78
其他贱金属、金属陶瓷及其制品	Other Base Metals,Cermets;Articles Thereof	27576	11276
贱金属工具、器具、利口器、餐匙、餐叉及其零件	Tools,Implements,Cutlery,Spoons and Forks, of Base Metal;Parts Thereof of Base Metal	4083	2777
核反应堆、锅炉、机器、机械器具及其零件	Nuclear Reactors ,Boilers, Machinery and Mechanical Appliances; and Parts Thereof	75911	52372
电机、电气设备及其零件；录音机及放声机、电视图像、声音的录制和重放设备及其零件、附件	Electrical Machinery and Equipment and Parts Thereof;Sound Recorders and Reproducers, Television Image and Sound Recorders and Reproducers, and Parts and Accessories of Such Articles	56758	53355
光学、照相、电影、计量、检验、医疗或外科仪器及设备、精密仪器及设备；上述物品的零配件、附件	Optical,Photographic,Cinematographic,Measuring, Checking,Precision Medical or Surgical Instruments and Apparatus;Parts and Accessories Thereof	6348	5255
家具、寝具、褥垫、弹簧床垫、软床垫及类似的填充制品；未列名灯具及照明装置；发光标志、发光铭牌及类似品；活动房屋	Furniture,Bedding,Mattresses,Mattress Supports,Cushions and Similar Stuffed Furnishings;Lamps and Lighting Fittings, not Elsewhere Specified or Included;Illuminated Signs,Illuminated	8296	4769

continued

(USD 10 000)

2010	2011	2012	2013	2014*	2015*	2016*	2017*	2018*	2019*	2020*	2021*
2633	2016	1961	2699	2686	2039	2555	1129	659	1337	1000	912
22189	36763	2576	49361	132663	112701	102768	149311	131711	79123	62463	22213
5247	4709	1679	1686	14977	96	178	346	25	2	4	8661
13645	11735	8911	12588	67764	44508	49950	52192	52289	61278	49903	67022
18881	20067	17890	28694	109986	109654	117162	148719	176287	185794	195107	223582
923	796	562	2433	15782	3005	5648	3153	5680	5731	1130	5934
3277	2628	2185	5827	9252	14309	6429	5301	5531	9583	3281	5580
1951	2586	2375	8245	13685	11581	11178	14502	12923	14903	14132	11360
3830	3366	12316	6491	29551	37030	31646	36441	30570	15335	12534	44913
3134	3262	7050	4861	33872	23610	19393	40633	52971	22579	54999	55359
3170	2838	4412	4471	18906	15677	15187	26219	19425	37534	137812	66968
544	1003	5252	6293	20186	5032	2292	18614	18514	19469	5553	13609
6691	8073	10995	13856	54453	45991	46764	46059	49904	44400	52181	67143
9622	16681	8407	6730	31854	20390	27589	28467	34424	26844	19000	28730
12149	25319	24259	33546	102720	88740	100956	164963	151403	132817	126743	143745
2	2	4913	16	3		26	19	1	12		4
10	10	11	59	109	93	20	334	48	83	95	238
20723	28092	21397	24030	106691	95442	83309	103608	115801	122230	93007	128297
3374	3641	5176	5992	30653	25321	24868	33582	41004	38312	42354	61952
102893	99631	127795	211009	1929864	2744726	3431041	6147739	8252801	4882165	4356460	5263898
118140	137105	183536	327931	3113155	3625079	4264312	7044093	8971300	10051890	10977973	15026069
9489	11066	14908	17879	112646	119117	107892	108613	149348	170976	247596	263762
4992	3860	25644	23595	52352	42140	40142	77439	83975	26295	28047	47977

17-8 主要年份主要商品分大类进口金额

Import Value of Major Merchandise by Type in Representative Years

单位：万美元 (USD 10 000)

商品分类	HS Section and Division	2000	2005	2010	2015*	2016*
无机化学品；贵金属、稀土金属、放射性元素及其同位素的有机及无机化合物	Inorganic Chemicals,Organic or Inorganic Compounds of Precious Metals,of Rare Earth Metals,of Radioactive Elements or of Isotopes	1467	317	7513	185175	299328
有机化学品	Organic Chemicals	7257	15237	13949	86359	154656
塑料及其制品	Plastic and Articles Thereof	2559	4317	4091	54103	76182
钢铁	Iron and Steel	2467	752	10949	17403	16093
铜及制品	Copper and Articles Thereof	2367	689	43343	484480	224287
铝及制品	Aluminium and Articles Thereof	2652	3627	3116	43935	34384
核反应堆、锅炉、机器、机械器具及其零件	Nuclear Reactors ,Boilers, Machinery and Mechanical Appliances; and Parts Thereof	12990	38050	134753	2021311	990108
电机、电气设备及其零件；录音机及放声机、电视图像、声音的录制和重放设备及其零件、附件	Electrical Machinery and Equipment and Parts Thereof;Sound Recorders and Reproducers, Television Image and Sound Recorders and Reproducers,and Parts and Accessories of Such Articles	5911	23337	207937	5011437	5272203
车辆及其零件、附件，但铁道及电车道车辆除外	Vehicles Other Than Railway or Tramway Rolling-Stock, and Parts and Accessories Thereof	1530	1387	3109	19700	22697
航空器、航天器及其零配件	Aircraft, Spacecraft and Parts Thereof	10443	8800	3620	35164	31933
光学、照相、电影、计量、检验、医疗或外科仪器及设备、精密仪器及设备；上述物品的零配件、附件	Optical,Photographic,Cinematographic,Measuring, Checking,Precision Medical or Surgical Instruments and Apparatus;Parts and Accessories Thereof	3673	10424	37414	542812	521411

17-8 续表 continued

单位：万美元 (USD 10 000)

商品分类	HS Section and Division	2017*	2018*	2019*	2020*	2021*
无机化学品；贵金属、稀土金属、放射性元素及其同位素的有机及无机化合物	Inorganic Chemicals,Organic or Inorganic Compounds of Precious Metals,of Rare Earth Metals,of Radioactive Elements or of Isotopes	246352	371885	346091	405611	580296
有机化学品	Organic Chemicals	123439	148022	114497	174149	184876
塑料及其制品	Plastic and Articles Thereof	103008	157809	198420	211050	213974
钢铁	Iron and Steel	16567	18717	21793	30309	23237
铜及制品	Copper and Articles Thereof	240188	571455	652623	603906	953700
铝及制品	Aluminium and Articles Thereof	32032	71631	100994	90818	73866
核反应堆、锅炉、机器、机械器具及其零件	Nuclear Reactors ,Boilers, Machinery and Mechanical Appliances; and Parts Thereof	926081	1056642	2881715	3286053	4658714
电机、电气设备及其零件；录音机及放声机、电视图像、声音的录制和重放设备及其零件、附件	Electrical Machinery and Equipment and Parts Thereof;Sound Recorders and Reproducers, Television Image and Sound Recorders and Reproducers,and Parts and Accessories of Such Articles	6510729	9406713	8561929	9033247	9478124
车辆及其零件、附件，但铁道及电车道车辆除外	Vehicles Other Than Railway or Tramway Rolling-Stock, and Parts and Accessories Thereof	26662	22430	23238	47976	54675
航空器、航天器及其零配件	Aircraft, Spacecraft and Parts Thereof	101247	31940	28326	24734	70321
光学、照相、电影、计量、检验、医疗或外科仪器及设备、精密仪器及设备；上述物品的零配件、附件	Optical,Photographic,Cinematographic,Measuring, Checking,Precision Medical or Surgical Instruments and Apparatus;Parts and Accessories Thereof	307404	341141	580507	680636	620101

注：本表数据来源于关中海关。2014年起数据计量单位由“万美元”更改为“万元”。本表数据为西安原口径数据。

17-9 按贸易方式分外贸出口总值（2021年）

Total Value of Exports in Foreign Trade by Type of Trade (2021)

单位：万元　　　　(10 000 yuan)

指　标	Item	2021	2021年比2020年增长（%）Growth Rate in 2021 over 2020(%)
出口总值	**Total Exports**	**23619210**	**33.0**
1.一般贸易	General Trade	5676103	35.0
2.国家间、国际组织无偿援助	Between Countries, International Organizations	724	-88.0
和赠送的物资	Aid and Donated Materials		
3.其他捐赠物资	Other Donated Materials	30	-99.3
4.来料加工装配贸易	Assembly Processing Trade	9114181	32.4
5.进料加工贸易	Processing With Imported Trade	5112933	24.8
6.对外承包工程出口货物	Exports Contracted Projects	39817	-12.6
7.租赁贸易	Lease Trade		
8.易货贸易	Barter		
9.出料加工贸易	Material Processing	421	151.1
10.保税监管场所进出境货物	Inward and Outward Goods of Free	433	51.2
（保税仓库进出境货物）	(Trade Storehouse)		
11.海关特殊监管区域物流货物	Re-export Goods of Free Trade Zone	3660170	46.2
12.其他	Others	14398	-12.9

注：本表数据来源于关中海关，为西安原口径数据。

17-10 按贸易方式分外贸进口总值（2021年）

Total Value of Imports in Foreign Trade by Type of Trade(2021)

单位：万元 (10 000 yuan)

指 标	Item	2021	2021年比2020年增长（%） Growth Rate in 2021 over 2020(%)
进口总值	**Total Imports**	**20380386**	**19.8**
1.一般贸易	General Trade	4877060	48.7
2.国家间、国际组织无偿援助和赠送的物资	Between Countries, Internationals Organization Aid and Donated Materials		
3.华侨、港澳台同胞、外籍华人捐赠物资	The overseas Chinese, Hong Kong, Macao, Taiwan,Chinese of foreign Donated Materials		
4.来料加工装配贸易	Assembly Processing Trade	7196075	13.8
5.进料加工贸易	Processing With Imported Trade	3797622	4.2
6.来料加工装配进口的设备	Assembly Processing Trade Equipment	92	
7.租赁贸易	Lease Trade	58040	
8.外商投资企业作为投资进口的设备、物品	Foreign-invested Enterprises as the Import Investment of Equipment, Goods	7523	
9.出料加工贸易	Material Processing	435	-37.8
10.易货贸易	Barter		
11.保税监管场所进出境货物（保税仓库进出境货物）	Inward and Outward Goods of Free (Trade Storehouse)	179775	136.9
12.海关特殊监管区域物流货物（保税区仓储转口货物）	Re-export Goods of Free Trade Zone (Re-exports)	1660188	5.9
13.海关特殊监管区域进口设备（出口加工区进口设备）	Export Processing Zones Imported (Equipment)	2527555	22.6
14.其他	Other	76008	15.9

注：本表数据来源于关中海关，为西安原口径数据。

17-11　主要年份旅游人数及收入

Number of Tourists and Tourism Earnings in Representative Years

年　份 Year	接待旅游者人数（万人次） Number of Tourists (10 000 person-times)	#国际旅游人数 Number of International Tourists	旅游总收入（万元） Total Tourism Earnings (10 000 yuan)	#国际旅游收入 Earning of International Tourists	国际旅游者在西安人均停留天数（天） Number of Days of Average International Tourists Staying in Xi'an(day)
1980	4.00	4.00	1757	1757	3.8
1985	21.15	21.15	7029	7029	2.2
1990	25.88	25.88	19628	19628	2.1
1995	791.35	41.35	440000	103818	2.0
1999	1260.40	55.41	830000	186282	2.5
2000	1567.00	65.03	1050000	224100	2.5
2001	1752.20	67.20	1130000	240700	2.4
2002	1984.13	74.13	1310000	260000	2.2
2003	1647.67	33.66	1064200	121200	2.5
2004	2149.03	65.03	1544000	273900	2.9
2005	2423.60	77.56	1785000	335380	2.9
2006	2738.70	86.73	2043000	378270	2.9
2007	3118.01	100.01	2372000	424263	2.9
2008	3232.20	63.20	2435200	287200	2.6
2009	3929.29	67.29	2974000	310500	2.9
2010	5285.18	84.18	4051800	424000	2.9
2011	6653.23	100.23	5301500	512800	2.9
2012	7978.35	115.35	6543900	598900	2.9
2013	10130.00	121.11	8114400	641600	2.9
2014	12000.00		9500000		
2015	13600.80		10736900		
2016	15012.56		12138100		
2017	18093.14		16333000		
2018	24738.75		25548100		
2019	30110.43		31460500		
2020	18417.41		18824200		
2021	24201.73		24452700		

注：1.本表数据来源于市文化和旅游局。2014年以后市文化和旅游局未发布国际旅游统计数据。2017年及以后数据包含西咸新区。
2.1980-1994年因未开展国内旅游统计，故接待旅游者人数和旅游总收入为国际旅游统计。
3.2021年接待旅游者人数与旅游总收入为西安市文化和旅游局测算结果，未经文化和旅游部认定。

17-12　主要年份旅行社及A级景点

Statistics of Travel Agencies and Level-A Scenic Spots in Representative Years

项　目	Item	2005	2010	2014	2015	2016	2017	2018	2019	2020	2021
旅行社数（个）	Number of Travel Agencies (unit)	221	334	385	353	410	452	583	574	550	656
旅行社营业收入（亿元）	Revenue of Travel Agencies (100 million yuan)	17.82	31.22	45.70	59.54	66.68	79.39	93.93	103.14	34.89	36.23
旅游A级景点数（个）	Number of Level-A Scenic Spots(unit)	18	34	67	74	72	77	77	77	83	91
旅游A级景点年接待游客人次（万人次）	Number of Tourists Received at Level-A Scenic Spots (10 000 person-times)	930	2726	7462	8553	10454	18120	24506	22596	10866	13124

注：本表数据来源于市文化和旅游局。2017年及以后所有指标均不包含西咸新区，但2018年旅行社数、旅行社营业收入来源于第四次全国经济普查583家有营业收入的企业数据，包含西咸新区。

主 要 统 计 指 标 解 释

进出口总值 指实际进出我国国境的货物总金额。包括对外贸易实际进出口货物，来料加工装配进出口货物，国家间、联合国及国际组织无偿援助物资和赠送品，华侨、港澳台同胞和外籍华人捐赠品，租赁期满归承租人所有的租赁货物，进料加工进出口货物，边境地方贸易及边境地区小额贸易进出口货物（边民互市贸易除外），中外合资企业、中外合作经营企业、外商独资经营企业进出口货物和公用物品，到、离岸价格在规定限额以上的进出口货样和广告品（无商业价值、无使用价值和免费提供出口的除外），从保税仓库提取在中国境内销售的进口货物，以及其他进出口货物。该指标可以观察一个国家在对外贸易方面的总规模。我国规定出口货物按离岸价格统计，进口货物按到岸价格统计。

商品经营单位所在地进、出口额 指在所在地海关注册登记的有进出口经营权的企业实际进、出口额。

商品目的地进口额和商品货源地出口额 目的地进口额指进口货物的消费、使用或最终抵运地的实际进口额；货源地出口额指出口货物的产地或原始发货地的实际出口额。

利用外资 指我国各级政府、部门、企业和其他经济组织通过对外借款、吸收外商直接投资以及用其他方式筹措的境外现汇、设备、技术等。

外商直接投资 指外国企业和经济组织或个人（包括华侨、港澳台胞以及我国在境外注册的企业）按我国有关政策、法规，用现汇、实物、技术等在我国境内开办外商独资企业、与我国境内的企业或经济组织共同举办中外合资经营企业、合作经营企业或合作开发资源的投资（包括外商投资收益的再投资），以及经政府有关部门批准的项目投资总额内企业从境外借入的资金。

旅游人数：

（1）入境旅游人数：指报告期内来我国观光、度假、探亲访友、就医疗养、购物、参加会议或从事经济、文化、体育、宗教活动的外国人、港澳台同胞、入境游客。统计时，外国人、港澳台同胞每入境一次统计1人次。

（2）出境人数：指中国（大陆）居民因公或因私出境前往其他国家、中国香港特别行政区、澳门特别行政区和台湾省观光、度假、探亲访友、就医疗养、购物、参加会议或从事经济、文化、体育、宗教活动的人数，即出境游客。统计时，按每出境一次统计1人次。

（3）国内旅游人数：指在报告期内在中国（大陆）观光游览、度假、探亲访友、就医疗养、购物、参加会议或从事经济、文化、体育、宗教活动的中国（大陆）居民人数，其出游的目的不是通过所从事的活动谋取报酬。统计时，国内游客按每出游一次统计1人次。

国际旅游（外汇）收入 指入境游客在中国（大陆）境内旅行、游览过程中用于交通、参观游览、住宿、餐饮、购物、娱乐等全部花费。

国内旅游收入 又称旅游总花费，指国内游客在国内旅行、游览过程中用于交通、参观游览、住宿、餐饮、购物、娱乐等全部花费。

国际旅行社 指经营业务范围包括入境旅游业务、出境旅游业务和国内旅游业务的旅行社。

国内旅行社 指经营范围仅限于国内旅游业务的旅行社。

星级饭店 指设备、设施、服务符合《旅游饭店星级的划分与评定》（GB/T14308—2010）标准，通过相关旅游管理部门评定，并取得星级饭店称号的饭店（含预备星级饭店）。

Explanatory Notes on Main Statistical Indicators

Total Imports and Exports at Customs refer to the real value of commodities imported and exported across the border of China. They include the actual imports and exports through foreign trade, imported and exported goods under the processing and assembling trades and materials, supplies and gifts as aid given gratis between governments and by the United Nations and other international organizations, and contributions donated by overseas Chinese, compatriots in Hong Kong and Macao and Chinese with foreign citizenship, leasing commodities owned by tenant at the expiration of leasing period, the imported and exported commodities processed with imported materials, commodities trading in border areas (excluding mutual exchange goods) , the imported and exported commodities and articles for public use of the Sino-foreign joint ventures, cooperative enterprises and ventures with sole foreign investment. Also included is import or export of samples and advertising goods for which CIF or FOB value are beyond the permitted ceiling (excluding goods of no trading or use value and free commodities for export) , imported goods sold in China from bonded warehouses and other imported or exported goods. The indicator of the total imports and exports at customs can be used to observe the total size of external trade in a country. In accordance with the stipulation of the Chinese government, imports are calculated at CIF, while exports are calculated at FOB.

Import Export Value by Location of China's Foreign Trade Managing Units refers to actual value of imports and exports carried out by corporations which have been registered by the local Customs house and are vested with right to run import export business.

Import Value of Commodities by Place of Destination and Export Value of Commodities by Place of Origin in China The former indicator refers to the value of import commodities of the places of their consumption, utilization or the places of their final destination. The latter indicator refers to the value of export commodities of the places of their origin or the places of the commodities dispatched.

Utilization of Foreign Capitals refers to remittance, equipment and technology financed from abroad, by loans, foreign direct investment and other forms undertaken by the Chinese governments at all levels, by various departments, enterprises and other economic units.

Foreign Direct Investment refers to the investments inside China by foreign enterprises and economic organizations or individuals (including overseas Chinese, compatriots from Hong Kong, Macao and Taiwan, and Chinese enterprises registered abroad) , following the relevant policies and laws of China, for the establishment of ventures exclusively with foreign own investment, Sino-foreign joint ventures and cooperative enterprises or for co-operative exploration of resources with enterprises or economic organizations in China.

Number of Tourists

(1) Visitor arrivals refer to the number of foreigners,Chinese compatriots from Hong Kong, Macao and Taiwan Chinese (mainland) who come to China (mainland) for sight-seeing,vacation,visiting relatives, medical treatment, shopping, attending conference, or to engage in economic, cultural, sports and religious activities. In compiling statistics, each time of entering China is counted as one person-time.

(2) Number of Chinese residents going abroad refer to the number of Chinese (mainland) residents going to other countries, Hong Kong Special Administrative region, Macao Special Administrative region and Taiwan for on official or private purposes, for sight-seeing, vacation, visiting relatives, medical treatment, shopping, attending conference, or to engage in economic, cultural , sports and religious activities. In compiling statistics, each time of leaving is counted as one person-time.

(3) Number of domestic tourists refers to the number of Chinese (mainland) residents who travel within China (mainland) for sight-seeing, vacation, visiting relatives, medical treatment, shopping, attending conference, or to engage in economic, cultural, sports and religious activities. In compiling statistics, each time of travelling is counted as one person-time.

Foreign Exchange Earnings from International Tourism refer to the total expenditure of foreigners, overseas Chinese,Chinese compatriots from Hong Kong,Macao and Taiwan during their stay in the mainland of China on transportation,sighting,accommodation, food,shopping and entertainment.

Income from Domestic Tourism refer to expenditure of domestic tourists on transportation,sighting, accommodation, food, shopping and entertainment while they travel.

International Travel Agencies refer to travel agencies engaged in tourism entering China, Chinese residents going abroad and domestic tourism.

Domestic Travel Agencies refer to travel agencies only engaged in domestic tourism.

Star-rated Hotels refer to hotels rated with stars as assessed by the relevant tourism authorities according to GB/T14308-2010 standard with reference to their infrastructure, facilities and service levels.

18 规模以上服务业

SERVICE INDUSTRY OBOVE DESIGNATED SIZE

资料整理：冯　乐　贾荟田
Data management：Feng Le　Jia Huitian
数据审核：刘栋婷
Data audit：Liu Dongting

第十八部分　规模以上服务业

一、简要说明

1.本章主要包括规模以上服务业（九个门类、四个中类）单位个数及主要经济指标，由西安市统计局服务业与社会科技统计处提供。

2.统计范围：辖区内年营业收入2000万元及以上服务业法人单位。包括：交通运输、仓储和邮政业，信息传输、软件和信息技术服务业，水利、环境和公共设施管理业三个门类和卫生行业大类。

辖区内年营业收入1000万元及以上服务业法人单位。包括：租赁和商务服务业，科学研究和技术服务业，教育三个门类，以及物业管理、房地产中介服务、房地产租赁经营和其他房地产业四个行业中类。

辖区内年营业收入500万元及以上服务业法人单位。包括：居民服务、修理和其他服务业，文化、体育和娱乐业两个门类，以及社会工作行业大类。

3.2021年数据不含西安（西咸新区）—咸阳共管区。

二、主要指标

规模以上服务业单位个数（个）	2366		
规模以上服务业资产总计（亿元）	10695.62	比上年增长	10.3%
规模以上服务业营业收入（亿元）	3367.34	比上年增长	17.2%
规模以上服务业利润总额（亿元）	250.92	比上年增长	19.1%

18 SERVICE INDUSTRY OBOVE DESIGNATED SIZE

Ⅰ. Brief Introduction

1. The data in this chapter consists of the number of service units and main economic indicators of Service enterprises above designated size (Including nine categories, four classes), data in this chapter is provided by Tertiary Industry and Social Science&Technology Division of Xi'an Bureau of Statistics.

2. Scope of statistics:The annual operating income of the service enterprise within the jurisdiction is 20 million yuan or more. It includes transportation, storage and postal services,information transmission, software and information technology services, water conservancy,environment and public facilities management, and health services. The annual operating income of the service enterprise within the jurisdiction is 10 million yuan or more. It includes: leasing and business services, scientific research and technology services, three categories of education, and property management, real estate intermediary services, real estate leasing and other real estate industry.

The annual operating income within the jurisdiction is 5 million yuan or more. Including: residential services, repair and other services, culture, sports and entertainment two categories, and social work industry categories.

3. The data in 2021 excludes areas mutually controlled by Xi'an(Xixian New Area)–Xian yang.

Ⅱ. Major Indicators

		Increase over Preceding Year
Number of Service Enterprises above the Designated Size(units)	2366	
Total Assets of Service Enterprises above the Designated Size(100 mil.yuan)	10695.62	10.3%
Operating Income of Service Enterprises above the Designated Size(100 mil.yuan)	3367.34	17.2%
Total Profits of Service Enterprises above the Designated Size(100 mil.yuan)	250.92	19.1%

18-1 主要年份规模以上服务业主要经济指标

Major Economic Indicators for Services above the Designated Size in Representative Years

单位：万元 (10 000 yuan)

指　标	Item	2015	2016	2017	2018	2019	2020	2021
企业单位数（个）	Number of Enterprises(unit)	1056	1229	1546	1670	2075	2222	2366
资产总计	Total Assets	62321993.9	70706084.2	81172689.4	83589990.5	104196300.9	125468817.0	106956191.5
固定资产原价	Original Value of Fixed Assets	34083410.8	37690984.8	42493526.7	47715297.2	52484267.4	56646202.8	33398462.3
负债合计	Total Liabilities	38612455.8	44500949.3	50412896.1	49777084.0	61769819.9	75768947.6	66376516.9
所有者权益合计	Total Owners' Equities	23706613.0	26205716.2	30759793.3	33812906.5	42426481.0	49699869.4	40579674.6
营业收入	Business Revenue	15622838.8	17699509.4	21146457.1	25887537.8	30847961.6	33014968.7	33673403.2
营业成本	Business Cost	11094383.8	13037904.8	15282402.8	19661919.2	23565609.4	26159714.2	27008664.2
销售费用	Selling Expenses	1138387.7	979373.2	1206035.9	1258937.1	1361655.9	1433201.2	1145401.8
管理费用	Administrative Expenses	1595009.8	1806745.9	2104498.2	2485578.9	2354924.6	2435128.3	2510557.0
研发费用	R&D Expenses					660652.9	854836.1	1116205.5
财务费用	Financial Expenses	974310.3	1032444.2	1191706.4	1256296.0	1403795.5	1280074.4	968130.7
投资收益	Investment Income	436577.4	382392.0	286218.3	223023.6	282996.3	694559.2	848883.3
营业利润	Operating Profits	1256825.3	1132716.0	1616118.6	1588474.9	1967982.6	1961738.3	2370531.7
利润总额	Total Profits	1559208.3	1422770.3	1701396.9	1582864.5	2052358.0	2058642.1	2509158.9
应付职工薪酬	Salary Payable	2823540.9	3362254.1	4228194.3	5114155.7	6346279.9	6856080.1	7255601.3
期末用工人数（人）	Year-end Employed Persons(person)	335722	359745	406270	478344	532203	550624	534987

注：期末用工人数为2021年新增指标，2015-2020年数据为平均用工人数。

18-2 规模以上服务业按登记注册类型分主要经济指标（2021年）

单位：万元

指 标	Item	企业单位数（个）Number of Enterprises (unit)	资产总计 Total Assets	固定资产原价 Original Value of Fixed Assets
总计	**Total**	**2366**	**106956191.5**	**33398462.3**
按登记注册类型分组	**Grouped by Registration Type**			
内资	Domestic Funded Enterprises	2284	103976398.6	32039600.1
国有	State-owned Enterprises	104	5989564.9	3165887.1
集体	Collective-owned Enterprises	12	75025.5	26971.3
股份合作	Cooperative Enterprises	1	1126.1	117.4
联营	Joint Ownership Enterprises	1	1768.4	130.1
有限责任公司	Limited Liability Corporations	918	81455923.2	22433880.4
股份有限公司	Share-holding Corporations	56	5049830.0	3967244.5
私营	Private	1178	11191156.7	2343388.0
其他	Other Enterprises	14	212003.8	101981.3
港澳台商投资	Enterprises with Funds from Hong Kong, Macao &Taiwan	33	2067430.3	974405.1
外商投资	Foreign Funded Enterprises	49	912362.6	384457.1

18-2 续表

单位：万元

指 标	Item	管理费用 Administrative Expenses	研发费用 R&D Expenses	财务费用 Financial Expenses
总计	**Total**	**2510557.0**	**1116205.5**	**968130.7**
按登记注册类型分组	**Grouped by Registration Type**			
内资	Domestic Funded Enterprises	2412350.7	1076574.7	941320.2
国有	State-owned Enterprises	217227.1	43362.2	34426.3
集体	Collective-owned Enterprises	15522.1	445.6	-977.3
股份合作	Cooperative Enterprises	147.1	1014.8	-2.4
联营	Joint Ownership Enterprises	139.8	174.5	-1.0
有限责任公司	Limited Liability Corporations	1078266.4	787776.4	807206.8
股份有限公司	Share-holding Corporations	145216.8	31623.9	19165.0
私营	Private	918124.9	212177.3	73562.5
其他	Other Enterprises	37706.5		7940.3
港澳台商投资	Enterprises with Funds from Hong Kong, Macao &Taiwan	48920.8	1074.2	11782.9
外商投资	Foreign Funded Enterprises	49285.5	38556.6	15027.6

Main Economic Indicators for Services above the Designated Size grouped by Registration Type (2021)

(10 000 yuan)

负债合计 Total Liabilities	所有者权益合计 Total Owners' Equities	营业收入 Business Revenue	营业成本 Business Cost	销售费用 Selling Expenses
66376516.9	**40579674.6**	**33673403.2**	**27008664.2**	**1145401.8**
64798320.5	39178078.1	32536147.3	26257945.6	1091919.0
3510774.6	2478790.3	2559990.7	2254740.7	70153.4
58060.6	16964.9	84509.1	58102.9	9268.2
155.3	970.8	1358.5		175.6
634.4	1134.0	2887.7	2203.1	101.2
52249127.5	29206795.7	18577009.8	15449018.2	425322.6
849211.1	4200618.9	2167955.2	1569203.5	149110.6
8010416.1	3180740.6	8897647.0	6737077.1	423552.6
119940.9	92062.9	244789.3	187600.1	14234.8
1110608.2	956822.1	598732.6	388849.3	41146.4
467588.2	444774.4	538523.3	361869.3	12336.4

continued

(10 000 yuan)

投资收益 Investment Income	营业利润 Operating Profits	利润总额 Total Profits	应付职工薪酬 Salary Payable	期末用工人数（人） Year-end Employed Persons (person)
848883.3	**2370531.7**	**2509158.9**	**7255601.3**	**534987**
693165.7	2065645.1	2200912.7	6959487.7	519650
193178.4	423488.0	440124.8	678782.2	45198
29.6	1977.1	1794.5	37461.5	4560
	4.3	144.6	358.5	27
	254.9	269.7	482.2	35
459467.0	844590.4	885739.1	4040599.2	237534
9067.2	253172.3	248785.3	377031.4	22713
31423.5	545412.4	627568.5	1721193.3	204717
	-3254.3	-3513.8	103579.4	4866
155564.6	242282.6	243815.2	84882.3	5538
153.0	62604.0	64431.0	211231.3	9799

18-3 规模以上服务业按规模分主要经济指标（2021年）

单位：万元

指 标	Item	企业单位数（个）Number of Enterprises (unit)	资产总计 Total Assets	固定资产原价 Original Value of Fixed Assets
总计	**Total**	**2366**	**106956191.5**	**33398462.3**
按企业规模分组	**Grouped by Size of Enterprises**			
大型企业	Large-size	180	36318915.0	21813736.4
中型企业	Medium-size	487	21993225.9	5421541.0
小型企业	Small-size	1292	42786328.4	5207554.1
微型企业	Microenterprise	407	5857722.2	955630.8

18-3 续表

单位：万元

指 标	Item	管理费用 Administrative Expenses	研发费用 R&D Expenses	财务费用 Financial Expenses
总计	**Total**	**2510557.0**	**1116205.5**	**968130.7**
按企业规模分组	**Grouped by Size of Enterprises**			
大型企业	Large-size	882946.2	744240.5	342547.1
中型企业	Medium-size	693136.8	243652.2	218652.6
小型企业	Small-size	811775.1	125478.2	366649.0
微型企业	Microenterprise	122698.9	2834.6	40282.0

Main Economic Indicators for Services above the Designated Size grouped by Size of Enterprises (2021)

(10 000 yuan)

负债合计 Total Liabilities	所有者权益合计 Total Owners' Equities	营业收入 Business Revenue	营业成本 Business Cost	销售费用 Selling Expenses
66376516.9	**40579674.6**	**33673403.2**	**27008664.2**	**1145401.8**
20243736.0	16075179.0	14854403.9	12049772.9	487178.0
13380872.6	8612353.3	7128502.0	5416478.0	345011.5
28268222.8	14518105.6	9311479.6	7412157.7	238420.9
4483685.5	1374036.7	2379017.7	2130255.6	74791.4

continued

(10 000 yuan)

投资收益 Investment Income	营业利润 Operating Profits	利润总额 Total Profits	应付职工薪酬 Salary Payable	期末用工人数（人） Year-end Employed Persons (person)
848883.3	**2370531.7**	**2509158.9**	**7255601.3**	**534987**
169801.3	996040.5	1029463.5	4544411.3	252538
390710.9	646085.3	663615.1	1658486.1	158153
202158.6	647250.9	721099.4	969371.2	115485
86212.5	81155.0	94980.9	83332.7	8811

18-4 规模以上服务业按行业分主要经济指标（2021年）

单位：万元

指标	Item	企业单位数（个）Number of Enterprises (unit)	资产总计 Total Assets	固定资产原价 Original Value of Fixed Assets
总计	**Total**	**2366**	**106956191.5**	**33398462.3**
按国民经济行业大类分组	**Grouped by sector categories**			
铁路运输业	Railway transport industry	3	4058017.8	4893503.1
道路运输业	The road transport industry	133	16257730.3	10417146.3
水上运输业	Water transportation			
航空运输业	The air transport industry	12	4673176.7	1894052.5
管道运输业	Pipeline transportation	1	57829.6	17166.9
多式联运和运输代理业	Handling and transport industry	45	314969.2	120902.0
装卸搬运和仓储业	Warehousing industry	35	1232504.9	214900.8
邮政业	The postal service	11	407209.3	208219.0
电信、广播电视和卫星传输服务	Telecommunication,broadcasting and satellite transmission services	22	3214491.4	4955531.7
互联网和相关服务	The Internet and related services	81	1434239.0	46811.2
软件和信息技术服务业	Software and information technology services	263	5370564.2	768461.5
物业管理	Property management	196	1840574.5	315121.5
房地产中介服务	Real estate intermediary service	23	165637.7	10550.0
房地产租赁经营	Owned Real Estate Business Activities	80	5571083.0	909773.8
其他房地产业	Other Real Estate			
租赁业	Leasing industry	31	293631.3	79834.6
商务服务业	Business services	449	21456178.3	3557626.3
研究和试验发展	Research and development	31	1814553.0	698271.7
专业技术服务业	Professional and technical services	391	16091255.1	1319585.2
科技推广和应用服务业	Promotion and application of science and technology services	26	561445.3	215145.5
水利管理业	Water resources management industry	2	1317.4	260.1
生态保护和环境治理业	Ecological protection and environmental control industries	8	204065.1	89934.9
公共设施管理业	Public facilities management industry	48	2880355.6	472792.0
土地管理业	Land Administration Industry	6	13438385.3	99028.2
居民服务业	Resident services	29	106063.2	44663.7
机动车、电子产品和日用产品修理业	Motor vehicles,electronics and household goods-repairing	21	39213.9	7451.3
其他服务业	Other service industries	23	59213.5	13617.1
教育	Education	27	232696.9	42048.1
卫生	Health	76	1621646.6	1077165.6
社会工作	Social work	1	130.3	18.0
新闻和出版业	Press and publishing industry	35	554129.1	74339.1
广播、电视、电影和录音制作业	Radio,television,film and video recordings	117	1289974.8	174739.2
文化艺术业	Culture and arts	68	722099.1	368283.6
体育	Physical education	6	46791.4	27576.4
娱乐业	The entertainment industry	66	945018.7	263941.4

注：物业管理、房地产中介服务、房地产租赁经营和其他房地产业为行业中类。

Main Economic Indicators for Services above the Designated Size grouped by Industry (2021)

(10 000 yuan)

负债合计 Total Liabilities	所有者权益合计 Total Owners' Equities	营业收入 Business Revenue	营业成本 Business Cost	销售费用 Selling Expenses	管理费用 Administrative Expenses
66376516.9	**40579674.6**	**33673403.2**	**27008664.2**	**1145401.8**	**2510557.0**
2570286.2	1487731.6	771118.5	629388.7	241.4	6512.3
9485713.8	6772016.5	2277478.8	2481032.8	13114.1	142034.3
2159346.9	2513829.8	405540.4	508542.6	13397.8	53891.1
44385.3	13444.3	47118.2	44992.8		2237.8
179193.5	135775.7	734418.5	691323.0	4377.1	25160.1
851773.6	380731.3	372006.3	316761.0	18254.7	26749.5
341053.7	66155.6	893621.1	812099.9	9326.4	61323.8
434247.8	2780243.6	2185293.9	1295953.4	183346.0	104840.2
847760.9	586478.1	1385540.0	942188.4	61322.5	103166.5
3184749.1	2185815.1	5416808.3	3893215.2	184994.3	333621.1
1296990.4	543584.1	1322055.9	1089449.4	14260.8	152414.3
110993.3	54644.4	232714.1	165714.3	22098.3	35292.0
4057544.7	1513538.3	425941.3	196940.1	28899.0	106838.6
246220.6	47410.7	118215.1	108179.3	3030.4	10464.5
14264262.2	7191916.1	5088059.3	4274729.0	153420.9	318774.3
752872.9	1061680.1	645414.9	464127.1	7807.6	69966.0
10024138.8	6067116.3	7622601.1	6191273.3	145317.4	485447.0
309301.9	252143.4	102280.6	71100.4	3713.2	15708.3
472.1	845.3	3187.5	2264.0		670.4
107918.9	96146.2	134733.8	110368.7	4249.2	5520.9
1886143.1	994212.5	472111.8	376480.2	12719.8	55429.0
9429693.6	4008691.7	302588.2	208324.2	49.3	17037.0
90856.3	15206.9	85045.8	42835.4	25069.0	16181.4
14638.9	24575.0	35247.6	26246.1	4914.3	4213.2
35671.5	23542.0	66131.2	49489.1	2572.6	11541.3
185269.3	47427.6	312030.2	215958.3	53705.4	62362.2
1127522.6	494124.0	1039100.6	807163.0	73754.6	137070.8
1404.5	-1274.2	910.7	543.6		311.6
259457.9	294671.2	354342.6	273644.7	25792.1	45161.8
861801.6	428173.2	273351.2	213194.5	27635.2	40824.5
385558.8	336540.3	136805.1	109643.8	26621.7	36790.3
46619.2	172.2	11832.0	3815.8	4952.1	2780.1
782653.0	162365.7	399758.6	391682.1	16444.6	20220.8

单位：万元

指 标	Item	研发费用 R&D Expenses	财务费用 Financial Expenses
总计	**Total**	**1116205.5**	**968130.7**
按国民经济行业大类分组	**Grouped by sector categories**		
铁路运输业	Railway transport industry	538.2	86357.9
道路运输业	The road transport industry	2116.8	239513.4
水上运输业	Water transportation		
航空运输业	The air transport industry		17196.4
管道运输业	Pipeline transportation	124.4	-114.4
多式联运和运输代理业	Handling and transport industry		2186.2
装卸搬运和仓储业	Warehousing industry	24.0	15433.7
邮政业	The postal service	346.6	3553.7
电信、广播电视和卫星传输服务	Telecommunication,broadcasting and satellite transmission services	2781.9	18137.9
互联网和相关服务	The Internet and related services	39313.7	5548.1
软件和信息技术服务业	Software and information technology services	728174.6	8390.2
物业管理	Property management	0.1	7051.6
房地产中介服务	Real estate intermediary service	0.2	281.6
房地产租赁经营	Owned Real Estate Business Activities	8312.2	72511.3
其他房地产业	Other Real Estate		
租赁业	Leasing industry	608.9	1607.4
商务服务业	Business services	11365.0	237332.3
研究和试验发展	Research and development	86675.3	5995.1
专业技术服务业	Professional and technical services	225131.3	53187.7
科技推广和应用服务业	Promotion and application of science and technology services	3641.0	5784.2
水利管理业	Water resources management industry		-1.8
生态保护和环境治理业	Ecological protection and environmental control industries	601.2	669.8
公共设施管理业	Public facilities management industry	70.8	22487.3
土地管理业	Land Administration Industry		105324.8
居民服务业	Resident services		-122.0
机动车、电子产品和日用产品修理业	Motor vehicles,electronics and household goods-repairing		303.7
其他服务业	Other service industries	487.2	136.8
教育	Education	2881.2	163.6
卫生	Health	719.4	28092.9
社会工作	Social work		1.3
新闻和出版业	Press and publishing industry	218.7	-1828.2
广播、电视、电影和录音制作业	Radio,television,film and video recordings	677.7	14473.6
文化艺术业	Culture and arts	1269.3	5135.7
体育	Physical education		408.0
娱乐业	The entertainment industry	125.8	12930.9

continued

(10 000 yuan)

投资收益 Investment Income	营业利润 Operating Profits	利润总额 Total Profits	应付职工薪酬 Salary Payable	期末用工人数（人） Year-end Employed Persons (person)
848883.3	**2370531.7**	**2509158.9**	**7255601.3**	**534987**
	46112.9	42007.5	6029.7	283
3115.1	-106422.9	-97615.8	564488.3	48282
25172.0	-111844.7	-113599.4	207010.4	10562
	-1063.0	-1197.8	10026.6	647
1212.3	12290.5	19753.3	31792.3	3781
6135.1	5730.6	17104.6	25428.2	3057
241.4	8010.0	9881.0	244383.0	26372
17.7	550861.7	546002.4	245764.8	15556
3010.4	235980.3	235060.5	181934.7	14292
83723.6	393565.3	409605.8	2289339.2	101456
2267.6	60966.1	66854.8	351458.8	57477
1401.8	10012.1	10252.2	66087.4	3946
51627.2	133506.0	182534.2	57406.2	4307
-29.8	-7525.9	-7069.6	13607.3	1505
329635.0	409422.5	415071.2	559619.7	79879
6066.8	13662.2	21028.6	188953.2	6823
256105.2	761662.7	775874.9	1317597.4	72295
2468.7	3749.7	4261.0	15864.3	994
	248.9	290.5	367.3	32
146.4	13684.7	14741.3	10651.8	1152
3975.9	9232.9	9619.6	108859.2	17542
60873.6	29023.6	29073.9	11094.1	364
16.0	954.8	1006.9	16781.0	3318
-233.6	-869.7	-711.7	6222.2	1022
1.6	1627.6	1863.7	29999.1	5876
3389.0	-19972.7	-28104.1	191199.6	10653
7359.9	-4348.1	-353.9	333329.0	27592
	54.1	80.2	292.2	48
992.1	9391.7	18806.5	61594.9	4342
5392.9	-12945.3	-10056.5	34981.1	3483
1703.5	-21169.4	-15013.3	47281.0	5297
	-168.2	-159.8	3785.5	515
-6904.1	-52889.3	-47733.8	22371.8	2237

18-5 规模以上服务业按隶属关系分主要经济指标（2021年）

单位：万元

指标	Item	企业单位数（个） Number of Enterprises (unit)	资产总计 Total Assets	固定资产原价 Original Value of Fixed Assets
总计	**Total**	**2366**	**106956191.5**	**33398462.3**
按隶属关系分	**Grouped by affiliation**			
中央	Central	90	13284945.4	7643709.4
地方	Region	165	20397210.5	2999206.2
其他	Others	2111	73274035.6	22755546.7

18-5 续表

单位：万元

指标	Item	管理费用 Administrative Expenses	研发费用 R&D Expenses	财务费用 Financial Expenses
总计	**Total**	**2510557.0**	**1116205.5**	**968130.7**
按隶属关系分	**Grouped by affiliation**			
中央	Central	272244.2	179251.6	59980.8
地方	Region	229842.0	68451.2	99286.7
其他	Others	2008470.8	868502.7	808863.2

Main Economic Indicators for Services above the Designated Size grouped by Affiliation (2021)

(10 000 yuan)

负债合计 Total Liabilities	所有者权益合计 Total Owners' Equities	营业收入 Business Revenue	营业成本 Business Cost	销售费用 Selling Expenses
66376516.9	**40579674.6**	**33673403.2**	**27008664.2**	**1145401.8**
6412125.3	6872820.1	7274011.3	5953822.3	173567.4
12088938.3	8308272.2	2973834.8	2273551.1	131830.3
47875453.3	25398582.3	23425557.1	18781290.8	840004.1

continued

(10 000 yuan)

投资收益 Investment Income	营业利润 Operating Profits	利润总额 Total Profits	应付职工薪酬 Salary Payable	期末用工人数（人） Year-end Employed Persons (person)
848883.3	**2370531.7**	**2509158.9**	**7255601.3**	**534987**
64984.8	655629.7	660927.7	980429.6	39940
232381.1	431445.4	441373.1	497545.6	34525
551517.4	1283456.6	1406858.1	5777626.1	460522

18-6 分区县、开发区规模以上服务业主要经济指标（2021年）

单位：万元

区县	Region	企业单位数（个） Number of Enterprises (unit)	资产总计 Total Assets	固定资产原价 Original Value of Fixed Assets
全市	**Total**	**2366**	**106956191.5**	**33398462.3**
新城区	Xincheng	114	3692983.9	1888184.1
碑林区	Beilin	169	5427833.2	4402840.9
莲湖区	Lianhu	148	4807712.1	1243019.6
灞桥区	Baqiao	172	9893753.9	2593850.5
未央区	Weiyang	424	28179661.8	12058854.5
雁塔区	Yanta	856	29759265.0	6832625.6
阎良区	Yanliang	29	885880.4	83985.7
临潼区	Lintong	31	1778211.8	269161.4
长安区	Chang'an	141	4144351.5	841924.2
高陵区	Gaoling	43	1105883.6	247416.3
鄠邑区	Huyi	12	107016.3	46021.0
蓝田县	Lantian	16	299657.7	141345.0
周至县	Zhouzhi	9	58658.4	16400.4
西咸新区	Xixian New Area	202	16815321.9	2732833.1
# 开发区	**Development Zones**			
高新区	Hi-Tech Industries Development Zone	460	18334945.5	5361814.6
经开区	Economic Development Zone	327	24735714.6	11462967.7
曲江新区	Qujiang New District	274	13248722.3	1726523.3
航空基地	National Aviation Hi-tech Industrial Base	15	793051.9	49680.4
航天基地	National Civil Aerospace Industrial Base	70	2786653.1	446089.3
浐灞生态区	Chan-ba Ecological District	69	1973837.6	300149.0
国际港务区	International Trade & Logistics Park	99	8063368.7	2209182.7

Major Economic Indicators for Services above the Designated Size by Region (2021)

(10 000 yuan)

负债合计 Total Liabilities	所有者权益合计 Total Owners' Equities	营业收入 Business Revenue	营业成本 Business Cost	销售费用 Selling Expenses
66376516.9	**40579674.6**	**33673403.2**	**27008664.2**	**1145401.8**
1072536.3	2620447.6	1162673.4	673262.9	113177.4
3414334.7	2013498.5	2418697.8	1942956.9	139096.7
2386141.3	2421570.8	1121195.5	915759.5	46280.0
6282883.5	3610870.4	2512386.6	2161081.0	34852.4
16918999.8	11260662.0	4474369.6	3932471.6	100419.5
19283653.6	10475611.4	16204978.5	12678115.9	537311.5
527456.0	358424.4	196142.2	163436.6	6522.8
1259427.3	518784.5	108273.3	64826.8	21804.5
2283029.6	1861321.9	2085358.4	1425505.0	55532.7
693265.3	412618.3	670831.3	596382.4	7338.6
98356.4	8659.9	122297.2	105730.2	6112.1
263738.1	35919.6	49853.9	37452.6	2942.1
39547.6	19110.8	17343.3	15128.8	550.1
11853147.4	4962174.5	2529002.2	2296554.0	73461.4
10929134.8	7405810.7	12273258.2	9285782.5	362906.4
14008393.0	10727321.6	4001710.9	3620341.7	83510.2
9299465.8	3949256.5	1874854.7	1437853.2	123982.3
455425.5	337626.4	125392.8	109310.2	1467.3
1447615.9	1339037.2	1007586.2	837989.2	20158.8
1095850.3	877987.3	429851.3	321000.7	10115.9
5294064.8	2769303.9	2125641.0	1882179.7	22025.4

18-6 续表

单位：万元

区 县	Region	管理费用 Administrative Expenses	研发费用 R&D Expenses	财务费用 Financial Expenses
全市	**Total**	**2510557.0**	**1116205.5**	**968130.7**
新城区	Xincheng	114954.5	3971.5	36026.3
碑林区	Beilin	184320.6	17049.2	64034.6
莲湖区	Lianhu	155906.6	6650.6	24741.4
灞桥区	Baqiao	112377.4	5011.2	112447.5
未央区	Weiyang	419281.2	69541.8	308630.0
雁塔区	Yanta	1077972.1	544499.5	221810.3
阎良区	Yanliang	29332.0		460.9
临潼区	Lintong	17920.1	199.6	22419.6
长安区	Chang'an	135443.5	417602.9	16317.2
高陵区	Gaoling	46274.2	13552.8	6326.4
鄠邑区	Huyi	8921.9		1426.3
蓝田县	Lantian	16875.3	447.0	9250.2
周至县	Zhouzhi	3499.1		801.8
西咸新区	Xixian New Area	187478.5	37679.4	143438.2
# **开发区**	**Development Zones**			
高新区	Hi-Tech Industries Development Zone	688866.4	782858.0	56562.2
经开区	Economic Development Zone	355170.4	71726.9	281296.2
曲江新区	Qujiang New District	239856.7	6697.2	211700.4
航空基地	National Aviation Hi-tech Industrial Base	15389.4		344.1
航天基地	National Civil Aerospace Industrial Base	77634.6	49643.3	9989.0
浐灞生态区	Chan-ba Ecological District	51178.9	9119.6	4420.3
国际港务区	International Trade & Logistics Park	55690.4	3360.6	107730.1

continued

(10 000 yuan)

投资收益 Investment Income	营业利润 Operating Profits	利润总额 Total Profits	应付职工薪酬 Salary Payable	期末用工人数（人） Year-end Employed Persons (person)
848883.3	**2370531.7**	**2509158.9**	**7255601.3**	**534987**
-64.1	216099.0	214821.7	169986.5	16583
4106.6	63511.7	64279.6	380447.5	31261
17793.7	21748.6	37520.3	278630.5	28827
61565.2	144886.3	157632.2	150987.4	16193
244701.9	311111.4	367578.4	1197729.1	116417
327215.6	1444071.9	1481145.6	3606363.3	210901
3425.3	1404.6	1863.6	49878.7	3871
425.1	-20844.9	-20656.1	33195.0	4169
168349.2	274142.4	282596.8	592968.2	27469
1358.4	89.3	3172.6	158103.0	16980
0.1	417.2	881.2	19729.2	3287
122.9	-16920.7	-17732.0	7642.2	1133
-39.7	-2651.8	-2401.9	5872.6	1038
19923.1	-66533.3	-61543.1	604068.1	56858
224504.6	1394184.9	1412480.3	3052478.5	158501
234642.9	249728.6	255007.4	1105239.1	103054
83051.6	-63932.4	-57586.3	371840.8	30060
3357.8	4259.0	4641.3	18440.7	2223
158325.1	157334.3	160751.4	217951.4	11676
8020.0	41387.6	46119.5	99079.8	9046
55897.4	107905.8	114394.2	59605.8	6327

主要统计指标解释

固定资产原价 指固定资产的成本，包括企业在购置、自行建造、安装、改建、扩建、技术改造某项固定资产时所发生的全部支出总额。根据会计“固定资产”科目的期末借方余额填报。

资产总计 指企业过去的交易或者事项形成的、由企业拥有或者控制的、预期会给企业带来经济利益的资源。包括企业拥有的土地、办公楼、厂房、机器、运输工具、存货等实物资产和现金、存款、应收账款和预付账款等金融资产。资产一般按流动性（资产的变现或耗用时间长短）分为流动资产和非流动资产。其中流动资产可分为货币资金、交易性金融资产、应收票据、应收账款、预付款项、其他应收款、存货等；非流动资产可分为长期股权投资、固定资产、无形资产及其他非流动资产等。根据会计“资产负债表”中“资产总计”项目的期末余额数填报。

负债合计 指企业过去的交易或者事项形成的，预期会导致经济利益流出企业的现时义务。包括银行贷款、借款、应付账款、应付职工工资、应付职工福利费、应交税金等企业负有偿还责任的债务。根据会计“资产负债表”中“负债合计”项目的期末余额数填报。

负债一般按偿还期长短分为流动负债和非流动负债。执行企业会计准则或《小企业会计准则》的企业：负债合计=流动负债合计+非流动负债合计；执行其他企业会计制度的企业负债包括流动负债和长期负债。

所有者权益合计 指企业资产扣除负债后由所有者享有的剩余权益。公司的所有者权益又称股东权益。包括实收资本、资本公积、盈余公积、未分配利润等。根据会计“资产负债表”中“所有者权益合计”项目的期末余额数填报。

营业收入 指企业从事销售商品、提供劳务和让渡资产使用权等生产经营活动形成的经济利益流入。营业收入包括“主营业务收入”和“其他业务收入”。根据会计“利润表”中“营业收入”项目的本年累计数填报。

营业成本 指企业从事销售商品、提供劳务和让渡资产使用权等生产经营活动发生的实际成本。“营业成本”应当与“营业收入”进行配比。包括“主营业务成本”和“其他业务成本”。根据会计“利润表”中“营业成本”项目的本年累计数填报。

销售费用 指企业在销售商品和材料、提供劳务的过程中发生的各种费用，包括保险费、包装费、展览费和广告费、商品维修费、预计产品质量保证损失、运输费、装卸费等以及为销售本企业商品而专设的销售机构（含销售网点、售后服务网点等）的职工薪酬、业务费、折旧费等经营费用。建筑业企业销售费用指企业从事施工生产活动过程中发生的各项费用，包括应由企业负担的运输费、装卸费、包装费、保险费、维修费、展览费、差旅费、广告费和其他经费。房地产企业销售费用指企业在从事主要经营业务过程中所发生的各项销售费用，包括转让、销售、结算和出租开发产品等。执行企业会计准则或《小企业会计准则》的企业，根据会计“利润表”中“销售费用”项目的本年累计数填报。执行其他企业会计制度的企业，根据会计“利润表”中“营业费用（或经营费用）”项目的本年累计数填报。

管理费用 指企业为组织和管理企业生产经营所发生的费用，包括企业在筹建期间内发生的开办费、董事会和行政管理部门在企业经营管理中发生的，或者应当由企业统一负担的公司经费等。为了与财政部《关于修订印发2019年度一般企业财务报表格式的通知》（财会〔2019〕6号）保持一致，“管理费用”不包含“研发费用”。执行企业会计准则的企业，根据会计“利润表”中“管理费用”项目的本年累计数填报。执行《小企业会计准则》的企业，应将会计“利润表”中“管理费用”项目本年累计数减“研究费用”项目本年累计数后填报。执行其他企业会计制度的企业以及未执行财政部《关于修订印发2019年度一般企业财务报表格式的通知》（财会〔2019〕6号）的企业，在会计“利润表”中“管理费用”项目的本年累计数的基础上，根据会计“管理费用”科目下的“研究费用”相关明细科目，将“研发费用”剔除后填报。

研发费用 指企业在新知识、新技术、新产品、新工艺等的研究与开发过程中发生的费用化支出，以及计入“管理费用”会计科目的企业自行开发无形资产的摊销。费用化支出主要包括研发活动的人工费用、直接投入费用、用于研发活动的仪器、设备的折旧费、用于研发活动的软件、专利权、非专利技术的摊销费用、新产品设计费、新工艺规程制定费以及其他研发活动相关费用。执行企业会计准则的企业，根据会计“利润表”中“研发费用”项目的本年累计数填报。执行《小企业会计准则》的企业，根据会计“利润表”中“研究费用”项目的本年累计数填报。执行其他企业会计制度的企业以及会计“利润表”未列示“研发费用”或“研究费用”的企业，根据会计“管理费用”科目下“研究费用”明细科目的本期发生额，以及“管理费用”科目下“无形资产摊销”明细科目的本期发生额分析填报。

财务费用 指企业为筹集生产经营所需资金等而发生的筹资费用，包括企业生产经营期间发生的利息支出

（减利息收入）、汇兑损失（减汇兑收益）以及相关的手续费等。根据会计“利润表”中“财务费用”项目的本年累计数填报。

投资收益 指企业确认的投资收益或投资损失，反映企业以各种方式对外投资所取得的收益。根据会计“利润表”中“投资收益”项目的本年累计数填报。如为投资损失以“-”号记。

营业利润 指企业从事生产经营活动所取得的利润。执行企业会计准则或《小企业会计准则》的企业，根据会计“利润表”中“营业利润”项目的本年累计数填报；执行其他企业会计制度的企业，根据会计“损益表”中“营业利润”项目、“投资收益”项目的本年累计数之和填报。

利润总额 指企业在一定会计期间的经营成果，是生产经营过程中各种收入扣除各种耗费后的盈余，反映企业在报告期内实现的盈亏总额。利润总额为营业利润加上营业外收入，减去营业外支出后的金额，根据会计“利润表”中“利润总额”项目的本年累计数填报。

应付职工薪酬（本期贷方累计发生额） 指企业为获得职工提供的服务或解除劳动关系而给予的各种形式的报酬或补偿。包括职工工资、奖金、津贴和补贴，职工福利费，医疗保险费、养老保险费、失业保险费、工伤保险费和生育保险费等社会保险费，住房公积金，工会经费和职工教育经费，带薪缺勤，利润分享计划，非货币性福利，辞退福利和其他为获得职工提供的服务而给予的报酬或补偿。其中，社会保险和住房公积金应包括单位和个人负担部分。

“应付职工薪酬”应包含“劳务派遣人员薪酬”。如果企业没有劳务派遣人员或“应付职工薪酬”会计科目核算范围已包含“劳务派遣人员薪酬”，但不设置明细科目单独核算，而是按类别拆分，分别计入“应付职工薪酬”会计科目下的工资、奖金、津贴和补贴、福利费等明细科目，执行企业会计准则或《小企业会计准则》的企业，根据财务报告“应付职工薪酬列示”合计项本期增加额，或会计“应付职工薪酬”科目本期贷方累计发生额填报；执行其他企业会计制度的企业或“应付职工薪酬”科目内容与统计口径不一致的，需按统计口径归并填报。如果企业“应付职工薪酬”会计科目的核算范围不包含“劳务派遣人员薪酬”，则应加“劳务派遣人员薪酬”后填报“应付职工薪酬”统计指标。“劳务派遣人员薪酬”不含因使用劳务派遣人员而支付的管理费用和其他用工成本。

无论用工单位是否直接支付劳动报酬，“劳务派遣人员薪酬”均由实际用工法人单位（派遣人员使用方）填报，而劳务派遣单位（派遣人员派出方）不填报。劳务外包人员薪酬由劳务承包法人单位（外包人员派出方）填报，劳务发包法人单位（外包人员使用方）不填报。

期末用工人数 指报告期最后一日24时企业实际拥有的、参与本企业生产经营活动的人员数，无论是否从本企业领取劳动报酬均视为用工人数。该指标为时点指标，不包括最后一日当天及以前已经不再参与本企业生产经营活动的人员。

包括企业的正式人员、劳务派遣人员和其他临时人员。具体包括直接参与加工、组装、维修、保养等本企业生产活动的人员；包括企业管理人员；包括对外安装本企业产品、保管、清洁、销售等与生产行为直接相关活动的人员；对于未参与本企业生产经营活动，但主要为本企业生产经营活动提供服务的人员，也视为参与生产经营活动人员，如利用本单位的车辆、仓储等设施进行运输、仓储活动的人员。不包括在本企业领取工资、股息、红利但未参加本企业生产经营活动的人员；不包括医疗、教育等为企业提供社会性服务活动的人员；不包括参加本企业建筑施工但所从事的工作与生产经营活动无关的人员，如参与企业厂房建筑施工的人员。

Explanatory Notes on Main Statistical Indicators

Total assets It refers to the resourcesformed by past transactions or events, that the enterprise owns or controls, is expected to bring economic benefits to the enterprise. Asset is classified into current assets and non-current assets by its liquidity (realization of assets or spent time). Current assets can be divided into currency, tradable financial assets, notes receivable, accounts receivable, prepayments, other receivables and inventory; and non-current assets can be classified as equity investments, fixed assets, intangible assets and other non-current assets. It depends on the "balance sheet" of "total assets" closing balance number of items.

Total liabilities It refers tothe present obligations of the enterprise that formed by past transactions or events and are expected to lead to an outflow of economic benefits. It depends onthe "balance sheets" in the "total" closing balance number of items.

Total owners' equity It refers to the residual rights and interests enjoyed by the owner after deducting the liabilities of an enterprise. The owner of the company is also called the shareholder's right. It includes the paid in capital, capital reserves, surplus reserves, undistributed profit and so on. According to the accounting "balance sheet", "the owner's equity total", the final balance of the project is reported.

Business revenue It refers to the total revenue recognized by the business and other business operations of the enterprise. Total operating income includes "main business income" and "other business income". It's reported according to the "business income" project of the "business income" in the accounting "profit statement".

Business cost It refers to the total cost incurred by the business and other business of the enterprise. It includes a variety of costs of enterprises (units) in the reporting period to engage in sales of goods, services and other daily activities provided.It includes"the main business costs" and "other business costs". According to the "operating cost" of the "business cost" of the project in accordance with the accounting statement.

Selling expenses It refers to the expenses of the enterprisein sales of goods and materials and providing services, including insurance, packing, exhibition fees and advertising fees, maintenance of commodity, expected to ensure product quality loss, transportation, loading and unloading charges and sales of the enterprise products and dedicated sales organizations (including sales network and after-sales service network) employee compensation, business expenses, depreciation charges and operating expenses. Construction enterprises selling expenses refers to expenses occurring in the process of production enterprises engaged in construction activities, including transportation fee shall be borne by the enterprise, handling, packing, insurance, maintenance, exhibition fees, poor travel costs, advertising costs and other expenses. Real estate enterprise sales cost refers to the business in the main business process of the sales costs, including transfer, sales, settlement and rental development products, etc.. According to the "sales expense" in accounting "profit statement", the amount of the item in this period of the project is reported. For business enterprises that didn't implement the 2006 accounting standard, according to the number of "operating expenses (or operating expenses)" of the project in accordance with the "profit statement".

Management expenses It refers to the expenses for the organization and management of enterprise production and management of the enterprises, And the amortization of intangible assets developed by enterprises themselves included in the accounting subject of "management expenses". including costs in construction occurred during the start-up costs, the board of directors and administrative departments in enterprise management, or shall be made by the enterprise unified burden of company funds. According to the "management fee" in the accounting "profit table", the amount of this period of the project is reported. And the analysis and reporting of the current amount of the detailed account of "amortization of intangible assets" under the account of "management expenses".

Financial expenses It refers to the costs of the enterprise to raise the production and business operation required capital and funding, including occurred during the production and operation of enterprises interest payments (a reduction in interest income), exchange loss (less exchange gains) and related fees. It is reported according to the amount of the "financial expense" in the project of "financial expense" in the accounting "profit statement".

Investment income It refers to the enterprise confirming the investment income or investment losses, reflecting the foreign investment income of the enterprise in various ways. According to the "investment income" in the accounting "profit statement", the amount of this period of the project is reported. Such as investment losses to "-".

Operating profit refers to the profits enterprises made through production and operation activities. For enterprises that implement the Accounting Standard for Enterprises or the Accounting Standards for Small Enterprises, it is reported according to the accumulative amount of operating profits in the income statement in this year. For enterprises that implement other corporate accounting standards, it is reported by adding up the accumulative amount of operating income and investment income in the income statement in this year.

Total profit It refers to the business results of the enterprise in a certain accounting period, and it is the production and operation of various kinds of income after deducting the cost of earnings, reflecting the enterprise in the reporting period to achieve total profit and loss. the total profit is operating profit plus operating income, andminus operating expenses; Fill in according to the accumulated amount of "total profit" item in the accounting income statement this year.

Employee compensation (accumulative credit account occurred during reporting period) refers to various forms of remunerations and compensations paid by the company for the services provided by employees or for layoffs. It includes wages, bonuses, allowances and subsidies, employee welfare benefits, medical insurance, endowment insurance, unemployment insurance, work-related injury insurance premiums and maternity insurance fees, housing provident fund, labor union fees, employee education expenditure, compensated absences, profit-sharing plan, non-monetary benefits, lay-off compensations, and other remunerations and compensations.Among them, social insurance and housing provident fund should include the portion covered by the company and the individual.

Employee compensation should include compensations for labor dispatch workers. If the company has no labor dispatch workers or has factored in compensation for labor dispatch workers in the accounting item of employee compensation through categories such as wages, bonuses, allowances and subsidies, and employee welfare benefits without setting up detailed accounts for independent calculation, the company should report the added amount or the accumulative credit amount of employee compensation occurred during the reporting period according to the Accounting Standard for Enterprises or the Accounting Standards for Small Enterprises. For companies implementing other corporate accounting standards or the statistic, caliber is inconsistent with the item of employee compensation, the item should be adjusted according to the statistic caliber and reported as such. If compensation for labor dispatch workers is not included in the accounting of employee compensation, it should be added and factored in. Compensation for labor dispatch workers does not include the management expenses and other employment costs paid for the use of labor dispatch workers.

No matter the compensation is paid directly by the employer or not, compensation for labor dispatch workers should be reported by the actual employing legal entity (the user of labor dispatch workers), other than the labor dispatch entity. The compensation for labor outsourcing workers should be reported by the labor contractor, rather than the labor outsourcing entity.

Number of persons engaged in service activities at balance sheet date refers to the number of persons the company has during the 24 hours of the balance sheet date and that participate in the company's production and operation activities, no matter they get paid or not by the company. The figure is a point-in-time indicator, excluding those who are no longer involved in the production and operation activities of the company on or before the balance sheet date.

It includes the regular workers, labor dispatch workers and other temporary persons. Specifically, it includes persons directly involved in the production activities such as processing, assembly, repair, and maintenance; it includes the management personnel; it includes persons directly related to the production activities, such as external installation of the company's products, storage, cleaning, and sales; for persons who are not involved in the production and operation activities but mainly provide services for the production and operation activities, like persons involved in the transportation and storage activities using the company's transportation and storage facilities, they are also regarded as persons involved in the production and operation activities. It excludes those who receive wages, dividends, and bonuses but do not participate in the production and operation activities, those who provide social services for the company, and those who participate in the construction of the company but are not involved in the production and operation activities, such as those who take part in the construction of the factories of the company.

19 金融业

FINANCIAL INDUSTRY

资料整理：孟　刚
Data management:Meng Gang
数据审核：罗延庆
Data audit:Luo Yanqing

第十九部分　金融业

一、简要说明

本章资料包括金融、证券和保险业情况，由西安市统计局综合处根据人民银行西安分行营业管理部和市金融工作局提供资料整理。本部分银行、保险类为西安原口径数据，证券类含西咸新区。

二、主要指标

金融机构人民币（含外资）存款余额（亿元）	28059.03	比上年增长	9.0%
金融机构人民币（含外资）贷款余额（亿元）	29124.00	比上年增长	13.9%
保费收入（亿元）	583.24	比上年增长	6.0%

19 FINANCIAL INDUSTRY

Ⅰ.Brief Introduction

This chapter includes information of the financial, securities and insurance, compiled by Integration Division of the Xi'an Bureau of Statistics, according to data from Xi'an Branch Management Department of the People's Bank of China, Provincial Banking Bureau and Xi'an Financial Office. Data in this chapter is based on original range.

Ⅱ.Major Indicators

		Increase over Preceding Year
Deposits in Financial Institution(100 mil. yuan)	28059.03	9.0%
Loans in Financial Institutions(100 mil.yuan)	29124.00	13.9%
Premiums(100 mil. yuan)	583.24	6.0%

19-1 西安银行系统机构、人员数（2020-2021年）

Number of Institution and Employed Person in Finance System in Xi'an(2020-2021)

机构名称	Name of Institution	2020		2021	
		机构数（个） Number of Institution (unit)	年末人数（人） Number of Employees at Year-End (person)	机构数（个） Number of Institution (unit)	年末人数（人） Number of Employees at Year-End (person)
合　计	**Total**	**2111**	**39355**	**2114**	**39626**
1. 人民银行西安分行营业管理部	Management Department of the People's Bank of China Xi'an Branch	1	356	1	352
2. 国家开发银行	National Development Bank	1	221	1	230
3. 中国进出口银行	Export Import Bank of China	1	81	1	81
4. 中国工商银行	Industrial and Commercial Bank of China	185	4292	187	4217
5. 中国农业银行	Agricultural Bank of China	165	3199	164	3198
6. 中国银行	Bank of China	131	3448	131	3397
7. 中国建设银行	Construction Bank of China	204	4508	205	4528
8. 交通银行	Bank of Communication	51	1206	50	1193
9. 中国邮政储蓄银行	The Postal Savings Bank of China	267	955	264	953
10. 中国农业发展银行	Agricultural Development Bank of China	11	277	11	264
11. 中信银行	China CITIC Bank	29	876	29	885
12. 中国光大银行	China Everbright Bank	41	935	43	921
13. 华夏银行	China Huaxia Bank	26	690	26	712
14. 广发银行	China Guangfa Bank	11	276	12	265
15. 平安银行	Pingan Bank	16	459	17	524
16. 招商银行	China Merchants Bank	55	1587	55	1716
17. 上海浦东发展银行	Pufa Bank	31	801	34	835
18. 兴业银行	Fujian Industrial Bank	62	820	56	861
19. 中国民生银行	China Minsheng Banking	24	1107	24	1134
20. 恒丰银行	Evergrowing Bank	17	475	17	491
21. 浙商银行	China Zheshang Bank	10	482	10	466
22. 渤海银行	China Bohai Bank	2	163	4	216
23. 北京银行	Bank of Beijing	26	808	26	768
24. 齐商银行	Qi Commercial Bank	7	194	7	185
25. 成都银行	Bank of Chengdu	6	186	6	200
26. 重庆银行	Bank of Chongqing	7	283	7	296
27. 宁夏银行	Bank of Ningxia	7	189	7	193
28. 昆仑银行	Bank of Kunlun	15	494	16	493
29. 西安银行	Bank of Xi'an	145	2609	145	2613
30. 长安银行	Bank of Changan	61	810	61	887
31. 农村商业银行	Rural Commercial Bank	404	5246	404	5304
其中：秦农银行	Qinnong Bank	298	4245	298	4293
32. 农村信用社	Rural Credit Cooperatives	67	780	67	735
33. 村镇银行	Village Bank	14	272	16	263
34. 香港汇丰银行	Huifeng Bank of Hong Kong	2	32	2	34
35. 香港东亚银行	Dongya Bank of Hong Kong	5	123	4	104
36. 新加坡星展银行	DBS Bank	1	13	1	13
37. 英国标准渣打银行	British Standard Chartered Bank	1	30	1	27
38. 韩亚银行	Hana Bank	1	43	1	42
39. 富邦华一银行	Fubon Bank	1	29	1	30

注：本表数据来源于人民银行西安分行营管部，本表为西安原口径数据（下同，除证券类）。

19-2 金融机构（含外资）本外币存贷款年末余额（2021年）

Deposits and Loans of Local Currency and Foreign Currency in Financial Institution (Including Foreign-Funded Institution)at Year-end (2021)

单位：万元　　(10 000 yuan)

指　标	Item	2021	比年初增减额 Increase or Decrease Compared with The Beginning of The Year
一、各项存款	**All Deposits**	**285100257**	**24641597**
（一）境内存款	Domestic Deposits	284716518	24581786
1. 住户存款	Household Deposits	120972706	10802569
（1）活期存款	Demand Deposits	42927984	3027665
（2）定期及其他存款	Time and Other Deposits	78044722	7774904
2. 非金融企业存款	Non Financial Enterprises Deposits	110008665	10928358
（1）活期存款	Demand Deposits	51054044	3637469
（2）定期及其他存款	Time and Other Deposits	58954621	7290889
3. 机关团体存款	Institution Deposits	38909186	63622
4. 财政性存款	Fiscal Deposits	2630571	1496478
5. 非银行业金融机构存款	Non Banking Financial Institution Deposits	12195390	1290759
（二）境外存款	Foreign Deposits	383739	59810
二、各项贷款	**All Loans**	**294112519**	**36183598**
（一）境内贷款	Domestic Loans	293969030	36247450
1. 住户贷款	Household loans	86785940	11923862
（1）短期贷款	Short-term Loans	9523363	1248994
消费贷款	Consumer loans	5780424	597273
经营贷款	Business loans	3742940	651722
（2）中长期贷款	Medium-term and Long-term loans	77262577	10674868
消费贷款	Consumer loans	70027316	9281734
经营贷款	Business loans	7235260	1393134
2. 非金融企业及机关团体贷款	Non Financial Enterprises and Institution Loans	207141372	24283597
（1）短期贷款	Short-term Loans	38750701	3836619
（2）中长期贷款	Medium-term and Long-term loans	153568999	15714599
（3）票据融资	Bill Financing	13535052	3596725
（4）融资租赁	Financial Leasing	27745	27538
（5）各项垫款	Various Advance Funds	1258875	1108116
3. 非银行业金融机构贷款	Non Banking Financial Institution Loans	41718	39991
（二）境外贷款	Foreign Loans	143489	-63853

注：本表数据来源于人民银行西安分行营管部。

19-3 金融机构（不含外资）本外币存贷款年末余额（2021年）

Deposits and Loans Domestic Funded Financial Institution of Local Currency and Foreign Currency at Year-end (2021)

单位：万元 (10 000 yuan)

指 标	Item	2021	比年初增减额 Increase or Decrease Compared with The Beginning of The Year
一、各项存款	**All Deposits**	**284011130**	**24999077**
（一）境内存款	Domestic Deposits	283670945	24953598
1. 住户存款	Household Deposits	120794883	10789111
（1）活期存款	Demand Deposits	42868620	3029626
（2）定期及其他存款	Time and Other Deposits	77926263	7759485
2. 非金融企业存款	Non Financial Enterprises Deposits	109143119	11315605
（1）活期存款	Demand Deposits	50856625	3623923
（2）定期及其他存款	Time and Other Deposits	58286493	7691682
3. 机关团体存款	Institution Deposits	38906983	61645
4. 财政性存款	Fiscal Deposits	2630571	1496478
5. 非银行业金融机构存款	Non Banking Financial Institution Deposits	12195390	1290759
（二）境外存款	Foreign Deposits	340185	45479
二、各项贷款	**All Loans**	**293278321**	**36418548**
（一）境内贷款	Domestic Loans	293139871	36462152
1. 住户贷款	Household loans	86648919	11870307
（1）短期贷款	Short-term Loans	9523363	1248994
消费贷款	Consumer loans	5780424	597273
经营贷款	Business loans	3742940	651722
（2）中长期贷款	Medium-term and Long-term loans	77125556	10621313
消费贷款	Consumer loans	69899492	9225054
经营贷款	Business loans	7226064	1396258
2. 非金融企业及机关团体贷款	Non Financial Enterprises and Institution Loans	206449234	24551854
（1）短期贷款	Short-term Loans	38478417	3839361
（2）中长期贷款	Medium-term and Long-term loans	153154296	15982217
（3）票据融资	Bill Financing	13529902	3594621
（4）融资租赁	Financial Leasing	27745	27538
（5）各项垫款	Various Advance Funds	1258875	1108116
3. 非银行业金融机构贷款	Non Banking Financial Institution Loans	41718	39991
（二）境外贷款	Foreign Loans	138450	-43603

注：本表数据来源于人民银行西安分行营管部。

19-4 主要年份金融机构（含外资）人民币存贷款年末余额

Deposits and Loans in Financial Institutions (Including Foreign-funded) in Representative Years

单位：亿元 (100 million yuan)

年 份 Year	存款年末余额 Balance of Deposit at Year-end	非金融企业存款 Non Financial Enterprises Deposits	住户存款 Household Deposits	贷款年末余额 Balance of Loan at Year-end
1978	11.66		2.57	21.72
1980	17.02		4.22	23.08
1985	40.64		14.26	49.08
1990	146.17	31.10	77.09	152.77
1995	471.89	114.54	291.46	403.16
1996	619.98	199.85	394.02	477.97
1997	686.72	227.61	433.56	503.32
1998	799.54	245.44	499.68	597.34
1999	1014.27	347.49	586.40	786.20
2000	1335.63	540.19	675.83	972.51
2001	1629.72	674.49	800.86	1185.97
2002	2191.47	884.69	988.04	1598.42
2003	2665.87	1041.43	1210.56	1954.18
2004	3061.66	1159.98	1432.86	2052.33
2005	3599.70	1237.37	1716.76	2158.10
2006	4066.16	1374.91	1950.53	2344.77
2007	4582.71	1702.12	2002.38	2683.77
2008	5749.37	2213.67	2513.70	3275.12
2009	7522.08	3077.99	3084.20	4482.63
2010	8933.23	3556.78	3641.09	6482.28
2011	10430.27	5997.60	4155.65	7564.93
2012	12125.53	6927.84	4787.03	8635.22
2013	13763.19	7759.61	5357.05	10023.63
2014	15166.78	8604.03	5698.15	11668.14
2015	17796.38	7031.75	6571.18	13714.02
2016	19073.96	7788.07	7035.81	15282.65
2017	20047.62	8203.27	7497.30	16954.81
2018	20948.18	8125.23	8360.33	19729.82
2019	23066.85	8756.48	9553.29	22264.12
2020	25730.51	9713.23	10913.05	25559.04
2021	28059.03	10669.69	11996.54	29124.00

注：本表数据来源于人民银行西安分行营管部，对部分历史年份数据进行了修订。

19-5 金融机构（含外资）人民币存贷款年末余额（2021年）

Year-end Balance of RMB Deposits and Loans in Financial Institutions(Including Foreign-funded)(2021)

单位：万元 (10 000 yuan)

指　标	Item	2021	比年初增减额 Increase or Decrease Compared with The Beginning of The Year
一、各项存款	**All Deposits**	**280590268**	**23285131**
（一）境内存款	Domestic Deposits	280367468	23246382
1. 住户存款	Household Deposits	119965430	10834886
（1）活期存款	Demand Deposits	42342519	3032782
（2）定期及其他存款	Time and Other Deposits	77622911	7802103
2. 非金融企业存款	Non Financial Enterprises Deposits	106696945	9565471
（1）活期存款	Demand Deposits	48652174	2505152
（2）定期及其他存款	Time and Other Deposits	58044771	7060319
3. 机关团体存款	Institution Deposits	38896247	70370
4. 财政性存款	Fiscal Deposits	2624926	1490833
5. 非银行业金融机构存款	Non Banking Financial Institution Deposits	12183919	1284822
（二）境外存款	Foreign Deposits	222800	38749
二、各项贷款	**All Loans**	**291240048**	**35649681**
（一）境内贷款	Domestic Loans	291234794	35650044
1. 住户贷款	Household loans	86784085	11923536
（1）短期贷款	Short-term Loans	9521614	1248613
消费贷款	Consumer loans	5778675	596891
经营贷款	Business loans	3742940	651722
（2）中长期贷款	Medium-term and Long-term loans	77262471	10674923
消费贷款	Consumer loans	70027211	9281789
经营贷款	Business loans	7235260	1393134
2. 非金融企业及机关团体贷款	Non Financial Enterprises and Institution Loans	204408990	23686517
（1）短期贷款	Short-term Loans	36827294	3156693
（2）中长期贷款	Medium-term and Long-term loans	152760024	15797445
（3）票据融资	Bill Financing	13535052	3596725
（4）融资租赁	Financial Leasing	27745	27538
（5）各项垫款	Various Advance Funds	1258875	1108116
3. 非银行业金融机构贷款	Non Banking Financial Institution Loans	41718	39991
（二）境外贷款	Foreign Loans	5254	-363

注：本表数据来源于人民银行西安分行营管部。

19-6 金融机构（不含外资）人民币存贷款年末余额（2021年）

Year-end Balance of RMB Deposits and Loans in Financial Institutions (Not Including Foreign-funded)(2021)

单位：万元 (10 000 yuan)

指　标	Item	2021	比年初增减额 Increase or Decrease Compared with The Beginning of The Year
一、各项存款	**All Deposits**	**279671489**	**23666228**
（一）境内存款	Domestic Deposits	279459108	23626561
1. 住户存款	Household Deposits	119824054	10814933
（1）活期存款	Demand Deposits	42303346	3032692
（2）定期及其他存款	Time and Other Deposits	77520708	7782241
2. 非金融企业存款	Non Financial Enterprises Deposits	105932165	9967580
（1）活期存款	Demand Deposits	48537371	2510106
（2）定期及其他存款	Time and Other Deposits	57394794	7457474
3. 机关团体存款	Institution Deposits	38894045	68393
4. 财政性存款	Fiscal Deposits	2624926	1490833
5. 非银行业金融机构存款	Non Banking Financial Institution Deposits	12183919	1284822
（二）境外存款	Foreign Deposits	212381	39667
二、各项贷款	**All Loans**	**290442046**	**35875013**
（一）境内贷款	Domestic Loans	290437034	35875340
1. 住户贷款	Household loans	86647064	11869981
（1）短期贷款	Short-term Loans	9521614	1248613
消费贷款	Consumer loans	5778675	596891
经营贷款	Business loans	3742940	651722
（2）中长期贷款	Medium-term and Long-term loans	77125450	10621368
消费贷款	Consumer loans	69899386	9225109
经营贷款	Business loans	7226064	1396258
2. 非金融企业及机关团体贷款	Non Financial Enterprises and Institution Loans	203748252	23965368
（1）短期贷款	Short-term Loans	36586409	3170030
（2）中长期贷款	Medium-term and Long-term loans	152345321	16065063
（3）票据融资	Bill Financing	13529902	3594621
（4）融资租赁	Financial Leasing	27745	27538
（5）各项垫款	Various Advance Funds	1258875	1108116
3. 非银行业金融机构贷款	Non Banking Financial Institution Loans	41718	39991
（二）境外贷款	Foreign Loans	5012	-326

注：本表数据来源于人民银行西安分行营管部。

19-7 主要年份保险业务情况

Indicators of Insurance Business in Representative Years

单位：万元 (10 000 yuan)

指　标	Item	2017	2018	2019	2020	2021
保费收入(万元)	**Premiums(10 000 yuan)**	**4211039**	**4785554**	**5228513**	**5504259**	**5832369**
一、财产险(万元)	**Property Insurance(10 000 yuan)**	**1037060**	**1125618**	**1062003**	**1162414**	**1222218**
(一) 财产保险	Property Insurance	916524	959618	868183	928967	1003003
1. 机动车辆及第三者责任	Motor Vehicle and Outside Person Liability	821186	862137	759314	795563	855592
2. 企业财产险	Enterprise Property Insurance	62226	65716	73996	85294	90369
3. 货物运输险	Freight Transport Insurance	5314	6777	7230	6749	6848
4. 家庭财产险	Family Property Insurance	1385	1772	1436	3259	2729
5. 建工及安工保险及其责任险	Construction and Installation Projects Insurance and Related Liability Insurance	20001	17174	17067	27392	25711
6. 其他	Others	6412	6042	9140	10710	21753
(二) 责任保险	Liability Insurance	32136	38508	54267	86279	95232
(三) 信用保险	Credit Insurance	14733	10114	9128	10741	13043
(四) 保证保险	Guarantee Insurance	60814	100393	112277	115323	88045
(五) 农业保险	Agriculture Insurance	12853	16985	18148	21104	22895
二、人身险(万元)	**Personnel Insurance(10 000 yuan)**	**3173979**	**3659936**	**4166510**	**4341845**	**4610151**
(一) 人寿保险	Life Insurance	2625509	3023129	3313934	3402702	3521424
1. 普通寿险	General Life Insurance	1554807	1355990	1653013	1902890	2327744
2. 分红保险	Dividend Insurance	1055099	1651416	1645508	1485230	1180966
3. 投资连接保险	Insurance Connection Insurance	217	212	280	326	233
4. 万能保险	Universal Insurance	15386	15512	15133	14256	12482
(二) 意外伤害险	Unforeseen Injury Insurance	84603	112382	145991	131819	135001
(三) 健康保险	Health Insurance	463867	524426	706585	807325	953725
赔款支出和各项给付(万元)	**Indemnity and Other Expenditure(10 000 yuan)**	**1187057**	**1308241**	**1414228**	**1577456**	**1765446**
一、财产险(万元)	**Property Insurance(10 000 yuan)**	**489353**	**553641**	**617430**	**700304**	**758608**
(一) 财产保险	Property Insurance	452892	497773	537006	574214	647786
1. 机动车辆及第三者责任	Motor Vehicle and Outside Person Liability	393011	459840	487263	526217	589170
2. 企业财产险	Enterprise Property Insurance	30811	20020	23175	21502	29576
3. 家庭财产保险	Family Property Insurance	757	4565	3255	788	2146
4. 货物运输保险	Freight Transport Insurance	2427	1376	864	3828	506
5. 建工及安工保险及其责任险	Construction and Installation Projects Insurance and Related Liability Insurance	12471	9663	8136	13154	15002
6. 其他	Others	13414	2309	14314	8725	11387
(二) 责任保险	Liability Insurance	12703	14948	20710	35618	34331
(三) 信用保险	Export Credit Insurance	3346	5273	3384	5602	6332
(四) 保证保险	Guarantee Insurance	11597	23608	48247	70146	54583
(五) 农业保险	Agriculture Insurance	8816	12039	8082	14723	15577
二、人身险(万元)	**Personnel Insurance(10 000 yuan)**	**697704**	**754600**	**796798**	**877152**	**1006838**
(一) 人寿保险	Life Insurance	557798	581062	565089	624946	685344
1. 普通寿险	General Life Insurance	136279	138591	136772	133902	126140
2. 分红保险	Dividend Insurance	418013	438997	424665	488409	555042
3. 投资连接保险	Insurance Connection Insurance	162	35	4	72	1144
4. 万能保险	Universal Insurance	3344	3438	3647	2564	3019
(二) 意外伤害险	Unforeseen Injury Insurance	19939	23621	30778	32710	33913
(三) 健康保险	Health Insurance	119967	149917	200930	219496	287581
退保金(万元)	**Withdrawal(10 000 yuan)**	**682534**	**762277**	**617446**	**452376**	**560710**
#人寿保险	Life Insurance	659965	751597	588932	437378	541237
1. 普通寿险	General Life Insurance	524211	582955	368570	271586	376192
2. 分红保险	Dividend Insurance	135723	168632	220354	165781	165032
3. 投资连接保险	Insurance Connection Insurance					
4. 万能保险	Universal Insurance	31	11	7	11	12

注：本表数据来源于市金融工作局。

19-8 西安地区证券期货系统机构、人员数（2020-2021年）

Number of Institution and Employed Person in Securities and Futures System in Xi'an (2020-2021)

机构名称	Name of Institution	2020		2021	
		机构数（个）Number of Institution (unit)	年末人数（人）Number of Employees at Year-End (person)	机构数（个）Number of Institution (unit)	年末人数（人）Number of Employees at Year-End (person)
一、证券经营机构总数	**Number of Securities Operating Institutions**	**399**	**8384**	**200**	**9118**
1. 证券公司机构总数	Number of Securities Companies	238	5503	41	6149
西部证券股份有限公司	Western Securities Company Ltd.	111	2410	22	2695
开源证券股份有限公司	KaiYuan Securities Company Ltd.	83	2236	14	2445
中邮证券有限责任公司	China Post Securities	44	857	5	1009
2. 外地驻我市证券机构总数	Number of Non-Local Securities Institutions In the City	161	2881	159	2969
二、期货公司机构总数	**Number of Futures Companies**	**30**	**513**	**7**	**508**
迈科期货股份有限公司	Maike Futures Company Ltd.	11	184	2	161
长安期货有限公司	ChangAn Company Ltd.	10	169	3	165
西部期货有限公司	Western Futures Brokerage Co., Ltd.	9	160	2	182

注：1.本表数据来源于市金融工作局。
2.证券公司包括三家公司及其在西安和外地的营业部。
3.中邮证券有限责任公司原为西安华弘证券经纪有限责任公司。

19-9 证券期货市场基本情况（2021年）

Basic Facts on Securities and Futures Markets (2021)

指　标	Item	2021
一、上市公司情况	**Listed Securities Companies**	
拥有境内上市公司（个）	Number of Listed Companies(unit)	48
上市公司总股本（亿股）	Total Capital of Listed Companies (100 millon shares)	856.84
#流通股（亿股）	Negotiable Shares(100 million shares)	726.43
总市值（亿元）	Total Market Capitalization(100 million yuan)	13697.47
本年度证券市场筹措资金（亿元）	Accumulated Securities Market Financing(100 millon yuan)	531.39
二、证券经营机构情况	**Securities Trading Organizations**	
拥有证券公司（个）	Number of Securities Companies(unit)	3
期末证券分公司（个）	Number of Securities branches(unit)	59
期末证券营业部（个）	Number of Sucurities Business Department(unit)	199
投资者开户数（万户）	Number of Investors Who have Opened an Account(10 000 accounts)	496.10
证券交易总额（亿元）	Total Turnover(100 million yuan)	72489.51
三、期货市场情况	**Futures Market**	
拥有期货公司（个）	Number of Futures Companies(unit)	3
期货分支机构（个）	Futures Branches(unit)	37
期货代理交易额（亿元）	Total Transaction Value in Futures Commissioning (100 million yuan)	63950.72
每个公司平均拥有注册资金（亿元）	Average Registered Capital of Each Company(100 million yuan)	5.40

注：本表数据来源于市金融工作局，期货分支机构、代理交易额数据为西安本市和外地公司在西安市口径数据。

主要统计指标解释

存款 指企业、机关、团体或居民根据资金必须收回的原则，把货币资金存入银行或其他信贷机构保管并取得一定利息的一种信用活动形式。根据存款对象或性质的不同可划分为企业存款、财政存款、机关团体存款、住户存款、信托及委托类存款、其他存款等科目。它是银行信贷资金的主要来源。

贷款 指银行或其他信贷机构根据资金必须归还的原则，按一定利率，为企业、个人等提供资金的一种信用活动形式。我国银行贷款分为短期贷款、中长期贷款、融资租赁、票据融资等。

保险金额 指保险人承担赔偿或者给付保险金责任的最高限额。

保费 指投保人为取得保险人在约定范围内所承担赔偿责任而支付给保险人的费用。

赔款 指保险人根据保险合同的规定，向被保险人支付的赔偿保险责任损失的金额。

给付 包括死伤医疗给付和满期给付。死伤医疗给付是指保险人根据人寿保险及长期健康保险合同的规定，因被保险人在保险期内发生保险责任范围内的保险事故支付给被保险人（或受益人）的金额。满期给付是指被保险人生存期满，保险人按人寿保险合同规定支付给被保险人的满期保险金额。

Explanatory Notes on Main Statistical Indicators

Deposit is a form of credit by which enterprises, institutions, organizations or households can put money into banks and other credit institutions for safekeeping and interest earning under the principle of free withdrawal. According to different depositors, deposits are divided into enterprise deposits, fiscal deposits, deposits of government agencies and organizations, savings deposits of rural and household deposits, agricultural savings deposits, entrusted deposits and other deposits. Deposits are major sources of the credit funds of banks.

Loan is a form of credit by which banks and other credit institutions provide funds at certain interest rate to enterprises and individuals in the light of the principle of unconditional repayment. Loans from Chinese banks include short-term loan, medium and long term loans, finance lease and other bill finance.

Amount Insured refers to the maximum that the insurant will get for the claim of the case insured.

Premium is the fee paid by the insurant to the insurer to obtain the obligation of compensation from the insurance within the agreed terms.

Settled Claim is the compensation paid by the insurer to the insurant in accordance with the insurance contract.

Payment includes payment for death, injury or medical treatment and payment at maturity. Payment for death, injury or medical treatment refers to the money paid to the insurant (or the beneficiary) in accordance with the life or health insurance contract when the insurant encounters accidents within the insured period covered in the contract. Payment at maturity refers to the payment to the insurant in accordance with the life insurance contract at the end of the insured period.

20 教育和科技

EDUCATION,SCIENCE AND TECHNOLOGY

资料整理：陈超毅　刘志杰　齐昆峰
Data management：Chen Chaoyi Liu Zhijie Qi Kunfeng
数据审核：刘栋婷
Data audit：Liu Dongting

第二十部分　教育和科技

一、简要说明

本章资料包括教育事业、科技事业基本情况，由西安市统计局服务业与社会科技统计处根据统计一套表资料和西安市教育局等有关部门提供资料整理。本章资料数据口径见表下备注。科技部分因数据反馈较晚，故从2018年起错年使用。

二、主要指标

普通高等学校数（所）	63	与上年	持平
普通高等学校（本专科）在校学生（万人）	81.69	比上年增加	3.30
高等学校研究生在校人数（万人）	16.37	比上年增加	1.63

20　EDUCATION,SCIENCE AND TECHNOLOGY

Ⅰ.Brief Introduction

Data in this chapter consists of primarily data of educational undertakings, science and technology activities of Xi'an city, compiled by Tertiary Industry and Social & Science and Technology Division of the Xi'an Bureau of Statistics according to data from units of "One Sheet" and Xi'an Bureau of Education concerned. Field and range of data are Listed in the explanatory notes below the chart. Due to late data feedback, science and technology has been used one year earlier data since 2018.

Ⅱ.Major Indicators

		Increase over Preceding Year
Number of Regular Institutions of Higher Education(unit)	63	essentially on a par with last year's
Student Enrollment of Regular Institutions of Higher Education (Universities and colleges) (10 000 persons)	81.69	3.30
Postgraduates Enrollment of Regular Institutions of Higher Education (10 000 persons)	16.37	1.63

20-1 主要年份各类普通教育基本情况

Basic Statistics on Regular Eduction in Representative Years

指　标	Item	2010	2014	2015	2016	2017	2018	2019	2020	2021
学校数（所）	**Number of Schools(unit)**									
普通高等学校	Regular Institutions of Higher Education	50	63	63	63	63	63	63	63	63
普通中等专业学校	Regular Specialized Secondary Schools	28	22	20	20	16	15	15	15	15
普通中学	Regular Secondary Schools	436	421	422	422	448	456	469	495	501
小学	Primary Schools	1531	1257	1234	1190	1125	1130	1145	1172	1170
幼儿园	Kindergarten	1004	1343	1417	1475	1605	1780	1839	1966	1987
毕业生人数（万人）	**Graduates(10 000 persons)**									
普通高等学校	Regular Institutions of Higher Education	18.3	21.27	23.23	24.06	23.07	23.21	22.02	22.67	29.39
普通中等专业学校	Regular Specialized Secondary Schools	2.5	1.76	1.32	1.25	1.06	0.84	0.72	0.81	0.41
普通中学	Regular Secondary Schools	17.0	14.54	13.92	13.96	13.89	13.50	13.89	13.89	14.00
小学	Primary Schools	9.6	8.29	7.85	8.46	9.06	9.32	10.17	10.75	10.96
幼儿园	Kindergarten	5.4	8.90	10.01	9.81	10.79	11.41	11.85	12.25	11.94
招生数（万人）	**New Enrollment(10 000 persons)**									
普通高等学校	Regular Institutions of Higher Education	21.7	23.58	23.41	23.08	23.70	23.67	26.88	29.26	28.18
普通中等专业学校	Regular Specialized Secondary Schools	2.1	1.25	0.95	0.88	0.96	0.83	1.12	1.16	0.78
普通中学	Regular Secondary Schools	16.2	13.97	13.41	13.72	14.08	14.37	15.29	16.20	16.99
小学	Primary Schools	8.6	10.13	10.51	11.65	13.13	15.16	15.80	16.92	15.83
幼儿园	Kindergarten	8.4	9.55	11.96	13.65	13.98	13.03	12.86	15.46	14.96
在校学生数（万人）	**Total Enrollment(10 000 persons)**									
普通高等学校	Regular Institutions of Higher Education	73.3	85.42	84.83	83.10	83.02	82.44	87.14	93.13	98.06
普通中等专业学校	Regular Specialized Secondary Schools	6.8	4.07	3.47	3.11	2.74	2.48	2.79	3.02	2.03
普通中学	Regular Secondary Schools	48.9	42.57	41.37	40.70	41.74	42.46	43.56	45.68	48.21
小学	Primary Schools	51.6	53.79	56.62	59.79	66.68	73.09	78.98	85.20	89.09
幼儿园	Kindergarten	18.4	28.95	30.90	31.80	34.81	35.40	36.05	39.64	40.40
教职工数（人）	**Staff and Teachers(person)**									
普通高等学校	Regular Institutions of Higher Education	72247	74954	74857	73686	74218	75609	73688	75213	78261
普通中等专业学校	Regular Specialized Secondary Schools	3249	2315	1991	1917	1556	1529	1386	1474	1517
普通中学	Regular Secondary Schools	39207	40576	40689	41352	44546	45390	47037	49388	52022
小学	Primary Schools	34118	32162	32585	34646	38494	41122	44511	48838	51649
幼儿园	Kindergarten	18710	33062	36004	39753	44895	49604	52442	59605	63745
专任教师（人）	**Number of Full-time Teachers(person)**									
普通高等学校	Regular Institutions of Higher Education	42098	46766	47768	47158	47917	49018	50236	51996	53139
普通中等专业学校	Regular Specialized Secondary Schools	1845	1346	1228	1210	998	958	918	970	974
普通中学	Regular Secondary Schools	31506	32615	33014	33962	36565	37539	39143	41133	38196
小学	Primary Schools	29944	28395	28748	30941	34163	36878	39836	43423	50767
幼儿园	Kindergarten	10638	17337	19096	21395	23789	25823	26496	29948	31222

注：1.本表数据来源于市教育局。
2.本表中普通高等学校毕业生、招生、在校生数含普通高等学校研究生及普通高等学校本、专科学生。
3.本表中小学的学校数是指独立小学个数，其在校生、教职工等指标均为普通初等教育；幼儿园的校数是指独立的幼儿园个数，其在校生、教职工等指标均为学前教育（下表同）。
4.本表中普通中学学生数据为普通中等教育口径，小学学生数为普通初等教育口径，幼儿园学生数为学前教育口径。
5.本表2017年及以后年份数据含西咸新区。

20-2 各级各类学校、教职工情况（2021年）

Situation of All Kinds of Schools and Staff Members at All Levels (2021)

指　标	Item	学校数（所）Number of Schools (unit)	教职工数（人）Number of Staff and Teachers (person)	专任教师数（人）Full-time Teachers (person)
一、高等教育	**Higher education**	**75**	**80220**	**54256**
（一）研究生培养机构	Postgraduate training institutions	(43)		
1. 普通高校	Institutions of Higher Schools	(22)		
2. 科研机构	Scientific Research Institution	(21)	-	-
（二）普通高等学校	Regular Institutions of Higher Schools	63	78261	53139
1. 本科院校	Universities and Colleges of Undergraduate Course	44	69012	46352
其中：独立学院	Non-university Tertiary	9	4288	2841
2. 专科院校	Higher Vocational Colleges	19	9249	6787
其中：高等职业学校	Higher Vocational College	17	7814	5943
（三）成人高等学校	Adult Higher Schools	12	1959	1117
二、中等职业教育	**Secondary Occupation Education**	**150**	**13758**	**9366**
（一）普通中等专业学校	Regular Specialized Secondary Schools	15	1517	974
（二）成人中等专业学校	Adult Secondary Specialized Schools	2	97	71
（三）职业高中学校	Vocational Hight Schools	55	5373	3767
其中：市属	Municipal schools	55	5373	3767
（四）技工学校	Technical Schools	78	6771	4554
其中：市属	Municipal schools	31	2588	2078
三、基础教育	**Elementary Education**	**3673**	**167953**	**120585**
（一）普通中等教育	Regular Institutions Education	501	52022	38196
1. 高中	Senior High Schools	167	25797	12934
完全中学	Complete Secondary Schools	105	16097	6154
高级中学	Senior Secondary Schools	54	7666	6391
十二年一贯制学校	Twelve-year Consistency Schools	8	2034	389
2. 初中	Junior Middle Schools	334	26225	25262
初级中学	Junior Middle Schools	255	16674	13821
九年一贯制学校	Nine-year Consistency Schools	79	9551	3430
完全中学	Complete Secondary school	-	-	513
十二年一贯制学校	Twelve-year Consistency schools	-	-	7498
附设普通初中班的学校	Senior Secondary Schools with Regular Junior Secondary Classes	(1)	-	
（二）普通初等教育	Regular Primary Education	1170	51649	50767
独立小学	Independent Primary Schools	1170	50568	44833
教学点	Teaching Points	(168)	1081	898
九年一贯制学校	Nine-year Consistency schools	-	-	4533
十二年一贯制学校	Twelve-year Consistency schools	-	-	495
附设小学班的学校	Schools with Primary Classes	(3)	-	8
（三）特殊教育	Special Education Schools	14	494	368
特殊教育学校	Special Education Schools	14	494	367
附设特教班的学校	Schools with Special Edution Classes	(1)	-	1
（四）工读学校	Reformatory Schools	1	43	32
（五）学前教育	Preschool Education	1987	63745	31222
幼儿园	Kindergarten	1987	63745	31166
附设幼儿班的学校	Schools with Nursery Classes	(53)	-	56
另有：职业技术培训机构	Vocational and Technical Institutions	(2815)	(27568)	(15910)

注：1.本表数据来源于市教育局。
2.本表为西安市行政区划内各级各类学校全口径数据（不含军事院校、党校）。
3.技工学校数据由西安市人力资源和社会保障局提供。
4.按照事业统计主体校原则，完全中学、十二年一贯制学校的学校数计入普通高中，九年一贯制学校的校数计入普通初中。
5.教职工和专任教师数按照办学类型划分。
6.( ) 内数据不计入总计，下表同。
7.本表数据包含西咸新区。

20-3 各级各类教育学生情况（2021年）

Basic Facts on Education Student by School Type (2021)

单位：人 (person)

指 标	Item	毕业生数 Number of Graduates	招生数 New Enrollment	在校学生数 Total Enrollment	女生 Female Students
一、高等教育	**Higher education**	**492581**	**474602**	**1470599**	**671600**
（一）研究生	Postgraduates	36075	54905	164406	78143
1. 高等学校	Institutions of Higher Schools	35905	54676	163685	77991
2. 科研机构	Scientific Research Institution	170	229	721	152
（二）普通高等教育	Regular Institutions of Higher Schools	257966	227161	816867	379473
1. 本科	Universities Course Schools	193744	149657	557039	275930
2. 专科	Junior Colleges	64222	77504	259828	103543
（三）成人高等教育	Higher Vocational Colleges	72018	88158	201082	96181
其中：成人高等学校	Contains:Adult Higher Education	12999	11553	39983	16014
（四）网络本专科生	Network Undergraduate and clooege students	126522	104378	288244	117803
1. 本科	Universities Course Schools	56280	79953	190549	80133
2. 专科	Junior Colleges	70242	24425	97695	37670
二、中等职业教育	**Secondary Occupation Education**	**60357**	**68898**	**201959**	**72309**
1. 普通中等专业学校	Regular Specialized Secondary Schools	4119	7776	20340	9019
2. 成人中等专业学校	Adult Secondary Specialized Schools	134	28	210	105
3. 职业高中学校	Vocational high Schools	16415	23364	64996	28412
其中：市属	Municipal schools	16415	23364	64996	28412
4. 技工学校	Technical Schools	39689	37730	116413	34773
其中：市属	Municipal schools	10712	14173	42193	13785
三、基础教育	**Elementary Education**	**369709**	**478335**	**1780580**	**847827**
（一）普通中等教育	Regular Institutions Education	140040	169862	482110	228719
1. 高中	Senior High Schools	50001	57209	161486	78839
完全中学	Complete Secondary Schools	25051	28909	80760	39512
高级中学	Senior Secondary Schools	23558	26610	75665	36845
十二年一贯制学校	Twelve-year Consistency schools	1392	1690	5061	2482
2. 初中	Junior Middle Schools	90039	112653	320624	149880
初级中学	Junior Middle Schools	46263	54954	156390	73239
九年一贯制学校	Nine-year Consistency Schools	10615	15544	42038	19432
十二年一贯制学校	Twelve-year Consistency Schools	2366	2459	7345	3306
完全中学	Complete Secondary school	30795	39696	114851	53903
（二）普通初等教育	Regular Primary Education	109617	158264	890921	423561
独立小学	Pricmary Schools	99084	140086	798494	379976
九年一贯制学校	Nine-year Consistency schools	9169	17012	83832	39762
十二年一贯制学校	Twelve-year Consistency Schools	1364	1166	8595	3823
（三）特殊教育	Special Education Schools	603	603	3493	1315
1. 特殊教育学校	Special Education Schools	153	212	1181	433
2. 小学附设特教班	Primary Schools with Special Education Classes		2	4	1
3. 小学随班就读	Elementary Inclusive	203	178	1331	514
4. 初中随班就读	Junior Mainstreaming	169	166	532	214
5. 小学送教上门	Primary School Delivery	55	21	346	118
6. 初中送教上门	Junior High School Delivery	23	24	99	35
（四）工读学校	Reformatory Schools	10	7	16	2
（五）学前教育	Preschool Education	119439	149599	404040	194230
1. 独立幼儿园	Independent Kindergartens	119263	149382	403520	193987
2. 附设幼儿园	Attached Kindergartens	176	217	520	243
另有：职业技术培训机构	Vocational and Technical Institutions				

注：1.本表数据来源于市教育局。
2.本表数据包含西咸新区。

20-4 主要年份普通高等学校和科研机构研究生情况

Basic Statistics of Postgraduates on Regular Institutions of Higher Education and Scientific Research Institution in Representative Years

单位：人 (person)

年 份 Year	毕业生数 Number of Graduates	高等学校 Higher Schools	招生数 New Enrollment	高等学校 Higher Schools	在校学生数 Total Enrollment	高等学校 Higher Schools
1978			232	232	232	232
1980			127	127	651	651
1985	754	754	2819	2819	4799	4799
1990	2051	2051	1662	1662	5275	5275
1995	1769	1769	2712	2712	7974	7974
2000	3236	3236	6924	6924	16620	16620
2001	3881	3770	9274	8966	22564	21855
2002	4103	3952	11282	10882	28446	27471
2003	5971	5765	14322	13882	36936	35790
2004	8384	8127	17310	16871	45402	44169
2005	10416	10127	18583	18106	52699	51310
2006	12914	12552	19581	19105	58433	56951
2007	15506	15124	20570	20167	64137	62801
2008	17234	16788	21892	21443	67296	65834
2009	19025	18574	24879	24400	72366	70908
2010	19526	19129	25971	25477	76993	75483
2011	20965	20605	26686	26256	81696	80332
2012	22963	22578	28065	27618	84712	83306
2013	24778	24385	28786	28333	87002	85570
2014	24092	23881	28636	28436	88518	87826
2015	25322	25104	29487	29293	91448	90790
2016	24779	24562	30263	30079	94720	94102
2017	25808	25616	36296	36084	104092	103458
2018	27276	27088	38582	38399	112250	111626
2019	28619	28448	42653	42439	131982	131325
2020	33355	33157	51726	51493	148025	147358
2021	36075	35905	54905	54676	164406	163685

注：1.本表数据来源于市教育局。
2.本表2017年及以后年份数据包含西咸新区。

20-5 主要年份普通高等学校基本情况（本专科）

Basic Statistics on Regular Institution of Higher Education in Representative Years

单位：所、万人 (units,10 000 persons)

年 份 Year	学校数 Number of Schools	毕业生数 Number of Graduates	招生数 New Enrollment	在校学生数 Total Enrollment	教职工数 Number of Staff and Teachers	专任教师数 Full-time Teachers
1978	21	0.60	1.31	2.88	2.24	0.87
1980	24	0.21	1.08	4.17	2.55	0.97
1985	28	1.17	2.28	6.49	3.40	1.28
1990	31	2.11	2.00	7.50	4.15	1.56
1995	32	2.87	3.13	10.07	4.21	1.59
2000	25	2.71	6.79	17.75	3.81	1.57
2001	32	3.31	8.31	23.24	4.30	1.75
2002	35	3.82	10.75	30.15	4.67	2.06
2003	37	5.89	12.21	36.42	4.92	2.21
2004	41	7.66	13.17	40.29	5.45	2.69
2005	44	10.08	14.68	47.79	5.73	2.95
2006	47	11.75	15.15	51.40	6.14	3.29
2007	48	14.33	16.96	56.03	6.56	3.67
2008	48	15.82	19.31	60.10	6.90	3.89
2009	49	15.04	18.84	63.22	7.08	4.06
2010	50	16.33	19.16	65.74	7.22	4.21
2011	61	17.68	20.52	68.52	7.27	4.27
2012	62	18.64	22.46	72.40	7.40	4.45
2013	63	17.73	21.05	75.27	7.50	4.64
2014	63	18.88	20.74	76.64	7.50	4.68
2015	63	20.72	20.49	75.75	7.49	4.78
2016	63	21.60	20.07	73.68	7.37	4.72
2017	63	20.50	20.10	72.68	7.42	4.79
2018	63	20.50	19.83	71.28	7.56	4.90
2019	63	19.18	22.63	74.01	7.37	5.02
2020	63	19.38	24.11	78.39	7.52	5.20
2021	63	25.80	22.72	81.69	7.82	5.31

注：1.本表数据来源于市教育局。
2.本表2017年及以后年份数据包含西咸新区。

20-6 主要年份普通中等专业学校基本情况

Basic Statistics on Regular Specialized Secondary Schools in Representative Years

年份 Year	学校数（所） Number of Schools (units)	毕业生数（万人） Number of Graduates (10 000 persons)	招生数（万人） New Enrollment (10 000 persons)	在校学生数（万人） Total Enrollment (10 000 persons)	教职工数（人） Number of Staff and Teachers(person)	专任教师数（人） Full-time Teachers(person)
1978	19	0.19	0.45	0.82	3937	1110
1980	31	0.18	0.42	1.50	3895	1474
1985	37	0.43	0.76	1.70	6071	2363
1990	44	0.56	0.68	2.09	7136	2891
1995	46	0.97	1.37	3.74	5903	2533
2000	47	1.63	1.90	6.02	6964	3172
2001	47	1.70	1.58	5.63	5252	2467
2002	46	1.60	1.69	5.57	5170	2508
2003	34	1.62	1.80	5.28	4562	2302
2004	35	1.40	2.09	5.71	4676	2388
2005	32	1.44	2.26	6.16	3924	2130
2006	31	1.84	2.61	7.30	3621	2014
2007	30	2.03	2.91	7.97	3548	2011
2008	29	2.58	2.55	8.06	3278	1814
2009	28	2.70	2.15	7.44	2965	1720
2010	28	2.45	2.08	6.75	3249	1845
2011	24	2.34	1.96	6.11	2868	1723
2012	24	2.15	1.67	5.43	2733	1595
2013	22	1.93	1.35	4.66	2599	1474
2014	22	1.76	1.25	4.07	2315	1346
2015	20	1.32	0.95	3.47	1991	1228
2016	20	1.25	0.88	3.11	1917	1210
2017	16	1.06	0.96	2.74	1556	998
2018	15	0.84	0.83	2.48	1529	958
2019	15	0.72	1.12	2.79	1386	918
2020	15	0.81	1.16	3.02	1474	970
2021	15	0.41	0.78	2.03	1517	974

注：1.本表数据来源于市教育局。
2.本表2017年及以后年份数据包含西咸新区。

20-7 主要年份普通中等教育基本情况

Basic Situation of General Secondary Education in Major Years

年　份 Year	学校数（所） Number of Schools (units)	毕业生数（万人） Number of Graduates (10 000 persons)	招生数（万人） New Enrollment (10 000 persons)	在校学生数（万人） Total Enrollment (10 000 persons)	教职工数（人） Number of Staff and Teachers(person)	专任教师数（人） Full-time Teachers(person)
1978	962	10.85		44.16	27380	20660
1980	1002	12.33	14.03	44.08	29867	22530
1985	563	10.72	13.05	38.24	30063	22050
1990	518	9.11	10.49	30.03	30739	22386
1995	485	8.13	12.40	32.32	30423	21984
2000	466	12.01	17.88	48.31	34385	26230
2001	470	13.85	18.98	52.50	35442	27190
2002	467	15.76	19.68	55.36	36706	28335
2003	467	16.76	18.78	56.44	38252	29887
2004	461	18.01	18.85	56.54	39121	30600
2005	460	18.82	18.83	55.74	39456	31094
2006	457	18.04	18.61	56.11	39341	31203
2007	453	18.37	17.96	54.68	39171	31373
2008	442	17.99	17.16	52.83	39088	31425
2009	439	17.80	16.57	50.63	39002	31415
2010	436	17.01	16.15	48.89	39207	31506
2011	423	16.44	15.42	47.20	41135	31675
2012	419	15.64	14.98	45.33	41197	31526
2013	418	15.24	14.47	43.73	41003	31419
2014	421	14.54	13.97	42.57	40576	32615
2015	422	13.92	13.41	41.37	40689	33014
2016	422	13.96	13.72	40.70	41352	33962
2017	448	13.89	14.08	41.74	44546	36565
2018	456	13.50	14.37	42.46	45390	37539
2019	469	13.89	15.29	43.56	47037	39143
2020	495	13.89	16.20	45.68	49388	41133
2021	501	14.00	16.99	48.21	52022	38196

注：1.本表数据来源于市教育局。
　　2.本表2017年及以后年份数据包含西咸新区。

20-8 各区县普通中等教育基本情况（2021年）

Basic Situation of Ordinary Secondary Education in Various Districts and Counties (2021)

单位：所、人 (unit, person)

区 县	Region	学校数 Number of Schools	毕业生数 Number of Graduates	高中 Senior	招生数 New Enrollment	高中 Senior	在校学生数 Total Enrollment	女生 Female Students	高中 Senior	教职工数 Number of Staff and Teachers	专任教师数 Full-time Teachers
合 计	**Total**	**501**	**140040**	**50001**	**169862**	**57209**	**482110**	**228719**	**161486**	**52022**	**38196**
新城区	Xincheng	23	10375	3844	11789	4411	34167	16448	12260	2655	2259
碑林区	Beilin	32	15459	6281	17872	7031	52389	23907	19968	4298	3480
莲湖区	Lianhu	21	9992	3441	10557	3503	32008	15187	10141	2508	2044
灞桥区	Baqiao	18	6129	1975	7799	2178	22125	10420	6215	2212	1743
未央区	Weiyang	21	7211	1996	7590	2273	24151	11449	6416	2737	1815
雁塔区	Yanta	35	10698	4048	13358	4627	37115	17616	12753	4103	2715
阎良区	Yanliang	11	3104	1079	3513	1157	10354	5299	3350	1054	927
临潼区	Lintong	33	8517	3163	8870	3306	26591	13078	9845	3449	2716
长安区	Chang'an	40	10448	3831	11853	4432	34961	16605	12459	3550	3042
高陵区	Gaoling	15	3569	1285	4360	1698	12453	6298	4525	1139	958
鄠邑区	Huyi	25	6769	3008	6140	2630	18610	8842	7378	2147	1785
蓝田县	Lantian	45	8457	3553	7538	3541	23262	11382	10153	3340	2411
周至县	Zhouzhi	35	8301	3202	8979	3775	25691	11644	11241	3002	2135
西咸新区	Xixian New Area	51	9353	2438	13688	3611	35816	16570	9073	5298	3364
高新区	Hi-Tech Industries Development Zone	49	9628	3541	13902	3929	37127	17541	11698	4175	2873
经开区	Economic Development Zone	13	4940	1893	8598	2604	22060	10428	7485	2704	1505
曲江新区	Qujiang New District	6	1459	215	3489	699	8817	4321	1614	1005	579
航空基地	National Aviation Hi-tech Industrial Base	1			152		152	73		32	22
航天基地	National Civil Aerospace Industrial Base	5	1404	150	2494	398	6022	2859	1177	554	465
浐灞生态区	Chan-ba Ecological District	13	2702	707	4553	800	11621	5637	2268	1201	866
国际港务区	International Trade & Logistics Park	9	1525	351	2768	606	6618	3115	1467	859	492

注：1.本表数据来源于市教育局。
2.专任教师按办学层次统计，不含一贯制学校小学部专任教师数。

20-9 主要年份职业高中基本情况

Basic Statistics on Vocational Secondary Schools in Representative Years

单位：所、人 (unit, person)

年 份 Year	学校数 Number of Schools	毕业生数 Number of Graduates	招生数 New Enrollment	在校学生数 Total Enrollment	教职工数 Number of Staff and Teachers	专任教师数 Full-time Teachers
1985	40	1661	8346	17621	1375	868
1990	58	5936	8095	20151	2674	1574
1995	71	8976	12490	32673	2394	1877
2000	95	9949	13903	32188	3311	1997
2001	85	10300	15591	34336	3517	2113
2002	78	8659	17231	39428	3461	2192
2003	87	10755	17310	44033	4036	2458
2004	83	12177	17865	46358	4101	2515
2005	91	15092	20603	51766	4750	2892
2006	96	14887	21158	53828	5193	3126
2007	86	14881	24434	56012	4899	3064
2008	84	15813	30201	62963	4878	3008
2009	84	14691	31042	72388	5129	3179
2010	84	18100	30042	78244	5222	3178
2011	78	22493	27641	75108	4849	3173
2012	77	24048	24995	67969	4775	3148
2013	74	21243	23043	61968	4699	3085
2014	81	19156	19508	60024	4860	3186
2015	80	18565	15060	49092	3239	2214
2016	64	17773	14305	43576	3126	2275
2017	62	14325	17080	45145	3318	2405
2018	60	14064	17295	46380	3499	2584
2019	60	12559	19797	52553	3801	2685
2020	57	16028	22359	58444	4790	3421
2021	55	16415	23364	64996	5373	3767

注：1.本表数据来源于市教育局。
2.本表2017年至2020年年份数据包含西咸新区。

20-10 各区县职业高中基本情况（2021年）

Basic Statistics on Vocational Secondary Schools by Region (2021)

单位：所、人 (unit, person)

区 县	Region	学校数 Number of Schools	毕业生数 Number of Graduates	招生数 New Enrollment	在校学生数 Total Enrollment	女生 Female Students	教职工数 Number of Staff and Teachers	专任教师数 Full-time Teachers
合 计	**Total**	**55**	**16415**	**23364**	**64996**	**28412**	**5373**	**3767**
新城区	Xincheng	4	553	2358	5696	2808	606	369
碑林区	Beilin	1	181	557	1205	622	109	90
莲湖区	Lianhu	5	1188	1352	3663	1695	294	239
灞桥区	Baqiao	4	3531	3434	10720	3640	671	380
未央区	Weiyang	2	391	416	1361	763	137	100
雁塔区	Yanta	7	1441	2063	5252	2541	444	320
阎良区	Yanliang	1	383	692	1710	770	167	132
临潼区	Lintong	4	764	1591	3784	1721	256	206
长安区	Chang'an	6	1701	3586	9326	4571	879	657
高陵区	Gaoling	1	314	672	1578	615	129	121
鄠邑区	Huyi	2	1039	1575	4337	2097	335	237
蓝田县	Lantian	3	645	1008	3265	1367	250	190
周至县	Zhouzhi	3	376	409	1303	578	69	54
西咸新区	Xixian New Area	3	334	462	1416	560	81	54
高新区	Hi-Tech Industries Development Zone	4	1793	1632	5433	1810	391	219
经开区	Economic Development Zone	2	458	513	1145	481	131	100
曲江新区	Qujiang New District							
航空基地	National Aviation Hi-tech Industrial Base	1	614	351	887	575	104	61
航天基地	National Civil Aerospace Industrial Base	1	690	637	2781	1100	298	224
浐灞生态区	Chan-ba Ecological District							
国际港务区	International Trade & Logistics Park	1	19	56	134	98	22	14

注：本表数据来源于市教育局。

20-11 主要年份普通初等教育基本情况

Basic Situation of General Primary Education in Major Years

年 份 Year	学校数（所） Number of Schools (units)	毕业生数（万人） Number of Graduates (10 000 persons)	招生数（万人） New Enrollment (10 000 persons)	在校学生数（万人） Total Enrollment (10 000 persons)	教职工数（人） Number of Staff and Teachers(person)	专任教师数（人） Full-time Teachers(person)
1978	2667	13.07	14.10	74.03	29744	26428
1980	2337	11.91	12.57	73.36	31770	28360
1985	2337	11.21	9.57	62.16	31075	26430
1990	2343	8.67	10.85	61.87	33788	29090
1995	2360	9.93	14.09	79.36	35568	30270
2000	2323	13.83	11.51	77.81	35336	30215
2001	2277	14.20	11.07	74.51	34257	29281
2002	2137	13.89	10.13	70.78	34143	29428
2003	2084	12.97	9.28	66.78	34080	29531
2004	2016	12.37	9.12	63.75	33794	29367
2005	1980	11.92	8.47	60.47	33907	29674
2006	1929	11.53	9.16	59.33	34460	30018
2007	1872	11.38	8.67	56.83	34901	30533
2008	1781	10.58	8.33	54.66	34653	30382
2009	1666	9.96	7.84	52.52	34389	30334
2010	1531	9.61	8.64	51.56	34118	29944
2011	1424	8.92	8.77	51.39	32457	29900
2012	1322	8.88	8.88	50.85	32208	29651
2013	1291	8.51	9.56	51.95	31863	29421
2014	1257	8.29	10.13	53.79	32162	28395
2015	1234	7.85	10.51	56.62	32585	28748
2016	1190	8.46	11.65	59.79	34646	30941
2017	1125	9.06	13.13	66.68	38494	34163
2018	1130	9.32	15.16	73.09	41122	36878
2019	1145	10.17	15.80	78.98	44511	39836
2020	1172	10.75	16.92	85.20	48838	43423
2021	1170	10.96	15.83	89.09	51649	50767

注：1.本表数据来源于市教育局。
　　2.本表2017年及以后年份数据包含西咸新区。

20-12 各区县普通初等教育基本情况（2021年）

Basic Situation of General Primary Education in Various Districts and Counties (2021)

单位：所、人 (unit, person)

区 县	Region	学校数 Number of Schools	毕业生数 Number of Graduates	招生数 New Enrollment	在校学生数 Total Enrollment	女生 Female Students	教职工数 Number of Staff and Teachers	专任教师数 Full-time Teachers
合 计	**Total**	**1170**	**109617**	**158264**	**890921**	**423561**	**51649**	**50767**
新城区	Xincheng	37	5715	6248	38617	18221	2332	2184
碑林区	Beilin	35	6064	8001	45669	21488	2668	2299
莲湖区	Lianhu	48	8266	10567	60509	28848	2952	2751
灞桥区	Baqiao	43	4800	6815	39123	18455	2054	2091
未央区	Weiyang	45	8740	10006	65040	30963	3250	3455
雁塔区	Yanta	46	9824	12945	74498	35535	3820	4040
阎良区	Yanliang	23	2575	2769	17192	8349	1030	968
临潼区	Lintong	105	6299	6487	43009	20630	3135	2764
长安区	Chang'an	109	8149	11930	67617	32033	4300	3969
高陵区	Gaoling	61	3270	4596	26474	12733	1874	1635
鄠邑区	Huyi	76	3521	4270	25749	12245	1783	1594
蓝田县	Lantian	83	4062	4115	27493	13209	2478	2344
周至县	Zhouzhi	111	5479	5732	35593	16768	2539	2343
西咸新区	Xixian New Area	117	9156	16109	84562	40175	4623	5158
高新区	Hi-Tech Industries Development Zone	106	8289	14186	74636	35340	4094	4298
经开区	Economic Development Zone	27	4560	9607	48338	23059	2064	2520
曲江新区	Qujiang New District	20	2664	6764	32485	15435	1907	1773
航空基地	National Aviation Hi-tech Industrial Base	1	83	397	1844	861	123	117
航天基地	National Civil Aerospace Industrial Base	12	1155	2890	13431	6422	817	756
浐灞生态区	Chan-ba Ecological District	43	5467	11303	56222	26654	3089	2891
国际港务区	International Trade & Logistics Park	22	1479	2527	12820	6138	717	817

注：本表数据来源于市教育局。

20-13 主要年份学前教育基本情况

Basic Conditions of Pre-school Education in Representative Years

年 份 Year	幼儿园（所） Number of Kindergartens (unit)	班数（个） Number of Class (unit)	在园幼儿数（万人） Student Enrollment (10 000 persons)	教职工数（人） Number of Staff and Teachers(person)	专任教师数（人） Full-time Teachers(person)
1978	191		4.44	3568	1315
1980	186		9.61	5525	2657
1985	310	3135	9.71	6887	2770
1990	256	3816	14.04	6123	2058
1995	257	4464	16.40	6173	2659
2000	367	4142	12.85	6346	2995
2001	366	4306	11.97	6224	3069
2002	378	4186	11.53	6541	3397
2003	610	4470	12.39	8959	4853
2004	660	4507	12.16	9870	5577
2005	737	4712	12.75	10528	5959
2006	863	5037	13.00	12335	7106
2007	830	5081	14.00	13468	7951
2008	905	5506	15.00	14932	8704
2009	896	5710	16.00	15928	9240
2010	1004	6420	18.00	18710	10638
2011	1122	8010	24.00	23680	12577
2012	1239	8729	27.10	27735	14293
2013	1295	9408	28.56	31989	16238
2014	1343	9782	28.95	33062	17337
2015	1417	10457	30.90	36004	19096
2016	1475	11090	31.80	39753	21395
2017	1605	12234	34.81	44895	23789
2018	1780	12970	35.39	49604	25823
2019	1839	13375	36.05	52442	26496
2020	1966	14612	39.64	59605	29948
2021	1987	15143	40.40	63745	31222

注：1.本表数据来源于市教育局。
2.本表2017年及以后年份数据包含西咸新区。

20-14 主要年份特殊教育基本情况

Basic Statistics on Special Education in Representative Years

单位：所、人 (unit, person)

年份 Year	学校数 Number of Schools	毕业生数 Number of Graduates	招生数 New Enrollment	在校学生数 Total Enrollment	教职工数 Number of Staff and Teachers	专任教师数 Full-time Teachers
1980	1	48	64	315	66	43
1985	2	14	36	318	94	59
1990	5	35	111	451	142	96
1995	5	27	147	1363	204	141
2000	5	269	145	1880	230	156
2001	5	237	209	1915	238	162
2002	5	216	148	1661	232	157
2003	5	156	161	1380	237	166
2004	5	137	142	1290	236	167
2005	5	184	182	1445	240	169
2006	6	171	143	1425	254	178
2007	6	169	114	1342	259	190
2008	6	83	96	1286	259	190
2009	7	311	202	1523	335	234
2010	8	214	402	1529	340	235
2011	8	280	222	1393	343	231
2012	8	197	220	1392	352	248
2013	8	194	212	1174	338	243
2014	8	172	222	1225	345	238
2015	8	168	338	1373	352	240
2016	8	214	327	1604	359	246
2017	9	237	774	2498	386	272
2018	9	352	461	2615	379	271
2019	10	435	541	2967	404	300
2020	11	508	589	3333	438	333
2021	14	603	603	3493	494	368

注：1.本表数据来源于市教育局。
2.包括盲、聋、哑、智力障碍者儿童教育。
3.本表2017年及以后年份数据包含西咸新区。

20-15　基础教育监测评价情况（2021年）

Monitoring and Evaluation of Basic Education (2021)

指　标	Item	2021
入学率（%）	Enrollment Rate(%)	
小学	Primary Schools	100.00
初中	Junior Middle Schools	100.00
巩固率（%）	The Consolidation Rate(%)	
小学（六年）	Primary Schools(six years)	100.53
初中（三年）	Junior Middle Schools(three years)	96.81
毕业率（%）	The Graduate Rate(%)	
小学	Primary school	98.34
初中	Junior middle school	97.85
专任教师学历合格率（%）	Qualified Rate of Full-time Teacher Education(%)	
小学	Primary Schools	100.00
初中	Junior Middle Schools	100.00
高中	Senior Middle Schools	99.21
幼儿园	Kindergartens	100.00
小学教师专科以上学历达到率（%）	Rate of Primary School Teachers with College degree or Above(%)	99.80
初中教师本科以上学历达到率（%）	Rate of Junior Middle SchoolTeachers with Bachelor degree or Above(%)	96.69
高中教师研究生以上学历达到率（%）	Rate of Senior Middle School Teachers with Postgraduate degree or Above(%)	23.84

注：1.本表数据来源于市教育局。
　　2.本表数据计算入学率和小学巩固率不包含西咸新区的咸阳部分。
　　3.2021年西咸新区两个街办划归咸阳市，毕业学生统计范围变化。

20-16 主要年份平均每万人口在校学生数及构成

单位：人、%

年 份 Year	平均每万人 高等学校在校学生 Per 10000 people on average Hight Education Students in the school	平均每万人 高中阶段在校学生 Per 10000 people on average Number of Senior high School Students in the school	平均每万人 初中在校学生 Per 10000 people on average Number of Junior Secondary School Students in the school	平均每万人 小学在校学生 Per 10000 people on average Number of Primary School Students in the school
1978	58			1486
1980	84			1434
1985	117			1124
1990	123			1016
1995	168			1224
2000	282			1131
2001	366			1072
2002	470			1007
2003	560			932
2004	618	463	517	879
2005	715	492	489	815
2006	760	534	484	788
2007	817	543	466	744
2008	863	571	444	708
2009	901	619	413	672
2010	939	635	361	660
2011	973	514	301	539
2012	986	471	278	518
2013	988	386	265	522
2014	983	352	256	532
2015	929	309	236	537
2016	865	288	224	513
2017	732	271	201	516
2018	741	260	209	566
2019	1044	277	215	600
2020	1106	279	233	657
2021	1142	293	249	692

注：1.本表数据来源于市教育局。
2.2011年起，表中三个比重指标数据参与计算的学生总数含普通教育、成人教育及网络教育数据。
3.2019年平均每万人高等学校在校学生包含全部高等教育在校生。
4.本表2017年及以后年份数据含西咸新区。
5.2020年，依据西安市常住人口数的修订，对2011年到2019年平均每万人在校学生数进行了修订。

The Average Number of Students in the School every 10000 Individuals in Representative Years

(persons,%)

平均每万人 学前教育在校学生 Average Number of Pre-school Students per 10,000 people	普通高等学校在校学生 占学生总数比重 Senior high School Students in the school in accounting for the proportion of the total number of students	中等学校在校学生 占学生总数比重 Junior Secondary School students in the school in accounting for the proportion of the total number of students	小学在校学生 占学生总数比重 Primary School students in the school in accounting for the proportion of the total number of students
	2.3	34.9	58.6
	3.1	33.2	55.3
	5.3	31.3	50.9
	6.7	25.1	51.7
	7.3	28.0	53.6
	11.5	34.8	46.0
	14.6	35.9	42.6
	18.2	36.4	39.0
	20.1	33.8	33.5
	22.2	35.2	31.6
	26.4	36.2	30.1
	27.7	37.1	28.7
	29.3	36.3	26.7
	30.8	36.1	25.2
	31.8	36.5	23.7
217	33.0	35.0	23.2
252	29.8	30.1	19.9
276	31.0	28.2	19.5
287	32.6	25.3	20.2
285	33.2	23.8	20.9
293	32.8	22.2	21.9
288	31.4	21.4	22.6
270	29.1	21.3	23.4
274	27.5	20.2	24.4
273	27.4	20.4	24.9
306	27.8	19.8	25.4
314	28.4	19.8	25.8

20-17 民办教育情况（2021年）

单位：所、人

指　标	Item	学校数 Number of Schools	毕业生数 Number of Graduates
一、民办高等教育(民办高校）	**Private higher Education(Institutions)**	**27**	**138049**
二、民办中等教育	**Private Secondary Education**	**99**	**45106**
民办普通高中	Ordinary High School	31	6972
民办普通中等专业学校	Ordinary Secondaru Vocational School	1	605
民办职业高中	Vocational high school	32	11761
民办普通初中	Ordinary Junior middle school	35	24495
民办的附设中职班	Schools with Vocational Secondary Class	(10)	1273
三、民办普通小学	**Private Primary School**	**92**	**19010**
四、民办幼儿园	**Private kindergarten**	**928**	**64583**
另有：民办培训机构	Private Training Institutions	(1968)	

注：1.本表数据来源于市教育局。
2.毕业生数中幼儿园为离园人数。
3.民办高等教育在校生为民办高校普通、成人本专科学生数。
4.聘请校外教师中，小学、中学、幼儿园为代课教师和兼任教师之和。
5.按照教育报表制度，民办的附设中职班教职工计入基础教育主体校教职工总数，专任教师为中职层次，故单独统计。
6.本表数据含西咸新区。

Private Education Situation (2021)

(unit, person)

招生数 New Enrollment	在校学生数 Total Enrollment	教职工数 Number of Teachers and Staff	专任教师 Full-time Teachers	校外教师 Teachers hired from Outside Schools
90746	**295016**	**19730**	**14038**	**2908**
57244	**162406**	**20581**	**9971**	**51**
9016	25003	5798	1985	
1765	4167	252	184	
15647	43206	3406	2115	51
28224	83088	11125	5402	
2592	6942		285	
26463	**162856**	**13960**	**8863**	
73896	**193797**	**31628**	**14660**	**928**
		24761	14756	6809

20-18 全市研究与试验发展（R&D）活动情况（2020年）

Scientific and Technological Activities in the Whole City (2020)

指　标	Item	2020
一、单位数（个）	**Number of Institutions(unit)**	**4111**
#有R&D活动单位数	The Number of R&D active units	1032
二、R&D人员（人）	**Personnel Engaged in R&D(person)**	**126471**
三、R&D人员折合全时当量（人年）	**R&D Stuff Equivalent to Full Time equivalent(person year)**	**92146**
四、R&D经费内部支出（万元）	**R&D Internal Expenditure(10 000 yuan)**	**5060593.9**

注：本表数据来源于省统计局反馈。

20-19 规模以上重点行业企业研究与试验发展（R&D）情况（2020年）

R&D Project Status of Key Enterprises above Designated Size (2020)

指　标	Item	2020
一、企业数（个）	**Number of Enterprises(unit)**	**3905**
工业	Industry	1671
非工业	Non-industry	2234
#有R&D活动的单位数	The number of R&D active units	868
工业	Industry	655
非工业	Non-industry	213
二、R&D人员（人）	**Personnel Engaged in R&D(person)**	**54869**
工业	Industry	40451
非工业	Non-industry	14418
三、R&D人员折合全时当量（人年）	**R&D Stuff Equivalent to Full Time equivalent(person year)**	**38744**
工业	Industry	29052
非工业	Non-industry	9692
四、R&D经费内部支出（万元）	**R&D Internal Expenditure(10 000 yuan)**	**2177725**
工业	Industry	1570544
非工业	Non-industry	607181

20–20 规模以上工业企业研究与试验发展（R&D）基本情况（2020年）

R&D Project Status of Industrial Enterprises above Designated Size (2020)

指　标	Item	企业数（个）Number of Enterprises (unit)	有R&D活动的企业数 The Number of R&D Enterprises
总计	**Total**	**1671**	**655**
按企业规模分	**Grouped by Size of Enterprises**		
大型企业	Large-size	69	47
中型企业	Medium-size	181	99
小型企业	Small-size	1299	499
微型企业	Microenterprise	122	10
按登记注册类型分	**Grouped by Registered Status**		
内资企业	Domestic Investment Enterprises	1547	612
国有企业	State-owned Enterprises	36	18
集体企业	Collective-owned Enterprise	3	
股份合作企业	Stock Cooperative Enterprises	5	2
联营企业	Affiliated Enterprises		
有限责任公司	Limited Liability Corporations	476	207
股份有限公司	Share-holding Corporations Ltd	100	74
私营企业	Private Enterprises	926	310
其他	Other Domestic Funded Enterprises	1	1
港、澳、台商投资企业	Enterprises with Funds from Hong Kong,Macao And Taiwan	21	4
外商投资企业	Foreign Funded Enterprises	103	39
按国民经济行业分	**Grouped by Sector**		
采矿业	Mining	12	2
煤炭开采和洗选业	Mining and Washing of Coal		
石油和天然气开采业	Extraction of Petroleum and Natural Gas	1	1

20-20 续表1 continued 1

指 标	Item	企业数（个）Number of Enterprises (unit)	有R&D活动的企业数 The Number of R&D Enterprises
黑色金属矿采选业	Mining of Ferrous Metal Ores		
有色金属矿采选业	Mining of Non-ferrous Metal Ores		
非金属矿采选业	Mining and Processing of Nonmetal Ores		
开采专业及辅助性活动	Mining Professional and Auxiliary Activity	11	1
其他采矿业	Mining of other Ores		
制造业	Manufacturing Industry	1591	647
农副食品加工业	Processing of Food from Agriculture Products	41	4
食品制造业	Manufacture of Food	49	12
酒、饮料和精制茶制造业	Manufacture of Beverages	16	1
烟草制品业	Manufacture of Tobacco	3	1
纺织业	Manufacture of Textile	18	3
纺织服装、服饰业	Manufacture of Textile Wearing,Apparel	3	
皮革、毛皮、羽毛及其制品和制鞋业	Manufacture of Leather,Furs,Feather, Related Products and Footware	2	1
木材加工和木、竹、藤、棕、草制品业	Processing of Timber,Manufacture of Wood, Bamboo,Rattan,Palm and Straw Products	3	
家具制造业	Manufacture of Furniture	12	
造纸及纸制品业	Manufacture of Paper And Paper Products	22	3
印刷和记录媒介复制业	Printing and Reproduction of Recording Media	29	9
文教、工美、体育和娱乐用品制造业	Manufacture of Articles for Culture, Education,Arts and Crafts,Sport and Entertainment Activities	8	1
石油、煤炭及其他燃料加工业	Processing of Petroleum,Coal and Other Fuels	7	3
化学原料和化学制品制造业	Manufacture of Raw Chemical Materials and Chemical Products	82	38
医药制造业	Manufacture of Medicines	70	43

20-20 续表2 continued 2

指 标	Item	企业数（个）Number of Enterprises (unit)	有R&D活动的企业数 The Number of R&D Enterprises
化学纤维制造业	Manufacture of Chemical Fiber	3	1
橡胶和塑料制品业	Manufacture of Rubber and Manufacture of Plastic	44	9
非金属矿物制品业	Manufacture of Non-metallic Mineral Products	194	33
黑色金属冶炼和压延加工业	Smelting and Pressing of Ferrous Metals	14	1
有色金属冶炼和压延加工业	Smelting and Pressing of Non-ferrous Metals	47	29
金属制品业	Manufacture of Metal Products	108	20
通用设备制造业	Manufacture of General Purpose Machinery	97	50
专用设备制造业	Manufacture of Special Equipment	141	83
汽车制造业	Manufacture of Motor Vehicle	73	22
铁路、船舶、航空航天和其他运输设备制造业	Manufacture of Railway,Ship,Aerospace and Other Transport Equipments	102	60
电气机械和器材制造业	Manufacture of Electric Equipment and Machinery	170	70
计算机、通信和其他电子设备制造业	Manufacture of Communication Equipment, Computers and Other Electronic Equipment	137	94
仪器仪表制造业	Manufacture of Measuring Instruments and Machinery	71	46
其他制造业	Other Manufacturing	8	6
废弃资源综合利用业	Comprehensive Utilization of Waste Resources	4	1
金属制品、机械和设备修理业	Metal Products,Machinery and Equipment Repair Industry	13	3
电力、热力、燃气及水生产和供应业	Production and Distribution of Electricity, Heat,Gas and Water	68	6
电力、热力生产和供应业	Production and Supply of Electric Power and Heat Power	33	3
燃气生产和供应业	Production and Supply of Gas	20	1
水的生产和供应业	Production and Supply of Water	15	2

20-21 规模以上工业企业研究与试验发展（R&D）人员和经费支出情况（2020年）

指　标	Item	R&D人员（人）R&D personnel (person)	研究人员 Researchers
总计	**Total**	**40451**	**37271**
按企业规模分	**Grouped by Size of Enterprises**		
大型企业	Large-size	21904	20174
中型企业	Medium-size	8351	7647
小型企业	Small-size	10130	9390
微型企业	microenterprise	66	60
按登记注册类型分	**Grouped by Ragistered Status**		
内资企业	Domestic Investment Enterprises	37109	34214
国有企业	State-owned Enterprises	4056	3592
集体企业	Collective-owned Enterprises		
股份合作企业	Stock cooperative enterprises	20	19
联营企业	Affiliated companies		
有限责任公司	Limited Liability Corporations	21369	19840
股份有限公司	Share-holding Corporations Ltd.	4932	4566
私营企业	Private Enterprises	6715	6181
其他	Other Domestic Funded Enterprises	17	16
港、澳、台商投资企业	Enterprises with Funds from Hong Kong,Macao and Taiwan	203	195
外商投资企业	Foreign Funded Enterprises	3139	2862
按国民经济行业分	**Grouped by Sector**		
采矿业	Mining	2055	1888
煤炭开采和洗选业	Mining and Washing of Coal		
石油和天然气开采业	Extraction of Petroleum and Natural Gas	1280	1183
黑色金属矿采选业	Mining of Ferrous Metal Ores		
有色金属矿采选业	Mining of Non-ferrous Metal Ores		
非金属矿采选业	Mining and Processing of Nonmetal Ores		
开采专业及辅助性活动	Mining Professional and Auxiliary Activity	775	705
其他采矿业	Mining of other Ores		
制造业	Manufacturing Industry	37998	35014
农副食品加工业	Processing of Food from Agricultural Products	42	38
食品制造业	Manufacture of Foods	307	272
酒、饮料和精制茶制造业	Manufacture of Beverages	5	5
烟草制品业	Manufacture of Tobacco	14	13
纺织业	Manufacture of Textile	21	21
纺织服装、服饰业	Manufacture of Textile Wearing Apparel		
皮革、毛皮、羽毛及其制品和制鞋业	Manufacture of Leather,Fur, Feather and Related Products and Footwear	57	37

R&D Personnel and Expenditure Conditions of Industrial Enterprises above Designated Size (2020)

R&D经费内部支出（万元） R&D Internal Expenditure (10 000 yuan)	政府资金 Government Funds	企业资金 Enterprise Funds	境外资金 Foreign Funds
1570544	**180905**	**1386990**	**912**
971994	165994	805823	82
290796	9887	280207	520
305472	5023	298678	310
2282	1	2282	
1364091	180234	1181691	429
111911	35332	76580	
425		425	
789380	129191	659791	119
184751	13830	170911	
276759	1805	273196	310
864	76	788	
11287	404	10883	
195167	268	194416	483
69792	15857	53935	
46067	9041	37026	
23725	6816	16909	
1496167	164972	1328546	912
1069		1069	
3962	23	3939	
227		227	
1135		1135	
1352	56	1296	
374		374	

20–21 续表

指 标	Item	R&D人员（人） R&D personnel (person)	研究人员 Researchers
木材加工和木、竹、藤、棕、草制品业	Processing of Timber,Manufacture of Wood, Bamboo,Rattan,aplam and Straw Products		
家具制造业	Manufacture of Furniture		
造纸及纸制品业	Manufacture of Paper and Paper Products	34	28
印刷和记录媒介复制业	Printing,Reproduction of Recording Media	374	324
文教、工美、体育和娱乐用品制造业	Manufacture of Articles for Culture, Education,Arts and Crafts,Sport and Entertainment Activities	13	12
石油、煤炭及其他燃料加工业	Processing of Petroleum,Coal and Other Fuels	55	45
化学原料及化学制品制造业	Manufacture of Raw Chemical Materials and Chemical Products	1548	1473
医药制造业	Manufacture of Medicines	1420	1323
化学纤维制造业	Manufacture of Chemical Fibers	64	54
橡胶和塑料制品业	Manufacture of Rubber and Manufacture of Plastics	286	268
非金属矿物制品业	Manufacture of Non-metallic Mineral Products	1037	955
黑色金属冶炼和压延加工业	Smelting and Pressing of Ferrous Metals	18	17
有色金属冶炼和压延加工业	Smelting and Pressing of Non-ferrous Metals	862	805
金属制品业	Manufacture of Metal Products	923	776
通用设备制造业	Manufacture of General Purpose Machinery	1601	1454
专用设备制造业	Manufacture of Special Equipment	2973	2735
汽车制造业	Manufacture of Motor Vehicle	4109	3886
铁路、船舶、航空航天和其他运输设备制造业	Manufacture of Railway,Ship,Aerospace and Other Transport Equipments	8677	7936
电气机械和器材制造业	Manufacture of Electric Equipment and Machinery	3066	2849
计算机、通讯和其他电子设备制造业	Manufacture of Communication Equipment, Computers and other Electronic Equipment	7068	6633
仪器仪表制造业	Manufacture of Measuring Instruments and Machinery	3219	2869
其他制造业	Other Manufacturing	155	147
废弃资源综合利用业	Comprehensive Utilization Of Waste Resources	4	4
金属制品、机械和设备修理业	Metal Products,Machinery and Equipment Repair Industry	46	35
电力、热力、燃气及水生产和供应业	Production and Distribution of Electricity,Heat,Gas and Water	398	369
电力、热力生产和供应业	Production and Supply of Electric Power and Heat Power	299	285
燃气生产和供应业	Gas mining and supplying industry	40	28
水的生产和供应业	Production and Supply of Water	59	56

continued

R&D经费内部支出（万元） R&D Internal Expenditure (10 000 yuan)	政府资金 Government Funds	企业资金 Enterprise Funds	境外资金 Foreign Funds
334		334	
9536		9536	
51		51	
714		714	
63715	4582	59117	
51863	116	51745	
1706		1706	
17033		17033	
32613	168	32446	
717		717	
37185	3689	33484	
35532	16960	18572	
34949	1673	33276	
102791	5260	97220	310
260282	407	259875	
269104	106942	161815	82
114706	3754	109835	37
399314	2389	396109	483
52343	18944	33372	
2391	9	2382	
62		62	
1108		1108	
4586	77	4509	
1438	76	1362	
2456	1	2455	
692		692	

20-22 规模以上工业企业新产品开发、生产及销售情况（2020年）

指 标	Item	新产品开发项目数（项）Number of New Product Development Projects(item)
总计	**Total**	**5849**
按企业规模分	**Grouped by Size of Enterprises**	
大型企业	Large-size	1588
中型企业	Medium-size	1100
小型企业	Small-size	3079
微型企业	microenterprise	82
按登记注册类型分	**Grouped by Ragistered Status**	
内资企业	Domestic Investment Enterprises	5529
国有企业	State-owned Enterprises	429
集体企业	Collective-owned Enterprises	
股份合作企业	Stock cooperative enterprises	2
联营企业	Affiliated companies	
有限责任公司	Limited Liability Corporations	2478
股份有限公司	Share-holding Corperation Ltd.	691
私营企业	Private Enterprises	1928
其他	Other Domestic Funded Enterprises	1
港、澳、台商投资企业	Enterprises with Funds from Hong Kong,Macao and Taiwan	64
外商投资企业	Foreign Funded Enterprises	256
按国民经济行业分	**Grouped by Sector**	
采矿业	Mining	147
煤炭开采和洗选业	Mining and Washing of Coal	
石油和天然气开采业	Extraction of Petroleum and Natural Gas	2
黑色金属矿采选业	Mining of Ferrous Metal Ores	
有色金属矿采选业	Mining of Non-ferrous Metal Ores	
非金属矿采选业	Mining and Processing of Nonmetal Ores	
开采专业及辅助性活动	Mining Professional and Auxiliary Activity	145
其他采矿业	Mining of other Ores	
制造业	Manufacturing Industry	5640
农副食品加工业	Processing of Food from Agricultural Products	17
食品制造业	Manufacture of Foods	61
酒、饮料和精制茶制造业	Manufacture of Beverages	17
烟草制品业	Manufacture of Tobacco	4
纺织业	Manufacture of Textile	27
纺织服装、服饰业	Manufacture of Textile Wearing Apparel	6
皮革、毛皮、羽毛及其制品和制鞋业	Manufacture of Leather,Fur, Feather and Related Products and Footwear	5

New Product Development, Production and Sales of Above-scale Industrial Enterprises (2020)

新产品开发经费支出（万元） New Product Development Expenditure (10 000 yuan)	新产品销售收入（万元） Sales Revenue of New Products (10 000 yuan)
2003117	**16061829**
1337566	11527067
306806	2552324
348391	1942325
10354	40113
1787229	15000996
122634	468908
151	2961
1277183	9748564
142898	1132371
243688	3645858
676	2335
12194	639296
203694	421536
36086	1238
310	
35776	1238
1962421	16060543
2564	23903
5480	55912
1457	3315
845	261203
4478	15590
707	2800
600	6058

20-22 续表

指　标	Item	新产品开发项目数（项）Number of New Product Development Projects(item)
木材加工和木、竹、藤、棕、草制品业	Processing of Timber,Manufacture of Wood, Bamboo,Rattan,aplam and Straw Products	1
家具制造业	Manufacture of Furniture	1
造纸及纸制品业	Manufacture of Paper and Paper Products	
印刷和记录媒介复制业	Printing,Reproduction of Recording Media	45
文教、工美、体育和娱乐用品制造业	Manufacture of Articles for Culture, Education,Arts and Crafts,Sport and Entertainment Activities	2
石油、煤炭及其他燃料加工业	Processing of Petroleum,Coal and Other Fuels	15
化学原料及化学制品制造业	Manufacture of Raw Chemical Materials and Chemical Products	373
医药制造业	Manufacture of Medicines	228
化学纤维制造业	Manufacture of Chemical Fibers	13
橡胶和塑料制品业	Manufacture of Rubber and Manufacture of Plastics	77
非金属矿物制品业	Manufacture of Non-metallic Mineral Products	232
黑色金属冶炼和压延加工业	Smelting and Pressing of Ferrous Metals	3
有色金属冶炼和压延加工业	Smelting and Pressing of Non-ferrous Metals	273
金属制品业	Manufacture of Metal Products	192
通用设备制造业	Manufacture of General Purpose Machinery	320
专用设备制造业	Manufacture of Special Equipment	629
汽车制造业	Manufacture of Motor Vehicle	251
铁路、船舶、航空航天和其他运输设备制造业	Manufacture of Railway,Ship,Aerospace and Other Transport Equipments	701
电气机械和器材制造业	Manufacture of Electric Equipment and Machinery	992
计算机、通讯和其他电子设备制造业	Manufacture of Communication Equipment, Computers and other Electronic Equipment	823
仪器仪表制造业	Manufacture of Measuring Instruments and Machinery	319
其他制造业	Other Manufacturing	11
废弃资源综合利用业	Comprehensive Utilization Of Waste Resources	
金属制品、机械和设备修理业	Metal Products,Machinery and Equipment Repair Industry	2
电力、热力、燃气及水生产和供应业	Production and Distribution of Electricity,Heat,Gas and Water	62
电力、热力生产和供应业	Production and Supply of Electric Power and Heat Power	54
燃气生产和供应业	Gas mining and supplying industry	8
水的生产和供应业	Production and Supply of Water	

continued

新产品开发经费支出（万元） New Product Development Expenditure (10 000 yuan)	新产品销售收入 （万元） Sales Revenue of New Products (10 000 yuan)
134	
314	27004
	8
7875	45000
54	27
647	4740
49224	352140
50168	312618
1937	
22253	228015
28266	248902
903	2636
47439	560654
56563	175255
64389	361338
110021	679975
284731	5830727
610100	2092225
156498	3836236
390906	725899
62419	193719
1172	14646
278	
4610	48
2198	
2412	48

20-23 规模以上非工业重点行业企业研究与试验发展（R&D）基本情况（2020年）

R&D Project Status of Non-Industrial Key Enterprises above Designated Size(2020)

指 标	Item	单位数（个）Number of Enterprises (unit)	#有R&D活动单位数（个）#The Number of R&D active units(unit)
总计	**Total**	**2234**	**213**
按企业规模分	**Grouped by Size of Enterprises**		
大型企业	Large-size	201	69
中型企业	Medium-size	521	64
小型企业	Small-size	1187	77
微型企业	Microenterprise	325	3
按登记注册类型分	**Grouped by Registered Status**		
内资企业	Domestic Investment Enterprises	2164	207
港、澳、台商投资企业	Enterprises with Funds from Hong Kong,Macao And Taiwan	25	3
外商投资企业	Foreign Funded Enterprises	45	3
按国民经济行业分	**Grouped by Sector**		
建筑业	Construction	405	39
交通运输、仓储和邮政业	Traffic,Transport,Storage and Post	237	3
信息传输、软件和信息技术服务业	Information Transmission,Computer Services and Software	333	66
租赁和商务服务业	Leasing and Business Services	444	6
科学研究和技术服务业	Scientific Research,Technical Services	406	96
水利、环境和公共设施管理业	Management of Water Conservancy, Environment and Public Facilities	68	1
卫生和社会工作	Health,Social Services	66	1
文化、体育和娱乐业	Culture,Sports and Entertainment	275	1

20-24 规模以上非工业重点行业企业研究与试验发展（R&D）人员和经费支出情况（2020年）

R&D Personnel and Expenditure of Non-Industrial Key Enterprises above Designated Size (2020)

指 标	Item	R&D人员（人）R&D personnel (person)	#研究人员 #Researchers
总计	**Total**	**14418**	**13737**
按企业规模分	**Grouped by Size of Enterprises**		
大型企业	Large-size	11438	11044
中型企业	Medium-size	2101	1908
小型企业	Small-size	855	766
微型企业	Microenterprise	24	19
按登记注册类型分	**Grouped by Registered Status**		
内资企业	Domestic Investment Enterprises	13998	13331
港、澳、台商投资企业	Enterprises with Funds from Hong Kong,Macao And Taiwan	11	11
外商投资企业	Foreign Funded Enterprises	409	395
按国民经济行业分	**Grouped by Sector**		
建筑业	Construction	2997	2795
交通运输、仓储和邮政业	Traffic,Transport,Storage and Post	48	43
信息传输、软件和信息技术服务业	Information Transmission,Computer Services and Software	5926	5778
租赁和商务服务业	Leasing and Business Services	27	23
科学研究和技术服务业	Scientific Research,Technical Services	5390	5075
水利、环境和公共设施管理业	Management of Water Conservancy, Environment and Public Facilities	21	16
卫生和社会工作	Health,Social Services	3	3
文化、体育和娱乐业	Culture,Sports and Entertainment	6	4

20-24 续表

指 标	Item	R&D经费内部支出（万元） R&D Internal Expenditure (10 000 yuan)
总计	**Total**	**607181**
按企业规模分	**Grouped by Size of Enterprises**	
大型企业	Large-size	530127
中型企业	Medium-size	46086
小型企业	Small-size	30502
微型企业	Microenterprise	466
按登记注册类型分	**Grouped by Registered Status**	
内资企业	Domestic Investment Enterprises	591611
港、澳、台商投资企业	Enterprises with Funds from Hong Kong,Macao And Taiwan	437
外商投资企业	Foreign Funded Enterprises	15132
按国民经济行业分	**Grouped by Sector**	
建筑业	Construction	174328
交通运输、仓储和邮政业	Traffic,Transport,Storage and Post	850
信息传输、软件和信息技术服务业	Information Transmission,Computer Services and Software	265348
租赁和商务服务业	Leasing and Business Services	1126
科学研究和技术服务业	Scientific Research,Technical Services	165427
水利、环境和公共设施管理业	Management of Water Conservancy, Environment and Public Facilities	42
卫生和社会工作	Health,Social Services	6
文化、体育和娱乐业	Culture,Sports and Entertainment	54

continued

#政府资金 #Government Funds	#企业资金 # Enterprise Funds
12143	**594743**
9833	520295
1651	44187
659	29795
	466
12143	579173
	437
	15132
85	174243
	850
722	264367
15	1111
11320	154070
	42
	6
	54

20-25 主要年份知识产权情况

Intellectual Property Rights in Major Years

指 标	Item	2015	2016	2017	2018	2019	2020	2021
一、专利申请合计数（件）	**Patents Application Accepted(piece)**	**60986**	**45417**	**81110**	**56408**	**72377**	**68353**	
发明专利	Inventions	14024	18282	40439	24074	29297	31376	
实用新型专利	Utility Models	15735	18087	22461	24313	28087	33406	
外观专利	Designs	31227	9048	18210	8021	14993	3571	
二、授权专利合计（件）	**Patents Application Granted(piece)**	**25103**	**37744**	**25042**	**31640**	**34123**	**45407**	**64131**
发明专利	Inventions	5873	6565	7902	8025	9017	11067	14055
实用新型专利	Utility Models	12030	12035	11595	17070	18937	29916	46123
外观专利	Designs	7200	19144	5545	6545	6169	4424	3953
三、注册商标（件）	**Registered Trade Mark(piece)**	**30527**	**23887**	**27060**	**43205**	**61692**	**58842**	**81879**

注：1.本表数据由市场监管局提供，并对历史数据进行了重新修订。
2.本表数据为西安原口径数据。
3.专利申请合计数中2020年的数据为截止到2020年11月底的数据，此数据国家以后不再公布。

20-26 主要年份民事知识产权维权情况

Protection of Civil Intellectual Property Rights in Major Years

单位：件 (piece)

指 标	Item	2015	2016	2017	2018	2019	2020	2021
1. 专利纠纷	Patent controversies	130	95	112	449	233	157	254
2. 商标纠纷	Trade mark controversies	277	353	404	892	744	1245	1399
3. 著作权纠纷	Copyright controversies	327	404	190	520	1852	1413	1216
4. 技术合同纠纷	Technological contract controversies	12	10	36	47	52	74	90
5. 其他知识产权纠纷	Others IPR controversies	67	25	110	182	366	667	352

注：1.本表数据由市中级人民法院提供。
2.本表数据为西安原口径数据。

20-27 规模以上工业企业自主知识产权情况（2020年）

The Independent Intellectual Property Rights of Industrial Enterprises above Designated Size (2020)

指 标	Item	专利申请数（件） Number of Patent Applications (piece)	#发明专利 Invention of Patent	期末有效发明专利数（件） Number of Valid Invention Patents At the End of the Term (piece)
总计	**Total**	**9399**	**4467**	**14892**
按企业规模分	**Grouped by Size of Enterprises**			
大型企业	Large-size	3446	1926	5073
中型企业	Medium-size	1853	922	3298
小型企业	Small-size	4051	1600	6329
微型企业	Microenterprise	49	19	192
按登记注册类型分	**Grouped by Registered Status**			
内资企业	Domestic Investment Enterprises	8975	4363	13891
国有企业	State-owned Enterprises	805	557	1625
集体企业	Collective-owned Enterprise			
股份合作企业	Stock Cooperative Enterprises	3	1	1
联营企业	Affiliated Enterprise			
有限责任公司	Limited Liability Corporations	4751	2289	6308
股份有限公司	Share-holding Corporation Ltd	1066	523	2005
私营企业	Private Enterprise	2345	993	3952
其他	Other Domestic Funded Enterprises	5		
港、澳、台商投资企业	Enterprises with Funds from Hong Kong,Macao And Taiwan	182	41	560
外商投资企业	Foreign Funded Enterprises	242	63	441
按国民经济行业大类分	**Grouped by Sector**			
采矿业	Mining	257	186	597
煤炭开采和洗选业	Mining and Washing of Coal			
石油和天然气开采业	Extraction of Petroleum and Natural Gas	34	26	56
黑色金属矿采选业	Mining of Ferrous Metal Ores			
有色金属矿采选业	Mining of Non-ferrous Metal Ores			
非金属矿采选业	Mining and Processing of Nonmetal Ores			
开采专业及辅助性活动	Mining Professional and Auxiliary Activity	223	160	541
其他采矿业	Mining of other Ores			
制造业	Manufacturing Industry	8795	4112	13844
农副食品加工业	Processing of Food from Agriculture Products	18	7	3
食品制造业	Manufacture of Food	65	8	50
酒、饮料和精制茶制造业	Manufacture of Beverages	52	10	42
烟草制品业	Manufacture of Tobacco	111	15	16
纺织业	Manufacture of Textile	14	6	40
纺织服装、服饰业	Manufacture of Textile Wearing,Apparel			4
皮革、毛皮、羽毛及其制品和制鞋业	Manufacture of Leather,Furs,Feather, Related Products and Footware	18	4	5

20-27 续表 continued

指 标	Item	专利申请数（件）Number of Patent Applications (piece)	#发明专利 Invention of Patent	期末有效发明专利数（件）Number of Valid Invention Patents At the End of the Term (piece)
木材加工和木、竹、藤、棕、草制品业	Processing of Timber,Manufacture of Wood, Bamboo,Rattan,Palm and Straw Products			
家具制造业	Manufacture of Furniture	34	34	294
造纸及纸制品业	Manufacture of Paper And Paper Products	11	6	11
印刷和记录媒介复制业	Printing and Reproduction of Recording Media	73	11	91
文教、工美、体育和娱乐用品制造业	Manufacture of Articles for Culture, Education,Arts and Crafts,Sport and Entertainment Activities	2		4
石油、煤炭及其他燃料加工业	Processing of Petroleum,Coking and Processing of Nuclear Fuel	54	24	50
化学原料和化学制品制造业	Manufacture of Raw Chemical Materials and Chemical Products	446	334	794
医药制造业	Manufacture of Medicines	139	70	646
化学纤维制造业	Manufacture of Chemical Fiber			69
橡胶和塑料制品业	Manufacture of Rubber and Manufacture of Plastic	80	15	174
非金属矿物制品业	Manufacture of Non-metallic Mineral Products	289	86	284
黑色金属冶炼和压延加工业	Smelting and Pressing of Ferrous Metals	5		17
有色金属冶炼和压延加工业	Smelting and Pressing of Non-ferrous Metals	367	238	847
金属制品业	Manufacture of Metal Products	252	132	398
通用设备制造业	Manufacture of General Purpose Machinery	575	216	733
专用设备制造业	Manufacture of Special Equipment	1300	566	2169
汽车制造业	Manufacture of Motor Vehicle	896	255	476
铁路、船舶、航空航天和其他运输设备制造业	Manufacture of Railway,Ship,Aerospace and Other Transport Equipments	1312	886	2153
电气机械和器材制造业	Manufacture of Electric Equipment and Machinery	932	316	1307
计算机、通信和其他电子设备制造业	Manufacture of Communication Equipment, Computers and Other Electronic Equipment	1182	594	1979
仪器仪表制造业	Manufacture of Measuring Instruments and Machinery	538	273	1098
其他制造业	Other Manufacturing	22	6	67
废弃资源综合利用业	Comprehensive Utilization Of Waste Resources			6
金属制品、机械和设备修理业	Metal Products,Machinery and Equipment Repair Industry	8		17
电力、热力、燃气及水生产和供应业	Production and Distribution of Electricity, Heat,Gas and Water	347	169	451
电力、热力生产和供应业	Production and Supply of Electric Power and Heat Power	320	167	420
燃气生产和供应业	Production and Supply of Gas	20	1	
水的生产和供应业	Production and Supply of Water	7	1	31

20–28　规模以上非工业重点行业企业知识产权（2020年）

Intellectual Property Rights of Non-Industrial Key Enterprises above Designated Size (2020)

指　标	Item	专利申请数（件）Number of Patent Applications (piece)	#发明专利 Invention of Patent	期末有效发明专利数（件）Number of Valid Invention Patents At the End of the Term (piece)
总计	**Total**	**7206**	**3343**	**6686**
按企业规模分	**Grouped by Size of Enterprises**			
大型企业	Large-size	6067	2876	4308
中型企业	Medium-size	482	176	955
小型企业	Small-size	653	288	1404
微型企业	Microenterprise	4	3	19
按登记注册类型分	**Grouped by Registered Status**			
内资企业	Domestic Investment Enterprises	7181	3336	6633
港、澳、台商投资企业	Enterprises with Funds from Hong Kong,Macao And Taiwan	11		14
外商投资企业	Foreign Funded Enterprises	14	7	39
按国民经济行业分	**Grouped by Sector**			
建筑业	Construction	1782	435	1219
交通运输、仓储和邮政业	Traffic,Transport,Storage and Post	3	2	18
信息传输、软件和信息技术服务业	Information Transmission,Computer Services and Software	954	566	2074
租赁和商务服务业	Leasing and Business Services	23	16	36
科学研究和技术服务业	Scientific Research,Technical Services	4415	2321	3322
水利、环境和公共设施管理业	Management of Water Conservancy, Environment and Public Facilities	1	1	8
卫生和社会工作	Health,Social Services			
文化、体育和娱乐业	Culture,Sports and Entertainment	28	2	9

20-29 规模（限额）以上企业创新活动总体情况（2020年）

指　标	Item	企业数（个）Number of Enterprises (unit)	开展创新活动企业数（个）Number of Innovation Activity Enterprises(unit)
总计	**Total**	**6346**	**2961**
按企业规模分	**Grouped by Size of Enterprises**		
大型企业	Large-size	340	258
中型企业	Medium-size	1577	756
小型企业	Small-size	3700	1798
微型企业	Microenterprise	729	149
按登记注册类型分	**Grouped by Registered Status**		
内资企业	Domestic Investment Enterprises	6063	2812
港、澳、台商投资企业	Enterprises with Funds from Hong Kong,Macao And Taiwan	76	34
外商投资企业	Foreign Funded Enterprises	207	115
按行业分	**Grouped by Sector**		
采矿业	Mining	12	7
制造业	Manufacturing Industry	1591	1114
电力、热力、燃气及水生产和供应业	Production and Distribution of Electricity, Heat,Gas and Water	68	29
建筑业	Construction	1073	358
批发和零售业	Wholesale and Retail Trades	2114	706
交通运输、仓储和邮政业	Traffic,Transport,Storage and Post	237	65
信息传输、软件和信息技术服务业	Information Transmission,Computer Services and Software	333	266
租赁和商务服务业	Leasing and Business Services	444	159
科学研究和技术服务业	Scientific Research,Technical Sevice	406	238
水利、环境和公共设施管理业	Management of Water Conservancy, Environment and Public Facilities	68	19

Basic Statistics on Enterprise Innovation Activities above Designated Size (2020)

#实现创新企业 Achieve Innovative Enterprise	#同时实现四种创新企业 Achieve Four Kinds of Innovative Enterprises At Same Time	#实现产品创新企业 Achieve Product Innovation Enterprises	#实现工艺创新企业 Achieve Process Innovation Enterprises	#实现组织创新企业 Achieve Organizational Innovation Enterprises	#实现营销创新企业 Achieve Marketing Innovation Enterprises
2843	**568**	**1264**	**1480**	**2136**	**1669**
249	78	147	175	193	143
730	131	296	352	568	416
1717	338	778	910	1261	1018
147	21	43	43	114	92
2706	542	1198	1398	2059	1594
32	5	12	14	18	20
105	21	54	68	59	55
7		2	5	6	3
1059	310	689	801	736	640
27	3	5	11	23	12
345	37	92	154	297	115
702	70	143	161	526	543
62	6	11	17	53	25
248	74	167	154	191	142
155	19	40	46	120	89
220	48	113	127	169	92
18	1	2	4	15	8

20-29 续表

指 标	Item	开展创新活动企业 Innovation Activity Enterprises
总计	**Total**	**46.7**
按企业规模分	**Grouped by Size of Enterprises**	
大型企业	Large-size	75.9
中型企业	Medium-size	47.9
小型企业	Small-size	48.6
微型企业	Microenterprise	20.4
按登记注册类型分	**Grouped by Registered Status**	
内资企业	Domestic Investment Enterprises	46.4
港、澳、台商投资企业	Enterprises with Funds from Hong Kong,Macao And Taiwan	44.7
外商投资企业	Foreign Funded Enterprises	55.6
按行业分	**Grouped by Sector**	
采矿业	Mining	58.3
制造业	Manufacturing Industry	70.0
电力、热力、燃气及水生产和供应业	Production and Distribution of Electricity, Heat,Gas and Water	42.6
建筑业	Construction	33.4
批发和零售业	Wholesale and Retail Trades	33.4
交通运输、仓储和邮政业	Traffic,Transport,Storage and Post	27.4
信息传输、软件和信息技术服务业	Information Transmission,Computer Services and Software	79.9
租赁和商务服务业	Leasing and Business Services	35.8
科学研究和技术服务业	Scientific Research,Technical Sevice	58.6
水利、环境和公共设施管理业	Management of Water Conservancy, Environment and Public Facilities	27.9

continued

在全部企业中占比（%） The Proportion in All Enterprises(%)					
#实现 创新企业 Achieve Innovative Enterprise	#同时实现四种创新企业 Achieve Four Kinds of Innovative Enterprises At Same Time	#实现产品创新企业 Achieve Product Innovation Enterprises	#实现工艺创新企业 Achieve Process Innovation Enterprises	#实现组织创新企业 Achieve Organizational Innovation Enterprises	#实现营销创新企业 Achieve Marketing Innovation Enterprises
44.8	**9.0**	**19.9**	**23.3**	**33.7**	**26.3**
73.2	22.9	43.2	51.5	56.8	42.1
46.3	8.3	18.8	22.3	36.0	26.4
46.4	9.1	21.0	24.6	34.1	27.5
20.2	2.9	5.9	5.9	15.6	12.6
44.6	8.9	19.8	23.1	34.0	26.3
42.1	6.6	15.8	18.4	23.7	26.3
50.7	10.1	26.1	32.9	28.5	26.6
58.3		16.7	41.7	50.0	25.0
66.6	19.5	43.3	50.3	46.3	40.2
39.7	4.4	7.4	16.2	33.8	17.6
32.2	3.4	8.6	14.4	27.7	10.7
33.2	3.3	6.8	7.6	24.9	25.7
26.2	2.5	4.6	7.2	22.4	10.5
74.5	22.2	50.2	46.2	57.4	42.6
34.9	4.3	9.0	10.4	27.0	20.0
54.2	11.8	27.8	31.3	41.6	22.7
26.5	1.5	2.9	5.9	22.1	11.8

20-30 规模以上工业企业创新活动总体情况（2020年）

指　标	Item	企业数（个） Number of Enterprises (unit)	开展创新活动企业数（个） Number of Innovation Activity Enterprises (unit)
总计	**Total**	**1671**	**1150**
按企业规模分	**Grouped by Size of Enterprises**		
大型企业	Large-size	69	60
中型企业	Medium-size	181	153
小型企业	Small-size	1299	905
微型企业	Microenterprise	122	32
按登记注册类型分	**Grouped by Registered Status**		
内资企业	Domestic Investment Enterprises	1547	1072
港、澳、台商投资企业	Enterprises with Funds from Hong Kong,Macao And Taiwan	21	11
外商投资企业	Foreign Funded Enterprises	103	67
按行业分	**Grouped by Sector**		
采矿业	Mining	12	7
煤炭开采和洗选业	Mining and Washing of Coal		
石油和天然气开采业	Extraction of Petroleum and Natural Gas	1	1
黑色金属矿采选业	Mining of Ferrous Metal Ores		
有色金属矿采选业	Mining of Non-ferrous Metal Ores		
非金属矿采选业	Mining and Processing of Nonmetal Ores		
开采专业及辅助性活动	Mining Professional and Auxiliary Activity	11	6
其他采矿业	Mining of other Ores		
制造业	Manufacturing Industry	1591	1114
农副食品加工业	Processing of Food from Agriculture Products	41	16
食品制造业	Manufacture of Food	49	30
酒、饮料和精制茶制造业	Manufacture of Beverages	16	11
烟草制品业	Manufacture of Tobacco	3	1
纺织业	Manufacture of Textile	18	10
纺织服装、服饰业	Manufacture of Textile Wearing,Apparel	3	2
皮革、毛皮、羽毛及其制品和制鞋业	Manufacture of Leather,Furs,Feather, Related Products and Footware	2	2
木材加工和木、竹、藤、棕、草制品业	Processing of Timber,Manufacture of Wood, Bamboo,Rattan,Palm and Straw Products	3	2
家具制造业	Manufacture of Furniture	12	5
造纸和纸制品业	Manufacture of Paper And Paper Products	22	9
印刷和记录媒介复制业	Printing and Reproduction of Recording Media	29	19

Basic Statistics on Industrial Enterprise Innovation Activities above Designated Size (2020)

#实现创新企业 Achieve Innovative Enterprise	#同时实现四种创新企业 Achieve Four Kinds of Innovative Enterprises At Same Time	#实现产品创新企业 Achieve Product Innovation Enterprises	#实现工艺创新企业 Achieve Process Innovation Enterprises	#实现组织创新企业 Achieve Organizational Innovation Enterprises	#实现营销创新企业 Achieve Marketing Innovation Enterprises
1093	**313**	**696**	**817**	**765**	**655**
57	28	46	50	48	37
148	50	112	120	107	81
858	228	524	632	591	519
30	7	14	15	19	18
1022	294	653	761	725	618
10	3	5	7	6	7
61	16	38	49	34	30
7		2	5	6	3
1			1	1	1
6		2	4	5	2
1059	310	689	801	736	640
15	2	8	7	5	12
30	8	16	16	19	25
11		5	4	3	10
1	1	1	1	1	1
10	4	8	8	7	8
2	1	1	2	2	2
2	1	2	2	2	1
2				2	2
5		1		2	4
8		2	5	3	4
17	4	8	15	9	7

20-30 续表1

指 标	Item	开展创新活动企业 Innovation Activity Enterprises
总计	**Total**	**68.8**
按企业规模分	**Grouped by Size of Enterprises**	
大型企业	Large-size	87.0
中型企业	Medium-size	84.5
小型企业	Small-size	69.7
微型企业	Microenterprise	26.2
按登记注册类型分	**Grouped by Registered Status**	
内资企业	Domestic Investment Enterprises	69.3
港、澳、台商投资企业	Enterprises with Funds from Hong Kong,Macao And Taiwan	52.4
外商投资企业	Foreign Funded Enterprises	65.0
按行业分	**Grouped by Sector**	
采矿业	Mining	58.3
煤炭开采和洗选业	Mining and Washing of Coal	
石油和天然气开采业	Extraction of Petroleum and Natural Gas	100.0
黑色金属矿采选业	Mining of Ferrous Metal Ores	
有色金属矿采选业	Mining of Non-ferrous Metal Ores	
非金属矿采选业	Mining and Processing of Nonmetal Ores	
开采专业及辅助性活动	Mining Professional and Auxiliary Activity	54.5
其他采矿业	Mining of other Ores	
制造业	Manufacturing Industry	70.0
农副食品加工业	Processing of Food from Agriculture Products	39.0
食品制造业	Manufacture of Food	61.2
酒、饮料和精制茶制造业	Manufacture of Beverages	68.8
烟草制品业	Manufacture of Tobacco	33.3
纺织业	Manufacture of Textile	55.6
纺织服装、服饰业	Manufacture of Textile Wearing,Apparel	66.7
皮革、毛皮、羽毛及其制品和制鞋业	Manufacture of Leather,Furs,Feather, Related Products and Footware	100.0
木材加工和木、竹、藤、棕、草制品业	Processing of Timber,Manufacture of Wood, Bamboo,Rattan,Palm and Straw Products	66.7
家具制造业	Manufacture of Furniture	41.7
造纸和纸制品业	Manufacture of Paper And Paper Products	40.9
印刷和记录媒介复制业	Printing and Reproduction of Recording Media	65.5

continued 1

在全部企业中占比（%） The Proportion in All Enterprises (%)					
#实现创新企业 Achieve Innovative Enterprise	#同时实现四种创新企业 Achieve Four Kinds of Innovative Enterprises At Same Time	#实现产品创新企业 Achieve Product Innovation Enterprises	#实现工艺创新企业 Achieve Process Innovation Enterprises	#实现组织创新企业 Achieve Organizational Innovation Enterprises	#实现营销创新企业 Achieve Marketing Innovation Enterprises
65.4	**18.7**	**41.7**	**48.9**	**45.8**	**39.2**
82.6	40.6	66.7	72.5	69.6	53.6
81.8	27.6	61.9	66.3	59.1	44.8
66.1	17.6	40.3	48.7	45.5	40.0
24.6	5.7	11.5	12.3	15.6	14.8
66.1	19.0	42.2	49.2	46.9	39.9
47.6	14.3	23.8	33.3	28.6	33.3
59.2	15.5	36.9	47.6	33.0	29.1
58.3		16.7	41.7	50.0	25.0
100.0			100.0	100.0	100.0
54.5		18.2	36.4	45.5	18.2
66.6	19.5	43.3	50.3	46.3	40.2
36.6	4.9	19.5	17.1	12.2	29.3
61.2	16.3	32.7	32.7	38.8	51.0
68.8		31.3	25.0	18.8	62.5
33.3	33.3	33.3	33.3	33.3	33.3
55.6	22.2	44.4	44.4	38.9	44.4
66.7	33.3	33.3	66.7	66.7	66.7
100.0	50.0	100.0	100.0	100.0	50.0
66.7				66.7	66.7
41.7		8.3		16.7	33.3
36.4		9.1	22.7	13.6	18.2
58.6	13.8	27.6	51.7	31.0	24.1

20-30 续表2

指 标	Item	企业数（个） Number of Enterprises (unit)	开展创新活动企业数（个） Number of Innovation Activity Enterprises (unit)
文教、工美、体育和娱乐用品制造业	Manufacture of Articles for Culture, Education,Arts and Crafts,Sport and Entertainment Activities	8	5
石油、煤炭及其他燃料加工业	Processing of Petroleum,Coking and Processing of Nuclear Fuel	7	4
化学原料和化学制品制造业	Manufacture of Raw Chemical Materials and Chemical Products	82	61
医药制造业	Manufacture of Medicines	70	59
化学纤维制造业	Manufacture of Chemical Fiber	3	2
橡胶和塑料制品业	Manufacture of Rubber and Manufacture of Plastic	44	26
非金属矿物制品业	Manufacture of Non-metallic Mineral Products	194	76
黑色金属冶炼和压延加工业	Smelting and Pressing of Ferrous Metals	14	5
有色金属冶炼和压延加工业	Smelting and Pressing of Non-ferrous Metals	47	39
金属制品业	Manufacture of Metal Products	108	57
通用设备制造业	Manufacture of General Purpose Machinery	97	80
专用设备制造业	Manufacture of Special Equipment	141	126
汽车制造业	Manufacture of Motor Vehicle	73	55
铁路、船舶、航空航天和其他运输设备制造业	Manufacture of Railway,Ship,Aerospace and Other Transport Equipments	102	84
电气机械和器材制造业	Manufacture of Electric Equipment and Machinery	170	122
计算机、通信和其他电子设备制造业	Manufacture of Communication Equipment, Computers and Other Electronic Equipment	137	124
仪器仪表制造业	Manufacture of Measuring Instruments and Machinery	71	65
其他制造业	Other Manufacturing	8	7
废弃资源综合利用业	Comprehensive Utilization Of Waste Resources	4	1
金属制品、机械和设备修理业	Metal Products,Machinery and Equipment Repair Industry	13	9
电力、热力、燃气及水生产和供应业	Production and Distribution of Electricity, Heat,Gas and Water	68	29
电力、热力生产和供应业	Production and Supply of Electric Power and Heat Power	33	16
燃气生产和供应业	Production and Supply of Gas	20	7
水的生产和供应业	Production and Supply of Water	15	6

continued 2

#实现创新企业 Achieve Innovative Enterprise	#同时实现四种创新企业 Achieve Four Kinds of Innovative Enterprises At Same Time	#实现产品创新企业 Achieve Product Innovation Enterprises	#实现工艺创新企业 Achieve Process Innovation Enterprises	#实现组织创新企业 Achieve Organizational Innovation Enterprises	#实现营销创新企业 Achieve Marketing Innovation Enterprises
5		2	3	2	5
4	3	3	4	4	3
58	22	45	45	44	38
56	14	30	42	42	42
2			2	1	1
26	5	14	13	15	14
71	9	20	44	52	41
5	2	4	4	5	2
39	15	32	35	25	22
54	6	23	35	38	27
73	24	51	59	54	39
119	41	85	99	79	76
51	17	38	39	39	27
80	22	55	68	56	37
119	38	78	98	84	78
117	45	101	96	85	67
63	24	51	44	47	38
7	2	5	5	5	6
7			6	4	1
27	3	5	11	23	12
15	1	2	4	13	7
6		1	3	5	2
6	2	2	4	5	3

20-30 续表3

指 标	Item	开展创新活动企业 Innovation Activity Enterprises
文教、工美、体育和娱乐用品制造业	Manufacture of Articles for Culture, Education,Arts and Crafts,Sport and Entertainment Activities	62.5
石油、煤炭及其他燃料加工业	Processing of Petroleum,Coking and Processing of Nuclear Fuel	57.1
化学原料和化学制品制造业	Manufacture of Raw Chemical Materials and Chemical Products	74.4
医药制造业	Manufacture of Medicines	84.3
化学纤维制造业	Manufacture of Chemical Fiber	66.7
橡胶和塑料制品业	Manufacture of Rubber and Manufacture of Plastic	59.1
非金属矿物制品业	Manufacture of Non-metallic Mineral Products	39.2
黑色金属冶炼和压延加工业	Smelting and Pressing of Ferrous Metals	35.7
有色金属冶炼和压延加工业	Smelting and Pressing of Non-ferrous Metals	83.0
金属制品业	Manufacture of Metal Products	52.8
通用设备制造业	Manufacture of General Purpose Machinery	82.5
专用设备制造业	Manufacture of Special Equipment	89.4
汽车制造业	Manufacture of Motor Vehicle	75.3
铁路、船舶、航空航天和其他运输设备制造业	Manufacture of Railway,Ship,Aerospace and Other Transport Equipments	82.4
电气机械和器材制造业	Manufacture of Electric Equipment and Machinery	71.8
计算机、通信和其他电子设备制造业	Manufacture of Communication Equipment, Computers and Other Electronic Equipment	90.5
仪器仪表制造业	Manufacture of Measuring Instruments and Machinery	91.5
其他制造业	Other Manufacturing	87.5
废弃资源综合利用业	Comprehensive Utilization Of Waste Resources	25.0
金属制品、机械和设备修理业	Metal Products,Machinery and Equipment Repair Industry	69.2
电力、热力、燃气及水生产和供应业	Production and Distribution of Electricity, Heat,Gas and Water	42.6
电力、热力生产和供应业	Production and Supply of Electric Power and Heat Power	48.5
燃气生产和供应业	Production and Supply of Gas	35.0
水的生产和供应业	Production and Supply of Water	40.0

continued 3

在全部企业中占比（%） The Proportion in All Enterprises (%)					
#实现创新企业 Achieve Innovative Enterprise	#同时实现四种创新企业 Achieve Four Kinds of Innovative Enterprises At Same Time	#实现产品创新企业 Achieve Product Innovation Enterprises	#实现工艺创新企业 Achieve Process Innovation Enterprises	#实现组织创新企业 Achieve Organizational Innovation Enterprises	#实现营销创新企业 Achieve Marketing Innovation Enterprises
62.5		25.0	37.5	25.0	62.5
57.1	42.9	42.9	57.1	57.1	42.9
70.7	26.8	54.9	54.9	53.7	46.3
80.0	20.0	42.9	60.0	60.0	60.0
66.7			66.7	33.3	33.3
59.1	11.4	31.8	29.5	34.1	31.8
36.6	4.6	10.3	22.7	26.8	21.1
35.7	14.3	28.6	28.6	35.7	14.3
83.0	31.9	68.1	74.5	53.2	46.8
50.0	5.6	21.3	32.4	35.2	25.0
75.3	24.7	52.6	60.8	55.7	40.2
84.4	29.1	60.3	70.2	56.0	53.9
69.9	23.3	52.1	53.4	53.4	37.0
78.4	21.6	53.9	66.7	54.9	36.3
70.0	22.4	45.9	57.6	49.4	45.9
85.4	32.8	73.7	70.1	62.0	48.9
88.7	33.8	71.8	62.0	66.2	53.5
87.5	25.0	62.5	62.5	62.5	75.0
53.8			46.2	30.8	7.7
39.7	4.4	7.4	16.2	33.8	17.6
45.5	3.0	6.1	12.1	39.4	21.2
30.0		5.0	15.0	25.0	10.0
40.0	13.3	13.3	26.7	33.3	20.0

20-31 资质等级以上建筑业企业创新活动总体情况（2020年）

指　标	Item	企业数（个）Number of Enterprises (unit)	开展创新活动企业数（个）Number of Innovation Activity Enterprises (unit)
总计	**Total**	**1073**	**358**
按企业规模分	**Grouped by Size of Enterprises**		
大型企业	Large-size	81	70
中型企业	Medium-size	412	152
小型企业	Small-size	500	123
微型企业	Microenterprise	80	13
按登记注册类型分	**Grouped by Registered Status**		
内资企业	Domestic Investment Enterprises	1069	358
港、澳、台商投资企业	Enterprises with Funds from Hong Kong,Macao And Taiwan	2	
外商投资企业	Foreign Funded Enterprises	2	
按行业分	**Grouped by Sector**		
建筑业	Construction	1073	358
房屋建筑业	Construction of Building	400	119
土木工程建筑业	Civil Engineering	335	127
建筑安装业	Architectural Installation	143	60
建筑装饰、装修和其他建筑业	Architectural Decoration and Other Construction	195	52

Basic Statistics on Service Enterprises Innovation Activities above Designated Size (2020)

#实现创新企业 Achieve Innovative Enterprise	#同时实现四种创新企业 Achieve Four Kinds of Innovative Enterprises At Same Time	#实现产品创新企业 Achieve Product Innovation Enterprises	#实现工艺创新企业 Achieve Process Innovation Enterprises	#实现组织创新企业 Achieve Organizational Innovation Enterprises	#实现营销创新企业 Achieve Marketing Innovation Enterprises
345	**37**	**92**	**154**	**297**	**115**
68	20	38	60	56	33
145	12	34	59	125	44
119	5	19	33	103	33
13		1	2	13	5
345	37	92	154	297	115
345	37	92	154	297	115
116	8	22	44	103	36
123	20	42	65	108	42
55	6	18	26	44	20
51	3	10	19	42	17

20-31 续表

指 标	Item	开展创新活动企业 Innovation Activity Enterprises
总计	**Total**	**33.4**
按企业规模分	**Grouped by Size of Enterprises**	
大型企业	Large-size	86.4
中型企业	Medium-size	36.9
小型企业	Small-size	24.6
微型企业	Microenterprise	16.3
按登记注册类型分	**Grouped by Registered Status**	
内资企业	Domestic Investment Enterprises	33.5
港、澳、台商投资企业	Enterprises with Funds from Hong Kong,Macao And Taiwan	
外商投资企业	Foreign Funded Enterprises	
按行业分	**Grouped by Sector**	
建筑业	Construction	33.4
房屋建筑业	Construction of Building	29.8
土木工程建筑业	Civil Engineering	37.9
建筑安装业	Architectural Installation	42.0
建筑装饰、装修和其他建筑业	Architectural Decoration and Other Construction	26.7

continued

在全部企业中占比（%） The Proportion in All Enterprises(%)					
#实现创新企业 Achieve Innovative Enterprise	#同时实现四种创新企业 Achieve Four Kinds of Innovative Enterprises At Same Time	#实现产品创新企业 Achieve Product Innovation Enterprises	#实现工艺创新企业 Achieve Process Innovation Enterprises	#实现组织创新企业 Achieve Organizational Innovation Enterprises	#实现营销创新企业 Achieve Marketing Innovation Enterprises
32.2	**3.4**	**8.6**	**14.4**	**27.7**	**10.7**
84.0	24.7	46.9	74.1	69.1	40.7
35.2	2.9	8.3	14.3	30.3	10.7
23.8	1.0	3.8	6.6	20.6	6.6
16.3		1.3	2.5	16.3	6.3
32.3	3.5	8.6	14.4	27.8	10.8
32.2	3.4	8.6	14.4	27.7	10.7
29.0	2.0	5.5	11.0	25.8	9.0
36.7	6.0	12.5	19.4	32.2	12.5
38.5	4.2	12.6	18.2	30.8	14.0
26.2	1.5	5.1	9.7	21.5	8.7

20-32 规模（限额）以上服务业企业创新活动总体情况（2020年）

指 标	Item	企业数（个） Number of Enterprises (unit)	开展创新活动企业数（个） Number of Innovation Activity Enterprises (unit)
总计	**Total**	**3602**	**1453**
按企业规模分	**Grouped by Size of Enterprises**		
大型企业	Large-size	190	128
中型企业	Medium-size	984	451
小型企业	Small-size	1901	770
微型企业	Microenterprise	527	104
按登记注册类型分	**Grouped by Registered Status**		
内资企业	Domestic Investment Enterprises	3447	1382
港、澳、台商投资企业	Enterprises with Funds from Hong Kong,Macao And Taiwan	53	23
外商投资企业	Foreign Funded Enterprises	102	48
按行业分	**Grouped by Sector**		
批发和零售业	Wholesale and Retail Trades	2114	706
批发业	Wholesale Trade	1209	383
零售业	Retail Trade	905	323
交通运输、仓储和邮政业	Traffic, Transport,Storage and Post	237	65
铁路运输业	Transport Via Railway	4	2
道路运输业	Transport Via Road	133	31
水上运输业	Water Transport		
航空运输业	Air Transport	11	5
管道运输业	Transport Via Pipeline	1	1
多式联运和运输代理业	Multimodal Transport and Transportation Agency	42	15
装卸搬运和仓储业	Loading,Unloading,Portage,Storge and Management of Land Industry	35	7

Basic Statistics on Service Enterprise Innovation Activities above Designated Size (2020)

#实现创新企业 Achieve Innovative Enterprise	#同时实现四种创新企业 Achieve Four Kinds of Innovative Enterprises At Same Time	#实现产品创新企业 Achieve Product Innovation Enterprises	#实现工艺创新企业 Achieve Process Innovation Enterprises	#实现组织创新企业 Achieve Organizational Innovation Enterprises	#实现营销创新企业 Achieve Marketing Innovation Enterprises
1405	**218**	**476**	**509**	**1074**	**899**
124	30	63	65	89	73
437	69	150	173	336	291
740	105	235	245	567	466
104	14	28	26	82	69
1339	211	453	483	1037	861
22	2	7	7	12	13
44	5	16	19	25	25
702	70	143	161	526	543
379	33	70	81	300	264
323	37	73	80	226	279
62	6	11	17	53	25
2	1	2	2	1	1
29	4	6	8	27	12
5		1	3	4	2
15	1	2	2	13	6
7			1	6	1

20-32 续表1

指标	Item	开展创新活动企业 Innovation Activity Enterprises
总计	**Total**	**40.3**
按企业规模分	**Grouped by Size of Enterprises**	
大型企业	Large-size	67.4
中型企业	Medium-size	45.8
小型企业	Small-size	40.5
微型企业	Microenterprise	19.7
按登记注册类型分	**Grouped by Registered Status**	
内资企业	Domestic Investment Enterprises	40.1
港、澳、台商投资企业	Enterprises with Funds from Hong Kong,Macao And Taiwan	43.4
外商投资企业	Foreign Funded Enterprises	47.1
按行业分	**Grouped by Sector**	
批发和零售业	Wholesale and Retail Trades	33.4
批发业	Wholesale Trade	31.7
零售业	Retail Trade	35.7
交通运输、仓储和邮政业	Traffic, Transport,Storage and Post	27.4
铁路运输业	Transport Via Railway	50.0
道路运输业	Transport Via Road	23.3
水上运输业	Water Transport	
航空运输业	Air Transport	45.5
管道运输业	Transport Via Pipeline	100.0
多式联运和运输代理业	Multimodal Transport and Transportation Agency	35.7
装卸搬运和仓储业	Loading,Unloading,Portage,Storge and Management of Land Industry	20.0

continued 1

在全部企业中占比（%） The Proportion in All Enterprises(%)					
#实现创新企业 Achieve Innovative Enterprise	#同时实现四种创新企业 Achieve Four Kinds of Innovative Enterprises At Same Time	#实现产品创新企业 Achieve Product Innovation Enterprises	#实现工艺创新企业 Achieve Process Innovation Enterprises	#实现组织创新企业 Achieve Organizational Innovation Enterprises	#实现营销创新企业 Achieve Marketing Innovation Enterprises
39.0	**6.1**	**13.2**	**14.1**	**29.8**	**25.0**
65.3	15.8	33.2	34.2	46.8	38.4
44.4	7.0	15.2	17.6	34.1	29.6
38.9	5.5	12.4	12.9	29.8	24.5
19.7	2.7	5.3	4.9	15.6	13.1
38.8	6.1	13.1	14.0	30.1	25.0
41.5	3.8	13.2	13.2	22.6	24.5
43.1	4.9	15.7	18.6	24.5	24.5
33.2	3.3	6.8	7.6	24.9	25.7
31.3	2.7	5.8	6.7	24.8	21.8
35.7	4.1	8.1	8.8	25.0	30.8
26.2	2.5	4.6	7.2	22.4	10.5
50.0	25.0	50.0	50.0	25.0	25.0
21.8	3.0	4.5	6.0	20.3	9.0
45.5		9.1	27.3	36.4	18.2
35.7	2.4	4.8	4.8	31.0	14.3
20.0			2.9	17.1	2.9

20-32 续表2

指　标	Item	企业数（个） Number of Enterprises (unit)	开展创新活动企业数（个） Number of Innovation Activity Enterprises (unit)
邮政业	Post	11	4
信息传输、软件和信息技术服务业	Information Transmission,Computer Services and Software	333	266
电信、广播电视和卫星传输服务	Telecom & Other Information Transmission Services	23	15
互联网和相关服务	Internet and Relevant Services	70	51
软件和信息技术服务业	Software Industry	240	200
租赁和商务服务业	Leasing and Business Services	444	159
租赁业	Leasing	25	12
商务服务业	Business Services	419	147
科学研究和技术服务业	Scientific Research,Technical Sevice	406	238
研究和试验发展	Research and Experimental Development	30	24
专业技术服务业	Professional Technical Services	348	196
科技推广和应用服务业	Services of Science and Technology Exchanges and Promotion	28	18
水利、环境和公共设施管理业	Management of Water Conservancy,Environment and Public Facilities	68	19
水利管理业	Management of Water Conservancy	4	1
生态保护和环境治理业	Environmental Management	7	5
公共设施管理业	Management of Public Facilities	51	12
土地管理业	Land management	6	1

continued 2

#实现创新企业 Achieve Innovative Enterprise	#同时实现四种创新企业 Achieve Four Kinds of Innovative Enterprises At Same Time	#实现产品创新企业 Achieve Product Innovation Enterprises	#实现工艺创新企业 Achieve Process Innovation Enterprises	#实现组织创新企业 Achieve Organizational Innovation Enterprises	#实现营销创新企业 Achieve Marketing Innovation Enterprises
4			1	2	3
248	74	167	154	191	142
14	2	7	9	9	9
46	10	24	21	37	29
188	62	136	124	145	104
155	19	40	46	120	89
11	2	4	3	10	7
144	17	36	43	110	82
220	48	113	127	169	92
23	7	18	14	17	10
181	35	84	103	139	73
16	6	11	10	13	9
18	1	2	4	15	8
1				1	
4	1	2	2	3	3
12			1	10	5
1			1	1	

20-32 续表3

指　标	Item	开展创新活动企业 Innovation Activity Enterprises
邮政业	Post	36.4
信息传输、软件和信息技术服务业	Information Transmission,Computer Services and Software	79.9
电信、广播电视和卫星传输服务	Telecom & Other Information Transmission Services	65.2
互联网和相关服务	Internet and Relevant Services	72.9
软件和信息技术服务业	Software Industry	83.3
租赁和商务服务业	Leasing and Business Services	35.8
租赁业	Leasing	48.0
商务服务业	Business Services	35.1
科学研究和技术服务业	Scientific Research,Technical Sevice	58.6
研究和试验发展	Research and Experimental Development	80.0
专业技术服务业	Professional Technical Services	56.3
科技推广和应用服务业	Services of Science and Technology Exchanges and Promotion	64.3
水利、环境和公共设施管理业	Management of Water Conservancy,Environment and Public Facilities	27.9
水利管理业	Management of Water Conservancy	25.0
生态保护和环境治理业	Environmental Management	71.4
公共设施管理业	Management of Public Facilities	23.5
土地管理业	Land management	16.7

continued 3

在全部企业中占比（%） The Proportion in All Enterprises(%)					
#实现 创新企业 Achieve Innovative Enterprise	#同时实现 四种创新企业 Achieve Four Kinds of Innovative Enterprises At Same Time	#实现产品 创新企业 Achieve Product Innovation Enterprises	#实现工艺 创新企业 Achieve Process Innovation Enterprises	#实现组织 创新企业 Achieve Organizational Innovation Enterprises	#实现营销 创新企业 Achieve Marketing Innovation Enterprises
36.4			9.1	18.2	27.3
74.5	22.2	50.2	46.2	57.4	42.6
60.9	8.7	30.4	39.1	39.1	39.1
65.7	14.3	34.3	30.0	52.9	41.4
78.3	25.8	56.7	51.7	60.4	43.3
34.9	4.3	9.0	10.4	27.0	20.0
44.0	8.0	16.0	12.0	40.0	28.0
34.4	4.1	8.6	10.3	26.3	19.6
54.2	11.8	27.8	31.3	41.6	22.7
76.7	23.3	60.0	46.7	56.7	33.3
52.0	10.1	24.1	29.6	39.9	21.0
57.1	21.4	39.3	35.7	46.4	32.1
26.5	1.5	2.9	5.9	22.1	11.8
25.0				25.0	
57.1	14.3	28.6	28.6	42.9	42.9
23.5			2.0	19.6	9.8
16.7			16.7	16.7	

主要统计指标解释

普通高等学校 指按国家规定的设置标准和审批程序批准举办的，通过全国普通高等学校统一招生考试，招收高中毕业生为主要培养对象，实施高等学历教育的全日制大学、独立设置的学院和高等专科学校、高等职业学校及其他机构（独立学院和分校、大专班）。

大学、独立设置的学院主要实施本科层次以上教育。高等专科学校、高等职业学校实施专科层次教育。其他机构是承担国家普通招生计划任务不计校数的机构，包括独立学院、普通高等学校分校、大专班和批准筹建的普通高等学校等。独立学院指由普通本科高校按新机制、新模式举办的本科层次的二级学院，一些普通本科高校按公办机制和模式建立的二级学院，“分校”或其他类似的二级办学机构不属此范畴。

成人高等学校 指按照国家规定的设置标准和审批程序批准举办的，通过全国成人高等教育统一招生考试，招收具有高中毕业或同等学历的人员为主要培养对象，利用函授、业余、脱产等多种形式对其实施高等学历教育的学校。包括职工高等学校、农民高等学校、管理干部学院、教育学院、独立函授学院、广播电视大学、其他机构等。其他机构是承担国家成人招生计划任务不计校数的机构。

研究与试验发展（R&D） 指在科学技术领域，为增加知识总量，以及运用这些知识去创造新的应用进行的系统的创造性的活动，包括基础研究、应用研究、试验发展三类活动。国际上通常采用R&D活动的规模和强度指标反映一国的科技实力和核心竞争力。

基础研究 指为了获得关于现象和可观察事实的基本原理的新知识（揭示客观事物的本质、运动规律，获得新发现、新学说）而进行的实验性或理论性研究，它不以任何专门或特定的应用或使用为目的。其成果以科学论文和科学著作为主要形式。用来反映知识的原始创新能力。

应用研究 指为获得新知识而进行的创造性研究，主要针对某一特定的目的或目标。应用研究是为了确定基础研究成果可能的用途，或是为达到预定的目标探索应采取的新方法（原理性）或新途径。其成果形式以科学论文、专著、原理性模型或发明专利为主。用来反映对基础研究成果应用途径的探索。

试验发展 指利用从基础研究、应用研究和实际经验所获得的现有知识，为产生新的产品、材料和装置，建立新的工艺、系统和服务，以及对已产生和建立的上述各项作实质性的改进而进行的系统性工作。其成果形式主要是专利、专有技术、具有新产品基本特征的产品原型或具有新装置基本特征的原始样机等。在社会科学领域，试验发展是指把通过基础研究、应用研究获得的知识转变成可以实施的计划（包括为进行检验和评估实施示范项目）的过程。人文科学领域没有对应的试验发展活动。主要反映将科研成果转化为技术和产品的能力，是科技推动经济社会发展的物化成果。

R&D人员 指参与研究与试验发展项目研究、管理和辅助工作的人员，包括项目（课题）组人员，企业科技行政管理人员和直接为项目（课题）活动提供服务的辅助人员。反映投入从事拥有自主知识产权的研究开发活动的人力规模。

R&D人员全时当量 指全时人员数加非全时人员按工作量折算为全时人员数的总和。例如：有两个全时人员和三个非全时人员（工作时间分别为20%、30%和70%），则全时当量为2+0.2+0.3+0.7=3.2人年。为国际上比较科技人力投入而制定的可比指标。

R&D经费内部支出 合计指调查单位用于内部开展R&D活动（基础研究、应用研究和试验发展）的实际支出。包括用于R&D项目（课题）活动的直接支出，以及间接用TR&D活动的管理费、服务费、与R&D有关的基本建设支出以及外协加工费等。不包括生产性活动支出、归还贷款支出以及与外单位合作或委托外单位进行R&D活动而转拨给对方的经费支出。

R&D经费内部支出中政府资金 指R&D经费内部支出中来自各级政府部门的各类资金，包括财政科学技术拨款、科学基金、教育等部门事业费以及政府部门预算外资金的实际支出。

R&D经费内部支出中企业资金 指R&D经费内部支出中来自本企业的自有资金和接受其他企业委托而获得的经费，以及科研院所、高校等事业单位从企业获得的资金的实际支出。

新产品销售收入 指报告期企业销售新产品实现的销售收入。

专利 是专利权的简称，是对发明人的发明创造经审查合格后，由专利局依据专利法授予发明人和设计人对该项发明创造享有的专有权。包括发明、实用新型和外观设计。反映拥有自主知识产权的科技和设计成果情况。

发明（专利） 指对产品、方法或者其改进所提出的新的技术方案。是国际通行的反映拥有自主知识产权技术的核心指标。

Explanatory Notes on Main Statistical Indicators

Regular Institutions of Higher Education refer to educational establishments set up according to the government evaluation and approval procedures, recruiting graduates from senior secondary schools as the main target by National Matriculation TEST. They include full-time universities, colleges, institutions of higher professional education, institutions of higher vocational education, institutions of higher vocational education and others (non-university tertiary, branch schools and undergraduate classes) .

Universities and colleges primarily provide undergraduate courses; institutions of higher professional education and institutions of higher vocational education primarily provide professional trainings; and others refer to educational establishments, which are responsible for enrolling higher education students under the State Plan but not enumerated in the total number of schools, including: branch schools of universities and colleges, and universities and colleges that have been approved and under plan for construction. Non-university tertiary refers to the regular undergraduate branch college which is running in new mechanism and mode, excluding the branch schools and other similar branches of educational institutions.

Institutions of Higher Education for Adults refer to educational establishments, set up in line with relevant rules approved by the government, enrolling staff and workers with senior secondary school or equivalent education, and providing higher education courses in many forms of correspondence, spare time, or full time for adults. Professionals thus trained receive a qualification equivalent to graduates studying regular courses at regular universities, colleges and professional colleges. Institutions of higher learning for adults include schools of higher education for staff and workers, schools of higher education for peasants, colleges for management cadres, pedagogical colleges, independent correspondence colleges, Radio and TV universities and other educational establishments. Other educational establishments have undertakings to enrol adult students but not enumerated in the schools under the State Plan.

Research and Development (R&D) refers to systematic and creative activities in the field of science and technology aiming at increasing the knowledge and using the knowledge for new application. R&D includes 3 categories of activities: basic research, applied research and experimentation for development. The scale and intensity of R&D are widely used internationally to reflect the strength of S&T and the core competitiveness of a country in the world.

Basic Research refers to empirical or theoretical research aiming at obtaining new knowledge on the fundamental principles regarding phenomena or observable facts to reveal the intrinsic nature and underlying laws and to acquire new discoveries or new theories. Basic research takes no specific or designated application as the aim of the research. Results of basic research are mainly released or disseminated in the form of scientific papers or monographs. This indicator reflects the innovation capacity for original knowledge.

Applied Research refers to creative research aiming at obtaining new knowledge on a specific objective or target. Purpose of the applied research is to identify the possible uses of results from basic research, or to explore new (fundamental) methods or new approaches. Results of applied research are expressed in the form of scientific papers, monographs, fundamental models or invention patents. This indicator reflects the exploration of ways to apply the results of basic research.

Experiments and Development refer to systematic activities aiming at using the knowledge from basic and applied researches or from practical experience to develop new products, materials and equipment, to establish new production process, systems and services, or to make substantial improvement on the existing products, process or services. Results of experiment and development activities are embodied in patents, exclusive technology, and monotype of new products or equipment. In social sciences, experiment and development activities refer to the process of converting the knowledge from basic or applied researches into feasible programmes (including conduct of demonstration projects for assessment and evaluation) . There are no experiment and development activities in the science of humanities. This indicator reflects the capability of transferring the results of S&T into technique and products, and measures the realization of S&T in spearheading the economic and social development.

R&D Personnel refer to persons engaged in research, management and supporting activities of R&D, including persons in the project teams, persons engaged in the management of S&T activities of enterprises and supporting staff providing direct service to the research projects. This indicator reflects the size of personnel engaged in R&D activities with independent intellectual property.

Full-time Equivalent of R&D Personnel refers to the sum of the full-time persons and the full-time equivalent of part-time persons converted by workload. For instance, if there are 2 full-time persons and 3 part-time workers (20%, 30% and 70% of working hours respectively on R&D activities) , the full-time equivalent are 2+0.2+0.3+0.7=3.2 person-years. This is an internationally comparable indicator of S&T manpower input.

Total Internal Expenditure of Funds on R&D refers to the real expenditure of surveyed units on their own R&D activities (basic research, application study, test and development) including direct expenditure on R&D activities, indirect expenditure of management and services on R&D activities, expenditure on capital construction and material processing by others. Excluding the expenditure on production activities, return of loan, and fees transferred to cooperated and entrusted agencies on R&D activities.

Internal Expenditure of Government Funds refersto the expenditure of funds on R&D activities from government agencies at different levels, including appropriate funds on science and technology from financial departments, scientific funds, operating expenses from education departments and the real expenditure of extra budgetary funds from government agencies.

Internal Expenditure of Funds of Enterprises refers to the expenditure of funds on R&D activities from self-raised funds of enterprises and funds from other enterprises through entrustment, and the expenditure of funds of institutions, such as institution of scientific research and universities, from enterprises.

Sales Income of New Products refers to the real sales income of new products of the enterprises at the reporting period.

Patent is an abbreviation for the patent right and refers to the exclusive right of ownership by the inventors or designers for the creation or inventions, given from the patent offices after due process of assessment and approval in accordance with the Patent Law. Patents are granted for inventions, utility models and designs. This indicator reflects the achievements of S&T and design with independent intellectual property.

Patented Inventions refer to new technical proposals to the products or methods or their modifications. This is universal core indicator reflecting the technologies with independent intellectual property.

21 文化、体育、卫生、社会福利和其他

CULTURE,SPORTS,PUBLIC HEALTH,SOCIAL WELFARE INSTITUTIONS AND OTHER SOCIAL ACTIVITIES

资料整理：陈超毅　陈春光
Data management：Chen Chaoyi Chen Chunguang
数据审核：刘栋婷
Data audit：Liu Dongting

第二十一部分　文化、体育、卫生、社会福利和其他

一、简要说明

本章资料主要包括文化、体育、卫生、社保、公检法等方面的内容，由西安市统计局服务业与社会科技统计处根据统计一套表资料和市委宣传部、市文化和旅游局、文物局、卫健委、民政局、体育局、人社局、公安局、医保局、退役军人事务局、团市委、司法局、妇联、应急管理局、消防救援支队、法院、检察院等部门及机构提供资料整理。本章资料数据口径见表下注释。

二、主要指标

公共图书馆藏量（千册件）	8628	比上年增加	651
医院数（个）	375	比上年增加	16
医院床位数（万张）	7.39	比上年增加	0.74

21　CULTURE,SPORTS,PUBLIC HEALTH,SOCIAL WELFARE INSTITUTIONS AND OTHER SOCIAL ACTIVITIES

I. Brief Introduction

Data in this Chapter primarily consists of data on culture, sanitation, civil administration, physical education, family planning, the Communist Youth League, the Women's Federation, public security organs, procuratorial organs and people's court, compiled by Tertiary Industry and Social Science Technology Division of Xi'an Bureau of Statistics according to data from units of "One Sheet" and Xi'an Bureau of Culture, Health and Family Planning Commission, Bureau of CivialAdministration, Bureau of PE, the Women's Federation, Municipal Committee of Communist Youth League, Bureau of Public Security, Procuratorate, People's Court and other department concerned. The field and range of data in this chapter are listed in the explanatory notes below the chart.

II. Major Indicators

		Increase over Preceding Year
Number of Collections in Libraries (1000 volume-times)	8628	651
Number of Hospitals(units)	375	16
Number of Beds(10000 units)	7.39	0.74

21-1 电影基本情况（2021年）

The Basic Situation of Film (2021)

指 标	Item	2021
全年上映本市生产的院线影片数量（个）	Number of Theatrical Films Produced In The Whole Year(unit)	3
电影发行放映管理机构（个）	Film Projection and Publication Administrating Institutions(unit)	2
电影发行放映管理机构从业人员（人）	Film Projection and Publication Administrating Institution Staff(person)	9
电影放映单位（个）	Unit of Film Shows(unit)	273
电影院	Cinema	121
放映队	File Projection Team	152
电影放映单位从业人员（人）	Staff of Unit of Film Shows(person)	2390
电影院	Cinema	2186
放映队	File Projection Team	204
电影放映场数（千场）	Number of Film Shows(1000 shows)	1534.1
电影观众人数（千人次）	Number of Spectators(1000 person-times)	20796
电影票房收入（万元）	Box-office Receipts(10 000yuan)	68548
平均每一放映场次的观众人次（人次）	Average Audience of Each Projection(person-times)	13
平均每一放映场次的放映收入（元）	Average Income of Each Projection(yuan)	456

注：本表数据来源于市委宣传部、市文化和旅游局。
本表数据含西咸新区。

21-2 图书馆基本情况（2021年）

The Basic Situation of Library (2021)

指　标	Item	2021
公共图书馆个数（个）	Number of Public Libraries(unit)	15
公共图书馆从业人员（人）	Public Library Practitioners (person)	450
公共图书馆藏量（千册件）	Public Library Reserves(1 000 volume-times)	8628
电子图书（千册）	E-books(1 000 volumes)	7133
阅览室坐席（个）	Number of Seating in Reading Room(unit)	6105
书刊文献外借人次（千人次）	Number of Books and literature Borrowed by Readers (1 000 person-times)	709
书刊文献外借册次（千册件）	Volumes of Books and literature Lent to Readers(1 000 volume-times)	2220
图书流通人次（千人次）	Book Circulation Person-time(1 000 person-times)	3062
县以上公共图书馆购书经费（万元）	Book-purchase Fund of Public Library above the County Level(10 000 yuan)	1800
公共图书馆建筑面积（万平方米）	Building Area of Public Library(10 000 sq.m)	10.88

注：本表数据来源于市文化和旅游局。
本表数据含西咸新区。

21-3 艺术表演基本情况（2021年）

The Basic Situation of Art Performance (2021)

指　标	Item	2021
艺术表演团体机构数（个）	Number of Organization of Art Performance Troupes(unit)	18
艺术表演团体从业人员（人）	Art Performance Troupes Practitioners (person)	891
艺术表演团体演出场次（场）	Number of Performances by Art Performance Troupes(show)	1283
#国内演出场次	Domestic Performance	1283
艺术表演观众人次（千人次）	Audience for the Art Performance(1 000 person-times)	75521
艺术表演团体本年创作首映剧目（个）	Art Performance Troupes Creative Premieres of the Year (unit)	13
艺术表演场馆数（个）	Number of Art Performance Places(unit)	14
艺术表演场馆从业人员（人）	Art Performance Place Practitioners (person)	89
艺术表演场馆坐席（个）	Art Performance Place Seatings(unit)	3468
艺术科研机构（个）	Art and Research Institutions(unit)	2
艺术科研机构从业人员（人）	Art and Research Institutions Practitioners(person)	52

注：本表数据来源于市文化和旅游局。
本表数据含西咸新区。
本表2021年起“艺术表演观众人次”统计口径调整。

21-4 主要年份文化馆（站）活动情况

Basic Statistics on Activities of Cultural Centers in Representative Years

指 标	Item	2010	2014	2015	2016	2017	2018	2019	2020	2021
机构数（个）	Number of Institutions(unit)	197	199	199	190	202	202	202	204	204
举办展览个数（个）	Number of Exhibitions(unit)	705	627	606	562	649	632	594	627	681
举办展览参观人次（千人次）	Number of Exhibition Visitors (1 000 person-times)		326	289	287	418	392	442	354	416
组织文艺活动次数（次）	Art Performances and Story-telling Sessions(times)	3729	3617	3811	4246	5498	6518	6589	5587	5525
组织文艺活动参加人次（千人次）	Number of Culture Activities attendees (1 000 person-times)		1576	1574	1688	2631	3322	2476	1668	2358
举办训练班班次（个）	Number of Training Courses(unit)	3018	1872	2126	1906	2597	3310	2608	2968	3008
举办训练班结业人次（千人次）	Number of Certificate Trained Persons (1 000 person-times)	133	156	207	149	188	209	174	239	222
组织各类理论研讨和讲座次数（次）	Number of Theoretical Discussion and Seminars(times)		254	216	189	101	113	144	148	217
组织各类理论研讨和讲座参加人次（千人次）	Number of Persons in Theoretical and Seminars(1 000 person-times)		28	25	18	17	15	20	27	35
本年收入（千元）	Income of this year(1 000 yuan)	42937	89520	102567	103706	133378	116324	115525	111177	129879
本年支出（千元）	Expenditure of this year(1 000 yuan)	45160	84827	100749	111942	141012	119354	123727	113812	130759

注：本表数据来源于市文化和旅游局。
本表2017年及以后年份数据含西咸新区。

21-5 文物保护基本情况（2021年）

Basic Statistics on Cultural Relics Protection (2021)

指 标	Item	机 构（个）Institutions (unit)	人 员（人）Personnel (person)	文物藏品 实际数量（件）Factual Number of Collections (piece)	一级品（件）Grade One (piece)	举办陈列展览次数(次) Times of exhibition (times)	参观人员（千人次）Number of Visitors (1000 person-times)
文物保护管理机构	Cultural Relics administrative Departments	30	517	10593	19		
其他文物机构	Other Agencies	3	53				
博物馆	Museums	133	3763	2139828	4198	304	14494
#免费开放馆	Museums Open Free	99	2277	2002657	2130	269	6050
文物科研机构	Scientific Research of Historical Relics Preservation	3	663	76460	186		

注：本表数据来源于市文物局。
本表数据含西咸新区。

21-6 主要年份广播电台及节目制作情况

Basic Statistics of Broadcasting Stations and Program Production in Representative Years

指 标	Item	2010	2015	2016	2017	2018	2019	2020	2021
省、地广播电台（座）	Broadcasting Stations at the Province and District Level(set)	2							
省、地广播电视台（座）	Broadcasting Station at Province and District Level(set)		2	2	2	2	1	4	4
县级广播电视台（座）	Number of Wire Broadcasting Stations and TV Relaying Stations(set)	6	6	6	6	6	8	6	6
中、短波转播发射台（座）	Medium and Short Wave Broadcast Transmitting Station (base)	55	13	13	13	13	13	13	13
节目套数（套）	Number of Programs(set)	18	20	20	20	20	25	19	19
全年播出时间（时）	Broadcasting Hours annually(hour)	124100	137075	139159	132252	132596	131122	143283	134373
广播节目综合人口覆盖率（%）	Broadcasts comprehensive population coverage（%）	99.40	99.55	99.62	99.65	100.00	99.99	100.00	100.00
制作广播节目（时）	Productions of Broadcasting(hour)	110639	116603	119424	100169	117418	112202	126748	118998
#新闻资讯类	News Programs	13786	12208	7590	6362	6761	6719	9303	7251
专题服务类	Special Subject Programs	24451	21864	26957	26907	28463	29278	38530	35866
综艺类	Variety Programs	37720	37885	39735	25793	41535	39475	34605	27264
广播剧类	Literature Programs	2406	6674	3990	4680	5404	4378	4614	4233
广告类	Advertisements	28339	15777	18363	15968	13627	10584	14192	9651
其他类	Service Programs	3937	22195	22787	20459	21628	21768	25504	34733

注：本表数据来源于市文化和旅游局。

中、短波转播发射台2014年之前统计口径为中短波、调频发射台及转播台。数据变化因指标含义变化所致。

本表2017年及以后年份数据含西咸新区。

21-7 主要年份电视台及节目制作情况

Basic Statistics of TV Stations and Production of TV Program in Representative Years

指 标	Item	2010	2015	2016	2017	2018	2019	2020	2021
调频电视转播发射台（座）	FM Television Relay Station (base)	10	48	48	47	48	43	39	39
全年播出时间（时）	Broadcasting Hours annually(hour)	141856	141839	140312	136960	128368	142289	121671	132044
电视节目综合人口覆盖率（%）	TV shows comprehensive population coverage(%)	98.57	99.01	99.11	99.13	100.00	99.99	100.00	100.00
制作电视节目（时）	Earth Stations of Satellite TV(hour)	29626	43563	54200	49001	45731	58427	30016	41152
#新闻资讯类	News and Information Programs	8930	11839	12891	10517	9387	14172	8358	13286
专题服务类	Special Subject Programs	7762	8073	9346	9769	10808	14581	10319	10757
综艺类	Variety Programs	3942	6242	7883	9080	8789	8728	4446	2481
影视剧类	Literature Programs	1729	462	490	870	363	3482	461	461
广告类	Advertisement	3313	7921	6198	6493	3981	6489	2620	7890
其他类	Service Programs	3950	9026	17390	12272	12403	10975	3812	6277

注：本表数据来源于市文化和旅游局。

电视转播发射台2014年之前统计口径为发射台及转播台，数字变化因指标含义变化所致。影视剧及广告类节目2019年数据变化较大，是因统计口径变化所致。

本表2017年及以后年份数据含西咸新区。

21-8 全市及各区县、开发区规模以上文化及相关产业法人单位数（2021年）

Number of Enterprises Culture and Related Industries above Designated Size by Region (2021)

单位：个 (unit)

区县、开发区	Region	法人单位数 Number of Enterprises	文化制造业 Culture Manufacture	文化批零业 Culture Whole and Retail Trade	文化服务业 Culture Service
西安市	**Total**	**749**	**42**	**97**	**610**
新城区	Xincheng	30		12	18
碑林区	Beilin	42		12	30
莲湖区	Lianhu	40	2	8	30
灞桥区	Baqiao	49	2	6	41
未央区	Weiyang	69	7	10	52
雁塔区	Yanta	360	6	33	321
阎良区	Yanliang	10	1	2	7
临潼区	Lintong	13		3	10
长安区	Chang'an	37	5	1	31
高陵区	Gaoling	12	5		7
鄠邑区	Huyi	10	5	3	2
蓝田县	Lantian	14	5	1	8
周至县	Zhouzhi	3		1	2
西咸新区	Xixian New Area	60	4	5	51
在总计中：	**In Total:**				
高新区	Hi-Tech Industries Development Zone	112	8	11	93
经开区	Economic Development Zone	43	6	6	31
曲江新区	Qujiang New District	229		13	216
航空基地	National Aviation Hi-tech Industrial Base	4		1	3
航天基地	National Civil Aerospace Industrial Base	11	2		9
浐灞生态区	Chan-ba Ecological District	28		2	26
国际港务区	International Trade & Logistics Park	17	2	4	11

21-9 全市及各区县、开发区规模以上文化制造业法人单位基本情况（2021年）

Basic Statistics on Culture and Related Manufacturing Corporate Enterprises above Designated Size by Region(2021)

单位：万元 (10 000yuan)

区县、开发区	Region	法人单位数（个）Number of Enterprises (unit)	从业人员期末人数（人）Engaged Persons at Year-end (person)	资产总计 Total Assets	营业收入 Total Revenue	营业利润 Operating Profit
西安市	**Total**	**42**	**7344**	**881281**	**617134**	**35312**
新城区	Xincheng	2	1797	327706	238379	29197
碑林区	Beilin					
莲湖区	Lianhu					
灞桥区	Baqiao	2	260	41763	54862	698
未央区	Weiyang	7	1335	108633	48376	-1370
雁塔区	Yanta	6	2124	244517	124002	5373
阎良区	Yanliang	1	95	5228	9814	573
临潼区	Lintong					
长安区	Chang'an	5	548	47502	59385	-1862
高陵区	Gaoling	5	389	20465	18592	771
鄠邑区	Huyi	5	397	53847	42924	2495
蓝田县	Lantian	5	203	14141	6975	-209
周至县	Zhouzhi	4	196	17480	13824	-354
西咸新区	Xixian New Area					
在总计中：	**In Total:**					
高新区	Hi-Tech Industries Development Zone	8	2389	279554	169189	2697
经开区	Economic Development Zone	6	1098	103612	43113	-1923
曲江新区	Qujiang New District					
航空基地	National Aviation Hi-tech Industrial Base					
航天基地	National Civil Aerospace Industrial Base	2	245	9983	12082	807
浐灞生态区	Chan-ba Ecological District					
国际港务区	International Trade & Logistics Park	2	260	41763	54862	698

21-10 全市及各区县、开发区限额以上文化批零业法人单位基本情况（2021年）

Basic Statistics on Culture Whole and Retail Trade Corporate Enterprises above Designated Size by Region (2021)

单位：万元 (10 000yuan)

区县、开发区	Region	法人单位数（个）Number of Enterprises (unit)	从业人员期末人数（人）Engaged Persons at Year-end (person)	资产总计 Total Assets	营业收入 Total Revenue	营业利润 Operating Profit
西安市	**Total**	**97**	**5660**	**981208**	**1385222**	**16075**
新城区	Xincheng	12	1232	194975	124776	1161
碑林区	Beilin	12	472	113915	472408	275
莲湖区	Lianhu	8	530	226709	318915	5444
灞桥区	Baqiao	6	145	127575	79621	763
未央区	Weiyang	10	565	24773	104438	155
雁塔区	Yanta	33	2165	244798	221051	11045
阎良区	Yanliang	2	11	933	1813	44
临潼区	Lintong	3	127	8988	10751	-1976
长安区	Chang'an	1	12	122	697	16
高陵区	Gaoling					
鄠邑区	Huyi	3	70	17643	26423	-206
蓝田县	Lantian	1		161	161	4
周至县	Zhouzhi	1	10	717	609	98
西咸新区	Xixian New Area	5	321	19898	23561	-747
在总计中：	**In Total:**					
高新区	Hi-Tech Industries Development Zone	11	400	113674	78372	1354
经开区	Economic Development Zone	6	518	17839	96068	88
曲江新区	Qujiang New District	13	1296	58645	107734	11359
航空基地	National Aviation Hi-tech Industrial Base	1	4	499	360	-14
航天基地	National Civil Aerospace Industrial Base					
浐灞生态区	Chan-ba Ecological District	2	102	5340	22905	433
国际港务区	International Trade & Logistics Park	4	53	121176	55450	316

21-11 全市及各区县、开发区规模以上文化服务业法人单位基本情况（2021年）

Basic Statistics on Culture Service Corporate Enterprises above Designated Size by Region(2021)

单位：万元 (10 000yuan)

区县、开发区	Region	法人单位数（个）Number of Enterprises (unit)	从业人员期末人数（人）Engaged Persons at Year-end (person)	资产总计 Total Assets	营业收入 Total Revenue	营业利润 Operating Profit
西安市	**Total**	**610**	**55864**	**15058355**	**4826973**	**194068**
新城区	Xincheng	18	632	57507	24163	-3158
碑林区	Beilin	30	3964	329818	195107	-10880
莲湖区	Lianhu	30	2425	225420	203480	4283
灞桥区	Baqiao	41	1454	897637	126273	-6126
未央区	Weiyang	52	6831	1246100	597746	25172
雁塔区	Yanta	321	27202	10321518	3030014	220701
阎良区	Yanliang	7	167	18929	5168	-931
临潼区	Lintong	10	2094	156678	43774	-13289
长安区	Chang'an	31	3434	303133	299730	6059
高陵区	Gaoling	7	377	15072	9491	69
鄠邑区	Huyi	2	77	1799	2239	230
蓝田县	Lantian	8	511	210524	11722	-19381
周至县	Zhouzhi	2	115	38622	2555	-1850
西咸新区	Xixian New Area	51	6581	1235599	275509	-6830
在总计中：	**In Total:**					
高新区	Hi-Tech Industries Development Zone	93	12687	1881046	1636388	288904
经开区	Economic Development Zone	31	5514	814017	523689	21102
曲江新区	Qujiang New District	216	13142	8228776	1395520	-70582
航空基地	National Aviation Hi-tech Industrial Base	3	98	13254	3285	-691
航天基地	National Civil Aerospace Industrial Base	9	1867	118483	168070	8718
浐灞生态区	Chan-ba Ecological District	26	1849	1100270	111150	2904
国际港务区	International Trade & Logistics Park	11	130	20773	33251	-2871

21-12 竞技体育情况（2021年）

The Situation of Competitive Sports(2021)

指 标	Item	2021
奥运会获得奖牌(枚)	Number of Medals Won in the Olympic Games(unit)	
金牌数	Gold	
银牌数	Silver	1
铜牌数	Bronze	
全运会获得奖牌(枚)	Number of Medals Won in the National Games(unit)	
金牌数	Gold	9
银牌数	Silver	8
铜牌数	Bronze	12
省运会获得奖牌(枚)	Number of Medals Won in the Provincial Games(unit)	
金牌数	Gold	
银牌数	Silver	
铜牌数	Bronze	
其他国际、国内赛事	Other International and Domestic Events	
金牌数(枚)	Gold(unit)	19
银牌数(枚)	Silver(unit)	25
体育传统项目学校(个)	Sports Traditional Project School(unit)	177
体育传统项目学校在校训练学生数(人)	Number of Students in the Sports Traditional Project School (person)	7450
高水平体育后备人才基地(个)	High Level Sports Reserve Base(unit)	7
省级示范性体校(个)	Provincial Demonstration Sports School(unit)	2
等级教练员人数(人)	Number of Graded Coaches(person)	71
国家级	National Level	1
高 级	Senior Level	18
一 级（中级）	One Level(Intermediate Level)	31
二 级（初级）	Two Level(Elementary Level)	21
三 级	Three Level	
二级运动员人数(人)	Second Grade Athletes (person)	429

注：本表数据来源于市体育局。
本表数据不含西咸新区。

21-13 群众体育情况（2021年）

The Situation of Mass Sports(2021)

指 标	Item	2021
全年承办的县级以上群众性体育赛事（个）	Mass Sports Events Held throughout the Year(unit)	636
国家级	National Level	4
省 级	Provincial Level	9
市 级	City Level	150
县 级	County Level	473
全年举办的社会体育指导员培训班（期）	Training Course for Social Sports Instructors Held throughout the Year(time)	27
社会体育指导员人数（名）	Social Sports Instructor(person)	29058
体育先进社区（个）	Advanced Sports Community(unit)	
#国家级	National Level	
省 级	Provincial Level	
群众体育先进单位（个）	Advanced Unit of Mass Sports(unit)	12
#国家级	National Level	12
省 级	Provincial Level	
晨晚健身站点（个）	Morning and Evening Fitness sites(unit)	1952
全民健身中心（个）	National Fitness Center(unit)	7
当年农民体育健身工程	Township Sports Fitness Project(unit)	23
累计村级农民体育健身工程（个）	Accumulative total Farmers' Sports Fitness Project(unit)	4303
体育人口（万人）	Sports Population(10 000 person)	650

注：本表数据来源于市体育局，数据不含西咸新区。
2021年“当年农民体育健身工程”“累计村级农民体育健身工程”统计指标名称变动，与往年不可比。

21-14 体育产业情况（2021年）

The Situation of Sport Industry (2021)

指 标	Item	2021
全市县级标准公共体育场地建设情况	Construction of Standard Public Sports Venues in the County Level	
已建场地个数（个）	Number of Built Sites(units)	6
在建场地个数（个）	Number of Sites in Construction(units)	1
全市全民健身设施建设情况	Construction of National Fitness Facilities in the City	
全民健身园区（个）	National Fitness Park(units)	34
多功能运动场（个）	Multifunction Playground(units)	73
全民健身室内健身房（个）	Fitness Indoor Gymnasium(units)	25
健身步道（千米）	Fitness Footpath(km)	50.2
全市体育彩票销售情况	Sales of Sports Lottery in the City	
体育彩票销售网点数量（个）	Number of Sales Outlets of Sports Lottery (units)	1518
体育彩票销售网点数量占全省的比重（%）	Proportion of Sports Lottery Sales Outlets Accounts for t he Proportion of the Whole Province(%)	32.1
本年体育彩票销售金额（万元）	Sales Amount of Sports Lottery in this Year(10 000 yuan)	265990.3
本年体育彩票销售金额占全省的比重（%）	Sales Amount of Sports Lottery in this year Accounts for the Proportion of the Whole Province(%)	44.6

注：本表数据来源于市体育局，数据不含西咸新区。

21-15 主要年份医疗卫生机构、床位、人员情况

Number of Health Care Institutions, Beds and Personnel in Health Care Institutions in Representative Years

年 份 Year	医疗卫生机构数（个） Number of Health Care Institutions (unit)	#医院数 Number of Health Care Hospital	医疗卫生机构床位数（张） Number of Health Care Bed (unit)	#医院床位数 Number of Hospital Bed	卫生技术人员数（人） Number of Medical Technical Personnel (person)
2009	5284	261	36849	32371	52620
2010	5632	258	39407	34274	57756
2011	5554	268	41010	35976	61281
2012	5576	276	44239	39213	66899
2013	5503	281	47867	42753	71134
2014	5554	281	51065	45561	76005
2015	5802	295	54708	49830	81462
2016	5869	292	56332	51508	86258
2017	6376	329	63942	58219	94221
2018	6638	343	68981	63365	101477
2019	7011	359	72549	67238	112243
2020	7129	359	75007	66506	117656
2021	7123	375	79426	73886	123293

注：本表数据来源于市卫生和健康委员会。
本表2017年及以后年份数据含西咸新区。

21-16 医疗卫生机构、床位及人员情况（2021年）

卫生机构	Health Care Institutions	机构数（个）Number of Institutions (unit)	床位数（张）Number of Beds (unit)
总计	**Total**	**7123**	**79426**
一、医院	**Hospitals**	**375**	**73886**
综合医院	General Hospitals	212	51705
中医医院	Hospitals Specialized in Traditional Chinese Medicine	50	7108
中西医结合医院	Hospitals Integrating Traditional Chinese Medicine with Western Therapeutics in Practice	5	1110
民族医院	Nationalities Hospitals		
专科医院	Specialized Hospitals	105	13754
护理院	Nursing centers	3	209
二、基层医疗卫生机构	**Commuting Health Hare Service Centre**	**6642**	**3743**
社区卫生服务中心(站)	Community Health Care Center(Station)	264	1919
社区卫生服务中心	Community Health Care Center	127	1918
社区卫生服务站	Community Health Care Station	137	1
卫生院	Health Center	113	1798
街道卫生院	Urban Health-center		
乡镇卫生院	Rural Health-center	113	1798
村卫生室	Village Clinics	2782	
门诊部	Outpatient Department	491	26
诊所、卫生所、医务室	Clinic, Health Center, Infirmary	2992	
三、专业公共卫生机构	**College of Public Health Institutions**	**52**	**1434**
疾病预防控制中心	Center for Disease Control and Prevention	16	
专科疾病防治院（所、站）	Specialized Disease Prevention and Cure Center(Place,Station)	1	800
健康教育所（站、中心）	Health Education Institute(Station,Center)	2	
妇幼保健院（所、站）	Maternal and Child Health Hospital(Station)	14	634
急救中心（站）	Emergency Center	2	
采供血机构	Blood Collection Agencies	1	
卫生监督所（中心）	Health Supervision Agencies(Center)	16	
计划生育技术服务机构	Institutions of Technical Service for Family Planning		
四、其他卫生机构	**Other Health Institution**	**54**	**363**
疗养院	Nursing Centre		
卫生监督检验(监测、检测)所(站)	Health Supervision and Inspection Agencies		
医学科学研究机构	Medical Scientific Research Institutions	3	
医学在职培训机构	Medical Training Institutions	3	
临床检验中心（所、站）	Clinical Testing Center(Place,Station)	8	
统计信息中心	Statistical Information Center	3	
其他	Other	31	

注：本表数据来源于市卫生健康委员会。
第四部分“其他卫生机构”分类发生变化，疗养院及卫生监督检验（监测、检测）所（站）2021年无数据。
本表数据含西咸新区。

Number of Health Care Institutions, Beds and Personnel in Health Care Institutions (2021)

人员合计（人）Total Number of Employed Persons (person)	卫生技术人员 Medical Technical Personnel	执业（助理）医师数 Licensed (Assistant) Doctors	#执业医师 Chartered Doctors
148657	**123293**	**43289**	**38228**
105930	**87460**	**27782**	**26657**
76458	63752	20362	19599
9341	7629	2390	2259
1315	1051	345	339
18713	14950	4663	4444
103	78	22	16
34897	**30133**	**14042**	**10237**
7556	6411	1985	1590
6208	5197	1516	1201
1348	1214	469	389
4073	3416	965	657
4073	3416	965	657
3520	2002	1919	277
7160	6307	2788	2326
12588	11997	6385	5387
5510	**4125**	**1058**	**972**
1314	1043	399	374
681	542	118	115
84	35		
2265	1687	465	408
264	151	67	67
324	225	9	8
578	442		
2320	**1575**	**407**	**362**
142	73	37	37
159	6	2	2
207	127	3	3
50			
1255	1093	305	268

21-16 续表

卫生机构	Health Care Institutions	人员合计（人） 卫生技术人员 注册护士 Registered Nurses	药师（士） Junior Paramedics
总计	**Total**	**57015**	**4833**
一、医院	**Hospitals**	**43939**	**3359**
综合医院	General Hospitals	32309	2274
中医医院	Hospitals Specialized in Traditional Chinese Medicine	3388	492
中西医结合医院	Hospitals Integrating Traditional Chinese Medicine with Western Therapeutics in Practice	504	72
民族医院	Nationalities Hospitals		
专科医院	Specialized Hospitals	7694	517
护理院	Nursing centers	44	4
二、基层医疗卫生机构	**Commuting Health Hare Service Centre**	**11182**	**1339**
社区卫生服务中心(站)	Community Health Care Center(Station)	2590	423
社区卫生服务中心	Community Health Care Center	2055	338
社区卫生服务站	Community Health Care Station	535	85
卫生院	Health Center	1078	211
街道卫生院	Urban Health-center		
乡镇卫生院	Rural Health-center	1078	211
村卫生室	Village Clinics	83	
门诊部	Outpatient Department	2752	240
诊所、卫生所、医务室	Clinic, Health Center, Infirmary	4679	465
三、专业公共卫生机构	**College of Public Health Institutions**	**1276**	**118**
疾病预防控制中心	Center for Disease Control and Prevention	77	12
专科疾病防治院（所、站）	Specialized Disease Prevention and Cure Center(Place,Station)	289	30
健康教育所（站、中心）	Health Education Institute(Station,Center)		
妇幼保健院（所、站）	Maternal and Child Health Hospital(Station)	709	69
急救中心（站）	Emergency Center	82	2
采供血机构	Blood Collection Agencies	119	5
卫生监督所（中心）	Health Supervision Agencies(Center)		
计划生育技术服务机构	Institutions of Technical Service for Family Planning		
四、其他卫生机构	**Other Health Institution**	**618**	**17**
疗养院	Nursing Centre		
卫生监督检验(监测、检测)所(站)	Health Supervision and Inspection Agencies		
医学科学研究机构	Medical Scientific Research Institutions	8	2
医学在职培训机构	Medical Training Institutions	3	
临床检验中心（所、站）	Clinical Testing Center(Place,Station)	5	1
统计信息中心	Statistical Information Center		
其他	Other	489	3

continued

Total Number of Employed Persons (person)				
Medical Technical Personnel		其他技术人员 Other Technical Personnel	管理人员 Administrative Personnel	工勤技能人员 Logistics Technical Workers
技师（士） Technicians	其他 Others			
8405	**9321**	**1556**	**14270**	**12074**
6120	**6260**	**970**	**11553**	**9284**
4151	4656	754	8049	6381
534	825	103	1043	877
80	50	5	202	97
1349	727	105	2246	1916
6	2	3	13	13
1323	**2247**	**158**	**1716**	**1893**
564	849	72	575	626
497	791	62	462	593
67	58	10	113	33
364	798	39	293	422
364	798	39	293	422
275	252	38	574	457
120	348	9	274	388
566	**678**	**124**	**676**	**709**
272	283	35	162	105
52	53	7	79	57
	35	32	17	
186	258	23	212	386
			77	64
56	36	27	49	27
	13		80	70
396	**136**	**304**	**325**	**188**
17	9	19	41	14
1		108	65	7
113	5	9	33	41
		23	25	2
204	91	19	90	65

21-17 各区县、开发区医疗卫生机构、床位及人员情况（2021年）

Number of Health Care Institutions, Beds and Employed Persons in Health Care Institutions By Region (2021)

区县、开发区	Region	机构（个）Number of Health Care Institutions (unit)	床位（张）Number of Beds (unit)	人员合计（人）Total Number of Employed Persons (person)	#卫生技术人员 Total Number of Medical Technical Personnel
全　市	**Total**	**7123**	**79426**	**148657**	**123293**
新城区	Xincheng	292	9497	17235	14582
碑林区	Beilin	472	9504	18731	15714
莲湖区	Lianhu	453	9560	17040	14044
灞桥区	Baqiao	455	3249	6218	5367
未央区	Weiyang	533	6971	14950	12976
雁塔区	Yanta	713	9312	23258	19073
阎良区	Yanliang	187	2136	3441	2791
临潼区	Lintong	530	3669	5204	4066
长安区	Chang'an	627	7116	11226	9181
高陵区	Gaoling	230	2994	4126	3447
鄠邑区	Huyi	430	3205	5443	4598
蓝田县	Lantian	570	2171	3146	2618
周至县	Zhouzhi	502	2628	4413	3311
西咸新区	Xixian New Area	590	2378	4404	3603
高新区	Hi-Tech Industries Development Zone	502	4948	9523	7684
国际港务区	International Trade & Logistics Park	37	88	299	238

注：本表数据来源于市卫生健康委员会。

21–18　各区县、开发区农村村级卫生组织情况（2021年）

Village Level Health Organization in the Rural Area by Region (2021)

区县、开发区	Region	村卫生室（个）Village Health Room（unit）	乡村医生和卫生员（人）Rural Doctors and Health Workers（person）	#乡村医生 Rural Doctors	#卫生员 Health Workers
全　市	**Total**	**2782**	**1518**	**1448**	**70**
新城区	Xincheng				
碑林区	Beilin				
莲湖区	Lianhu				
灞桥区	Baqiao	146	87	87	
未央区	Weiyang	45	9	9	
雁塔区	Yanta	12	6	6	
阎良区	Yanliang	80	87	87	
临潼区	Lintong	329	182	182	
长安区	Chang'an	298	128	128	
高陵区	Gaoling	121	85	84	1
鄠邑区	Huyi	323	102	102	
蓝田县	Lantian	468	175	173	2
周至县	Zhouzhi	387	343	281	62
西咸新区	Xixian New Area	344	181	178	3
高新区	Hi-Tech Industries Development Zone	197	118	116	2
国际港务区	International Trade & Logistics Park	32	15	15	

注：本表数据来源于市卫生健康委员会。

21-19 各区县、开发区社区卫生服务中心（站）情况（2021年）

Situations of Community Health Service Center（Station）by Region(2021)

区县、开发区	Region	社区卫生服务中心（站）（个） Community Health Care Center(Station) (unit)	床位数（张） Number of Beds (unit)	人员数（人） Personnel Number (person)	卫生技术人员（人） Medical Technical Personnel (person)	执业（助理）医师 Licensed (Assistant) Doctors	注册护士 Registered Nurses
全　市	**Total**	**264**	**1919**	**7556**	**6411**	**1985**	**2590**
新城区	Xincheng	17	20	279	243	83	101
碑林区	Beilin	22	110	438	372	161	133
莲湖区	Lianhu	29	250	1008	857	274	337
灞桥区	Baqiao	26	75	532	461	156	194
未央区	Weiyang	26	70	897	778	251	340
雁塔区	Yanta	46	106	1296	1154	343	516
阎良区	Yanliang	8	76	165	150	42	68
临潼区	Lintong	28	581	745	629	171	181
长安区	Chang'an	16	339	689	551	159	171
高陵区	Gaoling	8		55	50	12	26
鄠邑区	Huyi						
蓝田县	Lantian						
周至县	Zhouzhi	1		113	77	10	33
西咸新区	Xixian New Area	18	58	417	338	111	167
高新区	Hi-Tech Industries Development Zone	16	146	684	557	160	230
国际港务区	International Trade & Logistics Park	3	88	238	194	52	93

注：本表数据来源于市卫生健康委员会。

21-20 主要年份医疗卫生机构各类人员情况

Number of Personnel in Health Care Institutions in Representative Years

单位：人 (person)

指 标	Item	2010	2015	2016	2017	2018	2019	2020	2021
人员合计	**Total**	**71230**	**102684**	**107906**	**116939**	**125179**	**136333**	**142809**	**148657**
卫生技术人员	Medical Technical Personnel	56579	81462	86258	94221	101477	112243	117656	123293
执业（助理）医师	Licensed (Assistant) Doctors	18763	26626	27864	30820	33776	38469	40714	43289
#执业医师	Chartered Doctors	16613	23818	25023	27683	30322	34102	36086	38228
注册护士	Certified Assistant Doctors	22640	34819	37518	41603	46450	51882	54329	57015
药师（士）	Junior Paramedics	3030	3957	4075	4280	4423	4709	4814	4833
技师（士）	Technicians	4589	4690	5058	5593	6035	6633	6983	8405
卫生监督员	Health supervisors								430
其他	Others	7557	11370	11743	11925	10793	10550	10816	9321
其他技术人员	Other Technical Personnel	1156	816	835	839	925	936	937	1556
仅从事管理人员	Management Personnel only	6416	8248	8470	9003	9723	10229	10526	10216
工勤技能人员	Logistics Technical Workers	7079	8326	8913	9179	9707	9901	11061	12074

注：本表数据来源于市卫生健康委员会。
本表2011年及以后合计栏数据含乡村医生和卫生员。
本表2017年及以后年份数据含西咸新区。
本表“仅从事管理人员”指标数据2020年及以前为“管理人员”口径。
2021年卫健委制度变化，“卫生技术人员”分类中增加“卫生监督员”。

21-21 医疗卫生机构门诊、住院及病床使用情况（2021年）

指 标	Item	总诊疗人次数（人次） 总计 Total
总计	**Total**	**60810810**
一、医院	**Hospitals**	**42241543**
综合医院	General Hospitals	30215705
中医医院	Hospitals Specialized in Traditional Chinese Medicine	3575427
中西医结合医院	Hospitals Integrating Traditional Chinese Medicine with Western Therapeutics in Practice	343543
民族医院	Nationalities Hospitals	
专科医院	Specialized Hospitals	8084741
护理院	Nursing Centers	22127
二、基层医疗卫生机构	**Commuting Health Care Service Centre**	**17343308**
社区卫生服务中心（站）	Community Health Care Center(Station)	4326615
社区卫生服务中心	Community Health Care Center	3443000
社区卫生服务站	Community Health Care Station	883615
卫生院	Health Center	1684177
街道卫生院	Urban Health-center	
乡镇卫生院	Rural Health-center	1684177
村卫生室	Village Clinics	4272338
门诊部	Outpatient Department	2331180
诊所、卫生所、医务室	Clinic, Health Center, Infirmary	4728998
三、专业公共卫生机构	**College of Public Health Institutions**	**1163819**
专科疾病防治院（所、站）	Specialized Disease Prevention and Cure Center (Place, Station)	79217
妇幼保健院（所、站）	Maternal and Child Health Hospital (Place, Station)	910099
急救中心（站）	Emergency Center(Station)	174503
四、其他卫生机构	**Other Health Institution**	**62140**
疗养院	Sanatorium	62140

注：本表数据来源于市卫生健康委员会。
本表数据含西咸新区。

Medical and Health Institutions Outpatient, Inpatient and Utilization of Beds (2021)

Total Number of Clinics (person time)				观察室 Observation Room	
门、急诊人次数合计 Total Number of People In Outpatient and Emergency Department	门诊人次数 Number of Outpatients	急诊人次数 The Number of Emergency	死亡人数 Number of Deaths	留观病例数（人次） Number of Patients Receiving (person times)	死亡人数（人） Number of Deaths (persons)
59902928	**56004909**	**3898019**	**4180**	**123987**	**264**
42005517	**38394181**	**3611336**	**3898**	**101146**	**264**
30108488	27122973	2985515	3600	94796	264
3502609	3394391	108218	109	258	
335058	305420	29638	42		
8037674	7549709	487965	147	6092	
21688	21688				
16716158	**16673666**	**42492**	**282**	**22191**	
4084412	4050305	34107	282	21540	
3217291	3186199	31092	282	21477	
867121	864106	3015		63	
1668856	1660471	8385		651	
1668856	1660471	8385		651	
4106804	4106804				
2194445	2194445				
4661641	4661641				
1119809	**875747**	**244062**		**650**	
58994	58877	117			
886312	816870	69442		650	
174503		174503			
61444	**61315**	**129**			
61444	61315	129			

21-21 续表

指 标	Item	急诊死亡率（%） Emergency Mortality (%)	入院人数合计（人） Total Number of Admission Patients (person)
总计	**Total**	**0.11**	**2393911**
一、医院	**Hospitals**	**0.11**	**2332983**
综合医院	General Hospitals	0.12	1811558
中医医院	Hospitals Specialized in Traditional Chinese Medicine	0.10	185587
中西医结合医院	Hospitals Integrating Traditional Chinese Medicine with Western Therapeutics in Practice	0.14	27724
民族医院	Nationalities Hospitals		
专科医院	Specialized Hospitals	0.03	306532
护理院	Nursing Centers		1582
二、基层医疗卫生机构	**Commuting Health Care Service Centre**	**0.66**	**26208**
社区卫生服务中心（站）	Community Health Care Center(Station)	0.83	12521
社区卫生服务中心	Community Health Care Center	0.91	12521
社区卫生服务站	Community Health Care Station		
卫生院	Health Center		13687
街道卫生院	Urban Health-center		
乡镇卫生院	Rural Health-center		13687
村卫生室	Village Clinics		
门诊部	Outpatient Department		
诊所、卫生所、医务室	Clinic, Health Center, Infirmary		
三、专业公共卫生机构	**College of Public Health Institutions**		**30573**
专科疾病防治院（所、站）	Specialized Disease Prevention and Cure Center (Place, Station)		7485
妇幼保健院（所、站）	Maternal and Child Health Hospital (Place, Station)		23088
急救中心（站）	Emergency Center(Station)		
四、其他卫生机构	**Other Health Institution**		**4147**
疗养院	Sanatorium		4147

continued

出院人数合计（人） Total Number of Discharge Patients (person)	死亡人数（人） Number of Hospital Casualty (person)	病床周转次数（次） Number of Bed Remover (times)	病床使用率（%） Bed occupancy rate (%)	出院者平均住院（天） Average Stay Days in Hospital (day)
2407885	**10878**	**31.3**	**70.73**	**8.2**
2347324	**10839**	**32.8**	**73.69**	**8.2**
1822732	9588	36.5	76.21	7.6
186558	472	26.3	70.63	10.3
27950	102	25.6	68.20	9.7
308511	677	23.3	67.12	10.3
1573		7.5	17.41	8.4
26384	**12**	**7.5**	**16.51**	**8.0**
12477	12	7.1	14.99	7.5
12477	12	7.1	14.99	7.5
13651		7.7	18.00	8.6
13651		7.7	18.00	8.6
256				
30264	**27**	**21.1**	**69.46**	**11.8**
7322	27	9.2	83.99	32.7
22942		36.2	51.13	5.1
3913		**10.8**	**21.56**	**7.2**
3913		10.8	21.56	7.2

21-22 提供住宿的社会服务机构（2021年）

Social Welfare Institutions Providing Accommodation (2021)

指 标	Item	机构数（个）Number of Institutions (unit)	年末职工人数（人）Number of Staff and Workers at the End of Year(person)	#女性 Female	床位数（张）Number of Beds(unit)	年末在院人数（人）Number of Persons Housed at the Year-end(person)
1. 养老服务机构	Pension Service Institutions	143	3643	2003	28641	11485
2. 儿童福利院	Baby Welfare Homes	1	67	42	587	587
3. 社会福利医院	Social Welfare Hospitals	1	135	60	750	393
4. 救助站	Rescue Station	8	107	41	619	219

注：本表数据来源于市民政局。
　　本表数据含西咸新区。

21-23 主要年份社会福利事业单位机构及人员情况

Number of Social Welfare Institutions and Personnel

单位：个、人　　(unit, person)

指 标	Item	2010	2015	2016	2017	2018	2019	2020	2021
一、机构	**Insititutions**								
烈士纪念建筑物管理单位	Institutions Managing Memorial Buildings of Martyrs	2	2	2	2	2	2	2	2
救助类单位	Units Providing Assistance	8	9	9	9	9	9	8	8
殡仪服务单位	Funeral Service Units	22	26	25	27	25	26	25	26
殡仪馆	Funeral Homes	4	3	3	3	3	3	3	3
公墓	Cemeteries	14	16	16	19	18	19	19	20
殡葬管理单位	Funeral Management Units	4	7	6	5	4	4	3	3
二、人员	**Staff**								
烈士纪念建筑物管理单位	Institutions Managing Memorial Buildings of Martyrs	37	42	42	44	42	40	40	40
救助类单位	Units Providing Assistance	116	119	121	114	110	113	102	107
殡仪服务单位	Funeral Service Units	1371	1510	1510	1518	1337	1282	1299	1314
殡仪馆	Funeral Homes	375	497	481	484	458	476	461	469
公墓	Cemeteries	939	929	953	959	824	761	807	813
殡葬管理单位	Funeral Management Units	57	84	76	75	55	45	31	32

注：本表数据来源于市民政局、市退役军人事务局。
　　本表2017年及以后年份数据含西咸新区。

21-24 社会保障基本情况（2021年）

Basic Situation of Social Security (2021)

单位：万人、万户 （10 000 persons、10 000 households）

指 标	Item	2021
基本养老保险参保人数	Number of Basic Old-age Insurance	881.26
1.城镇企业职工养老保险参保人数	Number of Town Enterprise Worker Old-age Insurance	552.93
其中：离退休人员	Retired Personnel	72.98
2.机关事业单位养老保险参保人数	Number of Institution Old-age Insurance	31.83
其中：离退休人员	Retired Personnel	11.15
3.城乡居民养老保险参保人数	Number of Rural Residents Old-age Insurance	296.50
城乡基本医疗保险参保人数	Number of urban basic medical insurance	1094.10
失业保险参保人数	Number of unemployed insurance	259.76
生育保险参保人数	Number of Maternity insurance	317.08
工伤保险参保人数	Number of industrial injury insurance	299.27
城市居民最低生活保障户数	The Number of Minimum Living Guarantee for Urban Resident Households	1.39
城市居民最低生活保障人数	The Number of Minimum Living Guarantee for Urban Residents	1.98
农村居民最低生活保障户数	The Number of Minimum Living Guarantee for Rural Resident Households	2.98
农村居民最低生活保障人数	The Number of Minimum Living Guarantee for Rural Residents	7.84

注：本表数据来源于市人力资源和社会保障局、市民政局及市医疗保障局。

21–25 全市及各区县、开发区优抚对象人员情况（2021年）

Statistics on Persons Enjoying Favoured Treatment by Region (2021)

单位：人 (person)

区县、开发区	Region	伤残人员 Number of Disabled Veterans	烈军属人员 Number of Family Members of Martyrs and Soldiers	在乡复员军人 Demobilized Soldiers in Hometown	带病回乡退伍军人 Veterans Returning Home in Sick
全　市	**Total**	**5700**	**706**	**1669**	**902**
新城区	Xincheng	604	31	3	3
碑林区	Beilin	657	36	6	2
莲湖区	Lianhu	733	47	18	12
灞桥区	Baqiao	282	33	51	91
未央区	Weiyang	271	38	32	15
雁塔区	Yanta	750	59	23	14
阎良区	Yanliang	117	33	89	59
临潼区	Lintong	301	77	216	182
长安区	Chang'an	358	52	131	30
高陵区	Gaoling	165	29	106	86
鄠邑区	Huyi	239	43	239	52
蓝田县	Lantian	248	51	348	153
周至县	Zhouzhi	341	76	88	63
西咸新区	Xixian New Area	386	72	211	70
高新区	Hi-Tech Industries Development Zone	202	20	91	38
国际港务区	International Trade & Logistics Park	46	9	17	32

注：本表数据来源于市退役军人事务局。

21-26 全市及各区县、开发区计划生育和婚姻登记情况（2021年）

Conditions of Birth Control and Marriage Registration by Region (2021)

区县、开发区	Region	计划生育率（%）Family Planning Rate(%)	结婚对数（对）Marriages (couple)	再婚人数（人）Remarriages (person)	离婚对数（对）Divorced Couple (couple)
全 市	**Total**	**99.9**	**76004**	**38839**	**30108**
新城区	Xincheng	100.0	3989	1916	1519
碑林区	Beilin	100.0	5477	2448	1993
莲湖区	Lianhu	100.0	5366	2846	2599
灞桥区	Baqiao	100.0	4109	2172	1903
未央区	Weiyang	100.0	8064	3641	3260
雁塔区	Yanta	100.0	9069	4732	3980
阎良区	Yanliang	99.8	1787	1179	725
临潼区	Lintong	99.9	3790	1981	1622
长安区	Chang'an	99.9	7212	5088	3975
高陵区	Gaoling	99.9	2347	1453	892
鄠邑区	Huyi	99.8	2850	1340	1127
蓝田县	Lantian	99.9	3578	1659	1000
周至县	Zhouzhi	99.9	3486	1436	1304
西咸新区	Xixian New Area	99.9	6009	3330	1831
高新区	Hi-Tech Industries Development Zone	99.9	7750	2840	1983
国际港务区	International Trade & Logistics Park	99.9	1121	778	395

注：本表数据来源于市卫生健康委员会、市民政局、市中级人民法院。
本表中计划生育率、结婚对数、再婚人数含西咸新区，离婚对数含部分西咸新区数据。

21–27 全市及各区县、开发区妇幼卫生保健情况（2021年）

Care Health Conditions of Women and Child by Region (2021)

区县、开发区	Region	5岁以下儿童死亡率（‰） Mortality rate of Children under 5-year-old(‰)	新生儿死亡率（‰） Infant Mortality Ratio(‰)	婴儿死亡率（‰） Neonatal Mortality Ratio(‰)
全　市	**Total**	**2.15**	**0.97**	**1.45**
新城区	Xincheng	1.50	1.00	1.25
碑林区	Beilin	0.77	0.51	0.51
莲湖区	Lianhu	2.35	1.12	1.46
灞桥区	Baqiao	0.79	0.13	0.39
未央区	Weiyang	1.95	0.75	1.15
雁塔区	Yanta	1.80	1.04	1.52
阎良区	Yanliang	4.92	1.97	2.46
临潼区	Lintong	3.27	1.63	2.57
长安区	Chang'an	2.10	1.26	1.68
高陵区	Gaoling	3.84	1.92	2.88
鄠邑区	Huyi	2.65	0.66	1.65
蓝田县	Lantian	4.45	2.22	3.18
周至县	Zhouzhi	3.31	0.83	1.65
西咸新区	Xixian New Area	1.95	0.71	1.06
高新区	Hi-Tech Industries Development Zone	2.04	0.95	1.63
国际港务区	International Trade & Logistics Park	0.79		

注：本表数据来源于市卫生健康委员会。

21–27 续表 continued

区县、开发区	Region	孕产妇死亡率（1/10万） Maternal Mortality Ratio (one in hundred thousandth)	产妇住院分娩比例（%） Proportion of maternal Hospital Births (%)
全　市	**Total**	**12.25**	**99.99**
新城区	Xincheng		100.00
碑林区	Beilin	25.61	100.00
莲湖区	Lianhu	11.21	100.00
灞桥区	Baqiao	13.10	100.00
未央区	Weiyang	17.20	100.00
雁塔区	Yanta	6.91	100.00
阎良区	Yanliang		99.85
临潼区	Lintong	23.35	100.00
长安区	Chang'an	21.03	100.00
高陵区	Gaoling		100.00
鄠邑区	Huyi		100.00
蓝田县	Lantian		99.97
周至县	Zhouzhi		100.00
西咸新区	Xixian New Area	17.68	99.99
高新区	Hi-Tech Industries Development Zone		99.97
国际港务区	International Trade & Logistics Park	78.62	100.00

21-28 主要年份律师、公证及调解情况

Basic Statistics on Lawyer, Notaries and Mediation in Representative Years

指 标	Item	2010	2015	2016	2017	2018	2019	2020	2021
一、律师工作	**Lawyers**								
律师事务所（个）	Number of Law Offices (unit)	95	149	176	200	224	254	282	309
律师（人）	Lawyers(person)	1202	2198	2462	2836	3796	4220	4769	5608
#专职	Full-time	1139	2092	2337	2716	3476	3751	4222	4827
兼职	Part-time	63	91	84	120	148	188	141	140
刑事诉讼辩护及代理（件）	The Criminal suit Defence and agents(suit)		3524	3260	5872	5869	7481	7621	10119
民事诉讼代理（件）	Civil Litigation Agent(suit)		15308	16743	24593	28810	37116	40742	58489
行政诉讼代理（件）	Administrative litigation(suit)		532	601	1584	1256	1720	2248	3507
非诉讼法律事务(件)	Non-litigation legal affairs(suit)		2780	2840	4981	3900	5864	7127	6693
二、公证工作	**Notarization**								
公证处（个）	Number of Notary Offices (unit)	14	14	14	14	14	14	14	14
公证人员（人）	Notarial Personnel (person)	202	307	293	285	296	328	329	360
#公证员	Notaries	112	121	115	116	116	114	110	117
办理公证件数（件）	Number of Notarized Documents Issued (case)	106491	135622	144662	150300	161932	122152	96125	94875
三、人民调解工作	**Number of People Mediation**								
已建调委会数（个）	Number of Mediation Committees (unit)	3911	4052	4062	3903	3589	3411	3409	3526
调解人员数（人）	Number of Mediators (person)	15717	14838	14888	14295	14216	13895	13321	13320
调解纠纷数（件）	Number of Civil Disputes Mediated (case)	22247	31696	27455	48690	24868	22377	21209	26367
#调解成功数	Number of Cases Successfully Mediated	22164	30590	26426	47921	24364	21967	20830	24688

注：本表数据来源于市司法局。
本表2017年及以后年份数据含西咸新区。

21-29 主要年份共青团组织情况

Basic Facts on Communist Youth League in Representative Years

单位：个、人 (unit, person)

指 标	Item	2010	2015	2016	2017	2018	2019	2020	2021
一、基层团组织	Grass-root Youth League Organizations	7006	10074	10530	10237	9438	10359	11879	18181
二、共青团员	Youth League Members	308141	331261	251706	201789	162527	166284	206018	248604
三、专职团干部	Full Time Youth League Cadre	311	496	165	158	96	100	98	85

注：本表数据来源于共青团西安市委员会。
本表数据不含西咸新区。

21-30 妇联组织及工作情况（2021年）

The Basic Situation of Women's Federation（2021）

指 标	Item	2021
一、妇联组织	**Women's Organizations**	
市级妇联（个）	Municipal Women's Federation(unit)	1
街道妇联（个）	Street Women's Federation(unit)	144
社区妇联（个）	Community Women's Federation(unit)	1233
县（区）妇联（个）	County (district) Women's Federation(unit)	15
乡（镇）妇联（个）	Township (town) Women's Federation(unit)	41
村妇联（个）	Village Women's Representative Conference(unit)	1926
二、妇联工作	**Women's Work**	
巾帼建功标兵（个）	Women Business Model(unit)	172
巾帼建功集体（个）	Group of Women Business Model(unit)	62
巾帼文明岗（个）	Women's Civilized Model Post(unit)	66
三八红旗手标兵（人）	Models of "March 8 Red-Banner Holders" (person)	
三八红旗手（人）	March 8 Red-Banner Holders (person)	210
三八红旗集体（个）	March 8 Red-Banner Groups(unit)	106
五好家庭（户）	Five-virtue Family(household)	9
本级最美家庭（户）	The Best Family at the Present Level (household)	797
乡镇最美家庭（户）	The Best Family in the Town(household)	72
街道最美家庭（户）	The Best Family in the Street(household)	1346
村最美家庭（户）	The Best Family in the Village(household)	3794
社区最美家庭（户）	The Best Family in the Community (household)	466

注：本表数据来源于市妇联。
本表数据为西安原口径数据。

21-31 主要年份交通、火灾及安全生产情况

Transportation, Fire and Safety Production in Representative Years

指 标	Item	2010	2015	2016	2017	2018	2019	2020	2021
道路交通事故	**Road Accidents**								
事故数（起）	Number of Cases(case)	2323	2392	2943	2858	3153	2973	2835	2776
死亡人数（人）	Number of Deaths(person)	531	481	476	453	430	381	351	382
受伤人数（人）	Number of Injuries(person)	2520	2318	3012	2856	3219	3156	2978	2939
损失（万元）	Economic Loss(10 000yuan)	736.6	1470.2	1653.7	1777.3	2190.9	1808.5	1737.5	1547.6
火灾事故	**Fire Accidents**								
事故数（起）	Number of Cases(case)	1825	2590	3434	2353	2066	1871	3034	5348
死亡人数（人）	Number of Deaths(person)	13	20	16	8	26	18	27	23
受伤人数（人）	Number of Injuries(person)	7	7	7	2	37	2	2	18
损失（万元）	Economic Loss(10 000yuan)	2224.2	2401.5	1901.1	1659.1	1783.1	1886.6	2386.7	4461.8
农机事故	**Farm Machinery Accidents**								
事故数（起）	Number of Cases(case)	5	47	4	2	4	1	2	1
死亡人数（人）	Number of Deaths(person)		1	1		2	1	1	1
工矿商贸事故	**Accidents in Industry,Mine, Business and Trade**								
事故数（起）	Number of Cases(case)	20	10	33	36	33	28	45	66
死亡人数（人）	Number of Deaths(person)	24	11	35	43	41	31	53	67

注：本表2019年及以后年份数据来源于市公安局、市应急管理局及市消防救援支队。2011年及以前年份数据均来源于市安全生产监督管理局；2012–2018年交通、火灾数据来源于市公安局，农机和工矿商贸数据来源于市安全生产监督管理局。
2014年农机和工矿商贸事故发生起数统计口径变化，数据与以前年份不可比。
本表中交通和火灾数据为西安原口径，农机和工矿商贸事故2017年及以后年份数据含西咸新区。

21-32 主要年份刑事案件情况

Data on Criminal Cases in Representative Years

指 标	Item	2010	2015	2016	2017	2018	2019	2020	2021
一、案件数情况	**Data on Number of Cases**								
立案数（起）	Number of Registered Cases(case)	48566	108955	98056	79828	70332	69800	62738	67797
破案数（起）	Number of Cleared up Cases(case)	18906	28629	30730	33128	33616	36566	19540	25023
破案率（%）	Percent of Cleared up Cases(%)	38.9	26.3	31.3	41.5	47.8	52.4	31.3	36.9
抓获作案成员（人）	Number of Criminals Caught(person)	13104	12827	11982	12848	11153	15179	15196	30181
二、查获犯罪集团情况	**Data on Hunted down and Seized Criminal Gangs**								
查获犯罪集团个数（个）	Number of Hunted down and Seized Criminal Gangs (unit)	186	153	119	97	75	46	15	25
查获犯罪集团人数（人）	Number of Members of Hunted down and Seized Criminal Gangs (person)	939	680	492	418	359	254	62	131
涉及案件（起）	Number of Cases Involved(case)	1172	291	242	303	180	199	19	40
三、涉枪案件情况	**Data on Cases with Guns Involved**								
立案数（起）	Number of Registered Cases(case)	16	9	21	22	13	14	13	67
破案数（起）	Number of Cleared up Cases(case)	11	6	17	17	7	10	4	51
破案率（%）	Percent of Cleared up Cases(%)	68.8	66.7	81.0	77.3	53.8	71.4	30.8	76.1

注：本表数据来源于市公安局。
本表数据为西安原口径数据。

21-33 主要年份治安案件情况

Data on Public Order Cases in Representative Years

指 标	Item	2010	2015	2016	2017	2018	2019	2020	2021
受理数（起）	Number of Accepted(case)	58968	104553	109124	95821	92927	90250	77038	78360
查处数（起）	Number of Investigated and Prosecuted(case)	57151	100954	106999	93634	90563	88898	76345	77730
查处率（%）	Percent of Investigated and Prosecuted Cases(%)	96.9	96.6	98.1	97.7	97.5	98.5	99.1	99.2
查处违法人数（人）	Number of Investigated and Prosecuted Laws breakers and Crime Committer(person)	45856	40838	40126	34625	32185	31219	26155	28545

注：本表数据来源于市公安局。
本表数据为西安原口径数据。

21-34 主要年份西安市人民检察院案件办理情况

Data on Acceptance of Cases of Xi'an People's Procuratorate

指　标	Item	2010	2015	2016	2017	2018	2019	2020	2021
一、审查逮捕案件受理件数（件）	**Examination and Arresting(case)**	**4229**	**6545**	**7381**	**7184**	**7216**	**8345**	**5524**	**7018**
二、逮捕各类案件人数（人）	**Arresting of Criminals of each kind(person)**	**6183**	**6692**	**7763**	**7511**	**7162**	**9253**	**5523**	**6862**
决定逮捕贪污贿赂犯罪嫌疑人	Suspects of Corporation and Bribery to be Arrested	51	100	26	27	56	29		
决定逮捕渎职、侵权犯罪嫌疑人	Suspects of Misprision and Tort to be Arrested	2	4		22	2	5	1	1
批准逮捕刑事犯罪嫌疑人	Suspects of Criminal to be Arrested	6130	6588	7737	7462	7104	9219	5522	6861
三、刑事立案监督、侦查活动监督（件）	**Supervision of Acceptance of Criminal Cases and Investigation (case)**	**623**	**162**	**118**	**79**	**56**	**62**	**223**	**237**
四、审查起诉案件受理件数（件）	**Examination and Prosecution (case)**	**4662**	**6922**	**8090**	**8933**	**9288**	**11107**	**9017**	**11377**
五、起诉各类案件人数（人）	**Prosecution of Criminals of each kind(person)**	**5946**	**8018**	**9445**	**10365**	**10193**	**11894**	**9981**	**10962**
起诉贪污贿赂犯罪被告人	Prosecution of Criminals of Corruption and Bribery to be Defendants	163	153	154	179	101	102	87	89
起诉渎职、侵权犯罪被告人	Suspects of Misprision and Tort to be Defendants	22	17	39	38	12	8	8	9
起诉刑事犯罪被告人	Prosecution of Criminal to be Defendants	5761	7848	9252	10148	10080	11784	9886	10864

注：本表数据来源于市检察院。
本表数据为西安原口径数据。

21-35 西安市中级人民法院案件基本情况（2021年）

Law Cases Basic Data of Xi'an Intermediate People's Court（2021）

指　标	Item	全市结案（件） the whole City(case)	中级人民法院结案 the Intermediate People's Court	基层人民法院结案 the Basic People's Court
合　计	**Total**	**381321**	**39763**	**341558**
刑事	Criminal	10542	2159	8383
民事	Civil	230854	28834	202020
行政	Administration	1067	12	1055
执行	Execution	130953	6838	124115
其他类型	Other types	7905	1920	5985

注：本表数据来源于市中级人民法院。
本表数据为西安原口径数据。

主 要 统 计 指 标 解 释

艺术表演团体 指由文化部门主办或实行行业管理（经文化行政部门审批并领取营业性演出许可证），专门从事表演艺术等活动的各类专业艺术表演团体，含民间职业剧团（不包括群众业余文艺表演团队）。

艺术表演场馆 指由文化部门主办或实行行业管理（向文化行政部门备案或领取合资/合作演出场所许可证），有观众席、舞台、灯光设备，公开售票、专供文艺团体演出的文化活动场所。附属于文化部门机构内非独立核算的剧场、排演场，公开营业的也应单独统计。

图书馆 指各类图书馆的管理与服务（对文献和信息的搜集、整理、存储、利用和管理，向社会公众开放并提供科学、文化等各种知识普及教育）。包括公共图书馆和各类机构内部举办的或单独举办的图书馆的管理与服务。不包括部队系统以及文化馆（文化中心、群众艺术馆）、文化站内设的图书室。

群众文化活动 指开展群众文化活动的场所的管理和组织活动。包括文化馆（含综合性文化中心、群众艺术馆）、文化站、文化宫、少年宫等群众文化活动。在本制度中，目前暂不统计文化部门以外的文化宫和少年宫。

文化馆 （含综合性文化中心、群众艺术馆）、文化站：指专门从事群众文化活动的群众文化场馆。不包括临时抽调人员组成、没有编制的农村和街道文化工作队、服务站等。

广播/电视节目综合人口覆盖率 指根据国家广播电视总局制定的《广播电视人口覆盖率统计技术标准和方法》进行统计调查的，在对象区内能接收到由中央、省、地市或县通过无线、有线或卫星等各种技术方式转播的各级广播/电视节目的人口数占对象区总人口数的百分比。

博物馆 指为了研究、教育、欣赏的目的，收藏、保护、展示人类活动和自然环境的见证物，向公众开放，非盈利性、永久性社会服务机构，包括以博物馆（院）、纪念馆（舍）、科技馆、陈列馆等专有名称开展活动的单位。

等级运动员人数 指经考核正式批准授予等级运动员称号的人数。运动员等级分为国际级运动健将、运动健将、一级运动员、二级运动员、三级运动员、少年级运动员。

等级裁判员人数 指经考核正式批准授予等级裁判员称号的人数。裁判员等级分为国际裁判、国家级裁判、一级裁判、二级裁判、三级裁判。

医疗卫生机构 指从卫生（卫生健康）行政部门取得《医疗机构执业许可证》《中医诊所备案证》或从民政、工商行政、机构编制管理部门取得法人单位登记证书，为社会提供医疗服务、公共卫生服务或从事医学科研和在职培训等工作的单位。包括医院、基层医疗卫生机构、专业公共卫生机构、其他医疗卫生机构。

医院 包括综合医院、中医医院、中西医结合医院、民族医院、各类专科医院和护理院，不包括专科疾病防治院、妇幼保健院和疗养院，包括医学院校附属医院。

基层医疗卫生机构 包括社区卫生服务中心（站）、乡镇（街道）卫生院、村卫生室、门诊部、诊所（医务室）。

专业公共卫生机构 包括疾病预防控制中心、专科疾病防治机构、妇幼保健机构（含妇幼保健计划生育服务中心）、健康教育机构、急救中心（站）、采供血机构、卫生监督机构、取得《医疗机构执业许可证》或《计划生育技术服务许可证》的计划生育技术服务机构。

其他医疗卫生机构 包括疗养院、临床检验中心、医学科研机构、医学在职教育机构、卫生监督（监测、检测）机构、医学考试中心、农村改水中心、人才交流中心、统计信息中心等卫生事业单位。

卫生技术人员 包括执业医师、执业助理医师、注册护士、药师（士）、检验及影像技师（士）、卫生监督员和见习医（药、护、技）师（士）等卫生专业人员。包括从事临床或监督工作并同时从事管理工作的人员（如院长、副院长、党委书记等）。

提供住宿的社会服务机构 包括养老服务机构、精神疾病服务机构、儿童福利机构以及其他提供住宿机构。

烈士纪念建筑物管理机构 指民政部门管理的、独立核算的褒扬烈士的陵园、纪念馆等单位的总称。

殡葬服务机构 指为殡葬服务的单位总称。殡仪馆（含火葬场）、公墓、独立核算的骨灰堂、殡葬管理机构等。

公证人员 指在国家公证机关依法办理公证事务的司法人员，包括公证员、助理公证员和在公证处工作的其他人员。

办理公证文书 指公证处在一定时期内办结的公证文书件数。公证文书按司法部规定或批准的格式制作，包括国内公证和涉外公证两部分。国内公证分为经济合同公证和民事法律关系公证两大类。

调解人员 指在人民调解委员会担负调解民间一般民事纠纷和轻微违法行为引起纠纷的工作人员，包括调解委员会的委员和调解小组的调解员。

Explanatory Notes on Main Statistical Indicators

Arts Performance Troupes refer to the various professional performing arts groups, are sponsored by the cultural sectors or guided by the cultural society (Receive commercial performance license approved by the cultural administration authority), including non-governmental troupes(The mass amateur arts performance troupes are not included) .

Arts Performance Places refer to the various sites for cultural activities, are sponsored sponsored by the cultural sectors or guided by the cultural society (approved by the cultural market administration, or receive joint/ cooperative venues permit), with the facility of auditorium, stage, lighting, and selling tickets in public, including the opera halls and rehearse sites, etc. which are affiliated to the culture sectors without independent financial accounts and open to the public.

Library refers to all types of library management and services(collection, collation, storage, use and management of literature and information, open and providing scientific, cultural and other literacy education to the public). Including the management and services of public libraries and the libraries internally or separately organized by various sectors. Excluding the libraries the troops system and cultural palaces (cultural centers, mass art centers), cultural stations.

Mass Culture Center refers to the management and organization of the places where mass culture activities hold. Including cultural palaces (cultural center, mass art center), cultural stations, cultural palaces, youth palaces and other mass cultural activities. In this system, cultural palaces and youth palaces beyond cultural sectors are not counted at present.

Cultural Palaces (Cultural Centers, Mass Art Centers), Cultural Stations refers to the mass cultural venues specialized in mass cultural activities. Excluding rural and street cultural teams, service stations which made up of temporary without authorized strength.

Comprehensive Popularity of Radio/Television Programs refers to percentage of population at all levels that can receive radio/television programs transmitted by central, provincial, municipal or county through wireless, cable or satellite technologies in the target area, which is subject to statistical investigation according to the Technical Standards and Methods for the Statistics of Radio and Television Popularity formulated by National Radio and Television Administration.

Museum refers to the non-profit, permanent society service sectors which collect, protect, show human activities and the witnesses of natural environment, including the units that organize activities with the proper name such as museum, memorial hall, science and technology museum, exhibition hall, etc.

Number of Athletes in Grades refers to the number of athletes who have been given titles thorough examination. The titles of athletes include international masters of sports, masters of sports, first-grade, second-grade and third-grade athletes and young athletes.

Number of Referees in Grades refers to the number of referees who have been given titles after examination. They are classified as international referees, national referees and referees of the first, second and third grades.

Medical and health institutions are the organizations that have got the practice license of medical institution and record certificate of traditional Chinese medicine clinics from health administrative departments or have obtained legal entity registration certificates from civil, industrial and commercial administration, organization management departments, to provide medical services, public health services or engaged in medical research and medical job training. It includes hospitals, primary medical and health institutions, professional public health institutions, and other medical and health institutions.

Hospitals include general hospitals, hospitals of traditional Chinese medicine, hospitals of integrated traditional Chinese and Western Medicine, National Hospitals, various specialist hospitals, and nursing homes, excluding specialized disease prevention and treatment centers, Maternity and child care centers and sanatoriums, including hospitals affiliated to medical colleges and universities.

Primary medical and health institutions include community health service centers (stations), township (street) health centers, village clinics, outpatient departments, and clinics.

Professional public health institutions include the center for disease control and prevention, specialized disease prevention and treatment centers, maternity and child care centers (including maternal and child health family planning service centers), health education institutions, first aid agencies, collecting and supplying agencies, health supervision institutions, and family planning technical service institutions which have got the practice license of medical institution and family planning technical services license.

Other medical and health institutions include the sanatoriums, clinical inspection centers, medical research institutions, medical in-service education institutions, health supervision institutions, medical examination centers, Rural change water quality centers, personnel exchange centers, statistical information centers, and other health institutions.

Health technical personnel include practicing physicians, practicing assistant doctors, registered nurses, pharmacists, inspection and imaging technicians, health supervisors, clerks and other health professionals. It does include health technical personnel engaged in clinical or supervisory work and at the same time as management work such as Dean, vice president, Secretary of the Party committee, etc.

Social services providing accommodation include pension services, psychiatric care services, child welfare institutions, and other lodging establishments.

Martyr memorial buildings management organization refers to the floorboard of cemetery, memorial and other units which are independent accounting and managed by civil affairs departments to praise the Martyrs.

Funeral service agencies refer to the units that serve a funeral services. It includes a Funeral home (including crematorium), cemetery, independent accounting ashes hall, funeral and interment management organization, etc.

Notary Personnel refers to judicial workers of the state notary offices handling notarization work according to law. They include notaries, assistant notaries, and other people working for notary offices.

Notarized Documents refer to the documents settled by notary offices in a year. The notary documents are drawn up in accordance with the regulations of the Ministry of Justice, including domestic documents and foreign-related documents. Domestic documents are divided into two major categories, documents on economic contracts and documents on civil legal relations.

Mediators refer to workers on peoples mediation committees responsible for mediating civil disputes and cases of slight infractions of the law. They include members of the mediation committees and mediators of mediation groups.

22 企业调查

ENTERPRISES INVESTIGATION

资料整理：薛　燕
Data management：Xue Yan
数据审核：黄雪冰
Data audit：Huang Xuebing

第二十二部分　企业调查

一、简要说明

1.本章资料主要包括各行业企业景气调查指数和企业家信心指数等，由西安市统计局社会经济调查中心提供。

2.本章资料调查范围：包括规模以上工业、资质内建筑业、限额以上批发和零售业、限额以上住宿和餐饮业、房地产开发业和规模以上服务业。

3.调查方法：采用非全面调查的方法进行统计。

二、主要指标

企业景气指数（第四季度）	110.4
企业家信心指数（第四季度）	112.7

22　ENTERPRISES INVESTIGATION

Ⅰ.Brief Introduction

1.Data in this chapter consists prosperity survey indices of various industries and Entrepreneur Expectation Indicator, provided by Socio Economic Investigation Center of the Xi'an Bureau of Statistics.

2.The field of investigation and statistics range. The data in this chapter consists of industrial enterprises above designated size, construction enterprises which possess qualification grades, wholesaletrades and retail trades enterprises above designated size, hotels and catering services enterprises above designated size, real estate industry and services above designated size.

3.Methodology on survey. The survey is conducted bynon-overall investigation.

Ⅱ.Major Indicators

Business Climate Index（Fourth Quarter）	110.4
Entrepreneur Expectation Indicator（Fourth Quarter）	112.7

22-1 企业景气指数（2021年）

Business Climate Index (2021)

指　　标	Item	一季度 First Quarter	二季度 Second Quarter	三季度 Third Quarter	四季度 Fourth Quarter
企业景气指数	**Business Climate Index**	**129.3**	**126.3**	**121.0**	**110.4**
按行业门类分	**Grouped by Sector**				
工业	Industry	145.7	138.5	130.3	114.6
建筑业	Construction	116.1	114.2	112.9	104.0
批发和零售业	Wholesale and Retail Sales	127.7	122.0	122.5	98.8
住宿和餐饮业	Hotels and Catering Services	105.8	112.4	97.2	61.5
房地产开发业	Real Estate Development	132.1	134.9	125.2	121.9
规模以上服务业	Services above the Designated Size	122.3	121.5	116.8	114.1

22-2 企业家信心指数（2021年）

Entrepreneur Expectation Indicator (2021)

指　　标	Item	一季度 First Quarter	二季度 Second Quarter	三季度 Third Quarter	四季度 Fourth Quarter
企业家信心指数	**Entrepreneur Expectation Indicator**	**133.2**	**128.9**	**122.8**	**112.7**
按行业门类分	**Grouped by Sector**				
工业	Industry	148.2	140.1	131.4	116.0
建筑业	Construction	122.3	118.7	118.0	107.3
批发和零售业	Wholesale and Retail Sales	130.1	121.8	117.1	103.9
住宿和餐饮业	Hotels and Catering Services	120.0	114.8	104.1	67.9
房地产开发业	Real Estate Development	133.8	136.4	124.9	121.3
规模以上服务业	Services above the Designated Size	126.7	125.1	120.1	116.2

主 要 统 计 指 标 解 释

企业景气指数：是根据企业家对本企业综合生产经营情况所作的判断与预期（通常是对“良好”、“一般”、“不佳”的选择）而编制的指数，用以综合反映企业的生产经营状况。企业景气指数也称“企业综合生产经营景气指数”。

企业家信心指数：是根据企业家对企业外部市场经济环境与宏观政策的认识、看法判断和预期（通常是对“乐观”、“一般”、“不乐观”的选择）而编制的指数，用以综合反映企业家对宏观经济环境的感受与信心。企业家信心指数也称“宏观经济景气指数”。

景气指数的表示方式：景气指数的表示范围在0～200之间，其含义：100为景气指数的临界值，表明景气状况变化不大；100～200为景气区间，表明景气状况趋于上升或改善，越接近于200，状况越景气；0～100为不景气区间，表明经济状况趋于下降或恶化，越接近于0，状况越不景气。

Explanatory Notes on Main Statistical Indicators

Business Climate Index it is an index worked out according to the judgement and anticipation (normally a choice from good, ordinary, not good) of entrepreneurs made based on synthetic productive and operational situation of the enterprise. It is used to reflect synthetically the productive and operational situation of the enterprise. It is also referred to as synthetic and productive operational prosperity index of enterprise.

Confidence index of entrepreneur it is an index worked out according to the judgment and anticipation (normally a choice from optimistic , ordinary , not optimistic)of entrepreneurs made based on their understandings and views of the market and economic environment outside the enterprise and the macro policies. It is used to reflect synthetically the confidence and feelings of the entrepreneurs to the macro economic environment. It is also referred to as macro-economy prosperity index.

The way to express prosperity index the range of prosperity index is from 0 to 200; 100 is the critical value, and means economic situation didn't change largely; from 100 to 200 is the interval of prosperity; and from 0 to 100 is the interval of not prosperity, meaning economic situation is going down or worse, the closer to 0, the worse the economic situation.